D0718303

Collins
Welsh
Dictionary

HarperCollins Publishers
Westerhill Road
Bishopbriggs
Glasgow
G64 2QT
Great Britain

First Edition 1992

Latest Reprint 2005

© HarperCollins Publishers
1992

ISBN 0-00-719600-8

Collins Gem® and Bank of
English® are registered
trademarks of HarperCollins
Publishers Limited

www.collins.co.uk

A catalogue record for this
book is available from the
British Library

Printed in Italy by Legoprint
S.P.A.

Acknowledgements
We would like to thank those
authors and publishers who
kindly gave permission for
copyright material to be used
in the Collins Word Web. We
would also like to thank Times
Newspapers Ltd for providing
valuable data.

In collaboration with/
Mewn cydweithrediad â'r

Dr. David A. Thorne and the
Department of Welsh
Language and Literature,
St David's University College,
Lampeter

Dr. David A. Thorne ac Adran
Iaith a Llenyddiaeth Cymru,
Coleg Prifysgol Dewi Sant,
Llanbedr Pont Steffan

Editor/Golygydd
Anne Convery

Editorial staff/Staff golygyddol
Lesley Johnston

INTRODUCTION

The first Spurrell Welsh-English dictionary appeared in 1848 published by William Spurrell (1813–89) the Carmarthen printer and publisher. One of his sons, Walter Spurrell (1858–1934), joined his father in the business and the family firm published a series of distinguished Welsh-English, English-Welsh dictionaries and influential Welsh grammars during the latter part of last century and the first half of the present century. William Spurrell was advised by and well-acquainted with Daniel Silvan Evans (1818–1903), one of the father figures of Welsh lexicography, sometime lecturer in Welsh at St David's University College, Lampeter and the first professor of Welsh to be appointed by the University of Wales.

The Collins-Spurrell Welsh Dictionary was first published in 1960 and quickly became an essential tool of general reference for Welsh learners as well as those anxious to interpret literature. It was edited by Henry Lewis, Professor of Welsh Language and Literature at University College, Swansea. The staff of the Department of Welsh Language and Literature at St David's University College, Lampeter are happy to cooperate with the editorial staff at Collins to produce this latest edition of a famous dictionary.

D A THORNE

CONTENTS

THE WELSH LANGUAGE

MOST of the languages of Europe, and some of the languages of Asia, can be traced back to a common ancestor to which the name Indo-European is commonly given. From this ancestor were derived a dozen or so branches, one of which is called Celtic. This branch probably had its beginning in the upper Danube valley, and from there spread in many directions over Europe, and even to Galatia in Asia Minor. As the Celtic-speaking people became scattered, changes naturally occurred in the language, resulting in the growth of dialects. Of these the best known on the continent is that which was spoken in Gaul, to which the name Gaulish is given. Gaulish became extinct in the early Christian period, and was displaced by Latin.

In the meantime people speaking different forms of Celtic had crossed over from the Continent to the British Isles. One group established itself in Ireland. This is known as the Goidelic or Gaelic group, and from it descended the Irish language, which spread from Ireland to the Isle of Man, developing later to Manx, and also to Scotland, eventually becoming Scottish Gaelic. The other group prevailed in Britain and the language is called British or Brythonic or Brittonic. Prior to the Roman Conquest this language was spoken throughout what later became England, Wales and southern Scotland. It was from this descendant of the original Common Celtic language that ultimately sprang the Welsh, Cornish and Breton languages.

The language of the Goidelic group is referred to also as Q Celtic, and that of the British group as P Celtic. The reason for this is that the Indo-European consonant written 'qu' has given 'c' in the former and 'p' in the latter. An example is found in the forms corresponding to the English interrogative pronoun 'who', which in Irish is 'cia' or 'cé', in Welsh 'pwy', and in Latin 'quis'. It may be mentioned that Gaulish shows the same development as the British languages. Thus whereas the word for 'head, end' is in Irish 'ceann' (earlier 'cenn'), it is in Welsh 'pen', while the corresponding form is found in Gaulish 'penne' in a compound name.

One of the oldest poems in Welsh literature is a eulogy to Cynan Garwyn, son of Brochwel Ysgithrog. Cynan's son Selyf is known to have been killed as he led the Welsh in the battle of Chester about the year 615. The eulogy is attributed to Taliesin, whom persistent tradition acclaims as author of eulogies and elegies to princes in southern Scotland and northern England who struggled against the Saxon invader in the late sixth century. Another name that has been handed down from these early times is Aneirin, whose long poem *Y Gododdin* refers to a great tragic exploit at Catraeth, somewhere in the neighbourhood of Catterick. These early traditions have tenaciously persisted throughout the long story of Welsh poetic literature.

Recorded Welsh prose goes back to the early ninth century. The earliest remains are scanty, but it can hardly be contested that prose writing must have long preceded what little has had the good fortune to escape oblivion. It is free from the crudeness that would be expected from initial efforts, and the way in which difficult and somewhat abstruse material is expressed with clarity, economy and directness goes a long way to prove that the writers were inheritors rather than initiators. The splendour and exactness of medieval Welsh prose, quite apart from its literary content, is striking evidence of the mastery of the writers of the prose medium. These qualities appear not least in the unlikely realm of legal writing.

During its long history the Welsh language has naturally undergone changes, but far from the extent to which English, for example, has changed since the days of Chaucer. He was a contemporary of Dafydd ap Gwilym, but whereas Chaucer has to be practically translated into Modern English, Dafydd is using to all intents the same language as any present-day poet expressing himself in the same type of poem. Similarly, if most of the earlier prose literature were printed in accordance with modern orthographical usage, the reader would not experience excessive difficulty in comprehending it. There have been changes in syntax, and still more in vocabulary. Idiomatic expressions have become obsolete from age to age, and new ones have grown. But substantially the literary language has been strikingly uniform.

The vocabulary has naturally been greatly affected from time to time by contact with peoples speaking a different language. Like many other languages Welsh has rarely been afraid of borrowing words from foreign languages. In the period of Roman occupation, and later under the influence of the Church, hundreds of Latin words were borrowed and submitted to the same treatment as native words. The same is to a less extent true of the period of contact with Anglo-Saxons. Then came the influence of the Normans, followed ultimately by the great pressure of English. All these accretions have been from non-Celtic sources, but the Welsh vocabulary is not without borrowings taken from time to time from Irish.

The written, and especially the printed, literary language always tends to be more static and conservative than the spoken. This results in the retention in the literary language of forms which have long since vanished completely from everyday colloquial speech, thus giving the printed literary language a somewhat artificial appearance. But the spoken language also differs from area to area. Indeed a brook seems a sufficient barrier to create divergence in expression between the inhabitants on either side. It is well known that speakers of dialect in one locality can hardly understand compatriots speaking another dialect of the same language. To secure, therefore, that all speakers, of whatever dialects, should have access to all that is of value in enlightened minds, the standard literary language must retain a high level of permanence, but should also avoid pedantic rigidity and scholastic snobbery.

NOTES ON THE PRONUNCIATION OF WELSH

VOWELS

They are sounded, long or short, as the vowels in the English words given.

A   p*a*lm, p*a*t.
E   g*a*te (without diphthongization), g*e*t.
I   f*ee*t, f*i*t.
O   m*o*re, n*o*t.
U (1)   North Wales: like French *u* or German *ü* without rounding lips.
  (2)   South Wales: as I.
W   c*oo*l, f*u*ll.
Y (1)   In monosyllables generally, and in final syllables, as U (the 'clear' sound).
  (2)   In all but final syllables, and in **y**, **yr** (the), **fy** (my), **dy** (thy), **yn**, **yng**, **ym** (in), the adverbial **yn**, the preverbal and relative particle **y**, **yr** (**y'm**, **y'th** etc.), **syr** (sir), **nyrs** (nurse), as English f*u*n, (the 'obscure' sound).

DIPHTHONGS

(1)   Falling diphthongs, in which the second sound is consonantal: the two vowels have the sound noted above: **ae, oe, ai, oi,** the diphthong **ei** as English b*y*, **aw, ew, iw, ow, uw, ẁy, yw.**

(2)   Rising diphthongs, in which the first sound is consonantal: **ia, ie, io, iw, iy,** ('obscure' y); **wa, we, wi, wo, wy,** ('clear' y); **wy,** ('obscure' y).

viii

CONSONANTS

Only such as differ from English need be noted.

CH   (following C in the alphabet), as Scottish *loch*.
DD   (following D in the alphabet), as *th* in English *this*, breathe.
F   as English *v*.
FF   As English *f*.
G   always as in English *go*.
NG   (following G in the alphabet), as in English si*ng*. In some words (e.g. **dangos**), however, it is sounded *ng-g*, as in English lo*ng*er. Alphabetically this follows after N.
LL   produced by placing the tongue to pronounced *l*, then emitting breath without voice.
PH   (following P in the alphabet), as English *f*.
TH   always as th in English *thin*.

ACCENT

Welsh words are generally accented on the last syllable but one. There are certain exceptions:

(1) The reduplicated personal pronouns **myfi, tydi, efe, efô, hyhi, nyni, chwychwi, hwynt-hwy**, accented on the final syllable.

(2) Verbs in **-(h)au, -(h)oi, -eu**, accented on the final syllable.

(3) A few dissyllabic words beginning **y** + consonant, accented on the final syllable.

(4) Certain polysyllabic words with a diphthong resulting in contraction in the final syllable, such as **Cymraeg**.

(5) Some late borrowings accented as in the language of origin, generally English.

INITIAL MUTATIONS

Certain initial consonants are mutated under certain conditions, as shown in the following table. Only the radical form is given in the dictionary.

SOUNDS	EXAMPLES			
	Radical	*Soft*	*Nasal*	*Spirant*
p t c	*pren* *tad* *cam*	*bren* *dad* *gam*	*mhren* *nhad* *ngham*	*phren* *thad* *cham*
b d g	*baich* *dyn* *gŵr*	*faich* *ddyn* *-ŵr*	*maich* *nyn* *ngŵr*	
ll rh m	*llais* *rhes* *mam*	*lais* *res* *fam*		

ABBREVIATIONS

BYRFODDAU

abbreviation	**abbr**	byrfodd
adjective	**adj**	ansoddair
adverb	**adv**	adferf
collective noun	**coll n**	enw torfol
colloquial	**col**	tafodieithol
conjunction	**conj**	cysylltiad
contraction	**contr**	cywasgiad
demonstrative	**dem**	dangosol
dual noun	**dn**	enw deuol
emphatic	**emphat**	pwyslais
exclamation	**excl**	ebychiad
feminine	**f**	benywaidd
grammatical	**gram**	gramadegol
imperative	**imper**	gorchmynnol
masculine	**m**	gwrywaidd
mutation	**mut**	treiglad
noun dual	**nd**	enw deuol
plural	**pl**	lluosog
pronoun	**pron**	rhagenw
preposition	**prep**	arddodiad
relative	**rel**	perthynol
singular	**sg**	unigol
verb	**vb**	berf
intransitive verb	**vi**	berf gyflawn
transitive verb	**vt**	berf anghyflawn

GEIRIADUR CYMRAEG A SAESNEG

A

a *interrogative particle* ♦ *preverbal particle* ♦ *rel pron* who, that, which

a, ac *conj* and

â, ag *conj* as

â, ag *prep* with

a *excl* ah, oh

ab, ap *nm* son (*before name, in place of surname, like 'Mac', and 'Fitz'*)

abad (-au) *nm* abbot

abadaeth (-au) *nf* abbacy, abbotship

abades (-au) *nf* abbess

abatir (-oedd) *nm* abbey-land

abaty (abatai) *nm* abbey

aber (-oedd, ebyr) *nm* confluence; mouth of river, estuary; brook, stream

aberfa (-oedd) *nf* mouth of river, estuary

abergofiant *nm* forgetfulness, oblivion

aberth (-au, ebyrth) *nm* sacrifice

aberthged *nf* oblation; offering of fruits

aberthol *adj* sacrificial

aberthu *vb* sacrifice

aberthwr (-wyr) *nm* sacrificer

aberu *vb* flow into, disembogue

abid *nmf* apparel; dress of religious order

abiéc *nmf* alphabet

abl *adj* able; well-off

abladol *adj* ablative

abledd *nm* ability; plenty

abrwysg *adj* clumsy, drunken

absen *nm* absence; slander

absennol *adj* absent

absennu *vb* backbite, slander

absennwr (absenwyr) *nm* backbiter

absenoldeb *nm* absence

absenoli *vb* absent

absenoliaeth (-au) *nm* absenteeism

abwyd, -yn (-od) *nm* worm; fishing-bait

ac, a *conj* and

academaidd *adj* academic

academi (-iau) *nm* academy

acen (-ion) *nf* accent

aceniad *nm* accentuation

acennod *nm* accent mark

acennu *vb* accent, stress

acenyddiaeth *nf* accentuation

acer (-i) *nf* acre

acrilig *adj* acrylic

act (-au) *nf* act

actio *vb* act

actor (-ion) *nm* actor

actores (-au) *nf* actress

acw *adv* there, yonder

ach *excl* ugh

ach (-au, -oedd) *nf* degree of kinship; (*pl*) pedigree, ancestry

aches *nm* tide, flood; eloquence

achlân *adv* wholly, entirely

achles (-oedd) *nf* succour, protection; manure

achlesol *adj* succouring

achlesu *vb* succour, cherish; manure

achlod *nm* shame, disgrace

achlust *nm* rumour ♦ *adj* attentive

achlysur (-on) *nm* occasion

achlysuro *vb* occasion

achlysurol *adj* occasional

achos (-ion) *nm* cause, case

achos *conj* because, for

achosi vb cause

achres (-i, -au) nf genealogical table

achub vb seize, snatch; save, rescue. **a. y blaen** forestall. **a. y cyfle** seize the opportunity

achubiaeth nf salvation

achubol nf saving

achubwr (-wyr), **-ydd** (-ion) nm saviour, rescuer

achul adj thin, emaciated

achwre, ach(f)re n under-thatch, protection; covering, garment

achwyn vb complain ♦ (-ion) nm complaint, plaint

achwyngar adj querulous

achwyniad (-au) nm complaint, accusation

achwynwr (-wyr) nm complainer; complainant, plaintiff

achwynyddes (-au) nf complainant

achydd (-ion) nm genealogist

achyddiaeth nf genealogy

achyddol adj genealogical

ad- prefix very; second; bad, re-

adail nf building, edifice, structure

adain, aden (adenydd) nf wing; fin; spoke

adamant nm adamant, diamond

adamantaidd adj adamantine

adar npl (aderyn nm) birds, fowls. **a. drudwy, a. yr eira,** starlings. **a y to** sparrows

adara vb catch birds, fowl

adardy (-dai) nm aviary

adareg nf ornithology

adargi (-gwn) nm retriever, setter, spaniel

adargraffiad (-au) nm reprint

adarwr (-wyr) nm fowler

adarwriaeth nf fowling

adarydd (-ion) nm ornithologist

adaryddiaeth nf ornithology

ad-dalu vb repay, requite

ad-drefnu vb rearrange

adeg (-au) nf time, occasion,

opportunity

adeilad (-au) nmf building, edifice

adeiladaeth nf building; edification, construction

adeiladol adj edifying, constructive

adeiladu vb build, edify

adeiladwr (-wyr), **-ydd** (-ion) nm builder

adeiledd nm structure

adeiniog adj winged

aden (-ydd, edyn) nf wing (adain)

adenedigaeth nf regeneration

adeni vb regenerate

adennill vb regain, recover

aderyn (adar) nm bird

adfach (-au) nm barb; liver-fluke

adfail (-feilion) nm ruin

adfeddiannu vb repossess

adfeiliad nm decay, ruin

adfeiliedig adj decayed, in ruins

adfeilio vb decay, moulder

Adfent nm Advent

adfer, -u, -yd vb restore

adferf (-au) nf adverb

adferol adj adverbial

adferiad nm restoration

adferol adj restorative; remedial

adferwr (-wyr) nm restorer

adflas nm after-taste, bad taste

adfyd nm adversity

adfydus adj adverse, miserable

adfynach nm renegade monk

adfyw adj half alive, half dead

adfywhau vb revive, reanimate

adfywiad (-au) nm revival

adfywio vb revive, resuscitate

adfywiol adj refreshing

adg- see atg-

adiad nm drake

adio nm addition ♦ vb add

adiolyn (adiolion) nm additive

adladd, adlodd nm aftermath

adlais (-leisiau) nm echo

adlam (-au) nm home; rebound. **cic a.** drop-kick

adlamu vb rebound

adleisio vb resound

adlewyrch, -iad (-au) *nm* reflection

adlewyrchu *vb* reflect

adlewyrchydd (-ion) *nm* reflector

adlog (-au) *nm* compound interest

adloniadol *adj* of or for entertainment

adloniant *nm* recreation, entertainment

adlonni *vb* entertain, refresh

adlunio *vb* remodel, reconstruct

adnabod *vb* know, recognize

adnabyddiaeth *nf* knowledge, acquaintance

adnabyddus *adj* known, familiar

adnabyddwr *nm* knower

adnau (adneuon) *nm* deposit, pledge. **ar a.** on deposit

adneuo *vb* deposit

adneuol *adj* depositing

adneuwr (-wyr) *nm* depositor

adnewyddiad (-au) *nm* renewal, renovation

adnewyddu *vb* renew, renovate

adnewyddwr (-wyr) *nm* renewer, renovator

adnod (-au) *nf* verse

adnoddau *npl* resources

adolygiad (-au) *nm* review

adolygu *vb* review

adolygydd (-ion) *nm* reviewer

adran (-nau) *nf* division, section, department

adref *adv* homewards, home

adrodd *vb* relate, recite

adroddgan *nf* recitative

adroddiad (-au) *nm* report; recitation

adroddwr (-wyr) *nm* narrator, reciter

ads- see **ats-**

aduniad *nm* reunion

aduno *vb* reunite

adwaith (-weithiau) *nm* reaction

adweithiol *adj* reactionary

adweithydd (-ion) *nm* reactor

adwr *nm* coward, churl

adwy (-au, -on) *nf* gap, breach; pass

adwyth (-au) *nm* evil, misfortune, illness

adwythig *adj* cruel; evil, baneful; sore, sick; harmful

adyn (-od) *nm* wretch

adysgrif (-au) *nf* copy, transcript

adysgrifio *vb* copy, transcribe

addas *adj* suitable, proper

addasiad (-au) *nm* adjustment, adaptation

addasrwydd *nm* suitableness, fitness

addasu *vb* suit, adapt, fit

addawol *adj* promising

addef *vb* acknowledge, own, admit

addefiad *nm* admission, confession

addewid (-ion) *nf* promise

addfain *adj* slender, shapely

addfed see **aeddfed**

addfwyn *adj* gentle, meek, mild

addfwynder *nm* gentleness, meekness

addien *adj* fair, beautiful

addo *vb* promise

addod *nm:* **wy a.** nest-egg

addoed *nm* death, hurt

addoedi *vb* delay, postpone, prorogue

addoediad *nm* prorogation

addoer *adj* sad, cruel; chilling

addoldy (-dai) *nm* place of worship

addolgar *adj* devout, reverent

addolgarwch *nm* devoutness, reverence

addoli *vb* worship, adore

addoliad *nm* worship

addolwr (-wyr) *nm* worshipper

adduned (-au) *nf* vow

addunedu *vb* vow

addurn (-au, -iadau) *nm* ornament, adornment

addurnedig *adj* decorated

addurniad *nm* ornamentation

addurno *vb* adorn, ornament

addurnol adj ornamental, decorative

addurnwr (-wyr) nm decorator

addysg nf education, instruction

addysgiadol adj instructive, educational

addysgiaeth nf instruction, training

addysgol adj educational

addysgu vb educate, instruct

addysgwr (-wyr), -ydd (-ion) nm educator, instructor, tutor

aeddfed adj ripe, mature

aeddfedrwydd nm ripeness, maturity

aeddfedu vb ripen; mature

ael (-iau) nf brow

aele adj sad, wretched

aelgerth, -geth see **elgeth**

aelod (-au) nm member, limb. **A. Seneddol** Member of Parliament

aelodaeth nf membership

aelodi vb become a member; enrol

aelwyd (-ydd) nf hearth, fireside

aer (-ion) nm heir

aer nm air

aeres (-au) nf heiress

aerfa nf slaughter, battle

aerglo nm air-lock

aeron npl fruit, fruits, berries

aerwy (-au, -on) nm collar, torque; neck-chain

aes nf shield

aestheteg nf aesthetics

aesthetig adj aesthetic

aeth nm pain, grief, fear, shock

aethnen nf aspen, poplar

aethus adj poignant, grievous, severe

afal (-au) nm apple

afaleua vb gather apples

afallen (-au) nf apple-tree

afan npl (-en nf) raspberries

afanc (-od) nm beaver

afiach adj unwell, unhealthy, morbid

afiachus adj sickly; unwholesome

afiaith nm zest, mirth, glee

afiechyd (-on) nm disease, malady

afieithus adj mirthful, gleeful

aflafar adj harsh, unmelodious

aflan adj unclean, polluted, foul

aflawen adj fierce; sad, cheerless, dismal; awful

aflednais adj immodest, indelicate

afledneisrwydd nm immodesty, indelicacy

aflem adj obtuse

aflendid nm uncleanness; pollution

aflêr adj untidy, slovenly

aflerwch nm untidiness, slovenliness

afles nm disadvantage, hurt

aflesol adj disadvantageous, unprofitable

afliwiog adj pale, colourless

aflonydd adj unquiet, restless

aflonyddu vb disquiet, disturb, molest

aflonyddwch nm disturbance, unrest

aflonyddwr (-wyr) nm disturber

afloyw adj turbid; opaque

afluniaidd adj mis-shapen, deformed

aflunio vb disfigure, deform

aflwydd nm misfortune, calamity

aflwyddiannus adj unsuccessful

aflwyddiant nm failure

aflwyddo vb fail

aflywodraeth nf misrule, anarchy

aflywodraethus adj ungovernable, uncontrollable

afon (-ydd) nf river

afonig nf rivulet, streamlet, brook

afradlon adj wasteful, prodigal

afradlonedd nm prodigality

afradloni, afradu vb waste, lavish, squander

afraid adj unnecessary, needless

afrasol adj graceless, impious

afreidiau nm superfluity

afreidiol adj needless, superfluous

afreol nf misrule, disorder

afreolaidd adj irregular; disorderly

afreoleidd-dra nm irregularity

afreolus adj unruly, disorderly

afreswm nm absurdity

afresymol adj unreasonable

afresymoldeb nm unreasonableness

afrifed adj innumerable

afrllad, -en (-au, -ennau) nf wafer

afrosgo adj clumsy, unwieldy

afrwydd adj difficult, stiff, awkward

afrwyddineb nm difficulty

afrwyddo vb obstruct, hinder

afrywiog adj perverse, crossgrained, improper

afrywiogrwydd nm churlishness, roughness

afu liver ♦ nm/f **a. (g)las** gizzard

afwyn (-au) nf rein

affeithiad nm affection (in grammar)

afflau nm grip, hug, embrace

affliw nm shred, particle

Affrica nf Africa

affwysol adj abysmal

ag conj as ♦ prep with. see **â**

agen (-nau) nf cleft, chink, fissure

agendor nm/f gulf, abyss

agennu vb split, crack

ager, agerdd nm steam, vapour

agerfad (-au) nm steamboat

agerlong (-au) nf steamship, steamer

ageru vb steam, evaporate

agerw adj bitter, fierce

agor, -yd vb open, expand

agorawd (-au) nf overture

agored adj open; liable

agorfa (-oedd) nf opening, orifice

agoriad (-au) nm opening; key

agoriadol adj opening, inaugural

agorwr (-wyr), -ydd (-ion) nm opener.

agos adj near, nigh

agosaol adj approaching

agosatrwydd nm intimacy

agosáu vb draw near, approach

agosrwydd nm nearness, proximity

agwedd (-au) nf form; aspect; attitude

agweddi nm dowry, marriage gift

agwrdd adj strong, mighty

angall adj unwise, foolish

angau nm/f death

angel (angylion, engyl) nm angel

angen (anghenion) nm need, want

angenrheidiol adj necessary, needful

angenrheidrwydd nm necessity

angerdd nm heat; passion; force

angerddol adj ardent, intense, passionate

angerddoldeb nm vehemence, intensity

anghaffael nm mishap; defect, flaw

anghallineb nm unwisdom, imprudence

angharedig adj unkind

angharedigrwydd nm unkindness

anghelfydd adj unskilful, clumsy

anghenfil (angenfilod) nm monster

anghenraid (angenrheidiau) nm necessity

anghenus adj needy, necessitous, indigent

angheuol adj deadly, mortal, fatal

anghlod nm dispraise, dishonour

anghoelio vb disbelieve

anghofiedig adj forgotten

anghofio vb forget

anghofrwydd nm forgetfulness

anghofus adj forgetful, oblivious

anghred nf unbelief, infidelity

anghredadun (anghredinwyr) nm unbeliever

anghrediniaeth nf unbelief, infidelity

anghrediniol adj unbelieving

anghredu vb disbelieve

anghrefyddol adj irreligious

anghrist (-iau) *nm* antichrist
anghryno *adj* incompact, prolix
anghwrtais *adj* discourteous
anghwrteisi *nm* discourtesy
anghydbwysedd *nm* imbalance
anghydfod *nm* disagreement,
discord
Anghydffurfiaeth *nf*
Nonconformity
Anghydffurfiwr (-wyr) *nm*
Nonconformist
anghydnaws *adj* uncongenial
anghydsynio *vb* dissent, disagree
anghydweddol *adj* incompatible
anghyfaddas *adj* unsuitable, unfit
anghyfaddasu *vb* unfit, disqualify
anghyfamodol *adj* uncovenanted
anghyfanhedd-dra *nm* desolation
anghyfanheddle (-aneddleoedd)
nm desolate place
anghyfanheddol *adj* desolating;
desert
anghyfannedd *adj* uninhabited,
desert
anghyfansoddiadol *adj*
unconstitutional
anghyfartal *adj* unequal, uneven
anghyfartaledd *nm* disparity
anghyfarwydd *adj* unfamiliar,
unskilled
anghyfeillgar *adj* unfriendly
anghyfiaith *adj* foreign, alien
anghyfiawn *adj* unjust,
unrighteous
anghyfiawnder *nm* injustice
anghyflawn *adj* incomplete
anghyfleus *adj* inconvenient
anghyfleustra (-terau) *nm*
inconvenience
anghyflogaeth *nm* unemployment
anghyfnewidiol *adj* immutable
anghyfraith *nf* transgression,
crime
anghyfranogol *adj*
incommunicable
anghyfreithlon *adj* unlawful,
illegal, illegitimate

anghyfrifol *adj* irresponsible
anghyffredin *adj* uncommon, rare
anghyffwrdd *adj* intangible
anghyffyrddus *adj* uncomfortable
anghymedrol *adj* immoderate
anghymen *adj* rash, coarse, untidy
anghymeradwy *adj* unacceptable
anghymeradwyo *vb* disapprove
anghymesur *adj* inordinate
anghymharol *adj* incomparable
anghymharus *adj* ill-matched
anghymhendod *nm* foolishness,
indelicacy, untidiness
anghymhwyso *vb* unfit, disqualify
anghymhwyster *nm* incapacity,
disqualification
anghymodlon *adj* implacable
anghymwys *adj* unfit, unsuitable
anghynefin *adj* unfamiliar
anghynefindra *nm* unfamiliarity
anghynnes *adj* odious, loathsome
anghysbell *adj* out-of-the-way;
remote
anghyson *adj* inconsistent
anghysondeb, -der (-au) *nm*
inconsistency
anghysur (-on) *nm* discomfort
anghysuro *vb* discomfort
anghysurus *adj* uncomfortable
anghytbwys *adj* unbalanced,
lopsided
anghytgord (-iau) *nm* discord,
dissension
anghytûn *adj* not agreeing,
discordant
anghytundeb *nm* disagreement
anghytuno *vb* disagree
anghywair *adj* ill-equipped;
discordant ♦ *nm* disrepair
anghyweithas *adj* froward, uncivil
anghywir *adj* incorrect,
inaccurate, false
anghywirdeb (-au) *nm*
inaccuracy, falseness
anghywrain *adj* unskilful; slovenly
angladd (-au) *nm/f* burial, funeral

angladdol *adj* funereal

angof *nm* forgetfulness, oblivion

angor (-au, -ion) *nm* anchor

angorfa (-oedd, -feydd) *nf* anchorage

angori *vb* anchor

angylaidd *adj* angelic

angyles (-au) *nf* female angel

ai *adv* is it? what? **a. e?** is it so?

ai *conj* or; either; if

aidd *nm* zeal, ardour, zest

Aifft: yr A. *nf* Egypt

aig, eigiau *nf* host, shoal

aig *nf* (late corrupt form) sea, ocean

ail *adj* second † *adv* a second time, again

ailadrodd *vb* repeat

ailadroddiad (-au) *nm* repetition

ailenedigaeth *nf* rebirth

aileni *vb* bear again, regenerate

Ailfedyddiwr (-wyr) *nm* Anabaptist

ail-law *adj* second-hand

aillt *nm* vassal, villain, slave

ais *npl* (eisen *nf*) laths; ribs

alaeth *nm* wailing, lamentation, grief

alaethu *vb* lament

alaethus *adj* mournful, lamentable

alarch (-od, elyrch) *nm* swan

alaru *vb* surfeit; loathe

alaw (-on) *nf* lily; air, melody, tune

Alban: yr A. *nf* Scotland

Albanwr (-wyr) *nm* Scot

alcali (-iau) *nf* alkali

alcam *nm* tin

alcohol *nm* alcohol

alch (-au, eilch) *nf* grate, grill

ale (-au, -on) *nf* aisle; gangway; alley

algebra *nm* algebra

Algeria *nf* Algeria

Almaen: yr A. *nf* Germany

Almaeneg *nf* German

Almaenwr (-wyr) *nm* German

almon *nm* almond

aloi (aloeon) *nm* alloy

Alpau: yr A. *npl* the Alps

allan *adv* out

allanol *adj* outward, external

allblyg *adj* extrovert

allforio *vb* export

allfro *nm* foreigner; foreign land

allfudwr (-wyr) *nm* emigrant

allgarwch *nm* altruism

allor (-au) *nf* altar

allt (elltydd) *nf* hill; cliff; wood

alltud (-ion) *nm* alien; exile

alltudiaeth *nf* banishment, exile

alltudio *vb* banish, exile

allwedd (-au, -i) *nf* key, clef (music)

am *prep* round, about; for; at; on † *conj* for, because; so long as

am see **ym**

amaeth *nm* husbandman; agriculture

amaethdy (-dai) *nm* farm-house

amaethu *vb* farm, till

amaethwr (-wyr) *nm* farmer

amaethwraig *nf* farm-wife

amaethyddiaeth *nf* agriculture

amaethyddol *adj* agricultural

amarch *nm* disrespect, dishonour

amau *vb* doubt, suspect † (-heuon) *nm* doubt

ambell *adj* occasional. **a. waith** sometimes

amcan (-ion) *nm* purpose, aim; guess. **ar a.** at random, approximately, at a guess

amcangyfrif *vb* estimate † (-on) *nm* estimate

amcanu *vb* purpose; aim; guess

amdo (-oeau) *nm* shroud, winding-sheet

amdoi *vb* shroud, enshroud

amdorch (-dyrch) *nf* chaplet, wreath

amddifad *adj* destitute, orphan

amddifadrwydd *nm* destitution, privation

amddifadu vb bereave, deprive

amddifaty (-tai) nm orphanage

amddifedi nm destitution, privation

amddiffyn vb defend, protect, shield ♦ (-ion) nm defence

amddiffynfa (-feydd) nf fortress

amddiffyniad nm protection, defence

amddiffynnwr (-ynwyr), -ynnydd (-ynyddion) nm defender, protector

amddyfrwys adj mighty, rugged; marshy

America Ladin nf Latin America

Amerig: yr A. nf America

amfesur (-au) nm perimeter

amgáu vb enclose, shut in

amgen adj, adv other, else, otherwise; different. **nid a.** that is to say, namely

amgenach adj, adv otherwise; better

amgueddfa (-feydd) nf museum

amgyffred vb comprehend, comprise ♦ (-ion) nm comprehension

amgyffrediad nm comprehension

amgylch (-oedd) nm circuit; environs, surroundings. **o** (oddi) **amgylch** round about, about

amgylchedd nm circumference; environment

amgylchfyd nm environment

amgylchiad (-au) nm circumstance; occasion

amgylchiadol adj circumstantial

amgylchu vb surround

amgylchynol adj surrounding

amgylchynu vb surround

amharchu vb dishonour, disrespect

amharchus adj disrespectful, disreputable

amhariad nm impairment, damage

amharod adj unprepared, unready

amharodrwydd nm unreadiness

amharu vb impair, harm, injure, damage

amhendant adj indefinite, vague

amhenderfynol adj irresolute

amhenodol adj indefinite

amherchi vb dishonour, insult

amherffaith adj imperfect

amherffeithrwydd nm imperfection

amhersonol adj impersonal

amherth(yn)asol adj irrelevant

amheuaeth nf doubt, scepticism

amheugar adj suspicious; sceptical

amheuol adj doubting, doubtful

amheus adj doubting, doubtful, dubious

amheuthun adj dainty, savoury ♦ (-ion) nm dainty, delicacy, treat

amheuwr (-wyr) nm doubter, sceptic

amhlantadwy adj childless, barren

amhleidiol, amhleitgar adj impartial

amhoblog adj sparsely populated

amhoblogaidd adj unpopular

amhosibl adj impossible

amhriodol adj improper

amhrisiadwy adj priceless

amhrofiadol adj inexperienced

amhrydlon adj unpunctual

amhûr adj impure, foul

amhwrpasol adj irrelevant

amhwyllo vb lose one's senses, go mad

aml adj frequent, abundant ♦ adv often

amlder, amldra nm abundance

amldduwiad (-iaid) nm polytheist

amldduwiaeth nf polytheism

amleiriog adj wordy, verbose, prolix

amlen (-ni) nf envelope, wrapper

amlhad nm increasing, increase

amlhau vb increase, multiply

amlinelliad (-au) nm outline

aml-lawr adj multi-storey

amlochrog adj many-sided
amlosgfa nf crematorium
amlosgi vb cremate
amlwg adj plain, clear, manifest, evident, prominent
amlwreigiaeth nf polygamy
amlwreigiwr (-wyr) nm polygamist
amlygiad (-au) nm manifestation
amlygrwydd nm prominence, limelight
amlygu vb manifest, reveal, evince
amnaid (-neidiau) nf beck, nod
amneidio vb beckon, nod
amnest (-au) nm amnesty
amod (-au) nm/f condition
amodi vb covenant, stipulate
amodol adj conditional
amrant (-au, -rannau) nm eyelid
amrantiad nm wink, twinkling, second
amreiniol adj unprivileged
amrwd adj uncooked, raw, crude
amryddawn adj versatile
amryfal adj sundry, manifold
amryfus adj erroneous, inadvertent
amryfusedd (-au) nm error, oversight
amryliw adj variegated; multicoloured
amryw adj several, sundry, various
amrywiad (-au) nm variant
amrywiaeth nm variety, diversity
amrywio vb vary, differ
amrywiol adj sundry
amser (-oedd, -au) nm/f time
amseriad (-au) nm timing, dating, date
amserlen (-ni) nf time-table
amserol adj timely; temporal
amseru vb time, date
amserydd (-ion) nm chronologist
amseryddiaeth nf chronology
amseryddol adj chronological
amwisg (-oedd) nf covering, shroud

amwisgo vb enwrap, shroud
amwys adj ambiguous
amwysedd nm ambiguity
amyn conj, prep unless, except, but
amynedd nm patience
amyneddgar adj patient
an- prefix un-, in-, de-, dis-
anabl adj disabled
anabledd nm disability
anad adj: **yn a.** above all, more than
anadferadwy adj irreparable
anadl (-au, -on) nm/m breath
anadliad nm breath, breathing
anadlu vb breathe
anadnabyddus adj unknown
anaddas adj unfit, unsuitable
anaddasu vb unfit, disqualify
anaeddfed, anaddfed adj unripe, immature
anaeddfedrwydd nm unripeness, immaturity
anaele adj awful, direful; incurable
anaesthetig adj anaesthetic
anaf (-au) nm blemish, defect; wound
anafu vb blemish, maim, hurt
anafus adj maimed, disabled
anair (-eiriau) nm ill report, slander
anallu nm inability
analluog adj unable
analluogi vb disenable; disable
anaml adj infrequent, rare ♦ adv rarely, seldom
anamlwg adj obscure, inconspicuous
anamserol adj untimely, mistimed
anap (-hapon) nm/f mischance, mishap
anarchiaeth nm anarchy
anarchydd (-ion) nm anarchist
anarferol adj unusual, extraordinary
anarfog adj unarmed

anchwiliadwy adj unsearchable

ancr nm/f anchorite, anchoress

ancwyn (-ion) nm dinner, supper; delicacy

andras nm curse; devil, deuce

andwyo vb spoil, ruin, undo

andwyol adj harmful, ruinous

anedifeiriol adj impenitent

aneddfa see **anheddfa**

aneffeithiol adj ineffectual

aneglur adj indistinct; illegible

aneirif adj innumerable

anelu vb bend, aim

anenwog adj unrenowned, ignoble, mean

anerchiad (-au) nm salutation, address

anesboniadwy adj inexplicable

anesgusodol adj inexcusable

anesmwyth adj uneasy, restless

anesmwythder, -dra nm uneasiness, unrest

anesmwytho vb be or make uneasy

anesmwythyd nm uneasiness, disquiet

anewyllysgar adj unwilling

anfad adj wicked, nefarious

anfadrwydd nm wickedness, villainy

anfadwaith nm villainy; crime

anfadwr (-wyr) nm villain, scoundrel

anfaddeugar adj unforgiving

anfaddeuol adj unpardonable

anfantais (-teision) nf disadvantage

anfanteisiol adj disadvantageous

anfarwol adj undying, immortal

anfarwoldeb nm immortality

anfedrus adj unskilful

anfedrusrwydd nm unskilfulness

anfeidrol adj infinite

anfeidroldeb nm infinity

anferth adj huge, monstrous

anferthedd nm hugeness, monstrosity

anfodlon adj unwilling

anfodloni vb discontent, dissatisfy

anfodlonrwydd nm discontent

anfodd nm unwillingness, displeasure

anfoddio vb displease, disoblige

anfoddlon etc see **anfodlon**

anfoddog adj discontented, dissatisfied

anfoddogrwydd nm discontentment

anfoesgar adj unmannerly, rude

anfoesgarwch nm rudeness, incivility

anfoesol adj immoral

anfoesoldeb nm immorality

anfon vb send, transmit, dispatch

anfoneddigaidd adj ungentlemanly

anfonheddig adj ignoble, discourteous

anfoniad nm sending, transmission

anfri nm disrespect, dishonour

anfucheddol adj immoral

anfuddiol adj unprofitable

anfwriadol adj unintentional

anfwyn adj unkind, ungentle, uncivil

anfynych adj infrequent, seldom, rare

anffaeledig adj infallible

anffaeledigrwydd nm infallibility

anffafriol adj unfavourable

anffawd (-ffodion) nf misfortune

anffodus, anffortunus adj unfortunate

anffrwythlon adj unfruitful, barren

anffurfio vb disfigure, deform

anffurfiol adj informal

anffyddiaeth nf atheism

anffyddiwr (-wyr) nm infidel, atheist

anffyddlon adj unfaithful

anhaeddiannol adj unmerited, undeserved

anhaeddiant nm demerit, unworthiness

anhapus adj unhappy, unlucky

anhardd adj unhandsome, unseemly, ugly

anhawdd adj hard, difficult

anhawddgar adj unamiable, unlovely

anhawster (anawsterau) nm difficulty

anheddfa (aneddfaoedd) nf, -le (aneddleoedd) nm/f dwelling-place

anhepgor (-ion) nm essential

anhepgorol adj indispensable

anhoffter nm hatred, dislike

anhraethadwy adj unutterable

anhraethol adj unspeakable, ineffable

anhrefn nm disorder, confusion

anhrefnu vb disorder, disarrange

anhrefnus adj disorderly, untidy

anhreiddiol adj impervious, impenetrable

anhreuliedig adj undigested; unspent

anhrugarog adj unmerciful, merciless

anhuddo vb cover (a fire)

anhunedd nm wakefulness, disquiet

anhwyldeb nm disorder, complaint, illness

anhwylustod nm inconvenience

anhyblyg adj inflexible, stiff, rigid

anhydawdd adj insoluble

anhyder nm distrust, diffidence

anhyderus adj diffident

anhydrin adj unmanageable

anhydyn adj intractable, obstinate

anhyddysg adj unversed, ignorant

anhyfryd adj unpleasant

anhyfrydwch nm unpleasantness

anhygar adj unpleasant, unamiable

anhygoel adj incredible

anhygyrch adj inaccessible

anhylaw adj unhandy, unwieldy

anhynod adj indistinctive; uncertain

anhysbys adj unknown; unversed

anhywaith adj intractable, refractory

anial adj desert, wild ♦ nm wilderness

anialwch nm wilderness

anian (-au) nf nature, instinct, genius

anianawd nm temperament, disposition

anianol adj natural

anianyddol adj physical

anifail (-feiliaid) nm animal, beast

anifeilaidd adj beastly, brutish

anifeileiddio vb animalize, brutalize

anlwc nm bad luck, misfortune

anlwcus adj unlucky

anllad adj wanton, lascivious, lewd

anlladrwydd nm wantonness, lewdness

anlladu vb wanton

anllygredig adj incorrupt, incorruptible

anllygredigaeth nf incorruption

anllythrennog adj illiterate

anllywodraeth nf misrule, anarchy

annaearol adj unearthly, weird

annatodol adj indissoluble, that cannot be undone

annaturiol adj unnatural

annealladwy adj unintelligible

anneallus adj unintelligent

annedwydd adj unhappy, miserable

annedwyddwch nm unhappiness

annedd (anheddau) nf dwelling

anneddfol adj lawless

annefnyddiol adj useless; immaterial

annel (anelau) nm/f trap; purpose, aim

annelwig adj shapeless, unformed; vague

anner (aneirod, -i, -au) nf heifer

annerbyniol adj unacceptable

annerch vb salute, greet, address ♦ (anerchion) nm salutation,

greeting
annewisol adj ineligible, undesirable, unwelcome
annhebyg adj unlike, dissimilar
annhebygol adj unlikely, improbable
annhebygolrwydd nm improbability
annhebygrwydd nm unlikeness, unlikelihood
annheg adj unfair
annhegwch nm unfairness
annheilwng adj unworthy
annheilyngdod nm unworthiness
annherfynol adj endless; infinitive, infinite
annhirion adj ungentle, cruel
annhosturiol adj pitiless, ruthless
annhuedd nf disinclination
annhueddol adj disinclined, indisposed
anniben adj untidy, slovenly
annibendod nm untidiness
annibyniaeth nf independence
annibynnol adj independent
Annibynnwr (-ynwyr) nm Independent
annichellgar adj guileless, simple
annichon, -adwy adj impossible
anniddan adj comfortless, miserable
anniddig adj peevish, irritable, fretful
anniddigrwydd nm peevishness
anniddos adj leaky, comfortless
annifeiriol adj innumerable, countless
anniflanedig adj unfading, imperishable
annifyr adj miserable, wretched
annifyrrwch nm misery
anniffoddadwy adj unquenchable
annigonedd nm insufficiency
annigonol adj insufficient, inadequate
annigonolrwydd nm inadequacy
annileadwy adj indelible,

ineffaceable
annilys adj unauthentic, spurious, insincere
annillyn adj inelegant, clumsy
annioddefol adj unbearable, intolerable
anniogel adj unsafe, insecure
anniolchgar adj unthankful, ungrateful
anniolchgarwch nm ingratitude
annirnadwy adj incomprehensible
annisgrifiadwy adj indescribable
annisgwyliadwy adj unexpected
anniwair adj unchaste, incontinent, lewd
anniwall adj insatiable
anniweirdeb nm unchastity, incontinence
anniwylliedig adj uncultured
annoeth adj unwise, imprudent
annoethineb nm unwisdom, folly
annog vb incite, urge; exhort
annormal adj abnormal
annos vb incite, set (a dog) on
annosbarthus adj unruly, disorderly
annuw, -iad (-iaid) nm atheist
annuwiaeth nf atheism
annuwiol adj ungodly, godless
annuwioldeb nm ungodliness
annwn, annwfn nm the underworld; hell
annwyd (anwydau, -on) nm cold
annwyl adj dear, beloved
annyledus adj undue, wrongful
annymunol adj unpleasant, disagreeable
annynol adj inhuman, cruel
annysgedig adj unlearned
anobaith nm despair
anobeithio vb despair
anobeithiol adj hopeless
anochel, -adwy adj unavoidable, inevitable
anodd adj hard, difficult
anoddefgar adj impatient, intolerant

anogaeth (-au) *nf* exhortation
anolrheinadwy *adj* untraceable
anolygus *adj* unsightly
anonest *adj* dishonest
anonestrwydd *nm* dishonesty
anorchfygol *adj* irresistible;
  unconquerable
anorfod *adj* insuperable;
  unavoidable
anorffen *adj* endless, unending
anorffenedig *adj* incomplete,
  unfinished
anorthrech *adj* invincible
anrasol *adj* graceless
anrhaith (-rheithiau) *nf* prey, spoil,
  booty
anrheg (-ion) *nf* present, gift
anrhegu *vb* present, give
anrheithio *vb* prey, spoil, plunder
anrheithiwr (-wyr) *nm* spoiler,
  pillager
anrhydedd (-au) *nm* honour
anrhydeddu *vb* honour
anrhydeddus *adj* honourable
anrhydeddwr (-wyr) *nm* honourer
ansad *adj* unsteady, unstable
ansadrwydd *nm* instability
ansafadwy *adj* unstable; fickle
ansathredig *adj* untrodden,
  unfrequented
ansawdd (-soddau) *nm/f* quality,
  state
ansefydlog *adj* unsettled,
  unstable; fickle
ansefydlogi *vb* unsettle
ansicr *adj* uncertain, doubtful
ansicrwydd *nm* uncertainty, doubt
ansoddair (-eiriau) *nm* adjective
ansoddeiriol *adj* adjectival
ansyber *adj* untidy, slovenly
Antartica *nf* the Antarctic
anterliwt (-iau) *nm/f* interlude
anterth *nm* meridian, zenith,
  prime
antur (-iau) *nm* attempt, venture;
  adventure; enterprise. **ar a.** at
  random

anturiaeth (-au) *nf* adventure,
  enterprise
anturiaethus *adj* adventurous,
  enterprising
anturiaethwr (-wyr) *nm*
  adventurer
anturio *vb* venture, adventure
anturus *adj* adventurous
anthem (-au) *nf* anthem
anudon (-au) *nm* false oath,
  perjury
anudoniaeth *nf* perjury
anudonwr (-wyr) *nm* perjurer
anufudd *adj* disobedient
anufudd-dod *nm* disobedience
anufuddhau *vb* disobey
anundeb *nm* disunion
anunion *adj* crooked; unjust
anuniondeb *nm* injustice, iniquity
anurddo *vb* spoil, mar, disfigure
anwadal *adj* unstable, fickle,
  changeable
anwadalu *vb* waver, vacillate
anwadalwch *nm* fickleness
anwar *adj* wild, barbarous, savage
anwaraidd *adj* uncivilized,
  barbarous
anwarddyn (-wariaid) *nm*
  barbarian, savage
anwareidd-dra *nm* barbarity
anwastad *adj* uneven, unstable,
  fickle
anwe (-oedd) *nf* woof
anwedd *nm* vapour, steam
anweddaidd *adj* unseemly,
  indecent
anweddus *adj* improper, indecent
anweledig *adj* unseen, invisible
anwes *nm* indulgence; caress
anwesog *adj* pampered,
  affectionate
anwesu *vb* fondle, caress, pamper,
  indulge
anwir *adj* untrue, lying, false;
  wicked
anwiredd (-au) *nm* untruth;
  iniquity

anwireddu vb falsify

anwireddus adj untruthful, false, lying

anwr (-wyr) nm wretch, coward

anwybod nm ignorance

anwybodaeth nf ignorance

anwybodus adj ignorant

anwybyddu vb ignore

anwydog adj cold, chilly; having a cold

anwydwst nf influenza

anwyldeb nm belovedness, dearness

anwyliaid npl beloved ones, favourites

anwylo vb cherish, fondle, caress

anwylyd (-iaid) nm beloved

anwylyn nm favourite

anwythiad nm induction

anwytho vb induce

anwythol adj inductive

anymarferol adj impractical, impracticable

anymddiried vb, nm mistrust, distrust

anymwybodol adj unconscious

anymwybyddiaeth nf unconsciousness

anynad adj peevish, petulant; brawling

anysgrifenedig adj unwritten

anysgrythurol adj unscriptural

anystwyth adj stiff, rigid

anystwytho vb stiffen

anystyriaeth nf heedlessness, rashness

anystyriol adj heedless, reckless, rash

anystywallt, -ell adj unmanageable

apêl (apelion) nm/f, **apeliad** (-au) nm appeal

apelio vb appeal

apostol (-ion) nm apostle

apostolaidd, -ig adj apostolic

apostoliaeth nf apostleship

apwyntiad (-au) nm appointment

apwyntio vb appoint

âr nm ploughed land, tilth; ground

ar prep on, upon, over

arab adj facetious, merry, pleasant

arabedd nm facetiousness, wit

arabus adj witty

aradr (erydr) nm plough

araf adj slow, soft, gentle, still

arafu vb slow; quiet; moderate

arafwch nm slowness; moderation

arail vb guard, care for, foster ♦ adj attending, careful

araith (areithiau) nf speech

arall (eraill) adj, pron another, other; else

aralleg (-au) nm allegory

aralleiriad (-au) nm paraphrase

aralleirio vb paraphrase

araul adj sunny, sunlit; serene

arawd nf speech, oration

arbed vb spare, save

arbediad (-au) nm save, salvage

arbedol adj sparing, saving

arbenigaeth nf expertise; specialisation

arbenigo vb specialise

arbenigrwydd nm speciality, prominence

arbenigwr (-wyr) nm specialist

arbennig adj special

arbrawf (arbrofion) nm experiment

arbrofi vb experiment

arbrofol adj experimental

arch (eirchion) nf request, petition; bidding

arch (eirch) nf ark, coffin; trunk, waist

archaeoleg nf archaeology

archangel (-ylion) nm archangel

archddiacon (-iaid) nm archdeacon

archeb (-ion) nf order

archebu vb order

archen nf, **-ad** nm shoe; clothing

archesgob (-ion) nm archbishop

archesgobaeth (-au) nf archbishopric

archfarchnad (-oedd) nf

supermarket
archiad *nm* bidding
archif (**-au**) *nm* archive
archifdy (**-dai**) *nm* record office
archifydd (**-ion**) *nm* archivist
archoffeiriad (**-iaid**) *nm* high priest
archoll (**-ion**) *nf* wound
archolli *vb* wound
archwaeth *nm* taste, appetite
archwaethu *vb* taste, savour
archwilio *vb* examine, audit;
explore
archwiliwr (**-wyr**) *nm* examiner,
auditor; explorer
ardal (**-oedd**) *nf* region, district
ardalydd (**-ion**) *nm* marquis
ardreth (**-i**) *nf* rent
ardrethu *vb* rent
ardystiad (**-au**) *nm* pledge,
attestation
ardystio *vb* pledge, attest
arddangos *vb* show, exhibit,
indicate
arddangosfa (**-feydd**) *nf* show,
exhibition
arddegol *adj* teenage
arddel *vb* avow, own
arddeliad *nm* claim, avowal;
unction
ardderchog *adj* excellent, noble,
splendid
ardderchowgrwydd *nm*
excellency
arddodi *vb* prefix; impose
arddodiad (**-iaid**) *nm* preposition
arddu *vb* plough (*properly* **aredig**)
arddull (**-iau**) *nf* style
arddulleg *nf* stylistics
ardduniant *nm* sublimity
arddunol *adj* sublime
arddwr (**-wyr**) *nm* ploughman
arddwrn (**-ddyrnau**) *nm* wrist
arddywediad (**-au**) *nm* dictation
aredig *vb* plough
areitheg *nf* rhetoric
areithio *vb* speak, make a speech
areithiwr (**-wyr**) *nm* speaker,

orator
areithyddiaeth *nf* oratory;
elocution
arel *nm* laurel
aren (**-nau**) *nf* kidney; (*pl.*) reins
arestio *vb* arrest
arf (**-au**) *nm/f* weapon, (*pl.*) arms;
tool
arfaeth (**-au**) *nf* purpose; decree
arfaethu *vb* purpose, intend
arfbais (**-beisiau**) *nf* coat of arms
arfdy (**-dai**) *nm* armoury
arfer *vb* use, accustom ◆ (**-ion**)
nf/m use, custom, habit
arferiad *nm/f* use, custom, habit
arferol *adj* usual, customary
arfod *nf* stroke of a weapon, fight;
armour; opportunity
arfog *adj* armed
arfogaeth *nf* armour
arfogi *vb* arm
arfoll (**-au**) *nm* pledge, oath
arfordir (**-oedd**) *nm* coast
arforol *adj* maritime
arffed (**-au**) *nf* lap
argae (**-au**) *nm* dam,
embankment; enclosed place
argeisio *vb* seek
argel *nm/f* concealment, refuge ◆
adj hidden, occult
arglwydd (**-i**) *nm* lord
arglwyddaidd *adj* lordly
arglwyddes (**-au**) *nf* lady
arglwyddiaeth (**-au**) *nf* lordship,
dominion
arglwyddiaethu *vb* have dominion
argoed (**-ydd**) *nm* enclosure of
trees
argoel (**-ion**) *nf* sign, token, omen
argoeli *vb* betoken, portend, augur
argoelus *adj* ominous
argraff (**-ion, -au**) *nf* print,
impression
argraffdy (**-dai**) *nm* printing-house
argraffiad (**-au**) *nm* impression;
edition
argraffu *vb* print, impress

argraffwaith *nm* print, typography

argraffwasg *nf* printing-press

argraffwr (-wyr), -ydd (-ion) *nm* printer

argrwm, -wn *adj* convex

argyfwng (-yngau, -yngoedd) *nm* crisis

argyhoeddi *vb* reprove; convince, convict

argyhoeddiad (-au) *nm* conviction

argyhoeddiadol *adj* convincing

argymell *vb* urge, recommend

argymhelliad *nm* recommendation

arholi *vb* examine

arholiad (-au) *nm* examination

arholwr (-wyr) *nm* examiner

arhosfa *nf* abode; stopping-place (*bus*)

arhosiad *nm* staying, stay

arhosol *adj* abiding, permanent

arial *nm/f* vigour, mettle

arian *nm* silver ♦ *coll n* money, cash. **a. breiniol** currency. **a. byw** mercury. **a. gleision** silver. **a. parod** cash. **a. pen** exact money. **a. treigl** current money

ariandy (-dai) *nm* bank

ariangar *adj* fond of money, avaricious

ariangarwch *nm* love of money, avarice

ariannaid *adj* silver, silvern

ariannaidd *adj* silvery

arianneg *nm/f* finance

Ariannin *nf* Argentina

ariannog *adj* moneyed, wealthy, rich

ariannol *adj* financial, monetary

ariannu *vb* silver; finance/fund

ariannydd (ariannyddion) *nm* banker, investor, financier

arlais (-leisiau) *nf* temple

arloesi *vb* clear, prepare the way, pioneer

arloesydd (-wyr) *nm* pioneer

arluniaeth *nf* portraiture, painting

arlunio *vb* draw, paint, portray

arlunydd (-wyr) *nm* artist

arlwy (-au, -on) *nm/f* provision, feast, menu

arlwyaeth (-au) *nf* catering

arlwyo *vb* prepare, provide; cook

arlywydd (-ion) *nm* president

arlywyddiaeth *nf* presidency

arlywyddol *adj* presidential

arlliw (-iau) *nm* varnish, tint, shade, trace

arlliwio *vb* colour, tint, paint

arllwys *vb* pour out, empty

arllwysfa *nf* outfall, outlet, vent

armel *nm* second milk

armes *nf* prophecy; calamity

arobryn *adj* worthy, prize-winning

arofun *vb* intend, purpose

arogl (-au), **aroglau** (-euon) *nm* scent, smell

arogl-darth *nm* incense

arogldarthu *vb* burn incense

arogli, arogleuo *vb* scent; smell

arogliad *nm* smelling, sense of smell

arolwg *nm* survey

arolygiaeth *nf* superintendency

arolygu *vb* superintend

arolygwr (-wyr), -ydd (-ion) *nm* superintendent, inspector

aros *vb* wait, await, stay, stop, tarry, abide, remain

arswyd *nm* dread, terror, horror

arswydo *vb* dread; shudder

arswydus *adj* fearful, terrible, dreadful

arsyllfa (-feydd) *nf* observatory

arsylwi *vb* observe

artaith (-teithiau) *nf* torture, torment, pang

arteithio *vb* torture, rack

arteithiol *adj* racking, excruciating

arth (eirth) *nm/f* bear

arthes (-au) *nf* she-bear

arthio, -u *vb* bark, growl

Artig: yr A. *nf* the Arctic

artistig *adj* artistic

aruchel *adj* lofty, sublime

arucheledd nm loftiness, sublimity

aruthr adj marvellous, strange

aruthredd nm amazement, horror

aruthrol adj huge, prodigious

arwahanrwydd nm uniqueness, individuality

arwain vb conduct, lead, guide, carry

arwedd (-au, -ion) nf bearing, aspect

arweddu vb bear

arweddwr (-wyr) nm bearer

arweiniad nm guidance; introduction

arweiniol adj leading, introductory

arweinydd (-ion) nm guide, leader; conductor

arweinyddiaeth nf leadership

arwerthiant (-iannau) nm auction

arwerthu vb sell by auction

arwerthwr (-wyr) nm auctioneer

arwisgiad nm investiture

arwisgo vb enrobe, array, invest

arwr (-wyr) nm hero

arwraidd adj heroic, epic

arwres (-au) nf heroine

arwrgerdd (-i) nf epic poem

arwriaeth nf heroism

arwrol adj heroic, gallant

arwybod nm awareness

arwydd (-ion) nm/f sign, signal; ensign

arwyddair (-eiriau) nm motto

arwyddlun (-iau) nm emblem, symbol

arwyddluniol adj emblematic, symbolic

arwyddnod (-au) nm mark, token

arwyddo vb sign; signify

arwyddocâd nm signification, significance

arwyddocaol adj significant

arwyddocáu vb signify, denote

arwyl (-ion) nf funeral, funeral rites

arwylo vb mourn over the dead

arwynebedd nm surface, superficies

arwynebol adj superficial

arwyrain nm/f praise, panegyric ♦ vb rise, extol

arwystlo vb pledge, mortgage

arysgrif (-au), **-en** (-nau) nf inscription, epigraph

asb (-iaid) nf asp

asbri nm animation, vivacity, spirits

asen (-nau) nf rib

asen (-nod) nf she-ass

asesu vb assess

aseth nf stake, spar, lath

asgell (esgyll) nf wing, fin. **a. fraith** chaffinch

asgellog adj winged

asgellwr (-wyr) nm wing, outside-forward

asglod, asglodion npl (**asglodyn** nm) chips

asgre nf bosom, heart

asgwrn (esgyrn) nm bone

asiad (-au) nm joint, weld

asiant (-au) nm agent

asio vb join, weld; solder; cement

astell (estyll, ystyllod) nf plank, shelf

astroleg nf astrology

astrus adj abstruse, difficult

astud adj attentive

astudiaeth (-au) nf study

astudio vb study

astudrwydd nm attentiveness

aswy adj left

asyn (-nod) nm he-ass

asynnaidd adj asinine

at prep to, towards; for; at; by

atafaeliad nm confiscation, distraint

atafaelu vb distrain, confiscate

atal vb stop, hinder, withhold ♦ (-ion) nm hindrance, impediment. **a. dwedd** stammering

ataleb (-au) nf injunction

atalfa (-feydd) nf check; stoppage

ataliad nm stoppage

ataliol adj preventive
atalnod (-au) nf stop, point
atalnodi vb point, punctuate
atblygol adj reflexive
ateb vb answer, reply ♦ (-ion) nm answer
atebol adj answerable, responsible
ateg (-ion) nf prop, stay, support
ategiad (-au) nm affirmation
ategol adj confirming; auxiliary
ategu vb support
atgas adj odious, hateful
atgasedd nm hatred
atgasrwydd nm odiousness, hatefulness
atgenhedliad nm regeneration
atgenhedlu vb regenerate
atgno (-oeau, -oeon) nm remorse
atgof (-ion) nm remembrance, reminiscence
atgofio vb recollect, remember, remind
atgofus adj reminiscent
atgoffa vb recall, remind
atgyfnerthion npl reinforcements
atgyfnerthu vb reinforce
atgyfodi vb rise, raise again
atgyfodiad nm resurrection
atgynhyrchu vb reproduce
atgyweiriad (-au) nm repair
atgyweirio vb repair, mend
atgyweiriwr (-wyr) nm repairer, mender
Athen nf Athens
atig (-au) nm/f attic
atodi vb add, append, affix
atodiad (-au) nm addition, appendix
atodlen (-ni) nf supplement; schedule
atodol adj supplementary
atolwg, atolygu vb pray, beseech
atom (-au) nm atom
atomfa (-feydd) nf nuclear power station
atomig adj atomic
atsain (-seiniau) nf echo

atseinio vb resound, echo
atwf (atyfion) nm second growth
atyniad (-au) nm attraction
atyniadol adj attractive
atynnu vb attract
athletau npl athletics
athrawes (-au) nf teacher, governess
athrawiaeth (-au) nf doctrine
athrawiaethol adj doctrinal
athrist adj very sad, pensive, sorrowful
athro (-athrawon) nm teacher, master
athrod (-ion) nm slander, libel
athrodwr (-wyr) nm slanderer, libeller
athrofa (-feydd) nf college, academy, institute
athrofaol adj academic
athroniaeth nf philosophy
athronydd (-ion, -wyr) nm philosopher
athronyddol adj philosophical
athronyddu vb philosophize
athrylith (-oedd) nf genius
athrylithgar adj of genius, talented
athrywyn nm mediation, intervention ♦ vb mediate, arbitrate
aur nm gold
awch nm edge; ardour, zest; relish, appetite
awchlym adj sharp, keen, acute
awchlymu vb sharpen, whet
awchus adj sharp, keen; eager; greedy
awdl (-au, odlau) nf ode
awdur (-on, -iaid) nm author
awdurdod (-au) nm/f authority
awdurdodedig adj authorised
awdurdodi vb authorize
awdurdodol adj authoritative
awdures (-au) nf authoress
awduriaeth nf authorship
awel (-on) nf breeze, wind
awelog adj breezy, windy

awen (-au) *nf* muse
awen (-au) *nf* rein
awenydd (-ion) *nm* poet
awenyddiaeth *nf* poetry, poesy
awenyddol *adj* poetical
awenyddu *vb* poetize
awgrym (-au, -iadau) *nm* hint, suggestion
awgrymiadol *adj* suggestive
awgrymog *adj* suggestive
awgrymu *vb* hint, suggest
awr (oriau) *nf* hour
Awst *nm* August
Awstralia *nf* Australia
Awstria *nf* Austria
awtistig *adj* autistic
awydd (-au) *nm* desire, eagerness
awyddfryd *nm* vehement desire, zeal
awyddu *vb* desire
awyddus *adj* desirous, eager, zealous
awyr *nf* air, sky
awyrdrom (-au) *nf* aerodrome
awyren (-nau, -ni) *nf* balloon, aeroplane
awyrendy (-dai) *nm* hangar
awyrgylch (-au, -oedd) *nm/f* atmosphere
awyriad *nm* ventilation
awyrlong (-au) *nf* airship
awyro, -u *vb* air, ventilate

B

baban (-od) *adj* baby
babanaidd *adj* babyish
babandod *nm* babyhood, infancy
babi *nm/f* baby
bacas (bacs(i)au) *nf* footless stocking; hair on horse's fetlocks
baco *nm* tobacco
bacwn *nm* bacon
bach (-au) *nm* hook. **bachau petryal** square brackets
bach *adj* little, small

bachell (-au, -ion) *nf* nook, corner; snare
bachgen (bechgyn) *nm* boy
bachgendod *nm* boyhood
bachgennaidd *adj* boyish
bachgennyn (bechgynnos) *nm* little boy
bachigyn (bachigion) *nm* little bit, diminutive
bachog *adj* hooked
bachu *vb* hook, grapple
bachwr (-wyr) *nm* hooker (*rugby*)
bad (-au) *nm* boat. **b. achub** lifeboat
badwr (-wyr) *nm* boatman
badd (-au), **baddon** (-au) *nm* bath
bae (-au) *nm* bay
baedd (-od) *nm* boar
baeddu *vb* beat, buffet; soil
baetio *vb* bait, maltreat
bag (-iau) *nm* bag
bagad (-au) *nm* cluster; troop, multitude
bagl (-au) *nf* crook; crutch; leg
baglor (-ion) *nm* bachelor
bagloriaeth *nf* bachelorship
baglu *vb* entangle, ensnare, trip
bai (beiau) *nm* fault, vice; defect; blame
baich (beichiau) *nm* burden, load
bais *nm* bottom, ford; walking
bala *nm* efflux of river from lake
balch *adj* proud; glad
balchder *nm* pride
balchdra *nm* joy, gladness
balchio *vb* pride
baldordd *nm* babble, balderdash
baldorddi *vb* babble
bale *nm* ballet
baled (-i) *nf* ballad
baledwr (-wyr) *nm* ballad-monger
balm *nm* balm
balmaidd *adj* balmy
balog (-au, -ion) *nf* fly, cod-piece; flap
balleg *nf* hamper, net, purse
ballegrwyd (-au) *nf* drag-net

ban (-nau) *nm/f* peak; horn; corner; stanza

banadl *npl* (-**badlen** *nf*) broom

banc (-iau) *nm* bank

banc (**bencydd**) *nm* bank, mound, hill

bancaw (-iau) *nm* band, tuft

baner (-au, -i) *nf* banner, flag

banerog *adj* with banners, bannered

banerwr (-wyr) *nm* standard-bearer; ensign

banffagl (-au) *nf* bonfire, blaze

bangaw *adj* eloquent, melodious, skilful

bangor (-au, **bangyr**) *nf/m* upper row of rods in wattle fence; monastery

baniar (-**ieri**) *nm/f* shout; banner

banllawr (-**lloriau**) *nm* platform

banllef (-au) *nf* loud shout

bannod (**banodau**) *nf* article

bannog *adj* elevated, conspicuous; horned

bar (-rau) *nm* bar

bâr *nm* fury, greed

bara *nm* bread

barbaraidd *adj* barbarous

barbareidd-dra *nm* barbarity

barbareiddio *vb* barbarize

barbariad (-**iaid**) *nm* barbarian

barbariaeth *nm* barbarism

barbwr (-**wyr**) *nm* barber

barcer (-**iaid**) *nm* tanner

barclod (-iau) *nm* apron

barcud (-**iaid**), **barcutan** (-od) *nm* kite

bardd (**beirdd**) *nm* bard, poet

barddas *nm/f* bardism

barddol *adj* bardic

barddoni *vb* compose poetry, poetize

barddoniaeth *nf* poetry, verse

barddonol *adj* poetic, poetical

barf (-au) *nf* beard, whiskers

barfog *adj* bearded

bargeinio, bargenna *vb* bargain

bargen (-**einion**) *nf* bargain

bargod (-**ion**) *nm* eaves

bargyfreithiwr (-**wyr**) *nm* barrister

bariaeth *nf/m* evil, grief, wrath; greed

baril (-au) *nf* barrel

barilaid (-**eidiau**) *nf* barrelful

bario *vb* bar, bolt

barlad *nm* drake

barlys *nm* barley

barn (-au) *nf* judgment; opinion; sentence

barnais *nf* varnish

barnedigaeth (-au) *nf* judgment

barneisio *vb* varnish

barnol *adj* judicial, condemnatory, annoying

barnu *vb* judge

barnwr (-**wyr**) *nm* judge

baromedr *nm* barometer

barrug *nm* hoar-frost

barugo *vb* cast hoar-frost

barugog *adj* white with hoar-frost

barus *adj* voracious, greedy

barwn (-**iaid**) *nm* baron

barwnes (-au) *nf* baroness

barwniaeth (-au) *nf* barony

barwnig (-**iaid**) *nm* baronet

bas *adj* shallow ♦ (**bais, beis**) *npl* shallows

bas *adj, nm* bass

basged (-i, -au) *nf* basket

basgedaid (-**eidiau**) *nf* basketful

basgedwr (-**wyr**) *nm* basket-maker

basn (-au, -**ys**) *nm* basin

bastard (-**iaid**) *nm* bastard

bastardiaeth *nf* bastardy

batri *nm* battery

bath (-au) *nm* kind, sort; stamp; coin

bathdy (-**dai**) *nm* mint

bathodyn (-**odau**) *nm* medal, badge

bathol *adj* coin, coined

bathu *vb* coin

baw *nm* dirt, mire, dung, filth

bawaidd *adj* dirty, vile; sordid,

mean
bawd (**bodiau**) *nf* thumb, toe
bechan *adj* f. of **bychan**
bechgynnos *npl* little boys,
youngsters
bedw *npl* (**-en** *nf*) birch
bedydd *nm* baptism
bedyddfa (**-fâu, -feydd**) *nf*
baptistry
bedyddfaen (**-feini**) *nm* font
bedyddio *vb* baptize
bedyddiol *adj* baptismal; baptized
Bedyddiwr (**-wyr**) *nm* Baptist
bedd (**-au**) *nm* grave, tomb,
sepulchre
beddargraff (**-iadau**) *nm* epitaph
beddfaen (**-feini**) *nm* tombstone
beddgell (**-oedd**) *nf* vault,
catacomb
beddrod (**-au**) *nm* tomb, sepulchre
Beibl (**-au**) *nm* Bible
Beiblaidd *adj* Biblical
beichio *vb* burden; low; sob
beichiog *adj* pregnant
beichiogi *vb* conceive
beichus *adj* burdensome,
oppressive
beicio *vb* cycle
beiddgar *adj* daring, audacious
beiddgarwch *nm* daring, audacity
beiddio *vb* dare, presume
beili (**beiliaid**) *nm* bailiff
beio *vb* blame, censure
beirniad (**-iaid**) *nm* adjudicator;
critic
beirniadaeth (**-au**) *nf* adjudication;
criticism
beirniadol *adj* critical
beirniadu *vb* adjudicate; criticize
beisgawn (**-au**) *nf* stack, heap of
corn sheaves
beiston *nf* sea-shore, beach; surf
beius *adj* faulty; blameworthy
bellach *adv* now, at length
bendigaid, bendigedig *adj*
blessed
bendigedigrwydd *nm* blessedness

bendith (**-ion**) *nf* blessing,
benediction
bendithio *vb* bless
bendithiol *adj* conferring blessings
benthyca, -io *vb* borrow, lend
benthyciwr (**-wyr**) *nm* borrower,
lender
benthyg *nm* loan
benyw *adj* female ♦ (**-od**) *nf*
female, woman
benywaidd *adj* feminine;
effeminate
benywol *adj* feminine, female
ber *adj* f. of **byr**
bêr (**berau, -i**) *nm* spear; roasting-
spit
bera *nf/m* rick; pyramid
berdys *npl* (**-yn** *nm*, **-en** *nf*)
shrimps
berf (**-au**) *nf* verb. **b. anghyflawn**
transitive verb. **b. gyflawn**
intransitive verb
berfa (**-fâu, -feydd**) *nf* barrow
Berlin *nf* Berlin
berth *adj* beautiful, valuable
berthog *adj* wealthy, fair
berw *nm, adj* boiling, seething,
ebullition
berwedig *adj* boiling
berwedydd (**-ion**) *nm* boiler
berwedd-dy (**-dai**) *nm* brewery
berweddu *vb* brew
berwi *vb* boil, seethe, effervesce
berwr *coll n* cress
betgwn *nm/f* bedgown
betws *nm* oratory, chapel; birch
grove
beudy (**-dai**) *nm* cow-house, byre
beunoeth, beunos *adv* nightly,
every night
beunydd *adv* daily, every day,
always
beunyddiol *adj* daily, quotidian
bidog (**-au**) *nf* dagger; bayonet
bil (**-iau**) *nm* bill
bilidowcar *nm* cormorant
bilwg (**-ygau**) *nm* billhook

bing (-oedd) *nm* alley, bin
biocemeg *nm/f* biochemistry
bir (-oedd) *nm* beer
biswail *nm* dung
blaen *adj* fore, foremost, first; front ♦ (-au, -ion) *nm* point, end, top, tip; front, van, priority, precedence; edge
blaenasgellwr (-wyr) *nm* wing-forward
blaenbrawf (-brofion) *nm* foretaste
blaendal *nm* prepayment, deposit
blaendarddu *vb* sprout
blaenddalen (-nau) *nf* title page
blaenddodi *vb* prefix
blaenddodiad (-iaid) *nm* prefix
blaenffrwyth *nm* first-fruits
blaengar *adj* foremost, progressive
blaengroen (-grwyn) *nm* foreskin
blaenllaw *adj* forward, prominent
blaenllym *adj* sharp, keen
blaenllymu *vb* sharpen, whet
blaenor (-iaid) *nm* leader; elder
blaenori *vb* lead, precede
blaenoriaeth *nf* preference; precedence
blaenorol *adj* previous, antecedent
blaenu *vb* point; outrun; precede
blaenwr (-wyr) *nm* leader; forward
blagur *coll n* sprouts, buds, shoots
blaguro *vb* sprout, bud; flourish
blaguryn *nm* sprout, bud, shoot
blaidd (bleiddiaid, bleiddiau) *nm* wolf
blas *nm* taste, savour, relish
blasio, -u *vb* taste
blasus *adj* tasty, savory, delicious
blawd (blodion, -iau) *nm* flour, meal
blêr *adj* untidy, slovenly
blerwm *nm* blabberer; blab-blab
blew *npl* (-yn *nm*) hairs; hair; fur
blewog *adj* hairy, shaggy
bliant *nm* lawn, fine linen
blif (-iau) *nm* catapult

blingo *vb* skin, flay
blin *adj* tired, weary; peevish, irritable
blinder (-au) *nm* weariness; trouble
blinderog, -derus *adj* wearisome
blinfyd *nm* tribulation
blino *vb* tire, weary; trouble, vex
blith (-ion) *nm* milk ♦ *adj* milch
blith draphlith *adv* helter-skelter
blodeugerdd (-i) *nf* anthology
blodeuglwm *nm* bunch, nosegay
blodeuo *vb* flower, bloom, flourish
blodeuog *adj* flowery; flourishing
blodeuyn, blodyn (blodau) *nm* flower
blodiog *adj* floury, mealy
bloddest *nf* rejoicing, acclamation
bloedd (-iau, -iadau) *nf* shout
bloeddio, -ian *vb* shout, cry
bloeddiwr (-wyr) *nm* shouter
bloesg *adj* lisping, faltering, indistinct
bloesgi *vb* lisp, falter, speak indistinctly
bloneg *nm*, **-en** *nf* lard, grease
blwch (blychau) *nm* box
blwng *adj* angry, sullen, cheerless ♦ *nm* anger
blwydd (-au, -i) *nf*, *adj* year of age; year-old
blwydd-dal *nm* annuity, pension
blwyddiad (-iaid) *nm* yearling, annual
blwyddiadur (-on) *nm* yearbook, annual
blwyddyn (blynyddoedd) *nf* year
blychaid (-eidiau) *nm* boxful
blynedd *npl* years (*after numerals*)
blynyddol *adj* annual, yearly
blys *nm* craving, lust
blysig *adj* greedy, lustful
blysigrwydd *nm* greediness
blysio *vb* crave, lust
bocs (-ys) *nm* box
bocsach *nm* vaunt, boast, brag
boch (-au) *nm* check

bochgoch adj rosy-cheeked
bod vb be, exist ♦ (**-au**) nm being, existence. **Y Bod Mawr** nm God
boda nm/f buzzard
bodio vb thumb, finger
bodlon adj content, willing
bodloni vb satisfy, content; be content
bodlonrwydd nm contentment
bodolaeth nf existence
bodoli vb exist
bodd nm pleasure, will, consent
boddfa nf flood, drenching
boddhad nm pleasure, satisfaction
boddhaol adj pleasing, satisfactory
boddhau vb please, satisfy
boddhaus adj pleased
boddi vb drown; flood
boddio vb please, satisfy
boddlon etc see **bodlon**
bogail (**-eiliau**) nm/f navel; boss, hub
boglwm (**-lymau**), **-lyn** (**-lynnau**) nm boss, knob, stud, bud, bubble
bol, bola (**boliau**) nm belly
bolaid (**-eidiau**) nm bellyful
bolera vb gorge, guzzle; sponge (fig)
bolerwr (**-wyr**) nm sponge, parasite
bolgi (**-gwn**) nm gourmand, glutton
bolgno nm, **-fa** ny gripes, colic
bolheulo vb bask in the sun
bolio vb belly, gorge
boliog adj big-bellied, corpulent
boloch nm pain, anxiety, destruction
bolrwth adj gluttonous, greedy
bolrwym adj costive, constipated
bollt (**-au, -ydd, byllt**) nf bolt
bolwst nf/m gripes, colic
bol(y)sothach nm hotchpotch; jargon
bom (**-iau**) nm/f bomb
bomio vb bomb
bôn (**bonau, bonion**) nm bottom; stump

boncath (**-od**) nm buzzard
bonclust (**-iau**) nm box on the ear
boncyff (**-ion**) nm stump, trunk, stock
bondigrybwyll adv forsooth ♦ adj hardly mentionable
bondo nm eaves
bonedd nm gentility, nobility
boneddigaidd adj noble; gentlemanly
boneddigeiddrwydd nm gentlemanliness
boneddiges (**-au**) nf lady
bonesig nf lady; Miss
bonet (**-i**) nf bonnet
bongam (**-au**) adj bandy-legged
bonheddig adj noble, gentle, gentlemanly ♦ (**boneddigion**) nmpl gentlemen
bonheddwr (**-wyr**) nm gentleman
bonllef (**-au**) nf shout
bonllwm adj bare-bottomed, breechless; bare-backed
Bonn nf Bonn
bonyn (**bonion**) nm stump
bord (**-ydd, -au**) nf table, board
bore (**-au**) nm morning ♦ adj early
boreddydd nm day-break, morning
borefwyd nm breakfast
boreol nm morning
bors nf hernia
bos nf palm of the hand, fist
bost (**-iau**) nm boast, brag
bostio vb boast, brag
botas, en (**-asau**) nf boot
botwm (**-ymau**) nm button
botymog adj buttoned
botymu vb button
both (**-au**) nf nave of wheel; boss
brac adj free, frank, talkative
bracso vb wade, paddle
bracty (**-tai**) nm malt-house, brewery
brad (**-au**) nm treason; plot
bradfwriadu vb plot, conspire
bradlofrudd (**-ion**) nm assassin

bradlofruddiaeth (-au) *nf*
assassination

bradlofruddio *vb* assassinate

bradwr (-wyr) *nm* traitor

bradwriaeth (-au) *nf* treason,
treachery

bradwrus *adj* traitorous,
treacherous

bradychu *vb* betray

braen *adj* rotten, corrupt

braenar (-au) *nm* fallow

braenaru *vb* fallow, pioneer

braenu *vb* rot, putrify

braf *adj* fine

brag *nm* malt

bragad *nf* army, battle; offspring

bragaldian *vb* jabber, gabble,
prate

bragio *vb* brag, boast

bragiwr (-wyr) *nm* bragger,
boaster

bragod (-au, -ydd) *nm* bragget

bragu *vb* malt, brew

bragwair *nm* moorland hay, coarse
grass

bragwr (-wyr) *nm* maltster,
brewer

braich (breichiau) *nf* arm; branch,
handle; headland

braidd *adv* rather, somewhat

braint (breintiau) *nf* privilege

braisg *adj* gross, thick, large;
pregnant

braith *adj* f. of **brith**

brân (brain) *nf* crow, rook, raven

bras (breision) *adj* fat; coarse;
rich; luxuriant

brasáu *vb* grow fat or gross

brasbwytho *vb* baste, tack

brasgamu *vb* stride

Brasil *nf* Brazil

braslun (-iau) *nm* sketch, outline

braslunio *vb* sketch, outline

brasnaddu *vb* rough-hew

braster *nm* fat

brasterog *adj* fat, greasy

brat (-iau) *nm* rag, clout; pinafore

bratiaith *nf* debased language

bratiog *adj* ragged, tattered

brath (-au) *nm* stab, wound; sting;
bite

brathog *adj* that bites; biting

brathu *vb* stab, wound; sting; bite

brau *adj* brittle, frail, fragile;
kindly; prompt

braw (-iau) *nm* terror, dread,
fright

brawd (brodyr) *nm* brother; friar

brawd (brodiau) *nf* judgment

brawdgarwch *nm* brotherly love

brawdle (-oedd) *nf/m* judgement-
seat

brawdlys (-oedd) *nf/m* assize-court

brawdmaeth *nm* foster-brother

brawdol *adj* brotherly, fraternal

brawdoliaeth (-au) *nf*
brotherhood, fraternity

brawddeg (-au) *nf* sentence

brawddegu *vb* construct sentences

brawl *nm* boast, brag; gabble,
tattle

brawychu *vb* frighten, terrify

brawychus *adj* frightful, terrible

bre (-on, -oedd) *nf* hill, highland

brebwl (-yliaid) *nm* blockhead;
prattler

breci *nm* wort; spree

brecwast (-au) *nm/f* breakfast

brecwasta *vb* breakfast

brech *nf* eruption, pox

brech *adj* f. of **brych**

brechdan (-au) *nf* slice of bread
and butter

brechiad (-au) *nm* inoculation,
vaccination

brechu *vb* vaccinate, inoculate

bredych (-au, -ion) *nm* betrayal;
fear; rascal

bref (-iadau) *nf* lowing; bleat; bray

breferad (-au) *nm* bellowing

brefiad (-au) *nm* lowing; bleating

brefu *vb* low; bleat; bray

breg *nm* guile, blemish, breach ♦
adj fragile, faulty

bregliach vb jabber
bregus adj frail, brittle, rickety
breichled (-au) nf bracelet
breichrwy(f) (-au) nm/f bracelet
breinio vb privilege, enfranchise
breiniol adj privileged, free
breinlen (-ni) nf charter
breintal nm bonus; royalty
breintiedig adj patented, patent
breintio vb privilege, favour
brenhinaidd adj kingly, regal
brenhindod nm royalty
brenhindref (-i) nf royal city
brenhindy (-dai) nm royal palace
brenhines (breninesau) nf queen
brenhinfainc nf throne
brenhiniaeth (breniniaethau) nf
  kingdom
brenhinol adj royal, regal
brenin (-hinoedd) nm king
brest (-iau) nf breast, chest
bresych npl (-en nf) cabbages
brethyn (-nau) nm cloth
brethynnwr (-ynwyr) nm clothier;
  cloth-worker
breuan (-au) nf quern; print of
  butter
breuder nm brittleness, frailty
breuddwyd (-ion) nm/f dream. b.
  gwrach wishful thinking
breuddwydio vb dream
breuddwydiol adj dreaming,
  dreamy
breuddwydiwr (-wyr) nm dreamer
brëyr, brehyr (brehyrion, -iaid) nm
  nobleman, chief, baron
bri nm honour, renown, distinction
briallu npl (briallen nf) primroses
bribys npl fragments, scraps
brifo vb hurt
brig (-au) nm top; (pl) twigs
brigâd (-au) nf brigade. b. dân
  fire-brigade
briger (-au) nm hair of head; top
brigo vb top; branch
brigog adj branching; flourishing
brigwyn adj white-topped, white-

crested
brigyn (brigau) nm twig
brith adj mottled, speckled; f
  braith
britho vb mottle, speckle; dazzle
Brithwr (-wyr) nm Pict
brithyll (-od, -iaid) nm trout
briw adj broken, bruised, sore ♦
  (-iau) nm wound, sore
briwfwyd nm crumbs, mince
briwlaw nm drizzling rain
briwlio vb broil
briwo vb wound, hurt
briwsion npl (-yn nm) crumbs,
  fragments.
briwsioni vb crumble
briwsyn (briwsion) nm crumb,
  morsel
bro (-ydd) nf land; region; vale
broch nm badger
broch nm froth, anger, tumult
brochi vb chafe, fume; bluster
brochus adj fuming; blustering
brodio vb embroider; darn
brodor (-ion) nm native; fellow
  countryman
brodorol adj native, indigenous
broga (-od) nm frog
brol nf boast, brag
brolio vb boast, brag, vaunt
broliwr (-wyr) nm boaster,
  braggart
bron (-nau, -nydd) nf breast;
  hillside
bron adv almost, nearly. o'r b.
  completely, in succession
bronfraith (-freithod) nf thrush
brongoch (-iaid) nf/m robin
  redbreast
bronwen nf weasel
bru nm womb
brud (-iau) nm chronicle;
  divination
brudio vb prognosticate, divine
brudiwr (-wyr) nm wizard,
  soothsayer
brwd adj hot, fervent ♦ nm boil,

heat

brwdfrydedd nm ardour, enthusiasm

brwdfrydig adj ardent, enthusiastic

brwmstan nm brimstone, sulphur

brwmstanaidd adj brimstony, sulphury

brwnt adj foul, nasty, dirty; harsh; f **bront**

brwyd (-au) nm embroidering frame; skewer

brwyd adj variegated; bloodstained; shattered

brwydo vb embroider; tear, consume

brwydr (-au) nf battle, combat

brwydro vb battle, combat

brwydrwr (-wyr) nm fighter, combatant

brwydwaith nm embroidery

brwylio vb broil

brwyn nm grief, sadness

brwynen (brwyn) nf rush

brwynog adj rushy

brwysg adj drunk; vigorous

brycan, brecan (-au) nf/m blanket, rug

brych adj mottled, brindled, freckled; f **brech** ♦ nm the after-birth of a cow

brychau npl (-euyn nm) spots, freckles

brycheulyd adj spotted, brindled

brychni nm spots, freckles

brychu vb spot, freckle

bryd nm mind, heart, will

brydio vb burn, inflame, boil, throb

brygawthan vb jabber, prate, rant

bryn (-iau) nm hill

bryncyn (-nau) nm hillock

bryniog adj hilly

brynti, bryntni nm filthiness, filth

brys nm haste, hurry

brysio vb hasten, hurry

brysiog adj hurried, hasty

bryslythyr (-au) nm dispatch

brysneges (-au) nf telegram

brytheirio vb belch; utter oaths, threats etc

Brython (-iaid) nm Briton, Welshman

Brythoneg nf British language, Welsh

brythwch nm storm, tumult; groan

bryweddu vb brew

brywes nm brewis

bual (buail) nm buffalo, drinking horn

buan adj fast, quick, swift, fleet; soon

buander, -dra nm swiftness, speed

buandroed adj swift-footed

buarth (-au) nm yard

buchdraeth (-au) nf biography, memoir

buchedd (-au) nf life, conduct

bucheddol adj right-living, virtuous

bucheddu vb live, flourish

buches (-au) nf herd of cows

buchfrechu vb vaccinate

budr adj dirty, filthy, foul, vile

budreddi nm filthiness, filth

budro vb dirty, soil, foul

budd (-ion) nm benefit, profit, gain

buddai (-eiau) nf churn

buddel (-wydd) nm/f cow-house post, pillar

buddiant (-iannau) nm interest

buddio vb profit, avail

buddiol adj profitable, beneficial, useful

buddioldeb nm profitableness, expediency

buddsodd (-ion), **-iad** (-au) nm investment

buddsoddi vb invest

buddugol adj winning, victorious

buddugoliaeth (-au) nf victory

buddugoliaethus adj victorious, triumphant

buddugwr (-wyr) nm winner,

victor
bugail (**-eiliaid**) *nm* shepherd; pastor
bugeiles (**-au**) *nf* shepherdess
bugeiliaeth (**-au**) *nf* pastorate
bugeilio, -a *vb* watch, shepherd
bugeiliol *adj* pastoral
bugunad *nm* bellowing, roar
bun *nf* maid, maiden
burgyn (**-nod, iaid**) *nm* carcass, carrion
burman, burum *nm* barm, yeast
busnes (**-ion**) *nm/f* business
busnesa *vb* interfere, meddle
busnesgar, busneslyd *adj* meddlesome
bustach (**-tych**) *nm* bullock, steer
bustachu *vb* buffet about, bungle
bustl *nm* gall, bile
bustlaidd *adj* like gall; bitter as gall
buwch (**buchod**) *nf* cow. **b. goch gota** ladybird
bwa (**bwâu**) *nm* bow; arch
bwaog *adj* arched, vaulted
bwbach (**-od**) *nm* bugbear, bogey, scarecrow
bwced (**-i**) *nm/f* bucket
bwci (**-iod**) *nm* bugbear, bogey, ghost
bwcl (**byclau**) *nm* buckle
bwcled (**-au**) *nf* buckler
bwch (**bychod**) *nm* buck. **b. dihangol** scapegoat. **b. gafr** he-goat
bwgan (**-od**) *nm* bogey, ghost, scarecrow
bwgwl (**bygylau**) *nm* threat, menace
bwgwth see **bygwth, bygythio**
bwhwman *vb* beat about; vacillate
bŵl (**bylau**) *nm* globe, ball, knob
bwlch (**bylchau**) *nm* gap; pass; notch
bwled (**-i**) *nf* bullet
bwn (**bynnoedd, byniaid**) *nm* bittern
bwndel (**-i**) *nm* bundle
bwngler (**-iaid**) *nm* bungler
bwnglera *vb* bungle
bwngleraidd *adj* bungling, clumsy
bwnglerwaith *nm* bungle, botch
bwnglerwch *nm* clumsiness
bwr (**byr**) *adj* fat, big, strong
bwrdais (**-deisiaid**) *nm* burgess
bwrdeistref (**-i**) *nm* borough
bwrdd (**byrddau**) *nm* table; deck; board. **b. du** black-board
bwriad (**-au**) *nm* purpose, intention
bwriadol *adj* intentional
bwriadu *vb* purpose, intend
bwrlwm (**byrlymau**) *nm* bubble; gurgling
bwrn (**byrnau**) *nm* burden, incubus; bale
bwrw *vb* cast, shed; strike; imagine, suppose; spend ♦ *nm* cast, throw; woof
bwtler (**-iaid**) *nm* butler
bwtri *nm* buttery, pantry, dairy
bwth (**bythod**) *nm* hut, booth, cot
bwthyn (**bythynnod**) *nm* cottage, cabin, hut
bwyall, -ell (**-eill, -yll**) *nf* axe
bwyd (**-ydd**) *nm* food
bwyda, bwydo *vb* feed
bwyd-offrwm (**-ymau**) *nm* meat-offering
bwydwr (**-wyr**) *nm* feeder
bwygilydd *adv* (from one) to the other
bwylltid (**-au**) *nm* swivel
bwyllwr(w) (**-yriau**) *nm* provisions for journey
bwysel (**-au, -i**) *nm* bushel
bwystfil (**-od**) *nm* (wild) beast
bwystfilaidd *adj* beastly, brutish
bwystfiles (**-au**) *nf* beast
bwyta *vb* eat; corrode
bwytadwy *adj* eatable, edible
bwytawr (**-wyr**) *nm* eater
bwyteig *adj* greedy, voracious
bwyty (**-tai, -tyau**) *nm* restaurant

bychan adj little, small; f **bechan**

bychander, -dra nm littleness, smallness

bychanu vb belittle, minimize

bychanus adj derogatory

byd (-oedd) nm world; state; life

bydaf (-au) nm/f beehive

bydio vb live, fare

bydol adj worldly, secular

bydolddyn (-ion) nm worldling

bydolrwydd nm worldliness

bydwraig (-wragedd) nf midwife

bydweigiaeth nf midwifery

bydysawd nm universe

byddag (-au) nf running knot, noose

byddar adj deaf ♦ (**-iaid, byddair**) nm deaf person

byddardod nm deafness

byddarol adj deafening

byddaru vb deafen, stun

byddin (-oedd) nf army, host

byddino vb set army in array, embattle

byddinog adj with armies

bygwth vb threaten, menace ♦ (**-ython, -ythiau**) nm threat, menace

bygythiad (-au) nm threat

bygythio vb threaten, menace

bygythiol adj threatening, menacing

byl (-au) nm/f edge, brim (of vessel); **hyd y f.** to the brim

bylb (-au) nm bulb

bylchog adj gapped, gappy; notched

bylchu vb make a gap, breach; notch

byngalo (-s, -au) nm bungalow

bynnag pron -ever, -soever

byr adj short, brief; f **ber**

byrbryd (-iau) nm luncheon, snack

byrbwyll adj impulsive, rash

byrbwylltra nm impulsiveness

byrder, -dra nm shortness, brevity

byrdwn nm burden, refrain, chorus

byrddaid (-eidiau) nm tableful

byrddio vb board

byrddiwr (-wyr) nm boarder

byrfyfyr adj impromptu

byrgorn adj shorthorn

byrhau vb shorten, abridge

byrhoedlog adj short-lived

byrlymu vb bubble, gurgle

byrllysg (-au) nm/f mace

byrnio (-u) vb bale, bundle

byrnwr (-wyr) nm baler

bys (-edd) nm finger; toe; hand of dial, latch

bysaid (-eidiau) nm pinch

byseddu vb finger

bysled(r) (-au) nm finger-stall

byth adv ever, for ever ♦ nm eternity

bytheiad (-aid) nm hound

bytheirio vb belch, threaten

bythfywiol adj everliving

bythgofiadwy adj memorable

bythol adj everlasting, eternal, perpetual

bytholi vb perpetuate

bytholwyrdd (-ion) adj, nm evergreen

bythynnwr (-ynwyr) nm cottager

byw vb live ♦ adj alive, living, quick ♦ nm life

bywgraffiad (-au) nm biography

bywgraffiadol adj biographical

bywgraffiadur (-on) nm biographical dictionary

bywgraffydd (-ion) nm biographer

bywgraffyddol adj biographical

bywhau, bywiocáu vb animate, vivify, quicken

byw(i)ad nm soft part of bread

bywiog adj lively, animated, vivacious

bywiogi vb enliven, animate

bywiol adj living, animate

bywoliaeth (-iolaethau) nf living

bywyd (-au) nm life

bywydeg nf biology

bywydegwr (-wyr) *nm* biologist
bywydfad (-au) *nm* lifeboat
bywydol *adj* of life, vital
bywyn (-nau) *nm* pith, core

C

cabaets *npl* (**cabaetsen** *nf*) cabbage
caban (-au) *nm* cabin
cabidwl *nm* consistory, chapter
cabl (-au) *nm* blasphemy, reviling
cabledd (-au) *nm* blasphemy
cableddus *adj* blasphemous
cablu *vb* blaspheme, revile
cablwr (-wyr), -ydd (-ion) *nm* blasphemer
caboli *vb* polish
cacamwci *nm* burdock
cacen (-nau, -ni) *nf* cake
cacwn *npl* (**cacynen** *nf*) wasps; wild bees
cachfa (-feydd) *nf* excretion; closet
cachgi (-gwn) *nm* coward; sneak
cachiad *nm* excretion, jiffy; coward
cachlyd *adj* befouled, dirty
cachu *vb* defecate
cachwr (-wyr) *nm* coward; sneak; one who excretes
cad (-au, -oedd) *nf* battle; army, host
cadach (-au) *nm* cloth, kerchief, clout
cadair (-eiriau) *nf* chair, seat; cradle; udder
cadarn (cedyrn) *adj* strong, mighty; firm
cadarnhad *nm* affirmation, confirmation
cadarnhaol *adj* affirmative
cadarnhau *vb* strengthen, confirm
cadeirfardd (-feirdd) *nm* chaired bard
cadeirio *vb* chair
cadeiriog *adj* chaired
cadeiriol *adj* pertaining to a chair,

cathedral
cadeirydd (-ion) *nm* chairman
cadernid *nm* strength; stability
cadfarch (-feirch) *nm* war-horse
cadfridog (-ion) *nm* general
cadfwyall (-eill, -yll) *nf* battleaxe
cadlas (-lesydd) *nf* close, enclosure
cadlong (-au) *nf* warship, battleship
cadlys (-oedd) *nf* camp, headquarters
cadno (cadnoid, cadnawon) *nm* fox
cadnöes, cadnawes (-au) *nf* vixen
cadoediad (-au) *nm* armistice, truce
cadofydd (-ion) *nm* tactician, strategist
cadofyddiaeth *nf* tactics, strategy
cadofyddol *adj* tactical, strategic
cadw *vb* keep, preserve, save; hold
cadwedig *adj* saved
cadwedigaeth *nf* salvation
cadw-mi-gei *nm* money-box
cadwraeth *nf* keeping; observance; conservation
cadwyn (-au, -i) *nf* chain
cadwyno *vb* chain
cadwynog *adj* chained, in chains
caddug *nm* darkness; mist, fog
caddugo *vb* darken, obscure
cae (-au) *nm* field; fence, hedge; brooch
caead (-au) *nm* cover, lid ♦ *adj* shut, closed
caeadle (-oedd) *nm* enclosure
caeëdig *adj* closed, fenced
cael *vb* have; get; find
caen (-au) *nf* surface; peel; coating
caenen (-nau) *nf* layer, film, flake
caentach (-au) *nf* wrangle, grumbling ♦ *vb* wrangle, grumble
caenu *vb* coat, finish
caer (-au, ceyrydd) *nf* wall; castle; city
Caerdydd *nf* Cardiff

Caeredin *nf* Edinburgh
caeriwrch *nm* roebuck
caerog *adj* walled, fortified; brocaded
Caersalem *nf* Jerusalem
caeth *adj* bound, captive, confined
♦ (**-ion**) *nm* bondman, slave
caethder *nm* strictness; restraint; asthma
caethfab (**-feibion**) *nm* slave
caethfasnach *nf* slave-trade
caethferch (**-ed**) *nf* slave
caethforwyn (**-forynion**) *nf* slave
caethglud *nf* captivity
caethgludiad (**-au**) *nm* captivity
caethgludo *vb* lead captive
caethiwed *nm* slavery, bondage, captivity, detention
caethiwo *vb* bind, confine, enslave
caethiwus *adj* confining; confined, tied
caethlong (**-au**) *nf* slave-ship
caethwas (**-weision**) *nm* slave
caethwasanaeth, -wasiaeth *nm* slavery
cafell (**-au**) *nf* cell; sanctuary, oracle
cafn (**-au**) *nm* trough, gutter
cafnedd *nm* concavity
cafnio, -u *vb* hollow out, scoop, gouge
cafod see **cawod**
caffael *vb* get, obtain
caffaeledd *nm* availability; acquisitiveness
caffaeliad (**-au**) *nm* acquisition, asset; prey, spoil
caffe, -i (**-s**) *nm* café, restaurant
caffio *vb* snatch, grapple
cafflo *vb* cheat; entangle
cagl *nm* clotted dirt
caglu *vb* befoul, bedraggle
cangell (**-hellau**) *nf* chancel
cangelloriaeth *nf* chancellorship
cangen (**-hennau**) *nf* branch, bough
canghellor (**canghellorion**) *nm* chancellor

canghennog *adj* branching
canghennu *vb* branch, ramify
caib (**ceibiau**) *nf* pickaxe, mattock
cail (**ceiliau**) *nf* sheepfold, flock of sheep
caill (**ceilliau**) *nf* testicle
cain *adj* fair, fine, elegant
cainc (**cangau, ceinciau**) *nf* branch; strand; strain
cais (**ceisiadau**) *nm* application; attempt; try
cal(a) (**-iau**) *nf* penis
calan (**-au**) *nm* first day of month. Dydd C. New Year's Day
calch *nm* lime
calchaidd *adj* calcareous
calchbibonwy *nm* stalactite
calchbost (**-byst**) *nm* stalagmite
calchen *nf* limestone; lump of lime
calchfaen (**-feini**) *nm* limestone
calcho, calchu *vb* lime
calcwlws (**calcwli**) *nm* calculus
caled *adj* hard; severe; harsh; dry
caledfwrdd *nm* hardboard
caledi *nm* hardness; hardship
caledu *vb* harden, dry
caledwch *nm* hardness
calen (**-nau, -ni**) *nf* whetstone; bar
calendr *nm* calendar
calennig *nm/f* New Year's gift
calon (**-nau**) *nf* heart
calondid *nm* encouragement
calon-dyner *adj* tender-hearted
calon-galed *adj* hard-hearted
calon-galedwch *nm* hard-heartedness
calonnog *adj* hearty; high-spirited
calonogi *vb* hearten, encourage
calori (**-iau**) *nm* calorie
call *adj* wise, sensible, rational
callestr (**cellystr**) *nf* flint
callineb *nm* wisdom, sense
calsiwm *nm* calcium
cam (**-au**) *nm* step
cam *adj* crooked, wry; wrong ♦
(**-au**) *nm* injury, wrong
cam- *prefix* wrong, mis-

camarfer vb misuse, abuse ♦ (-ion) nm/f misuse, malpractice

camargraff nf/m wrong impression

camarwain vb mislead

camarweiniol adj misleading

Cambodia nf Cambodia

cambren (-ni) nm swingletree

camchwarae nm foul play

camdafliad (-au) nm foul throw

camdaflu vb foul throw

camder, -dra nm crookedness

cam-drefn nf disorder

camdreuliad nm indigestion

camdreulio vb mis-spend

cam-drin vb ill-treat, abuse

camdriniaeth (-au) nf ill-treatment

camdystiolaeth (-au) nf false witness

camdystiolaethu vb bear false witness

camddeall vb misunderstand

camddealltwriaeth nm misunderstanding

camddefnydd nm misuse

camddefnyddio vb misuse

camedd nm bend, curvature. **c. y droed** instep. **c. y gar** knee-joint

cameg (-au, cemyg) nf felloe

camel (-od) nm camel

camenw (-au) nm misnomer

camenwi vb misname

camfa (-feydd) nf stile

camfarnu vb misjudge

camgred (-oau, -au) nf misbelief, heresy

camgredu vb misbelieve

camgredwr (-wyr) nm heretic

camgwl nm penalty, fine; blame

camgyfrif vb miscalculate

camgyhuddiad (-au) nm false accusation

camgyhuddo vb accuse falsely

camgymeriad (-au) nm mistake

camgymryd vb mistake, err

camlas (-lesi, -lesydd) nf/m canal

camliwio vb misrepresent

camochri vb be offside

camog (-au) nf felloe

camp (-au) nf feat, exploit; game; prize

campfa (-feydd) nf gymnasium

campus adj excellent, splendid, grand

campwaith (-weithiau) nm masterpiece, feat

campwr (-wyr) nm champion

camre nm walk, footstep(s)

camsyniad (-au) nm mistake

camsynied vb mistake

camsyniol adj mistaken

camu vb bow, bend, stoop

camu vb step, stride

camwedd (-au) nm iniquity, transgression

camweddu vb transgress

camwri nm injury, wrong

camymddwyn vb misbehave

camymddygiad (-au) nm misconduct

cân (caniadau, caneuon) nf song

can adj white ♦ nm flour

Canada nf Canada

cancr nm canker; cancer

cancro vb canker, corrode

candryll adj shattered, wrecked

canfasio vb canvass

canfed adj hundredth

canfod vb see, perceive, behold

canfyddadwy adj perceptible

canfyddiad nm perception

canhwyllbren (canwyllbrenni, -au) nm/f candlestick

canhwyllwr (canwyllwyr) nm chandler

caniad nm singing; ringing; crowing

caniad (-au) nf song, poem

caniadaeth nf singing, psalmody

caniatâd nm leave, permission, consent

caniataol adj permissive; granted

caniatáu vb permit, allow

caniedydd (-ion) nm singer, songster; song-book

canlyn vb follow, pursue
canlyniad (-au) nm consequence, result
canlynol adj following, consequent
canlynwr (-wyr) nm follower
canllaw (-iau) nf/m hand-rail, parapet, aid
canmlwyddiant nm centenary
canmol vb praise, commend
canmoladwy adj praiseworthy
canmoliaeth (-au) nf praise, commendation
canmoliaethus adj eulogistic, complimentary
cannaid adj white, bright, luminous
cannu vb whiten, bleach
cannwr (canwyr) nm bleacher
cannwyll (canhwyllau) nf candle
canol adj ♦ (-au) nm middle, centre, midst
canolbarth (-au) nm middle part, midland
canolbwynt (-iau) nm centre, focus
canolbwyntio vb centre, concentrate
canoldir (-oedd) nm inland region
canolddydd nm mid-day, noon
canolfan (-nau) nm/f centre
canoli vb centre; arbitrate; centralize
canolig adj middling
canoloesol adj mediaeval
canolog adj central
canolradd (-ol) adj intermediate
canolwr (-wyr) nm mediator, referee; centrehalf, centre. **c. blaen** centreforward
canon (-au) nf/m, (-iaid) nm canon
canonaidd adj canonical
canoneiddio vb canonize
canoniaeth (-au) nf canonry
canonwr (-wyr) nm canon, canonist
canradd (-au) adj, nf centigrade, percentile

canran (-nau) nm percentage
canrif (-oedd) nf century
cansen (-ni) nf cane
canser nm cancer
canslo vb cancel
cant (-au) nm circle, ring, rim; tyre
cant (cannoedd) nm hundred
cantel (-au) nm rim, brim
cantîn (cantinoedd) nf canteen
cantor (-ion) nm singer
cantores (-au) nf songstress, singer
cantref (-i, -ydd) nm hundred
cantwr (-orion) nm singer, songster
cantwraig nf songstress, singer
canu vb sing, chant; play; crow; ring. **c. gwlad** country music
canŵ (-od) nm canoe
canŵo vb canoe
canwr (-wyr) nm singer
canwriad (-iaid) nm centurion
canwyr (-au, -ion) nm plane (in carpentry)
canys conj because, for
cap (-iau) nm cap
capan (-au) nm cap; lintel
capel (-i, -ydd, -au) nm chapel
capelwr (-wyr) nm chapel-goer
caplan (-iaid) nm chaplain
caplaniaeth (-au) nf chaplaincy
capteiniaeth nf captaincy
capten (-einiaid) nm captain
car (ceir) nm car. **c. campau** sports car
câr (ceraint) nm friend; relation
carafán (-au) nf caravan
carbohydrad (-au) nm carbohydrate
carbon (-au) adj, nm carbon
carbwl adj clumsy, awkward
carco vb take care
carcus adj solicitous, anxious, careful
carchar (-au) nm/m prison; restraint
carchardy (-dai) nm prison-house

carchariad *nm* imprisonment
carcharor (-ion) *nm* prisoner
carcharu *vb* imprison
carden (**cardiau**) *nf* card
cardigan (-au) *nf* cardigan
cardod (-au) *nf* charity, alms, dole
cardota *vb* beg
cardotyn (-wyr) *nm* beggar
cardydwyn, -odwyn, -wen *nf* weakest of brood or litter
caredig *adj* kind
caredigrwydd *nm* kindness
caregog *adj* stony
caregu *vb* stone; petrify; gather stones
carennydd *nm* friendship; kinship
caretsen (**carets**) *nf* carrot
carfaglog *adj* clumsy
carfan (-au) *nf* beam; swath; party, faction
cariad (-au) *nm* love
cariad (-au, -on) *nm/f* lover, sweetheart
cariadfab *nm* lover, sweetheart
cariadferch *nf* sweetheart, mistress
cariadlawn *adj* full of love, loving
cariadus *adj* loving, beloved, dear
caridým (-s) *nm* ragamuffin
cario *vb* carry, bear
carismatig *adj* charismatic
carlam (-au) *nm* prance, gallop
carlamu *vb* prance, gallop
carlwm (-lymod) *nm* ermine, stoat
carn (-au) *nm* hoof; hilt, haft, handle
carn (-au), **carnedd** (-au) *nf* cairn
cárnifal *nm* carnival
carniforus *adj* carnivorous
carnog, -ol *adj* hoofed
carol (-au) *nm/f* carol
carp (-iau) *nm* clout, rag
carped (-au, -i) *nm* carpet
carpiog *adj* ragged, tattered
carrai (**careiau**) *nf* lace, thong
carreg (**cerrig**) *nf* stone
cart (**ceirt**) *nm/f* cart

cartaid, certaid (-eidiau) *nf* cartful
cartilag (-au) *nm* cartilage
cartref (-i, -ydd) *nm* home, abode
cartrefle (-oedd) *nm* abode
cartreflu *nm* militia
cartrefol *adj* homely, domestic, home; civil
cartrefu *vb* make one's home, settle
cartŵn (**cartwnau**) *nm* cartoon
cartwnydd (-ion) *nm* cartoonist
carth (-ion) *nm* tow, oakum; off-scouring
carthen (-ni, -nau) *nf* Welsh blanket, coverlet
carthffos (-ydd) *nf* sewer
carthffosaeth *nf* sewage
carthu *vb* cleanse, purge, scavenge
caru *vb* love; like; court
caruaidd *adj* loving, kind
carw (**ceirw**) *nm* stag, deer
carwden (-ni) *nf* back-chain; tall awkward fellow
carwr (-wyr) *nm* lover, wooer
carwriaeth (-au) *nf* courtship
cas *adj* hateful, odious; nasty, disagreeable ♦ *nm* hatred, aversion
cas (**caseion**) *nm* hater, foe, enemy
casáu *vb* hate, detest, abhor
casbeth (-au) *nm* aversion, nuisance
caseg (**cesig**) *nf* mare
casét (-iau) *nm* cassette
casgen (-ni, **casgiau**) *nf* cask
casgl *nf/m* collection
casgliad (-au) *nm* collection; gathering
casglu *vb* collect, gather; infer
casglwr (-wyr), **-ydd** (-ion) *nm* collector
casineb *nm* hatred
cast (-iau) *nm* vice, knack
castan *nf* chestnut
castanwydd *npl* (-en *nf*) chestnut-trees

castell (**cestyll**) nm castle
castellog adj castled, castellated
castellu vb castle, encamp
castio vb trick, cheat; cast, calculate
castiog adj full of tricks, tricky
casul (-**(i)au**) nm/f chasuble, cassock
caswir nm unpalatable truth
casyn (**casiau**) nm case, casing
cat (-**iau**) nm bit, piece, fragment; pipe
catalog (-**au**) nm catalogue
catalogio vb catalogue
catalydd (-**ion**) nm catalyst
categori (-**ïau**) nm category
catel coll nf chattels; cattle
catgor (-**(i)au**) nm ember day(s)
catrawd (-**rodau**) nf regiment
cath (-**od, -au**) nf cat
cathl (-**au**) nf melody, hymn, lay
cathlu vb sing, hymn
cathod (-**au**) nf cathode
catholig adj catholic
Catholigiaeth nf Catholicism
catholigrwydd nm catholicity
cau adj hollow, concave
cau vb shut, close, enclose
caul (**ceulion**) nm maw; rennet; curd
caw (-**(i)au**) nm band, swaddling-clothes
cawdel nm hotchpotch, mess
cawell (**cewyll**) nm hamper, basket, cradle
cawellaid (-**eidiau**) nm hamperful
cawellwr (-**wyr**) nm basket-maker
cawg (-**iau**) nm basin, bowl, pitcher
cawl nm broth, soup; hotchpotch
cawn npl (-**en** nf) reeds
cawod (-**ydd**) nf shower
cawodi vb shower
cawodog adj showery
cawr (**cewri**) nm giant
cawraidd adj gigantic
cawres (-**au**) nf giantess

caws nm cheese; curd
cawsai, cawsi nf/m causeway
cawsaidd adj cheesy, caseous
cawsellt (-**ydd, -i, -au**) nm cheese-vat
cawsio vb curd, curdle
cawsiog adj curdled
cecian vb stammer
cecren (-**nod**) nf shrew, scold, cantankerous woman
cecru vb wrangle, bicker
cecrus adj cantankerous, quarrelsome
cecryn (-**nod**) nm wrangler, brawler
cedor nm/f pubic hair
cedrwydd npl (-**en** nf) cedars
cefn (-**au**) nm back; support
cefndedyn nm mesentery; diaphragm, pancreas
cefnder (-**dyr**) nm first cousin
cefndir (-**oedd**) nm background
cefnen (-**nau**) nf ridge
cefnfor (-**oedd**) nm main sea, ocean
cefngrwm adj hump-backed
cefnog adj well-off, well-to-do
cefnogaeth nf encouragement, support
cefnogi vb encourage, support
cefnogol adj encouraging
cefnu vb back, turn the back, forsake
cefnwlad (-**wledydd**) nf hinterland
cefnwr (-**wyr**) nm back, full-back
ceffyl (-**au**) nm horse
ceg (-**au**) nf mouth
cega vb mouth, prate
cegaid (-**eidiau**) nf mouthful
cegen (-**au**) nf gullet, windpipe
cegid, -en (-**au**) nf green woodpecker, jay
cegin (-**au**) nf kitchen
cegrwth adj gaping
cegyr npl hemlock
cengl (-**au**) nf band; girth; hank
cenglu vb hank; girth; wind

cei (-au) nm quay
ceibio vb pick with pickaxe
ceidwad (-aid) nm keeper, saviour
ceidwadaeth nf conservatism;
conservancy
ceidwadol adj conservative
Ceidwadwr (-wyr) nm
Conservative
ceiliagwydd (-au) nm gander
ceiliog (-od) nm cock. c. rhedyn
grasshopper
ceinach (-od) nf hare
ceincio vb branch out, ramify
ceinciog (-au) nf penny
ceinder nm elegance, beauty
ceiniog (-au) nf penny
ceiniogwerth (-au, -i) nf
pennyworth
ceinion npl beauties, gems
ceintach vb grumble, croak
ceintachlyd adj querulous
ceintachwr (-wyr) nm grumbler,
croaker
ceirch (-en nf) coll n oats
ceirios npl (-en nf) cherries
ceisbwl (-byliaid) nm catchpole,
bailiff
ceisio vb seek; ask; try, attempt,
endeavour; fetch, get
cêl adj hidden, concealed ♦ nm
concealment ♦ npl kale
celain (celanedd) nf dead body
celanedd coll nf carnage, slaughter
celc nm/f concealment; hoard
celf (-au) nf art, craft
celfi npl (-cyn cyn) tools, gear;
furniture
celfydd adj skilled, skilful
celfyddgar adj ingenious; artistic
celfyddwr (-wyr) nm artificer,
artist
celfyddyd (-au) nf art, craft; skill.
celfyddydau graffig graphic arts
celfyddydol adj relating to art/the
Arts
celu vb hide, conceal
celwrn (-yrnau) nm tub, bucket,
pail

celwydd (-au) nm lie, falsehood,
untruth
celwyddog adj lying, mendacious;
false
celwyddwr (-wyr) nm liar
celyn npl (-nen nf) holly
cell (-oedd, -au) nf cell, chamber.
celloedd cenhedlu germ cells.
enyniad y celloedd cellulitis
celli (celliau, -ioedd) nf grove
cellog adj cellular
cellwair vb jest, trifle ♦ nm fun
cellweiriwr (-wyr) nm jester,
trifler
cellweirus adj playful, jocular
cemeg nm chemistry
cemegol adj chemical
cemegwr, -ydd (-wyr) nm chemist
cemegyn (cemegau) nm chemical
cen coll n skin, peel, scales, scurf,
film, lichen
cenadwri nf message
cenau (cenawon) nm cub, whelp;
rascal
cenedl (-hedloedd) nf nation;
gender
cenedlaethol adj national
cenedlaetholdeb nm nationalism
cenedlaetholi vb nationalize
cenedlaetholwr (-wyr) nm
nationalist
cenedl-ddyn (-ion) nm gentile
cenfaint (-feiniau) nf herd
cenfigen (-nau) nf envy, jealousy
cenfigennu vb envy
cenfigennus, -enllyd adj envious,
jealous
cenhadaeth (cenadaethau) nf
mission
cenhadol adj missionary
cenhadu vb permit; propagate,
conduct a mission
cenhadwr (-hadon) nm missionary
cenhedlaeth (cenedlaethau) nf
generation
cenhedlig adj gentile, pagan

cenhedlu vb beget, generate

cenllif nm flood, torrent, deluge

cenllysg coll nm hailstones, hail

cennad (-hadau, -hadon) nf leave; messenger

cennin npl (-hinen nf) leeks

cennog adj scaly, scurfy

cennu vb scale, scurf

cêr nf gear, tools, trappings

cerameg nmf ceramics

ceramig adj ceramic

cerbyd (-au) nm chariot, coach, car

cerbydwr (-wyr) nm coachman

cerdyn (cardiau) nm card

cerdd (-i) nf song, poem; music, poetry

cerddbrenni npl woodwinds

cerddbresi npl brass section (orchestra)

cerdded vb walk; go; travel

cerddediad nm walking, going; pace

cerddgar adj harmonious, musical

cerddin, cerdin npl (-en nf) rowan

cerddor (-ion) nm singer, musician

cerddorfa (-feydd) nf orchestra

cerddorfaol adj orchestral

cerddoriaeth nf music

cerddorol adj musical

cerddwr (-wyr) nm walker

cerfddelw (-au) nf graven image, statue

cerfio vb carve

cerflun (-iau) nm statue; engraving

cerfluniaeth nf sculpture

cerflunydd (-lunwyr) nm sculptor

cerfwaith nm carving, sculpture

cern (-au) nf cheek, jaw

cernod (-iau) nf buffet

cernodio vb buffet, clout

cerpyn (carpiau) nm clout, rag

cerrynt nmf course, road; current

cert (-i) nf cart

certiwr (-wyr) nm carter

certh adj right; awful

cerub, ceriwb (-iaid) nm cherub

cerwyn (-i) nf tub; vat; winepress

cerydd (-on) nm correction, chastisement; rebuke, reproof, censure

ceryddol adj chastising, chastening

ceryddu vb correct, chastise; rebuke

ceryddwr (-wyr) nm chastiser; rebuker

cesail (-eiliau) nf arm-pit; bosom

cesair npl, coll n hailstones, hail

cest (-au) nf belly, paunch

cestog adj corpulent

cetyn (catiau) nm piece, bit; pipe

cethin adj dark, fierce, ugly

ceubren (-nau) nm hollow tree

ceubwll (-byllau) nm pit

ceudod nm cavity; abdomen; thought, heart

ceuffordd (-ffyrdd) nf tunnel

ceuffos (-ydd) nf drain, ditch

ceugrwm adj concave

ceulan (-nau, -lennydd) nf bank, brink

ceulo vb curdle, coagulate

ceunant (-nentydd) nm ravine, gorge

cewyn (-nau, cawiau) nm napkin

ci (cŵn) nm dog, hound

ciaidd adj dog-like, houndish; brutal

cib (-au) nm pod, husk

cibddall adj purblind

cibo vb frown, scowl

cibog adj scowling

cibws, cibwst nf kibes, chilblains

cibwts (-au) nm kibbutz

cibyn (-nau) nm shell; husk; half a bushel

cic (-iau) nmf kick

cicio vb kick

ciciwr (-wyr) nm kicker

cidwm (-ymiaid, -ymod) nm wolf; rascal

cieidd-dra nm houndishness, brutality

cig (-oedd) nm flesh, meat

cigfran (-frain) nf raven
cignoeth adj touching to the quick, caustic
cigog adj fleshy
cigwain (-weiniau) nf flesh-hook
cigydd (-ion) nm butcher
cigyddiaeth nf butchery
cigysol adj carnivorous
cigysydd (-ion) nm carnivore
cil (-iau, -ion) nm back; retreat; corner
cilagor vb open partly
cilagored adj ajar
cilbost (cilbyst) nm gate-post
cilchwyrn npl (-en nf), (-au, -od nm) glands
cildrem (-iau) nf leer
cildremio vb leer
cildroi vb reverse
cildwrn nm tip, bribe
cildyn adj obstinate, stubborn
cildynnu vb be obstinate
cildynnus adj obstinate, stubborn
cildynrwydd nm obstinacy
cilddant (-ddanedd) nm molar
cilfach (-au) nf nook; creek, bay
cilfilyn (-filod) nm ruminant
cilgnoi vb chew the cud, ruminate
cilgwthio vb push, shove, jostle
cilgynnyrch (-gynhyrchion) nm by-product
cilio vb retreat, recede, swerve
cilocalori (-au) nm kilocalorie
cilogram (-au) nm kilogram
cilomedr (-au) nm kilometre
cilwen (-au) nf half smile
cilwenu vb simper, smile, leer
cilwg (-ygon) nm frown, scowl
cilydd (-ion) nm fellow, companion
cilyddol adj reciprocal
cimwch (-ychiaid) nm lobster
cingroen nf stink-horn
ciniawa vb dine
cinio (ciniawu) nm dinner
cip (-ion) nm pluck, snatch; glimpse
cipdrem (-iau) nf/m glance,

glimpse
cipedrych vb glance, glimpse
cipio vb snatch
cipiwr (-wyr) nm snatcher
cipolwg nm/f glance, glimpse
ciprys vb, cribscramble
cis (-iau) nm/f buffet; slap, touch
cist (-iau) nf chest, coffer, box; bin
ciw (-iau) nm cue, queue
ciwb nm cube
ciwed coll nf rabble, mob, crew
ciwrad (-iaid) nm curate
ciwt adj cute, clever, ingenious
claddedigaeth (-au) nf/m burial
claddfa (-feydd) nf burial-ground, cemetery
claddu vb bury
claear adj lukewarm, tepid; mild; cool
claearineb nm lukewarmness
claearu vb make mild or tepid; soothe
claer adj clear, bright, shining
claerder nm clearness, brightness
claf (cleifion) adj sick, ill ♦ nm sick person, patient
clafdy (-dai) nm hospital, infirmary
clafr nm itch, mange
clafrllyd adj mangy
clafychu vb sicken, fall ill
clai (cleiau) nm clay
clais (cleisiau) nm stripe; bruise
clamp (-iau) nm mass, lump; monster
clap (-iau) nm lump
clapgi (-gwn) nm telltale
clapio vb lump; strike; gossip
clapiog adj lumpy
clas nm monastic community, cloister, college
clasur (-on) nm classic
clasurol adj classical
clau adj quick, swift, soon; true; audible
clawdd (cloddiau) nm hedge; dyke, embankment
clawr (cloriau) nm face, surface;

cover, lid; board
clebar, cleber *nf/m* idle talk, gossip, tattle
clebran *vb* chatter, gossip, tattle
clebryn *nm*, **clebren** *nf* tattler
clec (-iau, -s) *nf* click; clack; crack; gossip
cleci (-cwn) *nm* telltale
clecian *vb* click; clack; crack, snap
clecyn *nm*, **clecen** *nf* gossip, telltale
cledr (-au) *nf* pole; rail; palm (of hand)
cledren (-nau, -ni) *nf* pale, pole, rail
cleddyf, cleddau, cledd (cleddyfau) *nm* sword; brace
cleddyfwr (-wyr) *nm* swordsman
clefyd (-au) *nm* disease; fever. **c. melys** diabetes
clegar *vb* clack, cluck, cackle
clegyr, clegr *nm* rock; cairn, stony place
cleiog *adj* clayey
cleiriach *nm* decrepit one
cleisio *vb* bruise
cleisiog *adj* bruised
clem (-iau) *nf* notion, idea; look, gaze; *pl* grimaces
clep (-iau) *nf* clack, clap; gossip
clepgi (-gwn) *nm* babbler; telltale
clepian *vb* clap; slam; blab
clêr *coll nf* itinerant minstrels; bards
clêr *npl* (cleren *nf*) flies
clera *vb* stroll as minstrels
clerc (-od) *nm* clerk
clercio *vb* serve as clerk
clerigol *adj* clerical
clerigwr (-wyr) *nm* clergyman
clerwr (-wyr) *nm* itinerant minstrel
clerwriaeth *nf* minstrelsy
clewt (-iau) *nm* clout
clewtian *vb* clout
clic (cliciau) *nm* clique

clicied (-au) *nf* clicket; trigger
cliciedu *vb* latch, fasten
clindarddach *vb* crackle ♦ *nm* crackling
clinig (-au) *nm* clinic
clir *adj* clear
clirio *vb* clear
clo (cloeau, cloeon) *nm* lock, conclusion
clobyn *nm*, **cloben** *nf* monster
cloc (-iau) *nm* clock
clocian *vb* cluck
clocsiau *npl* (clocsen *nf*) clog
cloch (clych, clychau) *nf* bell. **o'r/ar gloch** o'clock
clochaidd *adj* sonorous, noisy
clochdar *vb* cluck, cackle
clochdy (-dai) *nm* belfry, steeple
clochydd (-ion) *nm* bell-man; sexton
clod (-ydd) *nm/f* praise, fame, renown
clodfori *vb* praise, extol
clodwiw *adj* commendable, praiseworthy
cloddfa (-feydd) *nf* quarry, mine
cloddio *vb* dig, delve; quarry, mine
cloddiwr (-wyr) *nm* digger, navvy
cloëdig *adj* locked, closed
cloer (-[i]au) *nm/f* locker; niche, embrasure; pigeon-hole
cloff *adj* lame
cloffi *vb* lame, halt ♦ *nm* lameness
cloffni *nm* lameness
cloffrwym (-au) *nm* fetter, hobble. **c. y cythraul, c. y mwci** great bindweed
clog (-au) *nm/f* cloak
clog (-au) *nf* rock, precipice
clogfaen (-feini) *nm* boulder
clogwyn (-i) *nm* cliff, crag, precipice
clogwynog *adj* craggy, precipitous
clogyn (-nau) *nm* cloak, cape
clogyrnaidd *adj* rough, rugged, clumsy

cloi vb lock

clonc nf clank; gossip ♦ adj addled

clopa (-âu) nf/m noddle; knob; club

cloren (-nau) nf rump, tail

clorian (-nau) nf/f pair of scales

cloriannu vb weigh, balance

clorin nm chlorine

clorinio, -adu vb chlorinate

clos (-ydd) nm yard

clos (closau) nm pair of breeches

clòs adj close

closio vb close, near

cludadwy adj portable

cludair (-eiriau) nf heap, load, wood-pile

cludiad nm carriage

cludiant (-nnau) nm transport, haulage

cludo vb carry, convey

cludwr (-wyr), -**ydd** (-ion) nm porter

clul (-iau) nm knell

clun (-iau) nf hip, haunch, thigh, leg; moor

cluro vb rub, smear

clust (-iau) nf/m ear; handle

clustfeinio vb prick up the ears; eavesdrop

clustfys nm little finger

clustffôn (-ffonau) nm earphone

clustlws (-lysau) nm earring

clustnod (-au) nm earmark

clustog (-au) nf/m cushion, pillow

clwb (clybiau) nm club

clwc adj addled

clwcian vb cluck

clwm (clymau) nm knot, tie

clwpa (-od) nm knob, boss; club; dolt

clws adj pretty, nice; f **clos**

clwstwr (clystyrau) nm cluster

clwt (clytiau) nm patch, clout, rag

clwyd (-au, -i, -ydd) nf hurdle; gate; roost

clwydo vb roost

clwyf (-au) nm wound; disease

clwyfo vb wound

clwyfus adj wounded; sore; sick

clybodeg nf acoustics

clybodig adj acoustic

clyd adj warm, sheltered, snug, cosy

clydwch, clydwr nm warmth, shelter

clyfar adj clever; pleasant, agreeable

clymblaid (-bleidiau) nf clique, cabal

clymog adj knotty, entangled

clymu vb knot, tie

clytio vb patch, piece

clytiog adj patched; ragged

clytwaith (-weithiau) nm patchwork

clyw nm sense of hearing

clywadwy adj audible

clywed vb hear; feel; taste; smell

clywedigaeth nf hearing

clywedol adj aural

clywedydd (-ion) nm hearer, auditor

clyweled adj audio-visual

cnaf (-on, -iaid) nm knave, rascal

cnafaidd adj knavish, rascally

cnaif (cneifion) nm shearing, fleece

cnap (-iau) nm lump, knob, boss

cnapan (-au) nm ball, bowl, kind of ball game

cnapiog adj lumpy

cnau npl (cneuen nf) nuts

cnawd nm flesh

cnawdol adj carnal, fleshly, fleshy

cneifio vb shear, fleece

cneifiwr (-wyr) nm shearer

cneua vb nut

cneuen (cnau) nf nut

cnewyllyn (cnewyll) nm kernel, nucleus

cnith (-iau, -ion) nm slight touch, blow; pluck

cno nm bite, chewing, gnawing

cnoc (-iau) nm/f knock

cnocio vb knock

cnofa (-feydd) nf gnawing, pang
cnofil (-od) nm rodent
cnoi vb gnaw, chew, bite; ache
cnot (-iau) nm knot, bunch
cnu (-au), **cnuf** (-iau) nm fleece
cnud (-oedd) nf pack (of wolves, etc.)
cnûl, cnul (-iau) nm knell
cnwd (cnydau) nm crop; covering
cnydfawr adj fruitful, productive
cnydio vb crop, yield increase
cnydiog adj fruitful, productive
cob (cobau) nf coat, cloak, robe
côb (-iau) nm embankment; miser; wag; cob
coban (-au) nf: c. nos nightshirt
coblyn (-nod) nm sprite, goblin, imp
cocos npl cogs. olwyn g. cog-wheel
cocos, cocs npl (cocsen nf) cockles
coch adj, nm red
coch-gam nf robin
cochi vb redden, blush
cochi, cochder nm redness
cochl (-au) nmf mantle, cloak
cod (-au) nf bag, pouch
codaid (-eidiau) nf bagful
codi vb rise, raise, lift, erect
codiad (-au) nm rise, rising; erection
codog adj baggy ♦ (-ion) nmf rich man; miser
codwm (codymau) nm fall, tumble
codwr (-wyr) nm riser; raiser, lifter. c. canu precentor
codymu vb wrestle
codymwr (-wyr) nm wrestler
codded nm anger; grief
coddi vb anger, offend
coed (-ydd) coll nm wood, timber, trees
coeden (coed) nf tree
coedio vb timber
coediog adj wooded, woody
coedwig (-oedd) nf wood, forest
coedwigaeth nf forestry

coedwigwr (-wyr) nm woodman, forester
coedd adj public
coeg adj empty, vain; one-eyed, blind
coegddyn (-ion) nm fop, coxcomb, fool
coegedd nm emptiness, silliness
coegen (-nod) nf minx, coquette
coegennaidd adj coquettish
coegfalch adj vain, foppish
coegi vb jeer at, mock
coeglyd adj vain, sarcastic
coegni nm vanity; spite; sarcasm
coegwr (-wyr) nm fool
coegwych adj gaudy, garish, tawdry
coegyn (-nod) nm coxcomb
coel (-ion) nf belief, trust, credit
coelbren (-nau, -ni) nm lot
coelcerth (-i) nf bonfire, blaze
coelgrefydd (-au) nf superstition
coelgrefyddol adj superstitious
coelio vb believe, credit, trust
coes (-au) nf leg, shank ♦ nmf handle; stem, stalk
coetgae nm hedge; enclosure
coetmon (-myn) nm lumberjack
coetref nf woodland, homestead
coeth adj fine, refined; elegant
coethder nm refinement, elegance
coethi vb refine; chastise; babble
coethwr (-wyr) nm refiner
cof (-ion) nm memory; remembrance
cofadail (-eiladau) nf monument
cofeb (-ion) nf memorandum; memorial
cofgolofn (-au) nf monument
cofiadur (-on, -iaid) nm recorder
cofiadwy adj memorable
cofiannydd (-anyddion) nm biographer
cofiant (-iannau) nm memoir, biography
cofio vb remember, recollect
cofl (-au) nf embrace; bosom

coflaid (-eidiau) nf armful; bundle
coflech (-au) nf memorial tablet
cofleidio vb embrace, hug
coflyfr (-au) nm record, chronicle
cofnod (-ion) nm memorandum, minute
cofnodi vb record, register
cofrestr (-au) nf register, roll
cofrestrfa nf registry
cofrestru vb register
cofrestrydd (-ion) nm registrar
cofus adj mindful
cofweini vb prompt
cofweinydd (-ion) nm prompter
coffa vb remember ♦ nm remembrance
coffâd nm remembrance
coffadwriaeth nf remembrance, memory
coffadwriaethol adj memorial
coffáu vb remember; remind; commemorate
coffi nm coffee
coffr (-au) nm coffer, trunk, chest
cog (-au) nf cuckoo
cog (-au) nm cook
coginiaeth nf cookery
coginio vb cook
cogio vb cog; sham, feign, pretend
cogiwr (-wyr) nm pretender, swindler
cogor vb chatter, caw, croak ♦ nm chattering
cogwrn (-yrnau, cegyrn) nm knob, cone; cock (of corn); shell
cogydd (-ion) nm, **cogyddes** (-au) nf cook
cogyddiaeth nf cookery
congl (-au) nf corner
côl nf bosom, embrace
col (-ion) nm awn, beard
coladu vb collate
coledd, -u vb cherish, foster
coleddwr (-wyr) nm cherisher, fosterer, patron, supporter
coleg (-au) nm college
colegol adj collegiate

colegwr (-wyr) nm collegian
coler (-i) nf/m collar
colfen (-nau, -ni) nf bough, branch; tree
colofn (-au) nf column, pillar
colomen (-nod) nf dove, pigeon
colomendy (-dai) nm dove-cot
colomennaidd adj dove-like
coluddion npl (-yn nm) bowels
colur (-au) nm make-up, colour
coluro vb make-up, paint; conceal
colwyn (-od) nm puppy
colyn (-nau) nm pivot; sting; tail
colynnog adj stinging; hinged
colynnu vb sting
coll (-iadau) nm loss; failing; defect
colladwy adj perishable
collddail adj deciduous
colled (-ion) nm/f loss
colledig adj lost, damned
colledigaeth nf perdition
colledu vb occasion loss
colledus adj fraught with loss
colledwr (-wyr) nm loser
collen (cyll) nf hazel
collfarn (-au) nf doom, condemnation
collfarnu vb condemn
colli vb lose; be lost, perish; spill, shed
collnod (-au) nm apostrophe
collwr (-wyr) nm loser
côma (-omâu) nm coma
coma (-s) nm comma
comed (-au) nf comet
comedi (-ïau) nf/m comedy
comig adj comic, comical ♦ nm comic (paper)
comisiwn (-iynau) nm commission
comisiynu vb commission
comiwnydd (-ion) nm communist
comiwnyddiaeth nf communism
comiwnyddol adj communist
conach vb grumble
conclaf nm conclave
concro vb conquer

concwerwr (-wyr) *nm* conqueror
concwest (-au) *nf* conquest, victory
condemniad *nm* condemnation
condemnio *vb* condemn
confensiwn (-iynau) *nm* convention
confederasiwn (-asiynau) *nm* confederation
conffirmasiwn *nm* confirmation
conffirmio *vb* confirm
conifferaidd *adj* coniferous
cono *nm* rascal; wag; old fogey
consesiwn (-iynau) *nf* concession
consuriaeth *nf* conjuring
consurio *vb* conjure
consuriwr (-wyr) *nm* conjurer
conwydd *npl* (-en *nf*) coniferous trees
cop, copyn (-nod, -nau) *nm* spider
copa (-âu) *nf* top, crest; head
copi (-ïau) *nm* copy; copy-book
copïo *vb* copy, transcribe
copïwr (-wyr) *nm* copyist, transcriber
copr *nm* copper
côr (corau) *nm* choir; stall, pew. **c. feistr** choirmaster
cor (-rod) *nm* dwarf; spider
corachaidd *adj* dwarfish, stunted
corawl *adj* choral
corbwll (-byllau) *nm* whirlpool; puddle
corcyn (cyrc) *nm* cork
cord (-iau) *nm* cord; chord
cordeddu *vb* twist, twine
corddi *vb* churn; turn; agitate
corddiad (-au) *nm* churning
corddwr (-wyr) *nm* churner
cored (-au) *nf* weir, dam
coreograffiaeth *nf* choreography
corfan (-nau) *nm* metrical foot
corff (cyrff) *nm* body
corfflu (-oedd) *nm* corps
corfflol *adj* corpulent; physical
corfolaeth *nf* bodily form; stature
corfforaeth (-au) *nf* corporation

corffori *vb* embody, incorporate
corfforiad (-au) *nm* embodiment
corfforol *adj* bodily, corporeal, corporal
corgan, côr-gân (-au) *nf* chant
corganu *vb* chant
corgi (-gwn) *nm* cur, corgi
corgimwch (-ychiaid) *nm* prawn
corhwyad (-aid) *nf* teal; moorhen
corlan (-nau) *nf* fold
corlannu *vb* fold
corn (cyrn) *nm* horn; pipe; tube; roll; corn; stethoscope. **c. gwddw(f), c. gwynt** windpipe. **c. siarad** loudspeaker
cornant (-nentydd) *nf* brook, rill
cornboer *nm* phlegm
cornchwiglen (-chwiglod) *nf* lapwing
cornel (-i, -au) *nf/m* corner
cornelu *vb* corner
cornicyll (-od) *nm* lapwing, plover, peewit
cornio *vb* horn, butt; examine with a stethoscope
corniog *adj* horned
cornwyd (-ydd) *nm* boil, abscess, sore
coron (-au) *nf* crown
coroni *vb* crown ♦ *nm* coronation
coroniad *nm* coronation
coronog *adj* crowned
corpws *nm* body (*facetious*)
corrach (corachod) *nm* dwarf, pygmy
corryn (corynnod) *nm* spider
cors (-ydd) *nf* bog, swamp
corsen (-nau, cyrs) *nf* reed; stem, stalk; cane
cortyn (-nau) *nm* cord, rope
corun (-au) *nm* crown of the head; tonsure
corwg(l) (-yg(l)au) *nm* coracle
corws *nm* chorus
corwynt (-oedd) *nm* whirlwind
cosb (-au) *nf* punishment, penalty. **c. ddihenydd** capital punishment

cosbadwy adj punishable
cosbedigaeth nf punishment
cosbi vb punish
cosbol adj punitive, penal
cosbwr (-wyr) nm punisher
cosfa (-feydd) nf itch, itching; thrashing
cosi vb scratch, itch ♦ nm itching
cosmetigau npl cosmetics
cosmig adj cosmic
cost (-au) nf cost, expense
costiad (-au) nm costing
costio vb cost
costiwm (-tiymau) nmf costume
costog (-ion) nm mastiff; cur ♦ adj surly
costowci (-cwn) nm mastiff, mongrel
costrel (-au, -i) nf bottle
costrelaid (-eidiau) nf bottleful
costrelu vb bottle
costus adj costly, expensive
cosyn (-nau, -nod) nm a cheese
côt, cot (cotiau) nf coat
cotwm nm cotton
cowlas (-au) nmf bay of building; hay-mow
cownter (-au, -i) nm counter
cowntio vb count, account, esteem
crac (-iau) nm crack
cracio vb crack
craciog adj cracked
crach npl (-en nf) scabs ♦ adj scabby; petty ♦ -ach npl snobs
crachboer nm phlegm
crachfardd (-feirdd) nm poetaster
crachfeddyg (-on) nm quack doctor
crachfonheddwr (-wyr) nm snob
crafangio, -u vb claw, grab
crafanc (-angau) nf claw; talon; clutch
crafiad (-au) nm scratch
crafog adj cutting, sarcastic
crafu vb scrape; scratch ♦ nm itch
crafwr (-wyr) nm scraper
craff adj close; keen; sagacious ♦

nm hold, grip
craffter nm keenness, sagacity
craffu vb look closely, observe intently
craffus adj keen, sagacious
cragen (cregyn) nf shell
crai adj new, fresh, raw
craidd (creiddiau) nm middle, centre
craig (creigiau) nf rock
crair (creiriau) nm relic
craith (creithiau) nf scar
cramen (-nau) nf crust, scab
cranc (-od) nm crab
crand adj grand
crandrwydd nm grandeur, finery
crap (-iau) nm hold; smattering
crapio vb grapple; pick up
cras (creision) adj parched, dry; harsh
crasiad nm baking
craslyd adj harsh, grating
craster nm dryness; harshness
crasu vb parch, scorch; bake
crau (creuau) nm hole, eye, socket
crau nmf blood, gore
crau (creuau) nm sty; stockade
crawcian, crawcio vb croak, caw
crawen (-nau) nf crust
crawn nm matter, pus
crawni vb gather, suppurate
crawnllyd adj purulent
cread nm creation
creadigaeth (-au) nf creation
creadigol adj creative
creadur (-iaid) nm creature; animal
creadures (-au) nf female creature
creawdwr (-wyr) nm creator
crebach adj shrunk, withered
crebachlyd adj crabbed, wrinkled
crebachu vb shrink, shrivel, wrinkle, pucker
crebwyll (-ion) nm invention, understanding, fancy
crecian vb cluck; crackle
crechwen nf loud laughter, guffaw

crechwenu vb laugh loud, guffaw
cred (-au) nf belief; trust; pledge, troth
credadun (**credinwyr**) nm believer
credadwy adj credible
crediniaeth nf belief
crediniol adj believing
credo (-au) nm/f creed, belief
credu vb believe
credwr (-wyr) nm believer
credyd (-on) nm credit
credydu vb credit
cref adj f. of **cryf**
crefu vb crave, beg, implore
crefydd (-au) nf religion
crefydda vb profess or practise religion
crefyddol adj religious, pious
crefyddolder nm religiousness, piety
crefyddwr (-wyr) nm religioner, religionist
crefft (-au) nf handicraft, trade
crefftus adj skilled, workmanlike
crefftwaith nm craftwork
crefftwr (-wyr) nm craftsman
cregyn npl (**cragen** nf) shells
creider nm freshness
creifion npl scrapings
creigiog adj rocky
creigiwr (-wyr) nm quarryman
creigle (-oedd) nm rocky place
creinio vb wallow, lie or fall down; cringe
creision npl flakes, crisps
crempog (-au) nf pancake
crensio vb grind (the teeth)
crepach adj numb ♦ nf numbness
crest nm crust, scurf
Creta nf Crete
creu vb create
creulon adj cruel
creulondeb (-derau) nm cruelty
crëwr (**crewyr**) nm creator
crëyr (**crehyrod**) nm heron
cri (-au) nm cry, clamour
cri adj new, fresh, raw; unleavened

criafol, -en nf mountain ash
crib (-au) nf/m comb, crest; ridge
cribddeilio vb grab, extort
cribddeiliwr (-wyr) nm extortioner; speculator
cribin (-iau) nf/m rake; skinflint
cribinio vb rake
cribo vb comb; card
criced nm cricket
cricedwr (-wyr) nm cricketer
crimog (-au) nf, **crimp** (-(i)au) nf shin
crin adj withered, sear, dry
crino vb wither, dry up
crintach, -lyd adj niggardly, stingy
crintachrwydd nm niggardliness
crintachu vb scrimp, skimp, stint
crio vb cry, weep
cripio vb scratch; climb, creep
cris-groes nf criss-cross
crisial (-au) nm, adj crystal
crisialu vb crystallise
Cristion (-ogion, **Cristnogion**) nm Christian
Cristionogaeth nf Christianity
Cristionogol adj Christian
criw (-iau) nm crew
criwr (-wyr) nm crier
crocbont (-ydd) nf suspension bridge
crocbren (-ni) nm/f gallows, gibbet
crocbris (-iau) nm exorbitant price
croch adj loud, vehement
crochan (-au) nm pot, cauldron
crochanaid (-eidiau) nm potful
crochenydd (-ion) nm potter
crochenwaith (-weithiau) nm pottery
croen (**crwyn**) nm skin; hide; peel, rind
croendenau adj thin-skinned
croeni, -io vb form skin, skin over
croes nf cross ♦ nm transept
croes (-au) adj cross, contrary
croesair (-eiriau) nm crossword
croesawgar adj hospitable
croesawiad nm welcome,

reception

croesawu vb welcome

croesawus adj hospitable

croesbren (-nau) nm/f cross

croesddweud vb contradict

croesfan (-nau) nf crossing

croesffordd (-ffyrdd) nf crossroad

croesgad (-au) nf crusade

croesgadwr (-wyr) nm crusader

croeshoeliad nm crucifixion

croeshoelio vb crucify

croesholi vb cross-examine

croesholiad (-au) nm cross-examination

croesi vb cross

croeso nm welcome

croesymgroes adj criss-cross; vice-versa

crofen (-nau, -ni) nf rind, crust

crog (-au) nf cross, rood ♦ adj hanging

crogi vb hang, suspend

croglath (-au) nf springe, snare, gibbet

Croglith nm/f: **Dydd Gwener y G.** Good Friday

croglofft (-ydd, -au) nf garret; rood-loft

crogwr (-wyr) nm hangman

cronglwyd (-ydd) nf: **tan fy ngh.** under my roof

crombil (-iau) nf crop; gizzard; bowels

cromen (-ni, -nau) nf dome

cromfach (-au) nf bracket, parenthesis

cromlech (-au, -i) nf cromlech

cromosom (-au) nm chromosome

cron adj f. of **crwn**

cronfa (-feydd) nf reservoir; fund

cronicl (-au) nm chronicle

croniclo vb chronicle

cronnell (cronellau) nf sphere, globe

cronni vb collect, hoard; dam

cronolegol adj chronological

cropian vb creep, crawl, grope

crosiet (-au, -i) nm crotchet

croth (-au) nf womb; calf (of leg)

croyw adj clear, plain, distinct; fresh

croywder nm clearness; freshness

croywi vb clear; freshen

crud (-au) nm cradle

crug (-iau) nm hillock; tumulus; heap; multitude; abscess, blister

cruglwyth (-i) nm heap, pile

cruglwytho vb heap, pile up; overload

crugo vb fester, vex, plague

crwban (-od) nm tortoise, turtle

crwca adj crooked, bowed, bent

crwm adj convex, curved, bowed; f **crom**

crwn adj round; complete; f **cron**

crwner (-iaid) nm coroner

crwsâd (-adau) nm/f crusade

crwst (crystiau) nm crust

crwt (cryts) nm boy, lad

crwth (crythau) nm crowd, fiddle; purring; hump

crwybr nm honeycomb; mist; hoarfrost

crwydr nm wandering. **ar g.** astray

crwydro vb wander, stray, roam

crwydrol, crwydrus adj wandering

crwydrwr (-wyr) nm wanderer, rover

crwydryn (-iaid) nm vagrant, tramp

crwys nf, npl cross, crucifix. **dan ei g.** laid out for burial

crybwyll vb mention ♦ (-ion) nm mention

crybwylliad nm mention, notice

crych adj rippling; curly; quavering ♦ (-au) nm crease, ripple, wrinkle

crychlais (-leisiau) nm trill, tremolo

crychlyd adj wrinkled, puckered

crychnaid (-neidiau) nf leap, gambol

crychneidio vb skip, frisk
crychni nm curliness; wrinkle
crychu vb wrinkle, pucker; ruffle, ripple
cryd (-iau) nm shivering; fever; ague
crydd (-ion) nm cobbler, shoemaker
crydda vb cobble
cryf adj strong; f **cref**
cryfder, -dwr nm strength
cryfhaol adj strengthening
cryfhau vb strengthen; grow strong
cryg adj hoarse; f **creg**
cryglyd adj hoarse, raucous
crygni nm hoarseness
crygu vb hoarsen
cryman (-au) nm reaping-hook, sickle
crymanwr (-wyr),nm reaper
crymu vb bow, bend, stoop
cryn adj considerable, much
crŷn, cryn nm, adj shivering
crynder nm roundness
cryndod nm trembling, shivering
crynedig adj trembling, tremulous
crynfa (-feydd) nf tremble, tremor
crynhoad (-noadau) nm collection, digest
crynhoi vb gather together, collect
cryno adj compact; neat, tidy
crynodeb (-au) nm summary
crynswth nm mass, bulk, whole
crynu vb shiver, tremble, quake
Crynwr (-wyr) nm Quaker
crys (-au) nm shirt
crysbaid (-beisiau) nf jacket, jerkin
crystyn (crystiau) nm crust
crythor (-ion) nm fiddler, violinist
cryw (-iau) nm creel; weir
cu adj dear, fond, kind
cuchio vb scowl, frown
cuchiog adj scowling, frowning
cudyll (-od) nm hawk
cudyn (-nau) nm lock (of hair),

tuft
cudd adj hidden, concealed
cuddfa (-feydd) nf hiding-place; hoard
cuddiad nm hiding
cuddiedig adj hidden, concealed
cuddio vb hide, conceal
cufydd (-au) nm cubit
cul (-ion) adj narrow, lean
culfor (-oedd) nm strait
culhau vb narrow; grow lean
culni nm narrowness
cun adj dear, beloved; lovely
cunnog (cunogau) nf pail
cur nm throb, ache, pain; care, trouble
curad (-iaid) nm curate
curadiaeth (-au) nf curacy
curfa (-feydd) nf beating, flogging
curiad (-au) nm beat, throb, pulse
curio vb pine, waste
curlaw nm pelting rain
curn (-au), **curnen** (-nau) nf mound, cone, rick
curnennu vb heap, stack
curo vb beat, strike, knock; throb; clap
curwr (-wyr) nm beater
curyll (-od) nm hawk
cusan (-au) nf/m kiss
cusanu vb kiss
cut (-iau) nm hovel, shed, sty
cuwch (cuchiau) nm scowl, frown
cwafrio vb quaver, trill
cwar (-au) nm quarry
cwb (cybiau) nm kennel, coop, sty
cwbl adj, nm all, whole, total
cwblhad nm fulfilment
cwblhau vb fulfil, complete, finish
cwcer (-au) nm cooker
cwcw nf cuckoo
cwcwallt (-iaid) nm cuckold
cwcwalltu vb cuckold
cwcwll (cycyllau) nm hood, cowl
cwch (cychod) nm boat; hive. **c. gwyllt** speed boat
cwd (cydau) nm pouch, bag

cweir (-iau) *nm* thrashing, hiding
cweryl (-on) *nm* quarrel
cweryla *vb* quarrel
cwerylgar *adj* quarrelsome
cwest (-au) *nm* inquest
cwestiwn (-iynau) *nm* question
cwestiynu *vb* question
cwffio *vb* fight, box
cwgn (cygnau) *nm* knot; knuckle; joint
cwilt (-iau) *nm* quilt
cwlbren (-ni) *nm* bludgeon
cwlff, -yn (cylffiau) *nm* chunk
cwlwm see **clwm**
cwlltwr (cylltyrau) *nm* coulter
cwm (cymau, cymoedd) *nm* valley
cwman *nm* rump; stoop; churn
cwmanu *vb* stoop
cwmni (-iau, -ïoedd) *nm* company
cwmnïaeth *nf* companionship
cwmpas (-oedd) *nm* round. **o.g.** about
cwmpasog *adj* round about, circuitous
cwmpasu *vb* round, wind, surround
cwmpawd (-odau) *nm* compass
cwmpeini, cwmpni *nm* company
cwmwd (cymydau) *nm* commot
cwmwl (cymylau) *nm* cloud
cwn see **ci**
cwndid (-au) *nm* song, carol
cwningen (-ingod) *nf* rabbit
cwnsel (-au, -oedd, -i) *nm* council; counsel, advice, secret
cwnsela *vb* counsel
cwnsler (-iaid) *nm* counsellor
cwnstabl (-iaid) *nm* constable
cworwm *nm* quorum
cwota (-au) *nm* quota
cwpan (-au) *nmif* cup, goblet; chalice
cwpanaid (-eidiau) *nm/f* cupful
cwpl (cyplau) *nm* couple; tie beam
cwplâd, cwpláu see **cwblhad, cwblhau**
cwpled (-i, -au) *nm* couplet

cwplws (cyplysau) *nm* coupling; brace
cwpwrdd (cypyrddau) *nm* cupboard
cwr (cyrrau) *nm* edge, border, skirt
cwrcwd *nm* stooping; squatting
cwrdd (cyrddau) *nm* meeting
cwrdd, cwrddyd *vb* meet, touch
cwrel *nm* coral
cwricwlwm (cwricwla) *nm* curriculum
cwrlid (-au) *nm* coverlet
cwrs (cyrsiau) *nm* course; fit
cwrt (cyrtiau) *nm* court
cwrtais *adj* courteous
cwrteisi, cwrteisrwydd *nm* courtesy
cwrw (cyrfau) *nm* ale, beer
cwrwg(l) see **corwg(l)**
cwsg *nm* sleep
cwsmer (-iaid) *nm* customer
cwsmeriaeth *nf* custom
cwstard (-au) *nm* custard
cwstwm (cystymau) *nm* custom, patronage
cwt (cytiau) *nf/m* tail, skirt, queue
cwt (cytiau) *nm* hut, sty
cwta *adj* short, curt
cwter (-i, -ydd) *nf* gutter, channel
cwtogi *vb* shorten, curtail
cwthr (cythrau) *nm* anus, rectum
cwthwm (cythymau) *nm* puff of wind, storm
cwympo *vb* fall, tumble
cwympo *vb* fall; fell
cwyn (-ion) *nm/f* complaint, plaint
cwynfan *vb* complain, lament
cwynfanllyd *adj* querulous
cwynfanus *adj* plaintive, mournful
cwyno *vb* complain, lament
cwyr *nm* wax
cwyro *vb* wax
cwys (-au, -i) *nf* furrow-slice, furrow
cybôl *nm* nonsense, rubbish
cybolfa *nf* hotchpotch, medley
cyboli *vb* muddle; talk nonsense;

mess, bother

cybydd (-ion) *nm* miser, niggard

cybydda *vb* stint, hoard

cybydd-dod, -dra *nm* miserliness

cybyddlyd *adj* miserly

cycyllog *adj* hooded, cowled

cychaid (-eidiau) *nm* boatful; hiveful

cychwr (-wyr) *nm* boatman

cychwyn *vb* rise, stir, start

cychwynfa *nf* start, starting-point

cychwyniad (-au) *nm* start, beginning

cyd *adj* joint, united, common; fellow ♦ *prefix* together

cydadrodd *vb* to recite together

cydaid (-eidiau) *nm* bagful

cydbwysedd *nm* balance

cyd-destun (-au) *nm* context

cydfod *nm* agreement, concord

cydfodolaeth *nf* coexistence

cydfyned *vb* go with, concur, agree

cydfyw *vb* cohabit

cydffurfio *vb* conform

cydgordio *vb* agree, harmonize

cydgwmni (-ïau) *nm* consortium

cydiedig *adj* adjoined

cydio *vb* join; bite; take hold

cydnabod *vb* acknowledge ♦ *nm* acquaintance

cydnabyddiaeth *nf* acquaintance; recognition

cydnabyddus *adj* acquainted; familiar

cydnaws *adj* congenial

cydnerth *adj* well set

cydol *nf/m, adj* whole

cydradd *adj* equal

cydraddoldeb *nm* equality

cyd-rhwng *prep* between

cydsyniad *nm* consent

cydsynio *vb* consent

cydwastad *adj* level (with), even

cydweddog *adj* conjugal

cydweddu *vb* accord, agree

cydweithfa (-feydd) *nf* co-operative

cydweithrediad *nm* co-operation

cydweithredol *adj* co-operative

cydweithredu *vb* co-operate

cydweled *vb* agree

cydwladol *adj* international

cyd-wladwr (-wyr) *nm* compatriot

cydwybod (-au) *nf* conscience

cydwybodol *adj* conscientious

cydwybodolrwydd *nm* conscientiousness

cydymaith (cymdeithion) *nm* companion

cydymdeimlad *nm* sympathy

cydymdeimlo *vb* sympathize

cydymffurfiad *nm* conformity

cydymffurfio *vb* conform

cydymgais *nm* competition, rivalry, joint effort

cydymgeisydd (-wyr) *nm* rival

cyddwysiad (-au) *nm* condensation

cyfadran (-nau) *nf* faculty (*in college*); period (*in music*)

cyfaddas *adj* fit, suitable, convenient

cyfaddasiad (-au) *nm* adaptation

cyfaddaster *nm* fitness, suitability

cyfaddasu *vb* fit, adapt

cyfaddawd (-odau) *nm* compromise

cyfaddawdu *vb* compromise

cyfaddef *vb* confess, own, admit

cyfaddefiad (-au) *nm* confession, admission

cyfaenad *nm, adj* harmonious song

cyfagos *adj* near, adjacent, neighbouring

cyfaill (-eillion) *nm* friend

cyfair (-eiriau) *nm* acre

cyfair, -er *nm* direction. **ar g.** for; opposite

cyfalaf *nm* capital

cyfalafiaeth *nf* capitalism

cyfalafol *adj* capitalistic

cyfalafwr (-wyr) *nm* capitalist

cyfamod (-au) *nm* covenant

cyfamodi *vb* covenant

cyfamodol adj federal; covenanted
cyfamodwr (-wyr) nm covenanter
cyfamser nm meantime
cyfamserol adj timely; synchronous
cyfan adj, nm whole
cyfandir (-oedd) nm continent
cyfandirol adj continental
cyfanfor (-oedd) nm main sea, ocean
cyfanfyd nm whole world, universe
cyfangorff nm whole, bulk, mass
cyfan gwbl adj: yn g. altogether, complete
cyfanheddol adj habitable, inhabited
cyfanheddu vb dwell, inhabit
cyfannedd adj inhabited ♦ (-anheddau) nf inhabited place, habitation
cyfannol adj integrated, integral
cyfannu vb make whole, complete
cyfanrwydd nm wholeness, entirety
cyfansawdd adj composite, compound
cyfansoddi vb compose, constitute
cyfansoddiad (-au) nm composition; constitution
cyfansoddiadol adj constitutional
cyfansoddwr (-wyr) nm composer
cyfansoddyn (-ion) nm constituent, compound
cyfanswm (-symiau) nm total
cyfantoledd (-au) nm equilibrium
cyfanwaith (-weithiau) nm complete composition, whole
cyfarch vb greet, salute, address
cyfarchiad (-au) nm greeting, salutation
cyfaredd (-ion) nf charm, spell
cyfareddol adj enchanting
cyfareddu vb charm, enchant
cyfarfod vb meet ♦ (-ydd) nm meeting
cyfarfyddiad (-au) nm meeting
cyfarpar nm provision, equipment;

diet. **c. rhyfel** munitions of war
cyfarparu vb equip
cyfartal adj equal, even
cyfartaledd nm proportion, average
cyfartalu vb proportion, equalize
cyfarth vb, nm bark
cyfarwydd adj skilled; familiar ♦ (-iaid) nm storyteller
cyfarwyddo vb direct; become familiar
cyfarwyddwr (-wyr) nm director
cyfarwyddyd (-iadau) nm direction, instruction
cyfatal adj unsettled, hindering
cyfateb vb correspond, agree, tally
cyfatebiaeth (-au) nf correspondence, analogy
cyfatebol adj corresponding, proportionate
cyfathrach (-au) nf affinity; intercourse
cyfathrachu vb have intercourse
cyfathrachwr (-wyr) nm kinsman
cyfathreb (-au) nm communication
cyfathrebu vb communicate
cyfddydd nm day-break, dawn
cyfeb, cyfebr adj pregnant (of mare, ewe)
cyfebol adj in foal
cyfeddach (-au) nf carousal
cyfeddachwr (-wyr) nm carouser
cyfeiliant nm musical accompaniment
cyfeilio vb accompany
cyfeiliorn nm error; wandering, lost (person etc). **ar g.** astray
cyfeiliornad (-au) nm error, heresy
cyfeiliorni vb err, stray
cyfeiliornus adj erroneous, mistaken
cyfeilydd (-ion) nm accompanist
cyfeillach (-au) nf fellowship; fellowship-meeting
cyfeillachu vb associate
cyfeilles (-au) nf female friend

cyfeillgar adj friendly
cyfeillgarwch nm friendship
cyfeiriad (-au) nm direction; reference; (postal) address
cyfeiriannu nm orienteering
cyfeirio vb point; direct; refer; address (letter)
cyfeirnod (-au) nm mark of reference; aim; direct (in music)
cyfeirydd (-ion) nm indicator, guide
cyfenw (-au) nm surname; namesake
cyfenwi vb surname
cyfer nm: **ar g.** for; opposite
cyferbyn adj opposite
cyferbyniad (-au) nm contrast
cyferbyniol adj opposing, opposite, contrasting
cyferbynnu vb contrast, compare
cyfethol vb co-opt
cyfiaith adj of the same language
cyfiawn adj just, righteous
cyfiawnder (-au) nm justice, righteousness
cyfiawnhad nm justification
cyfiawnhau vb justify
cyfieithiad (-au) nm translation, version
cyfieithu vb translate, interpret
cyfieithydd (-wyr) nm translator, interpreter
cyfisol adj of the present month, instant
cyflafan (-au) nf outrage; massacre
cyflafareddiad nm arbitration
cyflafareddu vb arbitrate
cyflafareddwr (-wyr) nm arbitrator
cyflaith nm toffee
cyflawn adj full, complete
cyflawnder nm fullness; abundance
cyflawni vb fulfil, perform, commit
cyflawniad (-au) nm fulfilment performance

cyfle (-oedd) nm place; chance, opportunity
cyfled adj as broad as
cyflegr (-au) nm gun, cannon, battery
cyflegru vb bombard
cyflenwad (-au) nm supply
cyflenwi vb supply
cyfleu vb place, set; convey
cyfleus adj convenient
cyfleustra (-terau) nm opportunity, convenience
cyflin adj parallel
cyfliw adj of the same colour
cyflo adj in calf
cyflog (-au) nmf hire, wage, wages
cyflogaeth nf employment
cyflogedig (-ion) nm employee
cyflogi vb hire; engage in service
cyflogwr (-wyr) nm hirer, employer
cyflwr (-lyrau) nm condition; case
cyflwyniad nm presentation; dedication
cyflwyno vb present; dedicate
cyflwynydd (-ion) nm compère, presenter
cyflychwr, -wyr nm evening twilight, dusk
cyflym adj quick, fast, swift
cyflymder, -dra nm swiftness, speed
cyflymu vb speed, accelerate
cyflynu vb stick together
cyflyru vb condition
cyflythreniad (-au) nm alliteration
cyfnerthu vb confirm; aid, help
cyfnerthydd (-ion, -wyr) nm strengthener, booster
cyfnesaf (-iaid, -eifiaid) nmf next of kin, kinsman ✝ adj next, nearest
cyfnewid vb change, exchange
cyfnewidfa (-oedd, -feydd) nf exchange
cyfnewidiad (-au) nm change,

alteration

cyfnewidiol *adj* changeable

cyfnewidiwr (-wyr) *nm* changer, trader

cyfnither (-oedd) *nf* female cousin

cyfnod (-au) *nm* period

cyfnodol *adj* periodic(al) ♦ **-yn** (-ion) *nm* periodical publication

cyfnos *nm* evening twilight, dusk

cyfochredd *nm* parallelism

cyfochrog *adj* parallel

cyfodi *vb* rise, arise; raise

cyfodiad *nm* rise, rising

cyfoed *adj* contemporary, of the same age ♦ (-ion) *nm* contemporaries

cyfoes *adj* contemporary

cyfoesi *vb* be contemporary

cyfoeswr (-wyr) *nm* contemporary

cyfoeth *nm* power; riches, wealth

cyfoethog *adj* powerful; rich, wealthy

cyfoethogi *vb* make or grow rich

cyfog *nm* sickness

cyfogi *vb* vomit

cyfor *nm* flood, abundance; rim, brim, edge ♦ *adj* entire, brim-full

cyforiog *adj* brim-full, overflowing

cyfosodiad *nm* apposition

cyfradd (-au) *nf* rate. **c. llog** rate of interest ♦ *adj* of equal rank

cyfraid (-reidiau) *nm* necessity

cyfraith (-reithiau) *nf* law

cyfran (-nau) *nf* part, portion, share

cyfranc (-rangau) *nf/m* meeting; combat; incident; story, tale

cyfranddaliad (-au) *nm* share

cyfranddaliwr (-wyr) *nm* shareholder

cyfraniad (-au) *nm* contribution

cyfrannog *adj* participating, partaking

cyfrannol *adj* contributing

cyfrannu *vb* contribute; impart

cyfrannwr (-anwyr) *nm* contributor

cyfranogi *vb* participate, partake

cyfranogwr (-wyr) *nm* partaker

cyfredol *adj* current, concurrent

cyfreithio *vb* go to law, litigate

cyfreithiol *adj* legal

cyfreithiwr (-wyr) *nm* lawyer

cyfreithlon *adj* lawful, legitimate

cyfreithlondeb *nm* lawfulness

cyfreithloni *vb* legalize; justify

cyfreithus *adj* legitimate

cyfres (-i) *nf* series

cyfresol *adj* serial

cyfresu *vb* serialise

cyfresymiad (-au) *nm* syllogism

cyfresymu *vb* syllogise

cyfrgolli *vb* lose utterly; damn

cyfrif *vb* count, reckon; account; impute ♦ (-on) *nm* account, reckoning

cyfrifeg *nm/f* accountancy

cyfrifiad (-au) *nm* counting; census

cyfrifiadur (-on) *nm* computer

cyfrifiadureg *nf* computer science

cyfrifianell *nf* calculator

cyfriol *adj* of repute; responsible

cyfrifoldeb (-au) *nm* responsibility

cyfrifydd (-ion) *nm* statistician, accountant

cyfrin *adj* secret, subtle

cyfrinach (-au) *nf* secret

cyfrinachol *adj* secret, private, confidential

cyfrinfa *nf* lodge of friendly society or trade union

cyfrin-gyngor (-nghorau) *nm* privy council

cyfriniaeth *nf* mystery; mysticism

cyfriniol *adj* mysterious, mystic

cyfriniwr (-wyr) *nm* mystic

cyfrodedd *adj* twisted, twined

cyfrodeddu *vb* twist, twine

cyfrol (-au) *nf* volume

cyfrwng (-ryngau) *nm* medium, means

cyfrwy (-au) *nm* saddle

cyfrwyo *vb* saddle

cyfrwys *adj* cunning

cyfrwystra *nm* cunning

cyfrwÿwr (-wyr) nm saddler
cyfryngdod nm mediation, intercession; mediatorship
cyfryngiad nm mediation; intervention
cyfryngol adj mediatorial
cyfryngu vb mediate; intervene
cyfryngwr (-wyr) nm mediator
cyfryngwriaeth nf mediatorship
cyfryw adj like, such
cyfuchlinedd (-au) nm contour
cyfuchliniau npl contours
cyfundeb (-au) nm union; connexion
cyfundebol adj connexional; denominational
cyfundrefn (-au) nf system
cyfundrefnol adj systematic
cyfundrefnu vb systematize
cyfuniad (-au) nm combination
cyfuno vb unite, combine
cyfunol adj united
cyfunrywiol adj homosexual
cyfuwch adj as high
cyfweld vb interview
cyfweliad (-au) nm interview
cyfwerth adj equivalent
cyfwng (-yngau) nm space; interval
cyfwrdd vb meet
cyfyng adj narrow, confined
cyfyngder (-au) nm trouble, distress
cyfyngdra nm narrowness; distress
cyfyngedig adj confined, restricted, limited
cyfyng-gyngor nm perplexity
cyfyngu vb narrow, confine, limit
cyfyl nm neighbourhood. ar ei g. near him
cyfyrder (-dyr) nm second cousin
cyfystlys adj side by side
cyfystyr adj synonymous
cyfystyron npl synonyms
cyff (-ion) nm stock
cyffaith (-ffeithiau) nm confection

cyffelyb adj like, similar
cyffelybiaeth (-au) nf likeness, similitude
cyffelybiaethol adj figurative
cyffelybrwydd nm likeness, similarity
cyffelybu vb liken, compare
cyffes (-ion) nf confession
cyffesgell (-oedd) nf confessional
cyffesu vb confess
cyffeswr (-wyr), **-ydd** (-ion) nm confessor
cyffin (-iau, -ydd) nf/m border, confine
cyffindir (-oedd) nm frontier, march
cyffio vb stiffen; fetter, shackle; beat
cyffion npl stocks
cyfford (-ffyrdd) nf junction
cyffredin adj common; general
cyffredinedd nm mediocrity, banality
cyffredinol adj general, universal
cyffredinoli vb universalize, generalize
cyffredinolrwydd nm universality
cyffredinwch nm commonness
cyffro (-adau) nm motion, stir; excitement
cyffroi vb move, excite; provoke
cyffrous adj exciting; excited
cyffur (-iau) nm/f ingredient, drug
cyffuriwr (-wyr) nm apothecary, druggist
cyffwrdd vb meet, touch
cyffylog (-od) nm woodcock
cyffyrddiad (-au) nm touch, contact
cyffyrddus adj comfortable
cygnog adj knotted, gnarled
cyngaf, cyngaw nm burdock; burs
cyngan adj suitable, harmonious
cynganeddol adj in cynghanedd
cynganeddu vb form cynghanedd; harmonize
cynganeddwr (-wyr) nm writer of

cynghanedd

cyngaws (**cynghawsau, -ion**) *nm* lawsuit, action; trial; battle

cyngerdd (**-ngherddau**) *nm/f* concert

cynghanedd (**cynganeddion**) *nf* music, harmony; Welsh metrical alliteration

cynghori *vb* counsel, advise; exhort

cynghorwr (**-wyr**) *nm* councillor; counsellor; exhorter

cynghrair (**-eiriau**) *nm/f* alliance, league

cynghreiriad (**-iaid**) *nm* confederate, ally

cynghreirio *vb* league, confederate

cynghreiriwr (**-wyr**) *nm* confederate, ally

cyngor (**-nghorion**) *nm* counsel, advice ♦ (**-nghorau**) *xm* council. **C. Bro** Community Council. **C. Tref** Town Council. **C. Sir** County Council

cyngres (**-au, -i**) *nf* congress

cyngresydd (**-wyr**) *nm* congressman

cyngwystl (**-(i)on**) *nm/f* wager, pledge

cyhoedd *adj, nm* public

cyhoeddi *vb* publish, announce

cyhoeddiad (**-au**) *nm* publication; announcement; (preaching) engagement

cyhoeddus *adj* public

cyhoeddusrwydd *nm* publicity

cyhoeddwr (**-wyr**) *nm* publisher

cyhuddiad (**-au**) *nm* accusation, charge

cyhuddo *vb* accuse, charge

cyhuddwr (**-wyr**) *nm* accuser

cyhwfan *vb* wave, heave

cyhyd *adj* as long, so long

cyhydedd *nm* equator

cyhydeddol *adj* equatorial, equinoctial

cyhyr (**-au**) *nm* flesh, muscle

cyhyrog *adj* muscular

cylch (**-au, oedd**) *nm* round, circle, sphere, hoop

cylchdaith (**-deithiau**) *nf* circuit

cylchdro (**-eon, -adau**) *nm* orbit

cylchdroi *vb* rotate, revolve

cylched (**-au**) *nm* coverlet, blanket

cylchedd (**-au**) *nm/f* compass, circle, circuit

cylchgrawn (**-gronau**) *nm* magazine

cylchlythyr (**-au**) *nm* circular

cylchredeg *vb* circulate

cylchrediad *nm* circulation

cylchres (**-i**) *nf* round, rota

cylchwyl (**-iau**) *nf* anniversary, festival

cylchynol *adj* surrounding

cylchynu *vb* surround, encompass

cylion *npl* (**-yn** *nm*, **-en** *nf*) flies, gnats

cylymu *vb* knot, tie

cyll *npl* (**collen** *nf*) hazel-trees

cylla (**-on**) *nm* stomach

cyllell (**-yll**) *nf* knife

cyllid (**-au**) *nm* revenue, income

cyllideb (**-au**) *nf* budget

cyllidol *adj* financial, fiscal

cyllidwr (**-wyr**), **cyllidydd** (**-ion**) *nm* taxgatherer, revenue or excise officer, financier

cymaint *adj* as big, as much, as many; so big, *etc*

cymal (**-au**) *nm* joint; clause (*gram.*)

cymalwst *nf* rheumatism

cymanfa (**-oedd**) *nf* assembly; festival

cymantoledd *nm* equilibrium

cymanwlad *nf* commonwealth

cymar (**-heiriaid**) *nf* fellow, partner

cymathiad *nm* assimilation

cymathu *vb* assimilate

cymdeithas (**-au**) *nf* society, association. **C. yr Iaith Gymraeg** The Welsh Language Society

cymdeithaseg nf/m sociology
cymdeithasegol adj sociological
cymdeithasgar adj sociable
cymdeithasol adj social
cymdeithasu vb associate
cymdogaeth (-au) nf neighbourhood
cymdogol adj neighbourly
cymedr (-au) nm mean (maths), average
cymedrol adj moderate, temperate
cymedroldeb nm moderation, temperance
cymedroli vb moderate
cymedrolwr (-wyr) nm moderator; moderate drinker
cymell vb urge, press, persuade, induce
cymen adj wise, skilful, neat, becoming
cymer (-au) nm confluence
cymeradwy adj acceptable, approved, commendable
cymeradwyaeth nf approval; applause
cymeradwyo vb approve; recommend
cymeradwyol aaj commendary
cymeriad (-au) nm character, reputation
cymesur adj proportionate, symmetrical
cymesuredd nm proportion, symmetry
cymesurol adj commensurate, proportionate
cymhareb (cymarebau) nf ratio
cymhariaeth (cymariaethau) nf comparison
cymharol adj comparative
cymharu vb pair; compare
cymhathu vb assimilate
cymhelliad (-hellion) nm motive, inducement
cymhelliant (-nnau) nm motivation
cymhendod nm knowledge; proficiency; tidiness; eloquence; affection

cymhennu vb put in order, trim; scold, reprove
cymhercyn adj limping, infirm ♦ nm valetudinarian
cymhleth (-au) adj complex, complicated
cymhlethdod (-au) nm complexity
cymhlethu vb complicate
cymhorthdal (cymorthdaloedd) nm subsidy, grant
cymhwysiad nm application, adjustment
cymhwyso vb apply, adjust
cymhwyster (cymwysterau) nm fitness, suitability; (pl) qualifications
cymod nm reconciliation
cymodi vb reconcile; be reconciled
cymodol adj reconciliatory, propitiatory
cymodwr (-wyr) nm reconciler
cymon adj orderly, tidy; seemly
cymorth vb assist, aid, help ♦ nm assistance, aid, help
Cymraeg nf/m, adj Welsh
Cymraes nf Welshwoman
cymrawd (-odyr) nm comrade, fellow
Cymreictod nm Welshness
Cymreig adj Welsh
Cymreigaidd adj Welshy
Cymreiges (-au) nf Welshwoman
Cymreigio vb translate into Welsh
Cymreigiwr (-wyr) nm one versed or skilled in Welsh; Welsh-speaking Welshman
Cymro (**Cymry**) nm Welshman
cymrodedd nm arbitration; compromise
cymrodeddu vb compromise, reconcile
cymrodor (-ion) nm consociate, fellow
cymrodoriaeth nf fellowship
Cymru nf Wales
cymrwd nm mortar, plaster

Cymry see **Cymro**
cymryd vb take, accept. **c. ar** pretend
cymun, -deb nm communion, fellowship
cymuned nf community
cymunedol adj community
cymuno vb commune
cymunwr (-wyr) nm communicant
cymwy (-au) nm affliction
cymwynas (-au) nf kindness, favour
cymwynasgar adj obliging, kind
cymwynasgarwch nm obligingness, kindness
cymwynaswr (-wyr) nm benefactor
cymwys adj fit, proper, suitable; exact
cymwysedig adj applied
cymwysiadol adj applicable
cymydog (cymdogion) nm neighbour; f **cymdoges**
cymylog adj cloudy, clouded
cymylu vb cloud, dim, obscure
cymyndod nm committal
cymynnu vb bequeath
cymynrodd (-ion) nf legacy, bequest
cymynroddi vb bequeath
cymynu vb hew, fell
cymynwr (-wyr) nm hewer, feller
cymysg adj mixed
cymysgedd nm/f mixture
cymysgfa nf mixture, medley, hotchpotch
cymysgliw adj motley
cymysglyd adj muddled, confused
cymysgryw adj mongrel; heterogeneous
cymysgu vb mix, blend; confuse
cymysgwch nm mixture, jumble
cymysgwr (-wyr) nm mixer, blender
cyn prefix before, previous, first, former, pre-, ex-
cyn adv: **cyn wynned â** as white as

cŷn (cynion) nm wedge, chisel
cynadledda vb meet in conference
cynaeafu vb harvest
cynamserol adj premature, untimely
cynaniad nm pronunciation
cynanu vb pronounce
cyndad (-au) nm forefather, ancestor
cynderfynol adj semi-final
cyndyn adj stubborn, obstinate
cyndynnu vb be obstinate
cyndynrwydd nm stubborness, obstinacy
cynddaredd nf madness; rabies
cynddeiriog adj mad, rabid
cynddeiriogi vb madden, enrage
cynddeiriogrwydd nm rage, fury
cynddrwg adj as bad
cynddydd nm day-break, dawn
cynefin nm acquainted, accustomed, familiar ♦ nm haunt, habitat
cynefindra nm use, familiarity
cynefino vb get used, become accustomed
cynefinol adj usual, accustomed
cynfas (-au) nf/m (bed) sheet; canvas
cynfyd nm primitive world, antiquity
cynffon (-nau) nf tail; tang
cynffonna vb fawn, toady, cringe
cynffonnwr (-onwyr) nm toady, sycophant; sneak
cyn-geni adj antenatal
cynhadledd (cynadleddau) nf conference
cynhaeaf (cynaeafau) nm harvest
cyn(h)aeafa vb dry in the sun
cyn(h)aeafu vb harvest
cyn(h)aeafwr (-wyr) nm harvester
cynhaliaeth nf maintenance, support
cynhaliol adj sustaining
cynhaliwr (-wyr) nm supporter, sustainer

cynhanesiol adj prehistoric
cynhebrwng (-yngau) nm funeral
cynhenid adj innate
cynhennu vb contend, quarrel
cynhennus adj contentious, quarrelsome
cynhennwr (-henwyr) nm wrangler
cynhesol adj agreeable, amiable
cynhesrwydd nm warmth
cynhesu vb warm, get warm
cynhorthwy (cynorthwyon) nm help, aid
cynhwynol adj natural, congenital, innate
cynhwysedd (cynwyseddau) nm capacity, capacitance
cynhwysfawr adj comprehensive
cynhwysiad nm contents
cynhyrchiad (-au) nm production
cynhyrchiol adj productive
cynhyrchu vb produce
cynhyrchydd (-ion, cynhyrchwyr) nm producer, generator
cynhyrfiad (cynyrfiadau) nm stirring, agitation
cynhyrfiol adj stirring, thrilling
cynhyrfu vb stir, agitate
cynhyrfus adj agitated; exciting
cynhyrfwr (-wyr) nm agitator, disturber
cynhysgaeth nf dower, portion, fortune
cyni nm anguish, distress, adversity
cynifer adj, nm as many, so many
cynigiad (-au) nm proposal, motion
cynigiwr (-wyr), **-ydd (-ion)** nm proposer, mover
cynildeb nm frugality, economy
cynilion npl savings
cynilo vb save, economise
cynio vb chisel, gouge
cyniwair vb go to and fro, frequent
cyniweirfa (-feydd) nf resort, haunt

cyniweirydd nm wayfarer
cynllun (-iau) nm pattern; plan
cynllunio vb plan, design
cynllunydd (-ion, -wyr) nm designer
cynllwyn vb plot, conspire ♦ (-ion) nm plot
cynllwynio vb conspire, plot
cynllwynwr (-wyr) nm conspirator
cynnal vb hold, uphold, support, sustain
cynnar adj early
cynnau vb kindle, light
cynneddf (cyneddfau) nf quality, faculty
cynnen (cynhennau) nf contention, strife. **asgwrn y g.** bone of contention
cynnes adj warm
cynnig vb offer; attempt; propose, move; bid; apply ♦ (cynigion) nm offer; attempt; motion
cynnil adj economical; delicate
cynnor (cynorau) nf door-post
cynnud nm firewood, fuel
cynnull vb collect, gather, assemble
cynnwrf nm stir, commotion, agitation
cynnwys vb contain, include, comprise, comprehend ♦ nm content(s)
cynnydd nm increase, growth, progress
cynnyrch (cynhyrchion) nm produce, product; (pl) productions
cynoesol adj primeval
cynorthwyo vb help, assist
cynorthwyol adj auxiliary; assistant
cynorthwywr (-wyr) nm helper, assistant
cynradd adj primary
cynrhon npl (-yn nm) maggots
cynrhoni vb breed maggots
cynrhonllyd adj maggoty

cynrychioladol adj representative
cynrychioliaeth nf representation
cynrychioli vb represent
cynrychiolwr (**-wyr**), **-ydd** (**-ion**) nm representative, delegate
cynt adj earlier, sooner, quicker ♦ adv see **gynt**
cyntaf adj, adv first
cyntedd (**-au**) nm court; porch, foyer
cyntefig adj prime, primitive
cyntun nm nap
cynulleidfa (**-oedd**) nf congregation
cynulleidfaol adj congregational
cynulliad (**-au**) nm gathering
cynuta vb gather fuel
cynyddol adj increasing, growing
cynyddu vb increase
cynysgaeddu vb endow, endue
cyplad nm copula
cypladu vb copulate
cyplu, cyplysu vb couple
cyraeddadwy adj attainable
cyraeddiadau npl attainments
cyrbibion npl atoms, smithereens
cyrcydu vb squat, cower
cyrch (**-au**) nm attack
cyrchfa (**-feydd**) nf resort
cyrchu vb go, resort, repair
cyrhaeddgar adj telling, incisive
cyrhaeddiad (**cyraeddiadau**) nm reach, attainment
cyrliog adj curly
cyrraedd vb reach, attain; arrive
cyrren npl (**cyrensen** nf) currants
cyrydiad nm corrosion
cyrydu vb corrode
cysawd (**-odau**) nm system; constellation
cysefin adj original, primordial
cysegr (**-au**, **-oedd**) nm sanctuary
cysegredig adj consecrated, sacred
cysegredigrwydd nm sacredness
cysegriad (**-au**) nm consecration
cysegr-ladrad nm sacrilege

cysegr-lân adj holy
cysegru vb consecrate, dedicate, devote
cyseinedd nm alliteration
cysetlyd adj fastidious
cysgadrwydd nm sleepiness, drowsiness
cysgadur (**-iaid**) nm sleeper
cysglyd adj sleepy
cysgod (**-au**, **-ion**) nm shade, shadow; shelter; type
cysgodi vb shadow, shade; shelter
cysgodol adj shady, sheltered
cysgu vb sleep
cysgwr (**-wyr**) nm sleeper
cysidro vb consider
cysodi vb set type, compose
cysodydd (**-ion**, **-wyr**) nm compositor
cyson adj consistent, constant
cysondeb nm consistency; regularity
cysoni vb harmonize; reconcile
cysonwr (**-wyr**), **-ydd** (**-ion**) nm harmonist
cystadleuaeth (**-au**) nf competition
cystadleuol adj competitive
cystadleuwr, **-ydd** (**-wyr**) nm competitor
cystadlu vb compete; compare
cystal adj as good, so good ♦ adv as well, so well
cystrawen (**-nau**) nf construction, syntax
cystudd (**-iau**) nm affliction; illness
cystuddiedig adj afflicted, contrite
cystuddio vb afflict, trouble
cystuddiol adj afflicted
cystuddiwr (**-wyr**) nm afflicter, oppressor
cystwyo vb chastise, castigate, trounce
cysur (**-on**) nm comfort, consolation
cysuro vb comfort, console
cysurus adj comfortable

cysurwr (**-wyr**) *nm* comforter
cyswllt (**-ylltiadau**) *nm* joint, junction
cysylltiad (**-au**) *nm* conjunction; joining, connexion
cysylltiol *adj* connecting; connected
cysylltnod (**-au**) *nm* ligature, hyphen
cysylltu *vb* join, connect
cysylltydd (**-ion**) *nm* connector, contact
cysyniad (**-au**) *nm* concept
cytbell *adj* equidistant
cytbwys *adj* of equal weight
cytbwysedd *nm* balance
cytew *nm* batter
cytgan (**-au**) *nm/f* chorus
cytgord *nm* concord
cytir (**-oedd**) *nm* common
cytras *adj* allied, related; cognate
cytsain (**-seiniaid**) *nf* consonant
cytûn *adj* agreed, of one accord, unanimous
cytundeb (**-au**) *nm* agreement, consent
cytuno *vb* agree, consent
cythlwng *nm* fasting, fast, hunger
cythraul (**-euliaid**) *nm* devil, demon
cythreuldeb *nm* devilment
cythreulig *adj* devilish, fiendish
cythru *vb* snatch, rush
cythruddo *vb* annoy, provoke, irritate
cythrwfl *nm* uproar, tumult
cythryblu *vb* trouble, agitate
cythryblus *adj* troubled, agitated
cyw (**-ion**) *nm* young bird, chick, chicken; baby
cywain *vb* convey, carry; garner
cywair (**-eiriau**) *nm* order; key; tune
cywaith (**-weithiau**) *nm* collective work, project
cywarch *nm* hemp
cywasg, -edig *adj* compressor, diminished

cywasgiad (**-au**) *nm* contraction, compression
cywasgu *vb* contract, compress
cywasgydd (**-ion**) *nm* compressor
cyweiriad (**-au**) *nm* repair
cyweiriadur (**-on**) *nm* modulator
cyweirio *vb* set in order; prepare, dress
cyweirnod (**-nod**) *nf* key-note
cywen (**-nod**) *nf* pullet, young hen
cywerth *adj* equivalent
cywilydd *nm* shame; shyness
cywilydd-dra *nm* shamefulness
cywilyddgar *adj* bashful, shy
cywilyddio *vb* shame; be ashamed
cywilyddus *adj* shameful, disgraceful
cywir *adj* correct, accurate, true, faithful
cywirdeb *nm* correctness; integrity
cywiriad (**-au**) *nm* correction
cywiro *vb* correct; make good; perform
cywirwr (**-wyr**) *nm* corrector
cywladu *vb* naturalize
cywrain *adj* skilful; curious
cywreinbeth (**-au, -einion**) *nm* curiosity
cywreindeb *nm* skill, ingenuity
cywreinrwydd *nm* skill; curiosity
cywydd (**-au**) *nm* alliterative Welsh poem
cywyddwr (**-wyr**) *nm* composer of *cywyddau*

CH

Chile *nf* Chile
China *nf* China
chwa (**-on**) *nf* puff, gust, breeze
chwaer (**chwiorydd**) *nf* sister
chwaeroliaeth *nf* sisterhood
chwaeth (**-au, -oedd**) *nf* taste
chwaethu *vb* taste
chwaethus *adj* tasteful; decent

chwaith *adv* nor either, neither
chwâl *adj* scattered, loose
chwalfa (-feydd) *nf* upset, rout
chwalu *vb* scatter, spread
chwalwr (-wyr) *nm* scatterer, demolisher
chwaneg *adj*, *nm* more
chwanegiad (-au) *nm* addition
chwanegol *adj* additional
chwanegu *vb* add, augment, increase
chwannen (chwain) *nf* flea
chwannog *adj* desirous; addicted; prone
chwant (-au) *nm* desire, craving, lust
chwantu *vb* desire, lust
chwap *nm* sudden blow, moment ♦ *adv* instantly
chwarae, chwarae *vb* play ♦ (-on) *nm* play
chwaraedy (-dai) *nf* playhouse, theatre
chwaraefa (-feydd) *nf* pitch, playground
chwaraegar *adj* playful, sportive
chwaraewr (-wyr) *nm* player, actor, performer
chwaraeydd (-ion) *nm* actor
chwarddiad (-au) *nm* laugh
chwarel (-au, -i, -ydd) *nf* quarry
chwarelwr (-wyr) *nm* quarryman
chwareus *adj* playful
chwarren (-arennau) *nf* gland; kernel
chwart (-iau) *nm* quart
chwarter (-i, -au) *nm* quarter
chwarterol *adj* quarterly
chwarterolyn (-olion) *nm* quarterly (magazine)
chwarteru *vb* quarter
chwe *adj* six (before a noun)
chweban (-nau) *nm* sestet, sextain
chwech *adj* six ♦ (-au) *nm* six; sixpence
chwechawd (-au) *nm* sextet
chwedl (-au) *nf* story, tale

chwedleua *vb* talk, gossip
chwedleuwr (-wyr) *nm* story-teller
chwedloniaeth *nf* mythology
chwedlonol *adj* mythical, mythological
chwedlonydd (-wyr) *nm* mythologist
chwedyn *adv*: na chynt na ch. neither before nor after
Chwefror, Chwefrol *nm* February
chwennych, chwenychu *vb* covet, desire
chwenychiad (-au) *nm* desire
chweongl (-au) *nm* hexagon
chwephlyg *adj* sixfold
chwerthin *vb* laugh ♦ *nm* laughter
chwerthiniad (-au) *nm* laugh
chwerthinllyd *adj* laughable, ridiculous
chwerthinog *adj* laughing, merry
chwerw *adj* bitter
chwerwder, -dod *nm* bitterness
chwerwedd *nm* bitterness
chwerwi *vb* grow bitter, embitter
chwi *pron* you
chwib (-iau) *nm* whistle
chwiban *vb*, *nm* whistle
chwibaniad *nm* whistling, whistle
chwibanogl (-au) *nf* whistle, flute
chwibanu *vb* whistle
chwibon (-iaid) *nm* curlew, stork
chwifio *vb* wave, flourish, brandish
chwiff (-iau) *nf* whiff, puff
chwiffiad *nm* whiff, jiffy
chwil (-od) *nm/f* beetle, chafer
chwil *adj* whirling, reeling
chwilboeth *adj* scorching, piping hot
chwildroi *vb* whirl, spin
chwilen (chwilod) *nf* beetle
chwilenna *vb* rummage; pry; pilfer
chwiler (-od) *nm* chrysalis, pupa
chwilfriw *adj* smashed to atoms
chwilfriwio *vb* smash, shatter
chwilfrydedd *nm* curiosity
chwilfrydig *adj* curious, inquisitive

chwilgar adj curious, inquisitive

chwilgarwch nm inquisitiveness

chwiliad (-au) nm search, scrutiny

chwilibawa(n) vb dawdle, trifle

chwilio vb search; examine

chwiliwr (-wyr) nm searcher

chwil-lys nm inquisition

chwilmantan vb pry, rummage

chwilolau (-oleuadau) nf searchlight

chwilota vb rummage, pry

chwilotwr (-wyr) nm searcher, rummager

chwim adj nimble, quick, agile

chwimder, -dra nm nimbleness

chwimio vb move, stir, accelerate

chwimwth adj nimble, brisk

chwinc nm wink

chwinciad nm twinkling, trice

chwiorydd see **chwaer**

chwip (-iau) nf whip; whipping

chwipiad (-au) nm whipping

chwipio vb whip

chwipyn adv instantly

chwirligwgan nf whirligig

chwisgi nm whisky

chwisl (-au) nf whistle

chwistrell (-au, -i) nf squirt, syringe

chwistrelliad (-au) nm injection

chwistrellu vb squirt, syringe, inject

chwit-chwat adj fickle, inconstant

chwith adj left; wrong; sad; strange

chwithau pron conj you (on your part), you also

chwithdod, -dra nm strangeness

chwithig adj strange, wrong, awkward

chwithigrwydd nm awkwardness

chwiw (-iau) nf fit, attack, malady

chwiwgar adj fickle

chwychwi pron you yourselves

chwyd, chwydiad nm vomit

chwydu vb vomit, spew

chwydd, chwyddi nm swelling

chwyddiant (-nnau) nm inflation; inflation

chwyddo vb swell, increase, magnify

chwyddwydr (-au) nm microscope

chwŷl (chwylion) nm/f turn, rotation

chwydro (-ion) nm rotation; orbit

chwydroad (-au) nm revolution

chwydroadol adj revolutionary

chwydroadwr (-wyr) nm revolutionary

chwyldroi vb whirl, revolve, rotate

chwyldrowr see **chwyldroadwr**

chwylolwyn (-ion) nf flywheel

chwyn (chwynnyn nm) coll n, npl weeds

chwynladdwr nm weed-killer

chwynnu vb weed

chwyrligwgan (-od) nm spinning top, whirligig

chwyrlïo vb whirl, spin, speed

chwyrlwynt (-oedd) nm whirlwind

chwyrn adj rapid, swift

chwyrnellu vb whirl, whiz

chwyrnu vb hum; snore; snarl

chwyrnwr (-wyr) nm snorer; snarler

chwys nm sweat, perspiration

chwysfa (-feydd) nf sweating

chwysiant nm exudation

chwysigen (-igod) nf blister, vesicle

chwyslyd adj sweaty

chwystyllau npl pores

chwysu vb sweat, perspire; exude

chwyswr (-wyr) nm sweater

chwyth, chwythad nm breath

chwythbib (-au) nf blowpipe

chwythbrenni npl woodwinds

chwythell (-i) nf jet

chwythiad (-au) nm blow, blast

chwythu vb blow, blast; breathe; hiss

chwythwr (-wyr) nm blower

D

da *adj* good, well ♦ (**-oedd**) *nm* good; goods; stock, cattle

da-da *nm* sweets

dacw *adv* there is, are; behold there

dad-, dat- *prefix* un-, dis- re-, back

dadansoddi *vb* analyse

dadansoddiad (**-au**) *nm* analysis

dadansoddol *adj* analytic(al)

dadansoddwr (**-wyr**) *nm* analyst

dadansoddydd (**-wyr**) *nm* analyser

dadchwyddiant (**-nnau**) *nm* deflation

dad-ddyfrio *vb* dehydrate

dadebriad *nm* resuscitation

dadebru *vb* resuscitate, revive

dadelfeniad (**-au**) *nm* decomposition

dadelfennu *vb* decompose; refine

dadeni *vb* regenerate, reanimate ♦ *nm* rebirth, renascence, renaissance

dadfachu *vb* unhook

dadfathiad *nm* dissimulation

dadfeiliad *nm* decay

dadfeilio *vb* fall to ruin, decay

dadflino *vb* rest (after exertion)

dadl (**-euon**) *nf* debate; doubt; plea

dadlaith *vb* thaw; dissolve

dadlau *vb* argue, debate; plead

dadleniad (**-au**) *nm* disclosure, exposure

dadlennol *adj* revealing, disclosing, exposing

dadlennu *vb* disclose, expose

dadleoli *vb* dislocate

dadleoliad *nm* dislocation

dadleuaeth *nf* polemics, controversy

dadleugar *adj* argumentative

dadleuol *adj* controversial, polemical

dadleuwr (**-wyr**), **-ydd** (**-ion**) *nm* debater, controversialist; advocate

dadluddedu *vb* rest (after exertion)

dadlwytho *vb* unload, unburden

dadlygru *vb* decontaminate

dadmer *vb* thaw; dissolve

dadnitreiddiad *nm* denitrification

dadolwch *nm* propitiation ♦ *vb* worship, seek forgiveness

dadorchuddio *vb* unveil, uncover

dadreolaeth *nf* decontrol

dadrewlifiant *nm* deglaciation

dadrithiad (**-au**) *nm* disillusionment

dadrithio *vb* disillusion

dadsefydlu *vb* disestablish

dadwaddoli *vb* disendow

dadwaddoliad *nm* disendowment

dadwneuthur, dadwneud *vb* undo, unmake

dadwrdd *nm* noise, uproar, hubbub

dadymchwel, -yd *vb* overturn, overthrow

daear (**-oedd**) *nf* earth, ground, soil

daeardy (**-dai**) *nm* dungeon

daeareg *nf* geology

daearegol *adj* geological

daearegwr (**-wyr**), **-ydd** (**-ion**) *nm* geologist

daearen *nf* the earth; land, country

daearfochyn (**-foch**) *nm* badger

daeargell (**-oedd**) *nf* dungeon, vault

daeargi (**-gwn**) *nm* terrier

daeargryd (**-iau**) *nm* earth tremor

daeargryn (**-fâu**) *nm/f* earthquake

daearol *adj* terrestrial, earthly, earthy

daearu *vb* earth; inter

daearyddiaeth *nf* geography

daearyddol *adj* geographical

daearyddwr (-wyr) nm geographer

dafad (defaid) nf sheep; wart

dafaden (-ennau) nf wart

dafn (-au) nm drop

dafnu vb trickle

dagr (-au) nm dagger, bayonet, dirk

dagrau npl (deigryn nm) tears

dagreuol adj tearful, sad

dangos see dan-

dail npl (dalen, deilen nf) leaves

daioni nm goodness, good

daionus adj good; beneficial; beneficent

dal, -a vb hold; catch; arrest; last

dalen (-nau, dail) nf leaf

dalfa (-feydd) nf hold; arrest, custody; prison

dalgylch (-oedd) nm catchment area

daliad (-au) nm holding; tenet; spell

daliwr (-wyr) nm jig, catcher

dall (deillion) adj blind

dallbleidiaeth nf bigotry

dallbleidiol adj bigoted

dallbleidiwr (-wyr) nm bigot

dallineb nm blindness

dallu vb blind; dazzle

damcaniaeth (-au) nf theory

damcaniaethol adj theoretical

damcaniaethwr (-wyr) nm theorist

damcanu vb theorize, speculate

dameg (-hegion) nf parable

damhegol adj parabolic(al), allegorical

damhegwr (-wyr) nm allegorist

damnedig adj damned, damnable

damnedigaeth nf damnation, condemnation

damnio vb damn

damniol adj damning, damnatory

damsang vb tread, trample

damwain (-weiniau) nf accident, chance, fate

damweinio vb befall, happen

damweiniol adj accidental, casual

dan see tan

danadl npl (danhadlen nf) nettles

danas coll n deer. bwch d. buck

danfon vb send, convey; escort

dangos vb show

dangoseg (-ion) nf index; indication

dangosol adj indicative, demonstrative

danheddog adj jagged, serrated, toothed

dannod vb reproach, upbraid, taunt, twit

dannoedd nf toothache

dansoddol adj abstract

dant (dannedd) nm tooth

danteithfwyd (-teithion) nm dainty

danteithiol adj dainty, delicious

danteithion npl delicacies

darbodus adj provident, thrifty

darbwyllo vb persuade, convince

darfod vb finish, end; perish; happen

darfodadwy adj transitory, perishable

darfodedig adj perishable, transient

darfodedigaeth nm consumption

darfudiad (-au) nm convection

darfudol adj convectional

darganfod vb discover

darganfyddiad (-au) nm discovery

darganfyddwr (-wyr) nm discoverer

dargludedd nm conductivity

dargludo vb conduct

dargludydd (-ion) nm conductor

dargyfeiredd nm divergence

dargyfeirio vb diverge, divert

darlith (-iau, -oedd) nf lecture

darlithfa (-feydd) nf lecture room

darlithio vb lecture

darlithiwr (-wyr), -ydd (-ion) nm lecturer

darlun (-iau) nm picture

darluniad (-au) nm portrayal, description

darluniadol *adj* pictorial, illustrated
darluniaeth *nf* imagery
darlunio *vb* portray, depict, describe
darluniol *adj* pictorial
darlleidiad (-au) *nm* broadcast
darlledu *vb* broadcast
darlledwr (-wyr) *nm* broadcaster
darllen *vb* read
darllenadwy *adj* readable, legible
darllenfa (-feydd) *nf* reading room; reading-desk; lectern
darllengar *adj* fond of reading, studious
darlleniad (-au) *nm* reading
darllenwr (-wyr), -ydd (-ion) *nm* reader
darn (-au) *nm* piece, fragment, part
darnguddio *vb* conceal *or* withhold a part
darniad (-au) *nm* fragmentation
darnio *vb* cut up, hack
darn-ladd *vb* beat mercilessly
darogan *vb* predict, foretell, forebode ♦ (-au) *nf* prediction, foreboding
daroganu *vb* predict, foretell
daroganwr (-wyr) *nm* predictor, prophet, soothsayer, forecaster
darostwng *vb* lower; subdue; subject, humiliate
darostyngiad *nm* humiliation; subjection
darpar (-ion, -iadau) *nm* preparation, provision ♦ *adj* intended, elect
darpariaeth (-au) *nf* preparation, provision
darparu *vb* prepare, provide
darparwr (-wyr) *nm* provider
darwden *nf* ringworm
das (-au, deisi) *nf* rick, stack
dat- *prefix* see **dad-**
data *nm* data
datblygiad (-au) *nm* development,

evolution
datblygol *adj* nascent, developing
datblygu *vb* develop, evolve
datblygus *adj* developmental
datblygydd (-ion) *nm* developer
datchwyddiant *nm* deflation
datgan *vb* declare; recount; render
datganiad (-au) *nm* declaration; rendering
datganoli *vb* devolve, decentralize
datganoli(ad) *nm* devolution
datganu *vb* declare; sing, render
datgeliad (-au) *nm* detection; revelation
datgelu *vb* detect; reveal
datgloi *vb* unlock
datglymu *vb* unhitch, undo
datgorffori *vb* dissolve *(parliament)*
datgorfforiad *nm* dissolution
datguddiad (-au) *nm* revelation, disclosure
datguddio *vb* reveal, disclose
datgyffesiad *nm* recantation
datgyffesu *vb* recant
datgymalu *vb* dislocate, dismember
datgysylltiad *nm* disestablishment
datgysylltu *vb* disconnect; disestablish
datod *vb* undo, untie, dissolve
datrannu *vb* dissect
datro *vb* change; undo
datru *vb* de-code
datrys *vb* solve
datrysiad (-au) *nm* solution, resolution
datseinio *vb* resound, reverberate
datsgwar (-au) *nm* square root
datysen (datys) *nf* date
dathliad (-au) *nm* celebration
dathlu *vb* celebrate
dau *adj, nm* two; *f* **dwy**
dau-, deu- *prefix* two, bi-
dauddyblyg *adj* twofold, double
daufiniog *adj* double-edged

dauwynebog *adj* two-faced
dawn (doniau) *nf/m* gift, talent
dawns (-iau) *nf* dance
dawnsio *vb* dance
dawnsiwr (-wyr) *nm* dancer
dawnus *adj* gifted, talented
de see **deau**
De Affrica *nf* South Africa
deall *vb* understand ♦ *nm* understanding, intellect, intelligence
dealladwy *adj* intelligible
deallgar *adj* intelligent
deallol *adj* intellectual
deallitwriaeth (-au) *nf* understanding, intelligence
deallus *adj* understanding, intelligent
deallusion *npl* intelligentsia
deallusrwydd *nm* intelligence
deau *adj, nm* right; south
debentur (-on) *nm* debenture
debyd (-au) *nm* debit
debydu *vb* debit
dec (-iau, -s) *nm* deck
decilitr (-au) *nm* decilitre
decimetr (-au) *nm* decimetre
decstros *nm* dextrose
dectant *nm* ten-stringed instrument, psaltery
dechrau *vb* begin ♦ *nm* beginning
dechreuad (-au) *nm* beginning
dechreunos *nf* nightfall, dusk
dechreuol *adj* initial
dechreuwr (-wyr) *nm* beginner
dedfryd (-au) *nf* verdict; sentence
dedfrydu *vb* sentence
dedwydd *adj* happy, blessed
dedwyddwch, -**yd** *nm* happiness, bliss
deddf (-au) *nf* law, statute, act
deddfeg *nf* jurisprudence
deddfegwr (-wyr) *nm* jurist
deddfol *adj* legal, lawful
deddfu *vb* legislate, enact
deddfwr (-wyr) *nm* legislator
deddfwriaeth *nf* legislation,

legislature
deddfwriaethol *adj* legislative
deddlyfr (-au) *nm* statute book
defni *vb* drip, trickle
defnydd (-iau) *nm* material, stuff; use
defnyddio *vb* use, utilize, employ
defnyddiol *adj* useful
defnyddioldeb *nm* usefulness, utility
defnyddiwr (-wyr) *nm* user, consumer
defnyn (-nau) *nm* drop
defnynnu *vb* drop, drip, dribble, distil
defod (-au) *nf* custom; rite, ceremony
defodaeth *nf* ritualism
defodol *adj* ritualistic
defosiwn (-ynau) *nm* devotion
defosiynol *adj* devotional, devout
deffiniad, -**io** see **diff-**
deffro, deffroi *vb* rouse; wake
deffroad (-au) *nm* awakening
deg *adj* ten ♦ (-au) *nm* ten
degawd (-au) *nm* decade
degaidd *adj* denary
degiad (-au) *nm* decimal
degol (-ion) *nm* decimal
degoli *vb* decimalise
degoliad *nm* decimalisation
degolyn (degolion) *nm* decimal
degwm (-ymau) *nm* tenth, tithe
degymu *vb* tithe
deng *adj* ten (*before certain words*)
dehau, deheu see **deau**
deheubarth, -**dir** *nm* southern region, south
deheuig *adj* dexterous, skilful
deheulaw *nf* right hand
deheuol *adj* southern
deheurwydd *nm* dexterity, skill
deheuwr (-wyr) *nm* southerner, southman
deheuwynt *nm* south wind
dehongli *vb* interpret
dehongliad (-au) *nm* interpretation

dehonglwr (-wyr), **-ydd** (-ion) *nm* interpreter

dehydrad (-au) *nm* dehydration

dehydru *vb* dehydrate

deial (-au) *nm* dial

deialog (-au) *nm/f* dialogue

deialu *vb* dial

deifio *vb* singe, scorch; blast; dive

deifiol *adj* scorching, scathing

deifiwr (-wyr) *nm* diver.

deigryn (**dagrau**) *nm* tear

deilbridd *nm* humus

deildy (-dai) *nm* bower, arbour

deilen (**dail**) *nf* leaf

deilgoll *adj* deciduous

deiliad (-on, **deiliaid**) *nm* tenant; subject

deiliant (-nnau) *nm* foliage

deilio *vb* leaf

deiliog *adj* leafy

deillio *vb* proceed, emanate, issue

deinameg *nf/m* dynamics

deinamig *adj* dynamic

deinamo (-s, -au) *nm* dynamo

deincod *nm* teeth on edge

deincryd *nm* chattering or gnashing of teeth

deintio *vb* nibble

deintrod (-au) *nf* cog

deintydd (-ion) *nm* dentist

deintyddiaeth *nf* dentistry

deintyddol *adj* dental

deiseb (-au) *nf* petition

deisebu *vb* petition

deisebwr, **-ydd** (-wyr) *nm* petitioner

deisyf, **deisyfu** *vb* desire, wish; beseech, entreat

deisyfiad (-au) *nm* request, petition

del *adj* pretty, neat

delfryd (-au) *nm* ideal

delfrydiaeth *nf* idealism

delfrydol *adj* ideal

delfrydwr (-wyr) *nm* idealist

delff *nm* churl, oaf, dolt, rascal

delio *vb* deal

delw (-au) *nf* image; form, mode, manner

delwedd (-au) *nf* image

delweddaeth *nf* imagery

delweddu *vb* portray

delwi *vb* be wool-gathering; pale, be paralysed with fright.

dellni *nm* blindness

dellt (**-en** *nf*) laths, lattice, splinters

democratiaeth (-au) *nf* democracy

democratig *adj* democratic

demograffeg *nf* demography

demograffig *adj* demographic

dengar *adj* attractive

dengarwch *nm* attractiveness

deniadau *npl* attractions, allurements

deniadol *adj* attractive

Denmarc *nf* Denmark

denu *vb* attract, allure, entice

deon (-iaid) *nm* dean

deondy (-dai) *nm* deanery

deoniaeth (-au) *nf* deanery

deor *vb* brood, hatch, incubate

deorfa (-fâu, -feydd) *nf* hatchery

deorydd (-ion) *nf* incubator

derbyn *vb* receive; accept; admit

derbyniad (-au) *nm* receipt; reception

derbyniadwy *adj* admissible

derbyniol *adj* acceptable

derbynnwr (-wyr), **-nnydd** (-ynyddion) *nm* receiver, acceptor

derbynneb (-ynebau, -ynebion) *nf* receipt, voucher

derbynnydd (-ynyddion) *nm* receiver

deri *npl* (**dâr** *nf*) oak-trees, oak

dernyn (-nau) *nm* piece, scrap

derwen (**derw**, **deri**) *nf* oak-tree, oak

derwydd (-on) *nm* druid

derwyddiaeth *nf* druidism

derwyddol *adj* druidic(al)

desg (-iau) *nf* desk

desgant (-au) *nm* descant

desibel (-au) nm decibel

destlus adj neat

destlusrwydd nm neatness

detector (-au) nm detector

dethol vb select, pick, choose ♦ adj select

detholedd nm selectivity

detholiad (-au, **detholion**) nm selection, anthology

deu- see **dau-**

deuawd (-au) nm/f duet

deublyg adj double, twofold

deuddeg adj, nm twelve

deufin adj two-edged

deuffocal adj bifocal

deugain adj, nm forty

deugraff nm digraph

deunaw adj, nm eighteen

deunydd (-iau) nm stuff, material

deuocsid nm dioxide

deuod (-au) nm diode, binary

deuol adj dual

deuoliaeth nf dualism, duality

deuparth nd two-thirds

deuris adj two-tier

deurudd nd the cheeks

deuryw adj bisexual

deusain nf diphthong

deutu nd: **o dd.** about

dewin (-iaid) nm diviner, magician, wizard

dewines nf witch, sorceress

dewiniaeth nf divination, witchcraft

dewinio vb divine

dewin(i)ol adj prophetic, divinatory

dewis vb choose, select ♦ nm choice

dewisiad nm choice, option

dewisol adj choice, desirable

dewr adj brave ♦ (-ion) nm brave man, hero

dewrder nm bravery, valour

di- neg prefix without, not, un-, non-, -less

diabetig adj, nm/f diabetic

diacon (-iaid) nm deacon

diacones (-au) nf deaconess

diaconiaeth nf diaconate

diadell (-au, **-oedd**) nf flock

diaddurn adj unadorned, plain, rude

diaelodi vb dismember; expel a member

diafael adj slippery, careless

diafol (**diefyl, dieifl**) nm devil

diaffram (-au) nm diaphragm

diagnosis nm diagnosis

diangen adj unnecessary, free from want

dianghenraid adj unnecessary, needless

di-ail adj unequalled, unrivalled

dial vb avenge, revenge ♦ nm vengeance, revenge

dialedd (-au) nm vengeance, nemesis

dialgar adj revengeful, vindictive

dialgarwch nm vindictiveness

di-alw-amdano adj redundant, uncalled for

dialwr (**-wyr**), **-ydd** (**-ion**) nm avenger

diamau adj doubtless

diamcan adj aimless, purposeless

diamedr (-au) nm diameter

diamedral adj diametral

diamheuol adj undoubted, indisputable

diamod adj unconditional, absolute

diamodol adj unconditional, unqualified

diamwys adj unambiguous

diamynedd adj impatient

dianc vb escape

dianwadal adj unwavering, immutable

dianwadalwch nm immutability

diarddel vb expel, excommunicate

diarddeliad nm expulsion, excommunication

diarfogi vb disarm

diarfogiad nm disarmament

diarffordd *adj* out of the way, inaccessible

diargyhoedd *adj* blameless

diarhebol *adj* proverbial

diaroglydd (**-ion**) *nm* deodorant

diarwybod *adj* unawares

diasbad *nf* cry, scream

diasbedain *vb* resound, ring

diatreg *adj* immediate

diau *adj* true, certain; doubtless

diawl (**-iaid**) *nm* devil

diawledig *adj* devilish

di-baid, dibaid *adj* unceasing, ceaseless

di-ball, diball *adj* unfailing, infallible, sure

diben (**-ion**) *nm* end, purpose, aim

di-ben-draw *adj* endless

dibeniad (**-au**) *nm* ending, conclusion, predicate

di-benllanw *adj* off-peak

dibennu *vb* end, conclude, finish

diberfeddu *vb* disembowel, eviscerate

dibetrus *adj* unhesitating

dibl (**-au**) *nm* border, edge

diboblogaeth *nf* depopulation

diboblogi *vb* depopulate

dibrin *adj* abundant, plentiful

dibriod *adj* unmarried, single

dibris *adj* reckless, contemptuous

dibrisio *vb* depreciate, despise

dibristod *nm* depreciation, contempt

dibwys *adj* trivial, unimportant

dibwysiant (**-nnau**) *nm* depression

dibyn (**-nau**) *nm* steep, precipice

dibynadwy *adj* reliable

dibynadwyedd *nm* reliability

dibyniad *nm* dependence

dibyniant *nm* dependence

dibynnedd *nm* reliability

dibynnol *adj* depending; subjunctive

dibynnu *vb* depend, rely

dibynnydd (**dibynyddion**) *nm* dependant

dicllon *adj* wrathful, angry

dicllonrwydd *nm* wrath, indignation

dicotomi (**-iau**) *nm* dichotomy

dicra *adj* squeamish, fastidious, slow

dicter *nm* anger, wrath, displeasure

dichell (**-ion**) *nf* wile, craft, guile

dichellgar *adj* wily, crafty, cunning

dichlyn *vb* choose, pick ♦ *adj* careful, circumspect, exact

dichon *vb* be able; it may be

di-dact *adj* tactless

didactig *adj* didactic

didaro *adj* unaffected, unconcerned, cool

di-daw *adj* ceaseless, clamant

diden (**-nau**) *nf* nipple, teat

diderfyn *adj* unlimited

didoli *vb* separate, segregate

didoliad *nm* separation, segregation

didolnod (**-au**) *nm/f* diæresis

di-dor, didor *adj* unbroken, uninterrupted

didoreth *adj* shiftless, silly, fickle

didoriad *adj* unbroken, untamed, rough

di-drais, didrais *adj* non-violent, meek

diduedd *adj* impartial, unbiassed

didwyll *adj* guileless, sincere

didwylledd *nm* guilelessness, sincerity

di-ddadl *adj* unquestionable, indisputable

diddan *adj* amusing, diverting, pleasant

diddanion *npl* pleasantries, jokes

diddanu *vb* amuse, divert; comfort

diddanwch *nm* comfort, consolation

diddanwr (**-wyr**), **-ydd** (**-ion**) *nm* comforter

diddarbod *adj* shiftless

di-dderbyn-wyneb *adj* outspoken
diddig *adj* contented, pleased
diddigrwydd *nm* contentment, placidity
diddim *adj, nm* void
diddordeb *nm* interest
diddori *vb* interest
diddorol *adj* interesting
diddos *adj* watertight, sheltered; snug
diddosi *vb* shelter
diddosrwydd *nm* shelter, safety
di-dduw, didduw *adj* ungodly ♦ *nm* atheist
di-ddweud *adj* taciturn, stubborn
diddwythiad *nm* deduction
diddwytho *vb* deduce
diddyfnu *vb* wean
diddymdra *nm* nothingness, void
diddymiad, -iant *nm* annihilation
diddymu *vb* annihilate, abolish
dieflig *adj* devilish, diabolical, fiendish
diegwyddor *adj* unprincipled
dieisiau *adj* unnecessary, needless
dieithr *adj* strange, alien, foreign ♦ (-iaid) *nm* stranger
dieithrio *vb* estrange, alienate
dieithrwch *nm* strangeness
dienaid *adj* soulless, senseless
dienyddiad (-au) *nm* execution
dienyddio *vb* put to death, execute
dienyddiwr (-wyr) *nm* executioner
dieuog *adj* guiltless, innocent
difa *vb* consume, destroy, devour
di-fai, difai *adj* blameless, faultless
difalch *adj* humble
difancoll *nf* total loss, perdition
difaol *adj* consuming, devouring
difater *adj* indifferent, unconcerned
difaterwch *nm* indifference, apathy
difeddiannu *vb* dispossess, deprive
di-feind *adj* heedless
difenwad (-au) *nm* defamation
difenwi *vb* revile, abuse, belittle
diferlif *nm* stream, issue

diferol *adj* dripping, dropping
diferu *vb* drip, drop, dribble, distil
diferyn (-nau, diferion) *nm* drop
difesur *adj* huge, immeasurable, unstinted
di-feth, difeth *adj* infallible, certain
difetha *vb* destroy, spoil, waste
difethwr (-wyr) *nm* destroyer
Difiau *nm* Thursday
difidend (-au) *nm* dividend
diflanbwynt *nm* vanishing point
diflanedig *adj* evanescent, fleeting
diflannu *vb* vanish, disappear
di-flas *adj* tasteless
diflas *adj* insipid, dull, wearisome
diflastod *nm* disgust
diflasu *vb* disgust; weary, surfeit
diflin, -o *adj* untiring, indefatigable
difodi *vb* annihilate, exterminate
difodiad, -iant *nm* annihilation
di-foes, difoes *adj* rude, unmannerly
difreiniad *nm* disfranchisement
difreinio *vb* disfranchise, deprive
difriaeth *nf* abuse, calumny
difrif *nm* seriousness, earnestness
difrifddwys *adj* solemn
difrifol *adj* serious, earnest, solemn, grave
difrifoldeb see **difrifwch**
difrifoli *vb* sober, solemnize
difrifwch *nm* seriousness, earnestness, solemnity
difrio *vb* scold, abuse, malign
difrod *nm* waste, havoc, damage
difrodi *vb* waste, spoil, ravage
difrodol *adj* destructive
difrodwr (-wyr) *nm* spoiler, devastator
difrycheulyd *adj* spotless, immaculate
di-fudd, difudd *adj* unprofitable, useless, futile
di-fwlch, difwlch *adj* without a break, continuous
difwyniad (-au) *nm* adulteration,

pollution
difwyniant *nm* defilement
difwyno *vb* mar, soil, sully, defile
difyfyr *adj* impromptu
difynio *vb* dissect, vivisect
difyr *adj* pleasant, diverting, amusing
difyrion *npl* diversions, amusements
difyrru *vb* divert, amuse, beguile
difyrrus *adj* diverting, amusing
difyrrwch *nm* diversion, amusement, fun
difyrrwr (-yrwyr) *nm* entertainer
difyrwaith (-weithiau) *nm* hobby
difywyd *adj* inert
diffaith *adj* waste, desert; base, mean ♦ (-ffeithydd) *nm* wilderness, desert
diffeithdra *nm* dereliction
diffeithio *vb* lay waste
diffeithwch (-ychau) *nm* desert, wilderness
diffiniad (-au) *nm* definition
diffinio *vb* define
diffodd, -i *vb* quench, extinguish
diffoddiad *nm* quenching, extinction
diffoddwr (-wyr), -ydd (-ion) *nm* quencher
diffrwyth *adj* barren; numb, paralysed
diffrwythder, -dra *nm* barrenness; numbness
diffrwytho *vb* make barren; paralyse
diffuant *adj* unfeigned, sincere, genuine
diffuantrwydd *nm* genuineness
di-ffurf *adj* amorphous
diffwys *adj* wild, waste; high, steep; huge, awful
diffyg (-ion) *nm* defect, want, lack; eclipse
diffygiant *nm* deficiency
diffygio *vb* fail; faint, weary
diffygiol *adj* defective; faint,

weary
diffyndoll (-au) *nf* tariff
diffyndollaeth *nf* protectionism
diffynnydd (-ynyddion) *nm* defendant
dig *adj* angry, wrathful ♦ *nm* anger, wrath
digalon *adj* disheartened, depressed, dejected, sad
digalondid *nm* depression, dejection
digalonni *vb* dishearten, discourage
digamsyniol *adj* unmistakable
digasedd *nm* hatred, enmity
digid (-au) *nm* digit
digidiad (-au) *nm* digitation
digidol *adj* digital
digio *vb* anger, offend; take offence
di-glem *adj* inept
digllon see **dicllon**
digofaint *nm* anger, wrath, indignation
digofus *adj* angry, indignant
digolledu *vb* indemnify, compensate
digon *nm, adj, adv* enough; done (*of cooking*)
digonedd *nm* abundance, plenty
digoni *vb* suffice; satisfy; cook
digonol *adj* satisfying; sufficient, adequate; satisfied
digonolrwydd *nm* sufficiency, abundance
digornio *vb* dehorn
di-gred *adj* infidel
di-grefft, digrefft *adj* unskilled
digrif, -ol *adj* mirthful, funny
digriflun (-iau) *nm* caricature, cartoon
digrifwas (-weision) *nm* clown, buffoon
digrifwch *nm* mirth, fun
digroeso *adj* inhospitable
digwydd *vb* befall, happen, occur
digwyddiad (-au) *nm* happening,

occurrence, event

digyfnewid adj unchangeable

digyffelyb adj incomparable

digymysg adj unmixed

digyswllt adj incoherent

digywilydd adj impudent

digywilydd-dra nm impudence

dihafal adj unequalled, peerless

dihangfa (dianghfâu) nf escape

dihangol adj escaped, safe

dihareb (diarhebion) nf proverb

dihatru vb strip, undress

dihefelydd adj unequalled

diheintio vb disinfect

diheintydd (-ion) nm disinfectant, sterilizer

di-hid(io) adj heedless, indifferent, reckless

dihidlo vb drop, distil; shed

dihidrwydd nm indifference, recklessness

dihiryn (-hirod) nm rascal, scoundrel

dihoeni vb languish, pine

dihuno vb wake, rouse

di-hwyl adj out of sorts

dihyder adj lacking confidence

dihydradu vb dehydrate

dihysbydd adj inexhaustible

dihysbyddu vb empty, exhaust

dil (-iau) nm: **d. mêl** honeycomb

dilead nm abolition, deletion

dilechdid nm dialectic

diledryw adj pure, genuine

dileu vb blot out, delete; abolish

dilewyrch adj dismal; unprosperous

dilorni vb abuse, revile

di-lun adj slovenly

diluw see **dilyw**

dilyffethair adj unencumbered, unfettered

dilyn vb follow, pursue; imitate

dilyniad nm following; imitation

dilyniant (-nnau) nm sequence, progression

dilynol adj following; consequent

dilynwr (-wyr) nm follower; imitator

dilys adj sure, certain; genuine

dilysiant (-nnau) nm validation

dilysnod (-au) nm hallmark

dilysrwydd nm genuineness

dilysu vb certify, warrant, guarantee

dilyw nm flood, deluge

dillad (dilledyn nm) npl clothes, clothing

dilladu vb clothe

dilledydd nm clothier

dilledyn nm garment

dim adj any; (with negative understood) no ♦ nm anything; none, nothing

dimensiwn (-iynau) nm dimension

dimensiynol adj dimensional

di-nam, dinam adj faultless

dinas (-oedd) nf city

dinasol adj municipal

dinasyddiaeth nf citizenship

dincod see **deincod**

dinesig adj civil, civic

dinesydd (dinasyddion) nm citizen

dinistr nm destruction

dinistrio vb destroy

dinistriol adj destroying, destructive

dinistrwr (-wyr) nm destroyer

dinistrydd (-ion) nm destroyer

diniwed adj harmless, innocent

diniweidrwydd nm innocence

di-nod, dinod, adj insignificant, obscure

dinodedd nm insignificance, obscurity

dinoethi vb bare, denude, expose

diod (-ydd) nf drink, beverage

diodi vb give drink

dioddef vb suffer, bear; wait ♦ (-iadau) nm suffering

dioddefaint nm suffering, passion

dioddefgar, -efus adj patient

dioddefgarwch nm patience

dioddefwr, -ydd (-wyr) nm

sufferer, patient
di-oed, dioed adj without delay, immediate
diofal adj careless
diofalwch nm carelessness
diog adj slothful, indolent, lazy
diogel adj safe, secure; sure, certain
diogelu vb make safe, secure
diogelwch nm safety, security
diogi vb be lazy, idle ♦ nm laziness
dioglyd adj lazy, sluggish, indolent
diogyn nm lazy one, idler, sluggard
diolch vb thank, give thanks ♦ (-iadau) nm thanks, thanksgiving
diolchgar adj thankful, grateful
diolchgarwch nm thankfulness, gratitude, thanksgiving
diolwg adj ugly
diorseddu vb dethrone, depose
di-os adj without doubt
diosg vb undress, put off, strip, divest
diota vb tipple
diotwr (-wyr) nm boozer, drunkard
dioty (-tai) nm ale-house, public-house
diploma (-âu) nm/f diploma
diplomateg nf diplomacy
diplomydd (-ion) nm diplomat
diplomyddol adj diplomatic
dipton (-au) nf diphthong
dir adj certain, necessary
diraddiad (-au) nm degradation
diraddio vb degrade
diraddiol adj degrading
di-raen adj shabby, dull
dirboeni vb torture, excruciate
dirdyniad (-au) nm convulsion
dirdynnol adj excruciating
dirdynnu vb rack, torture
direidi nm mischievousness, mischief
direidus adj mischievous
direol adj unruly, disorderly

direwydd nm defroster
direwyn nm antifreeze
dirfawr adj vast, huge, immense, enormous
dirgel adj secret ♦ (-ion) nm secret
dirgeledig adj hidden, secret; mystical
dirgeledigaeth (-au) nm/f mystery
dirgelu vb secrete, conceal, hide
dirgelwch nm secrecy, mystery, secret
dirgryniad (-au) nm tremor, vibration
dirgrynol adj vibrating
dirgrynu vb tremble, vibrate
diriaethol adj concrete
dirlawn adj saturated
dirmyg nm contempt, scorn
dirmygu vb despise, scorn
dirmygus adj contemptuous; contemptible
dirnad vb discern, comprehend
dirnadaeth nf discernment, comprehension
dirnadwy adj discernible
dirprwy (-on) nm deputy; delegate
dirprwyaeth (-au) nf commission; deputation
dirprwyo vb deputise, delegate
dirprwyol adj vicarious
dirprwywr (-wyr) nm commissioner
dirwasgiad (-au) nm depression
dirwest nm/f abstinence, temperance
dirwestol adj temperate
dirwestwr (-wyr) nm abstainer
dirwy (-on) nf fine
dirwyn vb wind, twist, twine
dirwynwr (-wyr) nm winder
dirwyo vb fine
di-rym adj powerless, void
dirymu vb nullify, annul, cancel
diryw adj neuter
dirywiad nm degeneration, deterioration
dirywiaeth nf degeneracy

dirywiedig *adj* degenerate
dirywio *vb* degenerate, deteriorate
dirywiol *adj* decadent, retrograde
dis (-iau) *nm* die, dice
di-sail *adj* groundless, baseless
disbaddu *vb* castrate, geld, spay
disbaddwr (-wyr) *nm* castrator
disberod *nm*: **ar dd.** wandering, astray
disbyddedig *adj* exhausted
disbyddu *vb* empty, exhaust
disbyddwr *nm* exhaust
disco (-au) *nm* disco
diserch *adj* sullen, sulky, loveless
disg (-iau) *nm* disk, record
disgen (disgiau) *nf* discus
disglair *adj* bright, brilliant
disgleirdeb, -der *nm* brightness, brilliance
disgleirio *vb* shine, glitter
disgloff *adj* free from lameness
disgownt (-iau, -s) *nm* discount
disgrifiad (-au) *nm* description
disgrifiadol *adj* descriptive
disgrifio *vb* describe
disgwyl *vb* look, expect, wait
disgwylfa (-feydd) *nf* watch-tower
disgwylgar *adj* watchful, expectant
disgwyliad (-au) *nm* expectation
disgybl (-ion) *nm* disciple, pupil
disgyblaeth *nf* discipline
disgyblu *vb* discipline
disgyblwr (-wyr) *nm* disciplinarian
disgyn *vb* descend; fall, drop; let down
disgynfa (-feydd) *nf* descent, declivity; landing place
disgyniad (-au) *nm* descent
disgynnol *adj* descending
disgynnydd (-ynyddion) *nm* descendant
disgyrchedd *nm* gravitation
disgyrchiad, -iant *nm* gravity. **craidd d.** centre of gravity
disgyrchu *vb* gravitate
di-sigl *adj* unshaken, steadfast, firm

disiog *adj* diced
disodli *vb* trip up, supplant
dist (-iau) *nm* joist, beam
distadl *adj* insignificant, low, base, mean
distadledd *nm* insignificance, obscurity
distain (-einiaid) *nm* steward
distaw *adj* silent, quiet
distawrwydd *nm* silence, quiet
distewi *vb* silence; calm, quiet
distryw *nm* destruction
distrywgar *adj* destructive, wasteful
distrywio *vb* destroy
distrywiwr (-wyr) *nm* destroyer
distyll *nm* ebb; **-iad** distillation
distyllio *vb* distil
di-sut *adj* unwell; small
diswta *adj* sudden, abrupt
diswyddiad (-au) *nm* dismissal
diswyddo *vb* dismiss from office, discharge
disychedu *vb* quench thirst
di-syfl *adj* immovable, impregnable
disyfyd *adj* sudden, instantaneous
disyml *adj* simple, artless, ingenuous
disymwth *adj* sudden, instantaneous
disynnwyr *adj* senseless
ditectif (-s) *nm* detective
diwahân *adj* inseparable, indiscriminate
diwair *adj* chaste
di-waith, diwaith *adj* unemployed, idle
diwall *adj* satisfied, full, perfect
diwallu *vb* satisfy, supply
diwarafun *adj* unforbidden, ungrudging
diwasgedd (-au) *nm* depression (*weather*)
diwedydd (-iau) *nm* evening, eventide
diwedd *nm* end, conclusion

diweddar adj late, modern
diweddaru vb modernize
diweddarwch nm lateness
diweddeb nf cadence
diweddglo nm conclusion
diweddu vb end, finish, conclude
diweirdeb nm chastity
diweithdra nm unemployment
diwelfa (-feydd) nf watershed
diwethaf adj last
diwinydd (-ion) nm divine,
    theologian
diwinyddiaeth nf divinity,
    theology
diwinyddol adj theological
diwreiddio vb uproot, eradicate
diwrnod (-iau) nm day
diwrthdro adj inexorable
diwyd adj diligent, industrious
diwydianfa nf industrial estate
diwydiannaeth nf
    industrialization, industrialism
diwydiannol adj industrial
diwydiannwr (-ianwyr) nm
    industrialist
diwydiant (-iannau) nm industry
diwydrwydd nm diligence,
    industry
diwyg nm form, dress, garb
diwygiad (-au) nm reform,
    reformation; revival
diwygiadol adj reformatory;
    revivalistic
diwygiedig adj reformed; revised
diwygio vb amend, reform, revise
diwygiol adj reformatory
diwygiwr (-wyr) nm reformer;
    revivalist
diwylliadol adj cultural
diwylliannol adj cultural
diwylliant (-nnau) nm culture
diwylliedig adj cultured
diwyllio vb cultivate
diymadferth adj helpless
diymadferthedd nm helplessness
diymdroi adj without delay
diymhongar adj unassuming

diymod adj steadfast, immovable
diymwad adj undeniable,
    indisputable
diysgog adj steadfast, firm, stable
diystyr adj contemptuous;
    contemptible; meaningless
diystyrllyd adj contemptuous,
    disdainful
diystyru vb disregard, despise
diystyrwch nm contempt, disdain,
    scorn
do adv yes (to questions in preterite
    tense)
doc (-iau) nm dock
docfa (-feydd) nf berth
docio vb shorten; dock, berth
doctor (-iaid) nm doctor
doctora vb doctor
dod see **dyfod**
dodi vb put, place; give
dodrefn npl (-yn nm) furniture
dodrefnu vb furnish
dodrefnwr (-wyr) nm furnisher
dodwy vb lay eggs
doe adv yesterday
doeth (-ion) adj wise
doethineb nm/f wisdom
doethinebu vb discourse wisely,
    pontificate
doethor (-iaid) nm doctor (of
    university)
doethur (-iaid) nm doctor (of
    university)
doethuriaeth (-au) nf doctorate
dof adj tame, domesticated;
    garden
dofednod npl fowls, poultry
dofi vb tame, domesticate;
    assuage
dofn adj f of **dwfn**
Dofydd nm God
dogfen (-ni, -nau) nf document
dogfennaeth nf documentation
dogfennen (-ennau) nf
    documentary
dogfennol adj documentary
dogn (-au) nm share, portion; dose

dogni vb ration

doili nm doyley

dol (-iau) nf doll

dôl nm dole

dôl (dolydd, dolau) nf meadow

dolbridd (-oedd) nm alluvium, meadow soil

doldir (-oedd) nm meadow-land

dolef (-au) nf cry

dolefain vb cry out

dolefus adj wailing, plaintive

dolen (-nau) nf loop, link, ring, bow

dolennog adj ringed, looped; winding

dolennu vb loop; wind, meander

doler (-i) nf dollar

dolffin nm dolphin

dolur (-iau) nm sore; ailment; grief

dolurio vb hurt, wound; grieve

dolurus adj sore

dominyddu vb dominate

donio vb endow, gift

doniol adj gifted; witty, humorous

donioldeb, -wch nm wit, humour

dôr (dorau) nf door

dos (-ys, -au) nf dose

dosbarth (au, -iadau) nm reason; class; district

dosbarthiad nm distribution

dosbarthu vb class, classify; distribute

dosbarthwr (-wyr) nm distributor

dosio vb dose

dosran (-nau) nf division, section

dosrannu vb separate, analyse

dot (-iau) nmf dot

dot nf giddiness, vertigo

dotio vb dote

drachefn adv again

dracht (-iau) nm draught (of liquor)

drachtio vb drink deep

draen (-iau) nf drain

draen (drain) nf prickle, thorn

draen, -en (drain) nf thorn

draeniad (-au) nm drainage

draenio vb drain

draenog (-od) nm hedgehog

drafft (-iau) nm draft, draught

draffts npl draughts

dragio vb drag, tear, mangle

draig (dreigiau) nf dragon

drain see draen, draenen

drama (dramâu) nf drama

dramateiddio vb dramatize

dramatig adj dramatic

dramodiad (-au) nm dramatization

dramodwr (-wyr) nm dramatist

draw adv yonder, away

dreflan vb dribble

dreng adj morose, surly, sullen, harsh

dresel, -er (-i, -ydd) nm dresser

drewdod (-au) nm stink, stench

drewi vb, nm stink

drewllyd adj stinking

driblo vb dribble

drifft (-iau) nm drift

dril (-iau) nm drill

drilio vb drill

dringad vb, nm climb

dringfa (-feydd) nf climb, ascent

dringo vb climb

dringwr (-wyr) nm climber

dripsych adj dripdry

drôr (drors) nm drawer

dros see tros

drud adj dear, precious, costly; reckless

drudfawr adj costly, expensive

drudwen nf, **drudwy** nm starling

drwg adj evil, bad, naughty, wicked ♦ (drygau) nm evil, harm, hurt

drwgdybiaeth (-au) nf suspicion

drwgdybio vb suspect

drwgdybus adj suspicious

drwglosgiad nm arson

drwgweithredwr (-wyr) nm evildoer

drwm (drymiau) nm drum

drws (drysau) nm door

drwy see **trwy**
drycin (-oedd) *nf* foul weather
drycinog *adj* stormy
drych (-au) *nm* spectacle; mirror; object, pattern
drychfeddwl (-yliau) *nm* idea
drychiolaeth (-au) *nf* apparition, phantom
drygair *nm* ill report; scandal
dryganadl *nm* halitosis
drygfyd *nm* adversity
drygioni *nm* badness, wickedness
drygionus *adj* bad, wicked
drygu *vb* hurt, harm, injure
dryll (-iau) *nm* piece; part ✝ *nm/f* gun, rifle
drylliad (-au) *nm* breaking; wreck
drylliedig *adj* broken
dryllio *vb* break in pieces, shatter
drylliog *adj* broken, contrite
drysi *npl* (-ien *nf*) thorns, briers
dryslwyn (-i) *nm* thicket
dryslyd *adj* perplexing; confused
drysu *vb* tangle; perplex; be confused
dryswch *nm* tangle; perplexity; confusion
dryw (-od) *nm/f* wren
du *adj, nm* black
duc, dug (-iaid) *nm* duke
dugiaeth *nf* duchy
dull (-iau) *nm* form, manner, mode
dullwedd (-au) *nm* mannerism
Dulyn *nf* Dublin
duo *vb* black, blacken
dur *nm* steel
duw (-iau) *nm* god. **Duw** God
dûwch *nm* blackness
duwdod *nm* godhead, divinity, deity
duwies (-au) *nf* goddess
duwiol (-ion) *adj* godly, pious
duwioldeb *nm* godliness, piety
duwiolfrydedd *nm* godliness, piety
duwiolfrydig *adj* god-fearing, pious
dwbio *vb* daub, plaster

dwbl *adj* double
dweud, dweyd see **dywedyd**
dwfn *adj* deep, profound; *f* **dofn**
dwfr, dŵr (dyfroedd) *nm* water
dwl *adj* dull, stupid, foolish
dwlu *vb* dote
dwmbwr-dambar *adv* helter-skelter
dwndwr *nm* din, babble, hubbub
dwnsiwn (-iynau) *nm* dungeon
dŵr see **dwfr**
dwrdio *vb* scold
dwrn (dyrnau) *nm* fist; knob, handle, hilt
dwsin (-inau) *nm* dozen
dwst *nm* dust, powder
dwster (-i) *nm* duster
dwthwn *nm* day
dwy see **dau**
dwyfol *adj* divine
dwyfoldeb *nm* divinity, deity
dwyfoli *vb* deify
dwyfron (-nau) *nf* breast, chest
dwyfronneg *nf* breastplate
dwyieithedd *nm* bilingualism
dwyieitheg *nf* study of bilingualism
dwyieithog *adj* bilingual, duoglot
dwyieithrwydd *nm* bilingualism
dwylaw, -lo *nd, pl* two hands, hands
dwyn *vb* bear; bring; steal
dwyochredd *nm* bilateralism
dwyochrol *adj* bilateral
dwyradd *adj* quadratic, two-tier
dwyrain *nm, adj* east. **D. yr Almaen** East Germany
dwyraniad *nm* dichotomy
dwyrannu *vb* bisect
dwyreiniol *adj* easterly, eastern, oriental
dwyreiniwr (-wyr) *nm* easterner, oriental
dwys *adj* dense, grave, deep, intense
dwysáu *vb* deepen, intensify
dwysbigo *vb* prick, sting

dwysedd (-au) *nm* density

dwyster *nm* gravity, solemnity

dwythell (-au) *nf* duct

dwywaith *adv* twice

dy *pron* thy, thine

dyblu *vb* double; repeat

dyblyg *adj* twofold, double

dyblygiad (-au) *nm* duplication, duplicate

dyblygu *vb* double, fold

dyblygydd (-ion) *nm* duplicator

dybryd *adj* sore, dire; flagrant

dychan (-au) *nf* lampoon, satire

dychangerdd (-i) *nf* satirical poem, satire

dychanol *adj* satirical

dychanu *vb* lampoon, satirize, revile

dychanwr (-wyr) *nm* satirist

dychmygadwy *adj* imaginable

dychmygol *adj* imaginary

dychmygu *vb* imagine

dychmygus *adj* imaginative, inventive

dychryn (-iadau) *nm* fright, terror
♦ *vb* frighten

dychrynllyd *adj* frightful, terrible

dychrynu *vb* frighten, be frightened

dychweledig *adj* returned

dychweliad (-au) *nm* return; conversion

dychwelyd *vb* return

dychymyg (dychmygion) *nm* imagination, fancy; riddle, device

dydd (-iau) *nm* day. **dyddiau cŵn** silly season

dyddfu *vb* flag, pine, faint

dyddiad (-au) *nm* date

dyddiadur (-on) *nm* diary, journal

dyddiedig *adj* dated

dyddio *vb* become day, dawn; date

dyddiol *adj* daily

dyddlyfr (-au) *nm* diary, journal

dyddodyn (-odion) *nm* deposit

dyfais (-feisiau) *nf* device,

invention

dyfal *adj* diligent

dyfalbarhad *nm* perseverance

dyfalbarhau *vb* persevere

dyfaliad (-au) *nm* guess, conjecture

dyfalu *vb* guess, conjecture

dyfalwch *nm* diligence, assiduity

dyfarniad (-au) *nm* decision, verdict

dyfarnu *vb* adjudge

dyfarnwr (-wyr) *nm* judge, umpire

dyfeisio *vb* devise, invent, imagine; guess

dyfeisiwr (-wyr) *nm* inventor

dyfnant (-nentydd) *nf* ravine

dyfnder (-au, -oedd) *nm* deep, depth

dyfnhau *vb* deepen

dyfod, dod *vb* come, become

dyfodfa *nf* access, entrance

dyfodiad *nm* coming, arrival, advent

dyfodiad (-iaid) *nm* incomer, stranger

dyfodol *adj* coming, future ♦ *nm* future

dyfradwy *adj* watered; watering

dyfredig *adj* irrigated

dyfrffos (-ydd) *nm* canal, watercourse

dyfrgi (-gwn) *nm* otter

dyfrhad *nm* irrigation

dyfrhau, dyfrio *vb* water

dyfrllyd *adj* watery

dyfyniad (-au) *nm* citation, quotation

dyfynnod (-ynodau) *nm* quotation mark

dyfynnol *adj* citatory, summoned

dyfynnu *vb* cite, quote; summon

dyffryn (-noedd) *nm* valley

dyffryndir (-oedd) *nm* low country; vale

dygn *adj* hard, severe, grievous, dire

dygnu *vb* strive, persevere

dygnwch *nm* perseverance, assiduity

dygwyl *nm* holiday, feast day

dygymod *vb* agree (with), put up (with)

dyhead (-au) *nm* aspiration

dyheu *vb* pant; long, yearn, aspire

dyhiryn see **dihiryn**

dyladwy *adj* due

dylanwad (-au) *nm* influence

dylanwadol *adj* influential

dylanwadu *vb* influence

dyled (-ion) *nf* debt, obligation

dyledog *adj* in debt, indebted

dyledus *adj* due

dyledwr (-wyr) *nm* debtor

dyletswydd (-au) *nf* duty, obligation

dylif *nm* flood, deluge ♦ *nf* warp

dylifo *vb* flow, stream, pour

dylni *nm* stupidity, dullness

dyluniad (-au) *nm* design, drawing

dylunio *vb* design

dylunydd (-ion) *nm* designer

dylyfu gên *vb* yawn, gape

dylluan see **tylluan**

dyma *adv* here is, here are; this is, these are

dymchweliad *nm* overthrow

dymchwelyd *vb* overthrow, upset, subvert

dymuniad (-au) *nm* wish, desire

dymuno *vb* wish, desire

dymunol *adj* desirable, agreeable, pleasant

dyn (-ion) *nm* man, person

dyna *adv* there is, there are; that is, those are

dynad *npl* nettles

dyndod *nm* manhood, humanity

dyneiddiaeth *nf* humanism

dyneiddiol *adj* humanistic

dyneiddiwr (-wyr) *nm* humanist

dynes *nf* woman

dynesiad *nm* approach

dynesu *vb* draw near, approach

dyngar *adj* humane

dyngarol *adj* philanthropic

dyngarwch *nm* philanthropy

dyngarwr (-wyr) *nm* philanthropist

dyniawed (-iewaid) *nm* yearling, steer

dyn-laddiad *nm* manslaughter

dynodi *vb* denote, signify

dynodiad (-au) *nm* denotation

dynol *adj* human; man-like; manly

dynoliaeth *nf* humanity

dynoliaethau *npl* humanities

dynolryw *coll n* mankind

dynwared *vb* imitate, mimic

dynwarededd *nm* mimicry

dynwarediad (-au) *nm* imitation, mimicry

dynwaredol *adj* imitative

dynwaredwr (-wyr) *nm* imitator, mimic

dyraddiant *nm* degradation

dyraniad (-au) *nm* allocation

dyrchafael *vb* rise, ascend ♦ *nm* ascension

dyrchafedig *adj* exalted

dyrchafiad *nm* elevation, promotion

dyrchafol *adj* elevating

dyrchafu *vb* raise, elevate; rise, ascend

dyri (-iau), **dyrif** (-au) *nf* ballad, lyric

dyrnaid (-eidiau) *nm* handful

dyrnio *vb* punch

dyrnod (-iau) *nm/f* blow, stroke

dyrnu *vb* thump; thresh

dyrnwr (-wyr) *nm* thresher

dyrnwr medi *nm* combine harvester

dyrys *adj* tangled; difficult; perplexing

dyryslyd, dyrysu, dyryswch see **dryslyd, drysu, dryswch**

dysg *nm/f* learning

dysgedig (-ion) *adj* learned

dysgeidiaeth *nf* teaching, doctrine

dysgl (-au) *nf* dish

dysglaid (-eidiau) *nf* dishful, dish

dysgu vb learn, teach
dysgwr (-wyr) nm learner, teacher
dywalgi (-gwn) nm tiger
dywediad (-au) nm saying
dywedwst adj taciturn ♦ nm taciturnity
dywedyd vb say, speak, tell
dyweddi (-ïau) nf betrothal, fiancé(e) ♦ n coll betrothed
dyweddïad nm betrothal
dyweddïo vb betroth

E

eang adj wide, broad, immense
eangder, eangu see ehangder, ehangu
eangfrydedd nm magnanimity
eangfrydig adj broad-minded, magnanimous
eb, ebe, ebr vb said, quoth
ebargofiant nm oblivion
ebill (-ion) nm auger, borer; peg
ebillio vb bore
ebol (-ion) nm colt, foal
eboles (-au) nf foal, filly
eboni nm ebony
ebran (-nau) nm provender, fodder
Ebrill nm April
ebrwydd adj quick, swift, soon
ebwch (-ychau) nm gasp
ebychiad (-au) nm interjection, ejaculation
ebychu vb gasp, interject, ejaculate
eciwmenaidd adj ecumenical
ecliptig adj, nm ecliptic
ecoleg (-au) nf/m ecology
ecolegol adj ecological
ecolegwr (-wyr) nm ecologist
economaidd adj economic
economeg nf economics
economegol adj economic
economegwr (-wyr) nm economist
economegydd (-ion) nm economist

economi (-ïau) nm economy
economydd nm economist
ecsbloetio vb exploit
ecsbloetiwr (-wyr) nm exploiter
ecseis nm excise
ecseismon (-myn) nm exciseman
ecsema nm eczema
ecsentredd (-au) nm eccentricity
ecsentrig adj eccentric (maths)
ecstasi nm ecstasy
ecstatig adj ecstatic
echblyg adj explicit, outward
echblygol adj extrovert
echdoe adv day before yesterday
echdoriad (-au) nm eruption
echel (-au) nf axle, axletree; axis
echelin (-au) nf axis
echnos adv night before last
echrydus adj fearful, frightful, shocking
echwyn (-ion) nm loan
echwynna vb borrow, lend
echwynnwr (-wynwyr) nm lender, creditor
edau (edafedd) nf thread; (pl) yarn, wool
edfryd vb restore
edifar adj penitent, sorry
edifarhau, -faru vb repent, be sorry
edifarus, -feiriol adj repentant, penitent
edifeirwch nm repentance, penitence
edliw vb upbraid, reproach, taunt
edmygedd nm admiration
edmygol adj admiring
edmygu vb admire
edmygwr, -ydd (-wyr) nm admirer
edrych vb look, examine
edrychiad nm look
edrychwr (-wyr) nm beholder, spectator
edwi, edwino vb fade, wither, decay
eddi npl thrums; fringe, nap

ef, efe *pron* he, him; it

efallai *adv* perhaps, peradventure

efengyl (**-au**) *nf* gospel

efengylaidd *adj* evangelical

efengyleiddio *vb* evangelize

efengyles (**-au**) *nf* female evangelist

efengylu *vb* evangelize

efengylwr, -ydd (**-wyr**) *nm* evangelist

efelychiad (**-au**) *nm* imitation

efelychiadol *adj* imitative

efelychu *vb* imitate

efelychwr (**-wyr**) *nm* imitator

efelychydd (**-ion**) *nm* simulator

eferw *adj* effervescent

eferwad (**-au**) *nm* effervescence

eferwi *vb* effervesce

efo *prep* with

efô *pron* he, him; it

efrau *npl* tares

Efrog Newydd *nf* New York

efrydiaeth (**-au**) *nf* study

efrydu *vb* study

efrydydd (**-ion, -wyr**) *nm* student

efydd *nm* bronze, copper, brass

effaith (**-eithiau**) *nf* effect

effeithio *vb* effect, affect

effeithiol *adj* effectual, effective, efficient

effeithioli *vb* render effectual

effeithiolrwydd *nm* efficacy

effeithion *adj* efficient

effeithlonedd *nm* efficiency (*of machines etc*)

effeithlonrwydd *nm* efficiency

effro *adj* awake, vigilant

eger (**-au**) *nm* bore, eagre

egin *npl* (**-yn** *nm*) germs, sprouts

eginhad, eginiad (**-au**) *nm* germination, sprouting

egino *vb* germinate, shoot, sprout

eginol *adj* germinal, shooting

eginyn (**egin**) *nm* sprout

eglur *adj* clear, plain, evident

eglurdeb, -der *nm* clearness

eglureb (**-au**) *nf* illustration

eglurhad *nm* explanation, demonstration

eglurhaol *adj* explanatory

egluro *vb* make clear, explain

eglwys (**-i, -ydd**) *nf* church

eglwysig *adj* church, ecclesiastical

eglwyswr (**-wyr**) *nm* churchman

eglwyswraig (**-wragedd**) *nf* churchwoman

egni (**-ion**) *nm* effort, might, energy

egnio *vb* endeavour, make an effort

egniol *adj* energetic

egnioli *vb* energise

ego *nm* ego

egoistiaeth *nm* egoism

egosentrig *adj* egocentric

egöydd *nm* egoist

egr *adj* sharp; sour; severe; savage; cheeky

egroes *npl* (**-en** *nm*) hips

egwan *adj* weak, feeble

egwyd (**-ydd**) *nf* fetlock; fetter

egwyddor (**-ion, -au**) *nf* rudiment; principle; alphabet

egwyddorol *adj* high-principled

egwyl *nf* lull, respite; opportunity

enghraiff (**-eifftiau**) *nf* example, instance

enghreifftiol *adj* exemplary, illustrative

englyn (**-ion**) *nm* Welsh alliterative stanza

englyna, -u *vb* compose *englynion*

englynwr (**-wyr**) *nm* composer of *englynion*

engyl see **angel**

ehangder (**eangderau**) *nm* breadth, immensity

ehangu *vb* enlarge, extend

ehedeg *vb* fly; run to seed

ehedfa (**-feydd**) *nf* flight

ehedfan *vb* hover, fly

ehediad (**-au**) *nm* flight

ehediad (**-iaid**) *nm* fowl, bird

ehedog *adj* flying

ehedydd (-ion) *nm* lark

ehofndra *nm* fearlessness, boldness

ei *pron* his, hers; its

eich *pron* your

Eidal: yr E. Italy

eidion (-nau) *nm* ox

eiddew *coll n* ivy

eiddgar *adj* zealous, ardent

eiddgarwch *nm* zeal, ardour

eiddigedd *nm* jealousy; zeal

eiddigeddu *vb* be jealous, envy; have zeal

eiddigeddus *adj* jealous, envious

eiddigus *adj* jealous; zealous

eiddil *adj* slender, feeble

eiddilwch *nm* slenderness, feebleness

eiddiorwg *coll n* ivy

eiddo *nm* property, possessions ♦ *pron* his, *etc*

eidduno *vb* desire, wish, pray

Eifftaidd *adj* Egyptian

Eifftiwr (-wyr), **Eifftiad** (-iaid) *nm* Egyptian

eigion *nm* depth, ocean

eigioneg *nf/m* oceanography

eigionol *adj* pelagic

eingion (-au) *nf* anvil

Eingl *npl* Angles, Englishmen

Eingl-Gymro (-Gymry) *nm* Anglo-Welshman

Eingl-Sais (-Saeson) *nm* Anglo-Saxon

Eingl-Seisnig *adj* Anglo-Saxon

eil- *prefix* second (ail)

eilchwyl *adv* again

eiliad (-au) *nmf* second, moment

eiliadur (-on) *nm* alternator

eilio *vb* weave, plait; sing; second

eiliwr (-wyr) *nm* seconder

eilradd (-ol) *adj* secondary, inferior

eilrif (-au) *nm* even number

eilun (-od) *nm* image, idol

eilunaddolgar *adj* idolatrous

eilunaddoli *vb* worship idols

eilunaddolwr (-wyr) *nm* idolator

eilwaith *adv* again

eilydd (-ion) *nm* seconder, reserve

eillio *vb* shave

eilliwr (-wyr) *nm* shaver, barber

ein *pron adj* our

einioes *nf* life, lifetime

einion (-au) *nf* anvil

eira *nm* snow

eirchion see **arch**

eirias *adj* burning, glowing, fiery

eirin *npl* (-en *nf*) plums. **e. gwlanog** peaches. **e. duon** damsons. **e. duon bach** sloes. **e. Mair** gooseberries

eiriol *vb* plead, pray, intercede

eiriolaeth *nf* intercession

eiriolwr (-wyr) *nm* intercessor, mediator

eirlaw *nm* sleet

eirlin (-iau) *nm* snowline

eirlithrad (-au) *nm* avalanche

eirlys (-iau) *nm* snowdrop

eironi *nm* irony

eisen (ais) *nf* rib; lath

eisglwyf *nm* pleurisy

eisiau *nm* want, need, lack

eisin *coll n* bran, husk

eising *nm* icing

eisio *vb* ice

eisoes *adv* already

eistedd *vb* sit, seat

eisteddfa (-oedd, -fâu) *nf* seat

eisteddfod (-au) *nf* session; eisteddfod

eisteddfodol *adj* eisteddfodic

eisteddfodwr (-wyr) *nm* frequenter of *eisteddfodau*

eisteddfota *vb* frequent *eisteddfodau*

eisteddiad (-au) *nm* sitting, session

eisteddle (-oedd) *nm* seat, sitting, pew

eitem (-au) *nf* item

eithaf (-ion) *adj*, *nm* extreme; superlative ♦ *adv* very, quite

eithafbwynt (-iau) *nm* extremity; apogee
eithafiaeth *nf* extremism
eithafion *npl* extremes, extremities
eithafol *adj* extreme
eithafwr (-wyr) *nm* extremist
eithin *npl* (-en *nf*) furze, gorse
eithinog *adj* furzy
eithr *prep* except; besides ♦ *conj* but
eithriad (-au) *nm* exception
eithriadol *adj* exceptional
eithrio *vb* except, exclude
elastig *adj, nm* elastic
elastigedd *nm* elasticity
electromagneteg *nf/m* electromagnetism
electromedr (-au) *nm* electrometer
electron (-au) *nm* electron
electroneg *nf/m* electronics
electronig *adj* electronic
elegeiog *adj* elegiac, mournful
eleni *adv* this year
elfen (-nau) *nf* element
elfennig *adj* elemental
elfennol *adj* elementary
eli (elïoedd) *nm* ointment, salve
elifiant (-nnau) *nm* effluence
elifyn (elifion) *nm* effluent
eliffant (-od, -iaid) *nm* elephant
eliffantaidd *adj* elephantine
elin (-au, -oedd) *nf* elbow; angle, bend
elips (-au) *nm* ellipse
eliptig *adj* elliptical
elor (-au) *nf* bier
elusen (-nau) *nf* alms
elusendy (-dai) *nm* almshouse
elusengar *adj* charitable, benevolent
elusengarwch *nm* charity, benevolence
elusennol *adj* eleemosynary
elusennwr (-enwyr) *nm* almoner
elw *nm* possession, gain, profit
elwa *vb* gain, profit

elwlen (-wlod) *nf* kidney
ellyll (-on) *nm* fiend; goblin
ellyllaidd *adj* fiendish; elfish
ellylles (-au) *nf* fury, she-goblin
ellyn (-au, -od) *nm* razor
embryo *nm* embryo
embryoleg *nf* embryology
emosiwn (-iynau) *nm* emotion
emosiynol *adj* emotional
empeiraeth *nf* empiricism
empeiraidd *adj* empirical
empirig *adj* empirical
emrallt *nm* emerald
emyn (-au) *nm* hymn
emyn-dôn (-au) *nf* hymn-tune
emyniadur (-on) *nm* hymnal
emynwr (-wyr) *nm* hymnist
emynydd (-ion, -wyr) *nm* hymnist
emynyddiaeth *nf* hymnody, hymnology
enaid (eneidiau) *nm* life, soul
enamel (-au) *nm* enamel
enamlio *vb* enamel
enbyd, -us *adj* dangerous, perilous
enbydrwydd *nm* peril, danger, jeopardy
encil (-ion) *nm* retreat, flight
encilfa (-feydd) *nf* retreat
enciliad (-au) *nm* retreat; desertion
encilio *vb* retreat; desert
enciliwr (-wyr) *nm* retreater; deserter
enclitig *adj* enclitic
encôr *nm* encore
encyd *nm* space; while
enchwythu *vb* inflate
endemig *adj* endemic
endid *nm* entity, existence
endothermig *adj* endothermic
eneidiog *adj* animate
eneidiol *adj* animate, living
eneiniad (-au) *nm* anointing, unction
eneinio *vb* anoint
Eneiniog *nm* The Messiah, Christ
eneiniog *adj, nm* anointed

enfawr *adj* enormous, huge, immense

enfys (**-au**) *nf* rainbow

engiriol *adj* nefarious, cruel, terrible

engrafiad (**-au**) *nm* engraving

engrafu *vb* engrave

enhuddo see **anhuddo**

enigma *nm* enigma

enigmatig *adj* enigmatic

enillfawr *adj* lucrative, remunerative

enillgar *adj* gainful; winsome

enillion *npl* profits, earnings

enillwr, -ydd (**-wyr**) *nm* gainer, winner

enllib (**-ion, -iau**) *nm* slander, libel

enllibaidd *adj* slanderous, libellous

enllibio *vb* slander, libel

enllibiwr (**-wyr**) *nm* slanderer, libeller

enllibus *adj* slanderous, libellous

enllyn *nm* relish eaten with bread

ennaint (**eneiniau**) *nm* ointment

ennill *vb* gain, win, earn ♦ (**enillion**) *nm* gain, profit; (*pl*) earnings

ennyd *nm/f* while, moment

ennyn *vb* kindle, burn, inflame; excite

ensyniad (**-au**) *nm* insinuation

ensynio *vb* insinuate

entrych (**-ion**) *nm* firmament, height, zenith

enw (**-au**) *nm* name; noun

enwad (**-au**) *nm* denomination, sect

enwadaeth *nf* sectarianism

enwadol *adj* sectarian; nominative

enwadwr (**-wyr**) *nm* sectarian, sectary

enwaediad *nm* circumcision

enwaedu *vb* circumcise

enwebai (**-eion**) *nm* nominee

enwebiad (**-au**) *nm* nomination

enwebu *vb* nominate

enwedig *adj*: **yn e.** particularly, especially

enwi *vb* name

enwog (**-ion**) *adj* famous, renowned, noted

enwogi *vb* make famous

enwogrwydd *nm* fame, renown

enwol *adj* nominal, nominative

enwyn *nm*: **llaeth e.** buttermilk

enynfa *nf* inflammation; itching

enyniad (**-au**) *nm* inflammation

enynnol *adj* inflammatory; inflamed

eofn *adj* fearless, bold

eog (**-iaid**) *nm* salmon

eos (**-au**) *nf* nightingale

eosaidd *adj* like a nightingale

epa (**-od**) *nm* ape, monkey

epidemig *adj*, *nm* epidemic

epig *nf* epic

epiglotis (**-au**) *nm* epiglottis

epigram (**-au**) *nm* epigram

epil *nm* offspring, brood

epilepsi *nm* epilepsy

epilgar *adj* prolific, teeming

epiliad (**-au**) *nm* reproduction

epilio *vb* bring forth, teem, breed

epilog *nm* epilogue

episeicloid (**-au**) *nm* epicycloid

epistol (**-au**) *nm* epistle

eples *nm* leaven, ferment

eplesiad *nm* fermentation

eplesu *vb* leaven, ferment

er *prep* for, in order to; since ♦ *conj* though

eraill see **arall**

erbyn *vb* receive, meet ♦ *prep* against, by

erch *adj* speckled; frightful

erchi *vb* ask, pray, command, demand

erchwyn (**-ion**) *nm* side, bed-side

erchyll *adj* hideous, horrible

erchyllter (**-au**) *nm* atrocity

erchylltod, -tra *nm* hideousness, horror

eres *adj* wonderful, strange

erestyn *nm* minstrel, buffoon

erfin *npl* (**-en** *nf*) turnips

erfyn *vb* beg, pray, implore, expect

erfyniad (**-au**) *nm* prayer, petition

ergyd (**-ion**) *nmf* blow, stroke; shot; cast

ergydio *vb* strike; throw, cast

ergydiwr (**-wyr**) *nm* striker

erial (**-au**) *nm* aerial

erioed *adv* ever

erledigaeth (**-au**) *nf* persecution

erlid *vb* persecute ♦ (**-iau**) *nm* persecution

erlidiwr (**-wyr**) *nm* persecutor

erlyn *vb* pursue, prosecute

erlyniad *nm* prosecution

erlynydd (**-ion**) *nm* prosecutor

ern, ernes (**-au**) *nf* earnest, pledge, deposit

ers *prep* since (**er ys**)

erthwch *nm* grunt, pant

erthygl (**-au**) *nf* article

erthyl (**-od**) *nm* abortion

erthylaidd *adj* abortive

erthyliad (**-au**) *nm* abortion, miscarriage

erthylu *vb* abort, miscarry

erw (**-au**) *nf* acre

erwain *npl* meadow-sweet

erwydd *npl* stave (*in music*)

erydiad (**-au**) *nm* erosion

erydol *adj* erosive

erydu *vb* erode

erydydd (**-ion**) *nm* erosive agent

eryr (**-od**) *nm* eagle; shingles

eryraidd *adj* eagle-like; aquiline

esblygiad (**-au**) *nm* evolution

esblygiadaeth *nf* evolutionism

esboniad (**-au**) *nm* explanation; commentary

esboniadaeth *nf* exposition, exegesis

esboniadol *adj* expository, explanatory

esbonio *vb* explain, expound

esboniwr (**-wyr**) *nm* expositor, commentator

esbonydd (**-ion**) *nm* exponent

esbonyddol *adj* exponential

escaladur (**-on**) *nm* escalator

esgair (**-eiriau**) *nf* shank, leg; ridge

esgeirlwm *adj* exposed, windswept

esgeulus *adj* neglectful, negligent

esgeuluso *vb* neglect

esgeulustod, -tra *nm* negligence

esgid (**-iau**) *nf* boot, shoe

esgob (**-ion**) *nm* bishop

esgobaeth (**-au**) *nf* bishopric, see, diocese

esgobyddiaeth *nf* episcopalianism

esgoli *vb* escalate

esgor *vb* bring forth, bear

esgud *adj* quick, swift, active

esgus (**-ion, -odion**) *nm* excuse, pretext

esgusodi *vb* excuse

esgusodol *adj* excusable, excused

esgymun *adj* execrable, excommunicate

esgymuno *vb* excommunicate

esgyn *vb* ascend, rise

esgynbren (**-nau**) *nm* perch

esgynfa (**-feydd**) *nf* ascent, rise

esgynfaen *nm* horse-block

esgyniad *nm* ascension

esgynneb (**esgynebau**) *nf* climax

esgynnol *adj* ascending

esgyrn see **asgwrn**

esgyrnog *adj* bony

esiampl (**-au**) *nf* example

esmwyth *adj* soft, smooth; easy

esmwythâd *nm* ease, relief

esmwythau *vb* soothe, ease

esmwythder, -dra *nm* ease

esmwytho, -áu *vb* ease, soothe, soften

esmwythyd *nm* ease, luxury

estron (**-iaid**) *nm* foreigner, alien

estron *adj* foreign, strange, alien

estrones (**-au**) *nf* alien woman

estronol *adj* strange, foreign, alien

estrys (**-od**) *nmf* ostrich

estyll *npl* (**-en** *nf*) planks, boards

estyn *vb* extend, reach; stretch, prolong

estynadwy *adj* extensible

estyniad *nm* extension, prolongation

estheteg *nm/f* aesthetics

esthetig *adj* aesthetic

etifedd (-ion) *nm* heir, inheritor

etifeddeg *nm/f* heredity

etifeddes (-au) *nf* heiress

etifeddiaeth (-au) *nf* inheritance

etifeddol *adj* hereditary

etifeddu *vb* inherit

eto *conj* yet, still ♦ *adv* again; yet, still

ether *nm* ether

ethnig *nm* ethnic

ethnoleg *nf* ethnology

ethol *vb* elect

etholaeth (-au) *nf* constituency

etholedig (-ion) *adj* elect

etholedigaeth *nf* election (*theol.*)

etholiad (-au) *nm* election

etholiadol *adj* electoral, elective

etholwr (-wyr) *nm* elector, voter

ethos *nm* ethos

eu *pron* their

euog *adj* guilty

euogrwydd *nm* guiltiness, guilt

euraid, -aidd *adj* golden, (of) gold

euro *vb* apply or bestow gold; gild

eurych (-od) *nm* goldsmith

ewig (-od) *nf* hind

ewin (-edd) *nm/f* nail, talon, claw; hoof

ewino *vb* claw

ewinog *adj* having nails or claws

ewinrhew *nf* frost-bite

Ewrop *nf* Europe

Ewropead (-aid) *nm* European

Ewropeaidd *adj* European

ewyllys (-iau) *nf* will

ewyllysio *vb* will, wish

ewyn *nm* foam, froth, surf

ewynnog *adj* foaming, foamy, frothy

ewynnu *vb* foam, froth

ewythr (-edd) *nm* uncle

F

fagddu *nf:* **y f.** gross darkness

falf (-iau) *nf* valve

fan (-iau) *nf* van

fandal (-iaid) *nm* vandal

fandaleiddio *vb* vandalise

fandaliaeth *nf* vandalism

farnais (-eisiau) *nf* varnish

farneisio *vb* varnish

fe *pron* he, him ♦ *preverbal particle*

feallai *adv* perhaps, peradventure

fel *adv, conj, prep* so, as, that, thus, like; how

felly *adv* so, thus

festri (-ioedd) *nf* vestry

ficer (-iaid) *nm* vicar

ficerdy (-dai) *nm* vicarage

finegr *nm* vinegar

fiola (-s) *nf* viola

firws (-au, fira) *nm* virus

fitamin (-au) *nm* vitamin

folt (-iau) *nm* volt

foltamedr (-au) *nm* voltameter

foltedd (-au) *nm* voltage

foltmedr (-au) *nm* voltmeter

fortais (-eisiau) *nm* vortex

fory *adv* tomorrow (**yfory**)

fry *adv* above, aloft

fwltur (-iaid) *nm* vulture

fy *pron* my

fyny *adv* up, upwards

FF

ffa *npl* (**ffáen, ffeuen** *nf*) beans. **ffa'r gors** buckbeans. **ffa pob** baked beans

ffabrigo *vb* fabricate

ffacbys *npl* fitches, vetches

ffactor (-au) *nm/f* factor. **ff. cyffredin mwyaf** highest common factor. **ff. cysefin** prime factor

ffactori, -o vb factorize
ffactri (-ioedd) nf factory, mill
ffaeledig adj fallible, ailing
ffaeledigrwydd nm fallibility
ffaeledd (-au) nm failing, defect, fault.
ffaelu vb fail
ffafr (-au) nf favour
ffafraeth nf favouritism
ffafrio vb favour
ffafriol adj favourable
ffagl (-au) nf blaze, flame; torch
ffagotsen (ffagots) nf faggot
ffair (ffeiriau) nf fair, exchange.
  ffair sborion jumble sale
ffaith (ffeithiau) nf fact
ffald (-au) nf fold; pound
ffals (ffeilsion) adj false, deceitful
ffalsedd nm falsehood, deceit
ffalster nm deceitfulness, cunning
ffalwm nm whitlow
ffan (-nau) nf fan
ffanatig nm fanatic
ffansi nf fancy
ffansio vb fancy
ffansiol adj fanciful, pleasing to the fancy
ffanatigiaeth nf fanaticism
ffantasi(a) (-iau) nf/m fantasy
ffarm (ffermydd) nf farm
ffarmio vb farm
ffarmwr (ffermwyr) nm farmer
ffarmwraig (-wragedd) nf farmwoman
ffârs (-iau) nf farce
ffarwél nf farewell
ffarwelio vb bid farewell
ffaryncs (-au) nm pharynx
ffas (-ys, -au) nf face, coal-face
ffasâd (ffasadau) nm facade
ffasiwn (-iynau) nm fashion
ffasiynol adj fashionable
ffasner (-i) nm fastener
ffasnin (-au) nm fastening
ffasno vb fasten
ffasnydd (-ion) nm fastener
ffatri (-ioedd) nf factory, mill

ffatrïaeth nf manufacturing
ffau (ffeuau) nf den
ffawd (ffodion) nf fortune, fate
ffawdheglu vb hitch-hike
ffawdheglwr (-wyr) nm hitch-hiker
ffawna nf fauna
ffawydd npl (-en nf) beech trees
ffederal adj federal
ffederaliaeth nf federalism
ffederasiwn (-iynau) nm federation
ffed(e)reiddio vb federate
ffefryn (-nau) nm favourite
ffeil nf file
ffein, ffeind adj fine
ffeirio vb barter, exchange
ffelt nm felt
ffelwm nm whitlow
ffemwr (ffemora) nm femur
ffendir nm fenland
ffenestr (-i) nf window
ffenigl nm fennel
ffenomen (-au) nf phenomenon
ffens (-ys) nf fence
ffensio vb fence
ffêr (fferau) nf ankle
fferdod nm numbness
fferi (-iau) nf ferry
fferins npl sweets
fferm (-ydd) nf farm
ffermdy (-dai) nm farm-house
ffermio vb farm
ffermwr (-wyr) nm farmer
fferru vb congeal, freeze; perish with cold
fferyllfa (-feydd) nf dispensary
fferylliaeth nf pharmacy
fferyllol adj chemical, pharmaceutical
fferyllydd (-wyr) nm chemist, pharmacist
ffesant (-s, -au) nm pheasant
ffest adj fast
ffest nf feast
ffetan (-au) nf sack, bag
ffi (-oedd) nf fee
ffiaidd adj loathsome, abominable
ffibr (-au) nm fibre

ffibrog, -us adj fibrous
Ffichtiad (-iaid) nm Pict
ffidil (ffidlau) nf fiddle
ffidlan vb fiddle, dawdle
ffidler (-iaid) nm fiddler
ffidlo vb fiddle
ffieiddbeth (-au) nm abomination
ffieidd-dra nm abomination
ffieiddio vb loathe, abominate, abhor
ffigur (-au) nf figure, type
ffigurol adj figurative
ffigys npl (**-en** nf) figs
ffigysbren (-nau) nm fig-tree
ffiled (-au, -i) nf fillet
ffilharmonig adj philharmonic
ffilm (-iau) nf film
ffilmio vb film
ffiloreg nf rigmarole, nonsense
ffilter (-au, -i) nm filter
ffin (-iau) nf boundary, limit
Ffindir: y **F.** nf Finland
ffindir (-oedd) nm borderland
ffinedig adj bounded
ffinio vb border (upon), abut
ffiniol adj bordering
ffiol (-au) nf vial; cup
ffiseg nm physics
ffisegol adj physical
ffisegwr (-wyr) nm physicist
ffisig nm physic, medicine
ffisigwr (-wyr) nm physician
ffisigwriaeth nm physic, medicine
ffisioleg nf/m physiology
ffit adj fit ♦ (**-iau**) nf fit, paroxysm
ffit-ffatio vb flip-flop
ffitrwydd nm fitness
ffiwdal adj feudal
ffiwg (-iau) nf fugue
ffiws (-iau) nf fuse
ffiwsio vb fuse
fflach (-iau) nf, **fflachiad (-au)** nm flash
fflachio vb flash
fflachiog adj flashing
fflag (-iau) nf flag
fflagen (-ni) nf flagon, flag-stone

fflangell (-au) nf scourge
fflangelliad (-au) nm flagellation
fflangellu vb scourge, whip, flog
fflam (-au) nf flame
fflamadwy adj (in)flammable
fflamio vb flame, blaze
fflamllyd adj flaming, blazing
fflan (-iau) nm flan
fflap (-iau) nm flap
fflasg (-iau) nf flask, basket
fflat adj flat ♦ (**-iau**) nm flat-iron ♦ (**-au, -iau**) nf a flat
fflatio vb flat, flatten
fflatwadn adj flatfooted
fflecs (-ys) nm flex
fflem, fflem nf phlegm
fflint nm flint
ffliwt (-iau) nf flute
ffloch (-au) nm floe. **ffloch iâ** ice floe
fflodiad, -iart nf floodgate
ffo nm flight
ffoadur (-iaid) nm fugitive, refugee
ffodus adj fortunate, lucky
ffoedigaeth nf flight
ffoi vb flee
ffôl adj foolish, silly ♦ (**ffols**) nf fall (in a slate quarry)
ffoledd nm foolishness, folly, fatuity
ffolen (-au) nf buttock
ffoli vb infatuate, dote; fool
ffolineb nm foolishness, folly
ffon (ffyn) nf stick, staff
ffonnod (ffonodiau) nf stroke, blow, stripe
ffonodio vb cudgel, beat
fforc (ffyrc) nf (table) fork
fforch (-au, ffyrch) nf fork
fforchi vb fork
fforchog adj forked, cleft, cloven
ffordd (ffyrdd) nf way, road; distance
fforddio vb afford
fforddol (-ion) nm wayfarer, passer-by
fforest (-ydd, -au) nf forest

fforffedu vb forfeit
ffortiwn (-iynau), **-un** (-au) nf fortune
fforwm (-ymau) nm forum
ffos (-ydd) nf ditch, trench
ffosffad (-au) nm phosphate
ffosil (-au) nm fossil
ffracsiwn (-iynau) nm fraction
ffrae (-au) nf quarrel
ffraeo vb quarrel
ffraeth adj fluent; witty, facetious
ffraetheb (-ion) nf joke, witticism
ffraethineb nm wit, facetiousness
Ffrangeg nf French (language)
Ffrainc nf France
ffrâm (fframiau) nf frame
fframio vb frame
fframwaith nm framework
Ffrances (-au) nf Frenchwoman
Ffrancwr (-wyr, Ffrancod) nm Frenchman
Ffrengig adj French. **llygod ff.** rats
ffrenoleg nm/f phrenology
ffres adj fresh
ffresgo (-au) nm fresco
ffresni nm freshness
ffretwaith nm fretwork
ffreutur nf refectory
ffrewyll (-au) nf whip, scourge
ffridd (-oedd) nf mountain pasture, sheep-walk
ffrimpan (-au) nf frying pan
ffrind (-iau) nm friend
ffrio vb fry; hiss
ffris (-iau) nf frieze
ffrit (-iau) nm frit, flop ♦ adj worthless, unsubstantial
ffrith (-oedd) nf mountain pasture, sheep-walk
ffrithiant (-nnau) nm friction
ffroch, ffrochwyllt adj furious
ffroen (-au) nf nostril; muzzle (of gun)
ffroenell (-au) nf nozzle
ffroeni vb snort, snuff, sniff
ffroenuchel adj haughty, disdainful
ffroes npl (-en nf) pancakes

ffrog (-iau) nf frock
ffrom adj angry, irascible, testy, touchy
ffromi vb fume, chafe, rage
ffrostgar adj boastful
ffrwd (ffrydiau) nf stream, torrent
ffrwgwd (ffrygydau) nm squabble
ffrwst nm hurry, haste, bustle
ffrwtian vb splutter
ffrwydriad (-au) nm explosion
ffrwydro vb explode
ffrwydrol adj explosive
ffrwydryn (-nau, ffrwydron) nm mine, explosive
ffrwyn (-au) nf bridle
ffrwyno vb bridle, curb
ffrwyth (-au, -ydd) nm fruit; vigour, use
ffrwythlon adj fruitful, fertile
ffrwythlondeb, -der nm fruitfulness, fertility
ffrwythlonedd nm fecundity
ffrwythloni vb become fruitful; fertilize
ffrwytho vb bear fruit
ffrydio vb stream, gush
ffrydlif nm/f stream, flood, torrent
ffug adj fictitious, false, sham ♦ (-ion) nm fiction, sham
ffug-bas (-ys) nf dummy (pass)
ffugbasio vb dummy
ffugenw (-au) nm pseudonym
ffugiad (-au) nm forgery
ffugio vb feign; forge
ffugiwr (-wyr) nm impostor; forger
ffuglen nf fiction
ffugliw (-iau) nm camouflage
ffugliwio vb camouflage
ffunud nm form, manner. **yr un ffunud â** exactly like
ffured (-au) nf ferret
ffureta vb ferret
ffurf (-iau) nf form, shape
ffurfafen nf firmament, sky
ffurfdro (-eon) nm inflection
ffurfeb (-au) nf formula

ffurfiad (-au) *nm* formation

ffurfiant (-nnau) *nm* accidence; formation

ffurfio *vb* form

ffurfiol *adj* formal

ffurfioiaeth *nf* formalism

ffurfioldeb *nm* formality, formalism

ffurflen (-ni) *nf* form (*to fill*)

ffurflin (-iau) *nm* formline

ffurfwasanaeth (-au) *nm* liturgy

ffurfwedd (-au) *nf* configuration

ffust (-iau) *nf* flail

ffustio, -o *vb* beat

ffwdan *nf* fuss, bustle, flurry

ffwdanllyd *adj* fussy, bustling

ffwdanu *vb* fuss, bustle

ffwdanus *adj* fussy, fidgety, flurried

ffwng (ffyngoedd, ffyngau) *nm* fungus

ffwngleiddiad (-au) *nm* fungicide

ffŵl (ffyliaid) *nm* fool

ffwlbart (-iaid) *nm* polecat

ffwlbri *nm* fudge, nonsense, tomfoolery

ffwlcyn *nm* fool, ninny, nincompoop

ffwndro *vb* founder, become confused

ffwndrus *adj* confused, bewildered

ffwndwr *nm* confusion, hurly-burly

ffwr *nm* fur

ffwrdd *nm* way, **i ff.** away

ffwrn (ffyrnau) *nf* furnace, oven

ffwrnais (-eisiau) *nf* furnace

ffwrwm (ffyrymau) *nf* form, bench

ffydd *nf* faith

ffyddiog *adj* strong in faith, trustful

ffyddlon *adj* faithful

ffyddlondeb *nm* faithfulness, fidelity

ffyddloniaid *npl* faithful ones

ffynhonnell (ffynonellau) *nf* fount, source

ffyniannus *adj* prosperous

ffyniant *nm* prosperity

ffynidwydd *npl* (-en *nf*) fir-trees, pine-trees

ffynnon (ffynhonnau) *nf* fountain, well, spring

ffynnu *vb* prosper, thrive

ffyrf *adj* thick, stout; *f* **fferf**

ffyrfder *nm* thickness, stoutness

ffyrling (-au, -od) *nf* farthing

ffyrnig *adj* fierce, savage, ferocious

ffyrnigo *vb* grow fierce; enrage

ffyrnigrwydd *nm* fierceness, ferocity

G

gadael, gadu *vb* leave, forsake; let, allow

gaeaf (-au, -oedd) *nm* winter

gaeafaidd, -ol *adj* wintry

gaeafu *vb* winter, hibernate

gafael, -yd *vb* hold, grasp ♦ (-ion) *nf* hold, grasp

gafaelgar *adj* gripping, tenacious

gafl (-au, geifl) *nf* fork, groin

gafr (geifr) *nf* goat

gafrewig (-od) *nf* gazelle, antelope

gagendor see **agendor**

gaing (geingau) *nf* chisel. **g. gau** gouge

gair (geiriau) *nm* word

galanas (-au) *nf* murder, massacre

galanastra *nm* slaughter; mess

galar *nm* mourning, grief, sorrow

galarnad (-au) *nf* lamentation

galarnadu *vb* bewail, lament

galaru *vb* mourn, grieve, lament

galarus *adj* mournful, lamentable, sad

galarwr (-wyr) *nm* mourner

galw *vb* call ♦ *nm* call, demand

galwad (-au) *nmf* call, demand

galwedigaeth (-au) *nf* occupation, vocation, calling

galwyn (-i) *nm* gallon

gallt (gelltydd) *nf* wooded slope;

hill, rise

gallu *vb* be able ♦ (**-oedd**) *nm* power, ability

galluog *adj* able, powerful, mighty

galluogi *vb* enable, empower

gan *prep* with; by; of, from

gar (**-rau**) *nf/m* thigh, shank

garan (**-od**) *nf* heron, crane

Garawys *nm* Lent

gardas, -ys (**-ysau**) *nm/f* garter

gardd (**gerddi**) *nf* garden; garth, yard

garddio *vb* garden ♦ *nm* gardening

garddwr (**-wyr**) *nm* gardener

garddwriaeth *nf* horticulture

gargam *adj* knock-kneed

garlant (**-au**) *nm* garland

garlleg *npl* (**-en** *nf*) garlic

gartref *adv* at home (*mut. of* **cartref**)

garth *nm* hill; enclosure

garw (**geirwon**) *adj* coarse, rough, harsh

garwedd *nm* roughness

garwhau *vb* roughen; ruffle

gast (**geist**) *nf* bitch

gau *adj* false; hollow

gefail (**-eiliau**) *nf* smithy

gefel (**-eiliau**) *nf* tongs, pincers

gefell (**-eilliaid**) *n* coll twin

gefeilldref (**-i**) *nf* twinned town

gefyn (**-nau**) *nm* fetter, shackle

gefynnu *vb* fetter, shackle

geingio *vb* chisel, gouge

geilwad (**-waid**) *nm* caller

geirfa (**-oedd**) *nf* vocabulary, glossary

geiriad *nm* wording, phraseology

geiriadur (**-on**) *nm* dictionary, lexicon

geiriadurol *adj* lexicographical

geiriadurwr (**-wyr**) *nm* lexicographer

geirio *vb* word, phrase

geirlyfr (**-au**) *nm* word-book, dictionary

geirwir *adj* truthful, truth-speaking

geirwiredd *nm* truthfulness

gelau, gelen (**gelod**) *nf* leech

gelyn (**-ion**) *nm* foe, enemy

gelyniaeth *nf* enmity, hostility

gelyniaethus *adj* hostile, inimical

gelynol *adj* hostile, adverse

gellyg *npl* (**-en** *nf*) pears

gem (**-au**) *nf* gem, jewel

gêm (**gêmau**) *nf* game

gemog *adj* gemmed, jewelled

gemydd (**-ion**) *nm* jeweller

gên *nf* jaw, chin

genau (**-euau**) *nm* mouth, orifice

genau-goeg, geneuoeg (**-ion**) *nf* lizard; newt

genedigaeth (**-au**) *nf* birth

genedigol *adj* native

Genefa *nf* Geneva

geneth (**-od**) *nf* girl

genethaidd *adj* girlish

genethig *nf* little girl, maiden

geni *vb* be born

genni *vb* be contained

genwair (**-eiriau**) *nf* fishing-rod

genweirio *vb* angle, fish

genweiriwr (**-wyr**) *nm* angler

ger *prep* by, near

gêr *coll n* gear, tackle

gerbron *prep* before (*place*); in the presence of

gerfydd *prep* by

geri *nm* bile, gall. **g. marwol** cholera morbus

geriach *coll n* gear, odds and ends

gerllaw *prep* near ♦ *adv* at hand

gerwin *adj* rough, severe, harsh

gerwindeb, -der *nm* roughness, severity

gerwino *vb* roughen

gewyn (**-nau, giau**) *nm* sinew, tendon

gewynnog *adj* sinewy

Ghana *nf* Ghana

giach (**-od**) *nm* snipe

Gibralter *n* Gibraltar

gieuwst *nf* neuralgia

gildio *vb* yield; gild

gilydd nm: **ei g.** each other. **gyda'i g.** together

gimbill nf gimlet

glafoerio vb drivel, slobber

glafoerion npl drivel, slobber

glaif, gleifiau nm lance, sword, glaive

glain (gleiniau) nm gem, jewel; bead

glan (-nau, glennydd) nf bank, shore

glân adj clean; holy; fair, beautiful

glanhad nm cleansing, purification

glanhaol adj cleansing, purging

glanhau vb cleanse, purify

glaniad nm landing, disembarkation

glanio vb land, disembark

glanwaith adj clean, tidy

glanweithdra nm cleanliness

glas (gleision) adj blue, green, grey, silver ♦ nm blue

glasgoch adj, nm purple

glaslanc (-iau) nm youth, stripling

glasog (-au) nf crop, gizzard

glastwr nm milk and water

glastwraidd adj watered down, feeble; muddled

glasu vb become blue, green or grey; turn pale

glaswellt coll n grass

glaswelltyn nm blade of grass; tigridia

glaw (-ogydd) nm rain

glawiad (-au) nm rainfall

glawio vb rain

glawlen (-ni) nf umbrella

glawog adj rainy

gleisiad (-iaid) nm sewin

gleision npl whey

glendid nm cleanness; fairness, beauty

glesni nm blueness, verdure

glew (-ion) adj brave, daring; astute

glewdra, -der nm courage,

resource

glin (-iau) nm knee

glo nm coal

gloddest (-au) nm carousal, revelling

gloddesta vb carouse, revel

gloddestwr (-wyr) nm reveller

gloes (-au, -ion) nf pang; qualm

glofa (-feydd) nf colliery

glöwr (-wyr) nm collier

glowty (-tai) nm cow-house, shippon

glöyn nm coal. **g. byw** butterfly

gloyw (-on) adj bright, clear; shiny, glossy

gloywder nm brightness, clearness

gloywi vb brighten, polish

glud (-ion) nm glue; bird-lime

gludio vb glue

gludiog adj sticky

glwth (glythau) nm couch

glwth (glython) adj gluttonous ♦ nm glutton

glwys adj fair; holy

glyn (-noedd) nm glen, valley

glynu vb stick, adhere, cleave

glythineb, glythni nm gluttony

glythinebu, glythu vb glut, gormandize

go adv rather, somewhat

goachul adj lean; puny; sickly, poorly

gobaith (-eithion) nm hope

gobeithio vb hope

gobeithiol adj hopeful

gobeithlu (-oedd) nm Band of Hope

gobennydd (-enyddiau) nm bolster, pillow

goblygu vb fold, wrap

gochel see **gochelyd**

gocheladwy adj avoidable

gochelgar adj wary, cautious

gocheliad nm avoidance. **ar ei o.** on his guard

gochelyd vb avoid, shun

godidog adj excellent, splendid

godidowgrwydd nm excellence
godineb nm adultery
godinebu vb commit adultery
godinebus adj adulterous
godinebwr (-wyr) nm adulterer
godre (-on) nm skirt, border, edge
godriad (-au) nm milking
godro vb milk
goddaith (-eithiau) nf fire, bonfire
goddef vb bear, suffer, allow, permit
goddefgar adj forbearing, tolerant
goddefgarwch nm forbearance, tolerance
goddefiad (-au) nm licence; toleration
goddefol adj tolerable; passive
goddiweddyd, goddiwes vb over-take
goddrych nm subject (in grammar)
goddrychol adj subjective
gof (-aint) nm smith
gofal (-on) nm care, charge
gofalu vb care, mind, take care
gofalus adj careful
gofaniaeth nf smith's craft
gofer (-oedd, -ydd) nm overflow of well; rill
gofid (-iau) nm grief, sorrow, trouble
gofidio vb afflict, grieve, vex
gofidus adj grievous, sad
gofod nm space. llong o. nf spaceship
gofodwr (-wyr) nm astronaut
gofyn vb ask, demand, require ♦ (-ion) nm demand, requirement
gofyniad (-au) nm question, query
gofynnod (-ynodau) nm note of interrogation, question-mark
gofynnol adj necessary, requisite; interrogative (pronoun etc)
gogan nf defamation, satire
goganu vb defame, satirize, lampoon
goganwr (-wyr) nm satirist
goglais vb, nm tickle

gogledd nm, adj north
Gogledd Iwerddon nf Northern Ireland
gogleddol adj northern
gogleddwynt nm north wind
gogleddwr (-wyr) nm northman; North Walian
gogleisio vb tickle
gogleisiol adj tickling, titillating, amusing
gogoneddu vb glorify
gogoneddus adj glorious
gogoniant nm glory
gogor (-ion) nf fodder, provender
gogr (-au) nm sieve, riddle
gogri, gogrwn, gogryn vb sift, riddle
gogwydd nm slant, inclination, bent
gogwyddiad (-au) nm inclination
gogwyddo vb incline, slope, lean
gogyfer adj opposite; for, by
gogyfuwch adj, prep of equal height
gogyhyd adj of equal length
gogymaint adj equal in size
gohebiaeth (-au) nf correspondence
gohebol adj corresponding
gohebu vb correspond (by letter etc); reply
gohebydd (-wyr) nm correspondent, reporter
gohiriad (-au) nm postponement
gohirio vb delay, postpone, defer
golau adj, nm, vb light
golau-leuad nm moonlight
golch (-ion) nm wash; coating; lye
golchdy (-dai) nm wash-house, laundry
golchfa nf wash; lathering
golchi vb wash; coat
golchiad (-au) nm washing; plating, coating
golchion npl slops; suds
golchwr (-wyr), -ydd (-ion) nm washer

golchwraig (**-wragedd**) *nf*
  washerwoman
golchyddes (**-au**) *nf* laundress
goledd(f) *nm* slant, slope
goledd(f)u *vb* slant, slope
goleuad (**-au**) *nm* light, luminary
goleudy (**-dai**) *nm* lighthouse
goleuni *nm* light
goleuo *vb* light, enlighten,
  illuminate
golosg *nm* coke, charcoal
golud (**-oedd**) *nm* wealth, riches
goludog *adj* wealthy, rich
golwg (**-ygon**) *nf/m* sight, look;
  (*pl*) eyes
golwr (**-wyr**) *nm* goalkeeper
golwyth (**-ion**) *nm* chop, slice, cut
golygfa (**-feydd**) *nf* scene, view;
  (*pl*) scenery
golygiad (**-au**) *nm* view
golygu *vb* view; mean; edit
golygus *adj* slightly, comely,
  handsome
golygwedd (**-au**) *nf* feature,
  aspect
golygydd (**-ion, -wyr**) *nm* editor
golygyddiaeth *nf* editorship
golygyddol *adj* editorial
gollwng *vb* drop, release, let go;
  discharge; dismiss; leak
gollyngdod *nm* release; absolution
gomedd *vb* refuse
gomeddiad *nm* refusal, omission
gonest, onest *adj* honest
gonestrwydd *nm* honesty
gôr *nm* pus
gor- *prefix* over-, super-
gorau (**-euon**) *adj* best. **o'r g.** very
  well
gorawen *nf* joy, ecstasy
gorblu *npl* immature feathers
gorboblogi *vb* overpopulate
gorbwyso *vb* outweigh, overweigh
gorchest (**-ion**) *nf* feat, exploit
gorchestol *adj* excellent, masterly
gorchfygu *vb* overcome, conquer
gorchfygwr (**-wyr**) *nm* victor;

conqueror
gorchudd (**-ion**) *nm* cover,
  covering, veil
gorchuddio *vb* cover
gorchwyl (**-ion**) *nm* task,
  undertaking
gorchymyn *vb* command ♦
  (**gorchmynion**) *nm* command,
  commandment
gordoi *vb* overspread, cover
gordyfu *vb* overgrow
gordd (**gyrdd**) *nf* sledge-hammer,
  mallet
gordderch (**-adon**) *nf* concubine;
  lover; bastard
goresgyn *vb* overrun, invade;
  conquer
goresgyniad *nm* invasion;
  conquest
goresgynnydd *nm* invader;
  conqueror
goreuro *vb* gild
gorfod *vb* be obliged ♦ *nm*
  obligation, necessity
gorfodaeth *nf* obligation,
  compulsion
gorfodi *vb* oblige, compel
gorfodol *adj* obligatory,
  compulsory
gorfoledd *nm* joy, rejoicing,
  triumph
gorfoleddu *vb* rejoice, triumph
gorfoleddus *adj* jubilant,
  triumphant
gorffen *vb* finish, complete,
  conclude
gorffeniad *nm* finishing, finish
Gorffennaf *nm* July
gorffennol *adj, nm* past
gorffwyll *adj* mad, frenzied
gorffwyllo *vb* rave
gorffwyllog *adj* mad, insane
gorffwylltra *nm* madness, insanity
gorffwys *vb, nm* rest, repose
gorffwysfa (**-oedd**) *nf* resting-
  place, rest
gorffwysiad (**-au**) *nm* rest, pause

gorffwyso, gorffwystra see
gorffwys

gorhendaid nm great-great-
grandfather

gorhennain nf great-great-
grandmother

gori vb hatch

gorifyny nm ascent, hill, steep
climb

goris prep below, beneath, under

goriwaered nm descent, declivity

gorlawn adj superabundant

gorlenwi vb overfill

gorliwio vb colour too highly,
exaggerate

gorllewin nm west. **G. yr Almaen**
West Germany

gorllewinol adj westerly, western

gorllewinwr (-wyr) nm westerner

gormes nm oppression, tyranny

gormesol adj oppressive,
tyrannical

gormesu vb oppress, tyrannize

gormeswr (-wyr), -ydd (-ion) nm
oppressor, tyrant

gormod (-ion) nm too much,
excess

gormodedd nm excess, superfluity

gormodiaith nf hyperbole,
exaggeration

gormodol adj excessive

gormwyth nm catarrh

gornest, ornest (-au) contest,
match

goroesi vb outlive, survive

goroesiad (-au) nm survival

goroeswr (-wyr) nm survivor

goror (-au) nm border, coast,
frontier

gorsaf (-oedd) nf station

gorsedd (-au) nf, **gorseddfa**
(-oedd) nf, **gorseddfainc**
(-feinciau) nf throne

gorseddu vb throne, enthrone,
install

gorsin, gorsing (-au) nf door-post

gorthrech nm oppression; coercion

gorthrechu vb oppress; coerce

gorthrwm nm oppression

gorthrymder nm oppression,
tribulation

gorthrymedig adj oppressed

gorthrymu vb oppress

gorthrymus adj oppressive

gorthrymwr, -ydd (-wyr) nm
oppressor

goruchaf adj most high, supreme

goruchafiaeth nf supremacy;
triumph

goruchel adj high, exalted

goruchwyliaeth (-au) nf oversight, supervision; dispensation

goruchwylio vb oversee, supervise

goruchwyliwr (-wyr) nm
supervisor, steward

goruwch prep above, over

goruwchnaturiol adj supernatural

goruwchreoli vb overrule

gorwedd vb lie

gorweddfa (-oedd), -fan (-nau) nf
bed, couch

gorweddian vb lounge, loll

gorweiddiog adj bedridden

gorwel (-ion) nm horizon

gorwych adj gorgeous

gorwyr (-ion) nm great-grandson

gorwyres (-au) nf great-grand-
daughter

gorymdaith (-deithiau) nf
procession

gorymdeithio vb walk in
procession

gorynys (-oedd) nf peninsula

gosber (-au) nm vespers

gosgedd (-au) nm form, figure

gosgeiddig adj comely, graceful

gosgordd (-ion) nf retinue, train,
escort

gosgorddlu (-oedd) nm body-
guard

goslef (-au) nf tone, intonation
(oslef)

gosod vb put, place, set; let ♦ adj
false, artificial

gosodiad (**-au**) *nm* proposition, statement

gosteg (**-ion**) *nf* silence; (*pl*) banns

gostegu *vb* silence, still, quell

gostwng *vb* lower, reduce; bow; put down, humble

gostyngedig *adj* humble

gostyngeiddrwydd *nm* humility

gostyngiad *nm* reduction; humiliation

gowt *nm* gout

gradell (**-gredyll**) *nf* griddle

gradd (**-au**) *nm/f* grade, degree, stage

graddedigion *npl* graduates

graddfa (**-feydd**) *nf* scale

graddio *vb* graduate

graddol *adj* gradual

graddoli *vb* grade, graduate

graean *coll n* (**greyenyn** *nm*) gravel

graeanu *vb* granulate

graeanwst *nf* gravel (*complaint*)

graen *nm* grain, gloss, lustre

graenus *adj* of good grain, glossy, sleek

graff (**-iau**) *nm* graph

gramadeg (**-au**) *nm* grammar

gramadegol *adj* grammatical

gramadegwr, **-ydd** (**-wyr**) *nm* grammarian

gran (**-nau**) *nm* cheek

gras (**-au**, **-usau**) *nm* grace

graslawn, **-lon** *adj* full of grace, gracious

graslonrwydd *nm* graciousness, grace

grasol, **grasusol** *adj* gracious

grât (**gratiau**) *nm* grate

grawn *npl* (**gronyn** *nm*) grain; grapes; roe

grawnfwyd (**-ydd**) *coll n* cereal

grawnwin *npl* grapes

Grawys *nm* Lent

gre (**-oedd**) *nf* stud, flock

greddf (**-au**) *nf* instinct, intuition

greddfol *adj* instinctive, intuitive,
rooted

greddfu *vb* become ingrained

grefi *nm* gravy

gresyn *nm* pity

gresyni, **-dod** *nm* misery, wretchedness

gresynu *vb* commiserate, pity

gresynus *adj* miserable, wretched

gridyll (**-au**) *nm/f* griddle

griddfan *vb* groan, moan ♦ (**-nau**) *nm* groan

grillian, **-io** *vb* squeak, creak; chirp; crunch

gris (**-iau**) *nm* step, stair

grisial *nm* crystal

grisialaidd *adj* crystal, crystalline

gro *coll n* (**gröyn** *nm*) gravel, pebbles

Groeg *nf* Greek language; Greece ♦ *adj* Greek

Groegaidd *adj* Grecian, Greek

Groeges (**-au**) *nf* Greek woman

Groegwr (**-wyr**, **-iaid**) *nm* Greek

gronell (**-au**) *nf* roe

Grønland *nf* Greenland

gronyn (**-nau**) *nm* grain, particle; while

grot (**-iau**) *nm* groat, fourpence

grual *nm* gruel

grud *nm* grit

grudd (**-iau**) *nf* cheek

gruddfan see **griddfan**

grug *nm* heather

grugiar (**-ieir**) *nf* moor-hen, grouse

grugog *adj* heathery

grwgnach *vb* grumble, murmur

grwgnachlyd *adj* given to grumbling

grwgnachwr (**-wyr**) *nm* grumbler

grwn (**grynnau**) *nm* ridge (*in ploughing*)

grŵn, **grwndi** *nm* purr

grwnan *vb* croon, purr

grwndwal (**-au**) *nm* foundation

grydian *vb* murmur; grunt

grym (**-oedd**) *nm* force, power, might

grymial *vb* mutter, murmur, grumble

grymus *adj* strong, powerful, mighty

grymuso *vb* strengthen

grymuster, -tra *nm* power, might

gwacáu *vb* empty

gwacsaw *adj* trivial, frivolous

gwacsawrwydd *nm* levity, vanity

gwacter *nm* emptiness, vacuity

gwachul see **goachul**

gwad, gwadiad *nm* denial, disavowal

gwadn (-au) *nm* sole

gwadnu *vb* sole; foot it

gwadu *vb* deny, disown; renounce, forsake

gwadwr (-wyr) *nm* denier

gwadd (-od) *nf* mole

gwadd see **gwahodd**

gwaddod (-ion) *nm* sediment, lees, dregs

gwaddodi *vb* deposit sediment

gwaddol (-ion, -iadau) *nm* endowment; dowry

gwaddoli *vb* endow

gwae (-au) *nm/f* woe

gwaed *nm* blood

gwaedlif, gwaedlyn *nm* hæmorrhage, dysentery

gwaedlyd *adj* bloody, sanguinary

gwaedoliaeth *nf* blood, consanguinity

gwaedu *vb* bleed

gwaedd (-au) *nf* cry, shout

gwaeddi see **gweiddi**

gwaeg (gwaegau) *nf* buckle, clasp

gwael *adj* poor, vile; poorly, ill

gwaelder, -dra *nm* poorness, vileness

gwaeledd *nm* illness

gwaelod (-ion) *nm* bottom; (*pl*) sediment

gwaelodi *vb* settle, deposit sediment

gwaelu *vb* sicken

gwaell (gwëyll, gweill) *nf* knitting-needle

gwaered *nm* descent. **I w.** down

gwaeth *adj* worse

gwaethwaeth *adj* worse and worse

gwaethygu *vb* worsen

gwaew see **gwayw**

gwag (gweigion) *adj* empty, vacant, vain

gwagedd *nm* vanity

gwagelog *adj* wary, circumspect

gwagen (-i) *nf* waggon

gwagenwr (-wyr) *nm* waggoner

gwagfa (-feydd) *nf* vacuum

gwagle (-oedd) *nm* space, void

gwagu *vb* empty

gwahadden (gwahaddod) *nf* mole

gwahan, gwahân *nm*: **ar w.** apart, separately

gwahangleifion *npl* lepers

gwahanglwyf *nm* leprosy

gwahanglwyfus *adj* leprous ♦ *nm* leper

gwahaniaeth (-au) *nm* difference

gwahaniaethol *adj* distinguishing

gwahaniaethu *vb* differ; distinguish

gwahanol *adj* different

gwahanu *vb* divide, part, separate

gwahardd *vb* forbid, prohibit

gwaharddiad (-au) *nm* prohibition, veto

gwahodd *vb* invite

gwahoddedigion *npl* guests

gwahoddiad (-au) *nm* invitation

gwahoddwr (-wyr) *nm* inviter, host

gwain (gweiniau) *nf* sheath, scabbard

gwair (gweiriau) *nm* hay

gwaith (gweithiau) *nm* work

gwaith (gweithiau) *nm* time, turn

gwal (-iau, gwelydd) *nf* wall

gwâl (gwalau) *nf* couch, bed; lair

gwala *nf* enough, plenty

gwalch (gweilch) *nm* hawk; rogue, rascal

gwaled (-au) nf wallet
gwalio vb wall, fence
gwall (-au) nm defect, want;
  mistake, error
gwallgof adj mad, insane
gwallgofdy (-dai) nm madhouse,
  lunatic asylum
gwallgofddyn (-gofiaid) nm
  madman
gwallgofi vb go mad, rave
gwallgofrwydd nm madness,
  insanity
gwallt (-iau) nm, coll n hair of the
  head
gwalltog adj hairy
gwallus adj faulty, incorrect,
  inaccurate
gwamal adj fickle, frivolous
gwamalio, -u vb waver; behave
  frivolously
gwamalrwydd nm frivolity, levity
gwan (gweiniaid, gweinion) adj
  weak, feeble
gwanaf (-au) nf layer; row, swath
gwanc nm greed, voracity
gwancus adj greedy, voracious
gwaneg (-au, gwenyg) nf wave,
  billow
gwangalon adj faint-hearted
gwangalonni vb lose heart
gwanhau vb weaken, enfeeble
gwanllyd, gwannaidd adj weakly,
  delicate
gwant nm caesura; division
gwantan adj unsteady, fickle;
  feeble, poor
gwanu vb pierce, stab
gwanwyn (-au) nm spring
gwanwynol adj vernal, spring-like
gwanychu vb weaken, enfeeble
gwar (-rau) nm/f (nape of) neck
gwâr adj civilised, tame, gentle
gwaradwydd (-iadau) nm shame,
  disgrace
gwaradwyddo vb shame, disgrace
gwaradwyddus adj shameful,
  disgraceful

gwarafun vb forbid, refuse,
  grudge
gwaraidd adj gentle, civilized
gwarant (-au) nf warrant
gwarantu vb warrant, guarantee
gwarchae vb besiege ♦ nm siege
gwarcheidiol adj guardian,
  tutelary
gwarcheidwad (-waid) nm
  guardian
gwarchod vb watch, ward, mind
gwarchodaeth nf ward, custody
gwarchodlu (-oedd) nm garrison,
  guards
gward (-iau) nm/f ward
gwarden (-deiniaid) nm warden
gwared vb rid; deliver, redeem
gwaredigaeth (-au) nf deliverance
gwaredigion npl redeemed,
  ransomed
gwaredu vb save, deliver,
  redeem; rid
gwaredwr (-wyr), -ydd (-ion) nm
  saviour
gwaredd nm mildness, gentleness
gwareiddiad (-au) nm civilization
gwareiddiedig adj civilized
gwareiddio vb civilize
gwargaled adj stiffnecked,
  stubborn
gwargaledwch nm stubbornness
gwargam adj stooping
gwargamu vb stoop
gwarged nm remains
gwargrwm adj round-shouldered
gwargrymu vb stoop
gwario vb spend
gwarogaeth see **gwrogaeth**
gwarth nm shame, disgrace
gwarthaf nm top, summit. **ar w.**
  on top of, upon
gwarthafl (-au) nf stirrup
gwartheg npl cows, cattle
gwarthnod (-au) nm stigma
gwarthnodi vb stigmatize
gwarthol (-ion) nf stirrup
gwarthrudd nm shame, disgrace

gwarthruddo *vb* shame, disgrace

gwarthus *adj* shameful, disgraceful

gwas (gweision) *nm* lad; servant

gwasaidd *adj* servile, slavish

gwasanaeth (-au) *nm* service

gwasanaethferch (-ed) *nf* handmaid

gwasanaethgar *adj* serviceable; obliging

gwasanaethu *vb* serve, minister

gwasanaethwr (-wyr) *nm* manservant, servant

gwasanaethwraig (-wragedd) *nf* maidservant

gwasanaethydd (-ion) *nm* servant

gwasanaethyddes (-au) *nf* handmaid

gwaseidd-dra *nm* servility

gwasg (-au, -oedd, gweisg) *nf* press ♦ *nm* waist; bodice

gwasgar *nm* dispersion. ar w. scattered, dispersed

gwasgaredig (-ion) *adj* scattered

gwasgarog *adj* scattered; divided

gwasgaru *vb* scatter, disperse; spread

gwasgarwr (-wyr) *nm* scatterer; spreader

gwasgfa (-feydd, -feuon) *nf* squeeze; fit

gwasgod (-au) *nf* waistcoat

gwasgu *vb* press, squeeze, crush, wring

gwasod *adj* in heat (*of a cow*)

gwastad *adj* level, flat; even; constant, continual

gwastadedd (-au) *nm* plain

gwastadol *adj* continual, perpetual

gwastadrwydd *nm* evenness

gwastatáu *vb* make even, level; settle

gwastatir (-oedd) *nm* level ground, plain

gwastraff *nm* waste, extravagance

gwastraffu *vb* waste, squander

gwastraffus *adj* wasteful, extravagant

gwastrawd (-odion) *nm* groom, ostler

gwastrodaeth, -odi *vb* grooming; discipline

gwatwar *vb* mock; mimic ♦ *nm* mockery

gwatwareg *nf* sarcasm, satire, irony

gwatwarus *adj* mocking, scoffing

gwatwarwr (-wyr) *nm* mocker, scoffer

gwau *vb* knit, weave

gwaun (gweunydd) *nf* moor, meadow

gwawch (-iau) *nf*, -io *vb* scream, yell

gwawd *nm* scoff, scorn, ridicule

gwawdiaeth *nf* ridicule

gwawdio *vb* mock, scoff, jeer, ridicule

gwawdiwr (-wyr) *nm* mocker, scoffer

gwawdlyd *adj* mocking, jeering, sneering

gwawl *nm* light

gwawn *nm* gossamer

gwawr *nf* dawn, day-break; hue, nuance

gwawrio *vb* dawn

gwayw (gwewyr) *nm* pang, pain, stitch

gwaywffon (-ffyn) *nf* spear

gwden (-ni, gwdyn) *nf* withe

gwdihŵ *nm* owl

gwddf (gyddfau) *nm* neck, throat

gwe (-oedd) *nf* web; texture

gwead *nm* weaving, knitting; texture

gwedd (-au) *nf* aspect, form; appearance

gwedd (-oedd) *nf* yoke; team

gweddaidd *adj* seemly, decent

gweddeidd-dra *nm* seemliness, decency

gwedder (gweddrod) *nm* wether. cig g. mutton

gweddgar adj plump, sleek
gweddi (-ïau) nm prayer
gweddigar adj prayerful
gweddill (-ion) nm remnant, remainder, rest; (pl) remains
gweddillio vb leave spare, leave a remnant
gweddïo vb pray
gweddïwr (-ïwyr) nm one who prays
gweddol adj fair, fairly
gweddu vb suit, become, befit
gweddus adj seemly, decent, proper
gweddustra nm decency, propriety
gweddw adj single; widow, widowed. gŵr g. widower ♦ (-on) nf widow
gweddwdod nm widowhood
gweddwi vb widow
gwefl (-au) nf lip (usu. of animal)
gwefr nm thrill, excitement; charge
gwefreiddio vb electrify, thrill
gwefreiddiol adj thrilling
gwefus (-au) nf (human) lip
gwefusol adj of the lip, labial
gwegi nm vanity, levity
gwegian vb sway, totter
gwegil nm back of head
gwehelyth nmf lineage, pedigree
gwehilion npl refuse, trash, riffraff
gwehydd (-ion) nm weaver
gwehynnu vb draw, pour, empty
gweiddi vb cry, shout
gweilgi nf sea, torrent
gweili adj empty, idle
gweini vb serve, minister; be in service
gweinidog (-ion) nm minister, servant
gweinidogaeth (-au) nf ministry, service
gweinidogaethol adj ministerial
gweinidogaethu vb minister

gweinio vb sheathe
gweinyddes (-au) nf attendant, nurse; waitress
gweinyddiaeth (-au) nf administration
gweinyddol adj administrative
gweinyddu vb administer, officiate
gweirglodd (iau) nf meadow
gweitied, -io vb wait
gweithdy (-dai) nm workshop
gweithfa (-oedd, -feydd) nf works
gweithfaol adj industrial
gweithgar adj hard-working, industrious
gweithgaredd (-au), -garwch nm activity
gweithio vb work; ferment; purge
gweithiwr (-wyr) nm workman, worker
gweithred (-oedd) nf act, deed, work
gweithrediad (-au) nm action, operation
gweithredol adj active, actual, virtual
gweithredu vb act, work, operate
gweithredwr (-wyr) nm doer
gweithredydd (-ion) nm doer, factor, agent
gweladwy adj perceptible, visible
gweled, gweld vb see, perceive
gwelediad nm sight, appearance
gweledig adj seen, visible
gweledigaeth (-au) nf vision
gweledydd (-ion) nm seer
gwelw adj pale
gwelwi vb pale
gwely (-au, gwelâu) nm bed; river basin; sea bed; stratum; flat surface
gwell adj better, superior
gwella vb better, mend, improve, recover
gwellau, gwellaif (-eifiau) nm shears
gwellen (gweill) nf knitting-needle
gwellhad nm recovery,

improvement
gwellhau *vb* better, improve
gwelliant (-iannau) *nm* amendment, improvement
gwellt *coll n* grass; sward; straw
gwelltglas *nm* grass, greensward
gwelltog *adj* grassy, green
gwelltyn *nm* blade of grass; a straw
gwellwell *adv* better and better
gwen *adj* f. of **gwyn**
gwên (**gwenau**) *nf* smile
gwenci (-iod) *nf* stoat, weasel
gwendid (-au) *nm* weakness, frailty
Gwener *nf* Venus. **Dydd G.** Friday
gwenerol *adj* venereal
gwenfflam *adj* blazing, ablaze
gweniaith *nf* flattery
gwenieithio *vb* flatter
gwenieithiwr (-wyr) *nm* flatterer
gwenieithus *adj* flattering
gwenith *npl* (-en *nf*) wheat
gwenithfaen *nm* granite
gwennol (**gwenoliaid**) *nf* swallow, martin; shuttle
gwenu *vb* smile
gwenwisg (-oedd) *nf* surplice
gwenwyn *nm* poison, venom; jealousy
gwenwynig, -wynol *adj* poisonous, venomous
gwenwynllyd *adj* peevish; jealous
gwenwyno *vb* poison; fret; be jealous
gwenyn *npl* (-en *nf*) bees
gwep *nf* visage, grimace
gwêr *nm* tallow, suet *etc*
gwêr *nm* shade
gwerchyr *nm* cover, lid, valve
gwerdd *adj* f. of **gwyrdd**
gwerin *coll n* f. of men, people; democracy; crew
gweriniaeth (-au) *nf* democracy; republic
Gweriniaeth Iwerddon *nf* Eire
gwerinlywodraeth (-au) *nf*

republic
gwerinol *adj* plebian, vulgar
gwerinos *coll nf* the rabble, the mob
gwerinwr (-wyr) *nm* democrat
gwern (-i, -ydd) *nf* swamp, meadow; alder-grove
gwern *npl* (-en *nf*) alder-trees
gwerog *adj* tallowy, suety
gwers (-i) *nf* verse; lesson
gwersyll (-oedd) *nm* camp, encampment
gwersyllu, -a *vb* encamp
gwerth *nm* worth, value. **ar w.** for sale
gwerthfawr *adj* valuable, precious
gwerthfawredd *nm* preciousness
gwerthfawrogi *vb* appreciate
gwerthfawrogiad *nm* appreciation
gwerthu *vb* sell
gwerthwr (-wyr) *nm* seller
gwerthyd (-au) *nf* spindle, axle
gweryd (-au) *nm* earth, soil; sward ♦ *nf* groin
gweryriad *nm* neighing
gweryru *vb* neigh
gwestai (-eion) *nm* guest
gwesty (-au, -tai) *nm* inn, hotel
gweu *vb* weave, knit
gwewyr *nm* anguish
gwg *nm* frown, scowl; disapproval
gwgu *vb* frown, scowl, lower
gwialen (**gwiail**) *nf* rod, switch
gwialennod (-enodiau) *nf* stroke, stripe
gwialenodio *vb* beat with a rod
gwib *nf* wandering, jaunt ♦ *adj* wandering
gwibdaith (-deithiau) *nf* excursion
gwiber (-od) *nf* viper
gwibio *vb* flash, flit, dart, wander
gwibiog *adj* flitting, darting, wandering
gwiblong (-au) *nf* cruiser
gwich *nf* squeak; creak; wheeze, wheezing
gwichiad (-iaid) *nm* periwinkle

gwichian vb squeak, squeal; creak; wheeze

gwichlyd adj creaking; wheezy

gwiddon (-od) nf witch

gwiddon npl mites

gwif (-iau) nm lever, crowbar

gwig (-oedd) nf wood

gwingo vb wriggle, fidget; writhe; kick, struggle

gwin (-oedd) nm wine

gwinau adj bay, brown, auburn

gwinc (-od) nf chaffinch

gwinegr nm vinegar

gwinllan (-noedd, -nau) nf vine-yard

gwinllannwr, -nydd nm vine-dresser

gwinwryf (-oedd) nm wine-press

gwinwydd npl (-en nf) vines

gwir adj true ♦ nm truth

gwireb (-au, -ion) nf truism, axiom

gwireddu vb verify, substantiate

gwirfodd nm goodwill; own accord

gwirfoddol adj voluntary, spontaneous

gwirfoddolwr (-wyr) nm volunteer

gwirio vb verify

gwirion (-iaid) adj innocent; silly

gwiriondeb (-au) nm innocence; silliness

gwirionedd (-au) nm truth, verity, reality

gwirioneddol adj true, real, genuine

gwirioni vb infatuate, dote

gwirionyn nm simpleton

gwirod (-ydd) nm liquor, spirits

gwisg (-oedd) nf dress, garment, robe

gwisgi adj brisk, lively, nimble; ripe

gwisgo vb dress; wear

gwisgwr (-wyr) nm wearer

gwiw adj fit, meet; worthy

gwiwer (-od) nf squirrel

gwlad (gwledydd) nf country, land

gwladaidd adj countrified, rustic

Gwlad Belg nf Belgium

Gwlad yr Iâ nf Iceland

Gwlad Thai nf Thailand

gwladfa (-oedd) nf colony, settlement

gwladgar see **gwlatgar**

gwladgarol adj patriotic

gwladgarwch nm patriotism

gwladgarwr (-wyr) nm patriot

gwladol adj of a country, civil, state

gwladoli vb nationalize

gwladweiniaeth nf statesmanship

gwladweinydd (-ion, -wyr) nm statesman

gwladwr (-wyr) nm countryman, peasant

gwladwriaeth (-au) nf state

gwladwriaethol adj state, political

gwladychfa (-oedd) nf settlement, colony

gwladychu vb inhabit, settle, colonize; rule

gwladychwr (-wyr) nm settler, colonist

gwlân (gwlanoedd) nm wool

gwlana vb gather wool

gwlanen (-ni) nf flannel

gwlanog adj woolly

gwlatgar adj patriotic

gwlaw see **glaw**

gwledig adj countrified, country, rural

gwledd (-oedd) nf feast, banquet

gwledda vb feast

gwleddwr (-wyr) nm feaster

gwleidydd (-ion) nm politician, statesman

gwleidyddiaeth nf politics

gwleidyddol adj political

gwleidyddwr (-wyr) nm politician

gwlith (-oedd) nm dew

gwlitho vb dew, bedew

gwlithog adj dewy; inspiring

gwlithyn nm dewdrop

gwlyb (-ion) adj wet, fluid, liquid ♦ nm fluid, liquid

gwlybaniaeth nm wet, moisture
gwlybwr nm wet, moisture, liquid, fluid
gwlybyrog adj wet, damp, rainy
gwlych nm wet. **rhoi yng ng.** steep
gwlychu vb wet, moisten; get wet; dip
gwlydd npl, coll n (-**yn** nm) haulm
gwn (**gynnau**) nm gun
gwn (**gynau**) nm gown
gwndwn see **gwyndwn**
gwneud, gwneuthur vb do, make
gwneuthuriad nm make, making
gwneuthurwr (-**wyr**) nm maker, doer, manufacturer
gwniad nm sewing, stitching, seam
gwniadur (-**iau, on**) nm/f thimble
gwniadwraig nf stitcher, seamstress
gwnio vb sew, stitch
gwniyddes (-**au**) nf seamstress
gwobr (-**au**) nf/m, **gwobrwy** (-**au, -on**) nm reward, prize
gwobrwyo vb reward
gwobrwywr (-**wyr**) nm rewarder
gŵr (**gwŷr**) nm man; husband
gwra vb seek or marry a husband
gwrach (-**iod, -od**) nf hag, witch. **breuddwyd g.** wishful thinking
gwrachiaidd adj old-womanish
gwraidd (**gwreiddiau**) coll n roots
gwraig (**gwragedd**) nf woman; wife
gwrandaw see **gwrando**
gwrandawiad nm listening, hearing
gwrandawr (-**wyr**) nm listener, hearer
gwrando vb listen, hearken
gwrcath (-**od**) nm tom-cat
gwregys (-**au**) nm girdle, belt, truss; zone
gwregysu vb girdle, gird
gwrêng nm, coll n (one of the) common people

gwreica vb seek or marry a wife
gwreichion npl (-**en** nf) sparks
gwreichioni vb emit sparks, sparkle
gwreiddio vb root
gwreiddiol adj radical, rooted; original
gwreiddioldeb nm originality
gwreiddyn (**gwreiddiau**) nm root
gwres nm heat, warmth
gwresfesurydd (-**ion**) nm thermometer
gwresog adj warm, hot; fervent
gwresogi vb warm, heat
gwrhyd (-**oedd**), **gwryd** nm fathom
gwrhydri nm exploit; valour
gwrid nm blush, flush
gwrido vb blush, flush
gwridog, gwritgoch adj rosy-cheeked, ruddy
gwrogaeth nf homage
gwrogi vb do homage
gwrol adj brave, courageous
gwroldeb nm bravery, courage
gwroli vb hearten
gwron (-**iaid**) nm hero
gwroniaeth nf heroism
gwrtaith (-**teithiau**) nm manure, fertiliser
gwrteithiad nm cultivation, culture
gwrteithio vb manure; cultivate, culture
gwrth- prefix counter-, contra-, anti-
gwrthban (-**au**) nm blanket
gwrthblaid nf (party in) opposition
gwrthbrofi vb disprove, refute
gwrthbwynt nm counterpoint
gwrthdaro vb clash, collide
gwrthdrawiad (-**au**) nm collision
gwrthdystiad (-**au**) nm protest
gwrthdystio vb protest
gwrthddadl (-**euon**) nf objection
gwrthddadlau vb object,

controvert

gwrthddywediad (**-au**) *nm*
contradiction

gwrthddywedyd *vb* contradict

gwrthgiliad (**-au**) *nm* backsliding

gwrthgilio *vb* backslide, secede

gwrthgiliwr (**-wr**) *nm* backslider,
seceder

gwrthglawdd (**-gloddiau**) *nm*
rampart

gwrthgyferbyniad (**-au**) *nm*
contrast, antithesis

gwrthgyferbynnu *vb* contrast

gwrthnaws *nm* antipathy ♦ *adj*
repugnant

gwrthnysig *adj* obstinate, stubborn

gwrthod *vb* refuse, reject

gwrthodedig *adj* rejected,
reprobate

gwrthodiad *nm* refusal, rejection

gwrthodwr (**-wyr**) *nm* refuser,
rejecter

gwrthol *nm, adv* back. **ôl a g.** to
and fro

gwrthrych (**-au**) *nm* object;
subject (*of biography*)

gwrthrychol *adj* objective

gwrthryfel (**-oedd**) *nm* rebellion,
mutiny

gwrthryfela *vb* rebel

gwrthryfelgar *adj* rebellious,
mutinous

gwrthryfelwr (**-wyr**) *nm* rebel,
mutineer

gwrthsafiad *nm* resistance

gwrthsefyll *vb* withstand, resist

gwrthun *adj* repugnant, odious,
absurd

gwrthuni *nm* odiousness, absurdity

gwrthuno *vb* mar, deform,
disfigure

gwrthweithio *vb* counteract

gwrthwyneb *nm* opposite,
contrary

gwrthwynebiad (**-au**) *nm*
objection

gwrthwynebol *adj* opposed

gwrthwynebu *vb* resist, oppose

gwrthwynebus *adj* repugnant;
antagonistic

gwrthwynebwr, -ydd (**-wyr**) *nm*
opponent, adversary

gwrych (**-oedd**) *nm* hedge

gwrych *npl, coll n* (**-yn** *nm*) bristles

gwryd see **gwrhyd**

gwryf (**-au**) *nm* press

gwrym (**-iau**) *nm* seam; wale

gwrysg *npl* (**-en** *nf*) stalks, haulm

gwryw *adj* male ♦ (**-od**) *nm* male

gwrywaidd, -ol *adj* masculine

gwrywgydiaeth *nm* homosexuality

gwrywgydiol *adj* homosexual

gwrywgydiwr (**-wyr**) *nm*
homosexual

gwth *nm* push, thrust, shove; gust

gwthio *vb* push, thrust, shove

gwthiwr (**-wyr**) *nm* pusher

gwyar *nm* gore, blood

gwybed *npl* (**-yn** *nm*) flies

gwybod *vb* know ♦ (**-au**) *nm*
knowledge. **gwybodau** studies

gwybodaeth (**-au**) *nf* knowledge

gwybodeg *nm* epistemology

gwybodus *adj* knowing, well-
informed

gwybyddus *adj* known, aware of

gwych *adj* fine, splendid, brilliant

gwychder *nm* splendour, pomp

gwŷd (**gwydiau**) *nm* vice

gwydn *adj* tough

gwydnwch *nm* toughness

gwydr (**-au**) *nm* glass

gwydraid (**-eidiau**) *nm* glassful,
glass

gwydro *vb* glaze

gwydrwr (**-wyr**) *nm* glazier

gwydryn (**gwydrau**) *nm* drinking-
glass

gwŷdd *nm* presence

gŵydd (**gwyddau**) *nm* goose

gwŷdd (**gwehyddion, gwyddion**)
nm loom; plough

gwŷdd *npl* (**gwydden** *nf*) trees

gwyddbwyll *nf* chess

Gwyddel (-od, Gwyddyl) *nm* Irishman

Gwyddeleg *nf* Irish language

Gwyddeles (-au) *nf* Irishwoman

Gwyddelig *adj* Irish

gwyddfa *nf* tumulus, grave

gwyddfid *nm* honeysuckle

gwyddfod *nm* presence

gwyddoniadur (-on) *nm* encyclopædia

gwyddoniaeth *nf* science

gwyddonol *adj* scientific

gwyddonydd (-wyr) *nm* scientist

gwyddor (-ion) *nf* rudiment; science. **yr w.** the alphabet

gwyddori *vb* instruct, ground

gwyfyn (-od) *nm* moth

gwyg *coll n* vetch

gŵyl (-iau) *nm* bashful, modest

gŵyl (-iau) *nf* holiday, feast, festival

gwylaidd *adj* bashful, modest

gwylan (-od) *nf* sea-gull

gwylder *nm* bashfulness, modesty

gwyleidd-dra *nm* bashfulness, modesty

gwylfa (-fâu, -feydd) *nf* watch; lookout

gwyliadwriaeth *nm* watchfulness, caution ♦ (-au) *nf* watch; guard

gwyliadwrus *adj* watchful, cautious

gwyliedydd (-ion) *nm* watchman, sentinel

gwylio *vb* watch, mind, beware

gwyliwr (-wyr) *nm* watchman, sentinel

gwylmabsant (-au) *nf* wake

gwylnos (-au) *nf* watch-night, wake, vigil

gwyll *nm* darkness, gloom

gwylliad (-iaid) *nm* robber, bandit

gwyllt *adj* wild, savage, mad; rapid ♦ (-oedd) *nm* wild

gwylltineb *nm* wildness; rage, fury

gwylltio, -u *vb* frighten; fly into a passion

gwymon *nm* seaweed

gwyn *adj* white; blessed; *f* **gwen**

gwŷn (gwyniau) *nm*/*f* ache, smart; lust

gwynder, -dra *nf* whiteness

gwyndwn *nm* unploughed land

gwynder, -dra *nf* whiteness

gwynder, -dra *nf* whiteness

gwynegon *nm* rheumatism

gwynegu *vb* throb, ache

gwynfa *nf* paradise

gwynfyd (-au) *nm* blessedness, bliss; (*pl*) beatitudes

gwynfydedig *adj* blessed, happy, beatific

gwyngalch *nm* whitewash

gwyngalchog *adj* whitewashed

gwyngalchu *vb* whitewash

gwynias (-iaid) *adj* white-hot

gwynias *adj* white-hot

gwyniedyn *nm* sewin

gwynio *vb* throb, ache

gwynnu *vb* whiten, bleach

gwynnwy *nm* white of egg

gwynt (-oedd) *nm* wind; breath; smell

gwyntell (-i) *nf* round basket without handle

gwyntio *vb* smell

gwyntog *adj* windy

gwyntyll (-au) *nf* fan

gwyntylliad *nm* ventilation

gwyntyllio, -u *vb* ventilate, winnow

gŵyr *adj* crooked, oblique, sloping

gwŷr see **gŵr**

gwyrdraws *adj* perverse

gwyrdro (-ion) *nm* perversion

gwyrdroi *vb* pervert, distort

gwyrdd (-ion) *adj*, *nm* green

gwyrddlas *adj* green, verdant

gwyrddlesni *nm* verdure

gwrddni *nm* greenness, verdure

gwyrgam *adj* crooked

gwyrni *nm* crookedness, perverseness

gwyro *vb* swerve; slope; stoop;

tilt; deviate
gwyrth (-iau) *nf* miracle
gwyrthiol *adj* miraculous
gwyry, gwyryf (gwyryfon) *nf* virgin
gwyryfdod *nm* virginity
gwyryfol *adj* virgin
gwŷs (gwysion) *nf* summons
gwysio *vb* summon
gwystl (-on) *nm* pledge; hostage
gwystlo *vb* pledge, pawn
gwystno *vb* dry, wither, flag
gwythien (gwythi, gwythiennau) *nf* vein, blood vessel, artery. **cwlwm gwythi** cramp
gwyw *adj* withered, faded, sere
gwywo *vb* wither, fade
gyda, -g *prefix* with
gyddfol *adj* guttural
gyferbyn *prefix* over against, opposite
gylfin (-od) *nm* bill, beak
gylfinir *nm* curlew
gynfad (-au) *nm* gunboat
gynnau *adv* a little while ago, just now
gynt *adv* formerly, of yore
gyr (-roedd) *nm* drove
gyrfa (-oedd, -feydd) *nf* race; course; career
gyriedydd (-ion) *nm* driver
gyrru *vb* drive; send; work, forge
gyrrwr (gyrwyr) *nm* driver; sender
gyrwynt (-oedd) *nm* hurricane, tornado
gysb *nm* staggers

H

ha *excl* ha
hac (-iau) *nf* cut, notch, hack
hacio *vb* hack
had (-au) *nm*, *coll n* (hedyn *nm*) seed
hadlif *nm* seminal fluid
hadog *nm* haddock

hadu *vb* seed
hadyd *coll n* seed-corn
haearn (heyrn) *nm* iron. **h. bwrw** cast iron. **h. gyr** wrought iron
haearnaidd *adj* like iron
haeddiannol *adj* meritorious; merited
haeddiant (-iannau) *nm* merit, desert
haeddu *vb* deserve, merit
hael *adj* generous, liberal
haelfrydedd *nm* liberality
haelfrydig *adj* generous, free
haelioni *nm* generosity
haelionus *adj* generous, liberal
haen (-au) *nf* layer, stratum; seam
haenen (-nau) *nf* layer, film
haenu *vb* stratify
haeriad (-au) *nm* assertion
haerllug *adj* importunate; impudent
haerllugrwydd *nm* importunity; impudence
haeru *vb* affirm, assert
haf (-au) *nm* summer
hafaidd *adj* summer-like, summery
hafal *adj* like, equal
hafaliad *nm* equation
hafan *nf* haven
hafn (-au) *nf* hollow, gorge, ravine
hafod (-ydd) *nf* summer dwelling, upland farm
hafog *nm* havoc
hafoty (-tai) *nm* summer residence
hagr *adj* ugly
hagru *vb* mar, disfigure
hagrwch *nm* ugliness
haid (heidiau) *nf* swarm, drove, horde
haidd (heiddiau) *nm*, *coll n* (heidden *nf*) barley
haig (heigiau) *nf* shoal
haint (heintiau) *nm/f* pestilence; faint
hala *vb* send, spend
halen *nm* salt, brine

halog, -edig *adj* defiled, polluted
halogi *vb* defile, profane, pollute
halogrwydd *nm* defilement, pollution
halogwr (-wyr) *nm* defiler, profaner
hallt *adj* salt, salty; severe
halltedd, -rwydd *nm* saltness, saltiness
halltu *vb* salt
halltwr (-wyr) *nm* salter
hambwrdd (-byrddau) *nm* tray
hamdden *nf* leisure, respite
hamddenol *adj* leisurely
hanerob (-au) *nf* flitch of bacon
haneru *vb* halve
hanes (-ion) *nm* history, story, account
hanesydd (-wyr) *nm* historian
hanesyddol *adj* historical
hanesyn (-nau) *nm* anecdote
hanfod *vb* descend from, issue ♦ *nm* essence
hanfodol *adj* essential
haniad *nm* derivation, descent
haniaeth *nf* abstraction
haniaethol *adj* abstract
hanner (hanerau, haneri) *nm, adj, adv* half
hanu *vb* proceed, be derived, be descended
hapus *adj* happy
hapusrwydd *nm* happiness
hardd *adj* beautiful, handsome
harddu *vb* beautify, embellish, adorn
harddwch *nm* beauty
harnais (-eisiau) *nm* harness
harneisio *vb* harness
hatling (-au, -od) *nf* mite, half a farthing
hau *vb* sow, disseminate
haul (heuliau) *nm* sun
hawdd *adj* easy
hawddamor *nm, excl* good luck, welcome
hawddfyd *nm* ease, prosperity

hawddgar *adj* amiable; comely
hawddgarwch *nm* amiability
hawl (-iau) *nf* claim; right. **h. ac ateb** question and answer
hawlio *vb* claim, demand
hawlydd (-ion) *nm* claimant, plaintiff
haws *adj* easier
heb *prep* without
heblaw *prep* beside(s)
hebog (-au) *nm* hawk, falcon
Hebraeg *nf, adj* Hebrew (*language*)
Hebreaidd, Hebreig *adj* Hebrew, Hebraic
Hebrees (-au) *nf* Hebrew woman
Hebreigydd (-ion) *nm* Hebraist
Hebrëwr (-wyr) *nm* a Hebrew
hebrwng *vb* accompany, conduct, convey, escort
hebryngydd (-ion) *nm* conductor, guide
hedeg *vb* fly; run to seed
hedegog *adj* flying; high-flown
hedfa (-fau) *nf* flight
hedfan *vb* fly, hover
hedydd (-ion) *nm* lark
hedyn (hadau) *nm* seed, germ
hedd *nm* peace, tranquillity
heddgeidwad (-waid) *nm* policeman
heddiw *adv* today
heddlu *nm* police force
heddwas (-weision) *nm* policeman
heddwch *nm* peace, quiet, tranquillity
heddychiaeth *nf* pacifism
heddychlon *adj* peaceful, peaceable
heddychol *adj* peaceable, pacific
heddychu *vb* pacify, appease
heddychwr (-wyr) *nm* pacifist, peace-maker
heddyw see **heddiw**
hefelydd *adj* similar
hefyd *adv* also, besides
heffer (heffrod) *nf* heifer
hegl (-au) *nf* leg, shank

heglog adj leggy, long-legged
heglu vb foot it, 'hook it'
heibio adv past
heidio vb swarm, throng, flock
heidden nf grain of barley
heigio vb shoal, teem
heini adj active, lively, nimble, brisk
heintio vb infect
heintus adj infectious, contagious
heislan (-od) nf hackle, hatchel
heislanu vb hackle flax
hel vb gather, collect; drive, chase
hela vb hunt, spend (money, time). **cwn h.** hounds
helaeth adj ample, abundant, extensive
helaethrwydd nm abundance
helaethu vb enlarge, extend, amplify
helaethwych adj sumptuous
helbul (-on) nm trouble
helbulus adj troubled, troublous
helcyd vb hunt ♦ nm worry, trouble
helfa (-fâu, -feydd) nf hunt, catch
helfarch (-feirch) nf hunter (horse)
helgi (-gwn) nm hound
heli nm salt water, brine
heliwr (-wyr) nm hunter, huntsman
helm (-au) nf helm, helmet, stack
help nm help, aid, assistance
helpio, -u vb help, aid, assist
helwriaeth nf game, hunting; chase
helyg npl (-en nf), willows
helynt (-ion) nf trouble, fuss, bother
helltni nm saltiness, saltness
hem nm rivet
hem (-iau) nf hem, border
hen adj old, aged, ancient, of old
henadur (-iaid) nm alderman
henaduriad (-iaid) nm Presbyterian, elder

henaduriaeth (-au) nf presbytery
henafgwr, henafol see hy-
henaint nm old age
hendaid (-deidiau) nm great-grandfather
hender nm oldness
hendref (-i, -ydd) nf winter dwelling, lowland farm
heneb (-ion) nf ancient monument
heneiddio vb grow old, age
henfam nf grandmother
henffasiwn adj old-fashioned
hennain (heneiniau) nf great-grandmother
heno adv tonight
henoed coll n elderly people, the aged
henuriad (-iaid) nm elder, presbyter
heol (-ydd) nf road
hepgor vb spare, dispense with ♦ (-ion) nm what may be dispensed with
hepian vb slumber, doze
her (-iau) nf challenge
herc (-iau) nf hop; limp
hercian vb hop, hobble, limp
heresi (-iau) nf heresy
heretic (-iaid) nm heretic
hereticaidd adj heretical
herfeiddio vb dare, brave, defy
herfeiddiol adj daring, defiant
hergwd nm push, thrust, shove
herio vb challenge, dare, brave, defy
herw nm raid; outlawry
herwa vb scout, prowl, raid
herwgipio vb kidnap
herwgipiwr (-wyr) nm kidnapper
herwhela vb poach (game)
herwr (-wyr) nm scout, raider; outlaw
herwydd see oherwydd
hesb adj f. of **hysb**
hesben (-nau) nf hasp
hesbin (-od) nf yearling ewe
hesbio vb dry up

hesbwrn (-yrniaid) *nm* young ram
hesg *npl* (-en *nf*), sedge, rushes
het (-iau) *nf* hat
heulo *vb* shine (*as the sun*); sun
heulog *adj* sunny
heulwen *nf* sunshine
heuwr (-wyr) *nm* sower
hi *pron* she, her; it
hidio *vb* heed
hidl *adj*: wylo yn h. weep
abundantly
hidl (-au) *nf* strainer, sieve
hidlen (-ni) *nf* strainer, sieve
hidlo *vb* distil; run; strain, filter
hil *nf* race, lineage, posterity
hilio *vb* bring forth, teem, breed
hiliogaeth *nf* offspring, issue,
posterity
hilydd (-ion) *nm* racist
hilyddiaeth *nf* racism
hin *nf* weather
hinfynegydd (-ion) *nm* barometer
hiniog (-au) *nf* threshold, door-
frame
hinon *nf* fair weather
hinsawdd (-soddau) *nf* climate
hinsoddol *adj* climatic
hir (hirion) *adj*, *prefix* long
hiraeth *nm* longing, nostalgia,
grief; homesickness
hiraethu *vb* long, yearn, sorrow
hiraethus *adj* longing; homesick
hirbell *adj*: o h. from afar
hirben *adj* long-headed, shrewd
hirhoedledd *nm* longevity
hirhoedlog *adj* long-lived
hirymarhous *adj* longsuffering
hirymaros *nm* longsuffering
hithau *pron conj* she (on her part),
she also
hobaid (-eidiau) *nf* peck
hobi (hobïau) *nm* hobby
hoced (-ion) *nf* deceit, fraud
hocedu *vb* cheat, deceive, defraud
hocedwr (-wyr) *nm* cheat, fraud
hoci *nm* hockey
hocys *npl* mallows

hodi *vb* shoot, ear, run to seed
hoe *nf* spell, rest
hoeden (-nau) *nf* hoyden
hoedl (-au) *nf* lifetime, life
hoel, -en (-ion) *nf* nail
hoelio *vb* nail
hoeliwr (-wyr) *nm* nailer
hoen *nf* joy, gladness; vigour
hoenus *adj* joyous, blithesome,
gay
hoenusrwydd *nm* liveliness,
sprightliness
hoenyn (-nau) *nm* snare
hoew see **hoyw**
hofran *vb* hover
hoff *adj* dear, fond; favourite
hoffi *vb* like, love
hoffter *nm* fondness; delight
hoffus *adj* lovable, amiable,
affectionate
hogen (-nod) *nf* girl; -naidd *adj*
girlish
hogfaen (-feini) *nm* whetstone,
hone
hogi *vb* sharpen, whet
hogyn (hogiau) *nm* boy, lad
hongiad (-au) *nm* suspension
hongian *vb* hang, dangle
holgar *adj* inquisitive, curious
holi *vb* ask, question, inquire
holiad (-au) *nm* interrogation,
question
holiadur (-on) *nm* questionnaire
holwr (-wyr) *nm* questioner,
interrogator; catechist, question-
master
holwyddoreg (-au) *nf* catechism
holwyddori *vb* catechize
holl *adj* all, whole
hollalluog *adj* almighty,
omnipotent
hollalluowgrwydd *nm*
omnipotence
hollbresennol *adj* omnipresent
hollbresenoldeb *nm* omnipresence
hollfyd *nm* universe
hollgyfoethog *adj* almighty

holliach *adj* whole, sound
hollol *adj* quite
hollt (-au) *nf* split, slit, cleft
hollti *vb* split, cleave, slit
hollwybodaeth *nf* omniscience
hollwybodol *adj* omniscient
homili (-iau) *nf* homily
hon *pron* f. of **hwn**
honcian *vb* waggle; jolt; limp
honedig *adj* alleged
honiad (-au) *nm* claim, assertion,
allegation
honni *vb* assert, allege, profess,
pretend
honno *pron* f. of **hwnnw**
hopran (-au) *nf* mill-hopper;
mouth
hosan (-au) *nf* stocking
hoyw *adj* alert, sprightly, lively,
gay
hoywdeb, -der *nm* sprightliness
hoywi *vb* brighten, smarten
hual (-au) *nm* fetter, shackle
hualu *vb* fetter, shackle
huan *nf* the sun
huawdl *adj* eloquent
hud *nm* magic, illusion, charm,
enchantment
hudlath (-au) *nf* magic wand
hudo *vb* charm, allure, beguile
hudol *adj* enchanting ♦ (-ion) *nm*
enchanter
hudoles (-au) *nf* enchantress,
sorceress
hudoliaeth (-au) *nf* enchantment,
allurement
hudolus *adj* enchanting, alluring
hudwr (-wyr) *nm* enticer, allurer
huddygl *nm* soot
hufen *nm* cream
hugan (-au) *nf* cloak, covering;
rug
hulio *vb* cover, spread
hun (-au) *nf* sleep, slumber
hun *pron* self. **yn ei dŷ ei h.** his
own house
hunan (-ain) *pron* self ♦ *prefix* self-

hunan-dyb *nm* self-conceit
hunangar *adj* self-loving, selfish
hunaniaeth *nf* identity
hunanladdiad *nm* self-murder,
suicide
hunanol *adj* selfish, conceited
hunanoldeb *nm* selfishness;
conceit
hunanymwadiad *nm* self-denial
hunanymwadu *vb* deny oneself
hunell (-au) *nf* wink (of sleep)
hunllef (-au) *nf* nightmare
huno *vb* sleep
huodledd *nm* eloquence
hur (-iau) *nm* hire, wage
hurio *vb* hire
huriwr (-wyr) *nm* hirer; hireling
hurt *adj* stunned, stupid
hurtio *vb* stun, stupefy
hurtrwydd *nm* stupidity
hurtyn (-nod) *nm* stupid,
blockhead
hwb (hybiau) *nm* push; effort; lift
hwde (hwdiwch) *vb imper* take,
accept
Hwngari *nf* Hungary
hwn *adj, pron* this (one); *f* **hon**
hwnnw *adj, pron* that one
(absent); *f* **honno**
hwnt *adv* beyond, away, aside. **tu
h.** beyond
hwp *nm* push; **-io, -o** *vb* push
hwrdd (hyrddod) *nm* ram
hwrdd (hyrddiau) *nm* impulse,
stroke
hwre *vb* see **hwde**
hwsmon (-myn) *nm* farm-bailiff
hwtio *vb* hoot, hiss
hwy *pron* they, them
hwyad, -en (hwyaid) *nf* duck
hwyhau *vb* lengthen, elongate
hwyl (-iau) *nf* sail; humour;
religious fervour
hwylbren (-nau, -ni) *nm* mast
hwylio *vb* sail; prepare, order
hwyliog *adj* fervent, eloquent
hwylus *adj* easy, convenient,

comfortable

hwyluso vb facilitate

hwylustod nm ease, facility, convenience

hwynt pron them, they

hwynt-hwy pron they, they themselves

hwyr adj late ♦ nm evening

hwyrach adv perhaps ♦ adj later

hwyrdrwm adj sluggish, drowsy, dull

hwyrfrydig adj slow, tardy, reluctant

hwyrfrydigrwydd nm tardiness, reluctance

hwyrhau vb get late

hwyrol adj evening

hwythau pron conj they (on their part), they also

hy adj bold

hybarch adj venerable

hyblyg adj flexible, pliant, pliable

hyblygrwydd nm flexibility, pliancy

hybu vb improve in health; promote

hyd (-au, -oedd) nm length ♦ prep to, till, as far as

hyder nm confidence, trust

hyderu vb confide, rely, trust

hyderus adj confident

hydred (-ion) nm longitude

hydredol adj longitudinal

hydref (-au) nm autumn. H. October

hydrefol adj autumnal

hydrin adj tractable, docile

hydwyll adj gullible

hydwylledd nm gullibility

hydwyth adj supple, elastic

hydwythedd nm elasticity

hydyn adj tractable, docile

hydd (-od) nm stag

hyddysg adj well versed, learned

hyf see **hy**

hyfder, -dra nm boldness

hyfedr adj expert, skilful, clever

hyfryd adj pleasant, delightful, agreeable

hyfrydu vb delight

hyfrydwch nm delight, pleasure

hyfwyn adj kindly, genial

hyfforddi vb direct, instruct, train

hyfforddiadol adj training

hyfforddiant nm instruction, training

hyfforddwr (-wyr) nm guide, instructor

hygar adj amiable

hygarwch nm amiability

hyglod adj celebrated, renowned, famous

hyglyw adj audible

hygoel adj credible

hygoeledd nm credibility; credulity

hygoelus adj credulous, gullible

hygyrch adj accessible

hyhi pron f emphat. of **hi**

hylaw adj handy, convenient; dexterous

hylif (-au) nm, adj fluid, liquid

hylithr adj slippery, fluent

hylosg adj combustible, inflammable

hylwydd adj prosperous

hyll adj ugly, hideous

hylltra nm ugliness

hyllu vb mar, disfigure

hyn adj, pron this; these; that

hynafgwr (-gwyr) nm old man, elder

hynafiad (-iaid) nm ancestor

hynafiaeth (-au) nf antiquity

hynafiaethol adj antiquarian

hynafiaethwr, -ydd (-wyr) nm antiquary

hynafol adj ancient

hynaws adj kind, genial

hynawsedd nm kindness, geniality

hynny adj, pron that; those

hynod adj noted, notable, remarkable

hynodi vb distinguish, characterize

hynodion *npl* peculiarities
hynodrwydd *nm* peculiarity
hynt (-iau, -oedd) *nf* way, course
hyrddio, -u *vb* hurl, impel
hyrddwynt (-oedd) *nm* hurricane
hyrwyddo *vb* facilitate, promote
hyrwyddwr (-wyr) *nm* sponsor,
  promoter
hysb *adj* dry, barren; *f* hesb
hysbio *vb* dry
hysbyddu *vb* exhaust, drain
hysbys *adj* known, evident. **dyn h.**
  nm wise man, sorcerer
hysbyseb (-ion) *nf* advertisement
hysbysebu *vb* advertise
hysbysebwr (-wyr) *nm* advertiser
hysbysiad (-au) *nm*
  announcement, advertisement
hysbysrwydd *nm* information
hysbysu *vb* inform, announce
hysbyswr (-wyr) *nm* informant,
  informer
hysian, -io *vb* hiss; set on, incite
hytrach *adv* rather
hywaith *adj* industrious, dexterous
hywedd *adj* trained, tractable

I

i *prep* to, into
i *pron* I, me
iâ *nm* ice
iach *adj* healthy, well
iachâd *nm* healing
iacháu *vb* heal; save
iachawdwr (-wyr) *nm* saviour
iachawdwriaeth *nf* salvation
iachawr (-wyr) *nm* healer
iachus, -ol *adj* healthy, healthful,
  wholesome
iad (-au) *nf* pate, cranium
iaith (ieithoedd) *nf* language. **yr i.**
  fain English
iâr (ieir) *nf* hen
iard (ierdydd) *nf* yard
iarll (ieirll) *nm* earl

iarllaeth (-au) *nf* earldom
iarlles (-au) *nf* countess
ias (-au) *nf* shiver; thrill
Iau *nm* Jupiter. **Dydd I.** Thursday
iau (ieuau) *nm* liver
iau (ieuau, ieuoedd) *nf* yoke
iawn *adj* right ♦ *nm* right;
  atonement ♦ *adv* very
iawndal *nm* compensation
iawnder (-au) *nm* right, equity
iawnol *adj* atoning, expiatory
idealaeth *nf* idealism
ideoleg (-au) *nf* ideology
idiom (-au) *nf* idiom
Iddew (-on) *nm* Jew
Iddewiaeth *nf* Judaism
Iddewes (-au) *nf* Jewess
Iddewig *adj* Jewish
iddwf *nm*: **tân i.** erysipelas
ie *adv* yes, yea
iechyd *nm* health
iechydaeth *nf* hygiene, sanitation
iechydol *adj* hygienic, sanitary
iechydwriaeth *nf* salvation
ieitheg *nf* philology
ieithegydd (-ion, -wyr) *nm*
  philologist
ieithwedd (-au, -ion) *nf* diction,
  (literary) style
ieithydd (-ion) *nm* linguist
ieithyddiaeth *nf* linguistics,
  philology
ieithyddol *adj* linguistic,
  philological
iet (-au, -iau) *nf* gate
ieuanc (-ainc) *adj* young
ieuenctid *nm* youth
ieuo *vb* yoke
ifanc (-ainc) *adj* young
ifori *nm* ivory
ig (-ion) *nm* hiccup
igam-ogam *adj* zigzag
igian *vb* hiccup
ing (-oedd) *nm* agony, anguish
ingol *adj* agonizing, agonized
ill *pron* they. **i. dau** they both
impio *vb* sprout, shoot; bud, graft

impyn nm graft; scion
inc nm ink
incil (-iau) nm tape
incwm nm income
India'r Gorllewin npl West Indies
iod nm iota, jot
lôn nm the Lord
lonawr nm January
lôr nm the Lord
lorddonen nf Jordan
iorwg nm ivy
ir adj fresh, green, raw
irai nm ox-goad
iraid (ireidiau) nm grease
iraidd adj fresh, succulent, luxuriant
Iran nf Iran
Iraq nf Iraq
irder nm freshness, greenness
ireidd-dra nm freshness, vigour
ireiddio vb freshen
iriad (-au) nm lubrication, greasing
iro vb grease, smear, rub, anoint
irwr (-wyr) nm greaser
is adj inferior, lower ♦ prep below, under ♦ prefix under-, sub-, vice-
isadran (-nau) nf subsection
Isalmaen nf Holland
isel adj low; base; humble; depressed
iselder (-au) nm lowness, depth; depression
iseldir (-oedd) nm lowland
Iseldiroedd: Yr I. npl Netherlands
iselfryd adj humble-minded
iselfrydedd nm humility, condescension
iselhau vb lower, abase, degrade
isetholiad (-au) nm by-election
is-gadeirydd nm vice-chairman
is-ganghellor nm vice-chancellor
is-gapten (-iaid, -einiaid) nm lieutenant
isgell nm broth, stock
isiarll (-ieirll) nm viscount
islaw prep below, beneath

isod adv below, beneath
isop nm hyssop
isosod vb sublet
isradd (-iaid) nm inferior, subordinate
israddol adj inferior
israddoldeb nm inferiority
Israel nf Israel
iswasanaethgar adj subservient
isymwybod nm subconscious
isymwybyddiaeth nf subconsciousness
ithfaen nm granite
Iwerddon nf Ireland
Iwerddon Rydd nf Eire
Iwerydd nm the Atlantic
Iwgoslavia nf Yugoslavia
iwrch (iyrchod) nm roebuck

J

jac codi baw nm JCB
jac-y-do nm jackdaw
jam nm jam ♦ -io vb preserve
Jamaica nf Jamaica
jar (-iau) nf jar, hot water bottle
jersi (-s) nf jersey
jest adv just, almost
jeti (-iau) nm jetty
jetlif nm jet stream
ji-binc (-od) nf chaffinch
jins npl jeans
job (-sys) nf job
jobyn nm job
jôc (-s) nf joke
jocan vb joke
joci (-s) nm jockey
jwg (jygiau) nf jug
jyngl (-oedd) nm jungle

L

label (-i) nf label
labelu vb label
labordy (-dai) nm laboratory

labro vb labour
labrwr (-wyr) nm labourer
lafant nm lavender
lamp (-au) nf lamp
lamplen (-ni) nf lampshade
lapio vb lap, wrap
larwm nm alarm
lawnt (-iau) nf lawn
lefain nm leaven
lefeinio vb leaven
lefeinllyd adj leavened
lefel (-au) nf level
leicio vb like
lein (-iau) nf clothes line, line-out
(rugby)
lesbiad (-iaid) nf lesbian
letys npl (-en nf) lettuce
Libanus nf Lebanon
libart nm back-yard
Libya nf Libya
lifft (-iau) nm lift
lifrai nm/f livery
lili nf lily
lindys npl (-yn nm) caterpillars
locust (-iaid) nm locust
lodes see **herlodes**
loetran vb loiter
lol nf nonsense
lolfa (-feydd) nf lounge
lolian vb talk nonsense
lôn (lonydd) nf lane
loncian vb jog
lonciwr (-wyr) nm jogger
lori (-iau) nf lorry
losin npl (-en nf) sweets
lot (-iau) nf lot
Luxembourg nf Luxembourg
lwans, lwfans nm allowance
lwc nf luck
lwcus adj lucky
lwmp (lympiau) nm lump

LL

llabed (-au) nf lappet, lapel, flap
llabwst (-ystiau) nm lubber, lout

llabyddio vb stone
llac adj slack, loose, lax
llacio vb slacken, loosen, relax
llacrwydd nm slackness, laxity
llacs nm mud, dirt
llacsog adj muddy, dirty
llach (-iau) nf lash, slash
llachar adj bright, brilliant,
flashing
llachio vb lash, slash
Lladin nf Latin
lladmerydd (-ion) nm interpreter
lladrad (-au) nm theft, robbery
lladradaidd adj stealthy, furtive
lladrata vb thieve, steal
lladron see **lleidr**
lladrones (-au) nf female thief
lladronllyd adj thievish, pilfering
lladd vb cut; kill, slay, slaughter
lladd-dy (-dai) nm slaughter-house
lladdedig (-ion) adj killed, slain
lladdedigaeth (-au), **lladdfa**,
(-fâu, -feydd) nf slaughter, a
tiring job
lladdwr (-wyr) nm killer, slayer
llaes adj long, loose. **Y treiglad ll.**
spirant mutation
llaesod(r) nf litter (for animals)
llaesu vb slacken, loosen, relax,
droop, flag
llaeth nm milk
llaetha vb yield milk
llaethdy (-dai) nm milk-house,
dairy
llaethog adj rich in milk; milky
llafar nm utterance, speech ♦ adj
vocal; loud
llafariad (-iaid) nf vowel
llafn (-au) nm blade
llafrwyn npl (-en nf) bulrushes
llafur (-iau) nm labour; corn
llafurfawr adj elaborate; laborious
llafurio vb labour, toil; till
llafurlu (-oedd) nm manpower,
labour force, workforce
llafurus adj laborious, toilsome,
painstaking

llafurwr (-wyr) *nm* labourer, husbandman
llai *adj* smaller
llaid *nm* mud, mire
llain (lleiniau) *nf* patch, piece, narrow strip
llais (lleisiau) *nm* voice, vote
llaith *adj* damp, moist
llall (lleill) *pron* other, another
llam (-au) *nm* stride, leap, jump, bound
llamhidydd (llamidyddion) *nm* porpoise
llamsachus *adj* prancing, frisky
llamu *vb* stride, leap, bound
llan (-nau) *nf* church; village
llanast(r) *nm* confusion, mess
llanc (-iau) *nm* young man, youth, lad
llances (-au, -i) *nf* young woman, lass
llannerch (llennyrch), **llanerchau** (-i, -ydd) *nf* spot, patch, glade
llanw *nm* flow (*of tide*) ♦ *vb* flow, fill
llaprwth *nm* lout
llariaidd *adj* mild, meek, gentle
llarieidd-dra *nm* meekness, gentleness
llarieiddio *vb* soothe, mollify
llarp (-iau) *nm* shred, clout
llarpio *vb* rend, tear, mangle, maul
llarpiog *adj* tattered, ragged
llaswyr (-au) *nm* psalter
llatai (-eion) *n coll* love-messenger
llath (-au) *nf* yard, wand
llathen (-ni) *nf* yard
llathr *adj* bright, glossy, smooth
llathraidd *adj* smooth; of fine growth
llathru *vb* polish
llau *npl* (lleuen *nf*) lice
llaw (dwylaw, dwylo) *nf* hand
llawcio *vb* gulp, gorge, gobble
llawchwith *adj* left-handed
llawdde *adj* dexterous
llawddryll (-iau) *nm* pistol, revolver

llawen *adj* merry, joyful, glad, cheerful
llawenhau *vb* rejoice, gladden
llawenychu *vb* rejoice
llawenydd *nm* joy, gladness, mirth
llawer (-oedd) *adj*, *adv* many, much
llawes (llewys) *nf* sleeve
llawfaeth *adj* reared by hand
llawfeddyg (-on) *nm* surgeon
llawfeddygaeth *nf* surgery
llawfeddygol *adj* surgical
llaw-fer *nf* shorthand
llawfom (-iau) *nf* grenade
llawforwyn (-forynion) *nf* handmaid
llawn *adj* full ♦ *adv* quite
llawnder, **-dra** *nm* fullness, abundance
llawr (lloriau) *nm* floor, ground, earth
llawryf (-oedd) *nm* laurel, bay
llawryfog, **-ol** *adj* laureate
llawysgrif (-au) *nf* manuscript
llawysgrifen *nf* handwriting
lle (-oedd, llefydd) *nm* place
llecyn (-nau) *nm* place, spot
llech (-au, -i) *nf* slab, flag, slate
llechgi (-gwn) *nm* sneak
llechres (-i) *nf* table, catalogue, list
llechu *vb* hide, shelter; lurk, skulk
llechwedd (-au, -i) *nf* slope, hillside
llechwraidd *adj* stealthy, underhand, insidious
lled (-au) *nm* breadth, width
lled *adv* partly, rather
lledaenu *vb* spread, disseminate, circulate
lleden (lledod) *nf* flat-fish
llediaith *nf/m* foreign accent
llednais *adj* modest, delicate; meek
llednant (-nentydd) *nf* tributary
lledneisrwydd *nm* modesty,

delicacy

lled-orwedd *vb* recline, lounge, loll

lledr (-au) *nm* leather. **ll. y gwefusau** gums

lledred (-ion) *nm* latitude

lledrith *nm* magic, illusion, phantasm

lledrithio *vb* appear, haunt

lledrithiol *adj* illusory, illusive

lledrwr (-wyr) *nm* leather-merchant

lledryw *adj* degenerate

lledu *vb* widen, broaden, expand, spread

lleddf *adj* slanting; flat, minor; plaintive

lleddfolyn (-olion) *nm* sedative

lleddfu *vb* flatten; soften, soothe, allay

llef (-au) *nf* voice, cry

llefain *vb* cry

llefareg *nf* speech training

llefaru *vb* speak, utter

llefarwr (-wyr), -ydd (-ion) *nm* speaker

lleferydd *nm/f* utterance, voice, speech

llefn *adj* f. of **llyfn**

llefrith *nm* sweet milk, new milk, milk

llegach *adj* weak, feeble, infirm, decrepit

lleng (-oedd) *nf* legion

lleiaf *adj* least, smallest

lleiafrif (-au) *nm* minority

lleian (-od) *nf* nun

lleiandy (-dai) *nm* nunnery, convent

lleibio *vb* lap, lick

lleidiog *adj* miry

lleidr (lladron) *nm* thief, robber

lleiddiad (-iaid) *nm* assassin

lleihad *nm* diminution, decrease

lleihau *vb* lessen, diminish, decrease

lleill see **llall**

lleisio *vb* sound, utter, voice

lleisiol *adj* vocal

lleisiwr (-wyr) *nm* vocalist

lleithder, -dra *nm* damp, moisture

lleithig *nf* couch; footstool

lleitho *vb* damp, moisten

llem *adj* f. of **llym**

llen (-ni) *nf* sheet; veil, curtain

llên *nf* literature, lore, learning

llencyn *nm* stripling, lad

llencyndod *nm* adolescence

llengar *adj* literary, learned

llengig *nf* diaphragm, midriff. **tor ll.** rupture

llên-ladrad (-au) *nm* plagiarism

llenor (-ion) *nm* literary man

llenwi *vb* fill; flow in

llenydda *vb* practise literature

llenyddiaeth (-au) *nf* literature

llenyddol *adj* literary

lleol *adj* local

lleoli *vb* locate; localize

lleoliad *nm* location; localization

llercian *vb* lurk, loiter

lles *nm* benefit, profit, good, advantage. **y wladwriaeth les** the welfare state

llesâd *nm* advantage, profit, benefit

llesáu *vb* benefit, advantage

llesg *adj* feeble, faint; languid, sluggish

llesgáu *vb* weaken, languish, faint

llesgedd *nm* weakness, languor, debility

llesmair (-meiriau) *nm* faint, swoon

llesmeirio *vb* faint, swoon

llesol *adj* advantageous, profitable, beneficial

llestair, llesteirio *vb* hinder, impede, baulk

llestr (-i) *nm* vessel

llesyddiaeth *nf* utilitarianism

lletbai *adj* askew, awry; oblique

lletchwith *adj* awkward, clumsy

lletem (-au) *nf* wedge, stud, rivet

lletraws *adj* diagonal

lletwad (-au) *nf* ladle

llety (**-au**) *nm* lodging(s)
lletya *vb* lodge
lletygar *adj* hospitable
lletygarwch *nm* hospitality
lletywr (**-wyr**) *nm* lodger; host
lletywraig (**-wragedd**) *nf* landlady
llethol *adj* oppressive, overpowering
llethr (**-au**) *nf* slope, declivity
llethrog *adj* sloping, steep, declining
llethu *vb* overlie; smother; oppress, overpower, overwhelm
lleuad (**-au**) *nf* moon
lleuog *adj* lousy
llew (**-od**) *nm* lion. **dant y ll.** dandelion
llewaidd *adj* lionlike, leonine
llewes (**-au**) *nf* lioness
llewpart (**-pardiaid**) *nm* leopard
llewych *nm* light, brightness
llewyg (**-on**) *nm* faint, swoon
llewygu *vb* faint, swoon
llewyrch *nm* brightness, radiance, gleam
llewyrchu *vb* shine
llewyrchus *adj* flourishing, prosperous
lleyg (**-ion**) *adj* lay
lleygwr (**-wyr**) *nm* layman
lliain (**-einiau**) *nm* linen; cloth; towel
lliaws *nm* host, multitude
llibin *adj* limp, feeble; awkward, clumsy
llid *nm* wrath; irritation, inflammation
llidiart (**-ardau**) *nm* gate
llidio *vb* be angry, chafe, inflame
llidiog *adj* angry, wrathful; inflamed
llidiowgrwydd *nm* wrath, indignation
llidus *adj* inflamed
llieiniwr (**-wyr**) *nm* linen-draper
llif (**-iau**) *nf* saw
llif (**-ogydd**) *nm* stream, flood, current

llifbridd *nm* alluvium
llifddor (**-au**) *nf* floodgate
llifddwfr (**-ddyfroedd**) *nm* flood, torrent
llifeiriant (**-iaint**) *nm* flood
llifeirio *vb* flow, stream
llifeiriol *adj* streaming, overflowing
llifio *vb* saw
llifiwr (**-wyr**) *nm* sawyer
llifo *vb* flow, stream
llifo *vb* grind (*tool*)
llifo *vb* dye
llifolau (**-euadau**) *nm* floodlight
llifwr (**-wyr**) *nm* dyer
llifyn (**-nau**, **-ion**) *nm* dye
llilinio *vb* streamline
llin *nm* flax. **had ll.** linseed
llinach (**-au**) *nf* lineage, pedigree
llindagu *vb* strangle, throttle, choke
llinell (**-au**) *nf* line. **ll. gais** try line. **ll. gwsg** touch-in-goal
llinelliad (**-au**) *nm* lineation, drawing
llinellog *adj* lined, ruled
llinellol *adj* lineal
llinglwm *nm*: **cwlwm ll.** tight knot
lliniaru *vb* ease, soothe, allay
llinorog *adj* eruptive; purulent, suppurating
llinos (**-od**) *nf* linnet
llinyn (**-nau**) *nm* line, string, twine
llinynnu *vb* string
llipa *adj* limp, weak
llipryn (**-nod**) *nm* hobbledehoy, weakling
lliprynnaidd *adj* limp, flabby
llith (**-iau**, **-oedd**) *nf* lesson, lecture; bait, mash
llithio *vb* entice, allure, seduce; feed
llithriad (**-au**) *nm* slip, glide
llithren (**-nau**) *nf* ·hute
llithrig *adj* slippery, glib, fluent
llithrigrwydd *nm* slipperiness, glibness

llithro *vb* slip, glide, slide

lliw (**-iau**) *nm* colour, hue, dye

lliwio *vb* colour, dye

lliwiog *adj* coloured

llo (**lloi**) *nm* calf

lloc (**-iau**) *nm* fold, pen

lloches (**-au**) *nf* refuge, shelter, den

llochesu *vb* harbour, shelter

llochi *vb* stroke, caress, fondle

llodig *adj* in heat (*of a sow*)

llodrau *npl* trousers, breeches

Lloegr *nf* England

lloer (**-au**) *nf* moon

lloeren (**-ni, -nau**) *nf* satellite

lloerig *adj, nm* lunatic

llofnod, -iad (**-au**) *nm* signature

llofnodi *vb* sign

llofrudd (**-ion**) *nm* murderer

llofruddiaeth (**-au**) *nf* murder

llofruddio *vb* murder

llofruddiog *adj* guilty of murder

lloffa *vb* glean

lloffion *npl* gleanings

llofft (**-ydd**) *nf* loft, bedroom, gallery

lloffwr (**-wyr**) *nm* gleaner

lloffyn *nm* bundle of gleanings

llog (**-au**) *nm* interest

llogi *vb* hire

llogwr (**-wyr**) *nm* hirer

llong (**-au**) *nf* ship

llongddrylliad (**-au**) *nm* shipwreck

llongwr (**-wyr**) *nm* sailor

llongwriaeth *nf* seamanship

llom *adj* f. of **llwm**

llon *adj* glad, merry

llonaid, llond *nm* full

llonder *nm* gladness, joy

llongyfarch *vb* congratulate

llongyfarchiad (**-au, -archion**) *nm* congratulation

lloniant *nm* joy, cheer

llonni *vb* cheer, gladden

llonydd *adj* quiet, still ♦ *nm* quiet, calm

llonyddu *vb* quiet, still, calm

llonyddwch *nm* quietness, quiet

llorgynllun (**-iau**) *nm* ground plan

llorio *vb* floor, ground (*rugby*)

llorwedd *adj* horizontal

llosg *nm. adj* burning

llosgach *nm* incest

llosgadwy *adj* combustible

llosgfa (**-fâu, -feydd**) *nf* burning, inflammation

llosgfynydd (**-oedd**) *nm* volcano

llosgi *vb* burn, scorch; smart

llosgwrn (**-yrnau**) *nm* tail

llosgydd (**-ion**) *nm* incinerator

llu (**-oedd**) *nm* host

lluched *npl* (**-en** *nf*) lightning

lluchfa (**-feydd**) *nf* snowdrift

lluchio *vb* throw, fling, pelt

lluchiwr (**-wyr**) *nm* thrower

lludlyd *adj* ashy

lludu, lludw *nm* ashes, ash

lludded *nm* weariness, fatigue

lluddedig *adj* wearied, tired, fatigued

lluddedu *vb* tire, weary

lluddias, -io *vb* hinder; forbid

lluest (**-au**) *nm* tent, booth

lluestfa (**-feydd**) *nf* encampment

lluestu *vb* encamp

lluesty (**-tai**) *nm* tent, booth

llugoer *adj* lukewarm

lluman (**-au**) *nm* banner, standard, ensign

llumanwr (**-wyr**) *nm* linesman

llumon *nm* chimney stack, peak

llun (**-iau**) *nm* form, image, picture

Llun, Dydd Llun *nm* Monday

Llundain *nf* London

lluniad (**-au**) *nm* drawing

lluniadaeth (**-au**) *nf* draughtsmanship

lluniaeth *nm* food, nourishment

lluniaethu *vb* order, ordain, decree

lluniedydd *nm* draughtsman

lluniaidd *adj* shapely

llunio *vb* form, shape, fashion

lluniwr (**-wyr**) *nm* former, maker

llun-recordydd (**-ion**) *nm* video-

tape recorder
lluosflwydd *adj* perennial
lluosi *vb* multiply
lluosiad *nm* multiplication
lluosill, -afog *adj* polysyllabic
lluosog *adj* numerous; plural
lluosogi *vb* multiply
lluosogiad *nm* multiplication
lluoswm *nm* product (*maths*)
lluosydd *nm* multiplier
llurgunio *vb* mangle, mutilate
llurguniwr (**-wyr**) *nm* mangler, mutilator
llurig (**-au**) *nf* coat of mail, cuirass
llurigog *adj* mail-clad
llus *npl* (**-en** *nf*) bilberries, whinberries
llusern (**-au**) *nf* lantern, lamp
llusg (**-ion**) *nm* draught; drag
llusgfad (**-au**) *nm* tugboat
llusgo *vb* drag; trail; crawl; drawl
llusgwr (**-wyr**) *nm* dragger, slowcoach
llutrod *nm* mire, ashes, debris
lluwch *nm* dust; spray; snowdrift
lluydd *nm* host, army
lluyddu *vb* mobilise
llw (**-on**) *nm* oath
llwch *nm* dust, powder
llwdn (**llydnod**) *nm* young of animals
llwfr *adj* timid, cowardly
llwfrdra *nm* cowardice
llwfrddyn, -gi *nm* coward
llwfrhau *vb* faint
llwglyd *adj* hungry, famished
llwgr *nm* corruption ♦ *adj* corrupt
llwgrwobrwy (**-on**) *nm* bribe
llwgrwobrwyo *vb* bribe
llwgu *vb* starve, famish
llwm *adj* bare; destitute, poor; *f* **llom**
llwnc *nm* gulp, swallow; gullet
llwncdestun *nm* toast (*health*)
llwr, llwrw *nm* track. II. **ei ben** heading. II. **ei gefn** backwards
llwy (**-au**) *nf* spoon, ladle

llwyaid (**-eidiau**) *nf* spoonful
llwybr (**-au**) *nm* path, track
llwybreiddio *vb* direct, forward
llwybro *vb* walk
llwyd *adj* brown; grey; pale; hoary
llwydaidd *adj* greyish, palish
llwydi, llwydni *nm* greyness; mould, mildew
llwydnos *nf* dusk, twilight
llwydo *vb* turn grey; become mouldy
llwydrew *nm* hoar-frost
llwydrewi *vb* cast hoar-frost
llwydd, -iant *nm* success, prosperity
llwyddiannus *adj* successful, prosperous
llwyddo *vb* succeed, prosper
llwyfan (**-nau**) *nmf* platform, stage
llwyfandir (**-oedd**) *nm* plateau
llwyfannu *vb* stage
llwyfen (**llwyf**) *nf* elm
llwyn (**-i**) *nm* grove; bush
llwyn (**-au**) *nf* loin
llwynog (**-od**) *nm* fox
llwynoges (**-au**) *nf* vixen
llwynwst *nf* lumbago
llwyo *vb* use a spoon; ladle
llwyr *adj* entire, complete, total ♦ *adv* entirely, altogether ♦ *prefix* total
llwyredd *nm* entireness, completeness
llwyrymatal, -ymwrthod *vb* abstain totally
llwyrymwrthodwr (**-wyr**) *nm* teetotaller
llwyth (**-au**) *nm* tribe, clan
llwyth (**-i**) *nm* load, burden
llwytho *vb* load, burden
llwythog *adj* laden, burdened
llychlyd *adj* dusty
Llychlyn *nf* Scandinavia
llychwino *vb* spot, tarnish, soil, sully
llychyn *nm* particle of dust, mote

llydan adj broad, wide
Llydaw nf Brittany
llydnu vb bring forth, foal
llyfn adj smooth, sleek; f **llefn**
llyfnder, -dra nm smoothness, sleekness
llyfndew adj plump, sleek
llyfnhau vb smooth, level
llyfnu vb smooth, level; harrow
llyfr (-au) nm book
llyfrbryf (-ed) nm bookworm
llyfrgell (-oedd) nf library
llyfrgellydd (-ion) nm librarian
llyfrifeg nmf book-keeping
llyfrnod (-au) nm bookmark
llyfrwerthwr (-wyr) nm bookseller
llyfrydd (-ion) nm bibliographer, transcriber of books
llyfryddiaeth nf bibliography
llyfrfa nf (-feydd) library; bookroom; official publishing house of religious denomination, government etc
llyfryn (-nau) nm booklet, pamphlet
llyfu vb lick
llyffant (-od, llyffaint) nm frog, toad
llyffethair (-eiriau) nf fetter, shackle
llyffetheirio vb fetter, shackle
llyg (-od) nmf shrew (-mouse)
llygad (llygaid) nm eye. **ll. y dydd** daisy
llygad-dynnu vb bewitch
llygadog adj eyed, sharp-eyed
llygadrwth adj wide-eyed, staring
llygadrythu vb stare
llygadu vb eye
llygatgraff adj keen-eyed, sharp-sighted
llygedyn nm ray of light
llygeidiog adj eyed
llygoden (-godydd) nf mouse. **ll. fawr, ll. ffrengig** rat
llygota vb catch mice
llygotwr (-wyr) nm mouser,

ratter; f **llygotwraig**
llygradwy adj corruptible
llygredig adj corrupt, depraved, degraded
llygredigaeth (-au) nf corruption
llygredd nm corruptness, depravity
llygriad (-au) nm corruption, adulteration
llygru vb corrupt, adulterate
llygrwr (-wyr) nm corrupter, adulterator
llynges (-au) nf fleet, navy
llyngeswr (-wyr) nm navy-man
llyngesydd (-ion) nm admiral
llyngyr npl (-en nf) (intestinal) worms
llym adj sharp, keen, severe; f **llem**
llymaid (-eidiau) nm sip, drink
llymarch (llymeirch) nm oyster
llymder nm sharpness, keenness, severity
llymder, -dra nm bareness, poverty
llymeitian, -io vb sip, tipple
llymeitiwr (-wyr) nm tippler, sot
llymhau vb make bare (from **llwm**)
llymhau vb sharpen (from **llym**)
llymriaid npl (-ien nf) sand-eels
llymru nm flummery
llymsur adj acrid
llymu vb sharpen, whet
llyn (-noedd) nm lake, pond, pool
llynciad (-au) nm draught, gulp
llyncu vb swallow, gulp, absorb
llyncwr (-wyr) nm swallower, guzzler
llynedd nf last year
llyo vb lick
llys (-oedd) nm court, hall, palace
llysaidd adj courtly, polite
llysblant npl step-children
llyschwaer nf step-sister
llysenw (-au) nm nickname
llysenwi vb nickname
llysfab nm step-son
llysfam nf step-mother

llysferch *nf* step-daughter
llysfrawd *nm* step-brother
llysgenhadaeth *nf* embassy,
legation
llysgenhadol *adj* ambassadorial
llysgenhadwr, llysgennad
(**-genhadon**) *nm* ambassador
llysiau *npl* (**-ieuyn** *nm*) herbs,
vegetables
llysieuol *adj* herbal, vegetable
llysieuydd (**-ion, -wyr**) *nm*
botanist; vegetarian
llysnafedd *nm* snivel, slime
llystad *nm* step-father
llyswenwyn *nm* herbicide
llysysol *adj* herbivorous
llysywen (**llysywod**) *nf* eel
llysywenna *vb* catch eels
llythrennol *adj* literal
llythyr (**-au**) *nm* letter, epistle
llythyrdy (**-dai**) *nm* post-office
llythyren (**llythrennau**) *nf* letter,
type
llythyrwr (**-wyr**) *nm* letter-writer
llyw (**-iau**) *nm* ruler; rudder, helm
llywaeth *adj* hand-fed, tame, pet
llywiawdwr (**-wyr**) *nm* ruler,
governor
llywio *vb* rule, govern, direct,
steer
llywiwr (**-wyr**) *nm* steersman,
helmsman
llywodraeth (**-au**) *nf* government
llywodraethol *adj* governing,
dominant
llywodraethu *vb* govern, rule
llywodraethwr (**-wyr**) *nm*
governor, ruler
llywydd (**-ion**) *nm* president
llywyddiaeth (**-au**) *nf* presidency
llywyddol *adj* presidential
llywyddu *vb* preside

M

mab (**meibion**) *nm* boy, son; man;
male
mabaidd *adj* filial
maban (**-od**) *nm* babe, baby
mabandod *nm* childhood, infancy
mabinogi *nm* tale, story
mablygad *nm* eyeball
mabmaeth (**-au, -od**) *nm* foster-son
maboed *nm* childhood, infancy,
youth
mabolaeth *nf* sonship; boyhood,
youth
mabolaidd *adj* youthful, boyish
mabolgamp (**-au**) *nf* game, sport,
feat
mabsant *nm* patron saint
mabwysiad *nm* adoption
mabwysiadol *adj* adoptive;
adopted
mabwysiadu *vb* adopt
macrell (**mecryll**) *n/m* mackerel
macsu *vb* to brew
macwy (**-aid**) *nm* youth, page
machlud, -o *vb* set, go down. **m.**
haul sunset
machludiad *nm* setting, going
down
machnïydd *nm* mediator
madarch *npl* (**-en** *nf*) mushrooms
madfall (**-od**) *nm* lizard
madrondod *nm* giddiness,
stupefaction
madroni *vb* make or become giddy
madru *vb* putrefy, fester, rot
madruddyn *nm* cartilage. **m. y**
cefn spinal cord
maddau *vb* pardon, forgive, remit
maddeuant *nm* pardon,
forgiveness
maddeugar *adj* of a forgiving
disposition
maddeuol *adj* pardoning, forgiving
maddeuwr (**-wyr**) *nm* pardoner

mae vb is, are; there is, there are
maeden nf slut, jade
maeddu see **baeddu**
maen (**meini**) nm stone
maenol, maenor (-au) nf manor
maentumio vb maintain
maer (-od, meiri) nm mayor
maeres (-au) nf mayoress
maerol adj mayoral
maeryddiaeth nf mayoralty
maes (meysydd) nm field. **i m.** out.
   m. glanio airport
maesglaf (-gleifion) nm outpatient
maeslywydd (-ion) nm field-
   marshal
maestir (-oedd) nm open country,
   plain
maestref (-i, -ydd) nf suburb
maeth nm nourishment, nutriment
maethlon adj nourishing,
   nutritious
maethu vb nourish, nurture
maethydd (-ion) nm nourisher
maethyn (-nau) nm nutrient;
   suckling
mafon npl (-en nf) raspberries
magl (-au) nf snare; mesh
maglu vb snare, mesh, trip
magnel (-au) nf gun, cannon
magnelaeth nf artillery
magnelwr (-wyr) nm gunner
magnesiwm nm magnesium
magnetedd nm/f magnetism
magneteiddio vb magnetise
magu vb breed, rear, nurse; gain,
   acquire
magwraeth nf nourishment,
   nurture
magwyr (-ydd) nf wall
maharen (meheryn) nm ram;
   wether
Mai nm May
mai conj that it is
maidd nm whey
main (meinion) adj fine, slender,
   thin. **m. y cefn** small of the back
mainc (meinciau) nf bench, form,
   seat

maint nm size, quantity, number
maintioli nm size, stature
maip npl (meipen nf) turnips
maith (meithion) adj long, tedious
mâl adj ground
malais nm malice
maldod nm dalliance, affection
maldodi vb pet, pamper, indulge
maleisus adj malicious
maleithiau npl chilblains
malio vb care, mind, heed
Malta nf Malta
malu vb grind, mince, chop, smash
malurio vb pound; crumble,
   moulder
malurion npl fragments, debris
malwod npl (-en, malwen nf)
   snails
malwr (-wyr) nm grinder
mall nf blight. **y f.** Belial, perdition
malltod nm rot, blight, blast
mallu vb rot, blast
mam (-au) nf mother. **mam-gu**
   grandmother
mamaeth (-od) nf nurse
mamal (-iaid) nm mammal
mamiaith (-ieithoedd) nf mother-
   tongue
mamog (-iaid) nf dam, sheep with
   young
mamolaeth (-au) nf maternity
mamwlad (-wledydd) nf
   motherland
man (-nau) nm/f place, spot;
   blemish
mân adj small, fine, petty
mandyllog adj porous
maneg (menig) nf glove, gauntlet
mangre nf place, spot
manion npl scraps, trifles, minutiæ
mantais (-eision) nf advantage
manteisio vb take advantage,
   profit
manteisiol adj advantageous
mantell (-oedd, mentyll) nf mantle
mantellog adj mantled

mantol (-ion) *nf* balance
mantolen (-ni) *nf* balance-sheet
mantoli *vb* turn scale, balance, weigh
manwaidd *adj* delicate, fine
mân-werthu *vb* retail
manwl *adj* exact, precise, strict, particular
manwl-gywir *adj* precise
manylion *npl* particulars, details
manylrwydd *nm* exactness, precision
manylu *vb* go into detail, particularize
manylwch *nm* exactness, precision
map (-iau) *nm* map
mapio *vb* map
mapiwr (-wyr) *nm* cartographer
marblen (marblys) *nf* marble
marc (-iau) *nm* mark
marcio *vb* mark
march (meirch) *nm* horse, stallion
marchlu (-oedd) *nm* cavalry
marchnad (-oedd) *nf* market
marchnadfa (-oedd) *nf* marketplace
marchnata *vb* market, trade
marchnatwr (-wyr) *nm* merchant
marchnerth (-oedd) *nm* horsepower
marchocáu *vb* ride a horse
marchog (-ion) *nm* horseman, rider; knight
marchogaeth *vb* ride
marchogwr (-wyr) *nm* rider, horseman
marchredyn *npl* (-en *nf*) polypody fern
marchwellt *nm* tall, coarse grass
marian *nm* holm, strand, moraine
marlad *nm* drake
marmalêd (-au) *nm* marmalade
marmor *nm* marble
marsialydd (-ion) *nm* marshal
marsiandïaeth *nf* merchandise
marsiandïwr (-wyr) *nm* merchant
marsipan *nm* marzipan

marw *vb* die
marw (meirw, meirwon) *n, adj* dead
marwaidd *adj* lifeless, sluggish, moribund
marwdon *nf* dandruff
marweidd-dra *nm* deadness, sluggishness
marwhad *nm* mortification
marwhau *vb* deaden, mortify
marwnad (-au) *nf* lament, elegy
marwol *adj* deadly, mortal, fatal
marwolaeth (-au) *nf* death
marwoldeb *nm* mortality
marwolion *npl* mortals
marwor *npl* (-yn *nm*) embers; charcoal
marwydos *npl* embers
masarnen (masarn) *nf* sycamore
masgl (-au) *nf* shell, pod
masglo, -u *vb* shell; interlace
masnach (-au) *nf* trade, traffic, commerce
masnachol *adj* commercial, business
masnachu *vb* do business, trade, traffic
masnachwr (-wyr) *nm* dealer, merchant
masw *adj* wanton
maswedd *nm* wantoness, ribaldry
masweddol *adj* wanton, ribald
maswr (-wyr) *nm* outside half
mat (-iau) *nm* mat
mater (-ion) *nm* matter
materol *adj* material; materialistic
materoliaeth *nf* materialism
matog (-au) *nf* mattock
matras (-resi) *nm* mattress
matrics (-au) *nm* matrix
matsien (matsys) *nf* match
math (-au) *nm* sort, kind
mathemateg *nm* mathematics
mathru *vb* trample, tread
mathrwr (-wyr) *nm* trampler
mawl *nm* praise

mawn *coll n* (**-en** *nf*) peat
mawnog *adj* peaty ♦ *nf* peat-bog
mawr (**-ion**) *adj* big, great, large
mawredd *nm* greatness, grandeur, majesty
mawreddog *adj* grand, majestic; grandiose
mawrfrydig *adj* magnanimous
mawrfrydigrwydd *nm* magnanimity
mawrhau *vb* magnify, enlarge
mawrhydi *nm* majesty
Mawrth *nm* Mars; March. **Dydd M.** Tuesday
mawrygu *vb* magnify, extol
mebyd *nm* childhood, infancy, youth
mecaneg *nf* mechanics
mecanwaith (**-weithiau**) *nm* mechanism
mecanyddol *adj* mechanical
mechniaeth *nf* surety, bail
mechnio *vb* go bail, become surety
mechniol *adj* vicarious
mechnïydd (**-ion**) *nm* surety, bail
medel (**-au**) *nf* reaping; reaping party
medelwr (**-wyr**) *nm* reaper
medi *vb* reap
Medi *nm* September
medr *nm* skill, ability
medru *vb* know, be able
medrus *adj* clever, skilful
medrusrwydd *nm* cleverness, skilfulness, skill
medrydd (**-ion**) *nm* gauge
medd *nm* mead
medd *vb* says
meddal *adj* soft, tender
meddalhau, meddalu *vb* soften
meddalwch *nm* softness
meddalwedd *nm* software
meddiannol *adj* possessing, possessive
meddiannu *vb* possess, occupy
meddiant (**-iannau**) *nm* possession

meddu *vb* possess, own
meddw (**-on**) *adj* drunk, intoxicated
meddwdod *nm* drunkenness, intoxication
meddwi *vb* get drunk, intoxicate, inebriate
meddwl *vb* think; mean ♦ (**-yliau**) *nm* thought; meaning; opinion
meddwol *adj* intoxicating
meddwyn (**-won**) *nm* drunkard, inebriate
meddyg (**-on**) *nm* physician, doctor
meddygaeth *nf* medicine
meddygfa (**-feydd**) *nf* surgery
meddyginiaeth (**-au**) *nf* medicine, remedy
meddyginiaethol *adj* medicinal, remedial
meddyginiaethu *vb* cure, remedy, heal
meddygol *adj* medicinal; medical
meddylfryd *nm* mind, affection, bent
meddylgar *adj* thoughtful
meddylgarwch *nm* thoughtfulness
meddyliol *adj* mental, intellectual
meddyliwr (**-wyr**) *nm* thinker
mefus *npl* (**-en** *nf*) strawberries
megin (**-au**) *nf* bellows
megino *vb* work bellows, blow
megis *conj, prep* as, so as, like a
Mehefin *nm* June
meicrobioleg *nm/f* microbiology
meicro-brosesydd *nm* microprocessor
meicroffon (**-au**) *nm* microphone
meicro-sglodyn (**-ion**) *nm* microchip
meicrosgop (**-au**) *nm* microscope
meichiad (**-iaid**) *nm* swineherd
meichiau (**-iafon**) *nm* surety, bail
meidrol *adj* finite
meidroldeb *nm* finiteness
meiddio *vb* dare, venture
meiddion *npl* curds and whey

meiddlyd adj wheyey, curdled
meilart nm drake
meillion npl (-en nf) clover
meim (-iau) nm/f mime
meimio vb mime
meinder nm fineness, slenderness
meindio vb mind, care
meinedd nm slender part, small
meingefn nm small of the back
meinhau vb grow slender, taper
meini see **maen**
meinllais nm shrill voice, treble
meintoli vb quantify
meintoliad nm quantification
meinwe (-bledd) nf tissue
meipen (maip) nf turnip
meirch see **march**
meirioli vb thaw
meirw see **marw**
meistr (-iaid, -i, -adoedd) nm
  master
meistres (-i) nf mistress
meistrolaeth nf mastery
meistrolgar adj masterful,
  masterly
meistroli vb master
meitin nm: ers m. some time since
meitr (-au) nm mitre
meithder nm length
meithrin vb nurture, rear, foster
meithrinfa (-oedd) nf nursery
mêl nm honey
mela vb gather honey
melan nf melancholy
melen adj f. of **melyn**
melfaréd nm corduroy
melfed nm velvet
melin (-au) nf mill
melinydd (-ion) nm miller
melodaidd adj melodious
melodi nm melody
melyn adj yellow; f **melen** ♦ nm
  yellow. **m. wy** yolk of egg. **Y
  clefyd m.** jaundice
melynaidd adj yellowish, tawny
melynder, -dra nm yellowness
melynddu adj tawny, swarthy

melyngoch adj yellowish red,
  orange
melyni nm yellowness; jaundice
melynu vb yellow
melynwyn adj yellowish white,
  cream
melys adj sweet ♦ (-ion) npl sweets
melyster, -tra nm sweetness
melysu vb sweeten
mellt npl (-en nf) lightning
melltennu vb flash lightning
melltigaid, -edig adj accursed,
  cursed
melltith (-ion) nf curse
melltithio vb curse
memorandwm (-anda) nm
  memorandum
memrwn (-rynau) nm parchment,
  vellum
men (-ni) nf wain, waggon, cart
mên adj mean
mendio vb mend, heal, recover
menestr nm cup-bearer
menig see **maneg**
mentr nf venture, hazard
mentro vb venture, hazard
mentrus adj adventurous
mentrwr (-wyr) nm entrepreneur
menyw (-od) nf woman
mêr (merion) nm marrow
mercwri nm mercury
merch (-ed) nf daughter, woman
Mercher nm Mercury. **Dydd M.**
  Wednesday
mercheta vb womanise
merchetaidd adj effeminate
merddwr (-ddyfroedd) nm stagnant
  water
merf, -aidd adj insipid, tasteless,
  flat
merfdra, merfeidd-dra nm
  insipidity
merlota vb pony-trek
merlyn (-nod, merlod) nm pony; f
  merlen
merllyd adj insipid
merthyr (-on, -i) nm martyr

merthyrdod *nm* martyrdom
merthyru *vb* martyr
merwindod *nm* numbness, tingling
merwino *vb* benumb, tingle, smart
meryw *npl* (-en *nf*) juniper trees
mes *npl* (-en *nf*) acorns
mesa *vb* gather acorns
mesur (-au) *nm* measure; metre;
 tune; bill
mesur, mesuro *vb* measure, mete
mesureg *nf* mensuration
mesuriad (-au) *nm* measurement
mesurwr (-wyr) *nm* measurer;
 surveyor
mesurydd (-ion) *nm* measurer,
 meter
metamorffedd *nm* metamorphism
metel (-oedd) *nm* metal; mettle
metelaidd *adj* metallic
metelydd (-ion) *nm* metallurgist
metelyddiaeth *nf* metallurgy
metr (-au) *nm* metre
metrig *adj* metric
metrigeiddio *vb* metricate
meth (-ion) *nm* miss, failure
methdaliad (-au) *nm* bankruptcy
methdalwr (-wyr) *nm* bankrupt
methedig (-ion) *adj* decrepit,
 infirm, disabled
methiannus *adj* failing, decayed
methiant *nm* failure
methodoleg *nf* methodology
methu *vb* fail, miss
meudwy (-aid, -od) *nm* hermit,
 recluse
meudwyaidd *adj* hermit-like,
 retiring
meudwyol *adj* eremitic
mewian *vb* mew
mewn *prep* in, within
mewnadlu *vb* inhale
mewnforio *vb* import ♦ (-ion) *npl*
 imports
mewnfudwr (-wyr) *nm* immigrant
mewnol *adj* inward, internal;
 subjective
mewnwr (-wyr) *nm* scrum-half

mewnyn (**mewnion**) *nm* filling
México *nf* Mexico
mi *pron* I, me
mieri *npl* (**miaren** *nf*) brambles
mig *nf*: **chwarae m.** play bo-peep
mign, -en *nf* bog, quagmire
migwrn (-yrnau) *nm* knuckle;
 ankle
mil (-od) *nm* animal
mil (-oedd) *nf* thousand
milain *adj* angry, fierce, savage,
 cruel
mileindra *nm* savageness, ferocity
mileinig *adj* savage, ferocious,
 malignant
milfed *adj* thousandth
milfeddyg (-on) *nm* veterinary
 surgeon
milfil *nf* million, an indefinite
 number
milflwyddiant *nm* millennium
milgi (-gwn) *nm* greyhound
miliast (-ieist) *nf* greyhound bitch
militariaeth *nf* militarism
militarydd *nm* militarist
miliwn (-iynau) *nf* million
miliynydd (-ion) *nm* millionaire
milodfa (-oedd, -feydd) *nf*
 menagerie
milwr (-wyr) *nm* soldier
milwraidd *adj* soldierly
milwriad (-iaid) *nm* colonel
milwriaeth *nf* warfare
milwriaethus *adj* militant
milwrio *vb* militate
milwrol *adj* military
milltir (-oedd) *nf* mile
min (-ion) *nm* edge; brink; lip
mindlws *adj* simpering, affected,
 precious
mingamu *vb* grimace
minio *vb* edge, sharpen; make
 impression
miniog *adj* sharp, keen, cutting
minlliw (-iau) *nm* lipstick
minnau *pron conj* I (on my part), I
 also

mintai (-eioedd) *nf* band, troop
mintys *nm* mint
mirain *adj* fair, beautiful, comely
mireinder *nm* beauty, comeliness
miri *nm* merriment, fun, festivity
mis (-oedd) *nm* month
misio *vb* miss, fail
misol (-ion) *adj* monthly
misolyn (-olion) *nm* monthly (magazine)
mitsio *vb* mitch, play truant
miwsig *nm* music
mo *contr. of* **dim o: nid oes mo'i debyg** there is none like him
moch *npl* (-yn *nm*) swine, pigs, hogs
mocha *vb* pig, litter
mochaidd *adj* swinish, hoggish
mochynnaidd *adj* piggish, swinish
modfedd (-i) *nf* inch
modrwy (-au) *nf* ring
modrwyo *vb* ring
modrwyog *adj* ringed
modryb (-edd) *nf* aunt
modur (-on) *nm* motor
modurdy (-dai) *nm* garage
modurwr (-wyr) *nm* motorist
modylu *vb* modulate
modylydd (-ion) *nm* modulator
modd (-ion, -au) *nm* mode, manner; means; mood
moddion *npl* means; medicine
moddol *adj* modal
moel (-ion) *adj* bare, bald; hornless, polled
moel (-ydd) *nf* hill
moeli *vb* make or become bald; hang (ears)
moelni *nm* bareness, baldness
moelyn *nm* bald-head
moes *vb imper* give, bring hither
moes (-au) *nf* morality; (*pl*) manners, morals
moeseg *nf* ethics
Moesenaidd *adj* Mosaic
moesgar *adj* mannerly, polite
moesgarwch *nm* politeness

moesol *adj* moral, ethical
moesoldeb *nm* morality
moesoli *vb* moralize
moesolwr (-wyr) *nm* moralist
moeswers (-i) *nf* moral
moesymgrymu *vb* bow
moeth (-au) *nm* luxury, indulgence
moethi *vb* pamper, indulge
moethlyd *adj* pampered, spoilt
moethus *adj* luxurious, pampered
moethusrwydd *nm* luxuriousness, luxury
molawd *nmf* eulogy, panegyric
molecwl (-cylau) *nm* molecule
molecwlar *adj* molecular
moled (-au) *nf* kerchief; muffler
moli, moliannu *vb* praise, laud
moliannus *adj* praised, praiseworthy
moliant (-iannau) *nm* praise
mollt (myllt) *nm* wether
molltgig *nm* mutton
moment (-au) *nf* moment
momentwm (**momenta**) *nm* momentum
monarchiaeth *nf* monarchy
monarchydd (-ion) *nm* monarchist
monni *vb* sulk, pout
monocsid (-au) *nm* monoxide
monópoli (-iau) *nm* monopoly
môr (**moroedd**) *nm* sea, ocean
Môr: Y M. Canoldir *nm* Mediterranean Sea. Y M. Coch *nm* Red Sea. Y M. Tawel *nm* Pacific Ocean. M. Udd *nm* English Channel. M. y Gogledd *nm* North Sea
mor *adv* how, so, as
moratoriwm (-atoria) *nm* moratorium
mordaith (-deithiau) *nf* voyage
mordeithiwr (-wyr) *nm* voyager
mordwyaeth *nf* navigation
mordwyo *vb* go by sea, voyage, sail
mordwywr (-wyr) *nm* mariner, sailor

morddwyd (-ydd) nf/m thigh

morfa (-feydd) nm moor, fen, marsh

morfil (-od) nm whale

môr-forwyn (-forynion) nf mermaid

morfran (-frain) nf cormorant

morffoleg nm/f morphology

morffolegol adj morphological

morgainc (-geinciau) nf gulf

morgais (-geisiau) nm mortgage

morgeisi nm mortgagee

morgeisio vb mortgage

môr-gerwyn nf whirlpool, vortex, abyss

morglawdd (-gloddiau) nm embankment, mole

morgrug (-yn nm) ants

morio vb voyage, sail

môr-ladrad (-au) nm piracy

môr-leidr (-ladron) nm pirate

morlen (-ni) nm chart

morlo (-loi) nm sea-calf, seal

morllyn (-noedd) nf/m lagoon

Moroco nf Morocco

morol adj maritime

moron npl (-en nf) carrots

mortais (-eisiau) nf mortise

morteisio vb mortise

morter (-au) nm mortar

morthwyl (-ion) nm hammer

morthwylio vb hammer

morthwyliwr (-wyr) nm hammerer

morwr (-wyr) nm seaman, sailor, mariner

morwriaeth nf seamanship, navigation

morwydd npl (-en nf) mulberry-trees

morwyn (-ynion) nf maid, virgin

morwyndod nm virginity

morwynol adj virgin, maiden

moryd (-iau) nf estuary

moryn (-nau) nm billow, breaker

mosaig (-au) nm, adj mosaic

Moscow nf Moscow

motif (-au) nm motive

motiff (-au) nm motif

muchudd nm jet

mud adj dumb, mute; dull

mudan (-od) nm mute

mudandod nm muteness

mudanes (-au) nf dumb woman

mudferwi vb simmer

mudiad (-au) nm removal; movement

mudo vb move, remove

mudol adj mobile, moving, migratory

mudwr (-wyr) nm remover

mul (-od) nm mule; donkey

mulaidd adj mulish, asinine

mules (-au) nf she-mule, she-ass

mulfran (-frain) nf cormorant

mun see bun

munud (-au) nm/f minute, moment

munud (-iau) nm sign, gesture; nod

munudio vb make gestures, gesticulate

mur (-iau) nm wall

murddun (-od) nm ruin, ruins

murio vb wall

murlun (-iau) nm mural

murmur vb murmur ♦ (-on) nm murmur

mursen (-nod) nf coquette; prude

mursendod nm prudery, affectation

mursennaidd adj prudish, affected

mursennu vb coquette, mince

musgrell adj feeble, decrepit

musgrellni nm feebleness, debility

mwd nm mud

mwdwl (mydylau) nm cock (of hay)

mwg nm smoke

mwgwd (mygydau) nm blind mask

mwng (myngau) nm mane

mwngial vb mumble

mwlsyn nm nincompoop; mule

mwlwg nm refuse, sweepings,

chaff
mwll adj close, warm, sultry
mwmian vb hum, mumble
mwn see **mwyn**
mwnci (-iod) nm monkey
mwnciaidd adj monkeyish, apish
mwnglawdd see **mwyn-**
mwnwgl (mynyglau) nm neck
mwnws coll n small particles, dust, debris
mwrdro vb murder
mwrllwch nm fog, mist, vapour
mwrn adj sultry, close, warm
mwrndra nm sultriness
mwrthwl (myrthylau) nm hammer
mws adj stale, rank, stinking
mwsg nm musk
mwsged (-i) nm/f musket
mwsogl, -wgl nm moss
mwstard, -tart nm mustard
mwstro vb fidget, hurry
mwstwr nm muster; bustle, commotion
mwy adj more, bigger ♦ adv more, again
mwyach adv any more, henceforth
mwyafrif (-au) nm majority
mwyalch, -en (-od) nf blackbird
mwyar npl (-en nf) blackberries
mwyara vb gather blackberries
mwydion npl crumb; pith, pulp
mwydo vb moisten, soak, steep
mwydro vb moider, bewilder
mwydyn (mwydod) nm worm
mwyfwy adv more and more
mwyhau vb increase, enlarge, magnify
mwyn nm sake
mwyn, mŵn (-au) nm ore, mineral
mwyn adj kind, gentle, mild; dear
mwynder (-au) nm gentleness; (pl) delights
mwyndoddi vb refine
mwyneidd-dra nm kindness, gentleness
mwynglawdd (-gloddiau) nm mine

mwyngloddio vb mine
mwynhad nm enjoyment, pleasure
mwynhau vb enjoy
mwyniant (-iannau) nm pleasure
mwynofydd (-ion) nm mineralogist
mwynoleg nf mineralogy
mwynwr (-wyr) nm miner
mwys adj ambiguous, equivocal
mwythau npl indulgence, caresses
mwytho vb pet, fondle, pamper
mwythus adj pampered
myctod nm asphyxia
mydr (-au) nm metre, verse
mydryddiaeth nf versification
mydryddol adj metrical
mydryddu, mydru vb versify
mydylu vb cock
myfi pron I, me, myself
myfiaeth nf egotism
myfiol adj egotistic
myfyrdod (-au) nm meditation
myfyrgar adj studious, contemplative
myfyrgell (-oedd) nf study
myfyrio vb meditate, study
myfyriol adj meditative
myfyriwr (-wyr) nm student
mygedol adj honorary
mygfa (-feydd) nf suffocation
myglyd adj smoky; close; asthmatic
myglys nm tobacco
mygu vb smoke; suffocate, stifle, smother
mygydu vb blindfold
mygyn nm a smoke
myngial vb mumble, mutter
myngog adj maned
myngus adj indistinct, mumbling
myllni nm sultriness
mympwy (-on) nm whim, caprice, fad
mympwyol adj arbitrary, capricious
mymryn (-nau) nm particle, bit, mite

myn prep by (in swearing)
myn (-nod) nm kid
mynach (-aich, -od) nm monk
mynachaeth nf monasticism
mynachdy (-dai) nm monastery, convent
mynachlog (-ydd) nf monastery, abbey
mynawyd (-au) nm awl
mynci (-iau) nm hame(s)
myned, mynd vb go, proceed
mynedfa (-oedd, -feydd) nf entrance, passage
mynediad nm going; access, admission
mynegai (-eion) nm index, exponent
mynegair (-eiriau) nm concordance
mynegfys (-edd) nm forefinger, index
mynegi vb tell, express, relate, declare
mynegiad (-au) nm statement, declaration
mynegiant nm expression
mynnu vb will, wish; insist; get, obtain
mynor (-ion) nm marble
mynwent (-au, -ydd) nf churchyard, graveyard
mynwes (-au) nf breast, bosom
mynwesol adj bosom
mynwesu vb cherish
mynych adj frequent, often
mynychiad nm frequenting; repetition
mynychu vb frequent, attend; repeat
mynydd (-oedd) nm mountain
mynydda vb mountaineer
mynydd-dir nm hill-country
mynyddig adj mountainous, hilly
mynyddwr (-wyr) nm mountaineer
myrdd, -iwn (-iynau) nm myriad
myrllyd adj myrrhy
myrndra nm sultriness
myrr nm myrrh

myrtwydd npl (-en nf) myrtles
mysg nm middle, midst. **ymysg** among
mysgu vb loose, undo
myswynog (-ydd) nf barren cow
mysglog adj mossy
mytholeg nf mythology
mytholegol adj mythological

N

na conj nor, neither; than ♦ adv no, not
nac adv no, not ♦ conj nor, neither
nacâd nm refusal, denial
nacaol adj negative
nacáu vb refuse, deny
nad adv not
nâd (nadau) nf cry, howl; clamour
Nadolig nm Christmas
Nadoligaidd adj Christmassy
nadu vb cry (out), howl
nadu vb stop, hinder
nadd adj hewn, wrought
naddion npl chips; shreds; lint
naddo adv no (to questions in preterite tense)
naddu vb hew, chip, whittle
Naf nm Lord
nag conj than
nage adv not so, no
nai (neiaint) nm nephew
naid (neidiau) nf jump, leap, bound
naïf adj naïve
naïfder nm naïveté
naill dem pron the one ♦ conj either
nain (neiniau) nf grandmother
nam (-au) nm mark, blemish, flaw
namyn prep except, but, save
nant (nentydd) nf brook; gorge, ravine
napcyn (-au) nm napkin
narcotig nm, adj narcotic
natur nf nature; temper
naturiaeth (-au) nf nature
naturiaethwr (-wyr) nm naturalist

naturiol *adj* natural
naturioldeb *nm* naturalness
naturus *adj* angry, quick-tempered
naw *adj, nm* nine
nawdd *nm* protection; patronage
nawddogaeth *nf* patronage, protection
nawfed *adj* ninth
nawn *nm* noon
naws *nf* nature, disposition; essence, tincture
nawseiddio *vb* temper, soften
neb *nm* any one; (*with negative understood*) no one
nedd *npl* (-en *nf*) nits
neddau, neddyf (**neddyfau**) *nf* adze
nef (-oedd) *nf* heaven
nefol, -aidd *adj* heavenly, celestial
nefoli *vb* make or become heavenly
nefrosis *nm* neurosis
neges (-au, -euau) *nf* errand, message
negesa, -eua *vb* run errands; trade
negeseuwr (-wyr) *nm* messenger
negodi *vb* negotiate
negyddiaeth *nf* negativism
negyddol *adj* negative
neidio *vb* leap, jump; throb
neidiwr (-wyr) *nm* leaper, jumper
neidr (**nadroedd, nadredd**) *nf* snake
neiedd *nm* nepotism
neillog (-ion) *nm* alternative
neilltu *nm* one side. **o'r n.** aside, apart
neilltuad *nm* separation
neilltuaeth *nf* separation, privacy, seclusion
neilltuedig *adj* separated, secluded
neilltuo *vb* set apart, separate
neilltuol *adj* particular, peculiar, special
neilltuolion *npl* peculiarities
neilltuolrwydd *nm* peculiarity, distinction

neis *adj* nice
neisied (-i) *nf* kerchief
neithdar *nm* nectar
neithior (-au) *nf* marriage feast
neithiwr *adv* last night
nemor *adj* few. **nid n.** hardly any
nen (-nau, -noedd) *nf* ceiling; heaven. **n. tŷ** house-top
nenbren *nm* roof-tree
nenfwd (-fydau) *nm* ceiling
nepell *adv* far. **nid n.** not far
nerf (-au) *nf* nerve
nerfwst *nm* neurasthenia
nerth (-oedd) *nm* might, power, strength
nerthol *adj* strong, powerful, mighty
nerthu *vb* strengthen
nes *adj* nearer. **yn n. ymlaen** further on
nes *adv* till, until
nesaf *adj* nearest, next
nesáu *vb* draw near, approach
nesnes *adv* nearer and nearer
nesu *vb* draw near. **n draw** move away
neu *conj* or
neuadd (-au) *nf* hall
newid *vb* change, alter ♦ *nm* change
newidiant *nm* variability
newidiol *adj* changeable, variable
newidydd (-ion) *nm* transformer
newidyn (-nau) *nm* variable
newydd *adj* new, novel; fresh ♦ (-ion) *nm* news
newyddbeth (-au) *nm* novelty
newydd-deb, -der *nm* newness, novelty
newyddiadur (-on) *nm* newspaper
newyddiaduriaeth *nf* journalism
newyddiadurwr (-wyr) *nm* journalist
newyddian (-od) *n coll* novice, neophyte
newyn *nm* hunger, famine
newynog *adj* hungry, starving

newynu vb starve, famish

ni pron we, us

ni, nid adv not

nifer (-oedd, -i) nm/f number

nifwl nm mist, fog; nebula

Nigeria nf Nigeria

Nihon nf Japan

ninnau pron conj we (on our part), we also

nionyn (nionod) nm onion

nis adv not ... it. **n. cafodd** he did not find it

nitrad (-au) nm nitrate

nith (-oedd) nf niece

nithio vb sift, winnow

nithiwr (-wyr) nm sifter, winnower

nithlen (-ni) nf winnowing-sheet

niwed (-eidiau) nm harm, injury

niwclear adj nuclear

niweidio vb harm, hurt, injure, damage

niweidiol adj harmful, injurious

niwl (-oedd) nm, **-en** nf mist, fog, haze

niwliog, niwlog adj misty, foggy, hazy

niwmatig adj pneumatic

niwmonia nm pneumonia

niwtral adj neutral

niwtraleiddio vb neutralise

niwtraliaeth nf neutrality

nobyn (nobiau) nm knob

nod (-au) nm/f note; mark, token

nodachfa (-feydd) nf bazaar

nodedig adj appointed, set; remarkable

nodi vb mark, note, appoint, state

nodiad (-au) nm note

nodiadur (-on) nm notebook

nodiant nm notation

nodwedd (-ion) nf character, characteristic, feature

nodweddiadol adj characteristic

nodweddu vb characterize

nodwydd (-au) nf needle

nodyn (-nau, nodau, nodion) nm note

nodd (-ion) nm moisture; juice, sap

nodded nm refuge, protection

noddfa (-fâu, -feydd) nf refuge

noddi vb protect

noddlyd adj juicy, sappy

noddwr (-wyr) nm protector; patron

noe (-au) nf dish; kneading-trough

noeth adj naked, bare, exposed, raw

noethder nm bareness, nakedness

noethi vb bare, denude

noethlymun adj nude

noethlymunwr (-wyr) nm streaker

noethlymunwraig nf stripper

noethni nm nakedness, nudity

noethwr (-wyr) nm nudist

nofel (-au) nf novel

nofelwr, -ydd (-wyr) nm novelist

nofiadwy adj swimmable

nofiedydd (-ion) nm swimmer

nofio vb swim; float

nofiwr (-wyr) nm swimmer

nogio vb jib

noglyd adj jibbing

nôl vb fetch, bring

Norwy nf Norway

nos (-au, nosweithiau) nf night

nosi vb become night

noson, noswaith (nosweithiau) nf a night, an evening

noswyl (-iau) nf eve of festival, vigil

noswylio vb cease work at eve

nudden nf fog, mist, haze

nwy (-on) nm gas

nwyd (-au) nm passion; emotion

nwydd (-au) nm substance, article; (pl) goods

nwyf nm vivacity, energy, vigour

nwyfiant nm vivacity, vigour

nwyfus adj sprightly, spirited, lively

nwyol adj gaseous

nychdod nm feebleness, infirmity

nychlyd adj sickly, feeble

nychu vb sicken, pine, languish

nydd-dro (-droeau, -droeon) nm twist

nydd-droi vb twist, screw

nyddu vb spin, twist

nyddwr (-wyr) nm spinner

nyf coll n snow

nyni pron we, us

nyrs (-ys) nmlf nurse

nyrsio adj nurse

nytmeg nm nutmeg

nyth (-od) nmlf nest

nythu vb nest, nestle

O

o prep from; of, out of; by

o excl oh!, O!

oblegid conj, prep because, for

obry adv beneath, below

obstetreg nm obstetrics

obstetregydd (-wyr) nm obstetrician

ocsid (-iau) nm oxide

ocsidiad nm oxidisation

ocsidio vb oxidise

ocsidydd (-ion) nm oxidising agent

ocsigen nm oxygen

och excl oh, alas, woe

ochenaid (-eidiau) nf sigh

ocheneidio, ochneidio vb sigh

ochr (-au) nf side

ochrgamu vb sidestep

ochri vb side

ôd nm snow

od adj odd, remarkable

odiaeth adj excellent, exquisite ♦ adv very, most, extremely

odid adv perchance, peradventure

odl (-au) nf rhyme; ode, song

odli vb rhyme

odrif (-au) nm odd number

odrwydd nm oddity

odyn (-au) nf kiln

oddeutu prep about

oddi prep out of, from

oddieithr, oddigerth prep except, unless

oed (-au) nm age; time

oed-dâl (-iadau) nm superannuation

oedfa (-on, -feuon) nf meeting, service

oedi vb delay; postpone, defer

oediad (-au) nm delay

oedran nm age, full age

oedrannus adj aged

oedd vb was, were

oen (ŵyn) nm lamb

oena vb lamb, yean

oenig nf ewe-lamb

oer adj cold, chill, frigid; sad

oeraidd adj coldish, cool, chilly

oerddrws (-ddrysau) nm wind gap

oerfel nm cold

oergell (-oedd) nf refrigerator

oeri vb cool, chill

oerllyd adj chilly, frigid; cool

oernad (-au) nf howl, wail, lamentation

oernadu vb howl, wail, lament

oerni nm cold, coldness, chilliness

oes (-oedd, -au) nf age, lifetime.
yn o. oesoedd for ever and ever

oes vb there is, there are; is there?

oesoffagws nm oesophagus

oesol adj age-long, perpetual

ofer adj vain, idle; prodigal; dissipated; waste

ofera vb waste, squander, idle

oferedd nm vanity, dissipation

ofergoel (-ion) nf superstition

ofergoeledd, -iaeth nm superstition

ofergoelus adj superstitious

oferwr (-wyr) nm idler, waster

ofn (-au) nm fear, dread

ofnadwy adj awful, terrible, dreadful

ofnadwyaeth nf awe, terror, dread

ofni vb fear, dread

ofnog *adj* fearful, timorous

ofnus *adj* timid, nervous

ofnusrwydd *nm* timidity, nervousness

ofwl (**-au**) *nm* ovule

ofydd (**-ion**) *nm* ovate

offeiriad (**-iaid**) *nm* priest, clergyman

offeiriadaeth *nf* priesthood

offeiriades (**-au**) *nf* priestess

offeiriadol *adj* priestly, sacerdotal

offeiriadu *vb* officiate, minister

offer *npl* implements, tools, gear

offeren (**-nau**) *nf* mass

offeryn (**-nau, offer**) *nm* instrument, tool

offerynnol *adj* instrumental

offerynoliaeth *nf* instrumentality

offrwm (**-ymau**) *nm* offering, oblation

offrymu *vb* offer, sacrifice

offrymwr (**-wyr**) *nm* offerer, sacrificer

offthalmia *nm* ophthalmia

offthalmosgop (**-au**) *nm* ophthalmoscope

og (**-au**), **oged** (**-au, -i**) *nf* harrow

ogof (**-au, -fâu, -feydd**) *nf* cave, cavern; den

ogylch *prep* about

ongl (**-au**) *nf* angle, corner

onglog *adj* angled, angular

oherwydd *conj, prep* because, for

ôl *adj* back, hind, hindmost ♦ (**olion**) *nm* mark, print, trace, track. **Yn ôl** according to; ago

ôl-ddâl (**-oedd**) *nm* back-pay

ôl-ddodiad (**-iaid**) *nm* suffix

ôl-ddyddio *vb* post-date

ôl-ddyled (**-ion**) *nf* arrears

olew (**-au**) *nm* oil

olewydd *npl* (**-en** *nf*) olive-trees

olifaid *npl* olive-berries

olrhain *vb* trace

olwr (**-wyr**) *nm* back (*rugby*)

olwyn (**-ion**) *nf* wheel

olwyno *vb* wheel, cycle

olwynog *adj* wheeled

olyniaeth *nf* succession, sequence

olynol *adj* successive, consecutive

olynu *vb* succeed (to)

olynwr (**-wyr**), **-ydd** (**-ion**) *nm* successor

ôlysgrif *nf* postscript

oll *adv* all, wholly; ever, at all

ombwdsman (**-myn**) *nm* ombudsman

omlet (**-i**) *nm* omelette

ond *conj* but, only ♦ *prep* except, save, but

onest *adj* honest

onestrwydd *nm* honesty

oni, onid *adv* not?, is it not? ♦ *conj* if not, unless ♦ *prep* except, save, but

onid e *adv* otherwise, else; is it not?

onis *conj* if it is not. **o. caiff** if he does not get it

onnen (**onn, ynn**) *nf* ash

opiniwn (**-ynau**) *nm* opinion

opiniynllyd, -iynus *adj* opinionated

optimistaeth *nf* optimism

optimistaidd *adj* optimistic

optimwm (**-tima**) *nm* optimum

oracl (**-au**) *nm* oracle

oraclaidd *adj* oracular

oraens *nm* orange

ordeiniad (**-au**) *nm* ordination, ordinance

ordeinio *vb* ordain

ordinhad (**-au**) *nf* ordinance, sacrament

oren (**-nau**) *nm/f* orange

organ (**-au**) *nf/m* organ

organaidd *adj* organic

organeb *nf* organism

organig *adj* organic

organydd (**-ion**) *nm* organist

orgraff (**-au**) *nf* orthography

orgraffyddol *adj* orthographical

oriawr (**oriorau**) *nf* watch

oriel (**-au**) *nf* gallery

orig *nf* little while

oriog *adj* fickle, changeable, inconstant

os *conj* if

osgo *nm* slant, slope, inclination

osgoi *vb* swerve, avoid, evade, shirk

oslef *nf* tone, voice

ow *excl* oh!, alas!

P

pa *adj* what, which

pab (-au) *nm* pope

pabaeth *nf* papacy

pabaidd *adj* papal, popish

pabell (pebyll) *nf* tent, tabernacle

pabellu *vb* tent, tabernacle, encamp

pabi *nm* poppy

pabwyr *npl* (-en *nf*, -yn *nm*) rushes

pabwyr *nm* wick, candle-wick

pabydd (-ion) *nm* Roman Catholic

pabyddiaeth *nf* Roman Catholicism

pabyddol *adj* Roman Catholic

pac (-iau) *nm* pack, bundle

pacio *vb* pack

padell (-au, -i, pedyll) *nf* pan, bowl

padellaid (-eidiau) *nf* panful

pader (-au) *nm* paternoster, Lord's Prayer

padera *vb* repeat prayers, patter

pae *nm* pay, wage

paediatreg *nm* paediatrics

paediatregydd *nm* paediatrician

paent *nm* paint

paentiad (-au) *nm* painting

pafiliwn *nm* pavilion

paffio *vb* box, fight

paffiwr (-wyr) *nm* boxer

pagan (-iaid) *nm* pagan, heathen

paganaidd *adj* pagan, heathen

paganiaeth *nf* paganism, heathenism

pang (-au) *nm*, **pangfa** (-feydd) *nf* pang, fit

paham *adv* why, wherefore

paill *nm* flour; pollen

pair (peiriau) *nm* cauldron, furnace

pais (peisiau) *nf* coat, petticoat

paith (peithiau) *nm* prairie

Pacistan *nf* Pakistan

pâl (palau) *nf* spade

paladr (pelydr) *nm* ray, beam, staff; stem

palaeolithig *adj* palaeolithic

palas (-au) *nm* palace

Palestina *nf* Palestine

palf (-au) *nf* palm, hand; paw

palfais (-eisiau) *nf* shoulder

palfalu *vb* feel, grope

palfod (-au) *nf* smack, slap, buffet

palff *nm* fine, well-built man

pali *nm* silk brocade

palis (-au) *nm* pale, partition, wainscot

palmant (-mentydd) *nm* pavement

palmantu *vb* pave

palmwydd *npl* (-en *nf*) palm-trees

palu *vb* dig, delve

palwr (-wyr) *nm* digger

pall (-au) *nm* mantle; tent

pall *nm* fail, failing; lack; lapse

pallu *vb* fail, cease; neglect; refuse

pam *adv* why, wherefore (**paham**)

pamffled (-i, -au), **-yn** *nm* pamphlet

pan *conj* when

pandy (-dai) *nm* fulling-mill

pannas *npl* (**panasen** *nf*) parsnips

pannu *vb* full cloth

pannwl (panylau) *nm* dimple, hollow

pannwr (panwyr) *nm* fuller

pant (-iau) *nm* hollow, valley

pantio *vb* depress, dent, sink

pantiog *adj* hollow, sunken; dimpled

papur (-au) *nm* paper

papuro *vb* paper

papurwr (-wyr) *nm* paperer, paperhanger

papuryn nm scrap of paper
pâr (parau) nm pair; suit
pâr (peri) nm spear, lance
para vb last, endure, continue
parabl (-au) nm speech, discourse
parablu vb speak
paradeim (-au) nm paradigm
paradwys nf paradise
paradwysaidd adj paradisean
paragraff (-au) nm paragraph
paratoad (-au) nm preparation
paratoawl adj preparatory
paratoi vb prepare, get ready
parc (-iau) nm park, field
parch nm respect, reverence
parchedig (-ion) adj reverend;
  reverent
parchedigaeth nf reverence
parchu vb respect, revere,
  reverence
parchus adj respectful;
  respectable
parchusrwydd nm respectability
pardwn (-ynau) nm pardon
pardynu vb pardon
parddu nm fire-black, smut; soot
pardduo vb blacken, vilify, defame
pared (parwydydd) nm partition
  wall, wall
paredd nm parity
parhad nm continuance,
  continuation
parhaol adj lasting, perpetual
parhau vb last, continue;
  persevere
parhaus adj lasting; continual,
  perpetual
Paris nf Paris
parlwr (-yrau) nm parlour
parlys nm paralysis, palsy
parlysu vb paralyse
parod adj ready, prepared; prompt
parodrwydd nm readiness,
  willingness
parôl (-ion) nm parole
parsel (-i, -ydd) nm parcel
parti (-ion) nm party

partïaeth nf partisanship
partïol adj partial, biassed,
  partisan
parth (-au) nm part, region; floor
parthed prefix about, concerning
parthu vb part, divide
parwyden (-nau) nf wall, side;
  breast
pas nm whooping-cough
Pasg nm Passover, Easter
pasgedig (-ion) adj fatted,
  fattened, fat
pasiant (-iannau) nm pageant
pasio vb pass
past nm paste
pastai (-eiod) nf pasty, pie
pastio vb paste
pasturedig adj pasteurised
pasturo vb pasteurise
pastwn (-ynau) nm baton, club,
  cudgel
pastynu vb club, cudgel, bludgeon
patriarch (-iaid, patrieirch) nm
  patriarch
patriarchaeth (-au) nf patriarchate
patriarchaidd adj patriarchal
patrwm (-ymau) nm pattern
patrymlun (-iau) nm template
pathew (-od) nm dormouse
patholeg nf pathology
patholegol adj pathological
patholegydd (-egwyr) nm
  pathologist
pau nf country
paun (peunod) nm peacock
pawb pron everybody, all
pawen (-nau) nf paw
pawl (polion) nm pole, stake
pe conj if
pebyll see **pabell**
pecyn (-nau) nm packet, package
pech-aberth (-au) nm sin-offering
pechadur (-iaid) nm sinner,
  offender
pechadures (-au) nf woman sinner
pechadurus adj sinful, wicked
pechadurusrwydd nm sinfulness

pechod (-au) *nm* sin, offence
pechu *vb* sin, offend
ped *conj* if
pedair *adj* f. of pedwar
pedeirongl *adj* foursquare
pedi *vb* worry, grieve
pedol (-au) *nf* horseshoe
pedoli *vb* shoe
pedrain *nf* haunches, crupper
pedrongl *adj* square ♦ (-au) *nf* square
pedronglog *adj* quadrangular
pedryfan *adj* four-cornered ♦ -noedd *nm* four quarters
pedrydwrdd (-fyrddau) *nm* quarter-deck
pedwar *adj* four; *f* pedair
pedwarawd *nm* quartette
pedwarcarnol (-ion) *adj* four-footed, quadruped
pedwaredd *adj* f. of pedwerydd
pedwarplyg *adj* fourfold, quarto
pedwerydd *adj* fourth; *f* pedwaredd
peddestr *nm* pedestrian
peddestrig *nm* walking; pedestrian
pefr *adj* radiant, bright, beautiful
pefrio *vb* radiate, sparkle
peg (-iau) *nm* peg
pegio *vb* peg
pegor (-au) *nm* manikin; dwarf; imp
pegwn (-ynau) *nm* pivot, pole, axis
Pegwn y Gogledd *nm* North Pole
pegynol *adj* axial, polar
peidio *vb* cease, stop, desist
peilon (-au) *nm* pylon
peilot (-iaid) *nm* pilot
peillio *vb* bolt, sift
peint (-iau) *nm* pint
peintiad (-au) *nm* painting
peintio *vb* paint
peintiwr (-wyr) *nm* painter
peipen (peipiau) *nf* pipe
peirianneg *nf* engineering
peiriannol *adj* mechanical
peiriannydd (-ianyddion) *nm* engineer
peiriant (-iannau) *nm* machine, engine. **p. golchi** washing machine
peirianwaith *nm* mechanism
peiswyn (-au) *nm* chaff
peithyn (-au) *nm* ridge-tile
Pecing *nf* Peking
pêl (pelau, peli) *nf* ball
pelawd (-au) *nf* over (*cricket*)
pêl-droed *nf* football
pêl-fasged *nf* basket-ball
pelferyn (-nau) *nm* ball-bearing
pêl-foli *nf* volley-ball
pêl-rwyd *nf* netball
pelten (pelts) *nf* blow
pelydr (-au) *nm* ray, beam
pelydru *vb* beam, gleam, radiate
pelydryn *nm* ray, beam
pell *adj* far, distant, remote, long
pellen (-nau, -ni) *nf* ball (of yarn)
pellennig *adj* far, distant, remote
pellhau *vb* put or remove far off
pellter (-au, -oedd) *nm* distance
pen (-nau) *nm* head; chief; end; top
pen *adj* head, chief, supreme
penadur (-iaid) *nm* sovereign
penaduriaeth *nf* sovereignty
penagored *adj* open, indefinite, undecided
penarglwyddiaeth *nf* sovereignty
penbaladr *adj* general, universal
penben *adv* at loggerheads
penbleth *nf* perplexity, quandary
pen-blwydd (-i) *nm* birthday
penboeth *adj* hot-headed, fanatical
penboethni *nm* fanaticism
penboethyn (-boethiaid) *nm* fanatic
penbwl (-byliaid) *nm* blockhead; tadpole
pencadlys *nm* head-quarters
pencampwr (-wyr) *nm* champion
pencampwriaeth (-au) *nf* championship
pencerdd (-ceirddiaid) *nm* chief musician

penchwiban *adj* giddy, flighty
pendant *adj* positive, emphatic
pendantrwydd *nm* positiveness
pendefig (-ion) *nm* prince, peer, noble
pendefigaeth *nf* aristocracy, peerage
pendefigaidd *adj* noble, aristocratic
pendefiges (-au) *nf* peeress
penderfyniad (-au) *nm* determination, resolution
penderfynol *adj* determined, resolute
penderfynu *vb* determine, resolve
pendew *adj* thick-headed, stupid
pendifaddau *adj*: **yn b.** especially
pendil (-iau) *nm* pendulum
pendramwnwgl *adj* topsyturvy; headlong
pendraphen *adj* helter-skelter, confused
pendro *nf* giddiness, vertigo; staggers
pendroni *vb* perplex oneself, worry over
pendrwm *adj* top-heavy; drowsy
pendrymu *vb* drowse, droop
pendwmpian *vb* nod, doze, slumber
penddaredd *nm* giddiness
penddaru *vb* make or become giddy
pendduyn (-nod) *nm* botch, boil
penelin (-oedd) *nm/f* elbow
penelino *vb* elbow
penffest (-au) *nm* headgear
penffol *adj* silly, idiotic
penffrwyn (-au) *nm/f* head-stall, halter
pengaled *adj* headstrong ♦ *nf* knapweed
pengaledwch *nm* stubbornness
pengam *adj* wrong-headed, perverse
pen-glin (-iau) *nf* knee
penglog (-au) *nf* skull

pengryf *adj* headstrong, stubborn
pengryniad (-iaid) *nm* roundhead
peniad (-au) *nm* header
penigamp *adj* excellent, splendid
penisel *adj* downcast, crestfallen
penlinio *vb* kneel
penllwyd *adj* grey-headed
penllwydni *nm* grey hair, white hair
penllywydd (-ion) *nm* sovereign
penllywyddiaeth *nf* sovereignty
pennaeth (**penaethiaid**) *nm* chief
pennaf *adj* chief, principal
pennawd (**penawdau**) *nm* heading; headline
pennill (**penillion**) *nm* verse, stanza
pennod (**penodau**) *nf* chapter
pennoeth *adj* bare-headed
pennog (**penwaig**) *nm* herring
pennu *vb* specify, appoint, determine
penodi *vb* appoint
penodiad (-au) *nm* appointment
penodol *adj* particular, specific
penrhydd *adj* unbridled, loose
penrhyddid *nm* licence, licentiousness
penrhyn (-noedd, -nau) *nm* cape, foreland
pensaer (-seiri) *nm* architect
pensaerniaeth *nf* architecture
pensil (-iau) *nm* pencil
pensiwn (-iynau) *nm* pension
pen-swyddog (-ion) *nm* chief officer
pensyfrdan *adj* stunned, dazed
pensyfrdandod *nm* giddiness, dizziness
pensyfrdanu *vb* stun, daze
pensyth *adj* perpendicular
pentan (-au) *nm* hob
penteulu (**pennau teuluoedd**) *nm* head of family
pentewyn (-ion) *nm* firebrand
pentir (-oedd) *nm* headland
pentis *nm* pentice, penthouse
pentref (-i, -ydd) *nm* village;

homestead
pentrefan (-nau) *nm* hamlet
pentrefol *adj* village
pentrefwr (-wyr) *nm* villager
pentwr (-tyrrau) *nm* heap, pile
penty (-tai) *nm* cottage, shed
pentyrru *vb* heap, pile, accumulate
penuchel *adj* proud, haughty
penwan *adj* weak-minded
penwyn *adj* white-headed
penwynni *nm* white hair, grey hair
penyd (-iau) *nm* penance, punishment
penyd-wasanaeth *nm* penal servitude
penysgafn *adj* light-headed, giddy, dizzy
penysgafnder *nm* giddiness, dizziness
pêr *adj* sweet, delicious, luscious
peraidd *adj* sweet, mellow
perarogl (-au) *nm* perfume, fragrance
perarogli *vb* perfume; embalm
peraroglus *adj* fragrant, scented
percoladur (-on) *nm* percolator
perchen, -nog (**perchenogion**) *nm* owner
perchenogaeth *nf* ownership
perchenogi *vb* possess, own
perchentywr (-wyr) *nm* householder
pereidd-dra *nm* sweetness
pereiddio *vb* sweeten
pererin (-ion) *nm* pilgrim
pererindod (-au) *nm*/*f* pilgrimage
pererinol *adj* pilgrim
perfedd (-ion) *nm* guts, bowels
perfeddwlad (-wledydd) *nf* interior, heartland
perffaith *adj* perfect
perffeithio *vb* perfect
perffeithrwydd *nm* perfection
perffeithydd (-ion) *nm* perfecter
perfformiad (-au) *nm* performance
perfformio *vb* perform

perfformiwr (-wyr) *nm* performer
peri *vb* cause, bid
perl (-au) *nm* pearl
perlewyg (-on) *nm* ecstasy, trance
perlysiau *npl* aromatic herbs; spices
perllan (-nau) *nf* orchard
perocsid (-au) *nm* peroxide
peroriaeth *nf* melody, music
persain *adj* euphonious, melodious
♦ (-seiniau) *nf* euphony
persawr (-au) *nm* fragrance
perseiniol *adj* melodious
persli *nm* parsley
person (-au) *nm* person
person (-iaid) *nm* parson, clergyman
personadu *vb* impersonate
personadwr (-wyr) *nm* impersonator
persondy (-dai) *nm* parsonage
personol *adj* personal
personoli *vb* personify
personoliad (-au) *nm* personification
personoliaeth (-au) *nf* personality
perswâd *nm* persuasion
perswadio *vb* persuade
pert *adj* quaint, pretty; pert
perth (-i) *nf* bush, hedge
perthnasedd (-au) *nm* relativity, relevance
perthnasiad (-au) *nm* affiliation
perthnasol *adj* relevant
perthyn *vb* belong, pertain, be related
perthynas (-au) *nf* relation; relationship
perthynol *adj* relative
perwyl *nm* purpose, effect
perygl (-on) *nm* danger, peril, risk
peryglu *vb* endanger, imperil
peryglus *adj* dangerous, perilous
pes *conj* if ... it. **p. adwaenasent** had they known him
pesgi *vb* feed, fatten
pesimist (-iaid) *nm* pessimist

pesimistaidd adj pessimistic
pesimistiaeth nf pessimism
pestl (-au) nm pestle
peswch nm cough
pesychiad (-au) nm cough
pesychu vb cough
petris npl (-en nf) partridges
petrocemegolau (**petrocemogolyn** nm) npl petrochemicals
petrol (-au) nm petrol
petroleg nm/f petrology
petrus adj hesitating; doubtful
petruso vb hesitate, doubt
petruster nm hesitation, doubt
petryal nm, adj square
peth (-au) nm thing; part; some
petheuach npl odds and ends, trifles
peunes (-od) nf peahen
pianydd (-ion) nm pianist
piau vb own, possess
pib (-au) nf pipe, tube; diarrhœa
pibell (-au, -i) nf pipe, tube
pibgorn (-gyrn) nm recorder (music)
pibo vb pipe; squirt
pibonwy (-en nf) npl icicles
pibydd (-ion) nm piper
picell (-au) nf dart, javelin, spear
picellu vb spear, stab
picfforch (-ffyrch) nf pitchfork
picil nm pickle, trouble
picio vb dart, hie
piclo vb pickle
pictiwr (-tiyrau) nm picture
picwns (-nen nf) npl wasps
piff (-iau) nm puff, sudden blast
piffian vb snigger, giggle
pig (-au) nf point, spike; beak; spout
pigan vb drizzle
pigdwr (-dyrau) nm spire, steeple
pigiad (-au) nm prick, sting; injection
pigion npl pickings, selections
pigo vb pick; peck; prick; sting
pigog adj prickly

pigyn nm thorn, prickle
pilcod npl (-yn nm) minnows
pilen (-nau) nf membrane, film; cataract
piler (-au, -i) nm pillar
pilio vb peel, pare
pili-pala nm butterfly
Pilipinas npl the Philippines
pilsen (pils) nf pill
pilyn nm garment, rag, clout
pin nm pine, fir
pin (-nau) nm/f pin ♦ nm pen
pinacl (-au) nm pinnacle
pinaclog adj pinnacled
pinafal (-au) nf pineapple
pinbwyntio vb pinpoint
pinc (-od) nm finch, chaffinch
pincio vb pink. **parlwr p.** beauty parlour
pincws (-cysau) nm pincushion
pindwll (-dyllau) nm pinhole
pinsiad (-au) nm pinch
pinsio vb pinch
pioden (piod) nf magpie
piser (-au, -i) nm pitcher, jug, can
pistyll (-oedd) nm spout; cataract
pistyllio vb spout, gush
pisyn (-nau, pisiau) nm piece
piti nm pity
pitw adj petty, puny, paltry
piw (-od) nm dug, udder
Piwritan (-iaid) nm Puritan
piwritanaidd adj puritan, puritanical
piwritaniaeth nf puritanism
pla (plâu) nm/f plague, pestilence; nuisance
pladur (-iau) nf scythe
pladurwr (-wyr) nm mower
plaen adj plain, clear
plaen (-au) nm plane
plaenio vb plane
plagio vb plague, tease, torment
plagus adj annoying, troublesome
plaid (pleidiau) nf side, party. **P. Cymru** The Welsh National Party
planced (-i) nf blanket

planed (-au) *nf* planet
planhigfa (-feydd) *nf* plantation
planhigyn (-higion) *nm* plant
plannu *vb* plant; dive
plannwr (planwyr) *nm* planter
plant *npl* (plentyn *nm*) children
planta *vb* beget or bear children
plantos *npl* (little) children
plas (-au) *nm* hall, mansion, palace
plasaidd *adj* palatial
plastr (-au) *nm* plaster
plastro *vb* plaster
plastrwr (-wyr) *nm* plasterer
plât, plat (-iau) *nm* plate
platŵn (-tynau) *nm* platoon
platwydr *nm* plate-glass
ple *nm* plea
pledio *vb* plead, argue
pledren (-nau, -ni) *nf* bladder
pleidgarwch *nm* partisanship
pleidio *vb* side with, support
pleidiol *adj* favourable, partial
pleidiwr (-wyr) *nm* partisan, supporter
pleidlais (-leisiau) *nf* vote, suffrage
pleidleisio *vb* vote
pleidleisiwr (-wyr) *nm* voter
plencyn (planciau) *nm* plank
plentyn (plant) *nm* child, infant
plentyndod *nm* childhood, infancy
plentyneiddiwch *nm* childishness
plentynnaidd *adj* childish, puerile
plentynrwydd *nm* childishness
pleser (-au) *nm* pleasure
pleserdaith (-deithiau) *nf* trip, excursion
pleserus *adj* pleasurable, pleasant
plesio *vb* please
plet, pleten (pletiau) *nf* pleat
pletio *vb* pleat
pletiog *adj* pleated
pleth (-au) *nf* plait
plethdorch (-au) *nf* wreath
plethu *vb* plait, weave, fold
plewra (-e) *nm* pleura
plicio *vb* pluck, peel, strip

plisg *coll n* (-yn *nm*) shells, husks, pods
plisgo *vb* shell, husk
plisman, -mon (-myn) *nm* policeman
plismones (-au) *nf* policewoman
plith *nm* midst
plocyn (plociau) *nm* block
plod *adj, nm* plaid, tartan
ploryn (-nod) *nm* pimple
plu *npl* (-en *nf*), **pluf** *npl* (-yn *nm*) feathers. **p. eira** snow-flakes
pluo, plufio *vb* pluck, deplume; plume
pluog *adj* feathered, fledged
plwc (plyciau) *nm* pluck; space, while
plwg (plygiau) *nm* plug
plwm *nm* lead
plws *nm* plus
plwtoniwm *nm* plutonium
plwyf (-i, -ydd) *nm* parish
plwyfol *adj* parochial
plwyfolion *npl* parishioners
plycio *vb* pluck
plyg (-ion) *nm* fold, double; hollow
plygain *nm* cock-crow, dawn; matins
plygeiniol *adj* dawning; very early
plygell (-au) *nm* folder
plygiad (-au) *nm* folding, fold
plygu *vb* fold; bend, stoop; bow
plymen *nf* plummet
plymio *vb* plumb, sound
plymwr (-wyr) *nm* plumber
po *particle used before superlative.*
gorau po gyntaf the sooner the better
pob *adj* each, every; all
pobi *vb* bake; roast; toast
pobiad (-au) *nm* baking, batch
pobl (-oedd) *nf* people
poblog *adj* populous
poblogaeth (-au) *nf* population
poblogaidd *adj* popular
poblogeiddio *vb* popularize

poblogi vb people, populate

poblogrwydd nm popularity

pobwr (-wyr), **-ydd** (-ion) nm baker

poced (-i) nf pocket

pocedu vb pocket

pocer (-i, -au) nm poker

poen (-au) nmf pain, torment

poenedigaeth nf torment

poeni vb pain, torment; worry, grieve

poenus adj painful

poenwr (-wyr) nm tormentor, torturer

poenydio vb torment, torture; fret, vex

poenydiwr (-wyr) nm tormentor

poer (-ion) nm spittle, saliva

poeri vb spit, expectorate

poeryn nm spittle

poeth adj hot; burning. **dŵr p.** heart-burn

poethder, -ni nm hotness, heat

poethdon (-nau) nf heatwave

poethi vb heat

pôl (polau) nm poll

polaredd nm polarity

polareiddiad nm polarisation

polareiddio vb polarise

polymorff nm polymorph

polymorffedd nm polymorphism

polyn (polion) nm pole

pomgranad (-au) nm pomegranate

pompiwn (-iynau) nm pumpkin, gourd

pompren nf plank bridge, footbridge

ponc (-iau), **-en** nf, **-yn** nm hillock, tump; bank

pont (-ydd) nf bridge, arch

pontffordd (-ffyrdd) nf fly-over, viaduct

pontio vb bridge

popeth nm everything

poplys npl (-en nf) poplar-trees

popty (-tai) nm bakehouse; oven

porc nm pork

porchell (perchyll) nm little pig

porfa (-feydd) nf pasture, grass

porffor adj, nm purple

pori vb graze, browse; eat

pornograffiaeth nf pornography

Portiwgal nf Portugal

portread (-au) nm portrayal, pattern

portreadu vb portray

porth nm aid, help, succour

porth (pyrth) nm gate, gateway; porch door. **p. awyr** airport

porthfa (-feydd) nf port, harbour; ferry

porthi vb feed

porthiannus adj well-fed, high-spirited

porthiant nm food, sustenance, support

porthladd (-oedd) nm port, harbour, haven

porthmon (-myn) nm cattle-dealer

porthor (-ion) nm porter, door-keeper, commissionaire

pôs (-au) nm riddle, conundrum, puzzle

posibilrwydd nm possibility

posib(l) adj possible

positif adj positive

positifiaeth nf positivism

post (pyst) nm post; pillar

poster (-i) nm poster

postfarc (-iau) nm postmark

postio vb post

postman, -mon (-myn) nm postman

postyn (pyst) nm post

pot (-iau) nm pot

potel (-i) nf bottle

potelaid (-eidiau) nf bottleful

potelu vb bottle

poten (-ni) nf paunch; pudding

potensial (-au) nm, adj potential

potes nm pottage, broth, soup

potio vb pot; tipple

potsiar (-s) nm poacher

potsio vb poach

pothell (-au, -i) *nf* blister
powdr (-au) *nm* powder
powl, -en (powliau) *nf* bowl, basin
powlio *vb* roll; wheel, trundle
powltis (-au) *nm* poultice
practis *nm* practice
praff *adj* thick, stout
praffter *nm* thickness, stoutness, girth
pragmatiaeth *nf* pragmatism
praidd (preiddiau) *nf* flock
pranc (-iau) *nm* frolic, prank
prancio *vb* caper, prance
pratio *vb* pat, stroke, caress
praw, prawf (profion) *nm* test, trial, proof
preblan *vb* chatter, babble
pregeth (-au) *nf* sermon, discourse
pregethu *vb* preach
pregethwr (-wyr) *nm* preacher
pregethwrol *adj* preacher-like
pregowtha *vb* jabber, rant
preifat *adj* private
preifatrwydd *nm* privacy
preimin *nm* ploughing match
prelad (-iaid) *nm* prelate
preladiaeth *nf* prelacy
preliwd (-au) *nm* prelude
premiwm (-iymau) *nm* premium
pren (-nau) *nm* tree, timber; wood
prentis (-iaid) *nm* apprentice
prentisiaeth *nf* apprenticeship
prentisio *vb* apprentice
prepian *vb* babble, blab
pres *nm* brass; bronze; copper; money
preseb (-au) *nm* crib, stall
presennol *adj* present
presenoldeb *nm* presence; attendance
presenoli *vb* be present (*reflexive*)
presgripsiwn (-iynau) *nm* prescription
preswyl *nm*, **-fa** (-feydd) *nf*, **-fod** *nm* abode, dwelling
preswylio *vb* dwell, reside, inhabit
preswylydd (-ion, -wyr) *nm* dweller, inhabitant
pric (-iau) *nm* stick, chip
prid *adj* dear, costly ♦ *nm* price, value
pridwerth *nm* ransom
pridd *nm* mould, earth, soil, ground
priddell (-au, -i) *nf* clod
priddglai *nm* loam
priddlech (-au, -i) *nf* tile
priddlestr (-i) *nm* earthenware vessel
priddlyd *adj* earthy
pridd(i)o *vb* earth
priddyn *nm* earth, soil, mould
prif *adj* prime, principal, chief
prifardd (-feirdd) *nm* chief bard
prifathro (-athrawon) *nm* . headmaster, principal
prifddinas (-oedd) *nf* metropolis, capital
prifiant *nm* growth
prifio *vb* grow
prifodl (-au) *nf* chief rhyme
prifysgol (-ion) *nf* university
priffordd (-ffyrdd) *nf* highway
prin *adj* scarce, rare ♦ *adv* scarcely
prinder, -dra *nm* scarceness, scarcity
prinhau *vb* make or grow scarce, diminish
print (-iau) *nm* print
printiedig *adj* printed
printio *vb* print
printiwr (-wyr) *nm* printer
priod *adj* own; proper; married ♦ *n coll* husband or wife
priodas (-au) *nf* marriage, wedding
priodasfab (-feibion) *nm* bridegroom
priodasferch (-ed) *nf* bride
priodasol *adj* matrimonial
priod-ddull (-iau) *nm* idiom
priodfab (-feibion) *nm* bridegroom
priodferch (-ed) *nf* bride

priodi *vb* marry
priodol *adj* proper, appropriate
priodoldeb (-au) *nm* propriety
priodoledd (-au) *nf* attribute
priodoli *vb* attribute
prior (-iaid) *nm* prior
priordy (-dai) *nm* priory
pris (-iau) *nm* price, value
prisiad, -iant *nm* valuation
prisio *vb* price, value; prize
prisiwr (-wyr) *nm* valuer
problem (-au) *nm/f* problem
proc (-iau) *nm* poke
procer (-au, -i) *nm* poker
procio *vb* poke; throb
procsi *nm* proxy
prodin (-au) *nm* protein
profedig *adj* approved, tried
profedigaeth (-au) *nf* trouble, tribulation
profedigaethus *adj* beset with trials
profi *vb* prove; taste; try; experience
profiad (-au) *nm* experience
profiadol *adj* experienced
profiannaeth (-au) *nf* probation
proflen (-ni) *nf* proof-sheet
profocio *vb* provoke, tease
profoclyd *adj* provoking, provocative
profwr (-wyr) *nm* taster, tester
proffes (-au) *nf* profession
proffesiwn (-iynau) *nm* profession
proffesu *vb* profess
proffid *nf* profit
proffidio *vb* profit, benefit
proffidiol *adj* profitable
proffwyd (-i) *nm* prophet
proffwydes (-au) *nf* prophetess
proffwydo *vb* prophesy
proffwydol *adj* prophetic
proffwydoliaeth (-au) *nf* prophecy
project (-au) *nm* project
proses (-au) *nm/f* process
prosesu *vb* process
prosesydd *nm* processor. **p. geiriau**
word processor
protest (-au) *nf* protest
Protestannaidd *adj* Protestant
Protestant (-aniaid) *nm* Protestant
protestio *vb* protest
protestiwr (-wyr) *nm* protestor
prudd *adj* grave, serious, sad; wise
pruddaidd *adj* sad, gloomy, mournful
prudd-der *nm* sadness, gloom
pruddglwyf *nm* depression, melancholy
pruddglwyfus *adj* depressed, melancholy
pruddhau *vb* sadden, depress
Prwsia *nf* Prussia
pryd (-iau) *nm* time; season ♦ (-au) *nm* meal
pryd *adv* while, when, since
pryd *nm* form, aspect; complexion
Prydain *nf* Britain
Prydeindod *nm* Britishness
Prydeinig *adj* British
Prydeiniwr (-wyr) *nm* Britisher
pryder (-on) *nm* anxiety, solicitude
pryderu *vb* be anxious
pryderus *adj* anxious, solicitous
pryderth *adj* beautiful, handsome
pryderthu *vb* beautify
pryderthwch *nm* beauty
prydles (-au, -i) *nf* lease
prydlon *adj* timely, punctual
prydlondeb *nm* punctuality
prydydd (-ion) *nm* poet
prydyddu *vb* compose poetry, poetize
pryddest (-au) *nf* poem in free metre
pryf (-ed) *nm* insect; worm; vermin
pryfedog *adj* verminous
pryfleiddiad (-au) *nm* insecticide
pryfyn *nm* worm
prŷn *adj* bought, purchased
prynedigaeth *nf/m* redemption
prynhawn (-au) *nm* afternoon

prynhawnol *adj* afternoon, evening

pryniad *nm* purchase

prynu *vb* buy, purchase; redeem

prynwr (-wyr) *nm* buyer; redeemer

prysg *nm* bush, wood

prysgwydd *npl* brushwood

prysur *adj* busy, hasty; diligent; serious

prysurdeb *nm* haste, hurry; busyness

prysuro *vb* hurry, hasten

publican (-od) *nm* publican (New Test.)

pulpud (-au) *nm* pulpit

pulsau *npl* pulses

pum, pump *adj* five

pumawd (-au) *nm* quintet

pumed *adj* fifth

pumongl (-au) *nm* pentagon

punt (punnoedd, punnau) *nf* pound (money)

pupur *nm* pepper

pur *adj* pure, sincere ♦ *adv* very, fairly

purdan *nm* purgatory

purdeb *nm* purity, sincerity

puredigaeth *nf* purification

puredd *nm* purity, innocence

purfa (-feydd) *nf* refinery

purion *adj* very well; right enough

puro *vb* purify, cleanse

puror *nm* harpist

purwr (-wyr) *nm* purifier, refiner

purydd (-ion) *nm* purist

putain (-einiaid) *nf* prostitute

puteindra *nm* prostitution

puteinio *vb* commit fornication

puteiniwr (-wyr) *nm* fornicator

pw *excl* pooh

pwbig *adj* pubic

pwdin *nm* pudding, dessert

pwdlyd *adj* sulking

pwdr *adj* rotten, corrupt, putrid

pwdu *vb* pout, sulk

pŵer (-au) *nm* power

pwerus *adj* powerful

pwff (pyffiau) *nm* puff, blast

pwffian *vb* puff

pŵl *adj* blunt, obtuse; dull, dim

pwl (pyliau) *nm* fit, attack, paroxysm

pwll (pyllau) *nm* pit, pool, pond. **p. glo** coal pit. **p. tro** whirlpool

pwmp (pympiau) *nm* pump

pwn (pynnau) *nm* pack, burden

pwnc (pynciau) *nm* point, subject, question

pwniad (-au) *nm* nudge, dig

pwnio *vb* nudge; beat, thump, wallop

pwrcas (-au) *nm* purchase

pwrcasu *vb* purchase

pwrffil *nm* purfle, train

pwrpas (-au) *nm* purpose

pwrpasol *adj* suitable

pwrpasu *vb* purpose, intend

pwrs (pyrsau) *nm* purse, bag; udder; scrotum

pwt (pytiau) *nm* anything short; stump

pwt, -ian *vb* prod, poke

pwti *nm* putty

pwy *pron* who

Pwyl *nf* Poland

pwyll *nm* sense, discretion

pwyllgor (-au) *nm* committee

pwyllgorwr (-wyr) *nm* committee-man

pwyllo *vb* pause, consider, reflect

pwyllog *adj* discreet, prudent, deliberate

pwynt (-iau) *nm* point

pwyntil *nm* tab, tag; pencil

pwyntio *vb* point; fatten

pwyo *vb* beat, batter, pound

pwys (-au, -i) *nm* weight, burden, pressure; pound (lb.); importance

pwysau *nm* weight

pwysedd *nm* pressure

pwysi (-iau) *nm* posy

pwysig *adj* important

pwysigrwydd *nm* importance

pwyslais (-leisiau) *nm* emphasis
pwysleisio *vb* emphasize
pwyso *vb* weigh, press; lean, rest; rely
pwyswr (-wyr) *nm* weigher
pwyth (-au) *nm* stitch. **talu'r p.** requite
pwytho *vb* stitch
pwythwr (-wyr) *nm* stitcher
pybyr *adj* strong, stout, staunch, valiant
pybyrwch *nm* stoutness, vigour, valour
pydew (-au) *nm* well, pit
pydredig *adj* rotten, putrid
pydredd *nm* rottenness, putridity, rot
pydru *vb* rot, putrefy
pyg *nm* pitch, bitumen
pygddu *adj* pitch-black
pygu *vb* pitch
pyngad, pyngu *vb* cluster
pylni *nm* bluntness, dullness
pylor *nm* dust, powder
pylu *vb* blunt, dull
pyllog *adj* full of pits
pyllu *vb* pit
pymtheg *adj, nm* fifteen
pymthegfed *adj* fifteenth
pyncio *vb* sing, play, make melody
pynfarch (-feirch) *nm* pack-horse; mill-race
pynio *vb* burden, load
pys *npl* (-en *nf*) peas
pysgod *npl* (-yn *nm*) fishes, fish. **p. a sglodion** fish and chips
pysgodfa (-feydd) *nf* fishery
pysgota *vb* fish
pysgotwr (-wyr) *nm* fisherman
pystylad *vb* stamp with the feet
pytaten (-tws) *nf* potato
pythefnos (-au) *nm/f* fortnight

PH

Pharisead (-aid) *nm* Pharisee
Phariseaeth *nf* Pharisaism
Phariseaidd *adj* Pharisaic(al)
Philistiad (-iaid) *nm* Philistine
Philistiaeth *nf* Philistinism

R

rabi (-niaid) *nm* rabbi
rabinaidd *adj* rabbinical
radio *nm* radio
radioleg *nf* radiology
radiws *nm* radius
ras (-ys) *nf* race
rasal, raser (-elydd, -erydd) *nf* razor
record (-iau) *nf/m* record
recordiad (-au) *nm* recording
reiat *nf* row, riot
reis *nm* rice
reit *adv* right, very, quite
ridens *nf* fringe, nap
riwl *nf* ruler
robin goch *nm* robin
robin y gyrrwr *nm* gadfly
roced (-i) *nf* rocket
România *nf* Romania
ruban (-au) *nm* ribbon
rŵan *adv* now
rwbel *nm* rubble, rubbish
rwber *nm* rubber
rwdins *npl* (rwden *nf*) swedes
Rwsia *nf* Russia
Rwsiad (Rwsiaid) *nm* Russian (citizen)
Rwsieg *nm* Russian (language)

RH

rhaca (-nau) *nf*, **-nu** *vb* rake
rhacs (rhecsyn *nm*) *npl* rags
rhad *adj* free; cheap

rhad (-au) *nm* grace, favour, blessing

rhadlon *adj* gracious, kind; genial

rhadlondeb, -rwydd *nm* graciousness, cheapness

rhadus *adj* economical

rhaeadr (-au) *nf* cataract, waterfall

rhaeadru *vb* pour, gush

rhaff (-au) *nf* rope, cord

rhaffo, -u *vb* rope

rhag *prep* before, against; from; lest ♦ *prefix* pre-, fore-, ante-

rhagafon (-ydd) *nf* tributary

rhagair (-au) *nm* preface

rhagarfaethiad *nm* predestination

rhagarfaethu *vb* predestine

rhagarweiniad *nm* introduction

rhagarweiniol *adj* introductory, preliminary

rhagarwyddo *vb* foretoken, portend

rhagbaratoawl *adj* preparatory

rhagbrawf (-brofion) *nm* foretaste; preliminary test

rhagdraeth (-au) *nm* preface, introduction

rhag-dyb (-ion) *nm* presupposition

rhagdybied, -io *vb* presuppose

rhagddodiad (-iaid) *nm* prefix

rhagddywedyd, rhagddweud *vb* foretell

rhagenw (-au) *nm* pronoun

rhagenwol *adj* pronominal

rhagfarn (-au) *nf* prejudice

rhagfarnllyd *adj* prejudiced

rhagferf (-au) *nf* adverb

rhagflaenor (-iaid) *nm* forerunner

rhagflaenu *vb* precede, anticipate, forestall

rhagflaenydd (-ion, -wyr) *nm* predecessor, precursor

rhagflas *nm* foretaste

rhagfur (-iau) *nm* bulwark

rhagfyfyrio *vb* premeditate

rhagfynegi *vb* foretell

Rhagfyr *nm* December

rhaglaw (-iaid, -lofiaid) *nm* prefect, viceroy, governor

rhaglawiaeth *nf* prefecture, governorship

rhaglen (-ni) *nf* programme

rhagluniaeth (-au) *nf* providence

rhagluniaethol *adj* providential

rhaglunio *vb* predestine, predestinate

rhagod *vb* ambush, hinder, waylay

rhagofnau *npl* forebodings

rhagolwg (-ygon) *nm* prospect, outlook

rhagor (-au, -ion) *nm* difference; more

rhagorfraint (-freintiau) *nf* privilege

rhagori *vb* exceed, excel, surpass

rhagoriaeth (-au) *nf* superiority; excellence

rhagorol *adj* excellent, splendid

rhagoroldeb *nm* excellence

rhagorsaf (-oedd) *nf* out-station; outpost

rhagredegydd (-ion) *nm* forerunner

rhagrith (-ion) *nm* hypocrisy

rhagrithio *vb* practise hypocrisy

rhagrithiol *adj* hypocritical

rhagrithiwr (-wyr) *nm* hypocrite

rhagrybuddio *vb* forewarn

rhagweld *vb* foresee

rhagwelediad *nm* foresight, prescience

rhagwybod *vb* foreknow

rhagwybodaeth *nf* foreknowledge

rhagymadrodd (-ion) *nm* introduction

rhai *pron* ones ♦ *some*

rhaib *nm* rapacity; greed; spell

rhaid (rheidiau) *nm* need, necessity

rhaidd (rheiddiau) *nf* antler

rhain *pron* these

rhamant (-au) *nf* romance

rhamantus *adj* romantic

rhan (-nau) *nf* part, portion; fate

rhanbarth *nm* division,

district

rhandir (-oedd) *nm/f* division, district

rhangymeriad (-iaid) *nm* participle

rhaniad (-au) *nm* division

rhannu *vb* divide, share, distribute

rhannwr (rhanwyr) *nm* divider, sharer

rhanrif *nm* fraction

rhathell (-au) *nf* rasp

rhathiad *nm* friction, chafing

rhathu *vb* rub, rasp, file

rhaw (-iau, rhofiau) *nf* spade, shovel

rhawd *nf* course, career

rhawg *adv* for a long time (to come)

rhawio, rhofio *vb* shovel

rhawn *coll n* coarse long hair, horse-hair

rhech *nf* fart

rhechain *vb* fart

rhedeg *vb* run; flow

rhedegfa (-feydd) *nf* racecourse, race

rhedegog *adj* running, flowing

rhedegydd (-ion, -wyr) *nm* runner

rhedfa *nf* running, course, race

rhediad *nm* running, trend; slope

rhedweli (-iau) *nf* artery

rhedyn *npl* (*-en nf*) fern

rheffyn (-nau) *nm* cord; string, rigmarole

rheg (-au, -feydd) *nf* curse

rhegen yr ŷd, rhegen ryg *nf* corncrake

rhegi *vb* curse

rheglyd *adj* given to cursing, profane

rheng (-au, -oedd) *nf* row, rank

rheibio *vb* raven, ravage, ravish

rheibus *adj* rapacious, of prey

rheidiol *adj* necessary, needful

rheidrwydd *nm* necessity, need

rheidus *adj* necessitous, needy

rheilffordd (-ffyrdd) *nf* railway

rheini *pron* those

rheitheg *nf* rhetoric

rheithfarn (-au) *nf* verdict

rheithgor (rheithwyr) *nm* jury

rheithiwr (-wyr) *nm* juryman, juror

rheithor (-ion, -iad) *nm* rector

rhelyw *nm* residue, rest, remainder

rhemp *nf* excess; defect

rhent (-i) *nm* rent

rhentu *vb* rent

rheol (-au) *nf* rule, regulation

rheolaeth *nf* rule, management, control

rheolaidd *adj* regular

rheoleiddio *vb* regulate; regularize

rheoli *vb* rule, govern, control

rheolwr (-wyr) *nm* ruler, controller

rhes (-i) *nf* line, stripe; row, rank

rhesen (rhesi) *nf* line, parting, streak, stripe

rhesin (-au, -ingau) *nm* raisin

rhesog *adj* striped; ribbed

rhestl (-au) *nf* rack

rhestr (-au, -i) *nf* list; row

rhestru *vb* list

rheswm (-ymau) *nm* reason

rhesymeg *nf* logic

rhesymegol *adj* logical

rhesymol *adj* reasonable, rational

rhesymoldeb *nm* reasonableness

rhesymolwr (-wyr) *nm* rationalist

rhesymu *vb* reason

rhetoreg, rhethreg *nf* rhetoric

rhew (-oedd, -ogydd) *nm* frost, ice

rhewfryn (-iau) *nm* iceberg

rhewgell (-oedd) *nf* freezer

rhewi *vb* freeze

rhewllyd *adj* icy, frosty, frigid

rhewyn (-au) *nm* ditch, stream

rhewynt (-oedd) *nm* freezing wind

rhi *nm* king, lord

rhiain (rhianedd) *nf* maiden

rhialtwch *nm* pomp; festivity, jollity

rhibidirês *nf* rigmarole
rhibin *nm* streak
rhic (-iau) *nm* notch, nick; groove
rhiciog *adj* notched; grooved; ribbed
rhidyll (-iau) *nm* riddle, sieve
rhidyllio, -u *vb* riddle, sift
rhieingerdd (-i) *nf* love-poem
rhieni *mpl* parents
rhif (-au) *nm*, **rhifedi** *nm* number
rhifo *vb* number, count, reckon
rhifol (-ion) *nm* numeral
rhifyddeg, -ddiaeth *nf* arithmetic
rhifyddwr (-wyr) *nm* arithmetician
rhifyn (-nau) *nm* number
rhigol (-au, -ydd) *nf* rut, groove
rhigwm (-ymau) *nm* rigmarole; rhyme
rhigymu *vb* rhyme, versify
rhigymwr (-wyr) *nm* rhymester
rhingyll (-iaid) *nm* sergeant, bailiff
rhimyn (-nau) *nm* strip, string
rhin (-iau) *nf* virtue, essence
rhincian *vb* creak; gnash
rhiniog (-au) *nm* threshold
rhinwedd (-au) *nm/f* virtue
rhinweddol *adj* virtuous
rhip *nm* strickle
rhisgl *nm* bark
rhith (-iau) *nm* form, guise, appearance, image; foetus
rhithio *vb* appear
rhithyn *nm* atom, particle, scintilla
rhiw (-iau) *nf* hill, acclivity
rhoch *nf* grunt, groan; deathrattle
rhochain, -ian *vb* grunt
rhod (-au) *nf* wheel, orb; ecliptic
rhodfa (-feydd) *nf* walk, promenade, avenue
rhodiad *nm* walk
rhodianna *vb* stroll
rhodio *vb* walk, stroll
rhodres *nm* ostentation, affectation
rhodresa *vb* behave ostentatiously
rhodresgar *adj* ostentatious, affected
rhodreswr (-wyr) *nm* swaggerer

rhodd (-ion) *nf* gift, present
rhoddi *vb* give, bestow, yield; put
rhoddwr (-wyr) *nm* giver, donor
rhoi *vb* give, bestow, yield; put
rhôl (-iau) *nf*, **rholyn** *nm* roll
rholbren (-ni) *nm* rolling-pin
rholio *vb* roll
rhombws (**rhombi**) *nm* rhombus
rhonc *adj* rank, stark, out-and-out
rhos (-ydd) *nf* moor, heath; plain
rhos (-yn *nm*) *nf* roses
rhost *adj* roast, roasted
rhostio *vb* roast
rhosyn (-nau) *nm* rose
rhuad (-au) *nm* roaring, roar
rhuadwy *adj* roaring
rhuchen (**rhuchion**) *nf* husk; film, pellicle
rhudd *adj* red, crimson
rhuddell *nf* rubric
rhuddem (-au) *nf* ruby
rhuddin *nm* heart of timber
rhuddion *npl* bran
rhuddygl *nm* radish
Rhufain *nf* Rome
Rhufeinaidd *adj* Roman
Rhufeiniad (-iaid), **-iwr** (-wyr) *nm* Roman
Rhufeinig *adj* Roman
rhugl *adj* free, fluent, glib
rhuglen (-ni) *nf* rattle
rhuglo *vb* rattle
rhuo *vb* roar, bellow, bluster
rhusio *vb* start, scare, take fright
rhuthr (-au) *nm* rush; attack; sally
rhuthro *vb* rush; attack, assault
rhwbio *vb* rub, chafe
rhwd *nm* rust
rhweng *prep* between, among
rhwnc *nm* snort, snore; death-rattle
rhwth *adj* gaping, distended
rhwyd (-au, -i) *nf* net, snare
rhwydo *vb* net, ensnare
rhwydog *adj* reticulated, netted
rhwydwaith (-weithiau) *nm*

network
rhwydd *adj* easy, expeditious, prosperous
rhwyddhau *vb* facilitate
rhwyddineb *nm* ease, facility
rhwyf (-au) *nf* oar
rhwyflong (-au) *nf* galley
rhwyfo *vb* row; sway; toss about
rhwyfus *adj* restless
rhwyfwr (-wyr) *nm* rower, oarsman
rhwyg (-iadau) *nf* rent, rupture; schism
rhwygo *vb* rend, tear
rhwyll (-au) *nf*, -**yn** *nm* buttonhole, aperture; lattice
rhwyllwaith *nm* fretwork, lattice-work
rhwym *adj* bound ♦ (-au) *nm* bond, tie; obligation
rhwymedig *adj* bound, obliged
rhwymedigaeth (-au) *nf* bond, obligation
rhwymedd *nm* constipation
rhwymiad (-au) *nm* binding
rhwymo *vb* bind, tie; constipate
rhwymwr (-wyr) *nm* binder
rhwymyn (-nau) *nm* band, bond, bandage
rhwysg (-au) *nm* sway; pomp
rhwysgfawr *adj* pompous, ostentatious
rhwystr (-au) *nm* hindrance, obstacle
rhwystro *vb* hinder, prevent, obstruct
rhwystrus *adj* embarrassed, confused
rhy *adv* too
rhybedio *vb* rivet
rhybudd (-ion) *nm* notice, warning
rhybuddio *vb* warn, admonish, caution
rhybuddiwr (-wyr) *nm* warner
rhych (-au) *nmf* furrow, rut, groove
rhychog *adj* furrowed, seamed

rhychwant (-au) *nm* span
rhychwantu *vb* span
rhyd (-au, -iau) *nf* ford
rhydio *vb* ford
rhydlyd *adj* rusty
rhydu *vb* rust
rhydd *adj* free; loose; liberal
Rhyddfrydiaeth *nf* Liberalism
rhyddfrydig *adj* liberal, generous
Rhyddfrydol *adj* liberal (in politics)
Rhyddfrydwr (-wyr) *nm* Liberal, Radical
rhyddhad *nm* liberation, emancipation
rhyddhau *vb* free, release, liberate
rhyddhawr (-wyr) *nm* liberator
rhyddiaith *nf* prose
rhyddid *nm* freedom, liberty
rhyddieithol *adj* prose, prosaic
rhyddni *nm* looseness, diarrhœa
rhyfedd *adj* strange, queer, wonderful
rhyfeddnod (-au) *nm* note of exclamation
rhyfeddod (-au) *nm/f* wonder, marvel
rhyfeddol *adj* wonderful, marvellous
rhyfeddu *vb* wonder, marvel
rhyfel (-oedd) *nm/f* war, warfare
rhyfela *vb* wage war, war
rhyfelgar *adj* warlike, bellicose
rhyfelgri *nm* war-cry, battle-cry
rhyfelgyrch (-oedd) *nm* campaign
rhyfelwr (-wyr) *nm* warrior
rhyferthwy *nm* torrent, inundation
rhyfon *npl* currants
rhyfyg *nm* presumption, foolhardiness
rhyfygu *vb* presume, dare
rhyfygus *adj* presumptuous; foolhardy
rhyg *nm* rye
rhyglyddu *vb* deserve, merit
rhygnu *vb* rub, grate, jar; harp
rhygyngu *vb* amble; caper, mince

rhyngu vb: **rh. bodd** please
rhyngwladol adj international
rhyndod nm shivering, chill
rhynion npl grits, groats
rhynllyd adj shivering, chilly
rhynnu vb starve with cold
rhysedd nm abundance, excess
rhython npl cockles
rhythu vb gape; stare
rhyw adj some, certain ♦ (**-iau**) nf/m sort; sex
rhywbeth nm something
rhywfaint nm some amount
rhywfodd, rhywsut adv somehow
rhywiog adj kindly, genial; fine; tender
rhywiol adj sexual
rhywle adv somewhere, anywhere
rhywogaeth (**-au**) nf species, sort, kind
rhywun (**rhywrai**) nm someone, anyone

S

Sabath, -oth (**-au**) nm Sabbath
Sabothol adj Sabbath, sabbatic(al)
sacrament nm/f sacrament
sacramentaidd adj sacramental
sach (**-au**) nf/m sack
sachaid (**-eidiau**) nf sackful
sachlen nf, **sachliain** nm sackcloth
sachu vb sack, bag
sad adj firm, steady, solid; sober
sadio vb firm, steady
sadistiaeth nf sadism
sadrwydd nm firmness, steadiness
Sadwrn (**-yrnau**) nm Saturn; Saturday
saer (**seiri**) nm wright, mason, carpenter
saerniaeth nf workmanship, construction
saernïo vb fashion, construct

Saesneg nf, adj English
Saesnes (**-au**) nf Englishwoman
saets nm sage
saeth (**-au**) nf arrow, dart
saethiad (**-au**) nm shooting
saethu vb shoot; dart; blast
saethwr (**-wyr**) nm shooter, shot
saethydd (**-ion**) nm shooter, archer
saethyddiaeth nf archery
saethyn (**-nau**) nm projectile
safadwy adj stable
safanna nm savannah
safbwynt (**-iau**) nm standpoint
safiad nm standing; stature; stand
safio vb save
safle (**-oedd**) nm position, station, situation
safn (**-au**) nf mouth, jaws
safnrhwth adj open-mouthed, gaping
safnrhythu vb gape, stare
safon (**-au**) nf standard, criterion
safoni vb standardise
safonol adj standard
saffir nm sapphire
saffrwm, saffron nm crocus
sagrafen (**-nau**) nf sacrament
sang (**-au**) nf pressure, tread
sangu, sengi vb tread, trample
saib (**seibiau**) nm leisure; pause, rest
saig (**seigiau**) nf meal, dish
sail (**seiliau**) nf base, foundation
saim (**seimiau**) nm grease
sain (**seiniau**) nf sound, tone
Sais (**Saeson**) nm Saxon, Englishman
saith adj, nm seven
sâl adj poor; poorly, ill
saldra nm poorness; illness
salm (**-au**) nf psalm
salmydd (**-ion**) nm psalmist
salw adj poor, mean, vile; ugly
salwch nm illness
Sallwyr nm Psalter
sampl (**-au**) nf sample

samplu vb sample
Sanct nm the Holy One
sanctaidd adj holy
sancteiddio vb sanctify, hallow
sancteiddrwydd nm holiness,
sanctity
sandal (-au) nm sandal
sant (saint, seintiau) nm saint
santes (-au) nf female saint
sarff (seirff) nf serpent
sarhad (-au) nm insult, disgrace,
injury
sarhau vb insult, affront, injure
sarhaus adj insulting, offensive,
insolent
sarn (-au) nf causeway ♦ nm litter,
ruin, destruction
sarnu vb trample; litter; spoil,
ruin
sarrug adj gruff, surly, morose
sarugrwydd nm gruffness,
surliness
sasiwn (-iynau) nm C.M.
Association
satan (-iaid) nm satan
sathredig adj common, vulgar
sathru vb tread, trample
Saudi Arabia nf Saudi Arabia
sawdl (sodlau) nm/f heel
sawl pron whoso, he that. **Pa s.**
how many
sawr, sawyr nm savour
sawrio, -u vb savour
sawrus adj savoury
saws nm sauce
sba (-on) nm spa
Sbaen nf Spain
sbageti nm spaghetti
sbaner (-i) nm spanner
sbâr (sbarion) nm spare; (pl)
leavings
sbario vb spare, save
sbectol nf spectacle(s)
sbeit nf spite
sbeitio vb spite
sbeitlyd adj spiteful
sbel (-iau) nf spell

sbon adv: **newydd s.** brand-new
sbonc (-iau) nm leap, jerk
sboncen nf squash
sbort nf sport, fun, game
sbri nm spree, fun
sbring nm spring
sbwylio vb spoil
sebon (-au) nm soap
seboni vb soap, lather; soft-soap,
flatter
sebonwr (-wyr) nm flatterer
sect (-au) nf sect
sectyddiaeth nf sectarianism
sectyddol adj sectarian
sech adj f. of **sych**
sedd (-au) nf seat, pew
sef conj that is to say, namely, to
wit
sefnig nm pharynx
sefydledig adj established
sefydliad (-au) nm establishment,
institution
sefydlog adj fixed, settled,
stationary, stable
sefydlo(w)grwydd nm stability
sefydlu vb establish, found, settle
sefyll vb stand; stop; stay
sefyllfa (-oedd) nf situation,
position
sefyllian vb stand about, loiter
sefyllwyr npl bystanders
segur adj idle
segura vb idle
segurdod nm idleness
segurwr (-wyr) nm idler
seguryd nm idleness
seguryn, segurwr (-wyr) nm idler
sengi vb tread, trample
sengl adj single
seiat (-adau) nf fellowship
meeting, 'society'
seibiant nm leisure, respite
seibio vb pause
seiciatreg nm psychiatry
seiciatrydd nm psychiatrist
seicoleg nf psychology
seidin nm sidings

seilio vb ground, found
seimio vb grease
seimllyd adj greasy
seinber adj melodious, euphonious
seindorf (-dyrf) nf band
seineg nf phonetics
seinfawr adj loud
seinfforch (-ffyrch) nf tuning-fork
seinio vb sound, resound;
pronounce
seintio vb saint, canonize
seintwar nf sanctuary
seinyddol adj phonetic
Seisnig adj English
Seisnigaidd adj English,
Anglicized
Seisnigeiddio, -igo vb Anglicize
seithblyg adj sevenfold
seithfed adj seventh
seithongl (-au) nf septangle,
heptagon
seithug adj futile, fruitless,
bootless
sêl nf zeal
sêl (seliau) nf seal
Seland Newydd nf New Zealand
seld (-au) nf dresser, sideboard,
bookcase
seler (-au, -i, -ydd) nf cellar
selio vb seal
selni nm illness
selog adj zealous, ardent
selsig (-od) nf black-pudding,
sausage
semanteg nf semantics
seml adj f. of **syml**
sen (-nau) nf reproof, rebuke,
censure, snub
senedd (-au) nf senate;
parliament
seneddol adj senatorial,
parliamentary
seneddwr (-wyr) nm senator
sennu vb rebuke, censure
sentimentaleiddiwch nm
sentimentality
sêr see **seren**

seraff (-iaid) nm seraph
serch conj, prep although,
notwithstanding
serch (-iadau) nm affection, love
serchog adj affectionate, loving
serchowgrwydd nm
affectionateness, love
serchu vb love
serchus adj loving, affectionate,
pleasant
sêr-ddewin (-iaid) nm astrologer
sêr-ddewiniaeth nf astrology
seremoni (-ïau) nf ceremony
seremoniol adj ceremonial
seren (sêr) nf star; asterisk
serennog adj starry
serennu vb sparkle, scintillate
serfyll adj unsteady
seri nm causeway, pavement
serio vb sear
sero (-au) nm zero
serth adj steep, precipitous;
obscene
serthedd nm ribaldry, obscenity
serwm nm serum
seryddiaeth nf astronomy
seryddol adj astronomical
seryddwr (-wyr) nm astronomer
sesbin nm shoehorn
set (-iau) nf set
sêt (seti) nf seat, pew. **s. fawr**
deacons' pew
setl (-au) nf settle
setlo vb settle
sethrydd (-ion) nm treader,
trampler
sew (-ion) nm juice; pottage;
delicacy
sffêr nf sphere
sg- see also **ysg-**
sgâm (sgamiau) nf scheme, dodge
sgamio vb scheme, dodge
sgarff (-iau) nf scarf
sgaprwth adj uncouth, rough
sgil nm pillion. **s. effaith** side effect
sgiw (-iau) nf settle. **ar y s.** askew
sglefren nf slide

sglefrio vb skate, slide

sgolor (-ion) nm scholar

sgôr nm score

sgrafell (-i) nf scraper

sgrech y coed nf jay

sgrechian vb shriek

sgrîn (-au) nf screen

sgriw (-iau) nf screw

sgwâr (sgydiau) nm square

sgwd (sgydiau) nf cataract, waterfall

sgwrs (sgyrsiau) nf talk, chat, conversation

sgwrsio vb talk, chat

si nm whiz, buzz; rumour, murmur

siaced (-i) nf jacket, coat

siâd (sidau) nf pate

sialc nm chalk

sialens nf challenge

sialensio vb challenge

siambr (-i, -ydd) nf chamber

siant (-au) nf chant

siâr nf share

siarad vb talk, speak ♦ nm talk

siaradus adj talkative, garrulous

siaradwr (-wyr) nm talker, speaker

siario vb share

siars nf charge, command

siarsio vb charge, enjoin, warn

siart (-iau) nm chart

siartr (-au) nf charter

siasbi nm shoehorn

siawns nf chance

siawnsio vb chance

sibrwd vb whisper, murmur ♦ (-ydion) nm whisper, murmur

sicr adj sure, certain; secure

sicrhau vb assure, affirm, confirm; secure

sicrwydd nm certainty, assurance

sidan (-au) nm silk

sidanaidd adj silky

sidanbryf (-ed) nm silkworm

siêd nm escheat, forfeit

sied (-au) nf shed

siesbin nm shoehorn

siew nf show

siffrwd vb rustle, shuffle

sigâr nf cigar

sigaret (sigaretau) nf cigarette

sigledig adj shaky, rickety, unstable

siglen (-nydd) nf swing; bog, swamp

siglo vb shake, quake, rock, swing, wag

sil (-od) nm spawn, fry

silff (-oedd) nf shelf

silwair nm silage

sill (-iau), **-af** (-au) nf syllable

sillafiaeth nf spelling

sillafu vb spell

sillgoll (-au) nf apostrophe

simnai (-neiau) nf chimney

simsan adj unsteady, tottering, rickety

simsanu vb totter

sinach (-od) nf balk, waste ground; skinflint

sinc nm zinc

sinema (sinemâu) nf cinema

sinig nm cynic

sinigaidd adj cynical

sinsir nm ginger

sio vb hiss, whiz; murmur, purl

sioe (-au) nf show

siôl (-au) nf skull, pate

siôl (siolau) nf shawl

siom (-au) nm disappointment

siomedig adj disappointed, disappointing

siomedigaeth (-au) nf disappointment

siomi vb disappoint; balk, thwart; deceive

siomiant nm disappointment

sionc adj brisk, nimble, agile, active

sioncio vb brisk

sioncrwydd nm briskness, agility

sioncyn y gwair nm grasshopper

siop (-au) nf shop

siopwr (-wyr) nm shopman, shopkeeper

sipian vb sip, sup, suck

siprys nm mixed corn (oats and barley)

sipsiwn npl gipsies

sir (-oedd) nf shire, county

siriol adj cheerful, bright, pleasant

sirioldeb nm cheerfulness

sirioli vb cheer, brighten

sirydd, -yf (-ion) nm sheriff

siryddiaeth nf shrievalty

sisial vb whisper

siswrn (-yrnau) nm scissors

siwgr nm sugar

siwmper (-i) nf jumper

siwr, siŵr adj sure, certain

siwrnai (-eiau) nf journey ♦ adv once

siwt (-iau) nf suit

slaf (slafiaid) nm slave, drudge

slei adj sly

sleifio vb slink

sleisen nf slice

slic adj slick

slotian vb paddle, dabble; tipple

slumyn see **ystlum**

slwt nf slut

smala adj droll

smalio vb joke

sment nm cement

smocio vb smoke (tobacco)

smociwr (-wyr) nm smoker

smotyn (smotiau) nm spot

smygu see **smocio**

snisin nm snuff

snwffian vb snuff, sniff; snuffle; whimper

sobr adj sober, serious

sobreiddio, sobri vb sober

sobrwydd nm sobriety, soberness

socas (-au) nf gaiter, legging

sodomiaeth nf sodomy

sodr nm solder

soddi vb submerge

soeg nm brewers' grains, draff

sofl npl (-yn nm) stubble

sofliar (-ieir) nf quail

sofraniaeth nf sovereignty

sofren (sofrod) nf sovereign (coin)

solas nm solace, joy

sol-ffa nm, **solffaeo** vb sol-fa

sôn vb, nm talk, mention, rumour

soned (-au) nf sonnet

sonedwr (-wyr) nm composer of sonnets

soniarus adj melodious, tuneful; loud

soriant nm indignation, displeasure

sorod npl dross, dregs, refuse

sorri (-ys) vb chafe, sulk, be displeased

sosban (-nau, -benni) nf saucepan

sosej (-s) nf sausage

soser (-i) nf saucer

sosialaeth nf socialism

sothach coll n refuse, rubbish, trash

st- see also **yst-**

stac (-iau) nf stack

staen (-au) nm, -**io** nf stain

stâl (-au) nf stall

stamp (-iau) nmf stamp

stampio vb stamp

starts nm starch

stên (stenau) nf pitcher

stesion (-au) nf station

sticil, -ill nf stile

stilio vb question

stiward (-iaid) nm steward

stiwdio nf studio

stoc (-au) nf stock

stomp nf bungle, mess, muddle

stompio vb beat, pound; bungle, mess

stompiwr (-wyr) nm bungler

stori (-iau, -iâu, straeon) nf story, tale

stormus adj stormy

stor(o)m (stormydd) nf storm

straegar adj gossiping, gossipy

strancio vb play tricks

strategaeth nf strategy

strategol adj strategic

strategydd (-ion) nm strategist

streic (**-iau**) nf strike
strwythur nm structure
stryd (**-oedd**) nf street
stwc (**stycau**) nm pail, bucket
stwff (**styffiau**) nm stuff
stwffio vb stuff, thrust
stwffwl (**styffylau**) nm post; staple
styffylydd (**-ion**) nm stapler
su nm buzz, murmur, hum
suad nm buzzing, lulling; hum
sucan nm gruel
sudd (**-ion**) nm juice, sap
suddgloch (**-glychau**) nf diving-bell
suddlong (**-au**) nf submarine
suddo vb sink, dive; invest (money)
sug (**-ion**) nm juice, sap
sugn nm suck; suction; sap
sugno vb suck, imbibe, absorb
Sul (**-iau**) nm Sunday
Sulgwyn nm Whitsunday
suo vb buzz, hum; lull, hush
sur (**-ion**) adj sour, acid
surdoes nm leaven
surni nm sourness, staleness, tartness
suro vb sour
suryn nm acid
sut nm manner; plight. **pa sut? sut?** how? what sort of?
swalpio vb flounder, jump, bounce
swci adj tame, pet
swcro vb succour
swcwr nm succour
swch (**sychau**) nf ploughshare; tip, grimble; lips
Sweden nf Sweden
swil adj shy, bashful
swilder nm shyness, bashfulness
swllt (**sylltau**) nm shilling
Swistir: y S. nf Switzerland
swm (**symiau**) nm sum, total
swmbwl (**symbylau**) nm goad
swmer (**-au**) nm beam; pack
swmp nm bulk
swmpus adj bulky
swn nm noise, sound

swnian vb murmur, grumble, nag
swnio vb sound, pronounce
swnllyd adj peevish, querulous
swnt nm sound, strait
swoleg nf zoology
swp (**sypiau**) nm mass, heap; cluster
swper (**-au**) nm/f supper
swpera, -u vb give or take supper
swrn (**syrnau**) nf fetlock, ankle ♦ nm good number
swrth adj heavy, sluggish; sullen
sws (**-ys**) nf kiss
swta adj abrupt, curt
swydd (**-au, -i**) nf office; county
swyddfa (**-feydd**) nf office
swyddog (**-ion**) nm officer, official
swyddogaeth nf office, function
swyddogol adj official
swyn (**-ion**) nm charm, fascination, spell, magic
swyngyfaredd (**-ion**) nf sorcery, witchcraft
swyngyfareddwr (**-wyr**) nm sorcerer
swyno vb charm, enchant, bewitch
swynol adj charming, fascinating
swynwr (**-wyr**) nm magician, wizard
swynwraig (**-wragedd**) nf sorceress
sy see sydd
syber adj sober, decent; clean, tidy
sych adj dry; f **sech**
sychder nm dryness, drought
sychdir (**-oedd**) nm dry land
syched nm thirst
sychedig adj thirsty, parched, dry
sychedu vb thirst
sychin nf drought
sychlyd adj dry
sychu vb dry, dry up; wipe dry, wipe
sychydd nm dryer
sydyn adj sudden, abrupt
sydynrwydd nm suddenness

sydd *vb* is, are
syfi *npl* (**syfien** *nf*) strawberries
syflyd *vb* stir, move, budge
syfrdan *adj* giddy, dazed, stunned
syfrdandod *nm* giddiness, stupor
syfrdanol *adj* stunning
syfrdanu *vb* daze, bewilder, stupefy, stun
sylfaen (-**feini**) *nf* foundation
sylfaenol *adj* basic
sylfaenu *vb* found
sylfaenwr (-**wyr**), -**ydd** (-**ion**) *nm* founder
sylw (-**adau**) *nm* notice, attention, remark
sylwadaeth *nf* observation
sylwebaeth *nf* commentary
sylwedydd (-**ion**) *nm* observer
sylwedd (-**au**) *nm* substance, reality
sylweddol *adj* substantial, real
sylweddoli *vb* realize
sylweddoliad *nm* realization
sylwi *vb* observe, regard, notice
syllu *vb* gaze
symbal (-**au**) *nm* cymbal
symbol *nm* symbol
symboliaeth *nf* symbolism
symbyliad *nm* stimulus, encouragement
symbylu *vb* goad, spur, stimulate
symbylydd (-**ion**) *nm* stimulant
symio *vb* sum
syml *adj* simple; *f* **seml**
symledd *nm* simplicity
symleiddiad *nm* simplification
symleiddio *vb* simplify
symlrwydd *nm* simplicity
symol *adj* middling, fair
symud *vb* move, remove
symudiad (-**au**) *nm* movement, removal
symudol *adj* moving, movable, mobile
syn *adj* amazed; astonishing, surprising
synagog (-**au**) *nm* synagogue

synamon *nm* cinnamon
syndod *nm* marvel, amazement, surprise
synfyfyrdod *nm* reverie
synfyfyrio *vb* muse
synhwyro *vb* sense
synhwyrol *adj* sensible
syniad (-**au**) *nm* notion, idea, view
syniadaeth *nf* conception
synied, -**io** *vb* think, believe, feel
synnu *vb* marvel, be amazed, surprise, be surprised
synnwyr (**synhwyrau**) *nm* sense
synwyroldeb *nm* sensibleness
synwyrusrwydd *nm* sensuousness
sypio *vb* pack, heap, bundle
sypyn (-**nau**) *nm* package, packet
syr *nm* sir
syrcas *nf* circus
syrffed *nm* surfeit
syrffedu *vb* surfeit
Syria *nf* Syria
syrthiedig *adj* fallen
syrthio *vb* fall, tumble
syrthni *nm* listlessness, sloth; inertia
system *nmf* system
systematig *adj* systematic
syth *adj* stiff; straight
sythu *vb* stiffen, straighten; starve with cold
sythelediad *nm* intuition

T

tabernacl (-**au**) *nm* tabernacle
tabl (-**au**) *nm* table
tablen *nf* ale, beer
tabŵ *nm* taboo
tabwrdd (-**yrddau**) *nm* drum
tabyrddu *vb* drum, thrum
taclau *npl* (**teclyn** *nm*) tackle, gear
taclo *vb* tackle
taclu *vb* put in order, trim
taclus *adj* neat, trim, tidy
tacluso *vb* trim, tidy

taclusrwydd nm tidiness

Tachwedd nm November

tacteg (-au) nf tactic

tad (-au) nm father. **tad-cu** grandfather

tadmaeth (-au, -od) nm fosterfather

tadogaeth nf paternity; derivation

tadogi vb father

tadol adj fatherly, paternal

taenelliad nm sprinkling, affusion

taenellu vb sprinkle

taenellwr (-wyr) nm sprinkler

taenu vb spread, expand, stretch

taenwr (-wyr) nm spreader, disseminator

taeog adj churlish, blunt ♦ (-au, -ion) nm churl

taeogaidd adj churlish, rude

taer adj earnest, importunate, urgent

taerineb, taerni nm earnestness, importunity

taeru vb insist, maintain; contend, wrangle

tafarn (-au) nf/m tavern, inn, public-house

tafarndy (-dai) nm public-house

tafarnwr (-wyr) nm inn-keeper, publican

tafell (-au, -i, tefyll) nf slice

tafl (-au) nf cast; scale. **ffon d.** sling

tafledigion npl projectiles

taflegryn (taflegrau) nm missile

tafleisiaeth nf ventriloquism

tafleisydd (-ion, -wyr) nm ventriloquist

taflen (-nau, -ni) nf table, list, leaflet

taflennu vb tabulate

tafliad (-au) nm throw; set-back

taflod (-ydd) nf loft. **t. y genau** palate

taflodol adj palatal

taflu vb throw, fling, cast, hurl

tafluniad nm projection

taflunio vb project

taflunydd nm projector

tafod (-au) nm tongue

tafodi vb berate, scold

tafodiaith (-ieithoedd) nf speech, language, dialect

tafod-leferydd nm speech, utterance, **ar d.** by rote

tafol nf scales, balance

tafol coll n dock

tafoli vb weigh up, assess

tafotrwg adj foul-mouthed, abusive

tafotrydd adj garrulous, flippant

tagell (-au, tegyll) nf gill; wattle; dewlap; double chin

tagellog adj wattled; doublechinned

tagfa (-feydd) nf choking, strangling

tagu vb choke, stifle; strangle

tangnefedd nm/f peace

tangnefeddu vb make peace; appease

tangnefeddus adj peaceable, peaceful

tangnefeddwr (-wyr) nm peacemaker

tai see **tŷ**

taid (teidiau) nm grandfather

tail nm dung, manure

tair adj f. of **tri**

taith (teithiau) nf journey, voyage, progress

tal adj tall, high, lofty

tâl (talau, taloedd) nm end, forehead

tâl (taliadau) nm pay, payment. **taloedd** rates

talaith (-eithiau) nf diadem; province, state

talar (-au) nf headland in field

talcen (-nau, -ni) nm forehead; gable

taldra nm tallness, loftiness, stature

taleb (-au, -ion) nf receipt, voucher

taledigaeth nf payment,

recompense

taleithiol *adj* provincial

talent (-au) *nf* talent

talentog *adj* talented

talfyriad (-au) *nm* abbreviation, abridgement

talfyrru *vb* abbreviate, abridge

talgryf *adj* sturdy, robust; impudent

taliad (-au) *nm* payment

talm *nm* space, while; quantity, number. **er ys t.** long ago

talog *adj* jaunty

talp (-au, -iau) *nm* mass, lump

talpiog *adj* lumpy

talu *vb* pay, render; answer, suit; be worth

talwr (-wyr) *nm* payer

talwrn *nm* threshing floor; poetic contest

tamaid (-eidiau) *nm* morsel, bit, bite

tan *prep* to, till, until, as far; under

tân (tanau) *nm* fire

tanbaid *adj* fiery, hot, fervent; brilliant

tanbeidrwydd *nm* fierce heat, ardour

tanchwa (-oedd) *nf* fire-damp, explosion

tanddaearol *adj* underground, subterranean

tanforol *adj* submarine

taniad *nm* ignition, firing

tanio *vb* fire, stoke

taniwr (-wyr) *nm* firer, fireman, stoker

tanlinellu *vb* underline

tanlwybr *nm* subway

tanlli *adj*: **newydd sbon danlli** brand new

tanllwyth (-i) *nm* blazing fire

tanllyd *adj* fiery

tannu *vb* adjust, spread, make (bed)

tanodd *adv* below, beneath

tant (tannau) *nm* chord, string

tanwent *nm* fuel

tanwydd *coll n* firewood, fuel

tanysgrifiad (-au) *nm* subscription

tanysgrifio *vb* subscribe

tanysgrifiwr (-wyr) *nm* subscriber

taradr (terydr) *nf* auger. **t. y coed** woodpecker

taran (-au) *nf* (peal of) thunder

taranfollt (-au) *nf* thunderbolt

taranu *vb* thunder

tarddell *nf* source, spring

tarddiad (-au) *nm* source, derivation

tarddle (-oedd) *nm* source

tarddu *vb* sprout, spring; derive, be derived

tarfu *vb* scare, scatter

targed (-au) *nm* target

tarian (-au) *nf* shield

tario *vb* tarry

taro *vb* strike, smite, hit, knock; tap; stick; hot; suit

tarren (tarenni, -ydd) *nf* knoll, rock

tarth (-oedd) *nm* mist, vapour

tarw (teirw) *nm* bull

tarwden *nf* ringworm

tas (teisi) *nf* rick, stack

tasel *nm* tassel

tasg (-au) *nf* task

tasgu *vb* task; start, jump; splash, spirt

tato, tatws *npl* (taten, tatysen *nf*) potatoes

taw *nm* silence. **rhoi t. ar** silence

taw *conj* that

tawch *nm* vapour, haze, mist, fog

tawdd *adj* melted, molten, dissolved

tawedog *adj* silent, taciturn

tawedogrwydd *nm* taciturnity

tawel *adj* calm, quiet, still, tranquil

tawelu *vb* calm; grow calm

tawelwch *nm* calm, quiet, tranquillity

tawelydd *nm* silencer

tawlbwrdd *nm* draughtboard, backgammon
tawtologiaeth *nf* tautology
te *nm* tea
tebot (-au) *nm* teapot
tebyg *adj* similar, like, likely
tebygol *adj* likely, probable
tebygolrwydd *nm* likelihood, probability
tebygrwydd *nm* likeness, resemblance
tebygu *vb* liken, resemble; suppose
tecáu *vb* beautify, adorn, embellish
teclyn (**taclau**) *nm* tool, instrument
techneg *nf* technique ♦ **-ol** *adj* technical
teg *adj* fair, beautiful, fine
tegan (-au) *nm* plaything, toy, bauble
tegell (-au, -i) *nm* kettle, teakettle
tegwch *nm* fairness, beauty
tei *nm/f* tie
teiar *nm* tyre
teigr (-od) *nm* tiger
teilchion *npl* fragments, atoms, shivers
teiliwr (-**eilwriaid**) *nm* tailor
teilo *vb* dung, manure
teilwng *adj* worthy; deserved
teilwra *vb* tailor
teilwres (-au) *nf* tailoress
teilwriaeth *nf* tailoring
teilyngdod *nm* worthiness, merit
teilyngu *vb* deserve, merit; deign
teim *nm* thyme
teimlad (-au) *nm* feel, feeling, sensation, emotion ♦ **-ol** *adj* emotional
teimladrwydd *nm* feelingness, sensibility
teimladwy *adj* feeling; sensitive
teimlo *vb* feel, touch, handle, manipulate
teimlydd (-ion) *nm* feeler, antenna, tentacle
teios *npl* cottages

teip (-iau) *nm* type
teipiadur (-ion) *nm* typewriter
teipio *vb* type
teipydd (-ion) *nm* typist
teisen (-nau) *nf* cake
teitl (-au) *nm* title
teithi *coll n* traits, characteristics, qualities
teithio *vb* travel, journey
teithiol *adj* travelling, itinerant
teithiwr (-**wyr**) *nm* traveller, passenger
telathrebiaeth *nf* telecommunication
teledu *nm* television ♦ *vb* televise
teleffon (-au) *nm* telephone
teler (-au) *nm* term, condition
teligraff *nm* telegraph
telm (-au) *nf* snare
telori *vb* warble; quaver
telyn (-au) *nf* harp
telyneg (-ion) *nf* lyric
telynegol *adj* lyrical
telynegwr *nm* lyric poet
telynor (-ion) *nm* harpist
telynores (-au) *nf* female harpist
teml (-au) *nf* temple
tempro *vb* temper
temtasiwn (-**iynau**) *nm/f* temptation
temtio *vb* tempt
temtiwr (-**wyr**) *nm* tempter
tenant (-iaid) *nm* tenant
tenantiaeth *nf* tenancy
tenau *adj* thin, lean; slender; rarified; sensitive
tendio *vb* tend, mind
teneuad *nm* dilution
teneuo *vb* thin, become thin, dilute
teneuwch *nm* thinness, leanness, tenuity
tenewyn (-nau) *nm* flank
tenis *nm* tennis
tenlli(f) *nm* lining
tennyn (**tenynnau**) *nm* cord, rope, halter
têr *adj* clear, refined, pure, fine

teras (-au) *nm* terrace
terfyn (-au) *nm* end, extremity, bound
terfyniad (-au) *nm* ending, termination
terfynol *adj* final; conclusive
terfynu *vb* end, terminate, determine
terfysg (-oedd) *nm* tumult, riot
terfysgaeth *nf* terrorism
terfysgaidd, -lyd *adj* riotous, turbulent
terfysgu *vb* riot, rage, surge
terfysgwr (-wyr) *nm* rioter, insurgent
term (-au) *nm* term
terminoleg *nf* terminology
tes *nm* sunshine, warmth, heat; haze
tesog *adj* sunny, hot, close, sultry
testament (-au) *nm* testament
testamentwr (-wyr) *nm* testator
testun (-au) *nm* text, theme, subject
testunio *vb* taunt, deride
tetanws *nm* tetanus
teth (-au) *nf* teat
teulu (-oedd) *nm* family
teuluaidd *adj* family, domestic
tew *adj* thick, fat, plump
tewdra, -dwr *nf* thickness, fatness
tewhau *vb* thicken, fatten
tewi *vb* keep silence, be silent
tewychu *vb* thicken, fatten; condense
tewychydd *nm* condenser
tewyn (-ion) *nm* ember, brand
teyrn (-edd, -oedd) *nm* monarch, sovereign
teyrnas (-oedd) *nf* kingdom, realm. **y Deyrnas Gyfunol** the United Kingdom
teyrnasiad (-au) *nm* reign
teyrnasu *vb* reign
teyrnfradwr (-wyr) *nm* traitor
teyrnfradwriaeth *nf* (high)

treason
teyrngar *adj* loyal
teyrngarwch *nm* loyalty
teyrnged (-au) *nf* tribute
teyrnwialen (-wiail) *nf* sceptre
ti *pron* you (*fam*)
ticed (-i) *nm/f* ticket
tician *vb* tick
tid (-au) *nf* chain
tila *adj* feeble, puny, insignificant
tim (timau) *nm* team
tin (-au) *nf* bottom; rump; tail
tinc (-iadau) *nm* clang, tinkle
tincian *vb* tinkle, chink, clink, clank
tip (-iadau) *nm* tick (of clock)
tipian *vb* tick
tipyn (-nau, tipiau) *nm* bit
tir (-oedd) *nm* land, ground, territory
tirio *vb* land, ground
tiriog *adj* landed
tiriogaeth (-au) *nf* territory
tiriogaethol *adj* territorial
tirion *adj* kind, tender, gentle, gracious
tiriondeb *nm* kindness, tenderness
tirlun (-iau) *nm* landscape
tirol *adj* relating to land
tirwedd *nf* relief (GEOG)
tisian *vb* sneeze
titw *nf* puss, pussy
tithau *pron conj* thou (on thy part), thou also
tiwmor *nm* tumour
tiwn (-iau) *nf* tune
tiwnio *vb* tune
tlawd (tlodion) *adj* poor
tlodaidd *adj* poorish, mean, dowdy
tlodi *vb* impoverish ♦ *nm* poverty
tlos *adj* f. of **tlws**
tloty (-ai) *nm* poorhouse, workhouse
tlotyn (tlodion) *nm* pauper
tlws *adj* pretty; *f* **tlos**
tlws (tlysau) *nm* jewel, gem; medal

tlysni nm prettiness

to (**toeau**) nm roof; generation

toc adv shortly, presently, soon

tocio vb clip, dock, prune

tocyn (**tociau**) nm pack, heap, hillock; slice of bread

tocyn (**-nau**) nm ticket

tocynnwr (**-ynwyr**) nm bus conductor

toddedig adj molten; melting

toddi vb melt, dissolve, thaw

toddiant (**-nnau**) nm solution

toddion npl dripping

toddwr (**-wyr**) **-ydd** (**-ion**) nm melter

toes nm dough

toi vb cover; roof; thatch

toili nm spectral funeral

tolach vb fondle

tolc (**-iau**) nm dent, dinge

tolchen (**-au**) nf clot

tolchennu vb clot

tolcio vb dent, dinge

tolciog adj dented, dinged

toll (**-au**) nf toll, custom

tolli vb take toll

tom nf dirt, mire, dung

tomen (**-nydd**) nf heap; dunghill

tomlyd adj dirty, miry

ton (**-nau**) nf wave, billow, breaker

ton (**-nau**) nm lay-land

tôn (**tonau**) nf tone; tune

tonc (**-iau**) nf tinkle, ring, clash

toncio, -ian vb tinkle, ring

tonfedd (**-i**) nf wavelength

tonig (**-iau**) adj tonic (MED) tonic (MUSIC)

tonnen (**tonennydd, -au**) nf skin; sward; bog

tonni vb wave, undulate

tonnog adj wavy, billowy

tonyddiaeth nf tone, intonation

topio vb plug, stop up

topyn nm plug, stopper

tor (**-ion**) nm break, interruption

tor (**-rau**) nf belly; palm (of hand)

torcalonnus adj heartbreaking

torch (**-au**) nf wreath; coil

torchi vb wreathe; coil; roll, tuck

torchog adj wreathed; coiled

tordyn adj tight-bellied; hectoring

toreithiog adj abundant, teeming

toreth nf abundance

torf (**-eydd**) nf crowd, multitude

torfynyglu vb break neck of; behead

torgoch (**-ion**) nm roach

torgwmwl nm cloudburst

torheulo vb bask, sunbathe

tori (**-iaid**) nm tory

toriad (**-au**) nm cut, break; fraction

toriaeth nf toryism

toriaidd adj tory, conservative

torlan (**-nau, -lennydd**) nf river bank

torllengig nm rupture

torllwyth (**-i**), **torraid** nf litter

torogen (**-ogod**) nf tick (in cattle)

torri vb break, cut; dig; write, trace

torrwr (**torwyr**) nm breaker, cutter

tors nmf torch

torsyth adj swaggering

torsythu vb strut, swagger

torth (**-au**) nf loaf

tost adj severe, sharp, sore; ill

tost nm toast

tosturi (**-aethau**) nm compassion, pity

tosturio vb be compassionate, pity

tosturiol adj compassionate

tosyn (**tosau**) nm pimple

tôwr (**towyr**) nm tiler

tra adv over; very ♦ conj while, whilst

tra-arglwyddiaeth (**-au**) nf tyranny

tra-arglwyddiaethu vb tyrannize

tra-awdurdodi vb lord it over, domineer

trabludd nm trouble, tumult, turmoil

trac (**-iau**) nm track

trachefn *adv* again
trachwant (-au) *nm* lust, covetousness
trachwanta, -tu *vb* lust, covet
trachwantus *adj* covetous
tradwy *adv* three days hence
traddodi *vb* deliver; commit
traddodiad (-au) *nm* tradition; delivery
traddodiadol *adj* traditional
traddodwr (-wyr) *nm* deliverer
traean *nm* one third, the third part
traed *see* **troed**
traeth (-au) *nm* strand, shore, beach
traethawd (-odau) *nm* treatise, essay; tract
traethell (-au) *nf* strand, sandbank
traethiad (-au) *nm* predicate
traethodydd (-ion) *nm* essayist
traethu *vb* utter, declare; treat
trafael (-ion) *nf* travail, trouble
trafaelio *vb* travel
trafaeliwr (-wyr) *nm* traveller
trafaelu *vb* travel; travail
traflyncu *vb* guzzle, gulp, devour
trafnidiaeth *nf* traffic
trafod *vb* handle; discuss; transact
trafodaeth (-au) *nf* discussion, transaction
trafodion *npl* transactions
trafferth (-ion) *nf/m* trouble
trafferthu *vb* trouble
trafferthus *adj* troublesome; troubled
tragwyddol *adj* everlasting, eternal
tragwyddoldeb *nm* eternity
tragwydd *adj* everlasting, eternal
traha *nm* arrogance, presumption
trahaus *adj* arrogant, haughty
trahauster *nm* arrogance, presumption
trai *nm* ebb
trais *nm* oppression, force, violence
trallod (-ion, -au) *nm* trouble, tribulation

trallodi *vb* afflict, vex, trouble
trallodus *adj* troubled; troublous
trallodwr (-wyr) *nm* troubler, afflicter
tramgwydd (-iadau) *nm* stumbling; offence
tramgwyddo *vb* stumble; offend; take offence
tramgwyddus *adj* scandalous; offensive
tramor *adj* foreign
tramorwr (-wyr) *nm* foreigner
tramwy, -o *vb* pass, traverse
tramwyfa (-feydd) *nf* passage, thoroughfare
tranc *nm* end, dissolution, death
trancedig *adj* deceased
trancedigaeth *nf* death, decease
trannoeth *adv* next day ♦ *nm* the morrow
trapio *vb* trap
traphlith *adv:* **blith d.** higgledy-piggledy
tras *nf* kindred, affinity
traserch *nm* great love, infatuation
trasiedi (trasiediau) *nf* tragedy
traul (treuliau) *nf* wear; cost, expense; digestion
trawiad (-au) *nm* stroke, beat, flash
trawiadol *adj* striking
traws *adj* cross; froward, perverse
trawsblannu *vb* transplant
trawsdoriad *nm* cross-section
trawsenwad *nm* metonymy
trawsfeddiannu *vb* usurp
trawsfudo *vb* transmigrate
trawsffurfio *vb* transform
trawsgludo *vb* transport, conduct
trawsgyweiriad *nm* transposition, modulation
trawsgyweirio *vb* transpose, change key
trawslif *nm* cross-saw
trawslythrennu *vb* transliterate
traws-sylweddiad *nm* transubstantiation

trawst (-iau) nm beam

trebl nm, adj treble

treblu vb treble

trech adj superior, stronger, mightier

trechu vb overpower, overcome, conquer

tref (-i, -ydd) nf home; town

trefedigaeth (-au) nf settlement, colony

trefgordd (-au) nf township

treflan (-nau) nf small town, townlet

trefn (-au) nf order, method, system

trefniad (-au) nm arrangement, ordering

trefniant nm arrangement, organization

trefnlen (-ni) nf schedule

trefnu vb order, arrange, dispose

trefnus adj orderly, methodical

trefnusrwydd nm orderliness

trefnydd (-ion) nm arranger; Methodist

trefol adj town, urban

treftadaeth nf patrimony, inheritance

trengi vb die, perish, expire

treial (-on) nm trial

treiddgar adj penetrating, keen

treiddgarwch nm penetration, acumen

treiddio vb pass, penetrate

treiddiol adj penetrating

treigl (-au) nm turn, revolution, course

treigl(i)ad (-au) nm mutation; inflection

treiglo vb roll; mutate; inflect; decline

treio vb ebb

treio vb try

treisiad (-iedi) nf heifer

treisio vb force, ravish, violate, oppress, rape

treisiwr (-wyr) nm violator,

oppressor; rapist

trem (-iau) nf sight, look, aspect

tremio vb look, gaze

trên (trenau) nm train

trennydd adv day after tomorrow

tres (-i) nf trace, chain; tress

tresbasu, tresmasu vb trespass

tresglen nf thrush

treth (-i) nf rate, tax, tribute. **t. y pen** community charge, poll tax

trethadwy adj rateable, taxable

trethdalwr (-wyr) nm ratepayer

trethu vb tax, rate, assess

trethwr (-wyr) nm taxer

treuliad nm digestion

treulio vb wear, consume; spend; digest

tri adj, nm three; f **tair**

triagl nm treacle, balsam, balm

triawd (-au) nm trio

triban (-nau) nm triplet (metre); Plaid Cymru badge

tribiwnlys (-oedd) nm tribunal

tric (-iau) nm trick

tridiau npl three days

trigain adj, nm sixty

trigfa (-feydd), **-fan** (-nau) nf dwelling-place, abode

trigiannol adj residentiary

trigiannu vb reside, dwell

trigiannydd (-ianwyr) nm resident

trigo vb stay, abide; dwell; die (animals)

trigolion npl inhabitants, dwellers

trimio vb trim

trin (-oedd) nf battle

trin vb handle; treat; dress; till; transact

trindod (-au) nf trinity

tringar adj skilful, tender

triniaeth (-au) nf treatment

trioedd npl triads

triongl (-au) nmlf triangle

trionglog adj triangular

trist adj sad, sorrowful

tristáu vb sadden, grieve

tristwch nm sadness, sorrow

triw adj loyal, faithful

tro (**troeau, troeon**) nm turn, twist; conversion

troad (**-au**) nm bend, turning; figure of speech

trobwll (**-byllau**) nm whirlpool

trobwynt (**-iau**) nm turning-point

trochfa (**-feydd**) nf plunge, immersion

trochi vb dip, plunge, immerse; soil

trochion npl lather, suds, foam

trochioni vb lather, foam

trochwr (**-wyr**) nm immerser, immersionist

troed (**traed**) nm/f foot, base; leg; handle

troedfainc (**-feinciau**) nf footstool

troedfedd (**-i**) nf foot (=12 inches)

troëdig adj turned, converted, perverse

troëdigaeth (**-au**) nf turning, conversion

troedio vb foot, tread, trudge

troednodyn nm footnote

troednoeth adj barefoot, barefooted

troedwst nf gout

troell (**-au**) nf wheel, spinning-wheel

troelli vb spin; twist, wind

troellog adj winding, tortuous

troellwr (**-wyr**) nm disc-jockey

troetffordd (**-ffyrdd**) nf footway, footpath

trofa (**-feydd**) nf turn; bend, turning

trofan (**-nau**) nf tropic

trofannol adj tropical

trofaus adj perverse

trofwrdd (**-fyrddau**) nm turntable

trogen see **torogen**

trogylch (**-au**) nm orbit

troi vb turn, revolve; convert; plough

trol (**-iau**) nf cart

trolian, -io vb roll

troliwr (**-wyr**) nm carter

trom adj f. of **trwm**

tros prep over, for, instead of, on behalf of

trosedd (**-au**) nm transgression, offence, crime

troseddol adj criminal

troseddu vb transgress, trespass, offend

troseddwr (**-wyr**) nm transgressor, trespasser, offender; criminal

trosgais (**trosgeisiau**) nm converted try

trosglwyddiad nm transference, transfer

trosglwyddo vb hand over, transfer

trosgynnol adj transcendental

trosi vb turn; translate; convert (a try)

trosiad (**-au**) nm translation; metaphor; conversion (rugby)

trosodd adv over, beyond

trosol (**-ion**) nm lever, crow-bar, bar; staff

trostan (**-au**) nf pole

trotian vb trot

trothwy (**-au**) nm threshold

trowr (**-wyr**) nm ploughman

trowsus (**-au**) nm trousers

trowynt (**-oedd**) nm whirlwind, tornado

truan (**truain**) adj poor, wretched, miserable ♦ (**trueiniaid**) nm wretch; f **truanes**

trueni nm wretchedness; misery; pity

truenus adj wretched, miserable

trugaredd (**-au**) nf/m mercy, compassion

trugarhau vb have mercy, take pity

trugarog adj merciful, compassionate

trugarowgrwydd nm mercifulness

trulliad (**-iaid**) nm butler, cupbearer

trum (-au, -iau) nm ridge

truth nm flattery; rigmarole

trwbl nm, -o vb trouble

trwch nm thickness. **t. y blewyn** hair's breadth

trwch adj broken; unfortunate; wicked

trwchus adj thick

trwm (trymion) adj heavy; f **trom**

trwnc (trynciau) nm trunk

trwodd adv through

trwsgl adj awkward, clumsy, bungling

trwsiad nm dress, attire

trwsiadus adj well-dressed, smart

trwsio vb dress, trim; mend, repair

trwsiwr (-wyr) nm mender, repairer

trwst nm noise, din, tumult

trwstan adj awkward, clumsy, untoward

trwstaneiddiwch nm awkwardness

trwy prep through, by, by means of

trwyadl adj thorough

trwydded (-au) nf leave, licence

trwyddedu vb license

trwyn (-au) nm nose, snout; point, cape

trwyno vb nose, nuzzle, sniff

trwynol adj nasal

trwynsur adj sour, morose

trwyth (-i) nm decoction, infusion, urine

trwytho vb steep, saturate, imbue

trybedd, trybed nf tripod, trivet

trybelid adj bright, brilliant

trybestod nm commotion, bustle, fuss

trybini nm trouble, misfortune, misery

tryblith nm muddle, chaos

trychfil (-od) nm insect, animalcule

trychiad (-au) nm cutting, fracture, section

trychineb (-au) nm/f disaster, calamity

trychinebus adj disastrous, calamitous

trychu vb cut, hew, pierce, lop

trydan nm electric fluid, electricity

trydaneg nm/f electrical engineering

trydaniaeth nf electricity; thrill

trydanol adj electric, electrical

trydanu vb electrify

trydar nm, vb chirp, chatter

trydydd adj third; f **trydedd**

tryfer (-i) nf harpoon, trident

tryferu vb spear, harpoon

tryfesur nm diameter

tryfrith adj speckled; swarming, teeming

trylediad (-au) nm diffusion

tryledu vb diffuse

tryloyw adj pellucid, transparent

tryloywder nm transparency

trylwyr adj thorough

trylwyredd nm thoroughness

trymaidd adj heavy, close, oppressive

trymder nm heaviness, drowsiness

trymfryd nm sadness, sorrow

trymhau vb make or grow heavy

trymllyd adj heavy, close, oppressive

tryryw adj thoroughbred

trysor (-au) nm treasure

trysordy (-dai) nm treasurehouse

trysorfa (-feydd) nf treasury, fund

trysori vb treasure

trysorlys nm treasury, exchequer

trysorydd (-ion) nm treasurer

trystio vb make a noise; trust

trystiog adj noisy, rowdy

trythyll adj wanton, lascivious

trythyllwch nm lasciviousness

trywanu vb transfix, stab, pierce

trywel nm trowel

trywydd nm scent, trail

Tseina nf China

Tsiecoslofacia nf Czechoslovakia

tu nm side, part, direction

tua, tuag prep towards; about

tuchan vb grumble, groan, murmur

tudalen (-nau) nmf page

tudded (-i) nf covering; pillowcase

tuedd (-iadau) nf tendency, inclination

tuedd (-au) nm district, region

tueddfryd nm inclination, bent

tueddol adj inclined, apt

tueddu vb incline, tend, trend

tufewnol adj inward, internal

tulath (-au) nf beam, rafter

Tunisia nf Tunisia

tunnell (tunelli) nf ton; tun

turio vb root up, burrow, delve

turn nm lathe

turniwr (-wyr) nm turner

turtur (-od) nf turtle-dove

tusw (-au) nm wisp, bunch

tuth (-iau) nm trot

tuthio vb trot

twb (tybiau) nm tub

twca nm tuck-knife

twffyn (twffiau) nm tuft

twlc (tylciau) nm sty

twlcio vb horn, butt, gore

twlciog adj given to horning

twll (tyllau) nm hole

twmpath (-au) nm tump, hillock; bush; folk-dance

twndis (-au) nm funnel

twndra (-âu) nm tundra

twnffed (-i) nm funnel

twnnel (twnelau) nm tunnel

twp adj stupid, dull, obtuse

twpdra nm stupidity

twpsyn nm stupid person

twr (tyrau) nm tower

twr (tyrrau) nm heap; group, crowd

Twrc (Tyrciaid) nm Turk

Twrci nf Turkey

twrci (-iod) nm turkey

twrch (tyrchod) nm hog. **t. daear** mole

twrf (tyrfau) nm noise; (pl.) thunder

twrnai (-eiod) nm attorney, lawyer

twrw nm noise (**twrf**)

twt excl tut!

twt adj tidy, neat, smart

twtio vb tidy

twyll nm deceit, deception, fraud

twyllo vb deceive, cheat, swindle

twyllodrus adj deceitful, false

twyllresymeg nf sophism

twyllresymiad (-au) nm sophistry

twyllwr (-wyr) nm deceiver

twym adj warm, hot, sultry

twymder, twymdra nm warmness, warmth

twymgalon adj warm-hearted

twymo, twymno vb warm, heat

twymyn (-au) nf fever. **y dwymyn goch** scarlet fever. **y dwymyn doben** mumps

twyn (-i) nm hill, hillock, knoll; bush

twysged nf lot, quantity

tŷ (tai, teiau) nm house

tyaid (-eidiau) nm houseful

tyb (-iau) nmf opinion, notion, surmise

tybaco nm tobacco

tybed adv I wonder; is that so?

tybiaeth (-au) nf supposition

tybied, tybio vb suppose, think, imagine

tybiedig adj supposed, putative

tycio vb prosper, succeed, avail

tydi pron thou, thyself

tyddyn (-nod) nm (small) farm, holding

tyddynnwr (-ynwyr) nm smallholder

tyfadwy adj growing

tyfiant nm growth

tyfu vb grow

tyfwr (-wyr) nm grower

tynged nf destiny, fate

tyngedfennol *adj* fateful, fatal
tynghedu *vb* destine, fate; adjure
tyngu *vb* swear, vow
tyngwr (-wyr) *nm* swearer
tylath see **tulath**
tyle *nm* slope, hill
tylino *vb* knead. **t. y corff** massage
tylinwr (-wyr) *nm* kneader, masseur
tylwyth (-au) *nm* household, family. **t. teg** fairies
tyllog *adj* holey
tyllu *vb* hole, bore, perforate, pierce
tylluan (-od) *nf* owl
tyllwr (-wyr) *nm* borer
tymer (-herau) *nf* temper
tymestl (-hestloedd) *nf* tempest, storm
tymheredd *nm* temperature
tymherus *adj* temperate
tymhestlog *adj* tempestuous, stormy
tymhoraidd *adj* seasonable
tymhorol *adj* temporal
tymor (-horau) *nm* season
tymp *nm* (appointed) time, season
tympan (-au) *nf* drum; timbrel
tyn *adj* tight
tynder, -dra *nm* tightness, tension
tyndro (tyndroeon) *nm* wrench
tyner *adj* tender, gentle
tyneru *vb* make tender, soften
tynerwch *nm* tenderness, gentleness
tynfa (-feydd) *nf* draw, attraction
tynfaen (-feini) *nm* loadstone, magnet
tynhau *vb* tighten, strain
tynnu *vb* draw, pull; take off, remove
tyno *nm* hollow; tenon
tyrchu *vb* root up, burrow
tyrchwr (-wyr) *nm* mole-catcher
tyrfa (-oedd) *nf* multitude, host, crowd
tyrfau *npl* thunder

tyrfedd (-au) *nm* turbulence, thunder
tyrfo, tyrfu *vb* make a noise or commotion
tyrpant *nm* turpentine
tyrpeg *nm* turnpike
tyrru *vb* heap, amass; crowd together
tyst (-ion) *nm* witness
tysteb (-au) *nf* testimonial
tystio *vb* testify, witness
tystiolaeth (-au) *nf* testimony, evidence
tystiolaethu *vb* bear witness, testify
tystlythyr (-au) *nm* testimonial
tystysgrif (-au) *nf* certificate
tywallt *vb* pour, shed, spill
tywalltiad *nm* outpouring
tywarchen (tywyrch) *nf* sod, turf
tywel (-ion) *nm* towel
tywod *nm* sand
tywodfaen *nm* sandstone
tywodlyd, -odog *adj* sandy
tywodyn *nm* grain of sand
tywydd *nm* weather
tywyll *adj* dark, obscure; blind
tywyllu *vb* darken, obscure
tywyllwch *nm* darkness
tywyn (-au) *nm* sea-shore, strand
tywynnu *vb* shine
tywys *vb* lead, guide
tywysen (-nau, tywys) *nf* ear of corn
tywysog (-ion) *nm* prince
tywysogaeth (-au) *nf* principality
tywysogaidd *adj* princely
tywysoges (-au) *nf* princess
tywysydd (-ion) *nm* leader, guide

TH

theatr (-au) *nf* theatre
thema (themâu) *nf* theme
theorem (-au) *nf* theorem
theori (-iau) *nf* theory

thermomedr *nm* thermometer
thesis (-au) *nm* thesis
thus *nm* frankincense

U

ubain *vb* howl, wail, moan; sob
uchaf *adj* uppermost, highest
uchafbwynt (-iau) *nm* climax; zenith
uchafiaeth *nf* supremacy; ascendancy
uchafion *npl* heights
uchafrif (-au) *nm* maximum
uchder *nm* height; top
uchel *adj* high, lofty; uppish; loud
uchelder (-au) *nm* highness, height
ucheldir (-oedd) *nm* highland
uchelfryd *adj* high-minded
uchelgais *nmf* ambition
uchelgeisiol *adj* ambitious
uchelion *npl* heights
uchelradd *adj* of high degree, superior
uchelseinydd (-ion) *nm* loudspeaker
uchelwr (-wyr) *nm* gentleman, nobleman
uchelwydd *coll n* mistletoe
uchgapten (-teiniaid) *nm* major
uchod *adv* above
udo *vb* howl
udd *nm* lord
ufudd *adj* obedient, humble
ufudd-dod *nm* obedience, humility
ufuddhau *vb* obey
uffern *nf* hell
uffernol *adj* infernal, hellish
ugain (ugeiniau) *adj, nm* twenty, score
Ulster *nf* Ulster
ulw *coll n* ashes, powder ♦ *adv* utterly
un *adj* one, only; same ♦ (-au) *coll n* one, unit
unawd (-au) *nm/f* solo

unawdydd (-wyr) *nm* soloist
unben (-iaid, unbyn) *nm* sovereign lord, despot
unbenaethol *adj* despotic
unbenaeth *nf* sovereignty, despotism
undeb (-au) *nm* unity, union. **yr U. Sofietaidd** the Soviet Union
undebaeth *nf* unionism
undebol *adj* united, union
undebwr (-wyr) *nm* unionist
undod (-au) *nm* unity; unit
Undodaidd *adj* Unitarian
Undodiaeth *nf* Unitarianism
Undodwr (-wyr, -iaid) *nm* Unitarian
undoned *nm* monotony
undonog *adj* monotonous
uned (-au) *nf* unit
unfan *nm* same place
unfarn *adj* unanimous
unfryd, -ol *adj* unanimous
unfrydedd *nm* unanimity
unffurf *adj* uniform
unffurfiaeth *nf* uniformity
ungell *adj* monocellular
uniaith *adj* monoglot
uniawn *adj* straight; right, upright; just
unig *adj* sole, only; alone, lonely
unigedd *nm* loneliness, solitude
unigol *adj* singular; individual ♦ (-ion) *nm* individual
unigoliaeth *nf*, **-rwydd** *nm* individuality
unigrwydd *nm* loneliness, solitude
union *adj* straight, direct; just, exact
uniondeb *nm* straightness; rectitude
uniongred *adj* orthodox
uniongrededd *nmf* orthodoxy
uniongyrch, -ol *adj* immediate, direct
unioni *vb* straighten; rectify; make for
unionsgwar *adj* perpendicular

unionsyth *adj* straight, direct; erect
unllygeidiog *adj* one-eyed
unman *adv* anywhere
unnos *adj* of one night
uno *vb* join, unit, amalgamate
unochrog *adj* unilateral, biased
unodl *adj* of the same rhyme
unol *adj* united. **yr U. Daleithiau** *npl* the United States
unoli *vb* unify
unoliaeth *nf* unity, oneness, identity
unplyg *adj* of one fold; folio; simple, ingenuous
unplygrwydd *nm* sincerity
unrhyw *adj* same; any
unrhywiol *adj* unisexual
unsain *adj* unison. **yn u.** in unison
unsill *adj* monosyllabic
unswydd *adj* of one purpose
unwaith *adv* once
unwedd *adj* like ♦ *adv* likewise
urdd (**-au**) *nf* order; rank
urddas (**-au**) *nf* dignity, honour
urddasol *adj* dignified, noble
urddo *vb* ordain, confer degree or rank
us *coll n* chaff
ust *excl*, *nm* hush
ustus (**-iaid**) *nm* justice, magistrate
usuriaeth *nf* usury
utganu *vb* sound a trumpet
utganwr (**-wyr**) *nm* trumpeter
utgorn (**-gyrn**) *nm* trumpet
uwch *adj* higher ♦ *prep* above, over
uwchbridd *nm* topsoil
uwchgapten (**-iaid**) *nm* major
uwchradd *nm*, *adj* superior
uwchsonig *adj* ultrasonic, supersonic
uwd *nm* porridge

W

wadi (**-iau**) *nm* wadi
wagen (**-ni**) *nf* truck, waggon
waldio *vb* wallop, beat
warws (**warysau**) *nm* warehouse
wats (**-iau**) *nm* watch
wedi *prep* after ♦ *adv* afterwards
wedyn *adv* afterwards, then
weiren *nf* wire
weir(i)o *vb* wire
weithian, **-ion** *adv* now, now at length
weithiau *adv* sometimes
wel *excl* well
wele *excl* behold, lo
wermod *nf* wormwood
wfft *excl* fie, for shame
wfftio *vb* cry fie, flout, scout
whado *vb* beat, thrash
wiced (**-i**) *nf* wicket
wicedwr (**-wyr**) *nm* wicket-keeper.
widw *nf* widow
Wien *nf* Vienna
wlser (**-au**) *nm* ulcer
wmbredd *nm* abundance
wraniwm *nm* uranium
wrth *prep* by; with; to; because, since
wy (**-au**) *nm* egg
wybr (**-au**), **wybren** (**-nau**, **-nydd**) *nf* sky; cloud
wybrol *adj* ethereal
wyf *vb* I am
wygell (**-oedd**) *nf* ovary
wylo *vb* weep, cry
wylofain *vb* wail, weep ♦ *nm* wailing
wylofus *adj* wailing, doleful, tearful
ŵyn see **oen**
wyna *vb* lamb
wyneb (**-au**) *nm* face, surface; front
wyneb-ddalen *nf* title-page

wynebgaled adj barefaced, impudent

wyneblun (-iau) nm frontispiece

wynebu vb face, front

wynepryd nm countenance

wynwyn npl onions

ŵyr (wyrion) n coll grandchild, grandson

wysg nm track. **yn w. ei gefn** backwards

wystrys npl, coll n oysters

wyth (-au) adj, nm eight

wythawd (-au, -odau) nf octave

wythblyg adj octavo

wythfed adj eighth

wythnos (-au) nf week

wythnosol (-ion) adj weekly

wythnosolyn (-olion) nm weekly paper

wythongl (-au) nf octagon

wythwr (-wyr) nm number eight (rugby)

Y

y, yr, 'r adj the

y, yr preverbal and relative particle

ych (-en) nm ox

ychwaith adv (nor) either, neither

ychwaneg nm more

ychwanegiad (-au) nm addition

ychwanegol adj additional

ychwanegu vb add, augment, increase

ychydig adj, adv, nm little, few

ŷd (ydau) nm corn

ydlan (-nau) nf stack-yard, rickyard

ydwyf vb I am

ydys vb: **yr ydys yn disgwyl** it is expected

ydyw vb is, are

yfed vb drink; absorb

yfory adv tomorrow

yfwr (-wyr) nm drinker

yfflon npl (yfflyn nm) shivers,

pieces, bits ♦ adj highly annoyed

yng prep in (mutation of **yn**)

yngan, -u vb utter, speak

ynghyd adv together

ynghylch prep about, concerning

ynglŷn â prep in connection with

ym prep in (mutation of **yn**)

ym- prefix (usu. reflexive or reciprocal)

yma adv here, in this place; this

ymadael, ymadaw vb depart

ymadawedig adj departed, deceased

ymadawiad nm departure; decease

ymadawol adj farewell, valedictory

ymado vb depart

ymadrodd (-ion) nm speech, saying, expression

ymadroddus adj eloquent

ymaddasu vb adjust, adapt

ymaelodi vb become a member, join

ymaelyd, ymafael, ymaflyd vb take hold

ymageru vb evaporate

ymagor vb open, unfold, expand

ymagweddiad (-au) nm demeanour, attitude

ymaith adv away, hence

ymarfer vb practise, exercise ♦ (-ion) nf practice, exercise

ymarferiad (-au) nm exercise

ymarhous adj dilatory; long-suffering, patient

ymaros vb bear with, endure ♦ nm long-suffering, patience

ymarweddiad nm conduct, behaviour

ymatal vb forbear, refrain, abstain

ymateb vb answer, respond, correspond

ymbalfalu vb grope

ymbaratoi vb get oneself ready

ymbarél nm umbrella

ymbelydredd nm radiation

ymbelydrol *adj* radioactive
ymbellhau *vb* go further away
ymbil (-iau) *vb* supplication, entreaty
ymbil, -io *vb* implore, beseech, entreat
ymboeni *vb* take pains
ymborth *nm* food, sustenance
ymbortheg *nf/m* dietetics
ymborthi *vb* feed
ymbriodi *vb* marry; intermarry
ymbwyllo *vb* pause, reflect
ymchwelyd *vb* turn, return; overturn
ymchwil *nf* search, research, quest
ymchwiliad (-au) *nm* investigation
ymchwydd (-iadau) *nm* swelling, surge
ymchwyddo *vb* swell; surge
ymdaith *vb* journey, march ♦ (-deithiau) *nf* journey, march
ymdebygu *vb* grow like; resemble
ymdeimlad *nm* feeling, sense
ymdeimlo *vb* feel; be conscious of
ymdeithio *vb* travel, journey; sojourn
ymdoddi *vb* melt, become dissolved
ymdopi *vb* manage
ymdrech (-ion) *nm/f* effort, endeavour, struggle
ymdrechgar *adj* striving, energetic
ymdrechu *vb* wrestle; strive, endeavour
ymdrin *vb* treat, deal with
ymdriniaeth *nf* treatment; discussion
ymdrochi *vb* bathe
ymdrochwr (-wyr) *nm* bather
ymdroi *vb* linger, loiter, dawdle
ymdrybaeddu *vb* wallow
ymdynghedu *vb* vow
ymddangos *vb* appear, seem
ymddangosiad (-au) *nm* appearance
ymddangosiadol *adj* seeming,
apparent
ymddarostwng *vb* submit
ymddarostyngiad *nm* humiliation, submission
ymddatod *vb* dissolve
ymddeol *vb* resign, retire
ymddeoliad (-au) *nm* retirement
ymddiddan *vb* talk, converse ♦ (-ion) *nm* talk, conversation
ymddihatru *vb* divest, undress
ymddiheuriad (-au) *nm* apology
ymddiheuro *vb* apologize
ymddiosg *vb* strip, undress
ymddiried *vb* trust ♦ *nm* trust, confidence
ymddiriedaeth *nf* trust, confidence
ymddiriedolwr (-wyr) *nm* trustee
ymddiswyddo *vb* resign
ymddwyn *vb* behave, act
ymddygiad (-au) *nm* behaviour, conduct; (*pl*) actions
ymddyrchafu *vb* exalt oneself; rise, ascend
ymegnïo *vb* exert oneself
ymehangu *vb* become enlarged, expand
ymennydd (ymenyddiau) *nm* brain
ymenyn *nm* butter
ymerawdwr (-wyr) *nm* emperor
ymerodraeth (-au) *nf* empire
ymerodres (-au) *nf* empress
ymerodrol *adj* imperial
ymesgusodi *vb* excuse oneself, apologize
ymestyn *vb* stretch, extend, reach
ymestyniad (-au) *nm* extension
ymfalchïo *vb* pride oneself
ymfodloni *vb* acquiesce
ymfudo *vb* emigrate
ymfudwr (-wyr) *nm* emigrant
ymffrost *nm* boast
ymffrostio *vb* boast, vaunt
ymffrostiwr (-wyr) *nm* boaster
ymgadw *vb* keep oneself (from), forbear
ymgais *nm/f* effort, attempt
ymgasglu *vb* gather together

ymgecru vb quarrel, wrangle

ymgeisio vb try, apply; aim at

ymgeisydd (-wyr) nm applicant, candidate

ymgeledd nm succour, care

ymgeleddu vb cherish, succour

ymgeleddwr (-wyr) nm succourer; tutor, guardian

ymgilio vb retreat, recede

ymgiprys vb, nm scramble

ymglymu vb involve, bind together

ymglywed vb feel (oneself), be inclined

ymgnawdoliad nm incarnation

ymgodymu vb wrestle, fight

ymgofleidio vb mutually embrace

ymgom (-ion) nf chat, conversation

ymgomio vb chat, converse

ymgorfforiad nm embodiment

ymgreinio vb prostrate oneself; grovel

ymgroesi vb cross oneself; beware

ymgryfhau vb strengthen oneself, be strong

ymgrymu vb bow down, stoop

ymguddfa nf shelter, hiding-place

ymguddio vb hide (oneself)

ymgydio vb copulate

ymgydnabod vb acquaint oneself

ymgyfathrachu vb have dealings with

ymgyfeillachu vb associate

ymgyfoethogi vb get rich

ymgynghori vb consult, confer

ymgynghoriad nm consultation

ymgymeriad (-au) nm undertaking

ymgymryd vb undertake

ymgynefino vb become familiar, get used to

ymgynnal vb bear up; support oneself; control oneself

ymgynnull vb assemble, congregate

ymgyrch (-oedd) nm/f campaign, expedition

ymgyrraedd vb stretch, strive after

ymgysegriad nm devotion, consecration

ymgysegru vb devote oneself

ymhél vb meddle

ymhelaethu vb abound; enlarge

ymhell adv far, afar

ymhellach adv further, furthermore

ymherodr etc see **ymerawdwr**

ymhlith prep among

ymhlyg adj implicit

ymhoelyd vb overturn, topple

ymhoffi vb take delight; boast

ymholi vb inquire

ymholiad (-au) nm inquiry

ymhonni vb lay claim to, pretend

ymhonnwr (-honwyr) nm pretender

ymhŵedd vb beseech, implore, crave

ymhyfrydu vb delight (oneself)

ymiacháu vb become healed, get well

ymlacio vb relax

ymladd vb fight ♦ (-au) nm fighting

ymládd vb kill oneself (with exertion), tire oneself out. **wedi y.** dead beat

ymladdfa (-feydd) nf fight

ymladdgar adj pugnacious, warlike

ymladdwr (-wyr) nm fighter, combatant

ymlaen adv on, onward

ymlafnio vb toil, strive, struggle

ymlawenhau vb rejoice

ymledu vb spread, expand

ymlenwi vb fill oneself

ymlid vb pursue, chase

ymlidiwr (-wyr) nm pursuer

ymlonyddu vb grow calm or still

ymlosgiad nm combustion

ymlusgiad (-iaid) nm reptile

ymlusgo vb creep, crawl

ymlwybro vb make one's way

ymlyniad nm attachment

ymlynu vb attach, adhere, cleave

(to)

ymlynwr (-wyr) *nm* adherent

Ymneillduaeth *nf* Nonconformity

ymneilltuo *vb* retire

Ymneilltuol *adj* Nonconformist

Ymneilltuwr (-wyr) *nm* Nonconformist

ymnesáu *vb* approach, draw near

ymochel, -yd *vb* shelter; beware

ymod, -i *vb* move, stir

ymofyn *vb* ask, inquire, seek ♦ (-ion) *nm* inquiry

ymofynnydd (-ofynwyr) *nm* inquirer

ymolchfa (-feydd) *nf* wash; lavatory

ymolchi *vb* wash oneself, bathe

ymollwng *vb* sink, drop, give way, collapse

ymorchestu *vb* strive, labour

ymorffwys *vb* rest, repose

ymorol *vb* seek; take care, attend to, see to it

ymosod *vb* attack, assail, assault

ymosodiad (-au) *nm* attack, assault

ymosodol *adj* aggressive, offensive, forward

ymosodwr (-wyr) *nm* attacker, assailant

ymostwng *vb* stoop; humble oneself; submit

ymostyngar *adj* submissive

ymostyngiad *nm* submission

ympryd (-ion) *nm* fast

ymprydio *vb* fast

ymprydiwr (-wyr) *nm* faster

ymrafael (-ion) *nm* quarrel, contention

ymrafaelgar *adj* quarrelsome, contentious

ymraniad (-au) *nm* division, schism

ymrannu *vb* part, divide, separate

ymrannwr (-ranwyr) *nm* separatist

ymreolaeth *nf* self-government, Home Rule

ymrestru *vb* enlist

ymresymiad (-au) *nm* reasoning, argument

ymresymu *vb* reason, argue

ymresymwr (-wyr) *nm* reasoner

ymrithio *vb* appear

ymroad *nm* application, devotion

ymroddedig *adj* devoted

ymroddgar *adj* of great application

ymroddi, ymroi *vb* apply or devote oneself; yield or resign oneself, surrender, do one's best

ymroddiad *nm* application, devotion

ymron *adv* nearly, almost

ymrous *adj* assiduous

ymrwyfo *vb* struggle, toss about

ymrwygo *vb* tear, burst

ymrwymiad (-au) *nm* engagement

ymrwymo *vb* bind or engage oneself

ymryson *vb* contend, strive ♦ (-au) *nm* contention, strife, rivalry

ymrysongar *adj* contentious

ymsefydlu *vb* establish oneself, settle

ymsefydlwr (-wyr) *nm* settler

ymserchu *vb* cherish, dote

ymson *vb* soliloquize ♦ (-au) *nm* soliloquy

ymsuddiant *nm* subsidence

ymswyno *vb* cross oneself; beware

ymsymud *vb* move

ymuno *vb* join, unite

ymwacâd *nm* kenosis

ymwacáu *vb* empty oneself

ymwadiad *nm* denial, abnegation

ymwadu *vb* deny (oneself); renounce

ymwahanu *vb* part, divide, separate

ymwahanwr (-wyr) *nm* separatist

ymwared *nm* deliverance

ymwasgu *vb* embrace, hug

ymweithydd (-ion) *nm* reactor

ymweld vb visit
ymweliad (-au) nm visit, visitation
ymwelwr, -ydd (-wyr) nm visitor, visitant
ymwrando vb hearken
ymwroli vb take heart, be of good courage
ymwrthod vb abstain; renounce
ymwrthodiad nm abstinence
ymwthgar adj pushing, obtrusive
ymwthio vb push oneself, obtrude
ymwthiol adj obtrusive, intrusive
ymwybodol adj conscious
ymwybyddiaeth nf consciousness
ymwylltio vb fly into a passion
ymyl (-au, -on) nmf edge, border, margin
ymylu vb border
ymylwe nf selvedge
ymyrgar adj meddlesome, officious
ymyrraeth, ymyrru, -yd vb meddle, interfere ♦ nf interference
ymyrrwr (-yrwyr) nm meddler
ymysg prep among, amid
ymysgaroedd npl bowels
ymysgwyd vb bestir oneself
yn prep in, at, into; for ♦ also introduces verb-nouns
yn adj particle
yna adv there; then; thereupon; that
ynad (-on) nm judge, justice, magistrate
yn awr adv now, at present
yndeintiad (-au) nm indentation
ynfyd (-ion) adj foolish, rash
ynfydrwydd nm foolishness, folly
ynfydu vb rave, be mad
ynfytyn (-fydion) nm fool, madman
ynni nm energy, vigour
yno adv there
yntau pron conj he (on his part), he also
ynteu, ynte conj or, or else, otherwise; then
Ynyd nm Shrovetide

ynys (-oedd) nf island, river meadow
ynysfor (-oedd) nm archipelago
Ynysoedd Dedwydd: yr Y. npl the Canary Islands
ynysol adj island, insular
ynyswr (-wyr) nm islander
ynysydd (-ion) nm insulator
yr see **y**
yrhawg adv for a long time (to come)
yrŵan adv now (N.W.)
ys vb it is ♦ conj as
ysbaddu vb castrate
ysbaid (-beidiau) nmf space (of time)
ysbail (-beiliau) nf spoil, plunder
ysbardun nmf spur
ysbarduno vb spur
ysbeidiol adj occasional, intermittent
ysbeilio vb spoil, plunder
ysbeiliwr (-wyr) nm spoiler, robber
ysbienddrych (-au) nm spying-glass
ysbio vb spy, look
ysbïwr (-wyr) nm spy
ysblander nm splendour
ysblennydd adj splendid
ysbonc (-iau) nf jump, bound; spurt
ysboncio vb jump, bounce; spurt, splash
ysborion npl cast-offs
ysbrigyn nm sprig, twig
ysbryd (-ion, -oedd) nm spirit, ghost
ysbrydegaeth nf spiritualism
ysbrydegol adj spiritualistic
ysbrydegydd (-ion) nm spiritualist
ysbrydiaeth nf encouragement, inspiration
ysbrydol adj spiritual; high-spirited
ysbrydoli vb spiritualize; inspire; inspirit

ysbrydoliaeth *nf* inspiration
ysbwng *nm* sponge
ysbwrial, -iel *nm* rubbish, refuse
ysbwylio *vb* spoil
ysbyty (-tai) *nm* hospital; hospice
ysfa (-feydd) *nf* itching; hankering
ysg- see **sg-**
ysgadan *npl* (-enyn *nm*) herrings
ysgafala *adj* secure, careless, free
ysgafn *adj* light ♦ *nm* stack
ysgafnder *nm* lightness, levity
ysgafnhau, ysgafnu *vb* lighten
ysgafnu *vb* heap, pile
ysgall *npl* (-en *nf*) thistles
ysgariad *nm*, **-iaeth** *nf* separation, divorce
ysgarlad *nm* scarlet
ysgarmes (-oedd, -au) *nf* skirmish
ysgaru *vb* part, separate, divorce
ysgatfydd *adv* perhaps, peradventure
ysgathru *vb* spread, scatter
ysgaw *coll n* (-en *nf*) elder
ysgeler *adj* wicked, villainous, infamous
ysgerbwd (bydau) *nm* skeleton, carcase
ysgithr (-edd) *nm* tusk, fang
ysgithrog *adj* fanged, tusked; craggy, rugged
ysgïw (-ion) *nf* settle
ysglefrio *vb* slide (on ice); skate
ysglyfaeth (-au) *nf* prey, spoil; carrion, filth
ysglyfaethus *adj* of prey; rapacious
ysgogi *vb* move, stir
ysgogiad (-au) *nm* movement, motion
ysgol (-ion) *nf* school; schooling
ysgol (-ion) *nf* ladder
ysgoldy (-dai) *nf* schoolhouse, schoolroom
ysgolfeistr (-i, -iaid) *nm* schoolmaster
ysgolfeistres (-i) *nf* schoolmistress
ysgolhaig (-heigion) *nm* scholar

ysgolheictod *nm* scholarship
ysgolheigaidd *adj* scholarly
ysgolor (-ion) *nm* scholar
ysgoloriaeth (-au) *nf* scholarship
ysgorpion (-au) *nm* scorpion
Ysgotyn (-gotiaid) *nm* Scot, Scotsman
ysgrafell (-od, -i) *nf* scraper; curry-comb
ysgrafeilu *vb* scrape, curry
ysgraff (-au) *nf* boat, barge, ferry-boat
ysgraffinio *vb* scarify, graze, abrade
ysgrech (-feydd) *nf* scream, shriek
ysgrechian, -in *vb* scream, shriek
ysgrepan (-au) *nf* wallet, scrip
ysgrif (-au) *nf* writing, article, essay
ysgrifbin (-nau) *nm*, **-grifell (-au)** *nf* pen
ysgrifen, -eniad (-iadau) *nf* writing
ysgrifennu *vb* write
ysgrifennwyr (-enwyr) *nm* writer
ysgrifennydd (-enyddion) *nm* scribe, secretary
ysgrifenyddiaeth *nf* secretaryship
ysgriw (-iau) *nf* screw
ysgriwio *vb* screw
ysgrwbio *vb* scrub
ysgryd *nm* shiver
ysgrythur (-au) *nf* scripture
ysgrythurol *adj* scriptural
ysgrythurwr (-wyr) *nm* scripturist
ysgub (-au) *nf* sheaf; broom
ysgubo *vb* sweep
ysgubol *adj* sweeping
ysgubor (-iau) *nf* barn, granary
ysgubwr (-wyr) *nm* sweeper, sweep
ysgutor (-ion) *nm* executor
ysguthan (-od) *nf* wood-pigeon; jade
ysgwâr *adj*, *nf* square
ysgwario *vb* square
ysgŵd *nm* jerk, toss, fling, shove

ysgwïer (-iaid) *nm* squire
ysgwrfa *nf* scouring, lathering
ysgwrio *vb* scour, scrub; lather
ysgwyd *vb* shake; flutter; wag
ysgwydd (-au) *nf* shoulder
ysgwyddo *vb* shoulder, jostle
ysgydwad *nm* shaking, shake
ysgyfaint *npl* lungs, lights
ysgyfarnog (-od) *nf* hare
ysgymun *adj* excommunicate, accursed
ysgymundod *nm* excommunication, ban
ysgymuno *vb* excommunicate
ysgyrion *npl* staves, splinters, shivers
ysgyrnygu *vb* grind the teeth, snarl
ysgytiad (-au) *nm* shock
ysgytio *vb* shake violently, shock
ysgythru *vb* cut, carve; prune
ysictod *nm* contusion; sprain
ysig *adj* bruised, sore, sprained
ysigo *vb* bruise, crush; sprain
yslotian *vb* dabble, tipple
ysmala *adj* droll, funny, amusing
ysmaldod *nm* fun, drollery
ysmalio *vb* joke, jest
ysmaliwr (-wyr) *nm* joker, wit
ysmotyn (ysmotiau) *nm* spot
ysmwddio *vb* iron
ysmygu *vb* smoke (tobacco)
ysmygwr (-wyr) *nm* smoker
ysol *adj* consuming, devouring; corrosive
yst- see also **st-**
ystabl (-au) *nf* stable
ystad (-au) *nf* state; estate; furlong
ystadegau *npl* statistics
ystadegol *adj* statistical
ystadegydd (-ion) *nm* statistician
ystafell (-oedd) *nf* chamber, room
ystalwyn (-i) *nm* stallion
ystanc (-iau) *nm* stake, bracket
ystarn (-au) *nf* stern
ystelcian *vb* skulk, loaf, loiter

ystelciwr (-wyr) *nm* loafer, loiterer
ystên (-enau) *nf* pitcher, ewer, milk-can
ystinos *nm* asbestos
ystiwart (-wardiaid) *nm* steward
ystlum (-od) *nm* bat
ystlys (-au) *nf* side, flank
ystlyswr (-wyr) *nm* linesman
ystod (-ion) *nf* course; swath. **Yn y. during**
ystof *nmf* warp
ystofi *vb* warp; weave, plan
ystôl (-olion) *nf* stool, chair
ystôr (-orau) *nm* store, abundance
ystordy (-dai) *nm* storehouse, warehouse
ystorfa (-feydd) *nf* store, storehouse
ystorio *vb* store
ystorïwr (-ïwyr) *nm* storyteller
ystorm (-ydd) *nf* storm
ystormus *adj* stormy
ystrad (-au) *nmf* vale, flat
ystranc (-iau) *nf* trick
ystrancio *vb* play tricks; jib
ystrodur (-iau) *nf* cart-saddle
ystryd (ystrydoedd) *nf* street
ystrydebol *adj* stereotyped
ystryw (-iau) *nf* wile, craft, ruse
ystrywgar *adj* wily, crafty
ystum (-iau) *nmf* bend; form; posture; (*pl*) grimaces
ystumio *vb* bend, distort; pose
ystumog (-au) *nf* stomach
ystŵr *nm* stir, noise, bustle, fuss
Ystwyll *nm* Epiphany
ystwyrian *vb* stretch and yawn, stir
ystwyth *adj* flexible, pliant, supple
ystwythder *nm* flexibility, pliancy
ystwytho *vb* make flexible; bend, soften
ystyfnig *adj* obstinate, stubborn
ystyfnigo *vb* behave obstinately
ystyfnigrwydd *nm* obstinacy
ystyr (-on) *nf/m* sense, meaning

ystyrgar *adj* thoughtful, meditative

ystyriaeth (-au) *nf* consideration, heed

ystyried *vb* consider, regard, heed

ystyriol *adj* mindful, heedful

ysu *vb* eat, consume; hanker; itch

yswain (-weiniaid) *nm* esquire

yswil *adj* shy, bashful, timid

yswildod *nm* shyness, bashfulness

yswiriant *nm* insurance

yswirio *vb* insure

yswywaeth *adv* more's the pity

yw *vb* is, are

yw *npl, coll n* (**-en** *nf*) yew

ENWAU PERSONAU PERSONAL NAMES

Adda Adam
Anghrist Antichrist
Andreas Andrew
Awstin Augustine
Bartholomeus Bartholomew
Beda Bede
Bedwyr Bedivere
Beti, Betsan, Betsi Betty, Betsy
Buddug Boadicea; Victoria
Bwda Buddha
Cadi Catherine, Kate
Cadog, Catwg Cadoc
Cai Kay
Caradog Caratacos, Caractacus
Caswallon Cassivellaunus
Catrin Catherine
Cesar Caesar
Crist Christ
Cystennin Constantine
Dafydd, Dewi David
Edmwnt, Emwnt Edmund
Efa Eve
Elen Helen, Ellen
Eleias Elijah, Elias
Eliseus Elisha, Eliseus
Emrys Ambrose
Ercwlff Hercules
Eseia, Esay Isaiah
Esyllt Iseult
Fychan Vaughan
Fyrsil, Fferyll Virgil
Ffowc Foulkes
Ffraid Bride, Bridget
Garmon Germanus
Geraint Gerontius
Gerallt Gerald
Glyndŵr Glendower
Gruffudd, Gruffydd Griffith
Gwallter Walter
Gwener Venus
Gwenffrewi, Gwenfrewi Winifred
Gwenhwyfar Guinevere
Gwilym William

Gwladus Gladys
Gwrtheyrn Vortigern
Harri Harry, Henry
Horas Horace
Hors Horsa
Hu, Huw Hugh
Iago James
Iau Jove, Jupiter
Iesu Grist Jesus Christ
Ieuan Evan
Ioan John
Iorwerth Edward
Iwan John
Lowri Laura
Luc Luke
Lleucu Lucy
Llwyd Lloyd
Llŷr Lear
Mabli Mabel
Mair Mary
Mali Molly
Mallt Maud, Matilda
Marc Mark
Marged, Margred Margaret
Mari Mary
Mawrth Mars
Mercher Mercury
Mererid Margaret
Meurig Morris
Mihangel Michael
Modlen, Magdalen Magdalene
Myrddin Merlin
Neifion Neptune
Ofydd Ovid
Oswallt Oswald
Owain Owen
Padrig Patrick
Pedr Peter
Peredur Perceval
Prys Price, Preece
Puw Pugh
Pyrs Pierce
Rheinallt Reginald

Rhisiart Richard
Rhobert Robert
Rhonwen Rowena
Rhydderch Roderick
Rhys Rees, Rice
Sadwrn Saturn
Sebedeus Zebedee
Selyf Solomon
Siân Jane
Siarl Charles
Siarlymaen Charlemagne

Sieffre Geoffrey
Siencyn Jenkin
Siôn John
Sioned Janet
Siôr, Siors George
Steffan Stephen
Timotheus Timothy
Tomos Thomas
Tudur Tudor
Twm Tom
Wmffre Humphrey

ENWAU LLEOEDD   PLACE NAMES

Aberdâr Aberdare
Aberdaugleddyf Milford Haven
Aberddawan Aberthaw
Abergwaun Fishguard
Aberhonddu Brecon
Abermo, Bermo Barmouth
Aberpennar Mountain Ash
Abertawe Swansea
Aberteifi Cardigan
Afon Menai Menai Straits
Amwythig Shrewsbury
Arberth Narberth
Babilon Babylon
Breudeth Brawdy
Brycheiniog Brecknock
Brynbuga Usk
Bryste, Caerodor Bristol
Caer Chester
Caerdroea Troy
Caerdydd Cardiff
Caerefrog York
Caerfaddon Bath
Caerfyrddin Carmarthen
Caergaint Canterbury
Caergrawnt Cambridge
Caergybi Holyhead
Caergystennin Constantinople
Caerhirfryn Lancaster, Lancashire
Caerliwelydd Carlisle
Caerloyw Gloucester
Caerlŷr Leicester(shire)
Caerllion Caerleon
Caernarfon Caernarvon
Caersallog Salisbury
Caerwrangon Worcester
Caer-wynt Winchester
Caer-Wysg Exeter
Caint Kent
Calfaria Calvary
Casllwchwr Loughor
Cas-mael Puncheston
Casnewydd Newport, Mon.
Castell-Nedd Neath

Castellnewydd Newcastle
Ceinewydd New Quay
Ceredigion Cardiganshire
Cernyw Cornwall
Clawdd Offa Offa's Dyke
Clwyd North East Wales
Coed-duon Blackwood
Conwy Conway
Côr y Cewri Stonehenge
Croesoswallt Oswestry
Crucywel Crickhowell
Cydweli Kidwelly
Dinas Basing Basingwerk
Dinbych Denbigh
Dinbych-y-pysgod Tenby
Donaw Danube
Drenewydd Newtown
Dyfed Demetia, South West Wales
Dyfnaint Devon
Dyfrdwy Dee
Efrog York
Eryri Snowdonia
Fflandrys Flanders
Fflint Flint
Gâl Gaul
Glynebwy Ebbw Vale
Gwent South East Wales
Gwlad-yr-haf Somerset
Gwy Wye
Gwynedd North West Wales
Gŵyr Gower
Hafren Severn
Hendy-gwyn Whitland
Henffordd Hereford
Hwlffordd Haverfordwest
Iâl Yale
Lacharn, Talacharn Laugharne
Lerpwl Liverpool
Llanandras Presteigne
Llanbedr Pont Steffan Lampeter
Llandaf Llandaff
Llandudoch St Dogmaels
Llaneirwg St Mellons

Llanelwy St Asaph
Llaneurgain Northop
Llanfair-ym-Muallt Builth
Llangatwg Cadoxton
Llangrallo Coychurch
Llanilltud Fawr Llantwit Major
Llanllieni Leominster
Llansawel Briton Ferry
Llanymddyfri Llandovery
Llwydlo Ludlow
Llyn Tegid Bala Lake
Maesyfed Radnor
Manaw Isle of Man
Manceinion Manchester
Meirionnydd Merioneth
Môn Anglesey
Morgannwg Glamorgan
Mynwy Monmouth
Mynyw St David's
Nanhyfer, Nyfer Nevern
Pennarlâg Hawarden
Pen-y-Fantach Mumbles Head
Penbedw Birkenhead
Pen-bre Pembrey
Penfro Pembroke
Penrhyn Gobaith Da Cape of Good Hope
Pen-y-bont ar Ogwr Bridgend
Pontarfynach Devil's Bridge
Pont-y-pŵl Pontypool
Porthaethwy Menai Bridge
Porthmadog Portmadoc
Powys Mid Wales
Rhuthun Ruthin
Rhydychen Oxford
Sain Ffagan St Fagans
Sili Sully
Solfach Solva
Tafwys Thames

Treamlod Ambleston
Trecelyn Newbridge
Trefaldwyn Montgomery
Trefdraeth Newport, Pem
Treforus Morriston
Trefyclo Knighton
Trefynwy Monmouth
Treffynnon Holywell
Tyddewi St David's
Tywi Towy
Wdig Goodwick
Wrecsam Wrexham
Wysg the Usk
Y Bont-faen Cowbridge
Y Fenni Abergavenny
Y Gelli (Gandryll) Hay
Y Gogarth Great Orme
Y Mot New Moat
Y Rhws Rhoose
Y Waun Chirk
Ynys Bŷr Caldey Island
Ynys Dewi Ramsey Island
Ynys Echni Flat Holm
Ynys Enlli Bardsey Island
Ynys Gybi Holy Island
Ynys Lawd South Stack
Ynys Seiriol Puffin Island
Ynysoedd Erch Orkney Islands
Ynysoedd Heledd The Hebrides
Ynysoedd y Moelrhoniaid The Skerries
Ynys y Garn Guernsey
Ynys Wyth Isle of Wight
Yr Wyddfa Snowdon
Yr Wyddgrug Mold
Ystrad-fflur Strata Florida
Ystrad Marchell Strata Marcella
Ystumllwynarth Oystermouth
Y Trallwng Welshpool

ENGLISH-WELSH DICTIONARY

A

a, an *adj*: **a man** dyn. **an ass** asyn

aback *adv* yn ôl. **taken a.** wedi synnu

abandon *vt* rhoi'r gorau i, gadael

abandoned *adj* wedi ei adael, ofer, afradlon

abase *vt* darostwng, iselhau, gostwng

abash *vt* cywilyddio

abate *vb* gostwng, lleihau; gostegu

abattoir *n* lladd-dy

abbess *n* abades

abbey *n* abaty, mynachlog

abbot *n* abad

abbreviate *vt* byrhau, talfyrru

abbreviation *n* byrfodd

abdicate *vb* ymddeol, ymddiswyddo

abdomen *n* bol

abdominal *adj* perthynol i'r bol

abduct *vt* dwyn ymaith drwy drais, cipio

aberration *n* cyfeiliorn, gwyriad

abet *vt* cefnogi, cynorthwyo, ategu

abeyance *n* dirymedd dros dro, oediad

abhor *vt* ffieiddio, casáu

abhorrence *n* ffieidd-dod, atgasrwydd, atgasedd

abide *vb* aros, trigo; goddef

abiding *adj* arhosol, gwastadol

ability *n* gallu, medr

abject *adj* distadl, dirmygedig

ablative *n* abladol

ablaze *adv* ar dân, yn wenfflam

able *adj* abl, galluog

ablution *n* golchiad; puredigaeth

abnormal *adj* anghyffredin, annormal

aboard *adv* ar fwrdd (llong)

abode *n* annedd, trigfa, cartrefle

abolish *vt* diddymu, dileu

abominable *adj* ffiaidd

abomination *n* ffieidd-dra

aborigines *npl* cyn-drigolion

abort *vb* erthylu, atal

abortion *n* erthyliad; erthyl

abortive *adj* seithug, ofer

abound *vi* amlhau, heigio; ymhelaethu

about *prep* am, oddeutu, tua ♦ *adv* oddeutu, o gwmpas

above *prep* uwch, uwchlaw ♦ *adv* fry

abrasive *adj* yn peri traul; annymunol

abreast *adj* ochr yn ochr, cyfystlys

abridge *vt* talfyrru, cwtogi

abroad *adv* allan, ar led, ar daen, dros y dŵr

abrogate *vt* diddymu, dileu

abrupt *adj* disymwth, sydyn, swta; serth

abscess *n* cornwyd, casgliad, crynhofa

abscond *vi* rhedeg i ffwrdd, dianc

absence *n* absenoldeb

absent *adj* absennol ♦ *vt* absenoli. **a.-minded** *adj* anghofus

absenteeism *n* absenoliaeth

absolute *adj* cwbl, hollol; diamodol ♦ *n* diamod, absolwt

absolutely *adv* yn hollol

absolution *n* gollyngdod; maddeuant

absolve *vt* rhyddhau, gollwng; maddau

absorb *vt* yfed, llyncu, sugno, sychu

absorbent *adj* amsugnol ♦ *n*

amsugnydd
absorption n llynciad, sychiad
abstain vb ymatal, ymgadw
abstemious adj cymedrol, sobr
abstention n ymataliad
abstinence n dirwest, ymataliad
abstinent adj cymedrol, sobr
abstract vt tynnu, haniaethu, crynhoi ♦ adj haniaethol ♦ n crynodeb
abstraction n haniaeth; synfyfyrdod
abstruse adj tywyll, dyrys, astrus
absurd adj gwrthun, afresymol
abundance n digonedd, helaethrwydd
abundant adj aml, helaeth, digonol
abuse vt camddefnyddio, camdrin; difrio
abuse n camddefnydd; difriaeth
abusive adj sarhaus, gwatwarus
abysmal adj diwaelod, dwys, enbyd
abyss n y dyfnder, agendor
academic, -al adj athrofaol, academig
academy n ysgol, athrofa, academi
accede vt cytuno, cydsynio
accelerate vt cyflymu, chwimio
accelerator n ysbardun, chwimiadur
accent n acen; lledaith ♦ vt acennu
accentuate vt acennu; pwysleisio
accept vt derbyn (yn gymeradwy)
acceptable adj derbyniol, cymeradwy
acceptance n derbyniad
access n dyfodfa, dyfodiad, mynedfa, mynediad
accessary n cynorthwywr, cefnogydd
accessible adj hygyrch; hawdd dod ato
accession n esgyniad (i'r orsedd)
accessory adj cynorthwyol,

cyfranogol; atodol
accidence n ffurfiant
accident n damwain, anap
accidental adj damweiniol
accidentally adv yn ddamweiniol
acclaim vt datgan cymeradwyaeth
acclamation n bloddest, cymeradwyaeth
accommodate vt cymhwyso; lletya
accommodating adj cyfaddasol
accommodation n lle, lletty
accompaniment n cyfeiliant
accompanist n cyfeilydd
accompany vb hebrwng; cyfeilio
accomplice n cynorthwywr mewn trosedd
accomplish vt cyflawni, cwblhau
accomplished adj medrus
accomplishment n medr, dawn, camp
accord vb cytuno; cyflwyno ♦ n cydfod
accordance n : **in a. with** yn unol â
according adv: **a. to** yn ôl
accordingly adv felly, gan hynny
accordion n acordion
accost vt cyfarch
account vb cyfrif ♦ n cyfrif; hanes
accountable adj cyfrifol, atebol
accountant n cyfrifydd
accountancy n cyfrifyddiaeth
account number n rhif cyfrif
accredit vt coelio, credu; awdurdodi
accrue vt deillio, codi, digwydd
accumulate vb casglu, pentyrru, cronni
accumulator n cronadur
accuracy n cywirdeb
accurate adj cywir
accurately adv yn gywir
accursed adj melltigedig, melltigaid
accusation n cyhuddiad
accusative adj gwrthrychol

(*gram.*); cyhuddol

accuse *vt* cyhuddo

accustom *vt* arfer, ymarfer, cynefino

accustomed *adj* cyfarwydd, cyffredin

ace *n* as; mymryn

ache *vi* poeni, gwynio ♦ *n* poen, cur

achieve *vt* cyflawni, gorffen, cwplâu, cwblhau

achievement *n* cyflawniad, camp

acid *adj* siarp, sur ♦ *n* suryn, asid

acidic *adj* asidig

acknowledge *vt* cydnabod, cyfaddef

acknowledgment *n* cydnabyddiaeth

acorn *n* mesen

acoustic *adj* clybodig

acoustics *npl* acwsteg

acquaint *vt* hysbysu, ymgydnabod

acquaintance *n* cydnabod, cydnabyddiaeth, adnabyddiaeth

acquainted *adj* cydnabyddus, cynefin, cyfarwydd

acquiesce *vi* dygymod, cydsynio

acquire *vt* cael, ennill

acquisition *n* caffaeliad

acquit *vt* rhyddhau

acre *n* erw, cyfair, acer

acrid *adj* chwerw, llymsur

acrimonious *adj* chwerw, sarrug, cecrus

acrobat *n* acrobat

across *adv*, *prep* yn groes, ar draws; trosodd

acrylic *adj* acrylig

act *vb* gweithredu, actio ♦ *n* act, gweithred, deddf

action *n* gweithred, gweithrediad

activate *vb* gweithredoli

active *adj* bywiog; gweithredol

activity *n* gweithgarwch, gweithgaredd

actor *n* actor, actiwr

actress *n* actores

actual *adj* gwir, gwirioneddol

actually *adv* mewn gwirionedd

actuary *n* ystadegydd, cyfrifydd

actuate *vt* ysgogi, cymell, cyffroi

acumen *n* treiddgarwch, craffter

acute *adj* llym, tost; craff

A.D. *abbr* O.C.

adage *n* dihareb, dywediad

adamant *n* adamant, diemwnt

adapt *vt* cyfaddasu

adapter *n* adaptydd

add *vb* chwanegu, atodi; adio

adder *n* neidr, gwiber

addict *vt* ymroddi, gorddibynnu

addiction *n* ymroddiad, gorddibyniaeth, tueddiad

addition *n* ychwanegiad

additional *adj* ychwanegol

additive *n* adiolyn

address *vb* annerch, cyfeirio ♦ *n* anerchiad; cyfeiriad

adduce *vt* dwyn ymlaen; nodi

adept *n* un cyfarwydd; campwr

adequate *adj* digonol

adhere *vi* ymlynu, glynu wrth

adhesion *n* glyniad, ymlyniad

adhesive *adj* glynol, ymlynol ♦ *n* adlyn, glud

adieu *excl* bydd wych! ffarwel!

adjacent *adj* cyfagos, gerllaw

adjective *n* ansoddair

adjoin *vt* cydio, cyffwrdd â

adjourn *vt* gohirio, oedi

adjudge *vt* dyfarnu, barnu

adjudicate *vt* beirniadu, barnu

adjudicator *n* beirniad

adjunct *n* atodiad, ychwanegiad

adjure *vt* tynghedu, tyngu

adjust *vt* cymhwyso, addasu, unioni

ad-lib *adv* yn rhydd, difyfyr

administer *vt* gweinyddu

administration *n* gweinyddiaeth

administrative *adj* gweinyddol

admirable *adj* rhagorol, campus

admiral *n* llyngesydd

admiralty *n* morlys

admiration n edmygedd
admire vt edmygu
admission n derbyniad; addefiad
admit vt derbyn; addef, cyfaddef
admittance n derbyniad; trwydded
admixture n cymysgiad, cymysgedd
admonish vt rhybuddio, ceryddu
admonition n rhybudd, cerydd
ad nauseam adv hyd syrffed
ado n helynt, heldrin, ffwdan
adolescence n llencyndod, adolesens
adolescent n adolesent, llencyn, llances
adopt vb mabwysiadu
adoption n mabwysiad
adore vt addoli
adorn vt addurno
adrift adv yn rhydd, diangor
adroit adj medrus, deheuig, hyfedr
adulation n gweniaith, truth
adult n (un) mewn oed, oedolyn
adulterate vt llygru
adulterer n godinebwr
adulteress n godinebwraig
adultery n godineb
advance vb symud ymlaen; dyrchafu; rhoi benthyg ♦ n benthyg, echwyn
advanced adj ar y blaen
advancement n dyrchafiad; lles, budd
advancing adj cynyddol, ar gynnydd
advantage n mantais
advantageous adj manteisiol
advent n dyfodiad; yr Adfent
adventure n antur, anturiaeth
adverb n adferf
adversary n gwrthwynebydd
adverse adj adfydus, gwrthwynebus, croes
adversity n adfyd, drygfyd
advert n hysbyseb
advertise vt hysbysu, hysbysebu
advertisement n hysbysiad,

hysbyseb
advertiser n hysbysydd
advertising adj hysbysebol
advice n cyngor, cyfarwyddyd
advisable adj doeth, buddiol
advise vt cynghori, annog; hysbysu
advisedly adv ar ôl ystyried, yn bwyllog
advisory adj ymgynghorol
advocate n eiriolwr, bargyfreithiwr ♦ vt eirioli, dadlau, cefnogi, pleidio
adze n neddau, neddyf
aerial adj awyrol, wybrol
aeroplane n awyren
aerosol n erosol
aesthetic adj esthetig
aesthetics n estheteg
afar adv pell, hirbell
affable adj hynaws, caruaidd, clên
affair n achos; mater; helynt
affect vt effeithio; cymryd arno, ffugio
affectation n mursendod, rhodres, ffug
affection n serch, cariad; clefyd, haint; affeithiad (gram.)
affectionate adj serchog, caruaidd
affiliate vt mabwysiadu, tadogi; uno
affinity n cyfathrach; tebygrwydd
affirm vb haeru, taeru; sicrhau, gwirio
affirmation n cadarnhad
affirmative adj cadarnhaol
affix vt sicrhau, gosod
afflict vt cystuddio
affliction n cystudd, adfyd
affluence n cyfoeth, digonedd
affluent adj goludog, cyfoethog, cefnog
afford vt rhoddi; fforddio
afforestation n coedwigaeth
affray n ymryson, ffrwgwd, ysgarmes
affront vt sarhau, tramgwyddo ♦ n

sarhad
afield *adv* : **far a.** ymhell i ffwrdd
aflame *adv* ar dân
afloat *adv* yn nofio; ar daen, ar led
afoot *adv* ar droed
afraid *adj* ag ofn arno, ofnus
afresh *adv* o'r newydd, eilwaith
Africa *n* Affrica
after *prep, conj* wedi, ar ôl, yn ôl ♦
adv wedyn
after-care *n* gofal wedyn, ôl-ofal
after-effects *n* ôl-effeithiau
afterlife *n* y byd a ddaw
aftermath *n* adladd, adlodd
afternoon *n* prynhawn
afters *n* y cwrs terfynol
afterthought *n* syniad diweddar
afterwards *adv* wedi hynny, wedyn
again *adv* eilwaith, drachefn, eto
against *prep* erbyn, yn erbyn
age *n* oed, oedran; oes; henaint ♦
vb heneiddio
aged *adj* hen, oedrannus
agency *n* goruchwyliaeth, cyfrwng,
asiantaeth
agenda *n* agenda
agent *n* goruchwyliwr;
gweithredydd, cynrychiolydd
aggravate *vt* gwneuthur yn waeth
aggregate *n* cyfanswm, crynswth
aggression *n* ymosodiad, gormes
aggressive *adj* ymosodol,
ymwthiol, gormesol
aggrieve *vt* blino, tramgwyddo
aghast *adj* syn, brawychedig
agile *adj* heini, sionc, gwisgi
agitate *vt* cynhyrfu, aflonyddu,
cyffroi
agnostic *n* agnostig, anffyddiwr
ago *adv* yn ôl. **long a.** ers talm
agog *adv* yn awchus
agonizing *adj* mewn gwewyr
meddwl
agony *n* ing, poen
agrarian *adj* tirol, gwledig
agree *vi* cytuno; dygymod; cyfateb
agreeable *adj* clên, dymunol,

hyfryd
agreement *n* cytundeb
agricultural *adj* amaethyddol
agriculture *n* amaethyddiaeth
aground *adv* ar lawr, ar dir, i dir
ahead *adv* ymlaen, o flaen
aid *vt* cynorthwyo, helpu ♦ *n*
cymorth, cynhorthwy
ail *vb* clafychu; blino, poeni
ailment *n* dolur, afiechyd,
anhwyldeb
aim *vb* anelu, amcanu ♦ *n* amcan,
nod
air *n* awyr; osgo; cainc, alaw ♦ *vt*
awyru
aircraft *n* awyren
airforce *n* llu awyr
airline *n* cwmni hedfan
airlock *n* aerglo
airport *n* maes glanio
air mail *n* post awyr
airtight *adj* aerglos, aerdyn
aisle *n* ystlys eglwys; llwybr; eil
ajar *adv* cilagored
akin *adj* perthynol, perthnasol
alack *excl* och fi!
alacrity *n* bywiogrwydd,
parodrwydd
alarm *vt* dychrynu ♦ *n* braw,
dychryn; rhybudd; larwm
alarm-clock *n* cloc larwm
alas *excl* och!
albeit *conj* er, er hynny, eto
album *n* albwm; record hir
alcohol *n* alcohol
alcoholic *adj*. *n* alcoholig,
meddwyn
alcove *n* cilfach wely; hafdy,
deildy, alcof
alder *n* gwernen
ale *n* cwrw
alert *adj* esgud, effro, gwyliadwrus
algebra *n* algebra
Algeria *n* Algeria
alias *adv* mewn modd, dan enw
arall
alibi *n* dadlau bod mewn man arall

alien adj estronol ♦ n estron
alight vi disgyn
align vb cyfunioni
alike adj yr un fath ♦ adv yn gyffelyb
aliment n maeth, ymborth
alimony n alimoni
alive adv, adj yn fyw, byw
alkali n alcali
alkaline adj alcaliaidd
all adj holl; oll, i gyd ♦ adv yn hollol ♦ n y cwbl, y cyfan; pawb
allay vt lleddfu, lliniaru; tawelu
all clear adv yn glir
allege vt honni, haeru
allegedly adv yn honedig
allegiance n teyrngarwch, gwrogaeth
allegory n alegori
allergic adj alergig
allergy n alergedd
alleviate vt ysgafnhau, esmwytho
alley n llwybr, ale
alliance n cyfathrach, cynghrair
allied adj cynghreiriol
alliteration n cyflythreniad, cyseinedd
all-night adv drwy'r nos
allocate vt cyfleu, rhannu, dosbarthu
allot vb gosod, penodi
allotment n cyfran; rhandir
all-out adv yn llwyr, a'i holl egni
allow vt caniatáu, goddef
allowance n goddefiad; dogn; lwfans
alloy n aloi
allude vi cyfeirio, sôn
allure vb hudo, denu, llithio
allusion n crybwylliad, cyfeiriad (at)
alluvium n llifbridd, dolbridd
ally vt cynghreirio ♦ n cynghreiriad
almighty adj hollalluog, holigyfoethog
almond n almon
almoner n elusennwr

almost adv bron, agos, braidd
alms n elusen; cardod
aloft adv yn uchel, fry, i fyny
alone adv, adj unig, ar ei ben ei hun
along adv ymlaen; ar hyd. **all a.** o'r cychwyn
aloof adv, adj yn cadw draw; pell
aloud adv yn uchel, yn groch
alphabet n egwyddor, abiéc
alphabetical adj yn nhrefn yr wyddor
Alps npl: **the A.** yr Alpau
already adv eisoes, yn barod
also adv hefyd
altar n allor
alter vb newid, altro
alteration n newid, cyfnewidiad
altercation n ymryson, ffrae
alternate adj bob yn ail ♦ vb digwydd bob yn ail; eilio
alternating adj bob yn ail
alternative n dewis arall
alternatively adv o ddewis arall
although conj er
altitude n uchder
alto n alto
altogether adv oll, i gyd, yn gyfan gwbl
aluminium n alwminiwm
always adv yn wastad(ol), bob amser
a.m. abbr a.m.
amalgamate vb cymysgu, cyfuno, uno
amanuensis n ysgrifennydd dros arall
amass vt casglu, cronni, pentyrru
amateur n amatur
amateurish adj trwsgl, anfedrus, amaturaidd
amatory adj carwriaethol
amaze vt synnu, rhyfeddu, aruthro
amazement n syndod
amazing adj rhyfeddol
ambassador n llysgennad
amber n ambr

ambidextrous adj deheuig â'i ddwy law

ambiguity n amwysedd

ambiguous adj amwys

ambition n uchelgais

ambitious adj uchelgeisiol

amble vi rhygyngu ♦ n rhygyng

ambulance n ambiwlans

ambush n, vb cynllwyn, rhagod

ameliorate vt gwella, diwygio

amenable adj hydrin; atebol; cyfrifol

amend vb gwella, diwygio, cywiro

amendment n gwelliant

amends n iawn

amenity n hyfrydwch; hynawsedd

America n yr Amerig

American adj Americanaidd ♦ n Americanwr

amiable adj hawddgar, serchus

amicable adj cyfeillgar

amid, -st prep ynghanol, ymhlith, ymysg

amiss adv ar fai, o'i le

amity n cyfeillgarwch

ammonia n amonia

ammunition n arlwy rhyfel; pylor, etc

amnesty n maddeuant

amok adv yn wyllt, dilywodraeth

among, -st prep ymhlith, ymysg, rhwng

amorous adj hoff o garu, carwriaethus

amorphous adj di-ffurf, amorffus

amount vi cyrraedd; codi ♦ n swm

amour n carwriaeth

ample adj helaeth, eang; cyflawn, digon

amplify vt helaethu, ehangu

amputate vt torri aelod, trychu

amulet n peth a wisgir fel swyn

amuse vt difyrru, diddanu

amusement n difyrrwch, digrifwch

an Gwêl a

anachronism n camamseriad

anaemia n diffyg gwaed

anaemic adj di-waed, diwryg

anaesthesia n dideimladrwydd

anaesthetic adj, n anesthetig

analogy n cyfatebiaeth, cydweddiad

analyse vt dadansoddi, dadelfennu

analysis (-yses) n dadansoddiad

analyst n dadansoddwr

analytical adj dadansoddol

anarchic, -al adj anarchol

anarchist n anarchydd, terfysgwr

anarchy n anhrefn, aflywodraeth, anarchaeth

anathema n anathema

anatomy n anatomeg

ancestor n cyndad, (pl) hynafiaid

ancestry n ach, achau; hynafiaid

anchor n angor ♦ vb angori

anchoress, -ite n meudwy, ancr

ancient adj hen, hynafol; oesol

ancillary adj ategol, cynorthwyol

and conj a, ac

anecdote n hanesyn, chwedl

anew adv o'r newydd

angel n angel

anger n dicter, llid ♦ vt digio, llidio

angle n ongl ♦ vi genweirio, pysgota

Anglican adj perthynol i Eglwys Loegr, Anglicanaidd

angling n pysgota

angry adj dig, llidiog

anguish n ing

angular adj onglog

animadvert vi beirniadu, ceryddu, sennu

animal n anifail, mil ♦ adj anifeilaidd

animate adj byw ♦ vt bywhau; ysgogi

animation n bywiogrwydd

animosity n gelyniaeth, digasedd

animus n drwgdeimlad, gelyniaeth

ankle n migwrn, ffêr, swrn

annals npl cofnodion blynyddol

annex vt cysylltu, cydio;

meddiannu
annihilate *vt* diddymu, difodi
annihilation *n* diddymiant,
difodiant
anniversary *n* pen blwydd;
cylchwyl flynyddol
annotate *vb* gwneud nodiadau
announce *vt* datgan, cyhoeddi
announcement *n* cyhoeddiad,
hysbysiad
announcer *n* cyhoeddwr
annoy *vt* poeni, blino, cythruddo
annoyance *n* blinder, poendod
annoying *adj* trafferthus, blinderus
annual *adj* blynyddol
annuity *n* blwydd-dal
annul *vt* diddymu, dileu, dirymu
anoint *vt* eneinio, iro
anomaly *n* peth croes i reol,
afreoleidd-dra
anon *adv* yn union, toc, yn y man
anonymity *n* cyflwr dienw
anonymous *adj* dienw, anhysbys
anorak *n* anorac
another *pron, n* arall
answer *vb* ateb ♦ *n* ateb, atebiad
answerable *adj* atebol, cyfrifol
ant *n* morgrugyn
antagonism *n* gelyniaeth,
gwrthwynebiaeth
antagonist *n* gwrthwynebydd
Antarctic *n*: **the A.** Antarctica
antarctic *adj* o gylch y pegwn
deheuol
ante- *prefix* cyn, o flaen, rhag- ♦ *n*
rhagflaenydd
antecedent *adj* blaenorol
antediluvian *adj* cynddilywaidd
antelope *n* gafrewig, antelop
antenatal *adj* cyn-geni
anterior *adj* blaen, blaenorol, cyn-
anthem *n* anthem
anthology *n* blodeugerdd
anthracite *n* glo caled, glo carreg
anthropology *n* anthropoleg
anti-, ant- *prefix* gwrth-, yn erbyn
antibiotic *n, adj* gwrthfiotig

antichrist *n* anghrist
anticipate *vt* achub y blaen,
disgwyl
anticlimax *n* disgynneb
antics *npl* munudiau, ystumiau,
maldod, stranciau
antidote *n* gwrthwenwyn
antifreeze *n, adj* gwrthrew,
direwyn
antipathy *n* gwrthnaws; casineb
antipodes *npl* pellafoedd byd,
eithafoedd
antiquarian *adj* hynafiaethol ♦ *n*
hynafiaethydd
antiquated *adj* hen a di-les
antique *adj* hen, hynafol,
henffasiwn
antique- *n* hen beth
antique-shop *n* siop hen bethau
antiquity *n* hynafiaeth; yr
cynoesoedd
anti-Semitism *n* gwrth-Iddewiaeth
antiseptic *adj, n* antiseptig
antisocial *adj* gwrthgymdeithasol
antithesis (-es) *n*
gwrthgyferbyniad
antler *n* cainc o gorn carw, rhaidd
anvil *n* eingion, einion
anxiety *n* pryder
anxious *adj* pryderus, awyddus
any *adj* un, unrhyw, rhyw, peth,
dim
anybody *pron* unrhyw un, rhywun
anyone *pron* rhywun
anything *pron* dim, rhywbeth,
rhywfaint
anywhere *adv* rhywle
apace *adv* ar garlam, ar ffrwst, ar
frys
apart *adv* o'r neilltu, ar wahân
apartheid *n* aparteid
apartment *n* rhandy, llety
apathetic *adj* difraw, difater,
didaro
apathy *n* difrawder, difaterwch
ape *n* epa ♦ *vt* dynwared
aperture *n* bwlch, twll, agorfa

apex n blaen, brig, pen, copa

aphis (aphides) n pryf gwyrdd

aphorism n gwireb, dihareb

apiece adv yr un, ar wahân, un bob un

apocalypse n datguddiad

apocryphal adj anghanonaidd, apocryffaidd

apologize vi ymddiheuro, ymesgusodi

apology n ymddiheuriad, esgusawd

apoplexy n parlys mud, strôc

apostasy n gwrthgiliad

apostate n gwrthgiliwr

apostle n apostol

apostolic, -al adj apostolaidd

apostrophe n sillgoll, collnod (')
fferyllydd

appal vt brawychu, digalonni

appalling adj arswydus, gwarthus

apparatus n offer, aparatws

apparel n dillad, gwisg

apparent adj amlwg, eglur

apparently adv mae'n debyg

apparition n drychiolaeth, ysbryd

appeal vi apelio, erfyn ♦ n apêl

appear vi ymddangos, ymrithio

appearance n ymddangosiad

appease vt llonyddu, tawelu, dofi

appellation n enw, teitl

append vt atodi, ychwanegu

appendicitis n enyniad y coluddyn crog, apendiseitis

appendix n atodiad, ychwanegiad

appertain vi perthyn

appetite n archwaeth, chwant, awydd

appetizer n lluniaeth i greu blas, blasyn

applaud vt cymeradwyo, curo dwylo

applause n cymeradwyaeth

apple n afal. **a. of the eye** cannwyll llygad

appliance n offeryn, dyfais

applicant n ymgeisydd

application n cymhwysiad; cais; ymroddiad

applied adj cymwysedig

apply vb cymhwyso; ymroi; cynnig (am), ymgeisio

appoint vb gosod, penodi, pennu

appointment n cyhoeddiad; penodiad

apportion vt rhannu, dosbarthu

apposite adj addas, priodol

appraise vt prisio

appreciate vt prisio, gwerthfawrogi

appreciation n gwerthfawrogiad

appreciative adj gwerthfawrogol

apprehend vt ymaflyd mewn; dirnad; ofni

apprehension n dirnadaeth; ofn

apprehensive adj ofnus, pryderus

apprentice n prentis, dysgwr ♦ vt prentisio

apprise vb hysbysu; tafoli

approach vb nesáu, dynesu ♦ n dyfodfa

approachable adj hawdd mynd ato

approbation n cymeradwyaeth

appropriate vt meddiannu ♦ adj priodol, addas

approval n cymeradwyaeth

approve vt cymeradwyo; profi

approximate vi agosáu ♦ adj agos

approximately adv oddeutu, tua, yn agos

appurtenance n peth perthynol

apricot n bricyllen

April n Ebrill

apron n (ar)ffedog, barclod

apt adj tueddol; cymwys, parod

aquarium n pysgodlyn, pysgoty

aquatic adj dyfrol, dyfriog

aqueduct n dyfrffos

arable adj: **a. land** tir âr

arbiter n dyddiwr, brawdwr, beirniad

arbitrament n rhaith, dedfryd

arbitrary adj gormesol, mympwyol

arbitrate vb cyflafareddu,
  athrywyn
arbour n deildy
arc n bwa, arc
arcade n arcéd
arch n bwa, pont; nen ♦ vt pontio
arch- prefix arch-, carn-, prif-
archaeology n archaeoleg
archaic adj hynafol, henaidd
archangel n archangel
archbishop n archesgob
archdeacon n archddiacon,
  archddiagon
archdruid n archdderwydd
archer n saethydd, saethwr
archery n saethyddiaeth
archipelago n twr ynysoedd,
  ynysfor
architect n pensaer
architecture n pensaerniaeth
archive n archif
archway n ffordd fwaol
Arctic n: **the A.** yr Artig
arctic adj gogleddol
ardent adj gwresog, poeth,
  angerddol
ardour n angerdd, aidd
arduous adj llafurus, blin, caled
area n arwynebedd, wyneb
Argentina n Ariannin
argue vb dadlau, ymresymu
argument n dadl, ymresymiad
arid adj sych, crin, cras, gwyw
aright adv yn iawn, yn briodol
arise vi cyfodi, codi
aristocracy n pendefigaeth
aristocrat n pendefig, gŵr mawr
aristocratic adj pendefigaidd,
  bonheddig
arithmetic n rhifyddeg
arithmetician n rhifyddgwr
ark n arch
arm n braich; cainc
arm n arf ♦ vb arfogi
armament n offer rhyfel;
  arfogaeth
armchair n cadair freichiau

armed adj arfog
armful adj coflaid, ceseiliaid
armistice n cadoediad
armour n arfogaeth, arfwisg
armoured adj wedi ei amddiffyn
armoury n arfdy
armpit n cesail
armrest n man i orffwys braich
army n byddin
aroma n perarogl(au)
aromatic adj perarogleidd, pêr,
  perswaus
around adv, prep am, o amgylch
arouse vt deffro(i), dihuno; cyffroi
arraign vt cyhuddo o flaen brawdle
arrange vb trefnu
arrangement n trefn, trefniad,
  trefniant
arrant adj dybryd, cywilyddus
array vt trefnu, cyfleu; gwisgo ♦ n
  trefn; gwisg
arrears npl ôl-ddyled
arrest vt atal; dal, dala, restio
arrival n dyfodiad, cyrhaeddiad
arrive vi cyrraedd, dyfod
arrogance n balchder, traha
arrogant adj balch, trahaus
arrogate vt hawlio, trawshawlio
arrow n saeth
arsenal n arfdy, ystordy neu ffatri
  arfau
arson n llosgiad, llosg
art n celfyddyd; ystryw
artefact n celfilun
artery n rhedweli
artful adj ystrywgar, dichellgar,
  cyfrwys
art gallery n oriel gelf
arthritis n gwynegon, crydcymalau
article n erthygl; nwydd; bannod
articulate vb cymalu; cynanu ♦ adj
  â meddwl clir, trefnus
artifice n dyfais; ystryw, dichell
artificer n saer, crefftwr,
  celfyddydwr
artificial adj celfyddydol; gosod,
  dodi, ffug

artillery n offer rhyfel, magnelau
artisan n crefftwr
artist n celfyddydwr, arlunydd, artist
artistic adj celfydd, celfyddgar, artistig
as conj, adv megis, fel; cyn, mor; á, ag
asbestos n ystinos, asbestos
ascend vb esgyn, dringo, dyrchafu
ascendancy n goruchafiaeth, uchafiaeth
ascension n esgyniad, dyrchafael
ascent n esgynfa, rhiw, gorifyny
ascertain vt cael gwybod, mynnu gwybod
ascetic n meudwy ♦ adj meudwyaidd, ymgosbol, asgetig
ascribe vt cyfrif i, priodoli, rhoddi
ash n onnen, onn
ash (-es) n lludw, ulw
ashamed adj ag arno gywilydd
ashore adv i'r lan, ar y lan
ashtray n plat lludw
aside adv o'r neilltu
ask vb gofyn, holi; ceisio
askance adv yn llygatraws, yn gam
askew adv ar osgo, ar letraws
aslant adv ar ei ogwydd, ar oledd
asleep adv yng nghwsg, yn cysgu
asparagus n merllys, asbaragws
aspect n golwg, golygwedd, wyneb, agwedd
aspen n aethnen
asperity n gerwindeb, llymder
asperse vt taenellu; gwaradwyddo
aspersion n difriad, enllib
asphyxiate vt mygu, tagu
aspirate vt seinio ag anadl ♦ n yr (h)
aspiration n dyhead
aspire vi dyheu
aspirin n asbrin
ass n asyn; asen
assail vt ymosod ar, rhuthro ar
assailant n ymosodwr

assassin n bradlofrudd, llofrudd
assassinate vt bradlofruddio
assault n ymosodiad ♦ vt ymosod
assay n praw(f) ♦ vb profi; cynnig, ceisio
assemble vb cynnull, ymgynnull
assembly n cynulliad, cymanfa
assent vi cydsynio ♦ n cydsyniad
assert vt haeru, honni, mynnu
assess vt trethu, prisio, asesu
assessment n asesiad
assessor n aseswr, cyfeisteddwr
asset n ased
assets npl eiddo, meddiannau
assiduous adj dyfal, diwyd
assign vt gosod, penodi; trosglwyddo
assimilate vb cymathu; tebygu
assist vb cynorthwyo, cymorth, helpu
assistance n cymorth
assistant n cynorthwyydd
assize n brawdlys
associate vb cymdeithasu, cyfeillachu, cysylltu ♦ n cydymaith
association n cymdeithas, cymdeithasfa
assort vb trefnu, dosbarthu
assorted adj amryfath
assortment n dosbarthiad, pigion
assuage vt llonyddu, lliniaru, lleddfu
assume vt cymryd ar; tybied; honni
assumption n tyb(iaeth), bwriant, honiad, dyrchafiad (Mair i'r nefoedd)
assurance n sicrwydd; hyder, hyfder
assure vt sicrhau; yswirio
asterisk n serennig, seren (*)
asthma n caethder, diffyg anadl, y fogfa
asthmatic adj byr ei wynt, caeth ei frest
astonish vt synnu

astound *vt* synnu, syfrdanu

astral *adj* serol

astray *adv* ar gyfeiliorn, ar grwydr

astride *adv* á'r traed ar led

astrologer *n* sêr-ddewin

astrology *n* sêr-ddewiniaeth

astronaut *n* gofodwr

astronomer *n* serydd, seryddwr

astronomy *n* seryddiaeth

astute *adj* craff, cyfrwys, call

asunder *adv* ar wahân, yn ddrylliau

asylum *n* noddfa. **lunatic a.** gwallgofdy

at *prep* yn, wrth, ger, ar

atheist *n* anffyddiwr

Athens *n* Athen

athlete *n* mabolgampwr

athletics *npl* mabolgampau

atlantic *adj* atlantaidd ♦ *n*: **the A. (Ocean)** Môr Iwerydd

atlas *n* llyfr mapiau, atlas

atmosphere *n* awyrgylch

atom *n* mymryn, gronyn, atom

atomic *adj* atomig

atone *vi* gwneuthur iawn

atonement *n* iawn, cymod

atrocious *adj* erchyll, anfad, ysgeler

attach *vb* gosod, glynu; atafaelu

attachment *n* ymlyniad, serch

attack *vt* ymosod ar ♦ *n* ymosodiad

attain *vt* ennill; cyrraedd; cael gafael

attainment *n* cyrhaeddiad

attempt *vt* ceisio, cynnig ♦ *n* cynnig, ymgais

attend *vb* gweini; ystyried; dilyn, mynychu

attendance *n* gwasanaeth; presenoldeb

attendant *n* gweinydd ♦ *adj* yn dilyn, ynghlwm wrth

attention *n* sylw, ystyriaeth

attentive *adj* astud, ystyriol

attenuate *vt* teneuo, lleihau

attest *vb* tystio, gwirio; ardystio

attic *n* nenlofft, nenlawr

attire *vt* gwisgo ♦ *n* gwisg, dillad

attitude *n* ystum, agwedd, osgo

attorney *n* twrnai

attract *vt* tynnu, atynnu, denu, hudo

attraction *n* atyniad

attractive *adj* atyniadol

attribute *n* priodoledd

attribute *vt* priodoli, cyfrif i

attrition *n* rhathiad, treuliad, traul

attune *vt* hwylio, cyweirio

auburn *adj* gwinau, browngoch

auction *n* arwerthiant, ocsiwn

auctioneer *n* arwerthwr

audacious *adj* hy, digywilydd, haerllug

audacity *n* hyfdra, ehofndra, beiddgarwch

audible *adj* hyglyw, clywadwy

audience *n* gwrandawyr, cynulleidfa

audio-visual *adj* clyweledol

audit *vt* archwilio cyfrifon ♦ *n* archwiliad

audition *n* clyweliadad

auditor *n* gwrandawr; archwilydd

auger *n* taradr, ebill

augment *vt* ychwanegu, atodi

augur *n* dewin ♦ *vb* darogan; argoeli

August *n* Awst

august *adj* urddasol, mawreddog

aunt *n* modryb

aura *n* naws, awyrgylch

aural *adj* clywedol

auspices *npl* nawdd

auspicious *adj* yn argoeli'n dda, ffafriol

austere *adj* gerwin, llym, tost, caled

austerity *n* gerwindeb, llymder

Australia *n* Awstralia

Australian *n* Awstraliad ♦ *adj* Awstralaidd

Austria *n* Awstria

Austrian *n* Awstriad ♦ *adj*

Awstriaidd
authentic adj dilys, gwir
author n awdur, awdwr
authoritarian adj awdurdodus
authoritative adj awdurdodol
authority n awdurdod
authorize vt awdurdodi
auto- prefix hunan-, ym-
autobiography n hunangofiant
autocracy n unbennaeth
autocrat n unben; dyn awdurdodol
autograph n llofnod
automatic adj hunanysgogol, awtomatig
automation n awtomasiwn
automobile n cerbyd, modur
autonomy n ymreolaeth
autumn n hydref
auxiliary adj cynorthwyol, ategol ♦ n cynorthwywr
avail vb llesáu, tycio ♦ n lles, budd
available adj ar gael
avalanche n syrthfa, cwymp (eira, etc)
avarice n cybydd-dod, trachwant
avaricious adj cybyddlyd, ariangar
avenge vt dial cam
avenue n mynedfa, rhodfa
aver vt gwirio, haeru
average n canolbris; cyfartaledd; cyffredin
averse adj gwrthwynebol, gelynol; croesi
aversion n gwrthwynebiad, casbeth
avert vt troi heibio, gochel, osgoi
aviary n adardy
avidity n awydd, awch, gwanc
avocation n gorchwyl, galwedigaeth
avoid vt gochel, osgoi, arbed
avouch vt gwirio, haeru; arddelwi
avow vt addef; cydnabod
await vt disgwyl, aros
awake vb deffro, dihuno ♦ adj effro
award vt dyfarnu ♦ n dyfarniad

aware adj hysbys, ymwybodol
awareness n arwybod, ymwybyddiaeth
awash adj llawn, cyforiog
away adv ymaith, i ffwrdd
awe n (parchedig) ofn ♦ vt rhoi arswyd
awful adj ofnadwy, arswydus
awhile adv am ennyd, am dro
awkward adj trwsgl, lletchwith, anghyfleus
awl n mynawyd
awning n cysgodlen, adlen
axe (axes) n bwyall, bwyell
axiom n gwireb
axis n echel, pegwn
axle n echel
ay adv ie
aye adv yn wastad(ol), byth
azure n glas y ffurfafen, asur ♦ adj asur

B

babble vb baldordd, clebran ♦ n baldordd
babe n baban, plentyn bach
baby n baban, maban, babi
babysitter n gwarchodwr babanod
bachelor n dyn dibriod, hen lanc; baglor
back n cefn ♦ vb cefnogi; bacio ♦ adv yn ôl
background n cefndir
backhander n tâl dirgel; ergyd â chefn y llaw
backpack n cefnbwn
backslide vi gwrthgilio
backward adv yn ôl, ar ôl ♦ adj hwyrfrydig; digynnydd; araf
backwater n dŵr disymud ar ymyl afon, lle o'r neilltu, dibwys, cwter gwsg
bacon n cig moch, bacwn
bad adj drwg, drygionus; gwael, sâl

badge *n* bathodyn
badger *n* mochyn daear, broch ♦ *vt* profocio, poeni
badminton *n* badminton
bad-tempered *adj* â thymer ddrwg
baffle *vt* drysu, siomi, trechu
bag *n* cwd, cod, bag
baggage *n* clud, celfi, pac
bagpipe *n* pibgod
bah *excl* pw!
bail *n* meichiau, gwystl ♦ *vt* mechnio
bail, bale *vt* hysbyddu cwch
bailiff *n* beili; hwsmon, goruchwyliwr
bait *vt* abwydo; baeddu, eirthio ♦ *n* abwyd
bake *vb* pobi, crasu
baker *n* pobydd
bakery *n* popty
balance *n* clorian, mantol; gweddill ♦ *vt* mantoli; cydbwyso
balanced *adj* cytbwys, cymesur
balcony *n* oriel, balcon
bald *adj* moel, penfoel
bale *n* pwn, sypyn, bwrn
baleful *adj* alaethus, gresynol, galarus
baler *n* byrnwr
balk, baulk *n* balc; siom ♦ *vt* balcio; siomi
ball *n* pêl, pellen
ball *n* dawns, dawnsfa
ballad *n* baled
ballast *n* balast
ball bearings *npl* berynnau pêl, pelferynnau
ballerina *n* balerina
ballet *n* bale
balloon *n* balŵn
ballot *n* balot, tugel
balm *n* balm, triagl
bamboozle *vb* twyllo, llygad-dynnu
ban *vt* gwahardd, ysgymuno
banal *adj* cyffredin, sathredig
banana *n* banana

band *n* band, rhwymyn; mintai; seindorf
bandage *n* rhwymyn ♦ *vb* rhwymo, rhwymynnu
bandbox *n* bocs hetiau
bandit *n* herwr, ysbeiliwr
bandy *vt* taflu (pêl, *etc*) yn ôl a blaen
bandy-legged *adj* coesgam
bane *n* dinistr, melltith
baneful *adj* dinistriol, andwyol
bang *vb* curo, dulio, clepian ♦ *n* ergyd, twrf
bangle *n* breichled
banish *vt* alltudio, deol
bank *n* mainc; rhes
bank *n* glan, torlan; traethell
bank *n* banc, ariandy ♦ *vb* bancio
banker *n* bancwr
bankrupt *n* methdalwr
bankruptcy *n* methdaliad
bank statement *n* datganiad banc, adroddiad banc
banner *n* baner, lluman
banns *npl* gostegion
banquet *n* gwledd ♦ *vb* gwledda
bantam *n* coriar, dandi
banter *n* ysmaldod, cellwair ♦ *vb* cellwair, profocio
baptism *n* bedydd
Baptist *n* Bedyddiwr
baptize *vt* bedyddio
bar *n* bar, bollt; rhwystr; traethell ♦ *vt* bario; eithrio
barb *n* barf; adfach
barbarian *n* barbariad, anwariad
barbaric *adj* barbaraidd
barbecue *n* rhostfa
barbed wire *n* weiar bigog
barber *n* barbwr
bard *n* bardd, prydydd
bare *adj* noeth, llwm, moel, prin ♦ *vt* dinoethi
barefooted *adj* troednoeth
barely *adv* prin, o'r braidd
bargain *n* bargen ♦ *vb* bargeinio
barge *n* bad mawr

bark *n* barc, llong, llestr

bark *vi* cyfarth, coethi ♦ *n* cyfarthiad

bark *n* rhisgl ♦ *vt* dirisglo, digroeni

barley *n* haidd, barlys

barm *n* burum, berem, berman

barmaid *n* barferch

barman *n* barmon

barn *n* ysgubor

barometer *n* hinfynegydd, baromedr

baron *n* barwn, arglwydd

baronet *n* barwnig

barrack *n* lluest, lluesty, gwersyllty

barrage *n* argae, clawdd

barrel *n* baril, casgen

barren *adj* diffrwyth; amhlantadwy

barricade *n* atalglawdd ♦ *vt* cau

barrier *n* atalfa, rhwystr, terfyn, ffin

barrister *n* bargyfreithiwr

barrow *n* berfa, whilber; crug

barter *vb* cyfnewid, ffeirio ♦ *n* cyfnewid

base *adj* isel, gwael, distadl, gau

base *n* sylfaen; bôn ♦ *vt* sylfaenu, seilio

baseball *n* pêl-fâs

basement *n* islawr

bashful *adj* swil, gwylaidd

basic *adj* gwaelodol, sylfaenol

basin *n* basn, cawg, dysgl

basis (**bases**) *n* sail, sylfaen

bask *vi* ymheulo, torheulo

basket *n* basged, cawell

basketful *n* basgedaid

bass *n* bas, isalaw; bàs, draenogiad y môr

bastard *n* bastard, plentyn gordderch/siawns

baste *vt* iro, brasteru; ffusto, ffonodio

bastinado *n, vt* ffonodio gwadnau'r traed

bat *n* ystlum

bat *n* bat ♦ *vi* batio

batch *n* pobiad, ffyrnaid; swp, sypyn

bath *n* ymolchfa, badd, baddon; bath

bathe *vb* ymdrochi, ymolchi, golchi

bathroom *n* ystafell ymolchi

baton *n* llawffon, baton, arweinffon

battalion *n* byddin, mintai, bataliwn

batter *vt* curo, pwyo ♦ *n* defnydd crempog, cytew

battery *n* magnelfa; batri

battle *n* brwydr, cad ♦ *vi* brwydro

battlefield *n* maes y gad

battlement *n* canllaw, murganllaw.

battleship *n* llongryfel

bauble *n* ffril, tegan

baulk Gwêl **balk**

bawdy *adj* anllad, anweddus

bawl *vi* gweiddi, crochlefain, bloeddio

bay *n* bae

bay *vb, n* cyfarth. **to hold at b.** rhoi cyfarth

bay *n* llawryf

bay *adj* gwinau, gwineugoch

bayonet *n* bidog ♦ *vt* bidogi

bazaar *n* basâr

be *vi* bod

beach *n* traeth, traethell ♦ *vt* gyrru ar y traeth

beacon *n* gwylfa, goleudy; coelcerth

bead *n* glain. **beads** paderau

beadle *n* rhingyll

beak *n* pig, gylfin, duryn

beaker *n* cwpan, diodlestr â phig, bicer

beam *n* trawst, paladr; pelydryn ♦ *vi* pelydru

bean *n* ffäen, ffeuen

bear *n* arth; arthes

bear *vt* dwyn, cludo; geni; dioddef, goddef

beard n barf; col ŷd
bearing n ymddygiad; traul
beast n bwystfil, anifail
beat vt curo ♦ n cur, curiad
beatitude n gwynfyd
beautiful adj prydferth, hardd, teg
beauty n prydferthwch, harddwch, tegwch. **b. parlour** parlwr pincio
beaver n afanc, llostlydan
becalm vt tawelu, llonyddu
because adv, conj oherwydd, oblegid, o achos; gan, am
beck n amnaid, awgrym
beckon vb amneidio
become vb dyfod; gweddu
becoming adj gweddus
bed n gwely; cefn, pâm
bedding n dillad gwely
bedeck vt addurno, trwsio
bedew vt gwlitho, gwlychu
bedfellow n cywely
bedlam n bedlam
bedraggled adj wedi caglo, dwyno; aflêr
bedrid(den) adj gorweiddiog
bedroom n ystafell wely, llofft
bedsitter n ystafell un gwely, ceginlofft
bedstead n pren neu haearn gwely
bee n gwenynen
beech n ffawydden
beef (**beeves**) n eidion; cig eidion, biff
beehive n cwch gwenyn
beeline n llinell unionsyth, ddiwyro
beer n cwrw
beestings npl llaeth newydd, llaeth toro
beet n betys
beetle n chwilen
beetroot n betys
befall vb digwyddd
befit vb gweddu
before prep o flaen, gerbron, cyn ♦ adv o'r blaen
beforehand adv ymlaen llaw
befriend vt ymgeleddu, bod yn

gefn
beg vb erfyn, deisyf, ymbil; cardota
beget vb cenhedlu, creu, peri
beggar n cardotyn ♦ vt tlodi, llymhau
begin vb dechrau
beginning n dechreuad
beguile vt hudo, twyllo; swyno, difyrru
behalf n plaid, rhan, achos, tu
behave vb ymddwyn
behaviour n ymddygiad
behead vt torri pen
behest n arch, archiad
behind adv, prep ar ôl, yn ôl, tu ôl, tu cefn
behold vt edrych, gweld ♦ vb imper wele
behove vt bod yn rhwymedig ar
beige adj beis
being n bod
belated adj diweddar; wedi ei ddal gan y nos
belch vb bytheirio
beleaguer vt gwarchae ar
belfry n clochdy
Belgium n Gwlad Belg
belie vt anwiredu, siomi
belief n cred, crediniaeth, coel
believe vb credu, coelio
believer n credwr, credadun
belittle vt bychanu
bell n cloch
belle n merch brydweddol, meinwen
bellicose adj rhyfelgar, ymladdgar
belligerent adj rhyfelog ♦ n rhyfelblaid
bellow vb rhuo, bugunad
bellows npl megin
belly n bol, bola; cest, tor ♦ vb bolio
belong vi perthyn
belongings n meddiannau, eiddo
beloved adj annwyl, cu ♦ n anwylyd

below *adv, prep* is, islaw, isod, obry, oddi tanodd

belt *n* gwregys

bemoan *vt* galaru am, arwylo

bemused *adj* syfrdan

bench *n* mainc

bend *vb* plygu, camu ♦ *n* tro, camedd

beneath *adv, prep* is, tan, oddi tanodd

benediction *n* bendith

benefactor *n* cymwynaswr, noddwr

benefice *n* bywoliaeth eglwysig

beneficent *adj* daionus, llesfawr

beneficial *adj* buddiol, llesol

benefit *n* budd, lles, elw ♦ *vb* llesáu, elwa

benevolent *adj* daionus, haelionus

benighted *adj* a ddaliwyd gan y nos; tywyll

benign *adj* tirion, mwyn

bent *n* tuedd, gogwydd

benumb *vt* merwino, fferru, diffrwytho

bequeath *vt* cymynnu, cymynroddi

bequest *n* cymynrodd

bereave *vt* difuddio, amddifadu

beret *n* bere

Berlin *n* Berlin

berry *n* aeronen, mwyaren

berserk *adj* gwyllt, aflywodraethus

berth *n* lle llong; gwely llongwr; swydd

beseech *vt* atolygu, deisyf, erfyn

beseem *vt* gweddu

beset *vt* cynllwyn; amgylchynu

beside *prep* gerllaw, wrth, yn ymyl. **to be b. oneself** o'i bwyll

besides *adv, prep* heblaw, gyda

besiege *vt* gwarchae ar

besmirch *vt* llychwino, pardduo

bespeak *vt* ymofyn ymlaen llaw

best *adj, adv* gorau

bestial *adj* bwystfilaidd

bestir *vt* cyffroi, ymysgwyd

bestow *vt* rhoddi, cyflwyno, anrhegu

bestride *vt* eistedd neu gamu yn groes i

bet *n* bet, cyngwystl ♦ *vb* betio, dal am

betoken *vt* arwyddo, argoeli

betray *vt* bradychu

betrayal *n* brad

betroth *vt* dyweddïo

better *adj* gwell, rhagorach ♦ *adv* yn well ♦ *vt* gwella

between, betwixt *prep* rhwng, cydrhwng

beverage *n* diod

bewail *vt* cwyno, cwynfan, galaru am

beware *vi* gochel, ymogelyd

bewilder *vt* drysu, mwydro, pensyfrdanu

bewitch *vt* rheibio

beyond *adv, prep* tu hwnt

bi- *prefix* dau-, deu-

bias *n* tuedd, gogwydd, rhagfarn ♦ *vt* tueddu

Bible *n* Beibl

bibliography *n* llyfryddiaeth

bibulous *adj* yfgar, llymeitgar

bicker *vi* ffraeo, ymrafaelio, ymgecru

bicycle *n* ceffyl haearn, deurod, beic

bid *vb* erchi; gwahodd; cynnig

bide *vb* aros, disgwyl

biennial *adj* dwyflynyddol

bier *n* elor

bifocals *npl* gwydrau deuffocal

big *adj* mawr; braisg

bigamy *n* dwywreigiaeth

bigheaded *adj* bras, mawreddog

bigot *n* penboethyn

bikini *n* bikini

bilberries *npl* llus

bile *n* bustl, geri

bilingual *adj* dwyieithog

bilingualism *n* dwyieithedd; dwyieitheg

bill *n* bil; mesur; rhaglen;

hysbyslen

bill *n* pig, gylfin, duryn
billet *n* llety (milwr) ♦ *vt* lletya
billiards *n* biliards
billion *n* biliwn
billow *n* ton, gwaneg, moryn ♦ *vi* tonni
billy-goat *n* bwch gafr
bin *n* cist
bind *vt* rhwymo, caethiwo
binge *n* gloddest, sbri
bingo *n* bingo
binoculars *n* deulygadur
biography *n* bywgraffiad, cofiant
biological *adj* biolegol
biology *n* bywydeg, bioleg
birch *n* bedw, bedwen; gwialen fedw ♦ *vt* chwipio
bird *n* aderyn
Biro *n* biro
birth *n* genedigaeth
birthday *n* pen-blwydd. **b. card** *n* carden pen-blwydd
birthmark *n* man geni
biscuit *n* bisgeden
bisect *vt* dwyrannu, rhannu
bisector *n* dwyrannydd
bisexual *adj* deurywiol
bishop *n* esgob
bishopric *n* esgobaeth
bison *n* ych gwyllt, bual
bit *n* tamaid; tipyn; dernyn; genfa, bit
bitch *n* gast
bite *vb* cnoi, brathu ♦ *n* cnoad, brath; tamaid
bitter *adj* chwerw, bustlaidd, tost
bittern *n* aderyn y bwn, bwmp y gors
bitterness *n* chwerwedd, chwerwder
bitumen *n* pyg
bituminous *adj* pyglyd
bizarre *adj* rhyfedd, od, chwithig
blab *vb* prepian, clepian ♦ *n* clepgi
black *adj* du ♦ *n* du, dyn du ♦ *vt* duo. **b. ice** *n* iâ du

blackberries *npl* mwyar duon
blackbird *n* aderyn du, mwyalchen
blackboard *n* bwrdd du
blackcurrant *n* cyrensen ddu ♦ *adj* cwrens du
blacken *vt* duo, pardduo; tywyllu
blackguard *n* dihiryn ♦ *vt* difrïo
blackleg *n* bradwr
blackmail *n* arian bygwth, blacmel
blacksmith *n* gof
bladder *n* pledren, chwysigen
blade *n* llafn; eginyn, blewyn
blame *vt* beio ♦ *n* bai
blameless *adj* di-fai
blanch *vt* gwynnu, cannu
bland *adj* mwyn, tyner, tirion
blandish *vt* gwenieithio, truthio
blank *adj* gwag, syn. **b. verse** mesur di-odl. **b. cheque** *n* siec wag
blanket *n* blanced, gwrthban
blare *vb* canu utgorn ♦ *n* sain utgorn
blarney *n* gweniaith, truth
blaspheme *vb* cablu, difenwi
blasphemy *n* cabledd, cabl
blast *n* chwa, chwythiad, deifiad ♦ *vt* deifio; saethu. **b. furnace** ffwrnais chwythu
blatant *adj* stwrllyd, digywilydd, haerllug
blaze *n* fflam, ffagl ♦ *vi* fflamio, ffaglu
bleach *vb* cannu, gwynnu
bleak *adj* oer, digysgod, noeth, noethlwm
blear *adj* pŵl, dolurus, dyfriog
bleat *vb* brefu ♦ *n* bref
bleed *vb* gwaedu
blemish *vt* anafu, anurddo ♦ *n* anaf, bai, mefl
blend *vb* cymysgu ♦ *n* cymysgedd
bless *vt* bendithio
blessed *adj* bendigedig, gwyn ei fyd
blessing *n* bendith
blight *n* malltod ♦ *vt* mallu, deifio

blind *adj* dall, tywyll ♦ *vt* dallu ♦ *n* llen, bleind

blindness *n* dallineb

blink *vb* cau'r llygaid, ysmicio, amrantu

bliss *n* gwynfyd, dedwyddyd

blister *n* chwysigen, pothell ♦ *vb* pothellu

blithe *adj* llawen, llon, hoenus

blitz *n* blits

blizzard *n* ystorm erwin o wynt ac eira

bloat *vb* chwyddo, chwythu

blob *n* ysmotyn, bwrlwm

block *n* plocyn, cyff ♦ *vt* cau, rhwystro

blockade *n* gwarchae ♦ *vb* gwarchae ar

blockhead *n* penbwl, hurtyn

blonde *adj* o bryd golau

blood *n* gwaed; gwaedoliaeth. **b. pressure** *n* pwysedd gwaed

bloody *adj* gwaedlyd

bloom *n* blodeuyn; gwawr, gwrid ♦ *vi* blodeuo

blossom *n* blodeuyn ♦ *vi* blodeuo

blot *n* ysmotyn du, blot, mefl ♦ *vb* blotio

blotch *n* ysmotyn, blotyn, ystremp

blouse *n* blows

blow *n* dyrnod, ergyd

blow *vb* chwythu

blow-dry *vb* chwythu'n sych

bludgeon *n* pastwn

blue *adj*, *n* glas ♦ *vt* glasu

bluff *adj* garw, brochus

blunder *n* amryfusedd ♦ *vb* amryfuso

blunt *adj* pŵl, di-fin; plaen ♦ *vt* pylu

blur *n* ysmotyn, ystaen

blurb *n* broliant

blurt *vt* rhuthro dywedyd

blush *vi* cochi, gwrido ♦ *n* gwrid

bluster *vi* trystio, brochi ♦ *n* brawl, broch

blustery *adj* stormus, rhuadus

boar *n* baedd

board *n* bwrdd, bord; ymborth ♦ *vb* byrddio

boarding house *n* llety

boast *n* ymffrost ♦ *vb* ymffrostio

boat *n* bad, cwch

bobbin *n* gwerthyd

bode *vt* darogan, argoeli

body *n* corff

bog *n* cors, mignen, siglen

boggle *vi* petruso; rhusio, ffwndro

bogus *adj* ffug, gau, ffuantus

bogy, -ey *n* bwbach, bwci, bwgan

boil *n* cornwyd, casgliad

boil *vb* berwi

boiler *n* pair, crochan

boisterous *adj* terfysglyd, trystiog, brochus

bold *adj* hy, eofn; hyderus; eglur

bollard *n* bolard

bolster *n* gobennydd ♦ *vt* ategu

bolt *n* bollt ♦ *vb* bolltio; dianc; trafluncu

bomb *n* bom

bombast *n* chwyddiaith

bombastic *n* chwyddedig

bona fide *adj* o'r iawn ryw, dilys, didwyll

bond *n* rhwymyn; ysgrifrwym ♦ *adj* caeth

bondage *n* caethiwed

bone *n* asgwrn

bonfire *n* coelcerth, banffagl

Bonn *n* Bonn

bonnet *n* bonet

bonny *adj* braf, nobl

bonus *n* bonws, ychwanegiad

booby *n* hurtyn, penbwl

book *n* llyfr

boom *n* bŵm

boom *vb* trystio, utganu ♦ *n* trwst, swae

boon *n* ffafr, bendith, caffaeliad

boor *n* taeog

boost *vb* gwthio, hybu

boot *n* botasen, esgid

booth n bwth, lluest, lluesty, caban

booty n ysglyfaeth, anrhaith, ysbail

booze vi diota, meddwi ♦ n diod feddwol

border n ffin, goror, ymyl ♦ vb ymylu

bore vb tyllu, ebillio ♦ n twll

bore n pla, dyn diflas ♦ vt blino, diflasu, llethu

bored adj wedi syrffedu ar beth, wedi alaru

boring adj diflas, annifyr, llethol

born adj wedi ei eni

borough n bwrdeistref

borrow vt benthyca

bosom n mynwes, côl

boss n meistr

botany n llysieueg

botch n ystomp ♦ vb ystompio, bwnglera

both adj, pron, adv y ddau, ill dau

bother vb blino, trafferthu ♦ n helynt, trafferth

bottle n potel, costrel ♦ vt potelu, costrelu. **b. opener** n agorwr poteli

bottom n gwaelod, godre, tin

bough n cainc, cangen

boulder n carreg fawr, clogfaen

bounce vb neidio, adlamu; bostio, ymffrostio

bound n terfyn, ffin, cyffin ♦ vt ffinio

bound vi llamu, neidio

boundary n ffin, terfyn

bounty n daioni, haelioni, ced

bouquet n blodeuglwm, pwysi

bout n sbel, term; ornest, ffrwgwd

bow n bwa; dolen

bow vb plygu, crymu, ymgrymu ♦ n moesymgrymiad

bow n pen blaen llong, bow

bowels npl ymysgaroedd, perfedd

bower n deildy

bowl n cawg, basn

bowler n het galed; bowliwr

box n bocs, pren bocs

box n bocs, blwch, cist; sedd, côr; bwth

box n bonclust ♦ vb taro bonclust; paffio. **b. office** n swyddfa docynnau

boy n bachgen, hogyn, mab, gwas

boycott n, vb ymwrthod â pherthynas a chydweithrediad, boicot(io)

boyfriend n cariadfab, anwylyd

boyhood n bachgendod, mebyd

brace n rhwymyn; pâr ♦ vt tynhau, cryfhau

bracelet n breichled

bracket n braced, cromfach

bracken n rhedyn ungoes

brag n brol, ymffrost, bocsach ♦ vb brolio, ymffrostio

braid n pleth, brwyd ♦ vt plethu, brwydo

brain n ymennydd

brake n dryslwyn, prysglwyn

brake n brêc ♦ vt brecio

bramble n miaren

bran n eisin, bran, rhuddion

branch n cangen, cainc ♦ vi canghennu

brand n pentewyn; nod ♦ vt gwarthnodi

brandish vb ysgwyd, chwifio

brandy n brandi

brash adj byrbwyll, ehud

brass n pres, efydd

brassière n bronglwm

brat n crwt, crwtyn; croten

bravado n gwag-ymffrost, bocsach, gorchest

brave adj dewr, gwrol, glew ♦ vt herio

bravo excl da iawn! campus!

brawl vi ffraeo, terfysgu ♦ n ffrae, ffrwgwd

brawn n cnawd

bray vt pwyo, briwio, malurio

bray vi brefu (megis asyn), nadu

brazen *adj* haerllug, hy
Brazil *n* Brasil
breach *n* adwy, rhwyg, tor; trosedd
bread *n* bara
breadth *n* lled
break *vb* torri ♦ *n* toriad, tor
breakdown *n* salwch, colli iechyd; (*car*) torri lawr
breakfast *n* brecwast ♦ *vb* brecwasta
breakwater *n* morglawdd
breast *n* bron, dwyfron, mynwes ♦ *vt* wynebu, ymladd â
breath *n* anadl, gwynt
breathalyser *n* anadlydd, anadliadur
breathe *vb* anadlu, chwythu
breathing *n* anadliad; anadlu
breech *n* tin, bôn
breeches *npl* llodrau, clos
breed *vb* magu; epilio; bridio ♦ *n* rhywogaeth, brid
breeze *n* awel, awelan, chwa
brethren *npl* brodyr (ffigurol yn bennaf)
brevity *n* byrder, byrdra
brew *vt* darllaw, bragu
brewer *n* darllawydd, bragwr
bribe *n* llwgrwobrwy ♦ *vt* llwgrwobrwyo
brick *n* bricsen, priddfaen ♦ *vt* bricio
bride *n* priodferch, priodasferch
bridegroom *n* priodfab
bridesmaid *n* morwyn briodas
bridge *n* pont ♦ *vt* pontio
bridle *n* ffrwyn ♦ *vt* ffrwyno
brief *adj* byr
brier, briar *n* miaren, drysien
brigade *n* brigâd, mintai, torf
brigand *n* ysbeiliwr, carnleidr, herwr
bright *adj* disglair, claer, gloyw, hoyw
brilliance *n* disgleirdeb
brilliant *adj* disglair, llachar ♦ *n* gem
brim *n* ymyl, min, cyfor; cantel
brimstone *n* brwmstan
brindled *adj* brith, brych
brine *n* heli
bring *vt* dwyn, cyrchu, dyfod â; dod â
brink *n* min, ymyl, glan
brisk *adj* bywiog, heini, sionc
bristle *n* gwrychyn, gwrych ♦ *vi* codi gwrychyn
Britain *n* Prydain
British *adj* Prydeinig, Brytanaidd
Briton *n* Brython, Prydeiniwr
Brittany *n* Llydaw
brittle *adj* brau, bregus
broach *vt* agor baril, gollwng; agor ymddiddan
broad *adj* llydan; eang; bras
broaden *vb* lledu, ehangu
broccoli *n* brocoli, math o fresych
brochure *n* llyfryn
brogue *n* llediaith (Gwyddelod)
broil *vt* briwlio
broken *adj* toredig, briw, drylliedig
broker *n* brocer, dyn canol
broll *n* terfysg, ymrafael, ymryson
bronchitis *n* bronceitis
bronze *n* pres, efydd
brooch *n* tlws
brood *n* nythaid; hil, epil ♦ *vi* deor; synfyfyrio
brook *n* nant, cornant, afonig
broom *n* banadl; ysgub, ysgubell
broth *n* potes, cawl
brothel *n* puteindy
brother (-s, brethren) *n* brawd
brotherly *adj* brawdol. b. **love** brawdgarwch
brow *n* ael, talcen; crib
brown *adj* brown, llwyd, gwinau. b. **paper** *n* papur llwyd. b. **sugar** *n* siwgr coch
browse *vi* brigbori, pori, blewynna
bruise *vb* cleisio, ysigo ♦ *n* clais
brunette *n* gwineuferch

brunt n pwys a gwres, ergyd
brush n brws ♦ vt brwsio, ysgubo
brushwood n manwydd, prysgwydd
brusque adj cwta, anfoesgar, taeog
Brussels sprouts npl ysgewyll Brysel
brutal adj creulon, bwysfilaidd
brute n anifail, creadur (direswm)
bubble n bwrlwm ♦ vb byrlymu
buccaneer n môr-leidr, môr-herwr
buck n bwch; coegyn ♦ vb llamsachu
bucket n bwced, ystwc
buckle n bwcl, gwäeg ♦ vb byclu, gwaegu
bud n blaguryn, eginyn ♦ vb blaguro, egino
budge vb syflyd, chwimio
budget n cwd, coden; cyllideb
buff adj llwydfelyn
buffalo n bual
buffet n cernod ♦ vt cernodio, baeddu
buffoon n digrifwas, croesan, ysgentyn
bug n drewbryf, bwg
bugbear n bwgan, bwbach, bwci
bugle n corn, utgorn
build vt adeiladu ♦ n corffolaeth
building n adail, adeilad, adeiladaeth
bulb n bwlb
bulge n chwydd ♦ vt chwyddo
bulk n swm, crynswth
bull n tarw
bulldozer n peiriant clirio ffordd, tarw dur
bullet n bwled, bwleden
bulletin n bwletin
bullfight n ymladd teirw
bullfinch n coch y berllan
bullion n aur neu arian clamp, bwliwn
bullock n bustach, eidion, ych
bull's eye n trawiad union

bully n gormeswr, bwli ♦ vt gormesu, erlid
bulrushes npl llafrwyn, hesg
bulwark n gwrthglawdd; canllaw
bumbailiff n bwmbeili
bumble-bee n cacynen
bump vb bwmpio, hergydio ♦ n bwmp, hergwd
bumper n llawn, helaeth
bumpkin n lleban, llabwst, llelo
bumptious adj hunandybus, rhodresgar
bumpy adj aflonydd, anwadal, garw
bun n bynsen, bynnen, teisen
bunch n swp; cwlwm, pwysi ♦ vt sypio
bundle n bwndel, coflaid ♦ vt bwndelu
bungalow n tŷ unllawr, byngalo
bungle vb bwnglera, ystompio ♦ n bwnglerwaith
bunion n corn ar fys troed
bunker n bwncer
bunkum n lol, ffiloreg, truth
bunting n (defnydd) banerau
buoy n bwi ♦ vt cynnal, cadw rhag suddo
buoyant adj hynawf; calonnog
burden n baich ♦ vt beichio, llwytho
bureau n ysgrifgist; swyddfa
bureaucracy n biwrocratiaeth
burgess, burgher n dinesydd, bwrdais
burglar n torrwr tŷ, bwrgler
burial n claddedigaeth, angladd
burlesque n digrifwawd, gwatwargerdd
burly adj corfful, praff, mawr
burn vb llosgi, ysu ♦ n llosg, llosgiad
burnish vt caboli, llathru, gloywi
burrow n twll cwningen ♦ vb tyllu, tyrchu
bursar n bwrser, swyddog ariannol
bursary n amneriaeth, ysgoloriaeth

burst vb byrstio, ymrwygo, ymddryllio, torri ♦ n rhwyg

bury vt claddu

bus n bws

bush n perth, llwyn; prysgwydd, drysi

bushel n bwysel, mesur wyth galwyn

business n busnes, masnach, gwaith. **b. trip** n taith fusnes

businessman/woman n gŵr busnes/gwraig fusnes

bus-stop n atalfa bws, arosfan

bust n penddelw; mynwes

bustle vi trafferthu, ffwdanu ♦ n ffwdan

busy adj prysur

busybody n ymyrrwr, dyn busneslyd, trwyn

but conj, prep ond, eithr

butcher n cigydd ♦ vt cigyddio, lladd

butler n trulliad, bwtler

butt n nod, targed; cyff clêr

butt vt cornio, hyrddu, twlcio, hwylio

butt n casgen, baril

butter n ymenyn ♦ vt rhoi ymenyn ar

buttercup n blodyn yr ymenyn

butterfly n glöyn byw, iâr fach yr haf, pili-pala

buttermilk n llaeth enwyn

buttery n bwtri

buttock n ffolen

button n botwm ♦ vt botymu

buttress n ateg, gwanas ♦ vt ategu

buxom adj glandeg, gweddgar, nwyfus

buy vt prynu

buzz vb suo, sisial, mwmian ♦ n su, swn gwenyn

by prep gan, wrth, trwy, ger, gerllaw ♦ adv heibio, yn agos ♦ prefix rhag-, is-

by-election n isetholiad

by(e)-law n is-ddeddf

by-gone n yr hyn a fu

bypass n ffordd osgoi

by-product n isgynnyrch

bystander n un yn sefyll gerllaw

byword n ymadrodd cynefin, cyffredin

C

cab n cab

cabal n clymblaid, cabal ♦ vi clymbleidio

cabaret n cabare

cabbage n bresychen, bresych

cabin n caban ♦ vt cabanu, caethiwo

cabinet n cell, cist; cabinet

cable n rhaff fferf; cebl tanfor

cackle vi clegar

cactus n mwll ysgallen, cactws

cad n taeog, bryntyn, cenau

caddie n gwas golffwr

cadence n goslef, diweddeb

cadet n mab ieuengaf; cadlanc

café n tŷ bwyta, caffe

cage n cawell, caets ♦ vt cau, carcharu

cairn n carn, carnedd, crug

cajole vt twyllo drwy weniaith

cake n teisen, cacen ♦ vb torthi; caglu

calamity n adfyd, trallod, trychineb

calcine vb llosgi'n galch

calculate vb cyfrif, bwrw cyfrif, clandro

calculation n cyfrif

calculator n cyfrifiannell

calendar n calendr, almanac

calf (calves) n llo

calf n (of the leg) croth (coes)

calibre n calibr

call vb galw ♦ n galwad, galw; ymweliad

calling n galwedigaeth

callous adj croendew, dideimlad,

caled
calm adj tawel ♦ n tawelwch ♦ vb tawelu
calorie n calori, uned gwres
calumny n anair, enllib, athrod, cabl
calve vi bwrw llo
Calvinism n Calfiniaeth
camber n camber
Cambodia n Cambodia
Cambrian adj Cymreig
camel n camel
cameo n cameo
camera n ystafell; teclyn tynnu lluniau, camera
camouflage n cuddliw, dull o ddieithrio ♦ vb dieithrio, cuddio
camp n gwersyll ♦ vi gwersyllu
campaign n ymgyrch, rhyfelgyrch
campbed n gwely plyg
campsite n maes gwersylla
campus n campws
can n tyn, piser, stên ♦ vb gallu. **c. opener** n agorwr caniau
Canada n Canada
Canadian adj Canadaidd ♦ n Canadiad
canal n camlas; pibell
canary n caneri
Canary Islands npl: the **C.I.** yr Ynysoedd Dedwydd
cancel vt dileu, dirymu, diddymu
cancer n dafad wyllt, cancr, cranc
candid adj teg, onest, plaen
candidate n ymgeisydd
candle n cannwyll
candlestick n canhwyllbren
candour n onestrwydd, didwylledd
candy n candi
cane n corsen, cansen ♦ vt curo â chansen
canine adj perthynol i'r ci
canister n tun cadw te, bocs (te)
canker n cancr ♦ vb cancro
canned adj ar gadw mewn can tun
cannibal n canibal
cannon n magnel

canny adj call, cyfrwys, ffel
canoe n ceufad, canŵ
canon n canon, rheol
canopy n gortho, nenlen
cant n ffugsancteidddrwydd, rhagrith ♦ vi rhagrithio
cantankerous adj cweryglar, cynhennus
cantata n cantata, cantawd
canteen n cantin
canter vi rhygyngu ♦ n rhygyng
canticle n cantigl, canig, cân, emyn
canto n cân, adran o gân
canton n rhandir, talaith
canvas n cynfas, lliain bras
canvass vb trafod; ymofyn pleidleisiau, canfasio
canyon n ceunant, canion
cap n cap, capan ♦ vt capio
capable adj galluog, cymwys, cyfaddas
capacity n gallu, cymhwyster; cynnwys
cape n penrhyn, pentir, trwyn
cape n mantell, cêp
caper n pranc ♦ vi prancio
capital adj prif, pen ♦ n priflythyren; prifddinas; cyfalaf
capitalism n cyfalafiaeth
capital punishment n y gosb eithaf
capitulate vi ymostwng ar amodau
caprice n mympwy, chwilen
capsize vb dymchwelyd, troi
capsule n capswl
captain n capten
caption n pennawd, teitl
captivate vt swyno, hudo, denu
captive adj caeth ♦ n carcharor
captivity n caethiwed; caethglud
captor n daliwr, deiliad
capture n daliad ♦ vt dal
car n car, cerbyd. **c. wash** golfcha geir
caravan n carafán; men. **c. site** n maes carafanau

carbine *n* dryll byr, byrddryll
carbohydrate(s) *n*
   carbohydrad(au)
carbon *n* carbon
carbuncle *n* carbwncl
carburettor *n* carburadur
carcass, -ase *n* celain, ysgerbwd
card *n* cerdyn, carden
card *vt* cribo gwlân
cardiac *adj* perthynol i'r galon
Cardiff *n* Caerdydd
cardigan *n* cardigan
cardinal *adj* prif, arbennig ♦ *n*
   cardinal
care *n* gofal, pryder ♦ *vi* gofalu,
   malio
career *n* gyrfa, hynt ♦ *vi* carlamu
careful *adj* gofalus, gwyliadwrus
careless *adj* diofal, esgeulus
caress *n* anwes, mwythau ♦ *vt*
   anwesu
caret *n* gwallnod, diffygnod (')
caretaker *n* gofalwr
cargo *n* llwyth (llong), cargo
caricature *n* gwawdlun, digrifllun
caring *adj* gofalus
carnage *n* galanastra, lladdfa
carnal *adj* cnawdol
carnation *n* blodyn cigliw
carnival *n* carnifal
carnivorous *adj* cigysol, rheibus
carol *n* carol ♦ *vi* caroli, canu
carouse *vi* gloddesta, cyfeddach
carp *vi* pigo beiau, cecru, cadw
   swn
car park *n* maes parcio
carpenter *n* saer coed
carpet *n* carped ♦ *vt* carpedu
carriage *n* cerbyd; cludiad;
   ymarweddiad
carrier *n* cariwr, cludydd. **c. bag** *n*
   cludfag
carrion *n* burgyn, celain, ysgerbwd
carrot *n* moronen
carry *vb* cario, cludo, cywain
cart *vb* men, troi, cert, cart, car
cartilage *n* madruddyn

carton *n* carton
cartoon *n* digrifllun, cartŵn
cartridge *n* cetrisen
carve *vt* cerfio, naddu; torri cig
cascade *n* rhaeadr
case *n* achos, cyflwr; dadl
case *n* cas, gwain; cist wydr
casement *n* ffenestr adeiniog,
   casment
cash *n* arian parod. **c. desk** *n* safle
   talu
cashier *n* ariannwr, trysorydd
cashier *vt* diswyddo
casing *n* plisgyn; casin
casino *n* casino
cask *n* casgen, baril
casket *n* cistan, prenfol, blwch
casserole *n* llestr coginio a dal
   bwyd
cassette *n* casét
cassock *n* llaeswisg ddu offeiriad,
   casog
cast *vb* bwrw, taflu ♦ *n* tafliad. **c.
   iron** haearn bwrw
caste *n* llwyth; gradd, braint; cast
castigate *vt* cystwyo
casting-vote *n* pleidlais y
   cadeirydd
castle *n* castell ♦ *vi* castellu
castrate *vt* disbaddu
casual *adj* damweiniol, achlysurol
casualty *n* un wedi ei anafu
casuistry *n* achosionaeth
cat *n* cath
cataclysm *n* dilyw, dylif,
   rhyferthwy
catacomb *n* claddgell, claddogof
catalogue *n* catalog
catapult *n* blif, catapwlt
cataract *n* rhaeadr, sgwd; pilen
catarrh *n* llif annwyd, gormwyth
catastrophe *n* trychineb
catch *vt* dal ♦ *n* bach, clicied;
   dalfa
catching *adj* heintus
catchment area *n* dalgylch
catechism *n* holwyddoreg,

catecism
category *n* trefn, dosbarth
cater *vi* arlwyo, darmerth, darparu
caterpillar *n* lindys
cathartic *n* carthlyn
cathedral *n* eglwys gadeiriol
catholic *adj* catholig: pabyddol ♦ *n* catholigydd; pabydd
catkins *npl* cenawon cyll, cywion gwyddau
cattle *npl* gwartheg, da
caucus *n* clymblaid
caudle *n* sucan
cauldron *n* crochan, pair, callor
cauliflower *n* blodfresychen
causality *n* achosiaeth
cause *n* achos ♦ *vt* achosi, peri
causeway *n* sarn, cawsai
caustic *adj* ysol, llosg, deifiol
cauterize *vt* serio
caution *n* pwyll, gwyliadwriaeth; rhybudd ♦ *vt* rhybuddio
cautious *adj* gwyliadwrus
cavalcade *n* mintai o farchogion
cavalier *n* marchog, marchfilwr
cavalry *n* gwŷr meirch
cave *n* ogof
cavern *n* ceudwll, ogof
caviar(e) *n* grawn pysgod, cafiâr
cavil *vi* cecru
cavity *n* ceudod, gwagle
caw *vi* crawcian
cease *vb* peidio, darfod
cedar *n* cedrwydden
cede *vt* rhoi i fyny, gildio, trosglwyddo
ceiling *n* nen, nenfwd
celebrate *vt* clodfori; dathlu; gweinyddu
celebrated *adj* clodfawr, enwog, hyglod
celebrity *n* bri, enwogrwydd; gŵr o fri
celery *n* seleri
celestial *adj* nefol, nefolaidd
celibate *adj* dibriod
cell *n* cell

cellar *n* seler
cement *n* sment ♦ *vt* smentio; cadarnhau
cemetery *n* mynwent, claddfa
censer *n* thuser
censor *n* beirniad; sensor
censure *n* cerydd, sen ♦ *vt* ceryddu
census *n* cyfrifiad
cent *n* y ganfed ran o ddoler
centenarian *n* canmlwyddiad
centenary *n* canmlwyddiant
centigrade *adj* canradd, sentigred
central *adj* canol, canolog. **c. heating** *n* gwres canolog
centre *n* canol, canolfan, canolbwynt ♦ *vb* canolbwyntio
centre-forward *n* canolwr blaen
centre-threequarter *n* canolwr
centrifugal *adj* allgyrchol
centripetal *adj* mewngyrchol
centurion *n* canwriad
century *n* canrif
ceramic *adj* perthynol i grefft y crochenydd, ceramig
cereal *n* grawn, ŷd
cerebral *adj* ymenyddol
ceremony *n* seremoni, defod
certain *adj* sicr; neilltuol; rhyw, rhai
certainly *adv* yn sicr, yn siwr
certainty *n* sicrwydd
certificate *n* tystysgrif
certify *vt* hysbysu, tystio
cesspool *n* carthbwll
chafe *vb* rhwbio; llidio ♦ *n* llid, cythrudd
chaff *n* us, manus, mân us
chaffer *vi* edwica, bargeinio, bargenna
chaffinch *n* pinc, asgell fraith
chagrin *n* cythrudd, siom
chain *n* cadwyn ♦ *vt* cadwyno
chair *n* cadair ♦ *vt* cadeirio
chairman *n* cadeirydd
chalet *n* bwthyn (haf)
chalice *n* cwpan cymun, caregl

chalk *n* sialc ♦ *vt* sialcio
challenge *n* her, sialens ♦ *vt* herio, sialensio
chamber *n* ystafell, siambr
chamberlain *n* gwas ystafell, siambrlen
champ *vt* cnoi, dygnoi
champagne *n* gwin Champagne
champion *n* pencampwr; pleidiwr ♦ *vt* cymryd plaid
chance *n* damwain, siawns ♦ *vt* digwydd
chancel *n* cangell
chancellor *n* canghellor
chandelier *n* canhwyllyr
chandler *n* canhwyllydd, masnachydd
change *n* newid, cyfnewid ♦ *n* newid
changing-room *n* ystafell newid
channel *n* sianel, gwely; rhigol
chant *vt* corganu ♦ *n* corgan, salmdon
chaos *n* tryblith, anhrefn
chap *vt* agennu, torri (am ddwylo)
chapel *n* capel
chaplain *n* caplan
chapter *n* pennod; cabidwl
char *vb* golosgi, deifio
character *n* cymeriad; nod, arwydd
characteristic *adj* nodweddiadol ♦ *n* nodwedd
charcoal *n* marwor, golosg, sercol
charge *vb* siarsio; cyhuddo; rhuthro; codi; llwytho ♦ *n* siars; gofal; cyhuddiad; rhuthr; pris; ergyd
charger *n* march rhyfel, cadfarch
chariot *n* cerbyd
charity *n* cariad; cardod, elusen
charlatan *n* un yn hônni gwybodaeth; cwac
charm *n* swyn, cyfaredd ♦ *vt* swyno
charming *adj* cyfareddol, swynol, cwrtais

chart *n* siart
charter *n* siarter, breinlen ♦ *vt* breinio; llogi. **c. flight** *n* hediad siartr
charwoman *n* morwyn wrth y dydd
chary *adj* gwagelog, gochelgar, gofalus
chase *vt* ymlid, erlid, hel ♦ *n* helwriaeth
chasm *n* hafn, ceunant, agendor
chaste *adj* diwair, pur, dillyn
chasten *vt* puro, coethi; ceryddu
chastise *vb* ceryddu, cosbi, cystwyo
chastity *n* diweirdeb, purdeb
chat *vi* sgwrsio, ymgomio ♦ *n* sgwrs, ymgom
chattel *n* catel
chatter *vi* trydar, cogor; clebran; rhincian
chatterbox *n* clebryn, clebren
chatty *adj* siaradus, parod am sgwrs
chauffeur *n* gyrrwr
cheap *adj* rhad, salw
cheat *n* twyll; twyllwr ♦ *vt* twyllo
check *n* rhwystr, atalfa ♦ *vt* atal, ffrwyno
cheek *n* grudd, boch; digywilydd-dra
cheeky *adj* digywilydd, haerllug, eg(e)r
cheer *n* calondid, cysur; arlwy ♦ *vb* llonni, sirioli, sirio
cheerful *adj* llon, siriol
cheers! *excl* iechyd da!
cheese *n* caws
chef *n* prif gogydd
chemical *adj* cemegol ♦ *n* cyffur
chemise *n* crys merch
chemist *n* fferyllydd; cemegwr
chemistry *n* cemeg
cheque *n* archeb (ar fanc), siec. **c. book** *n* llyfr siec; (col) llyfr main. **c. card** *n* carden siec
chequer *vt* amryliwio, britho

chequered adj brith, anwadal
cherish vt meithrin, coleddu, mynwesu
cherry n ceiriosen
cherub n ceriwb
chess n gwyddbwyll
chest n cist, coffr; brest
chestnut n castan
chevalier n marchog
chew vb cnoi. **c. the cud** cnoi cil
chewing gum n gwm cnoi
chick, chicken n cyw (iâr)
chicken-pox n brech yr ieir
chide vt ceryddu, dwrdio
chief adj pen, pennaf, prif ♦ n pennaeth
chieftain n blaenor, pennaeth
chilblain n llosg eira, cibwst, malaith
child (-ren) n plentyn
childhood n plentyndod, mebyd
Chile n Chile
chill n oerni, annwyd ♦ adj oer, anwydog ♦ vb oeri, fferru, rhynnu
chime n sain cloch neu gloc ♦ vb canu (clychau)
chimera n anghenfil; bwgan, bwbach
chimney n corn mwg, simnai
chin n gên
China n China, Tseina
china n llestri te (tsieni)
chink n agen, hollt
chip vb hacio, naddu ♦ n asglodyn, pric
chips npl sglodion
chiropodist n troedfeddyg
chirp vi yswitian, grillian, trydar
chisel n cŷn, gaing
chit n nodyn byr
chivalry n urddas marchog; sifalri
chives n cennin sifi
chocolate n siocled
choice n dewis, dewisiad ♦ adj dewisol, dethol
choir n côr; cafell
choke vb tagu; mygu; topio, cau

choler n geri, bustl; dicter, llid
cholera n y geri marwol, colera
choose vb dewis, dethol, ethol
chop vt torri ♦ n golwyth
choral adj corawl
chord n tant; cord
chore n y dwt
chorus n côr, cytgan, byrdwn, corws
Christ n Crist
christen vt bedyddio, enwi
Christendom n (gwledydd) Cred
Christian adj Cristnogol ♦ n Cristion
Christianity n Cristnogaeth
Christmas n Nadolig
Christmassy adj Nadoligaidd
chrome n crôm
chronic adj parhaol (am anhwyldeb)
chronicle n cronicl ♦ vt croniclo
chronology n amserydyddiaeth
chrysanthemum n ffarwel haf
chubby adj wynepgrwn, tew
chuck vt taro dan yr ên; taflu, lluchio
chuckle vi chwerthin yn nwrn dyn
chum n cyfaill mebyd ♦ vi cyfrinachu
chunk n tafell dew, toc
church n eglwys, llan ♦ vt eglwysa
churchyard n mynwent
churl n taeog, costog, cerlyn
churlish adj afrywiog, taeogaidd
churn n buddai ♦ vb corddi
chutney n picl cymysg
cider n seidr
cigar n sigâr
cigarette n sigarét
cincture n gwregys, rhwymyn
cinder n marworyn, colsyn
cine-camera n camera sine
cinema n sinema
cinnamon n sinamon
cipher n gwagnod (O); ysgrifen ddirgel ♦ vi cyfrif
circle n cylch ♦ vb cylchu

circuit n cylch; cylchdaith
circular adj crwn ♦ n cylchlythyr
circulate vb cylchredeg, lledaenu
circum- prefix cylch-, am-
circumcise vt enwaedu
circumference n cylchyn; cylchedd
circumflex n acen grom, to (^)
circumlocution n cylchymadrodd
circumscribe vt cyfyngu
circumspect adj gwyliadwrus, gofalus
circumstance n amgylchiad
circumstantial adj amgylchus
circumvent vb twyllo
circus n syrcas
cistern n dyfrgist, pydew, sistern
citadel n castell, amddiffynfa, caer
cite vt gwysio; dyfynnu
citizen n dinesydd
city n dinas
civic adj dinesig
civil adj gwladol; moesgar
civilian n dinesydd (anfilwrol)
civilization n gwareiddiad
civilize vt gwareiddio
civil service n gwasanaeth sifil, gwasanaeth gwladol
civil war n rhyfel cartref
clack vi clecian, clepian, clegar
claim vt hawlio ♦ n hawl
clamber vi dringo, cribo
clammy adj gludiog, cleiog, toeslyd
clamour n gwaedd, dadwrdd ♦ vi crochlefain
clamp n ystyffwl, craff
clan n tylwyth, llwyth
clandestine adj lladradaidd
clang, clank vb cloncio ♦ n clonc
clap n twrf, trwst ♦ vb curo; taro; clepian
claret n claret
clarify vt gloywi, puro; egluro
clarinet n clarinet
clarion n utgorn
clash vb taro, gwrthdaro ♦ n

gwrthdrawiad
clasp n gwaeg, bach, clesbyn ♦ vt gwaegu; cofleidio
class n dosbarth ♦ vt dosbarthu
classic n clasur, campwaith, llên goeth ♦ adj clasurol
classical adj clasurol
classics npl clasuron
classify vt dosbarthu
classroom n ystafell ddosbarth
clatter vb clewtian, clepian, trystio ♦ n trwst
clause n adran, cymal
claw n crafanc, ewin ♦ vt crafangu, cripio
clay n clai
clean adj glân, glanwaith ♦ vt glanhau
cleaner n glanhawr, glanheydd
cleaning n glanhad, glanheuad
cleanly adv yn lân
cleanse vt glanhau
cleanser n glanhawr
clear adj clir, eglur, gloyw; croyw ♦ vt clirio
cleave vi glynu (wrth)
cleave vi hollti; fforchogi
clef n allweddid, cleff
cleft n hollt, agen
clement adj tyner, tirion, trugarog
clench vt cau yn dynn, clensio
clergy n offeiriaid
clergyman n clerigwr, offeiriad
clerical adj clerigol; perthynol i glerc
clerk n clerc
clever adj medrus, deheuig, clyfar
cleverness n medr, deheurwydd, clyfrwch
click vi clician, clepian ♦ n clic
client n cyflogydd cyfreithiwr, cwsmer
cliff n clogwyn, allt
climate n hinsawdd
climax n uchafbwynt
climb vb dringo
climbing adj dringol

clinch vt clensio; cau, cloi
cling vi glynu, cydio
clinic n meddygfa, clinig
clinical adj clinigol
clink vi tincian
clip vt cneifio, tocio, clipio
clique n clic, clymblaid
cloak n mantell, clogyn, clog ♦ vt cuddio, celu
cloakroom n ystafell ddillad
clock n cloc
clod n tywarchen
clog n clocsen ♦ vt llesteirio; tagu; clocsio
cloister n clwysty
close vb cau; terfynu ♦ n diwedd, diweddglo
close adj agos, clòs; caeth, tyn
close n clas, clos, buarth, clwt, cae
closed shop n gwaith cyfyngedig, gwaith i rai yn unig
closet n cell, ystafell; geudy
close-up n llun agos
closure n cau, gorffen, darfod
clot n tolchen ♦ vb tolchi, ceulo
cloth n brethyn, lliain
clothe vt dilladu, gwisgo
clothes npl dillad, gwisgoedd
clothes peg n bachyn dillad
clothier n brethynnwr, dilledydd
clothing n dillad
cloud n cwmwl ♦ vt cymylu
clout n cernod, clewt; clwt ♦ vt clewtian; clytio
clover n meillion, clofer
clown n lleban; croesan, clown
club n pastwn; clwb ♦ vb pastynu; clybio
clue n pen llinyn, arwydd
clump n clwmp, clamp, cyff
clumsy adj trwsgl, anfedrus, lletchwith
cluster n clwstwr, swp ♦ vb casglu, tyrru
clutch n crafanc; gafael, (pl). hafflau ♦ vb crafangu

clutter n dadwrdd, helynt
co- prefix cyd-
coach n cerbyd; hyfforddwr ♦ vb hyfforddi
coagulate vb ceulo
coal n glöyn, glo
coalesce vi cyfuno, cyd-doddi
coalition n cyfuniad; cynghrair, clymblaid
coarse adj garw, aflednais; bras
coast n arfordir, glan ♦ vi hwylio gyda'r lan
coastal adj arfordirol
coastguard n gwyliwr y glannau
coastline n morlin
coat n cot. c. hanger n cambren (dillad). c. of arms n arfbais
coating n caen, golchiad
coax vb hudo, denu, perswadio
cobble, -stone n carreg balmant
cobbler n crydd, cobler
cobweb n gwe pryf cop, gwe'r cor
cock n ceiliog; mwdwl; cliced (dryll) ♦ vb mydylu; codi cliced
cockerel n cyw ceiliog, ceiliogyn
cock-eyed adj â llygad tro
cockles npl cocos, cocs, rhython
cockpit n sedd peilot; ymladdfan ceiliogod
cockroach n chwilen ddu
cock-sure adj gorbendant, gorhyderus
cocktail n coctêl
cocoa n coco
coconut n cneuen goco, coconyt
cod n y penfras; cod
code n côd
coerce vb gorfodi, gorthrechu
coercion n gorfodaeth, gorthrech
coffee n coffi
coffin n arch, ysgrin
cog n dant olwyn, còg
cogent adj cryf, grymus, argyhoeddiadol
cohabit vi cyd-fyw
cohere vb cydlynu
cohesion n cydlyniad

coil vb torchi ♦ n torch
coin n arian bath ♦ vb bathu
coincide vi cyd-ddigwydd, cyd-daro
coincidence n cyd-ddigwyddiad
coke n golosg, côc
colander n hidl
cold adj oer ♦ n oerfel, oerni,
  annwyd. **to catch a c.** dal annwyd
colic n bolwst, colig
collapse vb disgyn, cwympo ♦ n
  cwymp, methiant
collapsible adj plygadwy
collar n coler ♦ vb coleru. **c. bone**
  pont yr ysgwydd
collateral adj cyfochrog, cyfystlys
colleague n cydweithiwr
collect n colect ♦ vb crynhoi, hel,
  ymgynnull, casglu
collection n casgliad
collector n casglwr
college n coleg
collide vb gwrthdaro
collie n ci defaid
collier n glöwr; llong lo
colliery n gwaith glo, pwll glo,
  glofa
collision n gwrthdrawiad
colloquial adj llafar, tafodieithol
colon n gorwahannod, colon (:);
  coluddyn mawr
colonel n cyrnol
colonial adj trefedigaethol
colony n trefedigaeth, gwladfa
colossal adj cawraidd, anferth
colour n lliw, baner ♦ vb lliwio;
  cochi. **c. bar** gwahanfur lliw. **c.**
  blind lliwddall
coloured adj lliw
colourful adj lliwgar
colouring n lliwiad
colourless adj di-liw
colt n ebol
column n colofn
columnist n newyddiadurwr,
  colofnydd
coma n hunglwyf, côma
comb n crib ♦ vb cribo

combat n brwydr, gornest ♦ vb
  brwydro
combination n cyfuniad
combine vb cyfuno. **c. harvester**
  cynaeafydd, combein
come vi dod, dyfod. **to c. across**
  dod ar draws. **to c. to light** dod
  i'r golwg. **to c. to an end** dod i
  ben. **to c. by** meddiannu. **to c. to**
  pass digwydd
comedian n comedïwr
comedy n comedi
comfort n cysur, diddanwch ♦ vt
  cysuro, diddanu
comfortable adj cysurus,
  cyffyrddus
comfortably adv yn gysurus, yn
  gyffyrddus
comic adj comic, digrif, ysmala
comma n rhagwahannod, atalnod,
  coma
command vb gorchymyn ♦ n
  gorchymyn, awdurdod
commandeer vb meddiannu
commander n cadlywydd,
  comander
commandment n gorchymyn
commando n mintai (o filwyr), un
  o'r fintai
commemorate vt coffáu, dathlu
commence vb dechrau
commend vt cymeradwyo, canmol
commensurate adj cymesur
comment vi sylwi, esbonio ♦ n
  sylw
commentary n sylwebaeth
commentator n esboniwr,
  sylwebydd
commerce n masnach
commercial adj masnachol
commiserate vt cydymdeimlo â,
  cyd-dosturio â
commission n comisiwn,
  dirprwyaeth ♦ vb comisiynu
commissionaire n porthor
commissioner n comisiynydd
commit vt cyflawni; traddodi;

cyflwyno

commitment n ymrwymiad; traddodiad

committee n pwyllgor

commodity n nwydd (masnachol)

common adj cyffredin ♦ n tir cyffredin, cytir, comin. **the C. Market** y Farchnad Gyffredin

commoner n cominwr, gwerinwr

commonplace adj dibwys, cyffredin

commons npl y cyffredin. **House of C.** Tŷ'r Cyffredin

common sense n synnwyr cyffredin

commonwealth n cymanwlad

commotion n cyffro, terfysg

communal adj cymunol, cymunedol

commune vi ymddiddan; cymuno ♦ n cymundod; comun

communicate vb cyfathrebu; cymuno

communication n cyfathrebiad, cysylltiad, neges

communion n cymun, cymundeb

communism n comiwnyddiaeth

communist n comiwnydd

community n cymdeithas, cymuned. **c. centre** canolfan gymuned

commute vt cymudo, pendilio

commuter n cymudwr, pendiliwr

compact n cytundeb, cyfamod; bag bach, compact ♦ adj cryno ♦ vt crynhoi. **c. disc** cryno ddisg

companion n cydymaith

companionship n cwmniaeth, cyfeillach

company n cymdeithas, cwmni. **keep c. with** cadw cwmni â

comparative adj cymharol

comparatively adv yn gymharol

compare vt cymharu, cyffelybu

comparison n cymhariaeth

compartment n adran, cerbydran

compass n cwmpawd; cwmpas ♦

vt amgylchu

compassion n tosturi

compatible adj cydweddol, cyson

compatriot n cydwladwr

compel vt cymell, gorfodi

compendium n crynodeb, talfyriad

compensate vt talu iawn, digolledu

compensation n iawndal

compete vi cystadlu

competence n cymhwysedd

competent adj cymwys, digonol

competition n cystadleuaeth

competitive adj cystadleuol

competitor n cystadleuydd

complacency n ymfoddhad

complacent adj hunan-foddhaus, digonol

complain vi cwyno, achwyn, grwgnach

complaint n cwyn, achwyniad; anhwyldeb

complement n cyflawnder, cyflenwad

complementary adj cyflenwol

complete adj cyflawn ♦ vt cyflawni

completely adv yn llwyr

completion n cwblhad

complex adj cymhleth, dyrys

complexion n gwedd, pryd, gwawr

compliance n cydsyniad

complicate vt cymhlethu; drysu

complicated adj cymhleth, dyrys

complication n cymhlethdod

compliment n cyfarchiad; canmoliaeth

comply vi cydsynio, ufuddhau

component n cydran, cydelfen

compose vt cyfansoddi; cysodi; tawelu

composed adj hunanfeddiannol

composer n cyfansoddwr

composition n cyfansoddiad, traethawd

composure n tawelwch, hunanfeddiant

compound adj cyfansawdd ♦ n cymysg ♦ vb cymysgu
comprehend vt amgyffred, dirnad
comprehension n amgyffred, dirnadaeth
comprehensive adj cynhwysfawr. **c. school** Ysgol Gyfun
compress vt gwasgu, crynhoi ♦ n plastr
comprise vt amgyffred, cynnwys
compromise n cymrodedd, cyfaddawd ♦ vb cymrodeddu, cyfaddawdu
compulsion n gorfodaeth
compulsive adj trwy orfod, o anfodd
compulsory adj gorfodol
computer n cyfrifiadur. **c. operator** cyfrifiadurwr. **c. science** cyfrifianneg, cyfrifiadureg
comrade n cydymaith
concave adj ceugrwm
conceal vb cuddio, celu, dirgelu
concede vt caniatáu, addef
conceit n tyb, mympwy; hunandyb, hunanoldeb, cysêt
conceited adj hunandybus, hunanol, balch
conceive vb dirnad; tybied, synied; beichiogi
concentrate vt crynodi, canolbwyntio
concentration n crynodiad, ymroddiad
concept n cysyniad
conception n syniad; beichiogiad
concern vt perthyn, ymwneud (â), gofalu (am), pryderu, bod a wnelo â ♦ n busnes, diddordeb; gofal, pryder
concerned adj yn teimlo pryder, pryderus, gofalus, yn ymboeni
concerning prep ynglŷn â, ynghylch
concert n cyngerdd ♦ vt cyd-drefnu
concerted adj cydunol, wedi ei gyd-drefnu

concertina n consertina
conclude vb diweddu; casglu, barnu
conclusion n diwedd; casgliad
conclusive adj terfynol
concoct vt llunio, dyfeisio
concoction n cymysgedd
concourse n tyrfa, torf
concrete adj diriaethol ♦ n concrit
concur vi cydredeg; cydgroesi; cytuno
concurrently adv yn gyfredol
concussion n cyd-drawiad, ysgytiad
condemn vb condemnio, collfarnu
condensation n cywasgiad, cyddwysedd
condense vb cywasgu, cyddwyso, cwtogi
condensed adj cyddwys
condition n cyflwr, ansawdd; amod ♦ vb cyflyru; amodi
conditional adj amodol
conditionally adv ar amod
conditioner n cyflyrydd
condole vt cydofidio, cydymdeimlo
condolence n cydymdeimlad
condom n condom. **condoms** npl (col) sachau dyrnu
condominium n cydlywodraeth, condominiwm
condone vt maddau, esgusodi, cymeradwyo
conduce vi arwain, tueddu
conducive adj tueddol i, â thuedd i
conduct n ymddygiad, ymarweddiad, tywys
conduct vt arwain
conductor n arweinydd; tocynnwr
cone n pigwrn, côn
confection n cyffaith
confectioner n cyffeithiwr
confer vb ymgynghori, cyflwyno
conference n cynhadledd
confess vb cyffesu, cyfaddef
confession n cyffesiad, cyffes
confetti n confetti

confide vb ymddiried
confidence n ymddiried, hyder.
self-c. hunanhyder
confident adj hyderus
confidential adj cyfrinachol
confine vt cyfyngu, carcharu,
caethiwo
confined adj caeth, cyfyng
confinement n caethiwed, adeg
geni
confirm vt cadarnhau; conffirmio
confirmation n cadarnhad; bedydd
esgob, conffirmasiwn
confirmed adj cyson, arferol,
gwastadol, wedi ei gadarnhau
confiscate vt atafaelu
conflict n gwrthdrawiad, ymryson
conflict vi anghytuno, gwrthdaro
conflicting adj anghyson
conform vb cydymffurfio;
cydffurfio
confound vt cymysgu, drysu
confront vt wynebu
confrontation n gwrthdaro
confuse vt cymysgu, drysu
confused adj cymysg; didrefn;
dyrys; tywyll
confusion n anhrefn
confute vt gwrthbrofi, dymchwelyd
congeal vb rhewi, fferru, tewychu,
ceulo
congenial adj cydnaws, hynaws
congest vb cronni, gorlanw
congested adj gorlawn
congestion n gorlenwad, tagfa,
crynhoad
congratulate vt llongyfarch
congratulations n
llongyfarchiadau
congregate vb ymgynnull
congregation n cynulleidfa
congress n cyngres, cymanfa
conjunction n cysylltiad
conjunctivitis n llid yr amrant
conjure vb consurio
conjurer n consurwr
connect vb cysylltu, cydio

connected adj cysylltiedig,
cysylltiol
connection n cysylltiad,
perthynas. in c. with ynglŷn â
connive vi goddef, cau llygaid
rhag
conquer vt gorchfygu, trechu
conqueror n gorchfygwr,
concwerwr
conquest n buddugoliaeth,
concwest
conscience n cydwybod
conscientious adj cydwybodol
conscious adj ymwybodol
consciousness n ymwybyddiaeth
conscript n gorfodog, gwr rhif ♦
vb gorfodi
conscription n gorfodaeth filwrol
consecrate vt cysegru
consecutive adj olynol
consent vi cydsynio ♦ n cydsyniad,
caniatâd
consequence n canlyniad
consequently adv o ganlyniad
conservation n cadwraeth,
gwarchodaeth
conservative adj ceidwadol ♦ n
ceidwadwr
conservatory n tŷ gwydr
conserve vt cadw, diogelu,
amddiffyn
consider vb ystyried
considerable adj cryn
considerate adj ystyriol, tosturiol
consideration n ystyriaeth
considering prep ag ystyried
consign vt traddodi, trosglwyddo
consist vi cynnwys
consistency n cysondeb
consistent adj cyson
consolation n cysur, diddanwch
console vt cysuro, diddanu
consonant n cysain; cyson ♦ n
cytsain
conspicuous adj amlwg
conspiracy n bradwriaeth, brad,
cynllwyn

conspire *vb* bradwriadu, cynllwynio
constable *n* cwnstabl, heddgeidwad
constant *adj* cyson
constantly *adv* yn gyson
constipate *vt* rhwymo
constipated *adj* rhwym
constipation *n* rhwymedd
constituency *n* etholaeth
constituent *adj* cyfansoddol ♦ *n* etholwr; cyfansoddyn
constitution *n* cyfansoddiad
constitutional *adj* cyfansoddiadol
constraint *n* cyfyngydd, cyfyngiad
construct *vt* ffurfio, llunio, adeiladu, saernïo
construction *n* adeiladwaith, lluniad; cystrawen
constructive *adj* ymarferol, adeiladol
construe *vt* cyfieithu; dehongli
consul *n* ynad, conswl; consul
consulate *n* consuliaeth
consult *vb* ymgynghori
consultant *n* ymgynghorwr
consume *vb* treulio, difa, ysu; nychu
consumer *n* prynwr, treuliwr, defnyddiwr
consummate *adj* perffaith, cyflawn
consummate *vt* perffeithio, cyflawni
consumption *n* traul; darfodedigaeth
contact *n* cyffyrddiad, cyswllt. c. lenses *npl* gwydrau cyffwrdd
contagious *adj* heintus
contain *vt* cynnwys, dal
container *n* cynhwysydd
contaminate *vt* halogi, llygru, heintio
contemplate *vb* ystyried, myfyrio; bwriadu
contemporary *adj* cyfoes(ol) ♦ *n* cyfoeswr

contempt *n* dirmyg, diystyrwch. c. of court dirmyg llys
contemptuous *adj* dirmygus
contend *vb* ymryson, cystadlu
contender *n* cystadleuydd
content *adj* bodlon ♦ *vt* bodloni
content *n* cynnwys
contented *adj* bodlon
contention *n* cynnen, ymryson
contentment *n* bodlonrwydd
contents *npl* cynnwys, cynhwysiad
contest *n* cystadleuaeth, ymryson
contest *vb* amau, ymryson, ymladd
contestant *n* cystadleuydd
context *n* cyd-destun
continent *adj* cymedrol; diwair
continent *n* cyfandir
continental *adj* cyfandirol
contingency *n* damwain, digwyddiad
continual *adj* parhaus, gwastadol
continuation *n* parhad
continue *vb* parhau, para, dal (i)
continuous *adj* parhaol, di-fwlch, di-dor
contort *vt* gwyrdroi, dirdynnu
contour *n* amlinell, cyfuchlinedd
contra- *prefix* gwrth-, croes-
contraband *adj, n* (nwyddau) gwaharddedig
contraceptive *n* cyfarpar gwrth-genhedlu
contract *n* cytundeb, cyfamod
contract *vb* byrhau; cytuno, cyfamodi
contraction *n* talfyriad, cywasgiad
contractor *n* contractwr, adeiladydd
contradict *vt* gwrth-ddweud
contraption *n* dyfais
contrary *adj* gwrthwyneb, croes. on the c. i'r gwrthwyneb
contrast *n* gwrthgyferbyniad ♦ *vb* gwrthgyferbynnu
contribute *vb* cyfrannu
contribution *n* cyfraniad

contributor *n* cyfrannwr
contrive *vb* dyfeisio, llwyddo, trefnu
control *vt* llywodraethu, rheoli ♦ *n* rheolaeth, awdurdod. **self c.** hunan-reolaeth
controversial *adj* dadleuol
controversy *n* dadl
convalesce *vi* ymadfer, gwella
convene *vt* galw, gwysio, cynnull
convenience *n* cyfleustra, hwylustod
convenient *adj* cyfleus, gweddus, hwylus
convent *n* cwfaint, lleiandy
convention *n* confensiwn, cynhadledd
conventional *adj* confensiynol
conversant *adj* cyfarwydd, cynefin
conversation *n* ymddiddan, sgwrs
converse *vi* ymddiddan, ymgomio
converse *adj*, *n* gwrthwyneb, cyferbyniol
conversion *n* tröedigaeth, tro
convert *vt* troi, newid, trosi. **converted try** trosgais
convertible *adj* trosadwy
convex *adj* crwm
convey *vt* cludo; trosi, trosglwyddo; cyfleu
conveyor belt *n* cludfelt
convict *vt* barnu'n euog, euogfarnu; argyhoeddi
convict *n* troseddwr
conviction *n* euogfarn; argyhoeddiad
convince *vt* argyhoeddi
convincing *adj* argyhoeddiadol
convulse *vt* dirgrynu, dirdynnu
cook *n* cogydd, cogyddes ♦ *vb* coginio, gwneud bwyd
cooker *n* cwcer. **pressure c.** gwascogydd, sosban wyllt
cookery *n* coginiaeth
cooking *n* coginiaeth
cool *adj* oeri, oeraidd; hunanfeddiannol ♦ *vb* oeri,

claearu
coop *n* cawell, cut ieir ♦ *vt* cutio
co-operate *vi* cydweithio, cydweithredu
co-operation *n* cydweithrediad
co-operative *n* cydweithfa ♦ *adj* cydweithredol
co-opt *vt* cyfethol
co-ordinate *n* cyfesuryn ♦ *vb* cyfesur, cyd-drefnu
cop *n* plismon ♦ *vt* dal
cope *n* copa, crib
cope *vi* ymdaro â, ymdopi â
copious *adj* helaeth, dibrin
copper *n* copr, copor
copse *n* prysgwydd, prysglwyn
copy *n* copi ♦ *vt* copïo
copyright *n* hawlfraint
coracle *n* cwrwgl
coral *n* cwrel
cord *n* cortyn, rheffyn, tennyn ♦ *vt* rheffynnu
cordial *adj* o galon, calonnog ♦ *n* cordial, gwirod
cordon *n* rhes, cadwyn
corduroy *n* melfaréd, rib
core *n* calon, perfedd, craidd
cork *n* corc, corcyn ♦ *vt* corcio
corkscrew *n* corcsgriw
cormorant *n* mulfran, bilidowcar
corn *n* ŷd, llafur
corn *n* corn (ar droed)
corned beef *n* corn-biff
corner *n* congl, cornel, cil ♦ *vt* cornelu. **c. kick** cic gornel
cornet *n* corned
cornflakes *npl* creision ŷd
cornflour *n* blawd corn
coronation *n* coroniad
coroner *n* crwner
coronet *n* coronig
corporal *n* corfforol
corporate *adj* yn un corff, corfforedig
corporation *n* corfforaeth; cest
corporeal *adj* corfforol; materol
corps *n* corfflu

corpse n corff (marw), celain
corpuscle n corffilyn
correct adj cywir ♦ vt cywiro, ceryddu
correction n cywiriad; cerydd
correspond vi cyfateb; gohebu
correspondence n cyfatebiaeth; gohebiaeth
correspondent n gohebydd
corridor n coridor
corrode vb cyrydu, ysu, rhydu, treulio
corrugated adj rhychiog, gwrymiog
corrupt adj llygredig, pwdr ♦ vb llygru
corruption n llygredigaeth
corset n staes
cosmetic n cosmetig
cost vi costio ♦ n cost, traul
costly adj drudfawr, drud, prid
costume n gwisg, costiwm
cosy adj cysurus, clyd
cot n gwely bychan, cot
cottage n bwthyn
cotton n cotwm; edau. **c. wool** gwlân cotwm
couch n glwth, soffa ♦ vb gorwedd
cough n peswch ♦ vb pesychu
council n cyngor. **c. house** tŷ cyngor
councillor n cynghorwr
counsel n cyngor ♦ vt cynghori
counsellor n cynghorwr, cyfarwyddwr
count n cyfrif ♦ vb rhifo, cyfrif. **c. the cost** bwrw'r draul
count n iarll
countenance n wynepryd; cefnogaeth ♦ vt cefnogi
counter n cownter
counter- prefix gwrth- ♦ adj croes ♦ adv yn erbyn, yn groes
counteract vt gwrthweithio
counterfeit n ffug, twyll ♦ adj gau, ffug ♦ vt ffugio
counterfoil n gwrthddalen

countermand vt gwrthorchymyn
counterpane n cwrlid, cwilt gwely
counterpart n rhan gyfatebol, cymar
countess n iarlles
countless adj aneirif, di-rif
country n gwlad, bro ♦ adj gwladaidd, gwledig. **c. music** canu gwlad
countryman n gwladwr
countryside n cefn gwlad
county n sir, swydd
coup n ergyd, trawiad, dymchwel, llwyddiannus
couple n cwpl ♦ vt cyplu, cyplysu
couplet n cwpled
coupon n cwpon
courage n gwroldeb, dewrder
courier n cennad; tywyswr
course n cwrs, hynt ♦ vt hela, ymlid. **of c.** wrth gwrs. **in the c.** of yn ystod. **in due c.** yn ei bryd. **crash c.** cwrs carlam
court n llys; cwrt; cyntedd ♦ vt caru
courteous adj cwrtais
courtesy n cwrteisrwydd, cwrteisi
courtier n gŵr llys, llyswr
courtly adj llysaidd, boneddigaidd
court-martial n cwrt-marsial ♦ vb dodi ar brawf
courtship n carwriaeth
courtyard n buarth, cwrt, clos, iard
cousin n cefnder; cyfnither
cove n cil, cilfach
covenant n cyfamod ♦ vb cyfamodi
cover vt gorchuddio, toi; amddiffyn ♦ n gorchudd, clawr. **c. charge** n tâl am wasanaeth. **book c.** clawr llyfr. **to take c.** cuddio, cysgodi
covert adj cêl, cudd, dirgel
covert n lloches; prysglwyn
covet vt chwennych, chwenychu
cow n buwch. **barren c.** myswynog.

milking c. buwch odro. **c. in calf**
buwch gyflo
coward *n* llwfrddyn, llwfryn,
llwfrgi
cowardice *n* llwfrdra
cowardly *adj* llwfr
cowboy *n* cowboi
cower *vi* swatio, cyrcydu
cowl *n* cwcwll, cwfl
cowpox *n* brech y fuwch
cowslip *n* briallu Mair
coxwain *n* llywydd cwch, cocs
coy *adj* swil, gwylaidd
crab *n* cranc
crab (apple) *n* afal sur, afal
crabas
crack *vb* cracio, hollti ♦ *n* crac
cracker *n* cracer; bisgeden
crackle *vi* clindarddach
cradle *n* crud, cawell; cadair fagu
craft *n* crefft; cyfrwystra, dichell;
llong, bad
craftsman *n* crefftwr
craftsmanship *n* crefftwriaeth
crafty *adj* cyfrwys, dichellgar
crag *n* craig, clegr, clogwyn
cram *vb* gorlenwi, stwffio, saco
cramp *n* cwlwm gwythi, cramp;
creffyn ♦ *vt* caethiwo, gwasgu
cramped *adj* clòs
cranberries *npl* llugaeron
crane *n* garan, crëyr, crychydd,
craen ♦ *vt* estyn (gwddf)
cranium (**-ia**) *n* penglog
crank *n* cranc; mympwywr ♦ *vi*
cam-droi; troi
crankshaft *n* camwerthyd,
cranciasiafft
cranny *n* agen, hollt, agennig
crape *n* crêp
crash *vb* gwrthdaro, cwympo ♦ *n*
gwrthdrawiad, cwymp. **c. helmet**
n helmed ddiogelwch
crate *n* cawell
crater *n* safn llosgfynydd; ceudod,
cawg
cravat *n* cadach gwddf, crafat

crave *vb* crefu, deisyf, chwennych,
dyheu
craving *n* blys, chwant
crawl *vi* ymlusgo, cropian; crafu
crayon *n* creon
craze *n* ysfa
crazy *adj* penwan, gorffwyll, o'i gof
creak *vi* gwichian
cream *n* hufen
creamery *n* hufenfa
creamy *adj* hufennog
crease *n* ôl plygiad, plyg ♦ *vt*
crychu
create *vt* creu
creation *n* cread, creadigaeth
creative *adj* creadigol
creator *n* crëwr, creawdwr
creature *n* creadur
crèche *n* meithrinfa
credence *n* cred, coel, ffydd
credentials *npl* credlythyrau
credible *adj* credadwy, hygoel,
hygred
credit *n* coel, cred; clod, credyd ♦
vt coelio. **c. card** cerdyn credyd
creditor *n* credydwr
credulous *adj* hygoelus
creed *n* credo
creek *n* cilfach
creep *vi* ymlusgo, cropian
creeper *n* dringiedydd
creepy *adj* iasol
cremate *vt* amlosgi
crematorium *n* amlosgfa
crêpe *n* crêp
crescent *n* hanner lleuad;' cilgant
♦ *adj* cynyddol
cress *n* berwr
crest *n* crib; mwng; arwydd ar
arfbais
Crete *n* Creta
crevice *n* agen, hollt, rhigol
crew *n* criw, gwerin llong; haid
crib *n* preseb; caban; gwely
plentyn ♦ *vt* copïo
cricket *n* criced; cricsyn
crime *n* trosedd

criminal adj troseddol ♦ n
troseddwr
crimson adj, n rhuddgoch
cringe vi cynffonna, ymgreinio
crinkle vb crychu ♦ n crych, plyg
cripple n cloff, efrydd ♦ vt cloffi,
efryddu
crisis (**crises**) n argyfwng
crisp adj cras, crych
crisps npl creision tatws
criterion (**-ia**) n maen prawf, safon
critic n beirniad
critical adj beirniadol; pryderus;
peryglus
criticism n beirniadaeth
criticize vt beirniadu
croak vi crawcian ♦ n crawc
crochet vb crosio ♦ n crosiet,
gwaith crosio
crockery n llestri
crocodile n crocodil
crocus n saffrwn, crocus
croft n tyddyn, crofft
crony n cyfaill agos, cydymaith
crook n crwca, bagl, ffon fugail;
troseddwr
crooked adj crwca, cam
crop n cnwd, cynnyrch; crombil ♦
vt tocio, torri
cross n, adj croes ♦ vb croesi
cross-cut vb trawsdorri
cross-examine vb croesholi
crossing n croesfan
cross-road n croesffordd
cross-section n trawsdoriad
crosswise adv ar groes
crossword n croesair
crotchet n crosiet
crouch vi cyrcydu ♦ n cwrcwd
crow n brân
crow vi canu fel ceiliog;
ymffrostio
crow-bar n trosol, bar haearn
crowd n torf, tyrfa ♦ vb tyrru,
heidio
crowded adj llawn o bobl
crown n coron; corun ♦ vt coroni

crucial adj hanfodol, terfynol
crucifix n croeslun
crucifixion n croeshoeliad
crucify vt croeshoelio
crude adj cri, crai; llymrig,
amrwd
cruel adj creulon
cruelty n creulondeb
cruet n criwed
cruise vi morio ♦ n mordaith
cruiser n gwiblong
crumb n briwsionyn
crumble vb briwsioni, malurio ♦ n
briwsiongrwst
crumbly adj briwsionllyd
crumpet n crymped; lefren
crumple vb crychu, gwasgu
crunch vb creinsio
crupper n pedrain, crwper, pen ôl
crusade n rhyfel y groes, croesgad
crush vb gwasgu, llethu ♦ n
gwasgiad, torf
crust n crawen, crofen, crystyn
crutch n bagl, ffon fagl
crux n craidd
cry vb llefain, wylo, crio ♦ n llef,
sgrech, cri
cryptic adj dirgel, cyfrin
crystal n grisial ♦ adj grisialaidd
crystallisation n crisialiad
cub n cenau
cube n ciwb ♦ vb ciwbio
cubic adj ciwbig. **c. root** gwreiddyn
ciwb
cubicle n cuddygl
cuckoo n cog, cwcw; gwirionyn
cucumber n cucumer
cud n cil
cuddle vb anwylo, anwesu, tolach
cue n awgrym; ciw
cuff n torch llawes
cuff vt cernodio ♦ n cernod, dyrnod
cul-de-sac n pen ffordd, heol hosan
cull vt dewis, pigo
culminate vi cyrraedd ei anterth,
diweddu
culmination n anterth

culpable *adj* beius, camweddus
culprit *n* troseddwr, drwgweithredwr
cult *n* addoliad, cwlt
cultivate *vt* diwyllio, trin, meithrin
cultural *adj* diwylliannol
culture *n* diwylliant; gwrtaith
cultured *adj* diwylliedig, coeth
cumbersome *adj* afrosgo, beichus
cunning *adj* dichellgar, cyfrwys ♦ *n* cyfrwystra
cup *n* cwpan
cupboard *n* cwpwrdd
cup-tie *n* gornest gwpan
curate *n* curad
curator *n* curadur
curb *n* genfa, atalfa; cwrbyn ♦ *vt* ffrwyno
curd *n* caul, ceuled; caws
curdle *vb* ceulo, cawsio, cawsu
cure *n* iachád, gwellhad; meddyginiaeth ♦ *vb* iacháu, gwella; halltu
curfew *n* hwyrgloch
curiosity *n* cywreinrwydd, chwilfrydedd
curious *adj* cywrain; chwilfrydig; hynod
curl *n* cwrl, cudyn ♦ *vb* cyrlio
curlew *n* gylfinir
curly *adj* cyrliog, crych
currants *npl* grawn Corinth, cwrens. **currant bread** bara brith
currency *n* arian breiniol
current *adj* rhedegol, cyfredol, cyfoes ♦ *n* ffrwd, llif. **c. account** cyfrif cyfredol. **c. affairs** materion cyfoes
currently *adv* ar hyn o bryd
curriculum *n* cwricwlwm. **National C.** Cwricwlwm Cenedlaethol
curry *vt* trin lledr ♦ *n* cyrri. **to c. favour** cynffonna, ceisio ffafr
curse *n* melltith, rheg ♦ *vb* melltithio, rhegi
cursory *adj* brysiog, diofal
curt *adj* cwta, byr, cryno

curtail *vt* cwtogi, talfyrru; prinhau
curtain *n* llen
curtsy *n* cyrtsi
curve *vb* camu, gwyro, troi ♦ *n* tro; cromlin
cushion *n* clustog
custard *n* cwstard
custodian *n* ceidwad
custody *n* dalfa, cadwraeth
custom *n* defod; cwsmeriaeth; toll
customary *adj* arferol
customer *n* cwsmer
customs *npl* y tollau. **c. officer** *n* swyddog tollau
cut *vb* torri ♦ *n* toriad, archoll, briw. **c. back** torri yn ôl. **c. in** torri ar draws. **c. out** torri allan. **c. through** torri trwodd
cute *adj* ciwt, cyfrwys
cuticle *n* croen, pilen, cwticl
cutlery *n* cwtleri
cutlet *n* golwyth, cydled
cycle *n* cylch; cyfres; beic ♦ *vb* seiclo
cycling *n* beicio
cyclist *n* beiciwr
cyclone *n* trowynt
cygnet *n* cyw alarch, alarchen
cylinder *n* rhol; silindr
cymbal *n* symbal
cynic *n* gwawdiwr, sinig
cynical *adj* gwawdlyd, dirmygus
cynicism *n* coegni, gwawd
cyst *n* coden
cystitis *n* llid y bledren
Czechoslovakia *n* Tsiecoslofacia

D

dab *vt* dabio ♦ *n* dab
dabble *vb* dablo
dad, dada, daddy *n* tad, tada, tyta, dada
daffodil *n* cenhinen Bedr
daft *adj* hurt, gwirion
dagger *n* dagr, bidog

daily adj dyddiol, beunyddiol ♦ adv beunydd, bob dydd

dainty n danteithfwyd, amheuthun ♦ adj danteithiol, dillyn, del

dairy n llaethdy. **d. products** cynhyrchion llaeth

dais n esgynlawr, llwyfan

daisy n llygad y dydd

dale n dyffryn, glyn, dôl, cwm, bro

dam n argae, cronfa ♦ vt argáu, cronni

dam n mamog, mam (anifail)

damage n niwed, difrod ♦ vt niweidio, difrodi. **damages** npl iawn

damn vb damnio, rhegi, melltithio

damnation n damnedigaeth

damned adj colledig

damp adj llaith ♦ n lleithder ♦ vb lleitho

damson n eirinen ddu

dance vb dawnsio ♦ n dawns. **folk d.** dawns werin. **public folk d.** twmpath dawns

dancer n dawnsiwr

dandelion n dant y llew

dandruff n marwdon, cen

Dane n brodor o Ddenmarc, Daniad

danger n perygl, enbydrwydd

dangerous adj peryglus, enbyd

dangle vb hongian, siglo

dapper adj del, twt, sionc, heini

dare vb beiddio, mentro

dare-devil n un byrbwyll, un mentrus

daring adj beiddgar, mentrus ♦ n beiddgarwch

dark adj tywyll ♦ n tywyllwch, nos

darken vb tywyllu

darkness n tywyllwch

darling n anwylyd, cariad ♦ adj annwyl

darn vt cyweirio, trwsio ♦ n cyweiriad, trwsiad

dart n dart, picell, saeth ♦ vb dartio, rhuthro

dash vb rhuthro, chwalu, chwilfriwio ♦ n rhedr; llinell (—)

dashboard n dashfwrdd

data npl data

date n dyddiad, amseriad; datysen (ffrwyth) ♦ vb dyddio. **out of d.** henffasiwn, wedi dyddio. **up to d.** hyd yn hyn, cyfoes

dated adj dyddiedig

daub vb dwbio, iro

daughter n merch. **daughter-in-law** merch yng nghyfraith

dawdle vi ymdroi, swmera

dawn vi gwawrio, dyddio ♦ n gwawr

day n diwrnod, dydd. **by d.** liw dydd. **today** heddiw. **next d.** trannoeth. **d. before yesterday** echdoe

day-break n gwawr, toriad dydd

day-dream vb pensynnu, synfyfyrio

daylight n golau dydd

day-time n y dydd

daze vt synnu, syfrdanu; dallu

dazzle vb disgleirio, pelydru; dallu

dazzling adj disglair, llachar

deacon n diacon, blaenor

dead adj marw; difywyd ♦ adv hollol. **the d.** y meirw. **d. centre** yn ei ganol. **d. tired** wedi blino 'n lân. **d. heat** cwbl gyfartal

deaden vb lleddfu, marweiddio

deadlock n methu symud mlaen na nôl

deadly adj marwol, angheuol

Dead Sea n: the **D. Sea** y Môr Marw

deaf adj byddar

deafen vb byddaru

deafness n byddardod

deal vb delio; trin ♦ n trafodaeth, dêl. **a great d.** llawer iawn. **to d. with** ymwneud â

dealer n masnachwr

dean n deon

dear adj annwyl, cu, hoff; drud ♦ n

anwylyd, cariad. **d. me** o'r
annwyl!

death n angau, marwolaeth, tranc.
Black D. y Pla Du

deathly adj, adv fel angau,
angheuol, marwol

death rate n cyfradd marw

debar vt atal, lluddias, cau allan

debase vt iselu, darostwng, llygru

debate vb dadlau, ymryson ♦ n
dadl

debit n debyd

debt n dyled

debtor n dyledwr

decade n degawd

decadence n diryswiad, adfeiliad

decapitate vt torri pen

decay vi dadfeilio, pydru ♦ n
dadfeiliad

decease n tranc, marwolaeth ♦ vi
marw, trengi

deceased n ymadawedig,
trancedig

deceit n twyll, dichell, hoced

deceive vt twyllo, hocedu, siomi

December n Rhagfyr

decent adj gweddus, gweddaidd

deception n twyll, ffug, dichell

deceptive adj twyllodrus,
dichellgar

decide vb penderfynu

decided adj pendant, penderfynol

decidedly adv yn siŵr, yn ddiau

deciduous adj collddail

decimal adj degol ♦ n degolyn. **d.
system** system ddegol. **d. point**
pwynt degol. **recurring d.** degolyn
cylchol

decipher vt datrys, dehongli

decision n penderfyniad

decisive adj penderfynol, pendant

deck n bwrdd llong, dec. **d. chair** n
cadair haul

deck vt trwsio, addurno

declaration n datganiad; cau
batiad

declare vb mynegi, datgan,
cyhoeddi

decline vb dadfeilio; gwrthod ♦ n
dadfeiliad; darfodedigaeth

decompose vb pydru, braenu;
dadelfennu

decorate vt addurno, arwisgo

decoration n addurn, tlws

decorator n addurnwr, peintiwr tai

decoy n hud, magl ♦ vt hudo,
llithio

decrease vb lleihau, gostwng ♦ n
lleihad

decree n gorchymyn, dyfarniad ♦
vb gorchymyn, dyfarnu

dedicate vt cysegru, cyflwyno

dedication n cysegriad, cyflwyniad

deduce vt tynnu, casglu,
diddwytho

deduct vt tynnu ymaith, didynnu

deduction n diddwytiad, didyniad

deed n gweithred

deem vt meddwl, ystyried, barnu

deep adj dwfn; dwys ♦ n dwfn,
dyfnder. **d. freeze** n rhewgell. **d.
litter** gwasarn

deepen vb dyfnhau, trymhau,
dwysáu

deeply adv yn ddwys

deer (**deer**) n carw, hydd

deface vt difwyno, anurddo, hagru

default n diffyg, gwall, pall, meth
♦ vb methu, torri

defeat vt gorchfygu, trechu ♦ n
gorchfygiad

defect n diffyg, nam

defective adj diffygiol

defence n amddiffyn, amddiffyniad

defenceless adj diamddiffyn

defend vt amddiffyn

defendant n diffynnydd

defender n amddiffynnwr

defer vb oedi, gohirio

defiance n her, herfeiddiad

defiant adj herfeiddiol

deficient adj diffygiol, prin, yn
eisiau

deficit n diffyg

defile vi symud yn rhes ♦ n
culfforch, bwlch, ceunant
defile vt halogi, difwyno
define vt diffinio
definite adj penodol, pendant
definitely adv yn bendant, heb os
definition n diffiniad
deflate vb dadchwythu
deflect vb gwyro, osgoi
deform vt anffurfio, hagru,
aflunieiddio
deformed adj aflunaidd, anffurf
deformity n anffurfiad
defraud vt twyllo, hocedu; ysbeilio
defray vt talu (treuliau)
defrost vt dadrewi (fridge)
defroster n dadrewydd
deft adj medrus, hylaw, deheuig
defunct adj marw, trancedig
defy vt beiddio, herfeiddio, herio
degenerate vi dirywio ♦ adj
dirywiedig
degrade vt diraddio, difreinio
degree n gradd
dehydrate vb dihydradu
dehydration n dihydrad
de-ice vb toddi
deign vb ymostwng, teilyngu
deity n duwdod; duw
deject vt digalonni
dejected adj digalon
delay vb oedi, gohirio ♦ n oediad
delectable adj hyfryd, hyfrydlon
delegate vt dirprwyo ♦ n dirprwy,
cynrychiolydd
delete vt dileu
deliberate vi ystyried yn bwyllog
♦ adj pwyllog, bwriadol
deliberately adv yn fwriadol
delicacy n amheuthun,
danteithfwyd. **delicacies**
danteithion
delicate adj tyner; cain; gwanllyd
delicious adj danteithiol, blasus
delight vb difyrru; ymhyfrydu ♦ n
hyfrydwch
delightful adj hyfryd, braf

delinquency n bai, trosedd
delinquent n troseddwr,
tramgwyddwr ♦ adj troseddol,
tramgwyddus
delirious adj wedi drysu, yn drysu,
gwallgof
deliver vt traddodi; gwaredu,
danfon; cludo
deliverance n gwaredigaeth
delivery n traddodiad; danfoniad
dell n glyn, pant, ceunant, cwm
delude vt twyllo, hudo
deluge n dilyw, dylif ♦ vt gorlifo
delusion n twyll, cyfeiliornad;
lledrith
delve vb cloddio, palu, ymchwilio
demand vt gofyn, hawlio, mynnu ♦
n gofyn, hawl
demean vt ymddwyn
demeanour n ymddygiad
demented adj gwallgof, gorffwyll
demesne n treftadaeth, tiriogaeth;
bro
demi- prefix hanner
demise n marwolaeth
democracy n gweriniaeth,
democrat, democratiaeth
democrat n gwerinydd,
gweriniaethwr
democratic adj gwerinol,
democratig
demolish vt dymchwelyd,
distrywio
demonstrate vb arddangos, profi;
gwrthdystio
demonstration n arddangosiad;
gwrthdystiad
demonstrator n arddangoswr;
gwrthdystiwr
demote vb darostwng
demur vi codi gwrthwynebiad,
petruso
demure adj swil, gwylaidd
den n ffau, gwâl, lloches
denial n gwadiad; nacâd,
gwrthodiad. **self-d.**
hunanymwadiad

Denmark n Denmarc
denomination n enw, enwad
denote vt arwyddo, dynodi, hynodi
denounce vt lladd ar, cyhuddo, condemnio
dense adj tew, dwys; pendew, hurt
density n dwysedd, trwch
dent n tolc ♦ vt tolcio
dental adj deintiol
dentist n deintydd
dentistry n deintyddiaeth
dentures npl danedd gosod/dodi
deny vt gwadu, gomedd, gwrthod
deodorant n diaroglydd
depart vi ymadael; cychwyn
department n adran, dosbarth. **d. store** n siop adrannol
departure n ymadawiad; cychwyniad
depend vi dibynnu
dependable adj dibynadwy
dependant n dibynnydd
dependent adj dibynnol
depict vt darlunio
deplete vt gwacáu, gwagu, hysbyddu
depopulate vt diboblogi
deport vt alltudio
deportation n alltudiaeth
deportment n ymddygiad, ymarweddiad
deposit vt dodi i lawr; adneuo; gwaddodi ♦ n adnau, blaendal; gwaddod. **d. account** cyfrif cadw
depot n storfa; gorsaf
depreciate vb dibrisio
depredation n anrheithiad
depress vt gostwng, iselu; digalonni
depressed adj digalon, iselfryd
depression n iselder (ysbryd); dibwysiant (tywydd); pant; dirwasgiad (diwydiant)
deprivation n enbydrwydd, amddifadedd, colled
deprive vt amddifadu
deprived adj amddifadus

depth n dyfnder
deputation n dirprwyaeth
deputise vt dirprwyo
deputy n dirprwy
derail vb taflu oddi ar gledrau
derelict adj wedi ei adael, diberchen, diffaith
deride vt gwatwar, gwawdio
derision n gwatwar, gwawd, dirmyg
derive vb derbyn, cael; tarddu, deillio
derogatory adj amharchus, difriol, dilornus, gwawdus
descant vi desgant, cyfalaw
descend vi disgyn
descent n disgyniad, disgynfa; hil, ach
describe vt disgrifio, darlunio
description n disgrifiad, darluniad
desecrate vt digysegru, halogi
desert n haeddiant
desert adj diffaith, anial ♦ n diffeithwch
desert vb gadael, cefnu ar; encilio
deserter n enciliwr, ffoadur
deserve vb haeddu, teilyngu
deserving adj haeddiannol, teilwng
design n arfaeth; cynllun ♦ vb arfaethu; cynllunio
designer n cynllunydd, dylunydd
desirable adj dymunol, dewisol
desire vb dymuno ♦ n dymuniad, chwant
desk n desg
desolate adj anghyfannedd, diffaith ♦ vt anghyfanheddu
despair n anobaith ♦ vi anobeithio
desperate adj diobaith, anobeithiol; gorffwyll
desperation n anobaith, enbydrwydd, gorffwylltra
despicable adj dirmygedig, ffiaidd
despise vt dirmygu, diystyru
despite prep er, er gwaethaf
despoil vt anrheithio, ysbeilio
despondent adj digalon, isel-

ysbryd
despot n unben, gormeswr
dessert n pwdin, melysfwyd
destination n cyrchfan, pen y
daith
destiny n tynged, tynghedfen
destitute adj anghenus, amddifad
destroy vt distrywio, difetha,
dinistrio
destroyer n dinistrydd;
distrywlong
destruction n distryw, dinistr
detach vt datod, gwahanu,
dadgysylltu
detached adj ar wahân
detachment n adran; didoliad;
mintai (o filwyr)
detail n manylyn, (pl) manylion ♦
vb manylu, neilltuo. **in d.** yn
fanwl
detain vt cadw, atal, caethiwo
detect vt canfod, darganfod,
datgelu
detection n darganfyddiad,
datgeliad
detective n cuddswyddog, ditectif.
d. story stori dditectif
detention n carchariad, ataliad
deter vt cadw rhag, atal, rhwystro
detergent n golchydd
deteriorate vb dirywio, gwaethygu
determination n penderfyniad
determine vb penderfynu, pennu
determined adj penderfynol
deterrent n atalrym, ataliad
detest vt ffieiddio, casáu, atgasu
detour n cylch
detract vt tynnu oddi wrth,
bychanu
detriment n colled, niwed,
anfantais
detrimental adj niweidiol,
colledus, o anfantais
devaluation n gwerthostyngiad,
datbrisiad
devastate vt diffeithio, difrodi
devastating adj difrodus

develop vb datblygu
developing adj datblygol, ar ei
brifiant
development n datblygiad
device n dyfais
devil n diafol, diawl, cythraul
devilish adj dieflig
devious adj diarffordd, troellog;
cyfeiliornus
devise vt dyfeisio
devoid adj amddifad
devolution n datganoli
devote vt cysegru, cyflwyno,
ymroddi
devoted adj ffyddlon, ymroddgar
devotion n defosiwn, ymroddiad
devour vt ysu, difa, traflyncu
devout adj duwiol, crefyddol,
defosiynol
dew n gwlith ♦ vb gwlitho
diabetes n clefyd melys/siwgr
diabetic adj, n diabetig
diabolical adj dieflig
diagnosis n diagnosis
diagonal n croeslin ♦ adj croeslinol
diagram n darlun eglurhaol,
diagram
dial n deial ♦ vb deialu
dialect n tafodiaith
dialogue n ymddiddan, deialog,
sgwrs
diameter n tryfesur, diamedr
diamond n diemwnt
diaphragm n llengig; diaffram
diarrhoea n rhyddni, dolur rhydd
diary n dyddiadur, dyddlyfr
dice n dis
dictate vb arddywedyd, gorchymyn
dictate n arch, galwad, gorchymyn
dictation n arddywediad
dictatorship n unbennaeth
dictionary n geiriadur
diddle vt twyllo, hocedu
die vi marw, trengi, trigo, darfod
diehard n un di-ildio
diesel n disel
diet n ymborth, lluniaeth, deiet

dietetics n deieteg
differ vi gwahaniaethu
difference n gwahaniaeth
different adj gwahanol
differentiate vb gwahaniaethu
difficult adj anodd, caled
difficulty n anhawster
diffident adj petrusgar, anhyderus
dig vb palu, cloddio, ceibio
digest vb treulio, toddi; cymathu
digest n crynhoad
digestion n treuliad, traul
digit n digid, bys
digital adj digidol
dignified adj urddasol
dignify vt anrhydeddu, urddasu
dignity n urddas, teilyngdod
digress vi gwyro, crwydro
dike, dyke n clawdd, ffos; argae
dilapidate vb adfeilio, malurio
dilapidated adj adfeiliedig
dilemma n dilema
diligence n diwydrwydd, dyfalwch
diligent adj diwyd, dyfal
dilute vt cymysgu â dwfr, teneuo,
   gwanhau
dim adj pŵl, aneglur ♦ vb tywyllu,
   cymylu
dimension n mesur, maintioli,
   dimensiwn
diminish vb lleihau, prinhau
diminutive adj bychan; bachigol;
   n bachigyn
dimmer n pylydd
dimple n pannwl, pant ♦ vb panylu
din n twrf, dadwrdd, mwstwr
dine vi ciniawa
diner n ciniawr
dinghy n dingi
dingle n cwm, glyn, pant
dingy adj tywyll, dilewyrch;
   tlodaidd
dining room n ystafell fwyta
dinner n cinio. **D. jacket** n cot
   ginio, cot giniawa
dint n tolc; grym ♦ vt tolcio
diocesan adj esgobaethol ♦ n esgob

diocese n esgobaeth
dioxide n deuocsid
dip vb trochi, gwlychu; gostwng ♦
   n trochfa
diphthong n deusain, dipton
diploma n tystysgrif, diploma
diplomacy n diplomyddiaeth
diplomat n diplomydd
diplomatic adj diplomyddol
dire adj dygn, arswydus, echryslon
direct adj union, uniongyrchol ♦ vt
   cyfarwyddo, cyfeirio
direction n cyfarwyddyd; cyfeiriad
directly adv yn union, yn ddi-oed
director n cyfarwyddwr
directory n cyfarwyddiadur
dirge n galarnad, marwnad
dirt n baw, llaid, llaca
dirty adj budr, brwnt ♦ vt budro,
   diwyno, maeddu
disability n anabledd
disable vt analluogi
disabled adj anabl
disadvantage n anfantais
disagree vi anghytuno
disagreeable adj annymunol, cas
disappear vi diflannu
disappearance n diflaniad
disappoint vt siomi
disappointed adj siomedig
disappointment n siomedigaeth
disapprove vb anghymeradwyo
disarm vb diarfogi
disarmament n diarfogiad
disarray n anhrefn ♦ vb anrhefnu
disaster n trychineb, aflwydd
disband vb dadfyddino; gwasgaru
disbelief n anghrediniaeth, angoel
disc n disg(en)
discard vt rhoi heibio, gwrthod
discern vt canfod, dirnad
discerning adj deallus, craff
discharge vb dadlwytho, rhyddhau
   ♦ n gollyngdod, rhyddhad,
   gollwng
discipline n disgyblaeth ♦ vt
   disgyblu

disclaim vt diarddel, gwadu
disclose vt dadlennu, datguddio
disclosure n datguddiad, dadleniad
disco n disgo
discomfit vt gorchfygu, dymchwelyd
discomfort vt anghysuro ♦ n anghysur
discompose vt aflonyddu, cyffroi
disconcert vt aflonyddu, cyffroi, tarfu
disconnect vb datgysylltu
disconsolate adj digysur, anniddan, galarus
discontent n anfodlonrwydd
discontented adj anfodlon
discontinue vb torri, atal
discord n anghytgord
discount n disgwnt
discourage vt digalonni
discourteous adj anghwrtais
discover vt darganfod, canfod
discovery n darganfyddiad
discredit n anfri, anghlod, amarch ♦ vt anghoelio; amau, difrïo
discreet adj call, synhwyrol, pwyllog
discrepancy n anghysondeb
discretion n barn, pwyll, synnwyr
discriminate vb gwahaniaethu
discrimination n gwahaniaethu, rhagfarn, anffafriaeth
discursive adj crwydrol, anghysylltiol
discuss vt trin, trafod
discussion n trafodaeth, sgwrs
disdain vb distyru, dirmygu, diystyrwch ♦ n dirmyg
disease n afiechyd, clefyd, clwyf
disembark vb glanio
disengage vb datgyweddu, rhyddhau
disentangle vb datod, datrys
disestablish vt datgysylltu
disfigure vt anffurfio, anharddu, hagru
disgrace vt gwaradwyddo ♦ n

gwaradwydd, gwarth
disgraceful adj gwaradwyddus, gwarthus
disguise vt dieithrio, ffugio, lledrithio ♦ n rhith, dirithrwch
disgust n diflastod, ffieidd-dod ♦ vt diflasu, ffieiddio
disgusting adj ffiaidd, brwnt, gwrthun
dish n dysgl; dysglaid
dishcloth n cadach llestri
dishearten vt digalonni
dishevelled adj anhrefnus, aflêr, anniben
dishonest adj anonest
dishonour n amarch, gwarth ♦ vb amharchu
dishwasher n peiriant golchi llestri
disillusion vb dadrithio
disincentive n gwrthgymhelliant
disinfect vb diheintio
disinfectant n diheintydd
disintegrate vb datod, chwalu
disinterested adj heb ddiddordeb, diduedd
disjointed adj datgymalog
disk n disg(en)
dislike vt casáu ♦ n casineb
dislocate vt rhoi o'i le, datgymalu
dislodge vt symud, syflyd, gwared
dismal adj tywyll, dilewyrch, digalon
dismay vt brawychu, siomi, digalonni ♦ n braw, siom, chwithdod
dismiss vt gollwng; diswyddo
dismount vb disgyn, dymchwelyd
disobedience n anufudd-dod
disobedient adj anufudd
disobey vb anufuddhau
disorder n anhrefn; anhwyldeb ♦ vt anhrefnu
disorderly adj afreolus, anniben
disown vt gwadu, diarddel
disparage vt amharchu, bychanu, difrïo

disparaging adj amharchus, gwaradwyddus

disparity n anghyfartaledd, rhagor

dispatch vb anfon; diweddu ♦ n neges

dispel vt chwalu, gwasgaru

dispensary n fferyllfa

dispense vb rhannu; gweinyddu; hepgor

disperse vb gwasgaru, chwalu, taenu

dispirit vt digalonni, llwfrhau

dispirited adj digalon, gwangalon

display vt arddangos ♦ n arddangosiad

displease vt anfodloni, anfoddio, digio

displeasure n anfodlonrwydd, dicter

disposable nappies npl clytiau untro

dispose vt hepgor, gwaredu

disposition n anianawd

disprove vt gwrthbrofi

dispute vb dadlau, ymryson ♦ n dadl

disqualify vb difreinio, atal

disquiet vb anesmwytho

disregard vt diystyru, esgeuluso ♦ n diystyrwch, esgeulustra

disreputable adj gwarthus, amharchus

disrespect n amarch

disrupt vb rhwygo, amharu ar

dissatisfaction n anfodlonrwydd

dissatisfy vt anfodloni

dissect vt difynio, trychu; dadansoddi

disseminate vt hau, taenu, lledaenu

dissent vi anghytuno ♦ n anghytundeb; ymneilltuaeth

dissertation n traethawd

dissimilar adj annhebyg, gwahanol

dissipate vt chwalu, gwasgaru, afradloni

dissociate vt anghysylltu,

gwahanu, diaelodi

dissolute adj afradlon, ofer

dissolution n ymddatodiad, datodiad, diddymiad

dissolve vb toddi, datod; datgorffori, diddymu

distance n pellter

distant adj pell, pellennig, oeraidd

distaste n diflastod, cas

distend vt estyn, lledu, chwyddo

distil vb distyllu, dihidlo

distillery n distyllty

distinct adj gwahanol; eglur

distinction n arbenigrwydd, rhagoriaeth, gwahaniaeth

distinctive adj gwahanredol, arbennig

distinguish vb gwahaniaethu; hynodi

distinguished adj enwog, amlwg

distort vt ystumio, anffurfio, gwyrdroi

distract vb tynnu ymaith, drysu, mwydro

distraction n dryswch, diffyg sylw

distress n cyfyngder, ing, trallod

distressing adj trallodus, blin, poenus

distribute vt rhannu, dosbarthu

distribution n dosbarthiad, rhaniad

distributor n dosbarthydd, dosbarthwr

district n dosbarth, ardal, rhandir.
d. council cyngor dosbarth

distrust n drwgdybiaeth ♦ vb drwgdybio

disturb vt aflonyddu, cyffroi

disturbance n aflonyddwch, cyffro, terfysg

disturbed adj blinderus, cynhyrfus

ditch n ffos

ditto adv eto, yr un, yr un peth

dive vi ymsuddo, deifio

diverse adj gwahanol; annhebyg

diversion n difyrrwch, adloniant; dargyfeiriad

divert vt dargyfeirio, difyrru

divide vb rhannu, dosbarthu, gwahanu ♦ n gwahanfa

divided adj rhanedig

dividend n buddran; difidend

divine adj dwyfol ♦ n diwinydd ♦ vb dewinio, dyfalu

divinity n dwndod; diwinyddiaeth

division n rhan, rhaniad; cyfraniaeth. **long d.** n rhannu hir

divorce vt ysgar(u) ♦ n ysgariad

divorced adj wedi ysgaru

divulge vt datguddio, dadlennu

dizzy adj penysgafn, pensyfrdan

DJ n troellwr

do vb gwneud, gwneuthur

docile adj dof, hywedd, hydrin

dock n (dail) tafol

dock vt tocio, cwtogi

dock n doc, porthladd ♦ vt docio; cwtogi

dockyard n iard longau

doctor n doctor, meddyg; doethor, doethur

doctrine n athrawiaeth

document n ysgrif, gweithred, dogfen

documentary adj dogfennol

dodge vb osgoi, twyllo ♦ n cast, ystryw

doe n ewig

dog n ci ♦ vb dal i ddilyn

dogged adj cyndyn, ystyfnig

dogmatic adj athrawiaethol; awdurdodol, pendant

dole n dôl, dogn. **on the d.** yn ddi-waith, ar y clwt ♦ vt dogni, rhannu

doleful adj trist, prudd, galarus

doll n dol, doli

dollar n doler

dolphin n dolffin

domain n tiriogaeth, maes

dome n cromen, cryndo

domestic adj teuluaidd, cartrefol; gwâr, dof

dominant adj trech

dominate vb dominyddu

dominion n rheolaeth; dominiwn, tiriogaeth

don vt gwisgo (dilledyn) ♦ n athro (coleg)

donate vb rhoddi

donation n rhodd

donkey n asyn, mul

donor n rhoddwr

doodle vb dwdlan

doom n dedfryd, barn, tynged ♦ vt dedfrydu, tynghedu, collfarnu

doomsday n dydd barn

door n drws, dôr, dryslws

doorkeeper n porthor

door-step n rhiniog, trothwy

doorway n porth, drws

dope n cyffur ♦ vt rhoi cyffur

dormant adj ynghwsg; di-rym

dormitory n ystafell gysgu, hundy

dose n dogn ♦ vt dogni

dot n dot ♦ vb dotio

dote vi dotio, gwirioni, ffoli, dylu

double adj, n dwbl ♦ vb dyblu, plygu. **d. glazing** gwydro dwbl, ffenestri dwbl. **d. flat** meddalnod dwbl

double-bass n bas dwbl

double-dealing n twyll

doubt vb amau, petruso ♦ n amheuaeth, (pl) amheuon

doubtful adj amheus, petrus

doubtless adv yn ddiamau, diau

dough n toes

doughnut n toesen

douse vb trochi; diffodd

dove n colomen

dowdy adj aflêr, anniben

down n manblu

down n gwaun, rhos, mynydd-dir

down adv i lawr, i waered. **d. and out** digalon, truenus

downcast adj digalon, prudd

downfall n cwymp, codwm, dinistr

downpour n tywalltiad, pistylliad ♦ vb tywallt, pistyllio

downright adj diamheuol

downstairs *n* y llawr ♦ *adv* ar y llawr

downwards *adv* i lawr, i waered

dowry *n* gwaddol

doze *vi* hepian ♦ *n* cyntun

dozen *n* deuddeg, dwsin

drab *adj* llwydaidd, salw

draft *n* drafft, braslun ♦ *vb* drafftio braslunio

drag *vb* llusgo ♦ *n* car llusg

dragon *n* draig

dragon-fly *n* gwas y neidr

drain *n* traen, carthffos

drain *vb* draenio, diferu, yfed.
draining board bwrdd diferu

drainage *n* draeniad. **d. basin** dalgylch afon

drake *n* ceiliog hwyad, meilart

drama *n* drama

dramatic *adj* dramatig

dramatise *vb* dramateiddio, dramodi

dramatist *n* dramodydd

drape *vt* gwisgo, gorchuddio

draper *n* dilledydd

drastic *adj* cryf, llym, trwyadl

draught *n* dracht, llymaid, drafft(en); tynfa (llong)

draughts *npl* drafftiau

draughtsman *n* drafftsmon, lluniedydd

draw *n* atyniad, tynfa ♦ *vb* tynnu, llusgo; lluniadu, darlunio. **d. to scale** graddluniadu. **drawn game** gêm gyfartal

drawback *n* anfantais

drawer *n* drâr, drôr

drawing *n* lluniad, llun

drawing room *n* ystafell groeso

drawl *vb* llusgo (geiriau)

dread *vb* ofni, arswydo ♦ *n* ofn, arswyd

dreadful *adj* ofnadwy

dream *vb* breuddwydio ♦ *n* breuddwyd

dreamy *adj* breuddwydiol

dreary *adj* llwm, diflas, digysur

dredge *vb* glanhau

dregs *npl* gwaddod, gwaelodion, gwehilion

drench *vt* gwlychu; drensio

dress *vb* gwisgo, dilladu ♦ *n* gwisg

dresser *n* dreser, gwisgwr

dressing *n* dresin. **salad d.** dresin salad. **d. gown** gŵn gwisgo

dressmaker *n* gwniadwraig

dressmaking *n* gwniadwaith ♦ *vb* gwneud dillad

dribble *n* dribl(ad), drefl ♦ *vb* driblo, dreflu, glafoerio

drier *n* peiriant sychu

drift *n* drifft, lluwch; tuedd ♦ *vb* drifftio, lluwchio

drill *vb* drilio ♦ *n* dril

drink *vb* yfed ♦ *n* diod, llymaid

drinker *n* yfwr, diotwr

drinking water *n* dŵr yfed

drip *vb* diferu, defnynnu ♦ *n* diferiad

dripping *adj* diferol ♦ *n* toddion, saim

drive *n* dreif, gyriant, cymhelliad ♦ *vb* dreifio, gyrru

drivel *vi* glafoerio, driflan, dreflu ♦ *n* glafoerion

driver *n* gyrrwr

driving *adj* trwm, â grym y tu ôl iddo, grymus ♦ *n* gyrru

driving licence *n* trwydded yrru

drizzle *vb* briwlan ♦ *n* glaw mân

droll *adj* digrif, ysmala

drone *n* gwenynen ormes; diogyn

droop *vi* llaesu, ymollwng; nychu

drop *n* diferyn, dafn, cwympiad ♦ *vb* diferu, cwympo, gollwng. **d. goal** gôl adlam

drought *n* tywydd sych, sychder, sychdwr

drover *n* porthmon, gyrrwr

drown *vb* boddi

drowsy *adj* cysglyd, marwaidd, swrth

drudgery *n* caledwaith, slafdod

drug *n* cyffur

druid n derwydd
drum n tabwrdd, drwm ♦ vb
tabyrddu
drunk adj meddw, brwysg
drunkard n meddwyn
dry adj sych, hysb, cras ♦ vb
sychu. **d. cleaners** n sych
lanhawyr
dryness n sychder, craster
dry rot n sych-bydredd, tyllau
pryfed
dual adj deuol. **d. carriageway**
ffordd ddeuol
dub vt urddo, galw, llysenwi;
dwbio, lleisio (ffilm)
dubious adj amheus, petrus
Dublin n Dulyn
duchess n duges
duchy n dugiaeth
duck n hwyad, hwyaden
duck vb trochi; gostwng pen,
gwyro
duckling n cyw hwyaden
dud n ffugbeth
due adj dyledus, dyladwy ♦ n
dyled, haeddiant
duel n gornest
duet n deuawd
duke n dug
dull adj dwl, hurt; marwaidd;
diflas; cymylog; pŵl ♦ vb pylu,
lleddfu
dumb adj mud
dumbfound vt syfrdanu, drysu
dummy n dymi; delw; ffug-bas
(rygbi) ♦ vb ffug-basio
dump n dymp, storfa ♦ vb dympio
dumpling n tymplen, poten
dunce n hurtyn, twpsyn, penbwl
dune n twyn
dung n tom, tail
dungarees npl dyngaris
dungeon n daeardy, daeargell,
dwnsiwn
dupe n gwirionyn ♦ vt twyllo
duplex adj dwplecs
duplicate adj dyblyg ♦ n copi ♦ vt

dyblygu
duplicity n dichell, rhagrith
durable adj parhaol, parhaus, cryf
duration n parhad
during prep yn ystod
dusk n cyfnos, gwyll
dust n llwch ♦ vt taenu neu sychu
llwch, dwstio
dustbin n bin sbwriel
duster n cadach, dwster
dustman n dyn lludw
dusty adj llychlyd
Dutch n Iseldireg. **Dutchman** n
Iseldirwr
dutiful adj ufudd, ufuddgar
duty n dyletswydd; toll. **customs d.**
tolldal. **import d.** toll fewnforio.
export d. toll allforio
dwarf n cor, corrach ♦ adj
corachaidd
dwell vi trigo, preswylio
dwelling n annedd, preswyl
dwindle vi darfod, lleihau, dirywio
dye vb lliwio, llifo ♦ n lliw, lliwur
dyke n morglawdd, cob
dynamic adj dynamig
dynamics n dynameg

E

each adj, pron pob, pob un. **e. other**
ei gilydd
eager adj awyddus, awchus
eagle n eryr
ear n clust, dolen; tywysen.
earache clust dost
earl n iarll
early adj cynnar, bore, boreol ♦
adv yn fore
earmark n clustnod, nod clust ♦ vb
clustnodi, neilltuo
earn vt ennill, elwa
earnest adj difrif, difrifol, taer
earnest n ern, ernes ♦ vb gwystl
earnings npl enillion

earphone n ffôn clust
earring n clustlws
earshot n clyw
earth n daear, pridd ♦ vt priddo
earthenware npl llestri pridd
earthly adj daearol, ar wyneb
 daear
earthquake n daeargryn
ease n esmwythdra, esmwythyd;
 rhwyddineb ♦ vb esmwytho
easel n isl
east n dwyrain ♦ adj dwyreiniol. E.
 Germany Dwyrain yr Almaen
Easter n y Pasg
eastern adj dwyreiniol
eastwards adj, adv tua'r dwyrain
easy adj hawdd, rhwydd
easy-chair n cadair esmwyth
easy-going n didaro, di-hid
eat vt bwyta, ysu
eaves npl bargod, bondo
eavesdrop vb clustfeinio
ebb n trai ♦ vi treio
eccentric adj od, hynod;
 echreiddig
ecclesiastic adj eglwysig ♦ n
 clerigwr
echo n atsain, carreg ateb ♦ vb
 atseinio
eclipse n eclips, diffyg, clip ♦ vb
 tywyllu
ecology n ecoleg
economic adj economaidd
economical adj cynnil, darbodus
economics n economeg
economize vb cynilo
economy n cynildeb, darbodaeth,
 economi
ecstacy n gorfoledd, gorawen,
 hwyl
edge n min, ymyl ♦ vb minio,
 hogi; symud. to be on e. bod ar
 bigau'r drain
edible adj bwytadwy
edict n cyhoeddiad, gorchymyn
Edinburgh n Caeredin
edit vt golygu, paratoi i'r wasg

edition n argraffiad
editor n golygydd
editorial adj golygyddol
educate vt addysgu
education n addysg
educational adj addysgol
eel n llysywen
eerie adj iasol, annaearol
effect n effaith; canlyniad ♦ vt
 effeithio. after-effects sgil-
 effeithiau
effective adj effeithiol
effectiveness n effeithiolrwydd
effeminate adj merchetaidd
efficiency n effeithlonrwydd
efficient adj effeithiol, cymwys
effort n ymdrech, ymgais
effusive adj teimladol,
 arddangosiadol
e.g. adv abbr er enghraifft, e.e.
egg n wy. scrambled e. cymysgwy
egg vt annog, annos
egg cup n cwpan wy
egg shell n masgl/plisgyn wy
ego n ego, yr hunan
egoism n myfiaeth, egoistiaeth
egotism n hunanoldeb
egotist n un hunanol
Egypt n yr Aifft
eiderdown n cwrlid plu
eight adj, n wyth
eighteen adj, n deunaw, un deg
 wyth
eighth adj wythfed
eighty adj, n pedwar ugain, wyth
 deg
Éire n Iwerddon Rydd, Gweriniaeth
 Iwerddon
either adj un o'r ddau ♦ conj naill
 ai ♦ adv, conj na, nac, ychwaith
ejaculate vb saethu; gweiddi;
 ebychu
eject vt bwrw allan; diarddel
eke vt estyn allan; hel neu grafu
elaborate adj llafurfawr, manwl
elaborate vb manylu
elapse vi mynd heibio, treiglo

elastic *adj* hydwyth, ystwyth. **e. band** *n* cylch lastig
elated *adj* gorawenus, calonnog
elation *n* gorawen
elbow *n* elin, penelin
elder *n* henuriad, hynafgwr ♦ *adj* hŷn
elderly *adj* oedrannus
eldest *adj* hynaf
elect *vt* ethol, dewis ♦ *adj* etholedig
election *n* etholiad; etholedigaeth
elector *n* etholwr
electorate *n* etholaeth
electric *adj* trydanol, electrig. **e. blanket** *n* blanced drydan. **e. fire** *n* tân trydan
electrician *n* trydanwr
electricity *n* trydan
electrify *vt* gwefreiddio, trydanu
electronic *adj* electronig
elegant *adj* cain, dillyn, lluniaidd
elegy *n* marwnad, galarnad
element *n* elfen
elementary *adj* elfennol
elephant *n* cawrfil, eliffant
elevate *vt* dyrchafu, codi
eleven *adj, n* un ar ddeg
eleventh *adj* unfed ar ddeg
elf (elves) *n* ellyll, coblyn
elicit *vb* mynnu gan
eligible *adj* cymwys, etholadwy, dewisol
eliminate *vt* dileu, deol
elm *n* llwyf, llwyfen
elongate *vt* hwyhau, estyn
elongated *adj* hirgul
eloquent *adj* huawdl
else *adv* arall, amgen, pe amgen
elsewhere *adv* mewn lle arall
elude *vt* osgoi
elusive *adj* di-ddal, gwibiog, ansafadwy
emaciate *vt* teneuo, culhau, curio
emaciated *adj* tenau, curiedig
emanate *vi* deillio, tarddu, llifo
emancipate *vt* rhyddfreinio, rhyddhau

embankment *n* clawdd, cob
embargo *n* gwaharddiad
embark *vb* mynd neu osod ar long; hwylio. **to e. on** ymgymryd â, dechrau
embarrass *vt* rhwystro, drysu
embarrassed *adj* mewn penbleth, trafferthus
embarrassing *adj* dyrys, anffodus
embarrassment *n* chwithdod, embaras
embassy *n* llysgenhadaeth
embed *vb* mewnosod
embers *npl* marwor, marwydos
embezzle *vt* celcio, darnguddio, lladrata
embitter *vt* chwerwi
emblem *n* arwyddlun
embody *vt* corffori
emboss *vt* boglynnu
embrace *vt* cofleidio; cynnwys ♦ *n* cofleidiad
embroider *vt* brodio
embroidery *n* brodwaith
embryo *n* cynelwad, embryo
emend *vt* cywiro, diwygio
emerald *n* emrallt
emerge *vi* dyfod allan, dyfod i'r golwg, ymddangos
emergence *n* ymddangosiad
emergency *n* cyfyngder, taro, argyfwng. **in an e.** mewn taro
emigrate *vi* allfudo, ymfudo
eminent *adj* enwog, amlwg, o fri
emit *vt* rhoddi neu fwrw allan
emotion *n* cyffro, teimlad, emosiwn
emotional *adj* emosiynol
empathy *n* empathi
emperor *n* ymerawdwr, ymherodr
emphasis *n* pwys, pwyslais
emphasize *vt* pwysleisio
emphatic *adj* pwysleisiol, pendant
empire *n* ymerodraeth
empirical *adj* empeiraidd
employ *vt* cyflogi; arfer, defnyddio ♦ *n* gwasanaeth

employee n gŵr cyflog
employer n cyflogwr
employment n cyflogaeth, gwaith
empower vt awdurdodi, galluogi
empress n ymerodres
empty adj gwag, coeg ♦ vb gwagu, arllwys, gwacáu, dihysbyddu
empty-handed adj gwaglaw
emulate vt ymgystadlu á; efelychu
emulsion n emwlsiwn
enable vt galluogi
enact vt deddfu, ordeinio; cyflawni
enchant vt swyno, cyfareddu, hudo
enclose vt amgáu
enclosed adj amgaeëdig
enclosure n lle caeëdig, lloc
encompass vt amgylchu, cylchynu
encore n encôr ♦ adv eto
encounter vt cyfarfod, taro ar ♦ n ymgyfarfod, brwydr
encourage vt cefnogi, calonogi, annog
encouragement n cefnogaeth, calondid, anogaeth
encroach vi llechfeddiannu
encyclopaedia n gwyddoniadur
end n diwedd ; diben ♦ vb diweddu, dibennu, terfynu. **e. point** pwynt terfyn. **from e. to e.** o ben bwy gilydd
endanger vt peryglu
endear vt anwylo
endeavour vi ymdrechu ♦ n ymdrech
ending n diwedd, dibeniad, terfyniad
endless adj diddiwedd
endorse vt cefnogi, arnodi, ardystio
endorsement n arnodiad, ardystiad
endow vt gwaddoli, cynysgaeddu, donio
endowment n gwaddol, cynhysgaeth
endurance n dygnwch
endure vb parhau; dioddef,

goddef
enemy n gelyn
energetic adj grymus, egniol
energy n ynni, egni
enforce vt gorfodi
enforcement n gorfodaeth
engage vb ymrwymo, dyweddio; cyflogi; ymladd
engaged adj ymrwymedig, wedi dyweddio; prysur
engagement n ymrwymiad, dyweddiad; brwydr
engaging adj deniadol
engender vt achosi, peri
engine n peiriant, injan
engineer n peiriannydd
engineering n peirianneg
England n Lloegr
English adj Saesneg, Seisnig ♦ n Saesneg. **E. Channel** Môr Udd
Englishman (-men) n Sais (pl Saeson)
engrave vt ysgythru
engraving n ysgythrad
engulf vt llyncu
enhance vb chwanegu, mwyhau, chwyddo, hyrwyddo
enjoy vt mwynhau; meddu
enjoyable adj pleserus
enjoyment n mwynhad
enkindle vt ennyn
enlarge vt ehangu, helaethu
enlighten vt goleuo; hysbysu
enlightened adj goleuedig; golau
enlist vb ymrestru, listio; ennill
enmity n gelyniaeth
enormity n anfadrwydd, ysgelerder
enormous adj dirfawr, anferth, enfawr
enough adj, n, adv digon
enquire vb ymofyn, ymholi, gofyn, holi
enquiry n ymholiad
enrage vt ffyrnigo, cynddeiriogi
enrich vt cyfoethogi
enrol vt cofrestru

enrolment n cofrestrad
ensign n lluman, baner; llumanwr
enslave vt caethiwo
ensue vi dilyn, canlyn
ensure vt diogelu, sicrhau
entail vt gorfodi, gofyn
entangle vt drysu, maglu, rhwydo
enter vb mynd i mewn, treiddio;
cofnodi
enterprise n anturiaeth, menter
enterprising adj anturiaethus,
mentrus
entertain vt difyrru, adlonni;
croesawu
entertainer n difyrrwr, diddanwr
entertaining adj difyrrus, diddan
entertainment n difyrrwch,
adloniant
enthrall vb swyno
enthrone vt gorseddu
enthusiasm n brwdfrydedd
enthusiastic adj brwdfrydig,
eiddgar
entice vb hudo, denu, llithio
entire adj cyfan, hollol, llwyr
entirely adv yn gyfan gwbl, yn
llwyr
entirety n cyfanrwydd
entrails npl perfedd, ymysgaroedd
entrance n mynediad, mynedfa. **e.
fee** tâl mynediad
entrance vt swyno
entreat vt erfyn, ymbil, deisyf
entrust vt ymddiried
entry n mynediad, mynedfa;
cofnodiad
envelop vt amgáu
envelope n amlen
envious adj cenfigennus
environment n amgylchedd,
amgylchfyd
environmental adj amgylchol
envisage vb rhagweld
envoy n cennad, negesydd
envy n cenfigen, eiddigedd ♦ vt
cenfigennu, eiddigeddu
epic adj arwrol, arwraidd ♦ n

arwrgerdd, epig
epidemic adj heintus ♦ n haint
epiglottis n epiglotis
epilepsy n epilepsi
Epiphany n Yr Ystwyll
episcopate n esgobaeth
episode n digwyddiad, gogyfran,
episód
epistle n epistol, llythyr
epitaph n beddargraff
epitome n crynodeb, talfyriad
equable adj gwastad, cyson, tawel
equal adj cyfartal ♦ n cydradd ♦ vt
bod yn gyfartal. **without e.** heb ei
ail
equality n cydraddoldeb,
cyfartaledd
equalize vb cydraddoli, cyfartalu
equally adv yn ogystal â, yn llawn,
yn gyfartal
equanimity n tawelwch, anghyffro
equate vt cyfartalu, cymharu
equation n hafaliad. **simple e.** n
hafaliad syml. **quadratic e.** n
hafaliad dwyradd. **simultaneous e.**
n hafaliad cydamserol
equator n y cyhydedd
equatorial adj cyhydeddol
equestrian adj marchogol ♦ n
marchog
equilateral adj hafalochrog
equilibrium n cydbwysedd,
cymantoledd
equip vt taclu, paratoi, cymhwyso,
cyfarparu
equipment n cyfarpar, offer
equipoise n cydbwysedd
equivalent adj cyfwerth, cyfartal
equivocal adj amwys
era n cyfnod
eradicate vt difodi, difa
erase vt dileu, rhwbio allan
eraser n dilëydd, rwber
erect vt syth, unionsyth ♦ vt codi,
adeiladu
ermine n carlwm
erode vb ysu, treulio, erydu

erosion n erydiad

erotic adj serchol, nwydol, erotig

err vi cyfeiliorni

errand n neges, cenadwri

erratic adj ansefydlog, crwydraidd

error n cyfeiliornad, camgymeriad; bai, gwall. in e. ar gam

erupt vb echdorri, torri allan

eruption n echdoriad, tarddiad

escalator n escaladur

escapade n pranc, direidi

escape vb dianc, osgoi ♦ n dihangfa

escort vt hebrwng ♦ n gosgordd

especial adj arbennig, neilltuol

especially adv yn arbennig, yn enwedig

espionage n ysbiaeth

esquire n yswain, ysgwier

essay n ymgais; traethawd, ysgrif

essay vt profi, ymgeisio

essence n hanfod; rhinflas

essential adj hanfodol, anhepgor ♦ n hanfod, anghenraid

essentially adv yn hanfodol

essentials npl hanfodion, anhepgorion

establish vt sefydlu

establishment n sefydliad

estate n stad, ystad, eiddo. industrial e. stad ddiwydiannol

esteem vt parchu, edmygu, cyfrif ♦ n parch, bri

estimate vt, n amcangyfrif

estimation n amcangyfrif, parch, bri

estrange vt dieithrio

estuary n aber

et cetera adv ac yn y blaen

eternal adj tragwyddol, bythol

eternally adv yn dragwyddol, yn oes oesoedd, byth bythoedd

eternity n tragwyddoldeb

ethical adj moesegol

ethics npl moeseg

Ethiopia n Ethiopia

ethnic adj ethnig, cenhedlig

ethos n ethos, naws, natur

etiquette n moesau, arfer

etymology n geirdarddiad

eucharist n cymun, cymundeb

Europe n Ewrob, Ewrop

European adj Ewropeaidd ♦ n Ewropead

evacuate vt ymgilio, ymadael (â)

evade vt gochelyd, osgoi

evangelical adj efengylaidd

evangelist n efengylydd

evangelize vt efengylu

evaporate vb ymageru, anweddu

evaporated milk n llaeth anwedd(og)

evasion n osgoad, gocheliad

eve n min nos, noswyl

even adj gwastad, llyfn; cyfartal ♦ adv hyd yn oed. e. number eilrif

evening n noswaith, yr hwyr, min nos. e. class n dosbarth nos. e. dress n gwisg ffurfiol

evensong n prynhawnol weddi, gosber

event n digwyddiad. in the e. of os bydd

eventful adj llawn digwyddiadau

eventuality n achlysur, digwyddiad posibl

eventually adv o'r diwedd

ever adv bob amser, erioed, byth. e. and anon byth a hefyd

evergreen n, adj bythwyrdd, anwyw

everlasting adj tragwyddol, bythol

evermore adv byth, byth bythoedd

every adj bob

everybody pron pawb, pob un

everyday adj bob dydd, beunyddiol

everyone pron pawb, pob un

everything pron popeth

everywhere adv ym mhobman

evict vt troi allan, dadfeddiannu

evidence n tystiolaeth, prawf

evident adj amlwg, eglur

evil adj drwg, drygionus ♦ n drwg, drygioni

evoke *vt* galw neu dynnu allan; gwysio

evolution *n* esblygiad

evolve *vb* datblygu; esblygu

ewe *n* dafad, mamog

ex- *prefix* allan o; cyn-

exact *adj* manwl, cywir, union

exact *vt* hawlio, mynnu

exacting *adj* manwl, gorthrymus

exactly *adv* yn union, i'r dim

exaggerate *vt* chwyddo, gorliwio

exaggeration *n* gormodiaith, gorliwiad

exalt *vt* dyrchafu, mawrygu

examine *vt* arholi, archwilio

examination *n* arholiad, archwiliad

examiner *n* arholwr, archwiliwr

example *n* esiampl, enghraifft

exasperate *vt* llidio, cythruddo

exasperation *n* llid, cythrudd

excavate *vt* cloddio

exceed *vt* rhagori ar, bod yn fwy na

exceedingly *adv* tros ben, tra

excel *vb* rhagori

excellent *adj* rhagorol, ardderchog, godidog, campus

except *prep* ac eithrio, eithr, namyn, oddieithr, heblaw

exception *n* eithriad

exceptional *adj* eithriadol

excerpt *n* dyfyniad, detholiad

excess *n* gormod, gormodedd

excessive *adj* gormodol, eithafol

exchange *vt* cyfnewid, ffeirio ♦ *n* cyfnewid, cyfnewidfa. **e. rate** cyfradd cyfnewid

exchequer *n* trysorlys

excise *n* toll ♦ *vt* gosod toll

excite *vt* cynhyrfu, cyffroi

excited *adj* cynhyrfus

excitement *n* cynnwrf

exciting *adj* cyffrous

exclaim *vt* llefain, gweiddi, bloeddio, ebychu

exclamation *n* llef, gwaedd,

ebychiad. **e. mark** ebychnod

exclude *vt* cau allan, bwrw allan

exclusion *n* gwaharddiad, gwrthodiad

exclusive *adj* cyfyngedig

excommunicate *vt* esgymuno

excrement *n* carth, tom, baw

excrete *vt* ysgarthu

excruciating *adj* dirdynnol

excursion *n* gwibdaith, pleserdaith

excuse *vt* esgusodi ♦ *n* esgus

execute *vt* cyflawni, gweithredu; dienyddio

execution *n* cyflawniad, dienyddiad

executioner *n* dienyddiwr

executive *adj* gweithiol, gweithredol ♦ *n* gweithredwr. **e. committee** pwyllgor gwaith

executor *n* ysgutor

exemplify *vt* egluro, dangos, enghreifftio

exempt *adj* rhydd, esgusodol ♦ *vt* rhyddhau, esgusodi

exercise *n* ymarfer, ymarferiad ♦ *vb* ymarfer. **e. book** llyfr ysgrifennu, ymarfer

exert *vt* ymegnïo, ymdrechu

exertion *n* ymdrech, ymroddiad

exhale *vb* anadlu allan

exhaust *vt* disbyddu, diffygio, gwacáu ♦ *n* disbyddwr, gwacáwr. **e. (pipe)** *n* pibell nwyon

exhausted *adj* lluddedig, blin, disbyddedig, wedi ymládd

exhaustion *n* gorludded

exhaustive *adj* trwyadl

exhibit *vt* dangos, arddangos

exhibition *n* arddangosfa; ysgloriaeth

exhilarate *vt* llonni, sirioli, bywiogi

exile *n* alltud; alltudiaeth ♦ *vt* alltudio

exist *vi* bod, bodoli

existence *n* bod (olaeth), hanfod. **in e.** mewn bod, ar glawr

exit *n* allanfa ♦ *vb* mynd allan,

ymadael
exodus n ymadawiad
exonerate vt esgusodi
exorbitant adj afresymol, gormodol
exotic adj estron, egsotig
expand vb lledu, ehangu, datblygu
expanse n ehangder
expansion n ehangiad, ymlediad
expect vb disgwyl
expectancy n disgwyliad
expectation n disgwyliad
expediency n hwylustod
expedient adj, hwylus, cyfleus ♦ n ystryw
expedite vt hyrwyddo, hwyluso
expedition n ymgyrch, alldaith
expel vt bwrw allan, diarddel
expend vt gwario, treulio
expenditure n gwariant
expense n traul, cost
expenses npl treuliau
expensive adj drud, costus
experience n profiad ♦ vt profi
experienced adj profiadol
experiment n arbrawf ♦ vi arbrofi
expert n arbenigwr ♦ adj medrus, deheuig
expertise n medr, dawn, arbenigaeth
expire vb anadlu allan; darfod, marw
expiry n diwedd, terfyn
explain vt egluro, esbonio
explanation n eglurhad, esboniad
explanatory adj eglurhaol, esboniadol
explicit adj eglur, manwl, echblyg
explode vb ffrwydro, chwalu
exploit n camp, gorchest ♦ vt gweithio, gwneud elw o, ymelwa ar
exploitation n ymelwad
explore vt fforio, chwilio
explorer n fforiwr
explosion n ffrwydriad
explosive n ffrwydrydd/yn ♦ adj

ffrwydrol
exponent n esboniwr, dehonglwr
export vt allforio ♦ n allforyn
exporter n allforiwr
expose vt amlygu, dinoethi
expound vt esbonio
express vt mynegi, datgan ♦ adj cyflym, clir ♦ n trên cyflym
expression n mynegiant
expressly adv yn unig swydd, yn benodol
expulsion n diarddeliad
exquisite adj odiaeth, rhagorol; coeth
extempore adv, adj byrfyfyr, o'r frest
extend vb estyn, ymestyn; ehangu
extension n helaethiad, ehangiad, (ym)estyniad
extensive adj ymestynnol, helaeth
extent n ehangder, maint, hyd, mesur. **to some e.** i raddau
extenuate vt lleihau, lleddfu; esgusodi
exterior adj allanol ♦ n tu allan
exterminate vt difodi, dileu
external adj allanol
extinct adj wedi diffodd, wedi darfod, diflanedig
extinguish vt diffodd; diddymu, dileu
extinguisher n diffoddwr
extol vt moli, moliannu, clodfori
extort vt cribddeilio, gwasgu
extortionate adj gormodol
extra adj ychwanegol ♦ adv tu hwnt, dros ben ♦ n peth dros ben, ychwanegiad
extract vt echdynnu, tynnu; dyfynnu, rhinio ♦ n echdyniad; dyfyniad; rhin, darn
extracurricular adj allgyrsiol
extramural adj allanol
extraordinary adj hynod, anghyffredin
extravagant adj gwastraffus, afradlon

extreme adj i'r eithaf, eithafol ♦ n eithaf
extremely adv dros ben, gor-
extremity n pen, eithaf; cyfyngder
extrovert adj allblyg, alltro ♦ n alltröedydd, person allblyg
eye n llygad; crau; dolen ♦ vt llygadu, sylwi ar, gwylio
eyeball n cannwyll y llygad
eyebrow n ael
eyelashes npl blew yr amrant
eye-level n llinell orwel
eyelid n amrant
eye-opener n agoriad llygad
eyesight n golwg
eyesore n hyllbeth
eyewitness n llygad-dyst

F

fable n chwedl, dameg; anwiredd
fabric n adail, adeilad, defnydd
fabricate vt llunio, dyfeisio, ffugio
fabrication n ffug, anwiredd
fabulous adj chwedlonol, diarhebol
face n wyneb, wynepryd ♦ vb wynebu. **f. cloth** n clwtyn ymolchi. **f. value** arwynebwerth
facilitate vt hwyluso, hyrwyddo
facility n hwylustod, cyfleustra, rhwyddineb
fact n ffaith, gwirionedd. **as a matter of f.** mewn gwirionedd
factor n ffactor, elfen, nodwedd. **prime f.** ffactor cysefin
factory n ffatri
factual adj ffeithiol
faculty n cynneddf; cyfadran
fad n mympwy, chwiien
fade vb diflannu, gwywo; colli ei liw
fag vb slafio, ymládd, blino ♦ n caledwaith, lludded; gwas bach
fail vi ffaelu, methu, pallu, diffygio. **without f.** yn ddi-ffael
failure n methiant, pall,

aflwyddiant
faint adj llesmeiriol, gwan, llesg ♦ vi llewygu ♦ n llesmair, llewyg
fair n ffair
fair adj teg, glân; gweddol; golau
fairly adv yn deg/lân, yn weddol
fairness n glendid, tegwch
fairy n un o'r tylwyth teg
fairy-tale n stori hud, chwedl werin
faith n ffydd, cred, coel
faithful adj ffyddlon, cywir
faithfully adv yn ffyddlon, yn gywir. **yours f.** yr eiddoch yn gywir
fake n ffug ♦ vb ffugio
falcon n hebog, curyll
fall vi cwympo, syrthio ♦ n cwymp. **f. out** cweryla. **f. through** methu
fallacy n cyfeiliornad, gwall
fallow n braenar ♦ vt braenaru
false adj gau, ffug, ffals, twylodrus. **f. teeth** dannedd gosod/dodi
falter vb petruso, methu, pallu
fame n enwogrwydd, clod, bri
familiar adj cynefin, cyfarwydd
familiarity n cynefindra
family n teulu, tylwyth
famine n newyn
famish vb newynu, llwgu
famous adj enwog
fan n gwyntyll; ffan ♦ vt gwyntyllio, chwythu
fanatic n penboethyn, ffanatig
fanaticism n penboethni, ffanatigiaeth
fanciful adj ffansïol
fancy n dychymyg, ffansi, serch ♦ vt dychmygu, ffansïo, serchu. **f. dress** gwisg ffansi
fang n ysgithr, dant, pig, blaen
fantastic adj ffantastig, rhyfeddol
fantasy n ffantasi
far adj pell(ennig) ♦ adv ymhell. **as f. as** hyd at
farce n ffars
fare n cost, pris; ymborth ♦ vi bod,

dod ymlaen, byw

farewell *excl* yn iach, ffarwel ♦ *n* ffarwel. **to bid f.** canu'n iach

farm *n* fferm ♦ *vt* amaethu, ffarmio

farmer *n* ffarmwr, ffermwr, amaethwr. **Young Farmers' Club** Clwb y Ffermwyr Ifainc

farmhouse *n* ffermdy

farming *n* ffermio. **intensive f.** ffermio dwys

farmyard *n* buarth, clos

fascinate *vt* hudo, swyno

fascinating *adj* hudol, swynol

fascism *n* ffasgaeth

fashion *n* ffasiwn, arfer, dull ♦ *vt* llunio, gwneud

fashionable *adj* ffasiynol

fast *vi* ymprydio ♦ *n* ympryd

fast *adj* tyn, sownd; buan, cyflym, clau

fasten *vb* sicrhau, cau, clymu, ffasno

fastener *n* ffasnydd

fastening *n* ffasnin

fastidious *adj* cysetlyd

fat *adj* tew, bras ♦ *n* braster, bloneg, saim

fatal *adj* angheuol, marwol; andwyol

fatality *n* trychineb, marwolaeth

fate *n* tynged, ffawd ♦ *vt* tynghedu

fateful *adj* tyngedfennol

father *n* tad ♦ *vt* tadogi

father-in-law *n* tad-yng-nghyfraith

fatherly *adj* tadol

fathom *n* gwryd ♦ *vt* plymio

fatigue *n* lludded, blinder ♦ *vt* lluddedu, blino

fatten *vb* tewhau, pesgi

fatty *adj* seimlyd, brasterog

fatuous *adj* ynfyd, ffôl

fault *n* bai, diffyg, nam, anaf. **at f.** ar fai

faultless *adj* di-fai, perffaith

faulty *adj* gwallus, diffygiol

favour *n* ffafr, cymwynas ♦ *vt*

ffafrio. **in f. of** o blaid

favourable *adj* ffafriol

favourite *adj, n* ffefryn ♦ *adj* hoff

fawn *n* elain ♦ *adj* llwyd

fawn *vi* cynffonna, gwenieithio

fear *n* ofn, braw, arswyd ♦ *vb* ofni, arswydo

fearful *adj* ofnus, brawychus, arswydus

feasible *adj* dichonadwy

feast *n* gwledd, gŵyl ♦ *vb* gwledda

feat *n* camp, gorchest

feather *n* pluen, plufyn ♦ *vt* pluo, plufio

feature *n* arwedd, nodwedd

February *n* Chwefror, Mis Bach

federal *adj* cynghreiriol, ffederal

fee *n* ffi, tâl, cyflog

feeble *adj* gwan, eiddil

feed *vb* porthi, ymborthi, bwydo ♦ *n* porthiant, ffid, ymborth, gwledd

feedback *n* adborth, ymateb ♦ *vb* adborthi

feel *vb* teimlo, clywed, profi

feeler *n* teimlydd; ymchwiliad

feeling *n* teimlad; synhwyriad

feign *vb* cymryd arno, ffugio

fell *vb* cwympo, cymynu ♦ *n* croen; ffridd, rhos

fellow *n* cymar; cymrawd ♦ *prefix* cyd-

fellowship *n* cymdeithas, cyfeillach; cymrodoriaeth

felt *n* ffelt ♦ *vb* ffeltio

female *adj, n* benyw

feminine *adj* benywaidd, benywol

feminist *n* ffeminist

femur *n* ffemwr

fence *n* clawdd, ffens ♦ *vb* cau, amgáu

fencing *n* ffensio, cleddyfaeth

fend *vb* cadw draw; ymdaro, ymdopi

ferment *n* eples, cynnwrf ♦ *vb* eplesu, cynhyrfu

fermentation *n* eplesiad

fern *n* rhedynen, rhedyn

ferocious adj ffyrnig, gwyllt, milain

ferret n ffured ♦ vt ffuredu, chwilota

ferry n porth, fferi ♦ vb cludo dros

ferry-boat n ysgraff

fertile adj ffrwythlon, toreithiog

fertilisation n ffrwythloniad

fertility n ffrwythlonder

fertilize vb ffrwythloni; gwrteithio

fertilizer n gwrtaith

fervent adj brwd, gwresog, tanbaid, taer

fester vi crawni, gori, crynhoi

festival n gŵyl, dydd gŵyl. **singing f.** cymanfa ganu

festive adj llawen, llon

festivity n rhialtwch, miri, ysbleddach

fetch vt cyrchu, hôl, ymofyn, nôl

fête n gŵyl, miri ♦ vi gwledda

feud n cynnen, ffiwd

feudal adj ffiwdal

feudalism n ffiwdaliaeth

fever n twymyn, clefyd, gwres

feverish adj â thwymyn

few adj ychydig, prin, anaml

fiancé(e) n darpar-wr/wraig

fib n anwiredd, celwydd

fibre n edefyn, ffibr

fibreglass n ffibr gwydrog

fickle adj anwadal, oriog, gwamal

fiction n ffugien

fictitious adj ffug, ffugiol

fiddle n ffidil, crwth ♦ vi canu'r ffidl; ffidlan

fidelity n ffyddlondeb, cywirdeb

fidget vt ffwdanu, aflonyddu ♦ n un ffwdanus, un aflonydd

field n cae, maes ♦ vb maesu

field marshal n maeslywydd

field work n gwaith maes

fiend n cythraul, ellyll, ysbryd drwg

fierce adj ffyrnig, milain; tanbaid

fiery adj tanllyd, tanbaid

fifteen adj, n pymtheg

fifth adj, n pumed

fifty adj, n hanner cant, deg a deugain

fig n ffigysen

fight n ymladd, cwffio, brwydro, rhyfela ♦ n ymladdfa, brwydr

fighter n ymladdwr, brwydrwr

fighting n ymladd

figment n creadigaeth (y dychymyg)

figurative adj ffigurol, cyffelybiaethol

figure n ffigur; llun, ffurf ♦ vb cyfrif; llunio; ymddangos. **f. of speech** troad ymadrodd

figurehead n arweinydd (mewn enw)

file n ffeil, rhathell; rhes ♦ vb ffeilio, rhathu

fill vb llenwi ♦ n llenwad, llonaid, gwala

fillet n llain, ffiled. **f. steak** n stêc ffiled

filling n llenwad, mewnyn

filly n eboles

film n pilen, caenen; ffilm ♦ vb ffilmio, gwneud ffilm. **f. strip** stribed ffilm

filter n hidl, hidlydd ♦ vb hidlo, ffiltro. **f. tip** n hidl difaco

filth n brynti, budreddi, baw

filthy adj brwnt, budr, aflan

filtrate n hidlif ♦ vb hidlo

fin n adain, asgell, ffin

final adj terfynol, olaf. **semi-f.** cynderfynol

finale n ffinale, diweddglo

finally adv o'r diwedd, yn olaf

finance n cyllid ♦ vb cyllido, codi arian

financial adj cyllidol, ariannol

find vt darganfod ♦ n darganfyddiad

finding n darganfyddiad, dedfryd

fine adj main; mân; gwych; braf

fine n dirwy ♦ vt dirwyo

finery n gwychder

finger n bys ♦ vt bysio, bodio. **little f.** bys bach. **third f.** bys y fodrwy. **middle f.** y bys canol

fingerprint n bysbrint, ôl bys

finicky adj cysetlyd, gorfanwl

finish vb diweddu, gorffen, cwblhau ♦ n diwedd; gorffeniad

finished adj gorffenedig

finite adj meidrol

Finland n y Ffindir

fir n ffynidwydden

fire n tân ♦ vb tanio, ennyn. **wild f.** tân gwyllt. **f. precautions** rhagodion tân

firearm n arf-tân

firebrigade n brigâd dân

fire engine n peiriant tân

fire escape n grisiau tân

fire-extinguisher n diffoddydd tân

fireguard n sgrin dân

fireman n taniwr, diffoddwr tân

fireplace n lle tân

fireside n aelwyd

firewood n coed tân, cynnud

fireworks npl tân gwyllt

firm n cwmni, ffyrm ♦ adj cadarn, diysgog

firmly adv yn gadarn, yn ddiysgog

first adj cyntaf, blaenaf, prif ♦ adv yn gyntaf. **f. aid** n cymorth cyntaf. **f. class** adj dosbarth cyntaf. **f. floor** n llawr cyntaf. **f.-hand** adj o lygad y ffynnon. **f.-rate** adj campus, ardderchog, rhagorol

fish n pysgodyn, pysgod ♦ vb pysgota. **f. and chips** pysgodyn a sglodion

fisherman n pysgotwr

fishing n pysgota

fishing rod n genwair, gwialen bysgota

fishmonger n gwerthwr pysgod

fishy adj amheus; pysgodol

fist n dwrn

fit n llewyg, ffit, mesur

fit adj ffit, addas, cymwys, gweddus; abl, iach ♦ vb ffitio,

gweddu, taro

fitful adj anwadal, gwamal

fitment n cynhalydd

fitness n ffitrwydd, addasrwydd

fitter n ffitiwr

fitting n ffitiad ♦ vb ffitio ♦ adj priodol, gweddus, addas. **fittings** mân daclau, ffitiadau

five adj pum ♦ n pump

fix vb sicrhau, sefydlu, gosod ♦ n cyfyngder, cyfyng-gyngor

fixation n sefydlogiad, sefydledd

fixed n sefydlog

fixture n gosodyn, peniant (byd chwarae)

fizz vi sio

fizzle vb hisian, sio

fizzy adj byrlymog

flabbergast vt synnu, syfrdanu

flabby adj llipa, llac, llaes

flag n baner, lluman; fflagen ♦ vb llumanu; llaesu

flake n fflaw, caenen; pluen (eira)

flamboyant adj coegwych

flame n fflam ♦ vi fflamio, ffaglu

flame-resistant adj gwrthfflam

flan n fflan

flank n ystlys, ochr ♦ vb ymylu, ystlysu

flannel n gwlanen

flap n llabed, fflap ♦ vb fflapio

flare vb fflêr, fflach; fflerio, fflachio

flash vb fflachio ♦ n fflach

flashback n ôl-fflach

flashlight n fflachlamp

flashy adj gorwych

flask n costrel, fflasg

flat n fflat, gwastad; meddalnod ♦ adj fflat, gwastad, lleddf ♦ vb fflatio

flatten vb gwastatáu

flatter vt gwenieithio

flattery n gweniaith

flatulence n gwynt (yn y cylla)

flaunt vb fflawntio, rhodresa

flavour n blas, cyflas ♦ vt blasu, cyflasu

flavouring n cyflasyn

flaw n bai, diffyg, nam

flax n llin

flaxen adj golau, o lin

flay vt blingo

flea n chwannen

flee vb ffoi, cilio, dianc, diflannu

fleece n cnu ♦ vt cneifio; ysbeilio

fleet n llynges, fflyd ♦ adj cyflym, buan

fleeting adj diflanedig

flesh n cig, cnawd. **f. and blood** cig a gwaed. **f. and bones** cnawd ac esgyrn

flex n fflecs

flexible adj hyblyg, ystwyth

flick vt cyffwrdd â blaen chwip, cnithio

flier n ehedwr

flight n hediad, ffo, rhes

flighty adj gwamal, penchwiban

flimsy adj tenau, simsan, bregus

flinch vi cilio yn ôl, gwingo, llwfrhau

fling vt taflu, bwrw, lluchio ♦ n rhwysg, tafliad

flint n callestr, carreg dân, fflint

flip vb cnithio ♦ n cnith

flippant adj tafodrydd, gwamal

flipper n asgell

flirt vb cellwair caru, fflyrtan ♦ n fflyrten, fflyrtyn

flit vi gwibio

float n arnofyn, fflôt, trol ♦ vb arnofio

flock n diadell, praidd ♦ vi heidio

flog vt fflangellu, chwipio

flood n llif, dilyw, cenllif ♦ vt llifo, gorlifo

floodlight n llifolau ♦ vb llifoleuo

floor n llawr ♦ vt llorio; methu. **ground f.** daearlawr. **first f.** llawr cyntaf

flop n methiant, ymollwng

flora n fflora, planhigion

floral adj fflurol

florid adj blodeuog

florist n tyfwr neu werthwr blodau

flounce vi swalpio, ysboncio ♦ n llam, ysbonc

flounder n lleden fach ♦ vb ymdrybaeddu, ffwndro

flour n blawd, can

flourish vi blodeuo; ffynnu; ysgwyd ♦ n rhwysg; cân cyrn

flout vb gwawdio, wfftio, diystyru

flow vi llifo, llifeirio ♦ n llif, llanw

flow chart n siart rhediad

flower n blodeuyn, blodyn ♦ vi blodeuo. **flowerpot** pot blodau

flowery adj blodeuog

flu n ffliw, anwydwst

fluctuate vi codi a gostwng, amrywio, anwadalu

flue n pibell simnai, ffliw

fluency n huodledd, llithrigrwydd

fluent adj llithrig, rhugl

fluff n fflwcs, fflwff ♦ vb bwnglera, methu

fluid adj hylif, llifol ♦ n hylif, llifydd

fluke n pry'r afu; ffliwc, lwc

fluoride n ffliworid

flurry n cyffro, ffwdan

flush n gwrid; rhuthr dŵr ♦ adj cyfwyneb, gorlawn ♦ vb gwrido, cochi; gorlifo

fluster vb ffwdanu, cyffroi ♦ n ffwdan, cyffro

flute n ffliwt

flutter vb dychlamu, siffrwd ♦ n dychlamiad, siffrwd

fly n gwybedyn, cleren, pryf

fly vb ehedeg, ehedfan; ffoi ♦ n pryf, cleren, copis. **f. into a passion** ymwylltio, gwylltu

flying adj hedegog, cyflym

flyover n pontffordd, trosffordd

foal n ebol, eboles ♦ vb bwrw ebol. **in f.** cyfebol

foam n ewyn ♦ vi ewynnu, glafoerio

focus n canolbwynt, ffocws ♦ vb canolbwyntio

fodder n porthiant, ebran
foe n gelyn
fog n niwl
foggy adj niwlog
foil vt rhwystro, trechu ♦ n ffoil, ffwyl, dalen
fold n plyg; corlan ♦ vb plygu, corlannu
folder n plygell
folding n plygiant
foliage n dail, deiliant
folio n ffolio
folk npl pobl, gwerin
folklore n llên gwerin
folk song n cân werin
follow vb canlyn, dilyn
follower n dilynwr, canlynwr
following adj dilynol, canlynol ♦ n dilyniad, canlynwyr
folly n ffolineb, ynfydrwydd
fond adj hoff, annwyl
fondle vt anwylo, anwesu
font n bedyddfaen
food n bwyd, ymborth, lluniaeth.
   tinned f. bwyd tun. **f. poisoning** n gwenwyn bwyd
fool n ffŵl, ynfytyn ♦ vb ynfydu, twyllo
foolhardy adj rhyfygus
foolish adj ffôl, ynfyd, annoeth
foot (**feet**) n troed; troedfedd ♦ vb troedio. **f. and mouth disease** n clwyf y traed a'r genau. **f. rot** clwy'r traed
football n pêl-droed
footballer n peldroediwr
footbrake n brêc troed
footbridge n pont gerdded, pompren
foothold n gafael troed, troedle
footing n sylfaen, safle
footlights npl golau'r godre
footman n gwas (á lifrai)
footmark n ôl troed
footnote n troednodiad
footpath n llwybr troed
footprint n ôl troed

footstep n cam, ôl troed
footway n troedffordd
footwear n troedwisg
for prep i, at, am, dros, er ♦ conj canys, oblegid, oherwydd, gan, achos
forage n bwyd (anifail), porthiant ♦ vb chwilio am fwyd
forasmuch conj yn gymaint ag, am, gan, oherwydd
foray n cyrch, rhuthr ♦ vb gwneud cyrch, rhuthro
forbid vt gwahardd, gwarafun, gomedd
forbidden adj gwaharddedig
force n grym; trais ♦ vt gorfodi.
   centrifugal f. grym allgyrchol.
   centripetal f. grym mewngyrchol.
   the forces y lluoedd arfog
forceful adj grymus, egniol
forceps n gefel fain
forcible adj nerthol, effeithiol
ford n rhyd ♦ vt rhydio
fore adj blaen, blaenaf ♦ adv ymlaen ♦ prefix cyn-, rhag-, blaen-. **to the f.** amlwg, blaenllaw
forearm n elin ♦ vb rhagarfogi
forebode vt rhagargoeli, rhagarwyddo, darogan
foreboding n rhagargoel
forecast n rhagolygon, rhagolwg ♦ vb rhagddweud, darogan
forefather n cyndad
forefinger n mynegfys
forefront n lle blaen ♦ adj blaen
forego vb hepgor. **foregone conclusion** penderfyniad ymlaen llaw
foreground n blaendir
forehead n talcen
foreign adj estron, tramor. **f. affairs** materion tramor
foreigner n estron, tramorwr
foreman n fforman
foremost adj blaenaf ♦ adv ym mlaenaf
forensic adj fforensig

forerunner n rhagredegydd

foresee vt rhagweld, rhagwybod

foreseeable adj rhagweladwy

foreshadow vb rhagarwyddo, rhagargoeli

foresight n rhagwelediad

forest n coedwig, fforest ♦ vt coedwigo, fforestu

forestall vt achub y blaen

forestry n coedwigaeth. **f. commission** Comiswn Coedwigo

foretaste n rhagflas ♦ vt rhagbrofi

foretell vt rhagfynegi, darogan

forever adv am byth

foreword n rhagair, rhagymadroddi

forfeit n fforffed ♦ vt fforffedu, colli

forge n gefail, ffwrn ♦ vb gofannu; ffugio

forget vt anghofio

forgetful adj anghofus

forgive vt maddau

forgiveness n maddeuant

forgo vt gadael, hepgor, mynd heb

fork n fforch, fforc ♦ vb fforchio

forlorn adj amddifad, truan, anobeithiol

form n ffurf; mainc; fffurflen ♦ vb ffurfio. **application f.** ffurflen gais

formal adj ffurfiol, defodol

former adj blaenaf, blaenorol

formerly adv gynt, yn flaenorol

formidable adj arswydus, ofnadwy, grymus

formula n rheol, fformwla

forsake vt gadael, ymadael â, gwrthod, cefnu ar

fort n caer, castell, amddiffynfa

forte n cryfder ♦ adj uchel, cryf

forth adv allan, ymlaen. **and so f.** ac felly yn y blaen

forthcoming adj ar ddod, gerllaw

forthright adj union, plaen

forthwith adv yn ddioed, ar unwaith

fortify vt cadarnhau, cryfhau

fortitude n gwroldeb, dewrder

fortnight n pythefnos

fortnightly adj, adv bob pythefnos

fortress n amddiffynfa, caer, castell

fortunate adj ffodus, ffortunus

fortunately adv yn ffodus, yn lwcus

fortune n ffawd; ffortun

fortune teller n un sy'n dweud ffortun

forty adj, n deugain

forum n fforwm

forward n blaenwr ♦ adj eofn, hy; blaen ♦ adv ymlaen ♦ vb anfon ymlaen; hwyluso, hyrwyddo. **inside f.** mewnwr. **wing f.** blaenasgellwr

fossil n ffosil ♦ adj ffosilaidd

fossilise vb ffosileiddio

foster vt magu, meithrin, coleddu

foster-child n plentyn maeth

foster-mother n mamfaeth

foul adj aflan; annheg; afiach ♦ n ffowl(en) ♦ vb ffowlio, llychwino. **f. play** anfadwaith. **f. throw** camdaflu

found vt dechrau, sylfaenu, sefydlu

foundation n sail, sylfaen

founder vb ymddryllio, suddo ♦ n sylfaenydd

foundry n ffowndri, efail

fountain n ffynnon, ffynhonnell

four adj, n pedwar (f pedair)

foursome n pedwarawd

fourteen adj, n pedwar (pedair) ar ddeg

fourth adj pedwerydd (f pedwaredd)

fowl n dofedn, ffowlyn, ffowl

fox n cadno, llwynog

foyer n cyntedd

fraction n ffracsiwn. **improper f.** ffracsiwn pendrwm. **vulgar f.** ffracsiwn cyffredin. **proper f.** ffracsiwn bondrwm

fracture n toriad, drylliad ♦ vt torri, dryllio
fragile adj brau, bregus
fragment n dryll, darn, briwsionyn
fragrance n perarogl, persawr
frail adj brau, bregus, gwan, eiddil
frame n ffrâm; agwedd ♦ vt fframio, llunio. **f. of mind** agwedd meddwl
framework n fframwaith
franchise n etholfraint ♦ vb etholfreinio
frank adj didwyll, agored
frankincense n thus
frantic adj cyffrous, gwallgof
fraternal adj brawdol
fraternity n brawdoliaeth
fraud n twyll, hoced
fraudulent adj twyllodrus
fraught adj llwythog, llawn
fray n ymryson, ymgiprys, ffrae, rhaflad ♦ vb treulio, rhaflo
freak n mympwy, peth od
freckle n brych, brychni
free adj rhydd; hael; di-dâl, rhad ♦ vb rhyddhau
freedom n rhyddid, rhyddfraint
free expression n rhyddfynegiant
freehold adj rhydd-ddaliadol
free kick n cic rydd
freely adv yn rhydd, yn hael
freemason n saer rhydd
free trade n masnach rydd
free verse n mesur rhydd, y wers rydd
free will n ewyllys rydd, o'i fodd
freeze vb rhewi, fferru
freeze-dry vb sychrewi
freezer n rhewgist, rhewgell
freezing point n rhewbwynt
freight n llwyth llong ♦ vt llwytho llong
French adj Ffrengig ♦ n Ffrangeg. **F. beans** npl ffa Ffrengig
Frenchman n Ffrancwr
Frenchwoman n Ffrances
frenzy n gorffwylltra, cynddaredd

frequency n amider, mynychder
frequent adj mynych, aml ♦ vt mynychu
frequently adv yn fynych, yn aml
fresh adj ffres, crai, cri, croyw, newydd
freshen vb ffresáu, ireiddio
freshness n ffresni, creider, irder
fret vb sorri, poeni ♦ n soriant, trallod, ffret
friar n brawd, mynach
friction n ffrithiant, ymrafael
Friday n dydd Gwener
fridge n oergell, rhewadur
friend n cyfaill, ffrind
friendly adj cyfeillgar
friendship n cyfeillgarwch
frieze n ffris
fright n dychryn, ofn, braw
frighten vb dychrynu, brawychu, codi ofn ar
frightful adj dychrynllyd, brawychus
frigid adj oer, rhewllyd; oeraidd, oerllyd. **f. zone** n cylchfa rew
frill n ffril
fringe n ymyl, ymylwe, rhidens ♦ vb ymylu, rhidennu. **f. benefits** cilfanteision
frisk vt prancio
fritter vt afradu, ofera, gwastraffu
frivolous adj gwamal; diystyr, disylwedd
frizzy adj crychlyd
fro adv: **to and f.** yn ôl ac ymlaen
frock n ffrog
frog n llyffant (melyn), broga; bywyn, ffroga
frolic vi prancio, campio ♦ n pranc
from prep o, oddi, oddi wrth, gan
front n wyneb, blaen, ffrynt, talcen ♦ vb wynebu ♦ adj blaen. **f. door** drws ffrynt. **f. page** tudalen flaen. **f. room** ystafell (ffrynt)
frontier n ffin, terfyn, goror
frost n rhew
frostbite n ewinrhew

frosty *adj* rhewllyd
froth *n* ewyn ♦ *vi* ewynnu
frown *vi* cuchio, gwgu ♦ *n* cuwch, gwg
frozen *adj* wedi rhewi
frugal *adj* cynnil, darbodus
fruit *n* ffrwyth, ffrwythau. **f. juice** sudd ffrwyth. **f. salad** salad ffrwythau
fruiterer *n* gwerthwr ffrwythau
fruitful *adj* ffrwythlon, toreithiog
fruition *n* ffrwythloniad
frustrate *vt* rhwystro, llesteirio
frustration *n* llesteiriant
fry *vb* ffrio ♦ *n* afu, sil, silod. **small f.** *n* pobl ddibwys
frying-pan *n* ffrimpan, padell ffrio
fudge *n* cyffug
fuel *n* tanwydd; cynnud. **f. cell** cynudydd
fugitive *adj* ar ffo, diflanedig ♦ *n* ffoadur
fulfil *vt* cyflawni
fulfilment *n* cyflawniad
full *adj* llawn, cyflawn ♦ *n* llonaid
full-back *n* cefnwr
fuller *n* pannwr
full stop *n* atalnod
fulltime *adj* llawn amser
fully *adv* yn gyfan gwbl, yn gyflawn, yn hollol
fulsome *adj* ffiaidd, diflas (am weniaith, etc)
fumble *vb* palfalu, bwnglera
fume *n* tarth, mwg; llid ♦ *vb* mygu; llidio, sorri
fun *n* difyrrwch, digrifwch, hwyl
function *n* swydd, swyddogaeth; ffwythiant (mathemateg)
functional *adj* swyddogaethol, ffwythiannol, defnyddiol
fund *n* cronfa, trysorfa
fundamental *adj* sylfaenol
funeral *n* angladd, cynhebrwng, claddedigaeth
fungus *n* ffwng
funnel *n* twmffat, twndis, corn

funny *adj* digrif, ysmala; rhyfedd, hynod
fur *n* blew, ffwr; cen. **f. coat** *n* cot ffwr
furious *adj* cynddeiriog, ffyrnig, gwyllt
furlong *n* ystad, wythfed ran milltir
furnace *n* ffwrn, ffwrnais
furnish *vt* dodrefnu, rhoddi
furnishings *npl* dodrefn
furniture *n* dodrefn, celfi
furrow *n* cwys, rhych ♦ *vt* cwyso, rhychu
furry *adj* blewog
further *adj* pellach ♦ *adv* ymhellach ♦ *vt* hyrwyddo. **f. education** addysg bellach
fury *n* cynddaredd, ffyrnigrwydd
fuse *n* ffiws, toddyn, diogelydd ♦ *vb* ffiwsio
fuss *n* ffwdan, helynt, stŵr ♦ *vb* ffwdanu
fussy *adj* ffwdanus
futile *adj* ofer, di-les
future *adj*, *n* dyfodol
fuzzy *adj* blewog, aneglur

G

gabble *vb* bregliach, clebran ♦ *n* cleber
gable *n* piniwn, talcen tŷ
gadget *n* dyfais
Gaelic *n* Gaeleg ♦ *adj* Gaelaidd
gaff *n* bach pysgota
gag *n* smaldod; safnglo ♦ *vb* smalio; safngloi, cau ceg
gaiety *n* llonder, difyrrwch, miri
gaily *adv* yn llawen
gain *vb* ennill, elwa ♦ *n* ennill, elw, budd
gait *n* cerddediad, osgo
gale *n* awel, gwynt cryf; tymestl
gall *n* bustl, chwydd ♦ *vb* dolurio, blino. **g. bladder** *n* coden y bustl.

g. **stones** cerrig y bustl

gallant adj gwrol, dewr ♦ n carwr

gallery n oriel, llofft

galley n rhwyfIong; galí

gallon n galwyn

gallop n carlam ♦ vb carlamu

gallows n crocbren

galore n, adv digonedd

galvanize vt galfaneiddio, galfanu; symbylu

gamble vb hapchwarae, gamblo ♦ n gambl

game n chwarae, camp; helwriaeth ♦ adj calonnog, dewr, glew

game-keeper n cipar

gammon n palfais (mochyn); ffwlbri, lol

gander n ceiliagwydd, clacwydd

gang n mintai, torf, haid, gang

gangster n troseddwr

gangway n tramwyfa, eil, ale; pont

gaol n carchar ♦ vt carcharu

gap n bwlch, adwy

gape vi rhythu, syllu ♦ n rhythiad

garage n modurdy, garej

garbage n ysgarthion, ysbwriel, sothach

garble vt darnio, llurgunio

garden n gardd ♦ vi garddio

gardener n garddwr

gardening n garddwriaeth

gargle n golch gwddf ♦ vb golchi gwddf

garish adj coegwych

garland n coronbleth, garlant, talaith

garlic n garlleg

garment n dilledyn, gwisg

garnish vt addurno, harddu

garrison n gwarchodlu, garsiwn

garrulous adj tafodrydd, siaradus

garter n gardas, gardys ♦ vb gardysu

gas n nwy ♦ vb gwenwyno â nwy. g. **cooker** ffwrn nwy. g. **fire** tân

nwy. g. **ring** cylch nwy

gash n archoll, hollt, hac ♦ vt archolli, hacio

gasket n gasged

gas-mask n mwgwd nwy

gasometer n tanc nwy

gasp vb ebychu, anadlu'n drwm

gate n porth, llidiart, clwyd, gât, iet ♦ vb porthio, porthellu

gate-crasher n ymyrrwr

gatehouse n porthordy

gateway n mynedfa

gather vb casglu, cynnull, crynhoi, hel

gathering n casgliad, cynulliad

gaudy adj coegwych, gorwych

gauge n mesur; lled; meidrydd ♦ vt mesur, meidryddu

Gaul n Gâl

Gaulish n Galeg

gaunt adj llwm, tenau

gauntlet n dyrnfol, maneg ddur. **to throw down the g.** herio

gauze n rhwyllen, gaws, meinwe

gay adj llon, bywiog, ofer, hoyw

gaze vi edrych, syllu, tremio ♦ n golwg, trem

gazette n newyddiadur (swyddogol)

gazetteer n geiriadur daearyddol

GCSE n abbr TGAU = Tystysgrif Gyffredin Addysg Uwchradd

gear n gêr, offer, taclau ♦ vb taclu, harneisio

gearbox n gergist, blwch gêr, gerbocs

gelignite n geligneit

gem n glain, gem, tlws

gender n cenedl

genealogy n achau; achyddiaeth

general adj cyffredin, cyffredinol ♦ n cadfridog. g. **election** n etholiad cyffredinol

generalize vb cyffredinoli

generally adv yn gyffredinol

generate vt cenhedlu, cynhyrchu, generadu

generation n cenhedliad;
cenhedlaeth, tras

generator n cynhyrchydd;
generadur

generosity n haelioni

generous adj hael, haelionus,
haelfrydig

genetic adj genetig

genetics n geneteg

Geneva n Genefa

genial adj hynaws, rhadlon, tyner,
tirion

genital adj cenhedlol. **genitals** npl
organau cenhedlu

genius n athrylith

genteel adj bonheddig;
bonddigaidd

gentle adj bonheddig; mwyn, tyner

gentleman n gŵr bonheddig

gently adv yn dyner, addfwyn; gan
bwyll

gentry npl bonedd

gents npl toiledau dynion

genuine adj dilys, diffuant, pur

geography n daearyddiaeth

geology n daeareg

geometry n geometreg

geriatrics n geriatreg

germ n hedyn, eginyn, germ

German adj Almaenaidd ♦ n
Almaenwr; Almaeneg. **G. measles**
y frech Almeinig

Germany n yr Almaen

germinate vi egino, atyfu

germination n eginiad, atyfiant

gesture n ystum, arwydd, mosiwn

get vb cael, caffael, ennill. **to g. on
with it** bwrw arni, bwrw iddi

geyser n geyser

Ghana n Ghana

ghastly adj erchyll, gwelw

gherkin n gercin

ghost n ysbryd, drychiolaeth,
bwgan

giant n cawr ♦ adj cawraidd

gibberish n cleber, baldordd

gibe vb gwawdio ♦ n gwawd

giblets npl giblets, syrth gwydd

Gibraltar n Gibralter

giddiness n pendro

giddy adj penfeddw, penchwiban

gift n rhodd, dawn, anrheg, gwobr

gifted adj dawnus, talentog

gigantic adj cawraidd, dirfawr,
anferth

giggle vb lledchwerthin, giglan

gill n tagell; gil, chwarter peint

gimmick n gimig

gin n jin; hoenyn

ginger n sinsir

gingerly adj, adv gochelgar,
gwyliadwrus

gipsy, gy- n sipsi

giraffe n siráff

girder n trawst

girdle n gwregys, rhwymyn ♦ vt
gwregysu

girl n merch, geneth, hogen

girlfriend n cariadferch, anwylyd

girth n cengl; cylchfesur, cwmpas

gist n cnewyllyn pwnc, ergyd,
sylwedd

give vb rhoddi, rhoi. **g. up** rhoi'r
gorau i

glacier n rhewlif, iaen, glasier

glad adj llawen, llon, balch

gladiator n cleddyfwr, ymladdwr

gladly adv yn llawen, â phleser

glamorous adj swynol, cyfareddol,
hudol

glamour n swyn, cyfaredd, hud

glance vb cildrech, tremio ♦ n
cipolwg, trem, cip

gland n chwarren, cilchwyrnen,
gland

glare vb disgleirio; rhythu ♦ n
disgleirdeb, tanbeidrwydd

glass n gwydr; gwydraid; pl
gwydrau, sbectol

glassy adj gloyw, pŵl

glaze vt gwydro; sgleinio ♦ n
sglein, gwydredd

glazier n gwydrwr

gleam n pelydryn, llewyrch ♦ vi

pelydru, llewyrchu
glean vb lloffa
glebe n clastir, tir eglwys
glee n llonder, hoen; rhangan
glen n glyn, cwm, dyffryn
glib adj llyfn, llithrig, rhugl, ffraeth
glide vi llithro, llifo ♦ n llithr, llithrad
gliding n, vb llithran
glimmer vi llewyrchu'n wan ♦ n llewyrchyn, llygedyn
glimpse n trem, cipolwg
glint vb fflachio ♦ n fflach, llewyrch
glisten vi disgleirio
glitter vi tywynnu, pelydru ♦ n pelydriad
gloat vb llawenhau
global adj hollfydol, cyffredinol
globe n pêl, pelen
gloom n caddug, prudd-der, tywyllwch
gloomy adj prudd, digalon, tywyll
glorify vt gogoneddu
glorious adj gogoneddus
glory n gogoniant ♦ vi ymffrostio, gorfoleddu
gloss n disgleirdeb arwynebol, sglein; glòs, esboniad
glossary n geirfa
glossy adj llathraidd
glove n maneg
glow vi twymo, gwrido ♦ n gwres, gwrid
glower vi cuchio, gwgu
glue n glud ♦ vt gludio, asio
glum adj prudd, digalon, trist
glut vt gorlenwi, glythu ♦ n gormodedd, gorlawnder
glutton n glwth
gluttony n glythineb
gnarled adj cnotiog, ceinciog, garw
gnat n gwybedyn, cylionen
gnaw vb cnoi, deintio, cnewian
gnome n gwireb; ysbryd, coblyn
go vi mynd, cerdded, rhodio ♦ n

tro
goad n swmbwl ♦ vt symbylu
goal n gôl, nod, bwriad. **g. posts** npl pyst gôl. **g. shooter** saethwr
goalkeeper n golgeidwad, golwr
goat n gafr
goblin n ellyll, coblyn, bwgan
god n duw. **G.** Duw
godchild n mab bedydd, merch fedydd
goddess n duwies
godfather n tad bedydd
godhead n duwdod
godly adj duwiol
godmother adj mam fedydd
godsend n caffaeliad
goggles npl gwydrau
gold n aur ♦ adj aur, euraid
golden adj euraid
goldfish n eurbysg, pysgod aur
goldsmith n gof aur, eurych
golf n golff. **g. links** maes golff. **g. course** n maes golffio
golfer n golffwr
gong n gong, cloch fwyd
good adj da, daionus; cryn ♦ n da, daioni, lles. **g. morning** bore da. **g. afternoon** prynhawn da. **g. evening** noswaith dda. **g. night** nos da. **g. enough** digon da. **no g.** dim gwerth, da i ddim. **G. Friday** Dydd Gwener y Groglith. **g. humour** natur dda
good-bye excl, n da bo chi, yn iach! ffarwel
good-looking adj golygus
goodly adj hardd, teg
good-natured adj hynaws, rhadlon
goodness n daioni
goods npl nwyddau, eiddo
goodwill n ewyllys da; braint (masnachol)
goose (**geese**) n gŵydd
gooseberry n eirinen Fair, gwsbersen
gooseflesh n croen gŵydd
gore n gwaed, gôr ♦ vb cornio

gorge n hafn, ceunant ♦ vb safnio, traflyncu

gorgeous adj ysblennydd, gwych

gorilla n gorila

gorse n eithin

gory adj gwaedlyd

gosling n cyw gŵydd

gospel n efengyl

gossip n clec, clonc, clebryn, clebran ♦ vb clebran, clecian, hel straeon

gout n gowt, cymalwst

govern vb llywodraethu, rheoli, llywio

governess n athrawes

government n llywodraeth

governor n llywodraethwr

gown n gŵn

grab vb crafangu, cipio ♦ n gwanc, crap

grace n gras, rhad, graslonrwydd; gosgeiddrwydd ♦ vt harddu, prydferthu, addurno

graceful adj graslon, rhadlon; gosgeiddig, lluniaidd

gracious adj graslon, grasol, rhadlon, hynaws

grade n gradd, safon ♦ vb graddio

gradient n graddiant

gradual adj graddol

gradually adv yn raddol

graduate vb graddio, graddoli ♦ n gŵr gradd, graddedig

graduation n graddedigaeth, graddnod

graffiti n graffiti

graft n impyn, hunan-les ♦ vt impio, grafftio

grain n grawn, gronyn; mymryn; graen ♦ vb graenu, graenio

gram n gram

grammar n gramadeg. **g. school** n ysgol ramadeg

grammatical adj gramadegol

granary n ysgubor

grand adj mawreddog, ardderchog, crand; prif, uchel

grandchild n wyr, wyres. **great g.** n gorwyr(es)

granddaughter n wyres

grandfather n taid, tad-cu. **great g.** n hen daid, hen-dad-cu

grandmother n nain, mam-gu

grandson n wyr

granite n gwenithfaen, ithfaen

grant vt rhoddi, caniatáu ♦ n rhodd, grant. **to take for granted** cymryd yn ganiataol

granulated adj gronynnog

granule n gronynnell

grapefruit n grawnffrwyth

grapes n grawnwin

graph n graff

graphic adj graffig; byw

graphics npl graffigwaith, graffeg

grapple n gafl, gafaelfach ♦ vb gafaelyd, mynd i'r afael â

grasp vb gafael; amgyffred ♦ n gafael, amgyffrediad

grasping adj trachwantus

grass n glaswellt, porfa

grasshopper n ceiliog y rhedyn, sioncyn y gwair

grate n grat ♦ vb rhygnu, crafellu; merwino

grateful adj diolchgar; dymunol

grater n grater, crafellydd

gratify vt boddio, boddhau

grating adj garw, cras ♦ n gratin

gratitude n diolchgarwch

gratuity n cildwrn, rhodd

grave adj difrifol, dwys

grave n bedd, beddrod

gravel n graean, gro, grafel

gravestone n beddfaen, carreg fedd

graveyard n mynwent

gravitate vi disgyrchu, treiglo

gravity n disgyrchiant; pwysigrwydd. **centre of g.** craidd disgyrchiant

gravy n grefi, isgell, sew

graze vb pori; crafu, rhwbio, ysgythru

grease n saim, iraid ♦ vt iro, seimio

greaseproof adj gwrthsaim

greasy adj seimllyd, ireidlyd

great adj mawr. **a g. many** llawer iawn

greatly adv yn fawr

Greece n Groeg

greed n trachwant, gwanc

greedy adj barus, trachwantus, gwancus

Greek n Groeg; Groegwr ♦ adj Groegaidd

green adj gwyrdd, glas, ir ♦ vb glasu

greenery n gwyrddlesni

greengrocer n gringroser, gwerthwr llysiau

greenhouse n tŷ gwydr

Greenland n Grønland

greet vt annerch, cyfarch

greeting n cyfarchiad

grenade n grenâd

grey adj llwyd, llwydwyn, glas

greyhound n milgi

grid n grid, alch. **g. reference** cyfeirnod grid

grief n gofid, galar, hiraeth

grievance n cwyn

grieve vb gofidio, galaru, hiraethu

grievous adj gofidus, poenus, blin, dirifol

grill n gril, gridyll ♦ vb grilio, gridyllu. **mixed g.** gril cymysg

grille n gril, dellt

grim adj sarrug, milain, difrifol

grimace n ystum ♦ vi ystumio

grimy adj budr, brwnt, diraen

grin vb lledwenu ♦ n gwên

grind vb malu (ŷd etc); llifo (arf), llifanu

grip n gafael, gwasgu ♦ n gafael, crap

grisly adj erch, erchyll, hyll, milain

gristle n madruddyn, gwythi

grit n grit, grud, graean; pybyrwch

groan vi, n griddfan

grocer n groser

groceries npl nwyddau

groin n cesail morddwyd, gwerddyr

groom n priodfab; gwastrawd ♦ vb trwsio

groove n rhigol, rhych ♦ vt rhigoli, rhychu

grope vi ymbalfalu

gross n gros; crynswth ♦ adj bras, aflednais. **g. profit** elw gros

grotto n groto

ground n llawr, daear, tir; sail; gwaelod ♦ vt daearu, llorio. **g. floor** n daearlawr

groundless adj di-sail

groundwork n sylfaen, sail

group n grŵp, twr, bagad ♦ vt grwpio. **discussion g.** cylch trafod

grouse n grugiar ♦ vb grwgnach

grove n llwyn, celli

grovel vi ymgreinio

grow vb tyfu, prifio, cynyddu, codi

grower n tyfwr

growing adj yn tyfu

growl vi chwyrnu

growth n twf, tyfiant, cynnydd

grub n pryf, cynrhonyn; bwyd ♦ vb dadwreiddio

grubby adj budr, brwnt

grudge n gwarafun, grwgnach ♦ n dig, cenfigen, cas

gruesome adj erchyll, hyll, ffiaidd

gruff adj sarrug, garw, swta

grumble vi grwgnach, tuchan

grumpy adj sarrug, diserch

grunt vi rhochian ♦ n rhoch

guarantee n gwarant, ernes ♦ vt gwarantu, mechnïo

guard n gard, gwarchodydd; sgrin ♦ vb gwarchod

guarded adj gwyliadurus, gofalus

guardian n gwarcheidwad

guerilla n herfilwr

guess vb dyfalu, dyfeisio ♦ n

amcan
guesswork *n* dyfaliad
guest *n* gwestai, gŵr/gwraig
(g)wadd
guffaw *n* crechwen ♦ *vb*
crechwenu
guidance *n* cyfarwyddyd
guide *n* arweinydd ♦ *vt* arwain,
cyfarwyddo
guide book *n* teithlyfr
guide-dog *n* arweingi
guide-lines *npl* canllawiau
guild *n* cymdeithas, corfforaeth,
urdd
guile *n* twyll, dichell, ystryw
guillotine *n* gilotin
guilt *n* euogrwydd, bai
guilty *adj* euog
guinea pig *n* mochyn cwta
guise *n* dull, modd, rhith, diwyg
guitar *n* gitâr
gulf *n* gwlff, geneufor; gagendor
gull *n* gwylan; gwirionyn ♦ *vt*
twyllo
gullet *n* corn gwddf, sefnig
gullible *adj* hygoelus
gully *n* rhigol, ffos
gulp *vt* llawcian, traflyncu ♦ *n*
llawc, traflwnc
gum *n* gwm, glud ♦ *vt* gymio,
gludio
gumboots *npl* esgidiau rwber
gums *npl* cig y dannedd,
gorcharfanau, crib y dannedd,
gorfant
gun *n* gwn, dryll
gunner *n* gynnwr
gunpowder *n* powdr gwn
gunshot *n* ergyd gwn
gunsmith *n* gof gynnau (bach)
gurgle *vi* byrlymu
gush *vb* ffrydio, llifeirio ♦ *n* ffrwd,
hyrddwynt
gust *n* chwythwm
gusto *n* awch, blas, sêl
gut *n* perfeddyn, coluddyn ♦ *vt*
diberfeddu; difrodi, ysbeilio

gutter *n* ffos, cwter, cafn
guttural *adj* gyddfol
guzzle *vb* llawcio, traflyncu
gym *n* campfa
gymnasium *n* gymnasiwm,
campfa
gymnast *n* mabolgampwr
gynaecologist *n* gynaecolegydd
gynaecology *n* gynaecoleg
gypsy *n* sipsi
gyrate *vi* troi, chwyrlïo

H

ha *excl* ha!
haberdashery *n* dilladach, siop
ddillad
habit *n* arferiad; anian; gwisg ♦ *vt*
gwisgo, dilladu
habitable *adj* cyfannedd,
cyfanheddol
habitat *n* cartref, cynefin
habitation *n* trigfa, preswylfa
habitual *adj* arferol, cyson
habituate *vt* arfer, cynefino
hack *vb* hacio, torri ♦ *n* hac
hack *n* hurfarch; cystog, slâf
hackneyed *adj* ystrydebol,
cyffredin
hades *n* annwfn
haddock *n* corbenfras, hadog
haemorrhage *n* gwaedlif
haemorrhoids *npl* clwyf y
marchogion
haft *n* carn
hag *n* gwrach, gwiddon
haggard *adj* gwyllt, curiedig
haggle *vi* bargeinio'n daer
hail *n* cenllysg, cesair ♦ *vb* bwrw
cesair
hail *excl* henffych well ♦ *vb*
cyfarch, galw
hair *n* gwallt, blew, rhawn. **hair's
breadth** trwch y blewyn. **h.
splitting** hollti blew
hairbrush *n* brws gwallt

haircut n triniaeth gwallt, toriad, crop

hairdresser n triniwr gwallt

hair dryer n sychwr gwallt

hair spray n chwistrelliad gwallt; chwistrellydd gwallt

hairy adj blewog

hake n cegddu

hale adj iach, cryf, hoenus

half (halves) n hanner

half-back n hanerwr

half-breed adj cymysgryw

half-dead adj lledfyw

half-hearted adj diawydd, llugoer

halfpenny n dimai

halibut n halibwt

hall n llys, neuadd, plas; cyntedd

hallmark n dilysnod

hallo excl heló

hallow vt cysegru, sancteiddio

Halloween n nos Galangaeaf

hallucination n geuddrych, rhithwelediad

halo n corongylch, goroniant, halo, lleugylch

halt vb sefyll ♦ n safiad; gorsaf, arosfa

halter n cebystr, tennyn

halve vt haneru

ham n morddwyd, ham

hames npl mynci

hamlet n pentref

hammer n morthwyl, mwrthwl, gordd ♦ vb morthwylio

hammock n hamog, gwely crog

hamper vt rhwystro, llesteirio

hamstring n llinyn y gar

hand n llaw; (of clock) bys ♦ vt estyn, trosglwyddo. **hand-off** n hwp llaw. **in-hand** adj ar waith. **to be on h.** bod with law

handbag n bag llaw

handbook n llawlyfr

handbrake n brec llaw

handcuff n gefyn llaw

handful n dyrnaid, llond llaw

handicap n rhwystr, llestair,

anfantais; blaen. **handicapped children** plant dan anfantais

handicraft n crefft

handiwork n gwaith llaw

handkerchief n cadach poced, hances, macyn, neisied

handle n carn, coes, troed, dolen, clust, dwrn ♦ vt trin, trafod. **to fly off the h.** colli tymer

handlebars npl cyrn

handmade adj wedi ei wneud â llaw

handmaid, -en n llawforwyn

handrail n canllaw

handsome adj golygus, hardd, prydferth; hael

handwriting n llawysgrifen

handy adj hylaw, deheuig, cyfleus

hang vb crogi, hongian, dibynnu

hangar n awyrendy

hang-gliding vb barcuta

hangover n blinder ddoe, pen mawr

hank n cengl

hanker vi blysio, crefu, dyheu, hiraethu

hanky-panky n twyll, dichell ♦ adj twyllodrus, dichellgar

hap n hap, damwain

haphazard adj, adv damweiniol, ar siawns

happen vi digwydd

happily adv yn hapus

happiness n dedwyddwch, hapusrwydd

happy adj dedwydd, hapus

happy-go-lucky adj didaro, di-hid

harangue n araith, arawd ♦ vb areithio

harass vt poeni, blino, gofidio

harassment n poen, blinder

harbour n porthladd, harbwr ♦ vb llochesu

hard adj caled, anodd. **h. of hearing** trwm ei glyw. **to be h. done by** cael cam. **h. headed** hirben

hardboard n caledfwrdd

harden vb caledu

hardener n caledwr

hardness n caledwch

hardship n caledi

hard shoulder n llain galed

hard-up adj prin o arian

hardware n nwyddau metel

hardwood n pren caled

hardy adj caled, cryf, gwydn; hy, eofn

hare n ysgyfarnog, ceinach

harebrained adj byrbwyll, gwyllt

harelip n bylchfin, gwefus fylchog

hark excl gwrando! clyw! **h. back** dychwelyd

harlot n putain

harm n niwed, drwg, cam ♦ vt niweidio, drygu

harmful adj niweidiol

harmless adj diniwed, diddrwg

harmonious adj cytûn

harmonise vb cytgordio, cytuno

harmony n harmoni, cynghanedd

harness n harnais, gêr ♦ vt harneisio

harp n telyn ♦ vi canu'r delyn

harpoon n tryfer ♦ vt tryferu

harrow n og ♦ vt llyfnu; rhwygo, dryllio

harrowing adj dychrynllyd, ofnadwy, deifiol

harry vt difrodi, blino

harsh adj garw, gerwin, aflafar

harshness n craster, gerwinedd

hart n hydd

harvest n cynhaeaf ♦ vt cynaeafu

harvester n cynaeafwr. **combine h.** n combein

hash n briwgig; cymysgfa, cybolfa

hasp n hesben

haste n brys, hast ♦ vi brysio, prysuro

hasten vb brysio, prysuro, hastu

hastily adv yn frysiog

hasty adj brysiog, byrbwyll

hat n het

hatch vb deor, gori ♦ n deoriad

hatch n gorddrws, rhagddor, dôr

hatchery n deorfa

hatchet n bwyell (fach)

hate vt casáu ♦ n cas, casineb

hateful adj cas, atgas

hatred n cas, casineb, digasedd

haughtiness n balchder, traha, ffroenucheledd

haughty adj balch, ffroenuchel, trahaus

haul vb tynnu, llusgo, halio ♦ n dalfa

haulage n cludiad, cludiant

haulier n haliwr

haunch n morddwyd, pedrain

haunt vt cyniwair, mynychu; trwblu, aflonyddu ♦ n cyniweirfa, cynefin, cyrchfa

have vt cael, meddu. **I h. blue eyes** mae llygaid glas gennyf. **I h. a cold** mae annwyd arnaf

haven n hafan, porthladd

haversack n ysgrepan

havoc n hafog, difrod

hawk n hebog, cudyll, curyll ♦ vb heboca

hawk vt gwerthu o dŷ i dŷ, pedlera

haws npl crawel y moch, criafol y moch

hawthorn n draenen wen

hay n gwair

hayfever n clefyd y gwair

hayrick n tas wair

hazard n perygl, llestair, antur ♦ vt anturio, peryglu

hazardous adj peryglus, enbydus

haze n niwl, tarth, tawch

hazel n collen ♦ adj gwinau golau

haziness n aneglurder

hazy adj aneglur, niwlog

he pron ef, efe; efo, fo, o

head n pen ♦ vb blaenori, penio

headache n dolur (cur) yn y pen, pen tost

header n peniad

headgear n penffest, penwig

heading *n* pennawd
headlamp *n* lamp fawr
headland *n* pentir, penrhyn; talar
headline *n* pennawd, teitl, hedin
headlong *adv* pendramwnwgl
headmaster *n* prifathro
headmistress *n* prifathrawes
headphone *n* ffôn pen
headquarters *npl* pencadlys
headstrong *adj* cyndyn
headway *n* cynnydd
heal *vb* iachâu, meddyginiaethu
health *n* iechyd. **h. food shop** *n*
    siop bwyd iach. **H. Service** *n* y
    Gwasanaeth Iechyd
healthy *adj* iach, iachus
heap *n* crug, pentwr ♦ *vt* crugio,
    pentyrru
hear *vb* clywed
hearing *n* clyw
hearing aid *n* cymorth clywed
hearken *vi* gwrando, clustfeinio
hearsay *n* sôn, siarad ♦ *adj* o ben i
    ben, ail-law
hearse *n* hers
heart *n* calon
heart-ache *n* ing, dolur calon
heart attack *n* trawiad
heartburn *n* dwr poeth
hearten *vb* calonogi
hearth *n* aelwyd
heartland *n* perfeddwlad
hearty *adj* calonnog, cynnes
heat *n* gwres, poethder, *(sport)*
    rhagras ♦ *vb* twymo, poethi
heater *n* gwresogydd
heath *n* rhos, rhostir
heathen *adj* paganaidd ♦ *n* pagan
heather *n* grug
heating *n* gwres
heave *vb* codi, dyrchafu;
    chwyddo; taflu ♦ *n* hwb
heaven *n* nef, nefoedd
heavenly *adj* nefol, nefolaidd
heavily *adv* yn drwm, yn drymaidd
heavy *adj* trwm, trymaidd,
    trymllyd

heavyweight *n* *(SPORT)* pwysau
    trwm
Hebrew *n* Hebrëwr; Hebraeg ♦ *adj*
    Hebraeg; Hebreig
heckle *vb* ymyrryd
hectare *n* hectar
hedge *n* clawdd, gwrych, perth
hedgehog *n* draenog
heed *vt* ystyried, talu sylw ♦ *n*
    ystyriaeth
heel *n* sawdl ♦ *vb* sodli
heifer *n* anner, heffer, treisiad
height *n* uchder, uchelder, taldra
heinous *adj* dybryd, anfad, ysgeler
heir *n* etifedd, aer
heiress *n* etifeddes, aeres
helicopter *n* hofrennydd
hell *n* uffern
hellish *adj* uffernol
hello *excl* helô!, hylô!, clyw!,
    gwrando!
helm *n* llyw; llywyddiaeth
helmet *n* helm
help *n* helpu, cymorth,
    cynorthwyo ♦ *n* help, cymorth,
    cynhorthwy
helper *n* cynorthwywr, helpwr
helpful *adj* defnyddiol,
    cymwynasgar, gwasanaethgar,
    buddiol
helping *n* dogn, cyfran (o fwyd)
helpless *adj* diymadferth
helter-skelter *adv* blith-draphlith
hem *n* hem, ymyl ♦ *vt* hemio
hemi- *prefix* hanner
hemisphere *n* hemisffer
hemlock *n* cegid
hemp *n* cywarch
hen *n* iâr
hence *adv* oddi yma ♦ *excl* ymaith!
henceforth, -forward *adv* rhag
    llaw, mwyach, o hyn ymlaen
henchman *n* gwas, canlynwr,
    cefnogydd
hepatitis *n* llifi yr afu, hepatitis
her *pron* ei, hi, hithau
herald *n* herald ♦ *vt* cyhoeddi;

rhagflaenu
herb n llysieuyn, sawr-lysieuyn
herbal adj llysieuol
herbicide n llysleiddiad
herd n gyr, cenaint, gre ♦ vb heidio
here adv yma
hereditary adj etifeddol
heredity n etifeddeg
heresy n heresi, gau athrawiaeth
heretic n heretic, camgredwr
heritage n etifeddiaeth, treftadaeth
hermit n meudwy
hernia n bors, hernia, torllengig
hero n arwr, gwron
heroic adj arwrol
heroine n arwres
heron n crëyr, crychydd
herring n pennog, ysgadenyn
hesitant adj petrusgar
hesitate vi petruso
hesitation n petruster
heterodox adj anuniongred
heterodoxy n anuniongrededd
heterogeneous adj anghydryw, afryw, heterogenus
heterosexual n anghyfunryw
hew vt naddu, torri, cymynu
hewer n cymynwr, torrwr
hexa- prefix chwech
heyday n anterth
hiatus n hiatws
hibernate vi gaeafu
hiccup n yr ig ♦ vi igian
hide vb cuddio, celu, ymguddio
hide n croen
hide-and-seek n chwarae mig
hideous adj hyll, erchyll
hiding place n cuddfan, lloches
hierarchy n gradd, offeiriadaeth
higgle vi taeru, bargennna
high adj uchel; mawr; cryf; llawn
highbrow adj uchel-ael
high chair n cadair ar gyfer plentyn
highland n ucheldir
highly adv yn fawr, yn uchel

highness n uchelder
high-priest n archoffeiriad
high-spirited adj calonnog, nwyfus
high water n pen llanw
highway n priffordd, ffordd fawr
highwayman n lleidr penffordd
hijack vb cipio
hike vb crwydro ♦ n taith gerdded
hilarious adj llawen, llon, siriol, hoenus
hill n bryn, allt, gorifyny
hillock n bryncyn, ponc, twmpath
hilly adj bryniog, mynyddig
hilt n carn cleddyf
him pron ef, efe, yntau
hind adj ôl
hind n ewig
hinder vt rhwystro, atal, lluddias, llesteirio
hindrance n rhwystr, llestair, lludd
hinge n colyn drws ♦ vb troi, dibynnu
hint n awgrym ♦ vt awgrymu
hinterland n cefnwlad
hip n clun, pen uchaf y glun
hippie n hipi
hips npl egroes
hire vb cyflogi, hurio, llogi ♦ n cyflog, hur
hiss vb chwythu, sïo, hysio, hisian
historian n hanesydd
historic adj hanesyddol
historical adj hanesyddol
hit vb taro ♦ n ergyd, trawiad
hitch vb bachu ♦ n cwlwm; atalfa, rhwystr
hitchhike vb bodio
hitchhiker n bodiwr
hither adv yma, hyd yma, tuag yma
hitherto adv hyd yma, hyd yn hyn
hive n cwch gwenyn. **h. off** vb rhannu, trosglwyddo, newid
hoar adj llwyd, penllwyd ♦ n llwydrew, barrug
hoard n cronfa, cuddfa ♦ vt cronni

hoarfrost n barrug, llwydrew
hoarse adj cryg, cryglyd
hoax vt twyllo ♦ n cast, tric, twyll
hob n pentan
hobble vb hercian
hobby n difyrwaith, hobi
hobby horse n ceffyl pren; hoff beth
hobgoblin n bwbach, bwci, bwgan
hoe n hof ♦ vb hofio
hog n mochyn
hoist vt codi, dyrchafu
hold vb dal, credu; atal; cadw ♦ n gafael, dalfa
hold n ceudod llong, howld
holdall n celsach
holding n deiliadaeth; tyddyn
hold up n (robbery) lladrad arfog; (in traffic) rhwystr
hole n twll, ffau
holiday n gŵyl, dygwyl
holiness n sancteiddrwydd
Holland n Isalmaen
hollow adj cau, gwag ♦ n ceudod, pant ♦ vt tyllu, cafnio
holly n celyn, celynnen
holocaust n lladdfa
holster n gwain
holy adj sanctaidd, glân
Holy Ghost/Spirit n Ysbryd Glân
homage n gwrogaeth
home n, adj cartref ♦ adv adref. **at h.** gartref
homeland n mamwlad
homeless adj digartref
homely adj cartrefol
home rule n ymreolaeth, hunan-lywodraeth
homesick adj hiraethus
homestead n tyddyn
homework n gwaith cartref
homicide n dynleiddiad, llofruddiaeth
homily n pregeth, homili
homogeneous adj cydryw, homogenus
homosexual n gwrywgydiwr

homosexuality n gwrywgydiaeth
hone n carreg hogi, hôn ♦ vb hogi
honest adj (g)onest, didwyll
honesty n (g)onestrwydd
honey n mêl
honeycomb n dil mêl, crwybr ♦ vt tyllu, britho
honeymoon n mis mêl
honeysuckle n gwyddfid
honorary adj mygedol
honour n anrhydedd ♦ vt anrhydeddu
honourable adj anrhydeddus
hood n cwfl, cwcwll
hoodwink vt dallu, twyllo
hoof n carn
hook n bach; cryman ♦ vb bachu
hooker n bachwr
hooligan n adyn, dihiryn
hoop n cylch, cant ♦ vt cylchu, cantio
hoot vb hwtian, hwtio ♦ n hwt
hop vb hercian ♦ n llam, herc
hope n gobaith ♦ vb gobeithio
horde n torf, haid, mintai
horizon n gorwel
horizontal adj llorwedd
hormone n hormon
horn n corn ♦ vt cornio, twlcio
horned adj corniog
hornet n gwenynen feirch, cacynen
horoscope n horosgôp
horrible adj erchyll, ofnadwy
horrid adj erchyll, echrydus, anferth
horrify vt brawychu
horror n arswyd, erchylltod
horse n march, ceffyl
horsehair n rhawn
horseman n marchog
horsemanship n marchogaeth
horseplay n direidi
horseshoe n pedol
horticultural adj garddwriaethol
horticulture n garddwriaeth
horticulturist n garddwriaethwr
hose (hose) n hosan; (hoses)

pibell ddŵr
hospitable adj lletygar, croesawus
hospital n ysbyty
hospitality n lletygarwch, croeso
host n llu, byddin
host n lletywr, gwesteiwr
hostage n gwystl
hostel n llety efrydwyr, neuadd breswyl
hostess n croesawferch
hostile adj gelyniaethus
hot adj poeth, twym, brwd, gwresog
hotbed n magwrfa
hotch-potch n cymysgfa, cybolfa
hotel n gwesty
hotelier n gwestywr
hot-headed adj penboeth, byrbwyll
hot-water bottle n jar/potel dŵr twym
hound n bytheiad, helgi ♦ vt hela, erlid, annos
hour n awr
house n tŷ, annedd ♦ vb lletya
household n teulu, tylwyth
householder n deiliad tŷ
housekeeper n gofalyddes
housewife n gwraig tŷ
housing n tai
hovel n penty, hofel
hover vi hofran
hovercraft n hofrenfad
how adv pa mor, pa fodd, pa sut, sut
howbeit adv er hynny
however adv pa fodd bynnag, sut bynnag
howl vi udo, oernadu ♦ n udiad, oernad
hoyden n rhampen, hoeden
hub n both olwyn; canolbwynt
hubbub n mwstwr
huddle vb tyrru, gwthio
hue n gwawr
huff vb sorri, tramgwyddo ♦ n soriant
hug vt cofleidio, gwasgu

huge adj anferth, enfawr, dirfawr
hulk n corff llong, llong foel, hwlc
hull n corff llong; cibyn, plisgyn
hullabaloo n dadwrdd, helynt, halibalŵ
hum vb mwmian ♦ n si, sibrwd
human adj dynol
humane adj tirion, tosturiol, trugarog
humanism n dyneiddiaeth
humanist n dyneiddiwr
humanistic adj dyneiddiol
humanitarian n dyngarwr
humanitarianism n dyngaroldeb
humanity n dynoliaeth, dynolryw
humble adj gostyngedig, ufudd ♦ vt darostwng
humble-bee n cacynen
humbug n twyll, ffug, hoced; twyllwr ♦ vt twyllo
humdrum adj diflas
humid adj llaith
humiliate vt bychanu, gwaradwyddo, darostwng, iselu
humiliation n darostyngiad
humility n gostyngeiddrwydd
humour n hwyl, donioldeb ♦ vt boddio
hump n crwmach, crwmp, crwb
hunch n syniad, tybiaeth
hunch backed adj cefngrwm
hundred adj cant, can ♦ n cant; cantref
Hungary n Hwngari
hunger n newyn, chwant bwyd ♦ vi newynu
hungry adj newynog
hunk n cwlff(yn)
hunt vb hela, erlid ♦ n helwriaeth, hela
hunter n heliwr; ceffyl hela
hunting n hela
hurdle n clwyd
hurl vt hyrddio
hurly-burly n hwrli-bwrli, dwndwr
hurricane n corwynt
hurried adj brysiog

hurry *vb* brysio ♦ *n* brys
hurt *vb* niweidio, dolurio, brifo ♦ *n* niwed, dolur
hurtful *adj* niweidiol
hurtle *vb* gwrthdaro, chwyrlïo
husband *n* gŵr, priod ♦ *vt* cynilo
husbandry *n* amaethyddiaeth, hwsmonaeth
hush *excl* ust ♦ *vb* distewi ♦ *n* distawrwydd
husk *n* plisgyn, cibyn ♦ *vt* plisgo
husky *adj* sych, cryglyd
hussy *n* maeden
hustings *n* hwstyng, llwyfan etholiad
hustle *vb* gwthio, prysuro
hut *n* bwth, caban, cwt
hutch *n* cwt cwningen, cwb
hyacinth *n* croeso haf
hybrid *adj* croesryw
hydration *n* hydradiad
hydraulic *adj* hydrolig
hydraulics *n* hydroleg
hydro- *prefix* dwfr
hydroelectric *adj* hydroelectrig
hydrophobia *n* hydroffobia
hygiene *n* iechydaeth, gwyddor glendid
hymn *n* emyn ♦ *vb* emynu
hyper- *prefix* gor-, tra-
hyperbole *n* gormodiaith
hypermarket *n* archfarchnad
hyphen *n* cyplysnod, cysylltnod (-)
hypnotism *n* swyngwsg, hypnotiaeth
hypnotize *vt* swyno, rheibio
hypochondria *n* pruddglwyf, y felan
hypocrisy *n* rhagrith
hypocrite *n* rhagrithiwr
hypothesis (**-theses**) *n* damcaniaeth
hyssop *n* isop
hysteria *n* y famwst, hysteria
hysterical *adj* hysterig

I

I *pron* mi, myfi; fi, i; minnau, innau
ice *n* iâ, rhew ♦ *vt* taenu (megis) â rhew
iceberg *n* mynydd rhew
ice cream *n* hufen iâ
Iceland *n* Gwlad yr Iâ
ice lolly *n* loli iâ
ice rink *n* llain iâ
icicle *n* clöyn iâ, cloch iâ, pibonwy
icing *n* eising
icy *adj* rhewllyd
idea *n* drychfeddwl, syniad
ideal *adj* delfrydol, ideal ♦ *n* delfryd
idealism *n* delfrydiaeth
idealist *n* delfrydiwr
idealistic *adj* delfrydol
idealize *vb* delfrydu
identical *adj* yr un (yn union)
identify *vt* adnabod (fel yr un un); uniaethu
identikit (picture) *n* tebyglun
identity *n* unfathiant, hunaniaeth
idiocy *n* gwiriondeb, penwendid
idiom *n* priod-ddull, idiom
idiosyncrasy *n* tymer, anianawd
idiot *n* gwirionyn, hurtyn
idle *adj* segur, ofer ♦ *vb* segura, ofera
idleness *n* segurdod, diogi
idol *n* eilun
idolater *n* eilunaddolwr
idolatry *n* eilunaddoliaeth
idolise *vb* addoli, gwirioni
idyll *n* bugeilgerdd; canig
if *conj* os, pe
igloo *n* iglw
ignite *vb* ennyn, tanio, cynnau
ignition *n* taniad
ignoble *adj* anenwog, isel, gwael, salw
ignominious *adj* gwarthus,

gwaradwyddus

ignorance n anwybodaeth

ignorant adj anwybodus

ignore vt anwybyddu, diystyru

il- prefix di-, an-

ill adj drwg; gwael, claf ♦ adv yn ddrwg ♦ n drwg, niwed

ill-advised adj annoeth, ffôl

illegal adj anghyfreithlon

illegible adj annarllenadwy, aneglur

illegitimate, illicit adj anghyfreithlon

illiterate adj anllythrennog

illness n afiechyd, anhwylder, anhwyldeb

illogical adj afresymegol

ill-timed adj anamserol

ill-treat vb camdrin

illuminate vt goleuo, addurno

illumination n golau, esboniad

illusion n rhith, lledrith, rhithganfyddiad

illustrate vt egluro; darlunio

illustration n eglureb; darlun

illustrative adj darluniol, eglurhaol

illustrious adj enwog, hyglod

ill-will n gelyniaeth, casineb

im- prefix di, an-

image n delw, llun; delwedd

imagery n delweddaeth

imaginary adj dychmygol

imagination n dychymyg, darfelydd

imaginative adj dychmygus

imagine vt dychmygu, tybio

imbalance n anghydbwysedd

imbecile adj, n (un) penwan

imbue vt trwytho

imitate vt dynwared, efelychu

immaculate adj difrycheulyd, pur, glân

immaterial adj dibwys

immature adj anaeddfed

immediate adj agos, presennol

immediately adv ar unwaith

immemorial adj er cyn cof

immense adj anferth, eang, dirfawr

immerse vt trochi, suddo

immigrant n mewnfudwr

immigrate vi mewnfudo

imminent adj gerllaw, agos, wrth y drws

immobile adj diymod, disymud

immoral adj anfoesol

immortal adj anfarwol

immortality n anfarwoldeb

immortalize vb anfarwoli

immovable adj diysgog, ansymudol

immune adj rhydd rhag

immunization n gwrth-heintiad

immunize vb gwrtheintio

immure vt caethiwo, carcharu

immutable adj anghyfnewidiol, digyfnewid

imp n dieflyn, cenau

impact n ardrawiad, gwrthdrawiad

impair vt amharu

impale vt trywanu

impart vt cyfrannu, rhoddi

impartial adj diduedd, amhleidiol, teg

impassable adj na ellir mynd heibio iddo

impasse n ataliad, pen draw

impassioned adj brwd, hwyliog, cyffrous

impassive adj digyffro, didaro

impatient adj diamynedd

impeach vt cyhuddo, cwyno yn erbyn, uchelgyhuddo

impeccable adj di-fai

impede vt atal, rhwystro, llesteirio

impediment n atalfa, rhwystr, nam

impel vt gyrru, hyrddio, cymell

impending adj agos, gerllaw

imperative n gorchymyn ♦ adj gorchmynnol, gorfodol

imperfect adj amherffaith

imperial adj ymerodrol

imperil vt peryglu

imperious adj awdurdodol, trahaus

impermeable adj anathraidd
impersonal adj amhersonol
impersonate vt personoli, cynrychioli, portreadu (*person*)
impertinent adj amherthnasol; digywilydd
imperturbable adj tawel, digyffro
impervious adj na ellir ei dreiddio, anhydraidd
impetuous adj byrbwyll, nwydwyllt
impetus n cymhelliad, symbyliad
impinge vi taro yn erbyn, gwrthdaro, cyffwrdd â
impious adj annuwiol, diras
implacable adj anghymodlon
implant vt plannu, gwreiddio
implement n offeryn, arf ♦ vb gweithredu
implication n ymhlygiad, goblygiad
implicit adj dealledig; ymhlyg, goblygedig
implore vt atolygu, ymbil, erfyn, crefu
imply vt arwyddo, awgrymu
impolite adj anfoesgar
import vt mewnforio ♦ n (pl) mewnforion; arwyddocâd; pwys
importance n pwys, pwysigrwydd
important adj pwysig
importer n mewnforiwr
importune vt dyfal geisio, taer erfyn
impose vb gosod ar; twyllo
imposing adj llethol, mawreddog
impossibility n amhosibilrwydd
impossible adj amhosibl
impostor n twyllwr
imposture n twyll, hoced
impotence n anallu, analluedd
impotent adj di-rym, analluog
impound vi ffaldio; atafaelu
impoverish vt tlodi, llymhau
impracticable adj anymarferol
imprecate vt rhegi, melltithio
impregnable adj cadarn, di-syfl

impregnate vt ffrwythloni; trwytho
impress vt argraffu, pwyso, dylanwadu ♦ n argraffiad
impression n argraff
impressionable adj hawdd ei argyhoeddi
impressive adj trawiadol
imprint vt argraffu ♦ n argraff, delw
imprison vt carcharu
improbable adj annhebygol
impromptu adj, adv ar y pryd, byrfyfyr
improper adj anweddus
improve vb gwella, diwygio
improvement n gwelliant
improvise vb addasu ar y pryd
impudent adj digywilydd, haerllug
impulse n cymhelliad, ysgogiad
impulsive adj byrbwyll
impunity n bod heb gosb. **with i.** yn ddi-gosb
impure adj amhur, aflan
impute vt cyfrif i; priodoli; bwrw ar
in prep yn, mewn, i mewn, o fewn
in- prefix di-, an-
inability n anallu
inaccessible adj anhygyrch
inaccurate adj anghywir, anfanwl
inaction n segurdod
inadequate adj annigonol
inadmissible adj annerbyniol
inadvertent adj anfwriadol, amryfus
inane adj gwag, gwageddus, ofer
inanimate adj difywyd, dienaid
inappropriate adj anaddas
inasmuch adv yn gymaint (â)
inaudible adj anhyglyw, na ellir ei glywed
inaugurate vt urddo, cysegru, agor, dechrau
inauguration n agoriad, dechreuad
inborn adj cynhenid, greddfol
inbreed vb mewnfrido

incandescent *adj* gwynias

incantation *n* swyn, swyngyfaredd

incapable *adj* analluog

incapability *n* anallu

incapacitate *vt* anghymhwyso, analluogi

incarcerate *vt* carcharu

incarnation *n* ymgnawdoliad

incendiary *adj* llosg ♦ *n* bom tân

incense *n* aroglddarth

incense *vt* llidio, cythruddo

incentive *adj* cymelliadol ♦ *n* cymhelliad

inception *n* dechreuad, agoriad

incessant *adj* di-baid, di-dor

incest *n* llosgach

inch *n* modfedd

incident *n* digwyddiad

incidental *adj* digwyddiadol, achlysurol

incidentally *adv* gyda llaw

incinerate *vb* llosgi'n ulw

incineration *n* llosgiad llwyr

incinerator *n* llosgydd, ffwrnais

incipient *adj* dechreuol

incise *vt* torri, trychu

incisive *adj* llym, miniog

incite *vt* annog, cyffroi, annos

inclement *adj* gerwin, garw, drycinog

inclination *n* tuedd, gogwydd

incline *vb* tueddu, gogwyddo ♦ *n* llethr

include *vt* cynnwys

including *prep* gan gynnwys

inclusive *adj* cynwysedig, gan gynnwys

incognito *adj* yn ddirgel, dan ffugenw

incoherent *adj* digyswllt, anghysylltus

income *n* incwm. i. tax treth incwm

incompatible *adj* anghytûn

incompetent *n* anghymwys

incomplete *adj* anghyflawn

incomprehensible *adj*

annealladwy

incongruous *adj* anghydweddol, anaddas

inconsistency *n* anghysondeb

inconsistent *adj* anghyson

inconspicuous *adj* anamlwg

incontestable *adj* diymwad, diamheuol

inconvenience *n* anghyfleustra

inconvenient *adj* anghyfleus

incorporate *vb* corffori, ymgorffori

incorporated *adj* corfforedig

incorrect *adj* anghywir

incorrigible *adj* anwelladwy

increase *vb* cynyddu ♦ *n* cynnydd

incredible *adj* anhygoel, anghredadwy

incredulity *n* anghrediniaeth

incredulous *adj* anghrediniol

increment *n* cynnydd, ychwanegiad

incriminate *vt* cyhuddo, euogi

incubate *vb* gori, deor

incubator *n* deorydd

incumbent *adj* rhwymedig ar ♦ *n* periglor, offeiriad, clerigwr

incur *vt* rhedeg i ddyled; achosi

incursion *n* cyrch

indebted *adj* dyledus

indecent *adj* anweddus

indecision *n* petruster

indecisive *adj* amhendant

indeed *adv* yn wir; iawn, dros ben

indefatigable *adj* diflin, dyfal

indefinite *adj* amhenodol, amhendant

indelible *adj* annileadwy

indelicate *adj* aflednais

indemnify *vb* digolledu

indemnity *n* iawn

indented *adj* bylchog, danheddus

indenture *n* cytundeb, cyfamod

independence *n* annibyniaeth

independent *adj* annibynnol ♦ *n* annibynnwr

indescribable *adj* annisgrifiadwy

indeterminate *adj* amhenodol,

penagored

index n mynegai; mynegfys

India n India

Indian adj Indiaidd ♦ n Indiad

indicate vt dangos, arwyddo

indicative adj arwyddol, mynegol

indicator n dangosydd

indict vt cyhuddo

indifference n difaterwch, difrawder

indifferent adj difater; dibwys

indigenous adj cynhenid

indigent adj anghenus, tlawd, rheidus

indigestion n diffyg traul, camdreuliad

indignant adj dig, digofus, dicllon

indignation n dig, digofaint, llid

indignity n amarch, sarhad, anfri

indirect adj anuniongyrchol

indiscreet adj annoeth

indiscriminate adj diwahaniaeth

indispensable adj anhepgorol

indisposed adj anhwylus

indisputable adj diamheuol

indissoluble adj annatod

indistinct adj aneglur, anhyglyw, bloesg

indite vt cyfansoddi, traethu

individual adj unigol ♦ n un, unigolyn

indoctrinate vb trwytho (ag athrawiaeth), credorfodi

indoctrination n credorfodaeth

indolence n seguryd, syrthni

indolent adj segur, swrth, dioglyd

indomitable adj anorchfygol, di-ildio

indoor adj, adv dan do

indubitable adj diamheuol

induce vt darbwyllo, denu, cymell

inducement n anogiad

induct vt sefydlu; anwytho

induction n anwythiad

indulge vb boddio; maldodi

indulgence n ymfoddhad; maldod

indulgent adj ffafriol, maldodus

industrial adj diwydiannol, gweithfaol

industrialize vb diwydiannu

industrious adj diwyd, dyfal, gweithgar

industry n diwydrwydd; diwydiant

inebriate vt meddwi ♦ n meddwyn

inedible adj anfwytadwy

ineffable adj anhraethol, anhraethadwy

ineffective adj aneffeithiol

inefficiency n anallu

inefficient adj analluog

ineligible adj anghymwys

inept adj heb fod yn taro, gwrthun, gwirion

inequality n anghysondeb

inert adj swrth, diynni, diegni

inertia n anegni, inertia

inestimable adj amhrisiadwy

inevitable adj anochel, anesgorol

inexhaustible adj dihysbydd

inexorable adj di-ildio, anhyblyg

inexpensive adj rhad

inexperience n diffyg profiad

inexperienced adj amhrofiadol, dibrofiad

infallible adj anffaeledig

infallibility n anffaeledigrwydd

infamous adj gwaradwyddus, gwarthus

infancy n mabandod, mebyd, maboed

infant n maban, baban; un dan oed

infantry n gwŷr traed, milwyr traed

infatuate vt gwirioni, ffoli, dwlu

infatuated adj wedi ffoli, wedi gwirioni

infect vt heintio, llygru

infection n haint

infectious adj heintus

infer vt casglu

inferior adj is, israddol ♦ n isradd

inferiority n israddoldeb

inferiority complex n cymhleth y

taeog
infernal adj uffernol, dieflig
infertile adj anffrwythlon
infertility n anffrwythlondeb
infest vt bod yn bla, heigiannu
infidel n anffyddiwr
infidelity n anffyddlondeb
infield adj mewnfaes
infinite adj anfeidrol
infinitesimal adj anfeidrol fach, gorfychan
infinitive adj annherfynol ♦ n berfenw
infirm adj egwan, gwan, gwanllyd
infirmary n ysbyty, clafdy
infirmity n gwendid, llesgedd
inflame vb ennyn, cyffroi, llidio
inflamed adj llidus
inflammable adj hylosg, hyfflam
inflammation n enyniad, enynfa, llid
inflatable adj y gellir ei chwyddo neu ei chwythu
inflate vt chwyddo
inflation n chwyddiant
inflect vt ffurfdroi; treiglo
inflexible adj anhyblyg
inflexibility n anhyblygrwydd
inflict vt peri, gweinyddu (cosb, poen, etc)
influence n dylanwad ♦ vt dylanwadu
influenza n ffliw
influx n dylifiad
inform vb hysbysu
informal adj anffurfiol
information n gwybodaeth, hysbysrwydd
infra- prefix is-
infra-red adj is-goch
infrastructure n seilwaith
infrequent adj anaml
infringe vt torri, troseddu
infuriate vt ffyrnigo, cynddeiriogi
infuse vt tywallt, arllwys; trwytho
infusion n trwyth, hydreiddiad
ingenious adj medrus, cywrain,

celfydd
ingenuous adj didwyll, diddichell
ingenuousness n didwylledd, diffuantrwydd
ingrained adj wedi greddfu; cynhenid
ingratiate vt ennill ffafr
ingratitude n anniolchgarwch
ingredients npl cynhwysion, defnyddiau
inhabit vt cyfaneddu, trigo, preswylio
inhabitable adj cyfannedd, trigadwy
inhabitant n preswyliwr
inhale vt anadlu
inhere vi glynu, ymlynu, bod
inherent adj cynhenid, greddfol
inherit vt etifeddu
inheritance n etifeddiaeth
inheritor n etifedd, etifeddwr
inhibit vt gwahardd, atal
inhibition n ataliad, atalnwyd
inhibitor n atalydd
inhuman adj annynol, creulon
inimical adj gelyniaethus
inimitable adj digyffelyb
iniquitous adj drwg, traws
iniquity n anwiredd, camwedd
initial adj dechreuol ♦ n llythyren gyntaf
initiate vt egwyddori; derbyn; dechrau
initiative n cynhoredd, menter
inject vt chwistrellu
injection n chwistrelliad, pigiad
injunction n gorchymyn, gwaharddiad
injure vt niweidio, anafu
injury n niwed, cam, anaf
injustice n anghyfiawnder, cam
ink n inc ♦ vt incio
inkling n awgrym, arwydd
inland adj canoldirol ♦ n canoidir.
I. Revenue n Cyllid y Wlad
inlet n cilfach, bae
inmate n trigiannydd, preswylydd

inmost adj nesaf i mewn, dyfnaf
inn n tafarn, tafarndy, gwesty
innate adj cynhenid, cynhwynol, greddfol
inner adj mewnol
innings npl batiad
innkeeper n tafarnwr
innocence n diniweidrwydd
innocent adj diniwed, gwirion, dieuog
innocuous adj diniwed, diberygl
innovate vi newid, cyflwyno
innovation n newyddbeth
innuendo n ensyniad
innumerable adj aneirif, afrifed, dirifedi, di-rif
inoculate vt brechu
inoculation n brechiad
inoffensive adj di-ddrwg
inordinate adj anghymedrol, di-rôl
inorganic adj anorganig
input n mewnbwn, cyfraniad
inquest n cwest; trengholiad
inquire vb ymofyn, ymholi, gofyn, holi
inquiry n ymholiad
inquisition n ymchwiliad; chwil-lys
inquisitive adj ymofyngar, holgar
in-road n cyrch
insane adj gwallgof, gorffwyll, ynfyd
insanitary adj afiachus, brwnt
insatiable adj anniwall
inscribe vt arysgrifio
inscription n arysgrif
inscrutable adj anolrheiniadwy, anchwiliadwy
insect n pryf, trychfil
insensibility n dideimladrwydd
insensible adj dideimlad
insert vb mewnosod
in-service adj mewn swydd
inside n tu mewn ♦ adj mewnol ♦ prep y tu mewn i ♦ adv i mewn, o fewn
inside-forward n mewnwr

inside-half n mewnwr
inside-out adv o chwith
inside-right n mewnwr de
insidious adj llechwraidd
insight n mewnwelediad
insignificance n dinodedd
insignificant adj di-nod, distadl, dibwys
insincere adj annidwyll, ffuantus, rhagrithiol
insincerity n annidwylledd
insinuate vb ensynio
insipid adj diflas, merfaidd
insist vi mynnu
insolence n haerllugrwydd
insolent adj haerllug
insolvent adj methdalus, wedi torri
insomnia n anhunedd
inspect vt arolygu, archwilio
inspector n arolygwr
inspiration n ysbrydoliaeth
inspire vb ysbrydoli
instability n ansadrwydd
install vt sefydlu, gorseddu
instalment n cyfran, rhandal
instance n enghraifft ♦ vt enwi, nodi
instant adj taer, ebrwydd ♦ n eiliad, moment. **i. coffee** n coffi powdr
instantaneous adj yn y fan; disymwth
instantly adv ar drawiad
instead adv yn lle
instep n mwnwgl troed, cefn troed
instigate vt annog, cymell
instil vt argymell
instinct n greddf
institute n athrofa
institution n sefydliad
instruct vt hyfforddi
instruction n hyfforddiant
instructor n hyfforddwr
instrument n offeryn
insubordinate adj anufudd, gwrthryfelgar

insufferable *adj* annioddefol
insufficient *adj* annigonol
insular *adj* ynysol, cul
insulate *vt* ynysu, inswleiddio
insult *vt* sarhau ♦ *n* sarhad
insuperable *adj* anorfod,
anorchfygol
insurance *n* yswiriant. **i. policy** *n*
polisi yswiriant
insure *vb* yswirio
insurgent *adj* gwrthryfelgar ♦ *n*
gwrthryfelwr
insurrection *n* terfysg, gwrthryfel
intact *adj* cyfan, dianaf
integral *adj* cyfan, cyflawn
integrate *vb* cyfannu
integrity *n* cywirdeb, gonestrwydd
intellect *n* deall
intellectual *n* deallusyn ♦ *adj*
deallus, deallgar
intelligence *n* deallgarwch,
deallusrwydd; hysbysrwydd
intelligent *adj* deallus
intelligible *adj* dealladwy
intend *vt* bwriadu, amcanu, golygu
intense *adj* angerddol, dwys
intensive care unit *n* uned ofal
arbennig
intent *adj* dyfal, diwyd, astud
intent *n* bwriad, amcan; ystyr;
diben
intention *n* bwriad
intentional *adj* bwriadol
inter *vt* claddu, daearu
inter- *prefix* rhwng, cyd
interaction *n* rhyngweithiad
interbreed *vb* rhyngfridio
intercede *vi* cyfryngu, eirioli
intercept *vt* rhyng-gipio, rhwystro,
rhagod
intercession *n* cyfryngdod,
eiriolaeth
interchange *vt* cyfnewid,
ymgyfnewid
intercourse *n* cyfathrach
interdict *vt* gwahardd ♦ *n*
gwaharddiad

interest *n* budd, buddiant;
diddordeb; llog ♦ *vt* diddori
interested *adj* â chanddo
ddiddordeb
interesting *adj* diddorol
interests *npl* diddordebau
interface *n* cydwyneb
interfere *vt* cyfryngu, ymyrryd,
ymhél
interference *n* ymyrraeth
interim *adj* dros dro ♦ *n* cyfamser
interior *adj* mewnol ♦ *n* tu mewn,
canol, perfeddwlad
interject *vt* ebychu
interlock *vb* cyd-gloi
interloper *n* ymwthiwr, ymyrrwr
interlude *n* egwyl; anterliwt
intermediary *n* canolwr,
cyfryngwr
intermediate *adj* canol, canolradd
intern *vt* carcharu
internal *adj* mewnol
international *adj* cydwladol,
rhyngwladol
interpolate *vt* dodi i mewn,
rhyngosod
interpolation *n* rhyngosodiad
interpose *vb* gosod rhwng,
cyfryngu, rhyngwthio
interpret *vt* dehongli; cyfieithu
interpretation *n* dehongliad;
cyfieithiad
interpreter *n* lladmerydd,
cyfieithydd
interrelation *n* cydberthynas
interrogate *vt* holi
interrogative *adj* gofynnol
interrupt *vt* torri ar, torri ar
draws, ymyrryd
intersect *vb* croesi ei gilydd;
croesdorri
intersection *n* croesdoriad
intersperse *vb* gwasgaru, britho
interval *n* egwyl, saib
intervene *vi* ymyrryd
interview *n* cyfweliad ♦ *vb* cyfweld
intestines *npl* perfedd, coluddion

intimacy n agosatrwydd
intimate adj cyfarwydd, agos ♦ n cydnabod
intimate vt arwyddo, hysbysu
intimidate vt dychrynu, brawychu
into prep i, i mewn i
intolerable adj annioddefol
intonation n tonyddiaeth, goslef
intone vt llafarganu
intoxicate vt meddwi
intoxication n meddwdod
intractable adj anhydrin, afreolus
intransitive adj cyflawn (gramadeg)
intrepid adj di-ofn, diarswyd, gwrol, dewr
intricate adj dyrys, cymhleth, astrus
intrigue vi, n cynllwyn
intrinsic adj priodol, hanfodol
introduce vt cyflwyno
introduction n cyflwyniad, rhagarweiniad
introductory adj dechreuol, agoriadol, rhagarweiniol
introspection n mewnsylliad
introvert adj mewnblyg
intrude vb ymyrryd
intruder n ymyrrwr, ymwthiwr
intrusion n ymwthiad, ymyrraeth
intuition n sythwelediad
inundate vt gorlifo, boddi
inundation n gorlifiad
inure vt cyfarwyddo, caledu
invade vt goresgyn
invalid adj di-rym, annilys
invalid n un afiach, un methedig
invaluable adj amhrisiadwy
invariable adj gwastad, dieithriad
invariably adv yn ddieithriad
invasion n goresgyniad
invective n difriaeth, cabledd
invent vt dyfeisio, dychmygu
inventory n rhestr, stocrestr
inverse adj (yn y) gwrthwyneb, yn groes
inversion n gwrthdro

invert vt troi wyneb i waered, gwrthdroi
inverted commas npl dyfynodau
invest vt buddsoddi; arwisgo
investigate vt chwilio, archwilio, ymchwilio
investigation n ymchwiliad
investigator n ymchwiliwr
investiture n arwisgiad
investment n buddsoddiad
investor n buddsoddwr
invidious adj annymunol
invigilate vb arolygu
invigilator n arolygwr, gwyliwr
invigorate vt cryfhau, grymuso
invincible adj anorchfygol
inviolable adj dihalog, cysegredig
invisible adj anweledig, anweladwy
invitation n gwahoddiad
invite vt gwahodd
invoice n anfoneb
involuntary adj o anfodd, anfwriadol
involve vt drysu; cynnwys, ymwneud
involvement n ymwneud, ymglymiad
inward adj mewnol
iodine n iodin
ion n ïon
ionisation n ioneiddiad
ionise vb ioneiddio
iota n mymryn, iod, gronyn
ir- prefix di-, an-
Iran n Iran
Iraq n Iraq
irate adj dig, llidiog
Ireland n Iwerddon
iris n enfys; elestr
Irish adj Gwyddelig ♦ n Gwyddeleg
irksome adj blin, trafferthus, diflas
iron n, adj haearn ♦ vt smwddio
ironic adj eironig
ironing board n bwrdd smwddio
ironmonger n gwerthwr nwyddau haearn
irony n eironi

irradiate *vt* arbelydru

irradiation *n* arbelydredd

irrational *adj* direswm, afresymol

irreconcilable *adj* anghymodlon

irrefutable *adj* anatebadwy

irregular *adj* afreolaidd

irregularity *n* afreoleidd-dra

irrelevant *adj* amherthnasol

irreparable *adj* anadferadwy

irreproachable *adj* diargyhoedd, di-fai

irresistible *adj* anorchfygol

irretrievable *adj* anadferadwy

irrevocable *adj* di-alw-yn-ôl

irrigate *vt* dyfrhau

irritable *adj* croendenau, anniddig, llidiog

irritate *vt* blino, poeni, cythruddo

is *vi* mae, sydd, yw, ydy(w), oes

island, isle *n* ynys

islet *n* ynysig

isolate *vt* neilltuo, gwahanu

isolated *adj* wedi ei neilltuo, wedi ei wahanu

isolation *n* neilltuaeth, arwahanrwydd

Israel *n* Israel

Israelite *n* Israeliad

issue *n* llif; agorfa, arllwysfa; hilogaeth, plant; canlyniad, pwnc mewn dadl ♦ *vb* tarddu, deillio; rhoi allan, cyhoeddi

isthmus *n* culdir

it *pron* efe, fe, ef, efo, fo, o: hi

Italian *adj* Eidalaidd ♦ *n* Eidalwr; (*LING*) Eidaleg

italic *adj* italig

italicize *vb* italeiddio

italics *npl* llythrennau italaidd

Italy *n* Yr Eidal

itch *n* ysu, cosi ♦ *n* y crafu, ysfa

item *n* peth, pwnc, darn, tamaid

iterate *vt* ailadrodd

itinerant *adj* teithiol

itinerary *n* taith, teithlyfr

itinerate *vi* teithio, cylchdeithio

itself *pron* ei hun, ei hunan

ivory *n* ifori

ivy *n* eiddew, iorwg

J

jab *n* jab, pigiad ♦ *vb* procio, gwanu

jabber *vi* bragawthan, clebran ♦ *n* clebar

jack *n* jac

jackass *n* asyn gwryw; hurtyn

jackdaw *n* corfran, jac-y-do

jacket *n* siaced

jade *vt* blino, lluddedu

jagged *adj* danheddog, ysgithrog

jail *n* carchar

jam *n* jam; tagfa

jam *vt* jamio, tagu

Jamaica *n* Jamaica

jangle *vi* clochdar

janitor *n* porthor

January *n* Ionawr

Japan *n* Nihon, Japán, Siapán

Japanese *adj* Siapaneaidd ♦ *n* Siapanead; (*LING*) Siapaneg

jar *n* anghytsain; anghydfod ♦ *vb* rhygnu

jar *n* jar

jargon *n* ffregod, bregiaith, jargon

jaundice *n* y clefyd melyn

jaunt *vi* gwibio, rhodio ♦ *n* gwibdaith

jaunty *adj* llon, bywiog, talog

javelin *n* picell, gwaywffon

jaw *n* gên, cern; (*pl*) safn

jay *n* sgrech y coed

jazz *n* jas

jealous *adj* eiddigus, cenfigennus, gwenwynllyd

jealousy *n* cenfigen, eiddigedd

jeans *n* jîns

jeep *n* jip

jeer *vb* gwawdio, gwatwar

jelly *n* jeli

jellyfish *n* slefren fôr

jeopardy *n* perygl, enbydrwydd

jerk n plwc, ysgytiad ♦ vb plycio, ysgytio
jerkin n siercyn, siaced
jersey n siersi
Jerusalem n Caersalem, Jerwsalem
jest n cellwair, ysmaldod ♦ vi cellwair, ysmalio
Jesus n Iesu
jet n ffrwd, jet; muchudd ♦ vb ffrydio, pistyllio
jettison vt taflu (llwyth) dros y bwrdd
jetty n jeti, glanfa
Jew n Iddew
jewel n gem, tlws
jeweller n gemydd
jewellery n gemwaith, gemau
Jewish adj Iddewig
jib n hwyl flaen llong, jib
jib vi nogio, strancio
jig n dawns fywiog, jig
jig-saw n jig-so
jilt vt siomi cariad
jingle n rhigwm, tinc ♦ vb tincial
job n tasg, gorchwyl, gwaith
Job Centre n Canolfan Gwaith
jobless adj diwaith
jockey n joci
jocose adj cellweirus, direidus, ysmala
jocular adj ffraeth, ysmala
jog vb loncian
jogger n lonciwr
join vb cydio, cysylltu, uno, ymuno, asio
joiner n asiedydd, saer coed
joint n cyswllt, cymal ♦ adj cyd. **j. of meat** darn o gig
joist n dist, trawst
joke n cellwair, maldod ♦ vb cellwair, ysmalio
jolly adj braf, difyr, llawen
jolt n ysgytiad ♦ vb ysgytio
Jordan n Iorddonen
jostle n hergwd ♦ vb gwthio
jot n iod, tipyn ♦ vt nodi

jotter n nodlyfr
journal n newyddiadur
journalism n newyddiaduraeth
journalist n newyddiadurwr
journey n taith, siwrnai ♦ vt teithio
jovial adj llon, llawen
joy n llawenydd, gorfoledd
joyful adj llon, llawen, gorfoleddus
J.P. Gwêl justice of the peace
jubilant adj gorfoleddus
jubilee n jiwbili
Judaism n Iddewaeth
judge n barnwr, beirniad ♦ vb barnu, beirniadu
judg(e)ment n barn, brawd, dyfarniad; dedfryd
judicial adj barnwrol, ynadol
judiciary n barnwyr gwlad, barnwriaeth
judicious adj call, synhwyrol, doeth
jug n jwg
juggle vb siwglo
juggler n siwglwr
juice n sug, sugn, sudd, nodd
juicy adj llawn sudd
July n Gorffennaf
jumble vb cymysgu, cyboli ♦ n cymysgfa, cybolfa
jumble sale n ffair sborion
jump vb neidio, llamu ♦ n naid, llam
jumper n neidiwr; siwmper
jumpy adj ofnus
junction n cydiad; uniad; cyffordd
juncture n cyfwng, cyswllt
June n Mehefin
jungle n jyngl, coedwig; drysi
junior adj iau, ieuengach; ieuaf. **j. school** n ysgol iau
junk n sothach
jurisdiction n awdurdod
juror, juryman n rheithiwr
jury n rheithgor
just adj cyfiawn, uniawn, teg ♦ adv yn union; prin; braidd; newydd. **j. now** gynnau(fach)

justice *n* cyfiawnder; ynad, ustus.
  j. of the peace *n* ynad heddwch
justify *vt* cyfiawnhau
jut *vi* taflu allan, ymwthio
juvenile *adj* ieuanc

K

kale *n* cêl, celys
kangaroo *n* cangarŵ
keel *n* gwaelod llong, trumbren,
  cilbren
keen *adj* craff, llym, awchus, brwd
keep *vb* cadw, cynnal ♦ *n* cadw;
  amddiffynfa
keeper *n* ceidwad
keepsake *n* cofrodd
kennel *n* cenel, cwb ci, cwt ci
kerb *n* cwrbyn
kerchief *n* cadach, neisied, hances,
  macyn
kernel *n* cnewyllyn
kestrel *n* cudyll
kettle *n* tegell
kettle-drum *n* tympan
key *n* agoriad, allwedd; cywair. **k.
  ring,** *n* cylch allweddi. **k. worker**
  n gweithiwr allweddol
keyboard *n* allweddell
keyhole *n* twll clo
khaki *adj,* *n* caci
kick *vb* cicio, gwingo ♦ *n* cic
kid *n* myn; hogyn, plentyn, crwt
kidnap *vt* herwgipio
kidney *n* aren. **k. beans** *npl* ffa
  dringo, cidnebêns
kill *n* lladd
killer *n* lladdwr
killing *n* lladd
kiln *n* odyn
kilo *n* cilo
kilogram *n* cilogram
kilometre *n* cilomedr
kilowatt *n* cilowat
kin *n* perthynas, tras, carennydd
kind *n* rhyw, rhywogaeth, math

kind *adj* caredig
kindergarten *n* ysgol feithrin
kindle *vb* ennyn, cynnau
kindly *adj* caredig, hynaws, tirion
kindness *n* caredigrwydd
kindred *n* perthynas; perthynasau
  ♦ *adj* perthynol
king *n* brenin
kingdom *n* teyrnas
kingfisher *n* glas y dorlan
kink *n* cinc
kiosk *n* ciosg, bwth
kipper *n* ciper, ysgadenyn hallt
  (neu sych)
kirk *n* eglwys (Albanaidd)
kiss *vt* cusanu ♦ *n* cusan
kit *n* cit, pac
kitchen *n* cegin. **k. garden** *n* gardd
  lysiau
kitchenette *n* cegin fach
kite *n* barcut
kitten *n* cath fach ♦ *vb* bwrw
  cathod
kleptomania *n* ysfa ladrata
knack *n* cnac, medr
knacker *n* prynwr hen geffylau,
  nacer
knapsack *n* ysgrepan
knave *n* cnaf, dihiryn
knead *vt* tylino
knee *n* glin, pen-lin, pen-glin
kneel *vi* penlinio
knell *n* cnul
knickers *npl* nicers
knife (knives) *n* cyllell
knight *n* marchog ♦ *vt* urddo yn
  farchog
knighthood *n* urdd marchog
knit *vb* gwau; clymu
knitting needle *n* gwaell
knob *n* cnap, cnwc; dwrn
knock *vb* cnocio, taro, curo ♦ *n*
  cnoc, ergyd
knot *n* cwlwm; cymal, cwgn,
  cainc ♦ *vt* clymu
know *vb* gwybod, adnabod
knowing *adj* gwybodus

knowingly adv yn fwriadol
knowledge n gwybodaeth
knowledgeable adj gwybodus
knuckle n cymal, migwrn, cwgn

L

label n llabed, label ♦ vt llabedu, enwi
labial adj gwefusol
labialize vb gwefusoli
laboratory n labordy
laborious adj llafurus
labour n llafur; gwewyr esgor ♦ vb llafurio. **the L. Party** Y Blaid Lafur. **l. force** n llafurlu
labourer n gweithiwr, labrwr
labyrinth n drysfa
lace n las, les; carrai ♦ vb cau (esgidiau)
lacerate vt rhwygo, llarpio, dryllio darnio
lack n eisiau, diffyg, gwall ♦ vb bod mewn eisiau
lackadaisical adj diynni, llipa
laconic adj byreiriog, byr, cwta
lacquer n lacer ♦ vb lacro
lad n bachgen, hogyn, llanc
ladder n ysgol; rhwyg (mewn hosan)
lade vt llwytho
ladies npl toiledau merched
ladle n lletwad, llwy
lady n arglwyddes; boneddiges, bonesig
ladybird n buwch goch gota
lag vi llusgo ar ôl, ymdroi, llercian
lagging n ynysydd, lagin
lagoon n morlyn, llagwn
lair n gwâl, lloches, ffau
laity n lleygwyr
lake n llyn
lamb n oen ♦ vb bwrw ŵyn, wyna
lame adj cloff ♦ vt cloffi
lament vb galaru, cwynfan, cwyno
lamentation n galar, galarnad

laminate adj haenog ♦ vb haenogi, lamineiddio, laminadu
lamp n lamp, llusern
lampoon n dychangerdd, gogangerdd ♦ vb dychanu
lamppost n polyn lamp
lampshade n lamplen
lance n gwaywffon, picell ♦ vt lansio, agor dolur
lance corporal n is-gorpral
land n tir, gwlad ♦ vb tirio, glanio
landing n glaniad, glanio; glanfa; pen y grisiau
landlady n perchennog llety, gwraig llety
landlord n meistr tir; lletywr, tafarnwr
landscape n tirlun
lane n lôn, wtre, beidr
language n iaith. **l. laboratory** n labordy iaith
languid adj egwan, llesg
languish vi nychu, dihoeni, llesgáu
languor n llesgedd, nychdod
lank adj cul, tenau, main, llipa
lanky adj meindal
lantern n llusern
lap n arffed, glin
lap vb plygu, lapio ♦ n plyg, tro, cylch
lap vb llepian, lleibio
lapel n llabed
lapse n cwymp, methiant, gwall ♦ vi llithro, cwympo, methu
larceny n lladrad
larch n llarwydden
lard n bloneg ♦ vt blonegu
larder n bwtri, pantri
large adj mawr, helaeth, eang, maith
largely adv gan mwyaf
lark n ehedydd
lark n sbort, difyrrwch, miri ♦ vi cellwair, prancio
larva (-ae) n cynrhonyn, larfa
laryngitis n gwddf tost, laringitis
larynx n afalfreuant, bocs llais

lascivious adj anllad, trythyll, anniwair

lash n llach, fflangell ♦ vb llachio, fflangellu; rhwymo

lass n llances

lasso n dolenraff, lasw ♦ vt dolenraffu

last adj olaf, diwethaf ♦ adv yn olaf, yn ddiwetha. **at l.** o'r diwedd. **l. night** neithiwr. **l. week** yr wythnos ddiwethaf

last vi parhau, para

latch n clicied ♦ vt clicedu

late adj hwyr, diweddar. **l. developers** plant hwyrgynnydd

lately adv yn ddiweddar

latent adj dirgel, cudd

later adv wedyn, eto, yn ddiweddarach

lateral adj ochrol

latest adj diweddaraf

lath n eisen, dellten

lathe n turn

lather n trochion ♦ vb sebonì, trochioni; golchi

Latin adj, n Lladin

Latin America n America Ladin

latitude n lledred; penrhyddid

latter adj diwethaf

lattice n dellt, rhwyllwaith

laud vt canmol, clodfori, moli

laudable adj canmoladwy

laugh vb chwerthin ♦ n chwerthiniad

laughable adj chwerthinllyd, digrif

laughing stock n cyff gwawd

laughter n chwerthin

launch vb lansio

launderette n landret, golchdy

laundry n golchdy; dillad golch

laureate adj llawryfog

laurel n llawryf

lavatory n tŷ bach, ymolchfa, ystafell ymolchi

lavender n lafant

lavish adj hael, afradlon, gwastraffus ♦ vb afradu,

gwastraffu

lavishness n haelioni, afradlonedd

law n cyfraith, deddf. **l. and order** cyfraith a threfn. **l. of the land** cyfraith gwlad

lawful adj cyfreithlon

lawgiver adj deddfroddwr

lawless adj digyfraith

lawlessness n anghyfraith

lawn n lawnt, llannerch. **l. tennis** n tenis (lawnt)

lawnmower n peiriant torri porfa

lawsuit n cyngaws, cyfraith

lawyer n cyfreithiwr, twrnai

lax adj llac, esgeulus, diofal

laxative n carthlyn

lay n cân, cerdd

lay vt gosod, dodi; dodwy

lay adj lleyg

layby n gorffwysfan

layer n haen

laze vb diogi, segura

laziness n diogi

lazy adj diog, dioglyd

lea n doldir, dôl

lead n plwm

lead vb arwain, tywys ♦ n blaenoriaeth

leader n arweinydd; erthygl flaen

leadership n arweinyddiaeth

leaf (**leaves**) n deilen, dalen

leaflet n taflen

league n cynghrair ♦ vi cynghreirio

leak n agen, coll ♦ vi gollwng, diferu, colli

lean adj main, tenau, cul ♦ n cig coch

lean vb pwyso, gogwyddo

leap vb neidio, llamu ♦ n naid, llam. **l. year** n blwyddyn naid

leapfrog n chwarae naid

learn vb dysgu

learned adj dysgedig, hyddysg

learner n dysgwr

learning n dysg, dysgeidiaeth

lease n prydles ♦ vt prydlesu

leasehold n prydles
leash n cynllyfan, tennyn ♦ vt cynllyfanu
least adj lleiaf. **at l.** o leiaf
leather n lledr
leave n cennad, caniatád
leave vb gadael, ymadael
leaven n lefain ♦ vt lefeinio
Lebanon n Libanus
lecherous adj trythyll, anllad
lechery n trythyllwch, anlladrwydd
lectern n darllenfa
lecture n darlith ♦ vb darlithio
lecturer n darlithydd
ledge n silff, ysgafell; crib
ledger n llyfr cyfrifon
lee n ochr ysgodol, cysgod gwynt
leech n gelen
leek n cenhinen
leer vi cilwenu
lees npl gwaddod, gwaelodion
left adj aswy, chwith
left-handed adj llawchwith
left-handedness n llawchwithedd
left luggage n lle cadw bagiau
leg n coes
legacy n etifeddiaeth, cymynrodd
legal adj cyfreithiol, cyfreithlon
legalize vb cyfreithloni
legation n llysgenhadaeth
legend n chwedl
legible adj darllenadwy, eglur
legion n lleng, llu
legislate vi deddfu
legislation n deddfwriaeth
legislative adj deddfwriaethol
legitimate adj cyfreithlon
leisure n hamdden
leisurely adj hamddenol
lemon n lemwn
lemonade n diod lemwn, lemonêd
lend vt benthyca, rhoi benthyg
length n hyd, meithder
lengthen vb estyn, hwyhau
lengthy adj hir, maith
leniency n tiriondeb, tynerwch
lens n lens. **concave l.** lens

ceugrwm. **convex l.** lens amgrwm
Lent n y Grawys
lentil n corbysen, lentil
leonine adj llewaidd
leopard n llewpart
leper n dyn gwahanglwyfus, gwahanglaf
leprosy n gwahanglwyf
less adj, adv llai
lessee n prydlesai
lessen vb lleihau
lesson n gwers; llith
lest conj rhag, rhag ofn, fel na
let vt gadael, goddef; gollwng; gosod, rhentu
lethal adj marwol, angheuol
lethargy n cysgadrwydd, syrthni
letter n llythyren; llythyr
letterbox n bocs llythyrau
lettering n llythreniad
lettuce n letysen
level n, adj lefel, gwastad ♦ vt lefelu, gwastatáu. **spirit l.** n lefelydd
level crossing n croesfan
level-headed adj pwyllog
lever n trosol
leveret n ysgyfarnog ieuanc, lefren
Levite n Lefiad
levity n ysgafnder, gwamalrwydd
levy vt codi, trethu ♦ n treth
lewd adj anllad, anweddus
lexicographer n geiriadurwr
lexicon n geiriadur
liability n cyfrifoldeb, rhwymedigaeth
liable adj atebol
liaison n cyswllt
liar n gŵr celwyddog, celwyddgi
libel n athrod, enllib ♦ vt athrodi, enllibio
liberal adj hael, rhyddfrydig, rhyddfrydol ♦ n rhyddfrydwr
liberate vt rhyddhau
liberation n rhyddhad
liberty n rhyddid
librarian n llyfrgellydd

library n llyfrgell
Libya n Libya
licence n trwydded; penrhyddid.
driving l. n trwydded yrru
license vt trwyddedu
licensed adj trwyddedig
licentious adj penrhydd, ofer,
anllad
lick vt llyfu, llyo; curo
lid n caead, clawr
lie n celwydd, anwiredd ♦ vi dweud
celwydd
lie vi gorwedd
liege adj ffyddlon, ufudd
lieutenant n is-gapten; rhaglaw
life (**lives**) n bywyd, einioes, oes,
buchedd, hoedl
lifebelt n nofdorch, gwregys achub
lifeboat n bad achub
lifeguard n achubwr
life insurance n yswiriant bywyd
life jacket n siaced achub
lifeless adj difywyd, marw(aidd)
lifetime n oes, einioes, hoedl
lift vt codi, dyrchafu ♦ n codiad;
lifft
ligament n giewyn, gewyn
light n golau, goleuni ♦ adj golau ♦
vb goleuo, cynnau
light adj ysgafn
light bulb n bwlb golau
lighter n goleuydd, taniwr
light-footed adj ysgafndroed
light-headed adj penchwiban
light-hearted adj ysgafnfryd
lighthouse n goleudy
lightning n mellt, lluched
lightning conductor n cludydd
mellt
lightship n goleulong
like adj tebyg, cyffelyb
like vb caru, hoffi
likeable adj hoffus; dymunol
likelihood n tebygolrwydd
likely adj, adv tebygol, tebyg
liken vt cyffelybu
likeness n tebygrwydd

likewise adv yn gyffelyb, yn yr un
modd
lilac n lelog
lily n lili, alaw
lily-of-the-valley n lili'r
dyffrynnoedd
limb n aelod, cainc
lime n calch
limekiln n odyn galch
limelight n amlygrwydd
limestone n carreg galch
limit n terfyn, ffin ♦ vt cyfyngu
limited adj cyfyngedig
limp adj llipa, ystwyth, hyblyg
limp vi hercian, cloffi
limpet n brenigen, llygad maharen
line n llin, llinell, lein, rhes;
llinach ♦ vt llinellu, rhesu
lineage n ach, llinach
linear adj llinellog, llinellaidd,
llinol, unionlin. **l. equation**
hafaliad llinol
linen n lliain
line-out n lein, llinell
liner n leiner
linesman n llumanwr
linger vb ymdroi, aros
lingo n iaith ddieithr, cleber
linguist n ieithydd
linguistics n ieithyddiaeth
liniment n ennaint, eli
lining n leinin
link n dolen, cyswllt ♦ vb cydio,
cysylltu
linnet n llinos
lino n leino
linseed n had llin, llinad
lintel n capan drws, lintel
lion n llew
lip n gwefus, min, gwefl
lipstick n minlliw
liquid n llyn, hylif ♦ adj gwlyb,
hylif
liquidate vb talu, clirio (dyled),
dirwyn i ben, diddymu, dileu
liquidize vb hylifo
liquor n diod, gwirod

lisp *n* bloesgni ♦ *vb* siarad yn
   floesg
list *n* rhestr, llechres ♦ *vt* rhestru
list *n* gogwydd, goledd ♦ *vi* pwyso,
   gwyro, gogwyddo
listen *vi* gwrando
listener *n* gwrandawr
listless *adj* llesg, diynni
listlessness *n* llesgedd
litany *n* litani
literacy *n* llythrennedd
literal *adj* llythrennol
literary *adj* llenyddol
literature *n* llenyddiaeth
lithe, lithesome *adj* ystwyth,
   hyblyg
lithograph *n* lithograff
litigate *vb* cyfreithio
litmus *n* litmws
litre *n* litr
litter *n* elorwely; ysbwriel,
   gwasarn; torllwyth, tor
little *adj* bach, bychan; mân,
   ychydig ♦ *n* ychydig, tipyn
liturgy *n* litwrgi
live *adj* byw, bywiol, bywiog
live *vi* byw
livelihood *n* bywoliaeth
livelong *adj* maith, hirfaith
lively *adj* bywiog, hoyw, heini,
   sionc
liven *vb* bywiogi
liver *n* iau, afu
livery *n* lifrai
living *n* bywoliaeth; personiaeth
lizard *n* madfall, modrchwilen
load *n* llwyth ♦ *vb* llwytho
loaf (loaves) *n* torth
loaf *vb* ystelcian, sefyllian, diogi
loafer *n* diogyn, segurwr
loam *n* tywotglai, marl, priddglai
loan *n* benthyg, benthyciad
loath, loth *adj* anewyllysgar,
   anfodlon
loathe *vt* ffieiddio, casáu
loathsome *adj* atgas, ffiaidd
lobby *n* cyntedd, porth, lobi

lobster *n* cimwch
local *adj* lleol. **l. government** *n*
   llywodraeth leol
locality *n* lle, safle, ardal, cymdogaeth
locate *vt* lleoli, sefydlu, gosod
location *n* lleoliad
loch *n* llyn
lock *n* clo; lliffddor ♦ *vb* cloi, cau
lock *n* cudyn; (*pl*) gwallt
locked *adj* ar glo, ynghlo, dan glo
locker *n* cwpwrdd clo
locomotion *n* ymsymudiad
locomotive *adj* ymsymudol ♦ *n*
   peiriant rheilffordd
locust *n* locust
lodge *n* lluest, llety; cyfrinfa ♦ *vb*
   lletya
lodger *n* lletywr
lodging *n*, **lodgings** *npl* llety
loft *n* taflod, llofft
lofty *adj* uchel, aruchel,
   dyrchafedig
log *n* cyff, boncyff, pren
loggerheads *npl* benben
logic *n* rhesymeg
logical *adj* rhesymegol
loin *n* llwyn, lwyn
loiter *vi* ymdroi, loetran, sefyllian
loll *vi* gorweddian, diogi
lollipop *n* lolipop
London *n* Llundain
loneliness *n* unigrwydd
lonely *adj* unig
long *adj*, *adv* hir, maith, llaes
long *vi* hiraethu, dyheu
longevity *n* hirhoedledd, hiroes
long-headed *adj* call, hirben
longing *n* hireath, dyhead
longitude *n* hydred
longitudinal *adj* hydredol
long sight *n* golwg hir
long-suffering *adj* hirymarhous ♦
   n hirymaros
long-term *adj* yn y tymor hir
long-winded *adj* hirwyntog
look *vb* edrych, syllu ♦ *n*

edrychiad, golwg
looking-glass n drych
lookout n gwyliwr
loom n gw
dd
loom vi ymrithio, ymddangos
loon n gwirionyn, dihiryn
loop n dolen ♦ vb dolennu
loophole n dihangdwll
loose adj rhydd, llac ♦ vt gollwng
loosen vb rhyddhau, llacio
loot n anrhaith, ysbail ♦ vb
ysbeilio, anrheithio
looter n ysbeiliwr, anrheithiwr
lop vt tocio
lopsided adj unochrog,
anghymesur, anghyfartal
lord n arglwydd ♦ vb
arglwyddiaethu
lord mayor n arglwydd faer
lordship n arglwyddiaeth
lore n dysg, llên, traddodiad
lorry n lori. l. **driver** n gyrrwr lori
lose vb colli
loss n colled
lost property office n swyddfa
eiddo coll
lot n coelbren, rhan, tynged. a l.
llawer
lotion n golchdrwyth, eli
lottery n hapchwarae, raffl
lotus n alaw'r dŵr
loud adj uchel, croch. l. **speaker** n
corn siarad
lounge n lolfa ♦ vi segura,
gorweddian
louse (**lice**) n lleuen
lousy adj lleuog, brwnt
lout n lleban, llabwst, delff
love n cariad, serch ♦ vt caru
loveliness n prydferthwch
lovely adj hawddgar, teg, hyfryd
lover n cariad, carwr
loving adj cariadus, serchog
loving-kindness n trugaredd,
cariad
low adj isel
low vi brefu ♦ n bref (buwch)

lower vb gostwng, darostwng, iselu
lower vi gwgu, duo, hel cymylau
lowliness n gostyngeiddrwydd
lowly adj isel, iselfrydig,
gostyngedig
low tide n llanw isel; trai
low water n trai, distyll
loyal adj teyrngar
loyalty n teyrngarwch, ffyddlondeb
lozenge n losin
lubricate vt iro, llithrigo, seimio
lucid adj eglur, clir
luck n lwc, damwain, hap, ffawd
lucky adj ffodus, lwcus
ludicrous adj chwerthinllyd,
gwrthun
lug vb llusgo, tynnu
luggage n clud, bagiau, celfi
luggage rack n silff eiddo
lukewarm adj claear, llugoer
lull vt suo, gostegu ♦ n gosteg
lullaby n hwiangerdd
lumbago n llwynwst
lumber n llanastr, anialwch
lumber vb pentyrru; llusgo
luminous adj golau, disglair,
llachar
lump n lwmp, clamp, clap, talp. l.
sum cyfandaliad
lunacy n lloerigrwydd,
gwallgofrwydd
lunatic n lloerig, gwallgofddyn
lunch vb ciniawa (ganol dydd)
lunch, luncheon n byrbryd, cinio
canol dydd
lung n ysgyfaint
lunge n hergwd, gwth, rhuthr
lurch n cyfyngder, dryswch, trybini
♦ vi gwegian
lure n hud ♦ vt hudo, denu
lurid adj erchyll, erchlyw,
fflamgoch
lurk vi llercian, llechu
luscious adj melys
lush adj toreithiog, ffrwythlon
lust n chwant, trachwant ♦ vi
trachwantu

lustre n gloywder, disgleirdeb, llewyrch
lusty adj heini, cryf, pybyr, grymus
Luxembourg n Luxembourg
luxuriant adj toreithiog, bras, ffrwythlon
luxurious adj moethus
luxury n moeth, moethusrwydd, amheuthun
lying adj celwyddog
lyre n telyn gron
lyric adj telynegol ♦ n telyneg

M

mace n brysgyll, byrllysg
macerate vb meddalu, mwydo; nychu, curio
machine n peiriant
machinery n peiriannau
mackerel n macrell
mackintosh n cot law
mad adj cynddeiriog, gwallgof, gwyllt, ynfyd
madden vb gwallgofi, ffyrnigo
made-to-measure adj wedi ei dorri gan ddilynwr
madman n ynfytyn, gwallgofddyn
madness n ynfydrwydd, gwallgofrwydd
madrigal n madrigal
magazine n ystorfa, arfdy; cylchrawn
maggot n cynrhonyn
magic adj cyfareddol ♦ n hud, dewiniaeth, swyngyfaredd
magician n swynwr, dewin
magistrate n ynad
magnanimous adj mawrfrydig
magnet n magned
magnetic n magnetig
magnificent adj gwych, ysblennydd
magnify vt mawrhau, mwyhau, chwyddo

magnifying-glass n chwyddwydr
magnitude n maint, maintioli
magpie n pi, pia, pioden, piogen
maid n merch, morwyn
maiden name n enw morwynol
mail n y post
mail n arfwisg
maim vt anafu, anffurfio, llurgunio
main n prif bibell; prif gebl; cefnfor. **in the m.** yn bennaf, gan mwyaf
main adj pennaf, prif, mwyaf. **m. road** n priffordd, ffordd fawr
mainland n y tir mawr
mainly adv yn bennaf
mainstay n prif gynhaliaeth
maintain vt dal, cynnal, maentumio
maintenance n cynhaliaeth, gofalaeth
maize n indrawn, injan corn
majesty n mawrhydi, mawredd
majestic adj mawreddog, urddasol
major adj mwy, mwyaf, pennaf ♦ n uwchgapten
majority n mwyafrif; oedran llawn
make vt gwneud, gwneuthur, peri ♦ n gwneuthuriad
maker n gwneuthurwr, creawdwr
making n gwneuthuriad, ffurfiad
make-up n colur
malady n drwg, anhwyldeb, dolur
male n, adj gwryw
malevolence n malais
malevolent adj drygnaws, maleisus
malformation n camffurfiad
malice n malais
malign vt enllibio, difrïo, pardduo
malignant adj llidiog, adwythig, gwyllt
mallet n gordd
malnutrition n gwallfaethiad, camluniaeth
malt n brag ♦ vb bragu
maltreat vb cam-drin
maltreatment n camdriniaeth

mammal *n* mamal
mammoth *n* mamoth ♦ *adj* anferth
man (**men**) *n* dyn, gŵr
manacle *n* gefyn ♦ *vt* gefynnu
manage *vb* trin, llywodraethu, rheoli; ymdaro, ymdopi, llwyddo
manageable *adj* hydrin
management *n* rheolaeth, goruchwyliaeth
manager *n* goruchwyliwr, rheolwr
mandate *n* gorchymyn, arch
mane *n* mwng
mange *n* clafr, clefri, brech y cŵn
manger *n* mansier, preseb
mangle *vt* llurgunio
mangle *n* mangl
manhood *n* dyndod
mania *n* gwallgofrwydd, gorawydd
maniac *n* gwallgofddyn
manifest *adj* amlwg ♦ *vt* amlygu, dangos
manifesto *n* datganiad, maniffesto
manifold *adj* amryw, amrywiol
manipulate *vt* trin, trafod
mankind *n* dynolryw
manly *adj* dynol, gwrol
manner *n* modd; moes
mannerism *n* dullwedd
mannerly *adj* boneddigaidd, moesgar
manners *npl* moesau
manor *n* maenor, maenol
manse *n* tŷ gweinidog, mans
manservant *n* gwas
mansion house *n* trigfan y maer
manslaughter *n* dynladdiad
mantelpiece *n* silff ben tân
mantle *n* mantell ♦ *vt* mantellu
manual *adj* perthynol i'r llaw ♦ *n* llawlyfr
manufacture *n* gwaith, nwydd ♦ *vt* gwneuthur, gwneud
manure *n* tail, gwrtaith, achles ♦ *vt* teilo, gwrteithio, achlesu
manuscript *n* llawysgrif
many *adj* aml, sawl, llawer. **as m.** cymaint, cynifer. **how m.** sawl

map *n* map
maple *n* masarnen
mar *vt* difetha, andwyo, hagru
maraud *vb* ysbeilio, anrheithio
marble *n* marmor, mynor; marblen
March *n* (mis) Mawrth
march *vb* ymdeithio ♦ *n* ymdaith
march *n* mers, goror, cyffin
marchioness *n* ardalyddes
mare *n* caseg
margarine *n* margarîn
margin *n* ymyl, cwr, goror
marigold *n* gold Mair, gold
marine *adj* morol ♦ *n* môr-filwr; llynges
mariner *n* morwr, llongwr, mordwywr
marital *adj* priodasol
maritime *adj* morol, arforol
mark *n* nod, marc ♦ *vt* nodi, marcio, craffu, sylwi
market *n* marchnad ♦ *vb* marchnata
maroon *vb* rhoi a gadael ar ynys anial
marquis *n* ardalydd
marriage *n* priodas
married *adj* priod
marrow *n* mêr. **vegetable m.** *n* pwmpen
marry *vb* priodi
Mars *n* Mawrth
marsh *n* morfa, cors, mignen
marshal *n* cadlywydd, marsialydd ♦ *vt* byddino, trefnu
mart *n* mart
martial *adj* milwraidd, milwrol
martinet *n* disgyblwr llym
martyr *n* merthyr ♦ *vt* merthyru
martyrdom *n* merthyrdod
marvel *n* rhyfeddod ♦ *vi* rhyfeddu, synnu
marvellous *adj* rhyfeddol, gwych
marxism *n* marcsiaeth
marxist *adj* marcsaidd
mascara *n* masgara, colur llygaid

masculine adj gwryw, gwrywaidd

mash n cymysg, stwns ♦ vt stwnsio

mask n mwgwd ♦ vt mygydu, cuddio

mason n saer maen, masiwn, meiswn

mass n pentwr, talp, crynswth, mas; (pl) y werin

mass n offeren

massacre n cyflafan ♦ vt cyflafanu

massive adj anferth

mast n hwylbren

master n meistr, athro, capten (llong) ♦ vt meistroli

masterpiece n campwaith, gorchest

mastery n meistrolaeth, goruchafiaeth

masticate vt cnoi, malu

mastiff n gafaelgi, cystowci, catgi

mat n mat ♦ vt matio, plethu

match n matsen

match n cymar; priodas; ymrysonfa, gêm ♦ vb cystadlu; cyfateb

matchless n digymar, digyffelyb

mate n cymar, cydymaith; mêt ♦ vt cymharu

material adj materol; o bwys ♦ n defnydd

materialism n materoliaeth

maternal adj mamol; o du'r fam

maternity n mamolaeth

mathematics npl mathemateg

matins npl boreol weddi, plygain

matriculate vb ymaelodi mewn prifysgol, matricwleiddio

matrimony n priodas

matron n gwraig briod, meistres, matron, modron

matter n mater; crawn ♦ vi bod o bwys

mattock n caib, matog

mattress n matras

mature adj aeddfed; mewn oed ♦ vb aeddfedu

maturity n aeddfedrwydd

maul vt baeddu, pwyo ♦ n sgarmes

mauve n lliw porffor, piws

maxim n dihareb, gwireb, rheol

maximum n uchafswm, uchafrif, uchafbwynt

May n Mai. **M. Day** n Calan Mai

may n blodau drain gwynion

maybe adv efallai, hwyrach, dichon

mayor n maer

mayoress n maeres

me pron myfi, mi, fi, i; minnau

mead n medd

meadow n dôl, gwaun, gweirglodd

meagre adj cul, tenau, prin, tlodaidd, llwm

meal n blawd

meal n pryd o fwyd

meals on wheels npl pryd ar glud

mean n cyfrwng, modd; canol; cymedr

mean vt meddwl, golygu, bwriadu

mean adj gwael, isel, crintach, iselwael

meander n ystum (afon) ♦ vi dolennu, troelli, ymdroelli

meaning n ystyr, meddwl

meanness n cybydd-dod, crintachrwydd

means npl cyfrwng, modd(ion), cyfoeth. **by all m.** ar bob cyfrif, wrth gwrs

meantime, -while adv yn y cyfamser

measles npl y frech goch

measure vt, n mesur

measurement n mesur, mesuriad

meat n ymborth, bwyd; cig

mechanic n peiriannydd

mechanical adj peiriannol, peiriannyddol, mecanyddol

mechanics npl mecaneg

mechanism n peirianwaith

medal n bathodyn, medal

meddle vi ymyrryd, busnesa, ymhêl

media *npl* cyfryngau
mediaeval *adj* canoloesol
medial *adj* canol, canolog
mediate *vi* canoli, cyfryngu
medical *adj* meddygol
medicine *n* meddyginiaeth; ffisig, moddion
mediocre *adj* canolig, cyffredin
meditate *vb* myfyrio
meditation *n* myfyrdod
Mediterranean *n*: **the M. y Môr Canoldir**
medium *n* canol; cyfrwng ♦ *adj* canol, canolig
medley *n* cymysgfa, cybolfa; cymysgedd, cadwyn o alawon
meek *adj* llariaidd, addfwyn
meekness *n* addfwynder
meet *vb* cyfarfod, cwrdd ♦ *adj* addas
meeting *n* cyfarfod, cyfarfyddiad
melancholy *n* pruddder, prudd, pruddglwyfus ♦ *n* pruddglwyf, y felan
mêlée *n* ymgiprys, ysgarmes
mellifluous *adj* melyslais, melysber
mellow *adj* aeddfed, meddal ♦ *vb* aeddfedu
melody *n* peroriaeth, melodi
melt *vb* toddi, ymdoddi
member *n* aelod. **M. of Parliament** *n* Aelod Seneddol
membership *n* aelodaeth
membrane *n* pilen, croenyn
memento *n* cofarwydd
memoir *n* cofiant
memorable *adj* cofiadwy, bythgofiadwy
memorandum *n* cofnod, cofnodiad
memorial *adj* coffadwriaethol ♦ *n* coffadwriaeth; cofeb; deiseb
memorise *vt* dysgu ar gof
memory *n* cof; coffadwriaeth
menace *n* bygythiad ♦ *vt* bygwth
menagerie *n* milodfa, sioe (siew) anifeiliaid

mend *vb* gwella, cyweirio, trwsio, helpu
mendacity *n* anwiredd, celwydd
mendicant *adj* cardotaidd, cardotlyd ♦ *n* cardotyn
menial *adj* gwasaidd, isel ♦ *n* gwas
meningitis *n* llid yr ymennydd
menstruation *n* y misglwyf
mensuration *n* mesureg
mental *adj* meddyliol
mention *vt* crybwyll, sôn ♦ *n* crybwylliad
mentor *n* cynghorwr, cyfarwyddwr
menu *n* bwydlen, arlwy
mercantile *adj* marchnadol, masnachol
mercenary *adj* ariangar, chwannog i elw ♦ *n* huriwr, milwr cyflog
merchandise *n* marsiandiaeth
merchant *n* masnachwr, marsiandwr
merciful *adj* trugarog, tosturiol
mercifully *adv* drwy drugaredd
merciless *adj* didrugaredd
mercuric *adj* mercurig
mercury *n* arian byw, mercwri
mercy *n* trugaredd
mere *adj* unig, pur, moel, noeth, hollol
mere *n* llyn, llwch
merge *vb* soddi, suddo, colli, ymgolli, uno
merger *n* ymsoddiad, cyfuniad, ymdoddiad, uniad
meridian *n* nawn; cyhydedd; anterth
merit *n* haeddiant, teilyngdod ♦ *vt* haeddu, teilyngu
mermaid *n* môr-forwyn
merriment *n* digrifwch, difyrrwch
merry *adj* llawen, llon
merry-go-round *n* ceffylau bach
mesh *n* masgl, magl, rhwydwaith
mess *n* saig; llanastr, annibendod ♦ *vb* bwyta; ymhél; maeddu
message *n* cenadwri, neges
messenger *n* cennad, negesydd

messieurs (**Messrs**) *npl* meistri
metabolism *n* metaboleg, metabolaeth
metal *n* metel ♦ *adj* metelaidd
metamorphosis (**-ses**) *n* trawsffurfiad, metamorffosis
metaphor *n* trosiad
metaphysics *n* metaffiseg
mete *vb* mesur
meteor *n* seren wib
meter *n* mesurydd; medr
method *n* trefn, method, dull
meticulous *adj* gorfanwl
metonymy *n* trawsenwad
metre *n* mesur, mydr
metrical *adj* mydryddol
metric system *n* system fedrig
metropolis *n* prifddinas
mettle *n* metel, anian, ysbryd
mew *vi* mewian
Mexico *n* México
miasma *n* tawch heintus
Michaelmas *n* gŵyl Fihangel
microbe *n* trychfilyn, meicrob
micro-chip *n* meicro-sglodyn
microphone *n* meicroffon, meic
microscope *n* chwyddwydr, meicrosgop
microwave *n* meicrodon. **m. oven** *n* ffwrn meicrodon
mid *adj* canol
midday *n* canol dydd, hanner dydd
middle *n*, *adj* canol
middle-aged *adj* canol oed
middling *adj* canolig, gweddol, symol
midge *n* gwybedyn
midget *n* corrach
midnight *n* canol nos, hanner nos
midriff *n* llengig
midst *n* canol, plith
midsummer *n* canol haf. **M. Day** *n* gŵyl Ifan
midwife (**-wives**) *n* bydwraig
mien *n* golwg, pryd, gwedd, agwedd
might *n* nerth, cadernid, gallu

mighty *adj* cadarn, galluog, nerthol
migrant *n* mudwr, ymfudwr, crwydrwr ♦ *adj* mudol, crwydrol
migrate *vi* symud, mudo
migration *n* mudiad, ymfudiad
milch *adj* blith, llaethog
mild *adj* tyner, tirion, mwyn; gwan, ysgafn
mildew *n* llwydi, llwydni
mildness *n* tynerwch, tiriondeb, mwynder
mile *n* milltir
mileage *n* milltiredd
milestone *n* carreg filltir
militant *adj* milwriaethus
military *adj* milwrol
militate *vi* milwrio
milk *n* llaeth, llefrith ♦ *vt* godro
milkman *n* dyn llaeth
milkshake *n* ysgytlaeth, llaeth 'di guro
Milky Way *n*: **the M.W.** Y Llwybr Llaethog, Caer Wydion
mill *n* melin ♦ *vt* melino, malu
millennium *n* mil blynyddoedd
miller *n* melinydd
millimetre *n* milimedr
milliner *n* hetwraig
million *n* miliwn
millionaire *n* miliynydd
millstone *n* maen melin
mime *n* meim
mimic *vt* dynwared, gwatwar
mimicry *n* dynwarededd
mince *vt* malu ♦ *n* briwgig, briwfwyd
mind *vb* meddwl, bryd, cof ♦ *vb* gofalu, cofio
mine *n* mwynglawdd, pwll
miner *n* mwynwr, glöwr
mineral *adj* mwynol ♦ *n* mwyn
mineral water *n* dŵr pistyll
mingle *vb* cymysgu, britho
mingy *adj* cybyddlyd, crintach
miniature *n* mân ddarlun ♦ *adj* bychan

minimize vt lleihau, bychanu

minimum n lleiafswm, isafrif

mining n mwyngloddiaeth.
  opencast m. n mwyngloddio brig

minister n gweinidog ♦ vb
gwasanaethu, gweinidogaethu

ministry n gweinidogaeth,
gweinyddiaeth, gwasanaeth

minnow n pilcodyn, pilcyn, sildyn,
silcyn

minor adj llai, lleiaf, lleddf; un
dan oed

minority n maboed, mebyd;
lleiafrif

minster n mynachlog; eglwys
gadeiriol

minstrel n clerwr, cerddor

mint n bathdy ♦ vt bathu

mint n mintys

minus adj, pron llai, heb, yn fyr o
♦ n minws

minute adj bach, bychan, mân;
manwl

minute n munud; cofnod. **m. book**
n llyfr cofnodion

minx n coegen, mursen, maeden

miracle n gwyrth

miraculous adj gwyrthiol

mirage n rhithlun, lleurith

mire n llaid, llaca, tom, baw

mirror n drych ♦ vt adlewyrchu

mirth n llawenydd, digrifwch,
afiaith

mis- prefix cam-

misadventure n anffawd,
damwain

misanthropist n dyngasáwr

misapprehension n
camddealltwriaeth

misbehave vi camymddwyn

misbehaviour n camymddygiad

miscarriage n erthyliad. **m. of
justice** n aflwyddo cyfiawnder

miscarry vi erthylu; aflwyddo;
colli

miscellaneous adj amrywiol

mischance n anffawd, damwain

mischief n drwg, drygioni, direidi

mischievous adj drygionus,
direidus

misconception n camsyniad,
cam-dyb

misconduct n camymddygiad ♦ vb
camymddwyn

misdeed n drwgweithred,
camwedd

misdemeanour n camwedd,
trosedd

miser n cybydd

miserable adj truenus, gresynus,
anhapus

misery n trueni, gresyni, adfyd

misfortune n anffawd, aflwydd

misgivings npl amheuon, ofnau

misguide vb camarwain

mishandle vb cam-drin

mishap n anap, anffawd, aflwydd

misinterpret vb camesbonio

misjudge vb camfarnu, camddeall

mislead vb camarwain, twyllo

misnomer n camenw

misprint n cambrint ♦ vb
camargraffu

misread vb camddarllen

misrepresent vt camddarlunio,
camliwio

miss vt methu, ffaelu, colli ♦ n
meth

missal n llyfr offeren

missile n saethyn, tafleigryn

missing adj yn eisiau, yngholl, ar
goll

mission n cenhadaeth

missionary n cenhadwr ♦ adj
cenhadol

missive n llythyr

misspell vb camsillafu

mist n niwl, nudden; tarth; caddug

mistake n camgymryd, methu ♦ vb
camgymeriad, gwall

mistletoe n uchelwydd

mistress n meistres; athrawes;
Mrs

mistrust vt drwgdybio, amau

misty adj niwlog

misunderstanding n camddealltwriaeth

mite n hatling; mymryn, tamaid

mitigate vt lleddfu, lliniaru, lleihau

mitre n meitr

mix vb cymysgu

mixture n cymysgedd, cymysgfa

moan n, vb ochain, griddfan, udo

moat n ffos (castell)

mob n torf, tyrfa, haid ♦ vt ymosod ar, baeddu

mobile adj symudol, symudadwy; mudol (cemeg)

mobilize vt dygyfor, byddino

mock vb gwatwar ♦ adj gau, ffug

mockery n gwatwar; ffug

mode n modd, dull

model n cynllun, patrwm ♦ vt llunio

moderate adj cymedrol ♦ vt cymedroli

moderation n cymedroldeb

modern adj modern, diweddar

modernize vb moderneiddio

modest adj gwylaidd; diymhongar

modesty n gwylder, gwyleidd-dra

modify vt newid, lleddfu

modulate vb cyweirio neu reoli llais

moiety n hanner, hanereg

moist adj llaith, gwlyb

moisture n lleithder, gwlybaniaeth, gwlybwr

moisturizer n lleithydd

molar n cilddant

mole n man geni

mole n gwadd, twrch daear

mole n morglawdd

molecule n molecwl ♦ adj molecylig

molehill n pridd y wadd

molest vt molestu, aflonyddu, blino

mollify vt meddalu, tyneru, dyhuddo

mollycoddle vb maldodi

molten adj tawdd

moment n moment; pwys, pwysigrwydd

momentum n momentwm

monarch n brenin, teyrn, penadur

monarchy n brenhiniaeth

monastery n mynachlog, mynachdy

monastic adj mynachaidd

Monday n dydd Llun

monetary adj ariannol

money n arian, pres

mongrel adj cymysgryw ♦ n mwngrel

monitor n monitor

monk n mynach

monkey n mwnci

mono- prefix un-

monogamy n unwreigiaeth

monoglot adj uniaith ♦ n person uniaith

monolith n maen hir

monologue n ymson

monopoly n monopoli

monosyllable n gair unsill

monotheism n undduwiaeth

monotone adj, n unsain, un-dôn

monotonous adj undonog

monotony n undonedd, unrhywiaeth

monsoon n monsŵn

monster n anghenfil; clamp ♦ adj anferth

monstrous adj angenfilaidd, anferth, gwrthun

month n mis

monthly adj misol ♦ n misolyn

monument n cofadail, cofgolofn

mood n hwyl, tymer; modd

moody adj oriog, cyfnewidiol

moon n lleuad, lloer. **harvest m.** n lleuad fedi

moonlight n golau lleuad

moonshine n ffiloreg, ffwlbri, lol

moor n morfa, rhos, gwaun

moor vt angori, bachu, sicrhau

moorhen n iâr fach y dŵr

moorland n rhostir, gweundir
mop n mop ♦ vt mopio, sychu
mope vi pendrymu, delwi
moraine n marian
moral adj moesol ♦ n moeswers, addysg
morality n moesoldeb
morals npl moesau
morass n cors, mignen
morbid adj afiach
mordant adj brathog, llym
more adj mwy, ychwaneg, rhagor ♦ adv mwy, mwyach
moreover adv heblaw hynny, hefyd
moribund adj ar farw, ar dranc
morning n bore ♦ adj bore, boreol
Morocco n Moroco
morose adj sur, sarrug, afrywiog, blwng
morphology n ffurfianneg, morffoleg
morrow n trannoeth
morsel n tamaid, tameidyn
mortal adj marwol, angheuol ♦ n dyn marwol
mortar n cymrwd, morter; breuan, morter
mortgage n morgais, arwystl ♦ vt morgeisio, arwystlo
mortify vb marwhau; blino, siomi
mortise n mortais ♦ vt morteisio
mortuary n marwdy
mosaic adj brith, amryliw ♦ n brithwaith, mosaig
Moscow n Moscow
mosque n mosg
moss n mwswgl, mwsogl
most adj mwyaf, amlaf
mostly adv gan mwyaf, fynychaf
mote n brycheuyn, llychyn
moth n gwyfyn
mother n mam. **m.-in-law** n mam yng nghyfraith, chwegr
motion n symudiad, ysgogiad; cynigiad
motive adj symudol, ysgogol ♦ n

cymhelliad, amcan, motif
motley adj brith, cymysg
motor n modur
motor cycle n beic modur
motorist n modurwr
motorway n trafordd
mottle vt britho, brychu
motto n arwyddair
mould n pridd, daear, gweryd ♦ vt priddo
mould n mold; delw ♦ vt moldio, llunio, delweddu
mould n llwydni, llwydi
moulder vi malurio, adfeilio
moult vi bwrw plu, mudo
mound n twmpath, clawdd, crug
mount vb esgyn, dringo, codi, mynd ar gefn; gosod
mountain n mynydd
mountaineer n mynyddwr
mourn vb galaru
mournful adj galarus, dolefus, alaethus
mourning n galar; galarwisg
mouse (**mice**) n llygoden ♦ vb llygota
moustache n trawswch, mwstas
mouth n genau, safn, ceg ♦ vb cegu, safnu
move vb symud, syflyd; cymell; cynnig; cyffroi
movement n symudiad; ysgogiad
mow vt lladd (gwair) ♦ n mwdwl, medel
MP n abbr AS (aelod seneddol)
much adj llawer ♦ adv yn fawr
mucilage n glud, llys, llysnafedd
muck n tail, tom, baw ♦ vt tomi, baeddu
mucus n llys, llysnafedd
mud n mwd, llaid, llaca, baw
muddle vi drysu ♦ n dryswch
mug n cwpan, godart
mulberry n morwydden
mule n mul, bastart mul
mullion n post ffenestr

multi- *prefix* aml, lluosog

multifarious *n* amryfath, lluosog

multiple *adj* amryfal ♦ *n* cynhwysrif, lluosrif

multiplicand *n* lluosrif, lluosyn

multiplication *n* amlhad, lluosogiad, lluosiad

multiplicity *n* lluosowgrwydd

multiply *vb* amlhau, lluosogi, lluosi

multi-storey *adj* aml-lawr

multitude *n* lliaws, tyrfa

mumble *vb* grymial, myngial

mummy *n* mwmi

mumps *n* clwy'r pennau, y dwymyn doben

munch *vt* cnoi

mundane *adj* bydol, daearol

municipal *adj* dinesig, bwrdeisiol

munificent *adj* hael, haelionus

munitions *npl* arfau neu offer rhyfel

mural *adj* murol ♦ *n* murlun

murder *vt* llofruddio ♦ *n* llofruddiaeth

murderer *n* llofrudd

murky *adj* tywyll, cymylog, dudew

murmur *vb, n* murmur, grwgnach

muscle *n* cyhyr, cyhyryn

muscular *adj* cyhyrog

muse *n* awen, awenydd

muse *vi* myfyrio, synfyfyrio

museum *n* amgueddfa

mushroom *n* madarch

music *n* miwsig, cerdd, cerddoriaeth, peroriaeth

musical *adj* cerddorol

musician *n* cerddor

mussel *n* misglen. **mussels** *npl* cregyn gleision

must *vb* def rhaid

mustard *n* mwstart

muster *vb* casglu, cynnull, byddino ♦ *n* cynulliad, mwstwr

musty *adj* wedi llwydo, hendrwm, mws

mutable *adj* anwadal, cyfnewidiol

mutate *vb* treiglo (llythrennau)

mutation *n* cyfnewidiad, treiglad

mute *adj* mud ♦ *n* mudan

muteness *n* mudandod

mutilate *vt* anafu, hagru, llurgunio

mutiny *n* terfysg, gwrthryfel

mutter *vb* myngial, grymial, mwmian

mutton *n* cig dafad, cig mollt, cig gwedder

mutual *adj* cyd, o boptu, y naill a'r llall

muzzle *n* genau, ffroen; pennor ♦ *vt* cau safn, rhoi taw ar

my *pron* fy

myriad *n* myrdd

myrmidon *n* anfadwas, dihiryn

myrrh *n* myrr

myrtle *n* myrtwydd

myself *pron* myfi fy hun

mysterious *adj* dirgel, rhyfedd, dirgelaidd

mystery *n* dirgelwch

mystic *n* cyfriniwr, cyfrinydd

mystify *vt* synnu, syfrdanu

myth *n* dameg, chwedl, myth

mythology *n* chwedloniaeth

N

nab *vb* cipio, dal

nadir *n* isafbwynt, ory

nag *vb* cecru, ffraeo, cadw sŵn ♦ *n* ceffyl

nail *n* hoel, hoelen; ewin ♦ *vt* hoelio. **n. file** *n* ffeil/rhathell ewinedd

naïve *adj* diniwed, diddichell, gwirion

naked *adj* noeth

namby-pamby *adj* merf, merfaidd, llipa

name *n* enw ♦ *vt* enwi, galw

namely *adv* sef, nid amgen

namesake *n* cyfenw

nanny *n* nani

nap *vi* cysgu, pendwmpian ♦ *n*

cyntun

nape *n* gwar, gwegil

napkin *n* napcyn, cadach, cewyn

nappy *n* cewyn, clwt

narcotic *adj* narcotig ♦ *n* moddion cwsg

narrate *vt* adrodd (hanes)

narrative *n* hanes, chwedl, stori

narrow *adj* cul, cyfyng ♦ *vb* culhau, cyfyngu

nasal *adj* trwynol

nasty *adj* cas, brwnt, budr, ffiaidd

natal *adj* genedigol

nation *n* cenedl

national *adj* cenedlaethol

nationalism *n* cenedlaetholdeb

nationalist *n* cenedlaetholwr

nationality *n* cenedl, cenedligrwydd

nationalization *n* gwladoliad

nationalize *vb* gwladoli, cenedlaethol

native *n* brodor ♦ *adj* brodorol; cynhenid

nativity *n* genedigaeth

natural *adj* anianol, naturiol

naturalist *n* naturiaethwr

naturalize *vb* naturioli, breinio, cywladu, brodori

nature *n* anian, natur; naturiaeth

naught *n* dim

naughtiness *n* drygioni, direidi

naughty *adj* drwg, drygionus

nausea *n* clefyd y môr; cyfog; ffieidd-dod

nauseous *adj* cyfoglyd, ffiaidd, atgas

nautical *adj* morwrol, mordwyol

naval *adj* llyngesol, morol

nave *n* corff eglwys

nave *n* both, bŵl

navel *n* bogail

navigate *vt* morio, mordwyo, llywio

navvy *n* cloddiwr, ceibiwr

navy *n* llynges

nay *adv* na, nage; nid hynny yn

unig

naze *n* trwyn, penrhyn, pentir

neap *adj*, *n*: **n. tide** nêp, llanw isel

near *adj*, *adv*, *prep* agos, ger, gerllaw ♦ *vb* agosáu, nesu

nearby *adv* gerllaw, yn ymyl

nearly *adv* bron

nearness *n* agosrwydd

neat *adj* del, destlus, twt, trefnus; pur

nebula (-ae) *n* niwlen; niwl sêr

nebulous *adj* niwlog

necessarily *adv* o angenrheidrwydd

necessary *adj* angenrheidiol

necessitate *vt* gorfodi, gwneud yn angenrheidiol

necessitous *adj* anghenus, rheidus

necessity *n* angen, anghenraid, rhaid

neck *n* gwddf, mwnwgl, gwar

necklace *n* mwclis

necromancy *n* dewiniaeth

nectar *n* neithdar

need *n*, *vb* (bod mewn) angen, eisiau

needful *adj* rheidiol, angenrheidiol

needle *n* nodwydd; gwaell

needlework *n* gwniadwaith

needless *adj* afreidiol, dianghenraid

nefarious *adj* anfad, drygionus, ysgeler

negation *n* nacâd, gwadiad, negyddiad

negative *adj* nacaol, negyddol

neglect *vt* esgeuluso ♦ *n* esgeulustra

negligence *n* esgeulustod

negligent *adj* esgeulus

negotiate *vb* trafod, trefnu, negodi

negotiation *n* trafodaeth, cyd-drafodaeth

negro *n* dyn du, negro

neigh *vi* gweryru ♦ *n* gweryriad

neighbour *n* cymydog

neighbourhood *n* cymdogaeth

neither conj na, nac, ychwaith ♦ adj, pron na'r naill na'r llall, nid yr un o'r ddau
Nemesis n dialedd
neo- prefix newydd, diweddar
nephew n nai
nepotism n neigaredd
nerve n giewyn, gewyn, nerf ♦ vt gwroli
nervous adj gieuol; nerfus, ofnus
nest n nyth ♦ vb nythu
nestle vb nythu, gwasgu'n glos at
nestling n aderyn bach, cyw
net n rhwyd, rhwyden
net adj union, cywir, net ♦ vt rhwydo
netball n pêl rwyd
nether adj isaf
Netherlands npl: **the N.** yr Iseldiroedd
nettle n danadl ♦ vt pigo; llidio
network n rhwydwaith
neuralgia n gieuwst
neurasthenia n nerfwst
neuritis n newritis
neurosis n newrosis
neuter adj diryw
neutral adj amhleidiol ♦ n amhleidydd
neutrality n newtraliaeth, amhleidiaeth
neutralize vt dieffeithio, dirymu
never ni ... erioed, ni ... byth
nevertheless adv, conj eto, er hynny
new adj newydd. **N. Year** n Y Calan, Y Flwyddyn Newydd. **N. York** n Efrog Newydd. **N. Zealand** n Seland Newydd
newcomer n newydd-ddyfodiad
newness n newydd-deb
news n newydd, newyddion, hanes
newsagent n gwerthwr papurau newyddion
newspaper n papur newydd, newyddiadur
newt n madfall, genau-goeg,

modrchwilen
next adj nesaf ♦ adv yn nesaf
nib n blaen, nib
nibble vb deintio, cnoi
nice adj neis, hardd, tlws; manwl, cynnil
niche n cloer, cilfach
nickname n llysenw ♦ vt llysenwi
niece n nith
niggard n cybydd ♦ adj cybyddlyd, crintach
nigger n dyn du (mewn dirmyg)
nigh adj, adv agos
night n nos; noson, noswaith. **by n.** liw nos. **dead of n.** cefn nos. **n. club** n clwb nos
nightdress n gŵn nos, coban
nightfall n y cyfnos, yr hwyr
nightingale n eos
nightmare n hunllef
nil n dim
nimble adj gwisgi, heini, sionc
nimbleness n sioncrwydd
nincompoop n penbwl, gwirionyn
nine adj, n naw
nineteen adj, n pedwar (pedair) ar bymtheg, un deg naw
ninety adj, n deg a phedwar ugain, naw deg
ninth adj nawfed
nip vb brathu, cnoi; deifio
nipple n diden, teth, tethan
nit n nedden
nitrate n nitrad
nitre n neitr
nitrogen n nitrogen
nitrous n nitrus
no adj ni ... neb, dim ♦ adv ni, etc dim; nac oes, nage, naddo
nobility n bonedd, urddas, mawredd
noble adj ardderchog, urddasol, pendefigaidd ♦ n pendefig
nobleman n pendefig
nobody n neb
nocturnal adj nosol, gyda'r nos
nod vb amneidio; pendrymu ♦ n

amnaid

noise n swn, twrf, trwst

noisome adj niweidiol, atgas, ffiaidd

noisy adj swnllyd

nomad n nomad, crwydrwr ♦ adj crwydrol

nom de plume n ffugenw

nomenclature n cyfundrefn enwau

nominal adj enwol, mewn enw

nominate vt enwi, enwebu

nomination n enwebiad

nominative adj enwol

non- prefix an-, di-

nonagenarian n un deng mlwydd a phedwar ugain

non-alcoholic adj dialcohol

nonce n: for the n. am y tro

nonchalance n difrawder, difaterwch

nonchalant adj didaro, difater

nonconformist n anghydffurfiwr, ymneilltuwr

nonconformity n anghydffurfiaeth, ymneilltuaeth

nondescript adj anodd ei ddarlunio, od

none pron neb, dim, dim un

nonentity n dyn dibwys, neb

nonplus vt drysu, dymchwelyd

nonsense n lol, dyli, gwirionedb

non-violence n didreisedd

non-violent adj di-drais, didrais

noodle n gwirionyn, ffwlcyn; nwdl

nook n congl, cornel, cilfach

noon n nawn, hanner dydd, canol dydd

noose n cwlwm rhedeg, magl

nor conj na, nac

normal adj rheolaidd, cyffredin, safonol

normality n normalrwydd

north n gogledd ♦ adj gogleddol. **N. Pole** n Pegwn y Gogledd. **N. Sea** n Môr y Gogledd

northern adj gogleddol. **N. Ireland** n Gogledd Iwerddon

Norway n Norwy

nose n trwyn ♦ vb trwyno, ffroeni, gwyntio

nosebleed n gwaedlif o'r trwyn

nosegay n blodeuglwm, pwysi

nostalgia n hiraeth

nostril n ffroen

not adv na, nac, nad, ni, nid

notable adj nodedig, hynod, enwog

notary n nodiadur, nodiedydd

notation n nodiant

notch n rhic, bwlch, hecyn, rhwgn, rhint

note n nod, nodyn ♦ vt nodi, sylwi

noted adj nodedig, hynod, enwog

note pad n pad ysgrifennu

notepaper n papur ysgrifennu

noteworthy adj nodedig

nothing n dim. **n. at all** dim byd, dim o gwbl

notice n sylw, rhybudd ♦ vt sylwi

noticeboard n hysbysfwrdd

notify vt hysbysu, rhoi rhybudd

notion n tyb, amcan, syniad

notoriety n enw gwael

notorious adj hynod, carn, rhemp

notwithstanding conj er ♦ prep er, er gwaethaf

nought n dim; gwagnod (0)

noun n enw

nourish vt maethu, meithrin

nourishing adj maethlon

nourishment n maeth

novel adj newydd ♦ n nofel

novelist n nofelydd

November n Tachwedd

novice n newyddian, nofis

now adv, conj, n yn awr, yr awron, yrŵan, weithian, bellach. **just n.** gynnau. **n. and then** yn awr ac yn y man

nowadays adv yn y dyddiau hyn

nowhere adv dim yn unlle

noxious adj niweidiol, afiach

nozzle n ffroenell

nuclear adj niwclear

nucleus n cnewyllyn, bywyn

nude adj noeth, noeth lymun
nudge vt pwnio, penelino
nugatory adj ofer, disylwedd, dirym
nugget n clap aur
nuisance n pla, poendod, budreddi
null adj diddim, dirym, ofer
numb adj diffrwyth, cwsg ♦ vt fferru, merwino
number n nifer, rhif, rhifedi; rhifyn ♦ vt rhifo, cyfrif. **n. plate** n plat rhif car, plat cofrestru
numeral n rhifol, rhifnod
numeration n cyfrifiad
numerator n rhifiadur
numerical adj rhifiadol
numerous adj niferog, lluosog, aml
nun n lleian, mynaches
nurse n mamaeth, gweinyddes, nyrs ♦ vt magu, meithrin, nyrsio
nursery n magwrfa, meithrinfa
nurture n maeth, magwraeth, meithriniad ♦ vt maethu, meithrin
nut n cneuen; gwain, gweinell
nutcracker n gefel gnau
nutriment n maeth
nutrition n maeth, maethiad
nutritious adj maethlon
nutshell n plisgyn (masgl) cneuen
nuzzle vb trwyno, turio, ymwasgu
nylon n neilon

O

oaf n delff, hurtyn, awff, llabwst
oak n derwen; derw
oakum n carth, breisgion
oar n rhwyf
oat n ceirchen, (pl) ceirch
oatcake n bara ceirch, teisen geirch
oath n llw
oatmeal n blawd ceirch
obdurate adj caled, cyndyn,

ystyfnig, anhyblyg
obedience n ufudd-dod
obedient adj ufudd
obese adj tew, corffol
obey vb ufuddhau
obituary n marwgoffa
object n gwrthrych; amcan ♦ vb gwrthwynebu
objection n gwrthwynebiad
objectionable adj annymunol
objective adj gwrthrychol ♦ n amcan, nod
obligation n dyled, rhwymau
oblige vt rhwymo; boddio; gorfodi
obliging adj caredig, cymwynasgar
oblique adj lleddf, gŵyr, ar osgo
obliterate vt dileu
oblivion n angof, ebargofiant
oblong adj hirgul ♦ n oblong
obnoxious adj atgas, ffiaidd
obscene adj serth, anllad, anniwair, brwnt
obscure adj tywyll; anhysbys ♦ vt tywyllu
obsequious adj gwasaidd, cynffongar
observation n sylw; sylwadaeth
observatory n arsyllfa
observe vb sylwi, arsyllu; cadw
observer n sylwedydd, arsyllwr
obsolete adj anarferedig, ansathredig
obstacle n rhwystr, atalfa
obstinate adj cyndyn, ystyfnig, gwrthnysig
obstreperous adj trystiog, afreolus
obstruct vt cau, tagu; rhwystro, lluddio
obtain vt cael, caffael, ennill
obtrude vb gwthio ar, ymwthio
obtrusive adj ymwthgar
obtuse adj pŵl, di-fin, hurt. **o. angle** ongl aflem
obvious adj eglur, amlwg
occasion n achlysur ♦ vt achlysuro
occasional adj achlysurol, anaml

occidental adj gorllewinol

occult adj cudd, dirgel, cêl, cyfrin

occupation n gwaith, galwedigaeth; meddiant

occupy vt meddu, meddiannu; llenwi; dal

occur vi digwydd; taro i'r meddwl

occurrence n digwyddiad

ocean n môr, cefnfor, cyfanfor, eigion

o'clock adv o'r gloch

octagon n wythongl

octave n wythawd, octef

octavo n wythblyg ♦ n llyfr wythblyg

October n Hydref

octogenarian n gŵr pedwar ugain mlwydd oed

odd adj cⁱ, hynod. **o. number** odrif

odds npl ots, gwahaniaeth; mantais

ode n awdl

odious adj atgas, cas, ffiaidd

odium n atgasrwydd; gwaradwydd; bai

odour n arogl, aroglau, sawr

of prep o; gan; am; ynghylch. **o. course** wrth gwrs

off adv ymaith, i ffwrdd ♦ prep oddi, oddi wrth, oddi ar. **o. and on** yn awr ac yn y man

offal n syrth, gwehilion, perfedd

offence n tramgwydd, trosedd, camwedd

offend vb tramgwyddo, troseddu, pechu; digio

offender n troseddwr

offensive adj tramgwyddus, atgas, ffiaidd; ymosodol

offer vb cynnig, cyflwyno; offrymu ♦ n cynnig

offering n offrwm, aberth

office n swydd; swyddfa

officer n swyddog, swyddwr

official adj swyddogol ♦ n swyddog

officiate vi gweinyddu

officious adj ymyrgar, busneslyd

offside n camochr, camsefyll ♦ vb camochri, camsefyll

offspring n hiliogaeth, epil, hil, plant

oft, often adv yn aml, yn fynych

ogle vb cilwenu, ciledrych

ogre n anghenfil, bwystfil, cawr

oh excl O!

oil n olew, oel ♦ vt iro, oelio

oil rig n llwyfan olew

ointment n ennaint, eli

okay excl popeth yn iawn

old adj hen, oedrannus. **of o.** gynt. **o. age** henaint, henoed. **o. and infirm** hen a methedig. **o.-fashioned** adj henffasiwn, od. **o. stager** n hen law

olive n olewydden

omelette n crempog wyau

omen n argoel, arwydd, rhagarwydd

ominous adj argoelus, bygythiol

omission n gwall

omit vt gadael allan, esgeuluso

on prep ar, ar warthaf ♦ adv ymlaen

once adv unwaith; gynt

one adj, n un. **o.-way** adj unffordd (street, traffic)

onion n wynwynyn, wnionyn

only adj unig ♦ adv yn unig; ond

onset n ymosodiad, cyrch; cychwyn

onslaught n ymosodiad, rhuthr, cyrch

onus n baich, dyletswydd, cyfrifoldeb

onward adj, adv, **onwards** adv ymlaen

ooze n llaid, llysnafedd ♦ vi chwysu

opaque adj afloyw, tywyll

open adj agored ♦ vb agor, ymagor

open-air n, adj awyr agored

opencast n (coal) (glo) brig

opening n agoriad, agorfa

operate vb gweithredu, gweithio

operation n gweithrediad; gweithred, triniaeth lawfeddygol

operator n gweithredydd, trafodwr

opiate n cysglyn

opinion n tyb, meddwl, barn, opiniwn

opponent n gwrthwynebydd

opportune adj amserol, cyfleus

opportunity n cyfle, egwyl

oppose vt gwrthwynebu, cyferbynnu

opposite adj, adv, prep gwrthwyneb, cyferbynnu

opposition n gwrthwynebiad, gwrthblaid

oppress vt gorthrymu, llethu

optician n optegydd

optimism n optimistiaeth

optimist n optimist

option n dewisiad, dewis

or conj neu, ai, ynteu, naill ai

oracle n oracl

oral adj geneuol, llafar, anysgrifenedig

orally adv ar lafar

orange n oren, oraens ♦ adj melyngoch

oration n araith, anerchiad

orator n areithiwr, areithydd

orb n pêl, pelen, pellen; y llygad

orbit n rhod, tro, cylchdro, chwyldro

orchard n perllan

orchestra n cerddorfa

ordain vt ordeinio, urddo

ordeal n prawf llym

order n trefn; gorchymyn, archeb; urdd ♦ vb ordeinio, trefnu, gorchymyn; archebu; urddo. **in o. that** er mwyn

orderly adj trefnus ♦ n gwas milwr

ordinal adj trefnol

ordinarily adv fel rheol

ordinary adj cyffredin, arferol

ordination n ordeiniad, urddiad

ore n mwyn

organ n organ, offeryn

organist n organydd

organization n trefn; cyfundrefn; trefniadaeth

organize vb trefnu

organized adj trefnus. **o. by** trefnwyd gan

organizer n trefnydd

orgy n gloddest, cyfeddach

oriental adj dwyreiniol ♦ n dwyreiniwr

orientate vb cyfeirio

orifice n genau, ceg, agorfa

origin n dechreuad, tarddiad

original adj, n gwreiddiol

originality n gwreiddioldeb

originate vb dechrau, tarddu

ornament n addurn ♦ vt addurno

ornate adj addurnedig, mawrwych

ornithology n adaryddiaeth, adareg

orphan adj, n amddifad

orthodox adj uniongred

orthography n orgraff

oscillate vb siglo, dirgrynu, osgiladu

ostensible adj ymddangosiadol, proffesedig

ostentation n rhodres

ostentatious adj rhodresgar

ostracize vt diarddel, alltudio

ostrich n estrys

other adj, pron arall, llall, amgen

otherwise adv amgen

otter n dyfrgi, dwrgi

ounce n owns

our pron ein, ein ... ni

oust vt disodli

out adv allan, i maes

outcast n alltud, digartref, gwrthodedig

outcome n canlyniad, ffrwyth

outcrop n brig, cribell ♦ vb brigo

outcry n gwaedd; dadwrdd; gwrthdystiad

outdo vt rhagori ar, trechu

outdoor adj yn yr awyr agored

outer adj allanol, nesaf allan, cyrion

outing n pleserdaith, gwibdaith

outlandish adj dieithr, estronol, anghysbell, diarffordd

outlast vb goroesi

outlaw n herwr

outlay n traul, cost

outlet n allfa

outline n amlinelliad, braslun; amlinell ♦ vb amlinellu

outlive vb goroesi

outlook n rhagolwg, argoel; golygfa

outset n dechrau, dechreuad

outside n tu allan, tu faes ♦ adj, adv allan(ol), oddi allan ♦ prep tu allan i, tu faes i

outside-forward n blaenwr mas

outside-half n maswr

outside-left n asgellwr chwith

outside-right n asgellwr de

outskirts npl cyrrau, maestrefi

outstanding adj amlwg; dyledus

outward adj allanol

outwards adv tuag allan

outweigh vt gorbwyso

oval adj hirgrwn

ovary n wygell, wyfa, ofari

ovation n cymeradwyaeth

oven n ffwrn, popty

over prep uwch, tros ♦ adv gor, rhy, tra

overall adj o ben i ben ♦ n troswisg

overbearing adj gormesol

overcast adj cymylog

overcharge n gorbrisio, codi gormod

overcoat n cot fawr/uchaf

overcome vt gorchfygu, trechu, cael y goruu ar

overdo vt gorwneud

overflow n gorlif(iad) ♦ vb gorlifo

overhead adj, adv uwchben

overheat vi gorboethi

overload vb gorlwytho

overlook vb edrych dros; esgeuluso

overnight adv dros nos

overpopulate vb gorboblogi

overpower vb trechu

overrun vb goresgyn

overseas adv tramor, dros y môr

overtake vt goddiweddyd

overthrow n dymchweliad, dros y môr ♦ vt dymchwelyd

overture n cynnig; agorawd

overturn vt troi, dymchwelyd

overwhelm vt llethu, gorlethu

overwork vb gorweithio

owe vt bod mewn dyled

owl n tylluan, gwdihŵ

own adj eiddo dyn ei hun, priod ♦ vt meddu; arddel, addef

owner n perchen, perchennog

ox (-en) n ych, eidion

oxide n ocsid

oxygen n ocsigen

oyster n llymarch, wystrysen

P

pace n cam, camre; cyflymdra ♦ vb camu, cerdded

pacific adj heddychol, tawel

Pacific Ocean n Môr Tawel

pacifism n heddychiaeth

pacifist n heddychwr

pacify vt heddychu, tawelu

pack n pac, swp, pwn ♦ vb pacio, pynio

package n pecyn, bwndel, sypyn

packed lunch n tocyn, pryd wedi ei bacio

packet n sypyn, paced

pact n cyfamod, cynghrair

pad n pad ♦ vt padio

paddle n padl, rhodl, rhwyf ♦ vb rhodli, padlo

paddling pool n pwll padlo

paddock n marchgae, cae bach

padlock n clo clap, clo clwt, clo

egwyd

pagan n pagan ♦ adj paganaidd

page n tudalen

pageant n pasiant

pail n ystwc, crwc, bwced

pain n poen, gwayw, dolur ♦ vt poeni

painful adj poenus

painkiller n lleddfydd poen, lladdwr poen, dofydd poen

painstaking adj gofalus, trylwyr, diwyd

paint n paent, lliw ♦ vt peintio, lliwio

painter n peintiwr; arlunydd

painting n peintiad; arlunydd

pair n pâr, dau, cwpl ♦ vb paru

Pakistan n Pakistan

palace n plas, palas, palasty

palaeo-, paleo- prefix hen, hynafol

palatable adj archwaethus, blasus

palate n tafod y genau; blas, archwaeth

palatial adj palasaidd, gwych

palaver n cleber, baldordd ♦ vb clebran, baldorddi

pale adj gwelw, llwyd, glas, gwelwlas ♦ vb gwelwi

pale n pawl, cledr; clawdd, ffin

Palestine n Palestina

palisade n palis, gwalc

pall vb diflasu

pallet n gwely gwellt, matras

pallid adj gwelw, llwyd

pallor n gwelwedd

palm n palf, cledr llaw ♦ vt palfu

palm n palmwydden. **P. Sunday** Sul y Blodau

palpable adj amlwg, dybryd, teimladwy

palpitate vi curo, dychlamu

palsy n parlys ♦ vt parlysu, diffrwytho

paltry adj distadl, gwael, pitw

pamper vt mwytho, maldodi

pamphlet n pamffled, llyfryn

pan- prefix oll-

pan n padell

pancake n crempog, cramwythen, ffroisen

pandemonium n dadwrdd, terfysg, mwstwr

pander vb porthi, gweini

pane n cwar, cwarel, paen

panegyric n molawd

panel n panel

pang n gloes, gwasgfa, brath, gwayw

panic n dychryn, panig

pansy n trilliw, llysiau'r Drindod

pant vi dyheu

pantaloons npl llodrau

panties npl pantos

pantomime n pantomeim

pantry n bwtri, pantri

pants npl pants

papacy n pabaeth

papal adj pabaidd

paper n papur ♦ vb papuro. **blotting p.** n papur sugno. **tissue p.** n papur sidan. **brown p.** n papur llwyd

paperback n llyfr clawr meddal

paperclip n clip papur

papist n pabydd

papyrus (-i) n papurfrwyn

par n cyfartaledd, llawn werth

parable n dameg

parachute n parasiwt

parade n rhodfa; rhodres, rhwysg

paradise n paradwys, gwynfa, gwynfyd

paradox n gwrthddywediad, paradocs

paradoxical adj paradocsaidd

paradoxically adv yn baradocsaidd

paraffin n paraffin

paragraph n paragraff

parallel adj cyfochrog, cyflin, paralel

paralyze vt parlysu, diffrwytho

paralysis n parlys

paralytic adj, n claf o'r parlys

paramount adj pen, pennaf, prif

paramour n gordderch

parapet n canllaw, rhagfur

paraphernalia npl meddiannau, taclau, celfi, petheuach

paraphrase n araileiriad ♦ vt araileirio

parasite n un yn byw ar gefn un arall, cynffonnwr

parcel n parsel, swp, sypyn

parch vb crasu, deifio, golosgi, sychu

parched adj cras, crasboeth

parchment n memrwn

pardon n maddeuant, pardwn ♦ vt maddau, pardynu

parent n tad neu fam, (pl) rhieni

parenthesis (-ses) n sangiad, ymadroddi rhwng cromfachau

pariah n dyn sgymun

parings npl pilion, creifion

Paris n Paris

parish n plwyf ♦ adj plwyf, plwyfol

parishioner n plwyfolyn, (pl) plwyfolion

parity n cydraddoldeb, cyfartaledd

park n parc, cae, coetgae ♦ vb parcio

parking meter n amserydd parcio, rheolydd parcio

parking ticket n tocyn parcio

parlance n ymadrodd, iaith

parliament n senedd

parliamentary adj seneddol

parlour n parlwr

parochial adj plwyfol

parody n parodi ♦ vb gwatwar, dynwared

parole n gair, addewid, parôl

parricide n tadladdiad; tadleiddiad

parrot n parot, perot

parry vt osgoi, gochelyd, troi heibio

parse vt dosbarthu

parsimonious adj crintach, cybyddlyd

parsimony n crintachrwydd

parsley n persli

parsnip n panasen

parson n person, offeiriad

part n rhan; parth; plaid ♦ vb rhannu, parthu; gwahanu; ymadael

partake vb cyfrannu, cyfranogi

partial adj rhannol; pleidiol, tueddol

participate vb cyfranogi

participle n rhangymeriad

particle n mymryn, gronyn; geiryn

particular adj neilltuol, penodol; manwl ♦ n pwnc, (pl) manylion

parting n canolfur, gwahanfur, palis

partisan n pleidiwr

partition n canolfur, gwahanfur, palis

partly adv mewn rhan, yn rhannol

partner n partner; cymar

partridge n petrisen

part-time adj rhan amser

party n plaid; parti, mintai

pass vb myned heibio, llwyddo, pasio; treulio, bwrw ♦ n cyflwr, sefyllfa; bwlch; trwydded. **to p. away** vb marw. **reverse p.** n pas wrthol

passable adj y gellir mynd heibio iddo; purion

passage n tramwyfa; mordaith; cyfran

passenger n teithiwr

passing n ymadawiad, tranc, pasio ♦ adj yn pasio, diflannol

passion n dioddefaint; gwŷn, nwyd

passionate adj angerddol, nwydwyllt

passive adj goddefol

Passover n y Pasg

passport n trwydded deithio, pasbort

past adj, n gorffennol ♦ prep wedi ♦ adv heibio

paste n past ♦ vt pastio, gludio

pastern n egwyd

pasteurize vb pasteureiddio

pasteurized adj wedi ei

basteureiddio

pastime n difyrrwch, adloniant

pastor n bugail (eglwys), gweinidog

pastoral adj bugeiliol ♦ n bugeilgerdd

pastry n pasteiod, pasteiaeth, tarten; crwst

pasture n porfa ♦ vb porfelu, pori

pasty n pastai

pat vt patio, pratio, canmol ♦ adj parod, cymwys, priodol

patch n clwt, darn ♦ vt clytio

patchwork n clytwaith

paten n plat cymundeb

patent adj agored, cyhoedd, amlwg; breintiedig ♦ n breintlythyr

paternal adj tadol

paternoster n pader

path n llwybr

pathetic adj gresynus, pathetig

pathological adj patholegol

pathos n teimlad, dwyster

patience n amynedd

patient adj amyneddgar, dioddefus ♦ n dioddefydd, claf

patriarch n patriarch

patrimony n treftadaeth; gwaddol

patriot n gwladgarwr

patriotic adj gwladgarol

patrol n gwyliadwriaeth, gwylfa, patrôl

patron n noddwr

patronage n nawdd, nawddogaeth

patronize vt noddi, nawddogi

patronizing adj nawddogol

patronymic n tadenw

patter vb curo (fel glaw ar ffenestr)

patter vb padera ♦ n clebar, siaradach

pattern n patrwm, cynllun

paucity n prinder

paunch n bol, cest

pauper n dyn tlawd, tlotyn

pause n saib, seibiant, hoe ♦ vi

aros, sefyll, ymbwyllo

pave vt palmantu

pavement n palmant, pafin

pavilion n pabell, pafiliwn

paw n palf, pawen ♦ vb palfu, pawennu

pawky adj direidus

pawn n gwystl, (CHESS) gwerin ♦ vt gwystlo

pay vb talu ♦ n tâl, cyflog, pae, hur. **back p.** ôl-dâl

payment n taliad, tâl

pea n pysen

peace n heddwch, tangnefedd ♦ excl gosteg!, ust!

peaceful adj heddychol, tangnefeddus, llonydd

peach n eirinen wlanog

peacock n paun

peak n pig; crib, copa; uchafbwynt

peal n sain clychau; twrf (taran) ♦ vb canu

peanut n cneuen ddaear

pear n gellygen

pearl n perl

peasant n gwladwr, gwerinwr

peasantry n gwerin

peat n mawn

pebble n carreg lefn, cerrigyn, grôyn

peck vb pigo, cnocellu ♦ n cnoc, pigiad

peculiar adj priod, priodol; hynod

peculiarity n hynodrwydd

pecuniary adj ariannol

pedagogue n athro plant, ysgolfeistr

pedal n pedal ♦ vb pedalu

pedant n pedant

pedantic adj pedantig

peddle vb pedlera

pedestal n troed, bôn, gwaelod

pedestrian adj ar draed, pedestrig ♦ n gŵr traed, cerddwr. **p. crossing** n croesfan

pedigree n ach, achau, bonedd

pedlar *n* pedler
pee *n* pisiad ♦ *vb* pisio
peel *n* pil, croen, rhisgl ♦ *vb* pilio, plicio, crafu
peep *vi* cipedrych, sbio ♦ *n* cipolwg, cip
peer *vi* ciledrych, syllu
peer *n* gogyfurdd, cydradd; pendefig
peevish *adj* anniddig, blin, piwis
peg *n* hoel bren, peg ♦ *vt* pegio
Peking *n* Peking
pelf *n* golud
pellet *n* peled, pelen, haelsen
pelt *vt* lluchio, taflu, peledu, baeddu
pelvis *n* pelfis
pen *n* pin, ysgrifbin ♦ *vt* ysgrifennu
pen *n* lloc, ffald, cwt ♦ *vt* ffaldio, llocio
penal *adj* penydiol
penalize *vb* cosbi
penalty *n* cosb, cosbedigaeth. **p. (kick)** *n* cic gosb
penance *n* penyd
pence *npl* ceiniogau, pres
pencil *n* pwyntil, pensel, pensil. **p. sharpener** *n* naddwr pensiliau
pendant *n* tlws
pending *prep* hyd, nes, yn ystod
pendulous *adj* yn hongian, yn siglo
pendulum *n* pendil
penetrate *vb* treiddio; dirnad
penfriend *n* cyfaill llythyru
penguin *n* pengwin
penicillin *n* penisilin
peninsula *n* gorynys
penis *n* cala, pidyn
penitence *n* edifeirwch
penitent *adj* edifar, edifarus, edifeiriol
penitentiary *n* carchar
penknife (**-knives**) *n* cyllell boced
pen name *n* ffug enw
pennant, pennon *n* penwn, banner
penniless *adj* heb geiniog
penny (**pence, pennies**) *n* ceiniog
pension *n* blwydd-dal, pensiwn
pensioner *n* pensiynwr
pensive *adj* synfyfyriol, meddylgar
pent *adj* wedi ei gau i mewn, caeth
Pentateuch *n* pumllyfr Moses
penult *n* goben
people *n* pobl, gwerin ♦ *vt* pobli, poblogi
pepper *n* pupur
peppermint *n* mintys poethion; botwm gwyn
per *prep* trwy, wrth, yn ôl
peradventure *adv* efallai
perceive *vt* canfod, gweld, dirnad, deall
percentage *n* hyn a hyn y cant, canran
perceptible *adj* canfyddadwy
perception *n* canfyddiad, canfod
perceptive *adj* yn gallu dirnad
perch *n* perc; clwyd ♦ *vb* clwydo
perchance *adv* efallai, hwyrach
percolate *vb* hidlo, diferu
percussion *n* trawiad, gwrthdrawiad. **p. band** seindorf daro
peremptory *adj* pendant, awdurdodol
perennial *adj* drwy'r flwyddyn; bythol, lluosflwydd
perfect *adj* perffaith ♦ *vt* perffeithio
perfection *n* perffeithrwydd
perfectly *adv* yn berffaith
perfervid *adj* brwd, tanbaid
perfidy *n* brad, dichell, ffalster
perforate *vt* tyllu
perforated *adj* tyllog
perforation *n* twll
perforce *adv* o orfod, drwy drais
perform *vb* cyflawni; chwarae, perfformio
performance *n* perfformiad

performer n perfformiwr

perfume n perarogl, persawr ♦ vt perarogli

perfunctory adj o raid, diofal, esgeulus

perhaps adv efallai, hwyrach, ond odid, dichon

peril n perygl, enbydrwydd

perimeter n amfesur, perimedr

period n cyfnod; cyfradran (miwsig); diweddnod; misglwyf

periodic adj cyfnodol

periodical n cyfnodolyn

peripatetic adj crwydrol, cylchynol, peripatetig

peripheral adj ymylol

periphery n ymylon, cylchfesur

periphrastic adj cwmpasog

perish vi colli, trengi, marw, darfod; llygru

periwinkle n gwichiad

perjure vt: **p. oneself** tyngu anudon

perjury n anudon, anudoniaeth

perk n mantais. **to p. up** bywhau, adfywio

perky adj bywiog, eofn, hyf

permanent adj parhaol, arhosol, sefydlog

permeate vt treiddio, trwytho

permissible adj wedi ei ganiatáu

permission n caniatâd, cennad

permissive adj goddefol. **the p. society** y gymdeithas oddefol

permit vb caniatáu ♦ n trwydded

peroration n diweddglo araith, perorasiwn

perpendicular adj syth, unionsyth

perpetrate vt cyflawni (rhyw ddrwg)

perpetual adj parhaol, parhaus, bythol

perpetuate vt parhau, anfarwoli

perplex vt drysu, cythryblu, trallodi

persecute vt erlid

persevere vi dyfalbarhau

persist vi dal ati; mynnu, taeru,

dyfalbarhau

persistent adj dyfal, taer, cyndyn, parhaus

person n person

personable adj golygus, prydweddol, hawddgar

personal adj personol. **p. assistant** n cynorthwyydd personol

personality n personoliaeth

personally adv yn bersonol

perspective n persbectif, safbwynt

perspiration n chwys

perspire vb chwysu

persuade vt darbwyllo, perswadio

pert adj eofn, tafodrydd

pertain vi perthyn

pertinent adj perthynol, cymwys

perturb vt cyffroi, aflonyddu, cythruddo

peruse vt darllen, chwilio

pervade vt treiddio, trwytho

perverse adj gwrthnysig, trofaus, croes

pervert vt gwyrdroi, llygru, camdroi ♦ n cyfeiliornwr

pessimism n pesimistiaeth

pessimist n pesimist

pest n pla, haint, poendod

pester vt blino, aflonyddu, poeni

pestilence n haint, pla

pet n anwylyn, ffafryn ♦ adj llywaeth, swci ♦ vt anwesu, canmol

petal n petal

petite adj bychan

petition n deisyfiad; deiseb, petisiwn

petitioner n deisebwr

petrel n aderyn drycin

petrified adj stond

petrify vb parlysu

petroleum n petroliwm

petrol pump n pwmp petrol

petrol station n gorsaf betrol

petticoat n pais

petty adj bach, bychan, mân, gwael

petulant adj anniddig, anfoddog, anynad

pew n eisteddle, côr, sedd

pewit, peewit n cornicyll, cornchwiglen

pewter n pfiwter

phantom n rhith, drychiolaeth

Pharisee n Pharisead

pharmacy n fferylliaeth; fferyllfa

pharynx n sefnig

phase n golwg, gwedd, agwedd; tro

pheasant n ceiliog coed, coediar, ffesant

phenomenon (-na) n ffenomen; rhyfeddod

phial n ffiol

philander vi gwamalio caru

philanthropist n dyngarwr

philanthropy n dyngarwch

Philippines n Pilipinas

Philistine n Philistiad

philology n ieitheg

philosopher n athronydd

philosophical adj athronyddol

philosophy n athroniaeth

phlegm n cornboer, llysnafedd, fflem

phlegmatic adj difraw, digyffro, diflyswyd

phobia n ffobia

phone n ffôn, teleffon ♦ vb ffonio.
p. book n cyfeiriadur ffôn. **p. box**
n caban ffôn. **p. call** n galwad ffôn

phonetic adj seinegol

phonetician n seinegydd

phonetics n seineg

phoney adj ffug

phonology n ffonoleg

phosphorus n ffosfforws

photocopier n llungopïydd

photocopy n llungopi ♦ vb
llungopïo

photograph n llun, ffotograff

photographer n ffotograffydd

photography n ffotograffiaeth

phrase n ymadrodd; cymal ♦ vt

geirio

phraseology n geiriad, geirweddiad

physical adj corfforol, materol; ffisegol. **p. education** n addysg gorfforol

physician n meddyg, ffisigwr

physicist n ffisegydd/wr

physics n ffiseg

physiology n ffisioleg

physiotherapy n ffisiotherapi

physique n corffolaeth, cyfansoddiad

piano n piano

pick n caib ♦ vb ceibio

pick vb pigo, dewis, dethol ♦ n
dewis

pickaxe n caib

picket n polyn, cledren; gwyliwr, gwyliadwriaeth, picedwr ♦ vb
picedu

pickle n picl, heli ♦ vt piclo, halltu

picnic n picnic

pickpocket n pigwr pocedi, codleidr

pictorial adj darluniadol

picture n llun, darlun, pictiwr. **p.
book** n llyfr lluniau

picturesque adj darluniaidd, gwych, byw

pie n pastai. **p. chart** n siart olwyn

piebald adj brith; brithryw

piece n darn, dryll, rhan ♦ vt
clytio, asio, uno

piecemeal adv bob yn damaid

pied adj brith, brithliw

pier n piler; pier

pierce vb brathu, gwanu, trywanu

piety n duwioldeb

piffle n lol, oferedd, gwegi

pig n mochyn ♦ vb porchellu, bwrw perchyll

pigeon n colomen

pigeonhole n cloer

pigeon-house n colomendy

piggy bank n cadw-mi-gei, blwch cynilo

pig-headed adj pendew, ystyfnig

pigment n paent, lliw

pigsty n twlc mochyn

pigtail n pleth

pike n gwaywffon; penhwyad

pile n crug, pentwr ♦ vt pentyrru

pile n pawl, cledr

pile n blew, ceden

piles npl clwyf y marchogion

pilfer vb chwiwladrata

pilgrim n pererin

pilgrimage n pererindod

pill n pelen, pilsen

pillage n ysbail, anrhaith ♦ vt ysbeilio, anrheithio

pillar n colofn, piler. **p. box** n bocs postio

pillion n sgil

pillory n rhigod, pilwri

pillow n gobennydd, clustog. **p. case** n cas gobennydd

pilot n cyfarwyddwr llongau, peilot

pimple n ploryn, tosyn

pin n pin ♦ vt pinio, hoelio

pinafore n brat, piner

pincers npl gefel, pinsiwrn

pinch vb pinsio, gwasgu; cynilo ♦ n pins, pinsiad; gwasgfa, cyfyngder

pincushion n pincas, pincws

pine n pinwydden

pine vi dihoeni, nychu, curio

pineapple n afal pîn

pinion n asgell, adain ♦ vt torri esgyll

pink adj, n pinc

pinpoint vb pinbwyntio

pint n peint

pioneer n arloeswr, arloesydd

pious adj duwiol, duwiolfrydig, crefyddol

pip n hedyn afal, etc

pipe n pib, pibell ♦ vb canu pibell

piping adj: **p. hot** chwilboeth

piquant adj pigog, llym, tost

pique vt llidio, cyffroi; ymfalchïo ♦ n soriant

pirate n môr-leidr

piss vb pisio

pissed adj meddw

pistol n llawddryll, pistol

pit n pwll, pydew ♦ vt pyllu. **coal p.** pwll glo

pitch n pyg ♦ vt pygu

pitch vb bwrw; gosod; taro (tôn) ♦ n gradd, mesur, traw

pitcher n piser, ystên, cawg

pitchfork n picfforch, picwarch; seinfforch

piteous adj truenus, gresynus

pitfall n magl, perygl

pith n bywyn; mwydion; mêr; grym, sylwedd

pithy adj cryno, cynhwysfawr

pitiful adj truenus, tosturiol

pitiless adj didostur, didrugaredd

pittance n dogn, cyfran (annigonol)

pity n tosturi, trueni, gresyn ♦ vt tosturio, gresynu

pivot n colyn, pegwn

placable adj cymodlon, hynaws

placard n murlen, hysbyslen

placate vt cymodi, heddychu, dyhuddo

place n lle, man, mangre ♦ vt cyflew, gosod. **to take p.** digwydd. **in the first p.** yn y lle cyntaf

placid adj araf, tawel, llonydd

plagiary n llên-ladrad; llên-leidr

plague n pla, haint ♦ vt poeni, blino

plaice n lleden

plaid n plod

plain adj plaen, eglur ♦ n gwastadedd

plaintiff n achwynwr, hawlydd

plait n pleth ♦ vt plethu

plan n cynllun, plan ♦ vt cynllunio, planio

plane adj, n gwastad, lefel

plane n plaen; awyren ♦ vt plaenio

planet n planed

plank n astell, estyllen, planc

planning n cynllunio. **p. permission** n caniatâd cynllunio

plant n planhigyn, llysieuyn; offer; ffatri ♦ vt plannu

plaster n plaster ♦ vt plastro

plastic n, adj plastig. **p. bag** cwdyn plastig

plat n darn o dir, clwt, lawnt

plate n plat; llestri aur, etc ♦ vt golchi â metel

plateau n gwastatir uchel

platform n llwyfan, esgynlawr

platitude n sylw hen a diflas, gwireb

platoon n platŵn

platter n plat, dysgl, noe

plaudit n banllef o gymeradwyaeth

plausible adj teg neu resymol yr olwg, ffals

play vb chwarae; canu (offeryn) ♦ n chwarae

player n chwaraewr

playful adj chwareus

playground n chwaraele

playgroup n grŵp chwarae

playing field n maes chwarae

plaything n tegan

playwright n dramodydd

plea n ple, dadl, hawl; esgus

plead vb pledio, dadlau, eiriol, ymbil

pleasant adj hyfryd, pleserus, difyr, siriol

please vb boddhau, boddio, rhyngu bodd. **if you p.** os gwelwch yn dda

pleased adj boddhaus, bodlon, hapus. **p. to meet you** mae'n dda gen i gwrdd â chi

pleasing adj dymunol

pleasure n pleser, hyfrydwch

pleat n plet, pleten ♦ vt pletio

plebeian n gwerinwr, gwrêng

plebiscite n pleidlais y bobl

pledge n gwystl, ernes ♦ vt gwystlo

plenary adj llawn, cyflawn, diamodol

plenty n digon, helaethrwydd

plethora n gorgyflawnder

pleurisy n eisglwyf, plewrisi

pliable, pliant adj ystwyth, hyblyg

pliers npl gefel fechan

plight n cyflwr, drych, anghyflwr

plight vt addo, gwystlo

plod vb troedio, ymlafnio, llafurio, slafio

plot n darn o dir; brad, cynllwyn; cynllun, plot, ystofiad ♦ vb cynllwyn; cynllunio

plotter n cynllwynwr

plough n aradr, gwŷdd ♦ vb aredig, troi

ploy n cynllun, strategaeth

pluck vt tynnu; pluo ♦ n glewder

plucky adj dewr, gwrol, glew

plug n topyn, plwg ♦ vt topio, plygio

plum n eirinen

plumage n plu

plumber n plymwr

plumbing n gwaith plymwr

plume n pluen, plufyn ♦ vt pluo, plufio

plummet n plymen

plump adj tew, llyfndew, graenus ♦ vb pleidleisio i un (yn unig)

plunder n ysbail, anrhaith ♦ vt ysbeilio, anrheithio

plunge n plymiad ♦ vb plymio, trochi, bwrw

pluperfect adj gorberffaith

plural adj lluosog

plus n plws, ychwaneg ♦ prep, adj ychwanegol

plush n plwsh

ply vb arfer, defnyddio, gyrru; poeni

plywood n pren haenog (tair-haen, pum-haen)

pneumatic adj â'i lond o wynt, awyrog

pneumonia n llid yr ysgyfaint, niwmonia

poach vb herwhela, potsio

poach vt berwi (wy) heb ei blisg

poacher n herwheliwr, potsiwr

pock n brech, ôl brech

pocket n poced, llogell ♦ vt pocedu. **p. knife** cyllell boced. **p. money** arian poced

pod n coden, plisgyn, masgl, cibyn

podgy adj byrdew

poem n cerdd, cân

poet n bardd, prydydd

poetry n barddoniaeth, prydyddiaeth

poignant adj llym, tost, ingol, aethus, awchlym

point n pwynt; man; blaen ♦ vb pwyntio; blaenllymu; dangos. **p. of view** n safbwynt. **to be on the p.** of doing sth bod ar fin gwneud rhywbeth. **to get the p.** deall. **there's no p.** (in doing) does dim diben gwneud. **to p.** out nodi

pointed adj pigfain

pointedly adv yn llym

pointer n cyfeirydd; mynegfys

pointless adj dibwynt, diystyr, gwag

poise vb mantoli; hofran ♦ n ystum, osgo

poison n gwenwyn ♦ vt gwenwyno

poisoning n gwenwyno

poisonous adj gwenwynig

poke vb gwthio, pwnio, procio

poker n pocer

poky adj cyfyng, gwael

polar adj pegynol

pole n pawl, polyn; pegwn

polemic adj dadleuol ♦ n dadl

police n heddlu. **p. car** n car heddlu. **p. station** n gorsaf heddlu

policeman n heddwas, heddgeidwad, plismon

policewoman n heddferch, plismones

policy n polisi

polish vb cwyro, caboli, gloywi, llathru ♦ n cwyr

polite adj moesgar, boneddigaidd

politic adj call, cyfrwys, doeth, buddiol

political adj gwleidyddol

politician n gwleidydd, gwleidyddwr

politics n gwleidyddiaeth

poll n pen, copa; pôl ♦ vb cneifio; pleidleisio, polio. **p. tax** treth y pen, treth gymunedol

pollen n paill

polling booth n bwth pleidleisio

polling day n dydd pleidleisio

polling station n gorsaf bleidleisio

pollute vt halogi, difwyno, llygru

pollution n llygredd

polo neck n jersi polo

polygamy n amlwreigiaeth

polysyllable n gair lluosill

polytechnic n polytechnig

pomegranate n pomgranad

pomp n rhwysg

pompous adj rhwysgfawr, balch

pond n llyn, pwll

ponder vb ystyried, myfyrio, pwyso

ponderous adj pwysfawr, trwm

pong n drewdod

pontiff n archoffeiriad; y Pab

pontoon n ysgraff

pony n merlyn, poni, merlen. **p. trekking** merlota

pooh excl pw!

pool n pwll, llyn

pool n cronfa; pwll ♦ vt cydgyfrannu

poor adj tlawd, truan, gwael, sâl

poorly adj sâl, gwael, claf

pop vb ffrwydro, ysgortio; picio; plannu, taro

pope n pab

popery n pabyddiaeth

pop-gun n gwn clats

poplar n poplysen

poppy n pabi (coch), llygad y bwgan

populace n gwerin, gwerinos

popular adj poblogaidd

population n poblogaeth
populous adj poblog
porcelain n porslen
porch n porth, cyntedd
porcine adj mochaidd
porcupine n ballasg
pore n twll chwys
pore vi astudio, myfyrio, synfyfyrio
pork n cig moch, porc
porker n mochyn, porcyn
porous adj tyllog
porpoise n llamhidydd
porridge n uwd
port n porth, porthfa, porthladd
port n ochr aswy llong wrth edrych ymlaen
port n gwin Oporto, gwin coch
portable adj cludadwy
portcullis n porthcwlis
portent n argoel; rhyfeddod, gwyrth
porter n porthor
portfolio n cas papurau, portffolio; swydd
porthole n ffenestr llong; gyndwll
portion n rhan, cyfran, gwaddol
portly adj tew, corffol
portrait n llun, darlun
portray vt portreadu, darlunio
Portugal n Portiwgal
pose vb sefyll, ymddangos, cymryd ar ♦ n ystum, rhodres
posh adj hardd, coeth
position n safle, sefyllfa, swydd
positive adj cadarnhaol, pendant, posidiol
posse n mintai, torf
possess vt meddu, meddiannu
possession n meddiant
possessor n perchen, perchennog
possibility n posibilrwydd
possible adj posibl, dichonadwy
possibly adv dichon, efallai
post n post, cledr ♦ vt gosod, cyhoeddi
post n post, llythyrfa; safle, swydd

♦ vb postio
post- prefix wedi, ar ôl
postage n cludiad (llythyr, etc.)
postal adj post
postal order n archeb bost
postbox n bocs postio
postcard n cerdyn post
postcode n côd post
poster n hysbyslen, poster
posterior adj ar ôl, ôl
posterity n cenedlaethau'r dyfodol, hiliogaeth
postgraduate adj graddedig
posthumous adj ar ôl marw
postman n postmon
postmark n postfarc
postmaster n postfeistr
post office n llythyrdy, swyddfa'r post
postpone vt gohirio, oedi
postscript n ôl-ysgrif
posture n agwedd, ystum, osgo
postwar adj ar ôl y rhyfel
posy n blodeuglwm, pwysi
pot n pot, potyn; crochan ♦ vb potio
potato (-oes) n taten, pytaten
potency n nerth, grym
potent adj cryf, galluog, grymus, nerthol
potential adj dichonadwy, dichonol ♦ n potensial
pothole n ceubwll
potion n dogn, llymaid, llwnc
pottage n cawl, potes
potter n crochenydd
potter vb diogi, ymdroi, sefyllian, swmera
pottery n llestri pridd; gwaith llestri pridd; priddweithfa
potty n pot
pouch n cod, coden, cwd ♦ vb cydu
poultice n powltis
poultry n dofednod, ffowls
pounce vb disgyn ar, dyfod ar warthaf
pound n pwys; punt

pound n ffald ♦ vt ffaldio
pound vb pwyo, pwnio, malu, malurio
pour vb tywallt, arllwys; bwrw
pout vi pwdu, sorri, terru, monni
poverty n tlodi
poverty-stricken adj tlawd, llwm
powder n powdr, llwch, pylor ♦ vt powdro
powdered milk n llaeth powdr
powder room n ystafell bincio
power n gallu, nerth, grym, awdurdod; pŵer
power cut n toriad yn y cyflenwad
power failure n pall ar y cyflenwad
powerful adj nerthol, grymus
powerless adj dirym
power station n pwerdy
pox n brech
practicable adj dichonadwy
practical adj ymarferol
practice n arfer, arferiad, ymarferiad
practise vb arfer, ymarfer
practising adj ymarferol; yn dilyn ei swydd
practitioner n meddyg; cyfreithiwr
prairie n gwastatir, gweundir, paith
praise vt canmol, moli ♦ n canmoliaeth, mawl
pram n coets, pram
prance vi prancio
prank n cast, ystranc, pranc
prawn n corgimwch
pray vb gweddïo. **I p. thee** atolwg
prayer n gweddi
pre- prefix cyn-, rhag-, blaen-
preach vb pregethu
preacher n pregethwr
preamble n rhagymadrodd, rhaglith
precarious adj ansicr, peryglus, enbyd
precaution n rhagofal, rhagocheliad, gofal

precede vb blaenori, blaenu, rhagflaenu
precedence n blaenoriaeth
precedent n cynsail
precentor n arweinydd y gân, codwr canu
preceptor n athro, hyfforddwr
precinct n cyffin, rhodfa
precious adj gwerthfawr, prid, drud
precipice n dibyn, diffwys, clogwyn
precipitate vt bwrw, hyrddio ♦ vi gwaddodi, gwaelodi ♦ adj byrbwyll, anystyriol
précis n crynodeb
precise adj penodol, manwl
preclude vt cau allan, atal, rhwystro
precocious adj hen o'i oed, henaidd, henffel
precondition n rhagamod
precursor n rhagredegydd, rhagflaenydd
predatory adj anrheithgar, ysglyfaethus
predecessor n rhagflaenydd
predestination n rhagarfaethiad
predicament n cyflwr, helynt, sefyllfa
predicate vt haeru, honni ♦ n traethiad
predict vt rhagfynegi, rhagddywedyd, proffwydo
predilection n hoffter, tuedd, tueddfryd
predominate vi bod yn bennaf neu yn fwyaf, arglwyddiaethu, rhagori
pre-eminent adj ar y blaen i bawb
preen vb pincio, harddu
preface n rhagymadrodd, rhaglith
prefect n rhaglaw; swyddog
prefer vt dewis yn hytrach, bod yn well gan
preferable adj gwell
preference n dewis, hoffter,

ffafraeth, blaenoriaeth
preferential *adj* ffafriol
preferment *n* dyrchafiad, codiad
prefix *vt* rhagddodi ♦ *n* rhagddodiad
pregnancy *n* beichiogaeth
pregnant *adj* beichiog, llawn
prehistoric *adj* cynhanesol
prejudice *n* rhagfarn; niwed ♦ *vt* rhagfarnu, niweidio
prejudiced *adj* rhagfarnllyd
prelate *n* esgob, prelad
preliminary *adj* arweiniol, rhagarweiniol
prelude *n* rhagarweiniad; preliwd (cerdd.)
premarital *adj* cyn priodi
premature *adj* anaeddfed, cynamserol
premier *adj* blaenaf, pennaf, prif ♦ *n* prifweinidog
première *n* blaenberfformiad
premise *n* rhagosodiad; (*pl*) adeiladau, *etc* ♦ *vt* rhagosod
premium *n* gwobr, tâl, taliad
preoccupied *adj* wedi ymgolli
preoccupy *vt* rhagfeddiannu; llenwi, ymgolli
prepaid *adj* wedi ei dalu ymlaen llaw, rhagdalwyd
preparation *n* paratoad, darpariaeth
preparatory *adj* rhagbaratoawl
prepare *vb* paratoi, darparu, darbod, arlwyo
prepared *adj* parod; effro
preposition *n* arddodiad
preposterous *adj* afresymol, gwrthun
prerequisite *n* rhaganghenraid
prerogative *n* braint, rhagorfraint
presage *n* argoel, rhagargoel ♦ *vt* argoeli
presbyter *n* henuriad, offeiriad
Presbyterian *adj* Henadurol, Presbyteraidd ♦ *n* Presbyteriad
presbytery *n* henaduriaeth; tŷ

offeiriad Pabyddol
prescience *n* rhagwybodaeth
prescribe *vb* gorchymyn, cyfarwyddo
prescription *n* cyngor, cyfarwyddyd, presgripsiwn
presence *n* gwydd, presenoldeb
present *adj*, *n* presennol
present *n* anrheg ♦ *vt* anrhegu; cyflwyno; dangos
presentiment *n* rhagargoel
presently *adv* yn fuan
preserve *vt* cadw, diogelu ♦ *n* jam
preside *vi* llywyddu
president *n* llywydd, arlywydd
press *vb* gwasgu ♦ *n* gwasg; gwrŷf; cwpwrdd
pressing *adj* taer, dwys
pressure *n* gwasgiad, gwasgfa, pwys
prestige *n* bri, dylanwad, braint
presumable *adj* y gellir ei dybio
presumably *adv* yn ôl pob tebyg, gellid tybio
presume *vb* tybio, tebygu; beiddio, rhyfygu
presumption *n* rhyfyg; tyb
presumptuous *adj* rhyfygus
pretence *n* rhith, esgus, ffug
pretend *vb* ffugio, cymryd ar, cogio; proffesu; honni hawl
pretension *n* honiad, hawl
preter- *prefix* tu hwnt i, mwy na
pretext *n* esgus, cochl
pretty *adj* tlws, del, pert ♦ *adv* cryn, go
prevail *vi* tycio, ffynnu; gorfod, trechu
prevalent *adj* cyffredin; nerthol
prevent *vt* rhagflaenu; atal, rhwystro
preview *n* rhagolwg
previous *adj* blaenorol, cynt
prey *n* ysglyfaeth, aberth ♦ *vi* ysglyfaethu
price *n* pris, gwerth ♦ *vt* prisio. **p. list** *n* rhestr prisiau, taflen

brisiau; telerau *npl*

prick *n* pigyn, swmbwl ♦ *vb* pigo; picio, codi

prickle *n* draen ♦ *vb* pigo, tymhigo

pride *n* balchder ♦ *vt* balchïo, ymfalchïo

priest *n* offeiriad

priesthood *n* offeiriadaeth

prig *n* sychfoesolyn, mursennwr, coethyn

prim *adj* cymen, cymhenllyd

primary *adj* prif, cyntaf, cysefin; cynradd. **p. school** *n* ysgol gynradd

primate *n* archesgob

prime *adj* prif, cyntaf; gorau ♦ *n* anterth

prime *vt* llwytho, llenwi, cyflenwi

primer *n* llyfr cyntaf, cynlyfr

primeval *adj* cynoesol, cyntefig

primitive *adj* cyntefig; garw, amrwd

primordial *adj* cyntefig, cysefin

primrose *n* briallen, (*pl*) briallu

prince *n* tywysog

principal *adj* prif ♦ *n* pen; prifathro; corff

principality *n* tywysogaeth

principle *n* egwyddor, elfen

print *n* argraff, print, ôl ♦ *vb* argraffu, printio

printed *adj* argraffedig, wedi ei argraffu

prior *adj* cynt, blaenorol ♦ *n* prior, priol

priority *n* blaenoriaeth

priory *n* priordy, mynachdy

prise, prize *n* dryllio'n agored â throsol

prism *n* prism

prison *n* carchar, carchardy

prisoner *n* carcharor

pristine *adj* hen, cyntefig, cysefin

private *adj* preifat, cyfrinachol, personol. **p. enterprise** *n* ymroddiad unigol

privation *n* amddifadrwydd, diffyg

privilege *n* braint, rhagorfraint

privy *adj* dirgel, cudd, cyfrin ♦ *n* geudy

prize *n* gwobr ♦ *vt* prisio, gwerthfawrogi

prize *n* ysbail, caffaeliad, gwobr

pro- *prefix* am, yn lle; o blaid

probability *n* tebygolrwydd

probable *adj* tebygol, tebyg

probate *n* prawf ewyllys

probation *n* prawf

probe *n* profiedydd ♦ *vt* profi, chwilio

probity *n* uniondeb, cywirdeb

problem *n* pwnc, drysbwnc, problem

procedure *n* trefn, arfer, defod, dull

proceed *vi* myned, deillio, tarddu; erlyn ♦ *n* (*pl*) enillion, elw

process *n* gweithrediad, goruchwyliaeth, dull

procession *n* gorymdaith; deilliad

proclaim *vt* cyhoeddi, datgan

proclamation *n* cyhoeddiad, proclamasiwn

proclivity *n* gogwydd, tuedd

proconsul *n* rhaglaw

procrastinate *vi* oedi, gohirio

procreate *vt* cenhedlu

procure *vb* ceisio, caffael, cael

prod *vt* pigo, pwnio, symbylu

prodigal *adj* afradlon, hael

prodigious *adj* aruthrol, anferth

prodigy *n* rhyfeddod, gwyrth

produce *vt* cynhyrchu, epilio; dwyn ♦ *n* cynnyrch, ffrwyth

product *n* cynnyrch, ffrwyth

production *n* cynhyrchiad; (*pl*) cynhyrchion

profane *adj* anghysegredig, halogedig ♦ *vt* anghysegru, halogi

profess *vb* proffesu, arddel

profession *n* proffes, galwedigaeth

professional *adj* proffesiynol

professor *n* proffeswr; athro

proffer *vt*, *n* cynnig

proficient adj hyddysg, cyfarwydd

profile n ystlyslun, cernlun

profit n budd, lles, elw, proffid ♦ vb llesáu, proffidio

profiteer vi gwneud elw

profligate adj afradlon, ofer

profound adj dwfn, dwys, angerddol

profundity n dyfnder

profuse adj hael, helaeth, toreithiog

progenitor n cyndad

progeny n hil, epil, hiliogaeth

prognostic n argoel, rhagarwydd

programme n rhaglen

progress n cynnydd; taith ♦ vi cynyddu

progressive adj cynyddgar, progresif

prohibit vt gwahardd

project n bwriad, cynllun; project

project vb bwrw; bwriadu; ymestyn; taflunio (ffilm)

projectile n teflyn

projector n taflunydd

proletariat n gwerin, gwrêng

prolific adj epiliog, ffrwythlon, toreithiog

prolix adj maith, amleiriog

prologue n rhagair, prolog

prolong vt hwyhau, estyn

promenade n rhodfa ♦ vb rhodianna

prominent adj yn sefyll allan, amlwg

promise n addewid ♦ vb addo, argoeli

promissory adj addewidiol

promontory n pentir, penrhyn

promote vt hyrwyddo, meithrin, dyrchafu

promoter n hyrwyddwr

prompt adj parod, buan ♦ vt cofweini; cymell

promptitude n parodrwydd

promulgate vt cyhoeddi, lledaenu

prone adj â'i wyneb i waered; tueddol

prong n fforch, pig fforch

pronominal adj rhagenwol

pronoun n rhagenw

pronounce vb cynanu, yngan; cyhoeddi, datgan

pronunciation n cynaniad

proof n prawf; profien

prop n ateg, post, prop ♦ vt ategu

propaganda n propaganda

propagate vt epilio, cenhedlu; lledaenu

propel vt gyrru ymlaen, gwthio

propensity n tuedd, tueddfryd, gogwydd

proper adj priod, priodol, gweddus

property n priodoledd; eiddo; priodwedd (cemeg)

prophecy n proffwydoliaeth

prophesy vb proffwydo

prophet n proffwyd

propinquity n agosrwydd, cyfnesafrwydd

propitiate vt cymodi, dyhuddo

propitiation n cymod, iawn

propitious adj tirion, ffafriol

proportion n cyfartaledd, cyfrannedd

proportional adj cyfrannol

proportionate adj cymesur

proposal n cynnig

propose vb cynnig, bwriadu

proposition n cynigiad; gosodiad

propound vt cynnig, gosod gerbron

proprietor n perchen, perchennog

propriety n priodoldeb, gwedduster

propulsion n gwthiad, gyriad

prorogue vt gohirio

prosaic adj rhyddieithol, cyffredin

proscribe vt deol, diarddel, gwahardd

prose n rhyddiaith

prosecute vt erlyn, dilyn, dwyn ymlaen

prosecutor n erlynydd

proselyte n proselyt

prosody n mydryddiaeth

prospect n rhagolwg, golwg, golygfa

prospectus n rhaglen, hysbyslen, prosbectws

prosper vb llwyddo, tycio, ffynnu

prosperity n llwyddiant, hawddfyd, ffyniant

prostitute n putain ♦ vt darostwng

prostrate adj yn gorwedd ar ei wyneb; ar lawr yn lân ♦ vt bwrw i lawr; ymgrymu

protect vt amddiffyn, noddi

protection n amddiffyn, nawdd, diogelwch

protective adj amddiffynnol

protector n amddiffynnydd

protest n vb gwrthdystio ♦ n gwrthdystiad

prototype n cynddelw, cynllun

protract vt estyn, hwyhau

protrude vb gwthio allan

protuberance n chwydd

proud adj balch

prove vb profi

provender n ebran, gogor, porthiant

proverb n dihareb

provide vt darparu

providence n rhagluniaeth, darbodaeth

provident adj darbodus

providential adj rhagluniaethol

province n talaith, tiriogaeth; cylch, maes

provision n darpariaeth. **provisions** npl darbodion; ymborth

proviso n amod

provocation n anogaeth, cyffroad, cythrudd

provoke vt annog, cyffroi, cythruddo, profocio

provost n maer, profost

prow n pen blaen bad neu long

prowess n dewrder, glewder, grymuster

prowl vi ysglyfaetha, prowlan

proximate adj nesaf, agos at; agos

proximity n agosrwydd

proxy n dirprwy

prude n mursen, coegen

prudence n pwyll, synnwyr, callineb

prudent adj pwyllog, synhwyrol, call, doeth

prune n eirinen sech

Prussia n Prwsia

pry vi chwilota, chwilenna

psalm n salm

psalmody n caniadaeth y cysegr, salmdyddiaeth

psalter n llyfr salmau, sallwyr

pseudo- prefix gau, ffug

pseudonym n ffugenw

pshaw excl wfft, pw, och, ffei

psychiatrist n seiciatrydd

psychological adj seicolegol, meddyliol

psychology n seicoleg

puberty n aeddfedrwydd oed, blaenlencyndod, puberdod

public adj cyhoeddus ♦ n y cyhoedd. **p. house** n tŷ tafarn. **p. library** n llyfrgell gyhoeddus

publican n publican; tafarnwr

publicity n cyhoeddusrwydd

publish vt cyhoeddi

pucker vb crychu, crybachu

pudding n pwdin

puddle n corbwll; pydew, llaca

puerile adj bachgennaidd, plentynnaidd

puff n pwff, chwa, chwyth ♦ vb pwffio, chwythu

pugilist n paffiwr, ymladdwr

pugnacious adj ymladdgar, cwerylgar

puissant adj galluog, grymus, nerthol

pull vt tynnu ♦ n tynfa, tyniad

pullet n cywen

pulley n chwerfan, troell, pwli

pullover n gwasgod wlân

pulmonary adj ysgyfeiniol

pulp n bywyn, mwydion

pulpit n pulpud

pulsate vb curo (megis y galon)

pulse n curiad y galon, curiad y gwaed

pulse n pys, ffa, etc

pulverize vt malu yn llwch, chwilfriwio

pummel vt pwnio, dyrnodio, curo

pump n sugnedydd, pwmp ♦ vb pwmpio

pumpkin n pwmpen

pun n gair mwys, mwysair

punch n pwns; dyrnod ♦ vb pwnsio, dyrnodio

punctilious adj cysetlyd, gorfanwl

punctual adj prydlon

punctuate vt atalnodi

puncture n twll ♦ vt tyllu

pundit n ysgolhaig, doethwr

pungent adj llym, llymdost, siarp

punish vt cosbi, ceryddu; poeni

punishment n cosb, cosbedigaeth

punitive adj cosbol

puny adj eiddil, bychan, tila, pitw

pupil n ysgolhaig, ysgolor, disgybl; cannwyll llygad

puppet n delw, dol, pyped; gwas

puppy n ci bach

purblind adj cibddall, coegddall

purchase vt prynu, pwrcasu ♦ n pryniant, pwrcas

pure adj pur, noeth

purgative adj carthol ♦ n carthlyn

purgatory n purdan

purge vt puro, glanhau, carthu, coethi ♦ n carthlyn

purification n puredigaeth

purify vt puro, coethi, glanhau

Puritan n Piwritan

purity n purdeb

purl n crychleisio, byrlymu

purlieu n cyffin, ffin, cymdogaeth

purloin vt lladrata, dwyn

purple adj, n porffor

purport n ystyr, rhediad, ergyd ♦ vt arwyddo, proffesu, honni

purpose n pwrpas, bwriad, arfaeth ♦ vt bwriadu, arfaethu

purr vb canu crwth, grwnan

purse n pwrs, cod ♦ vb crychu

pursue vb dilyn, erlyn, erlid, ymlid

pursuit n ymlidiad; ymchwil, gorchwyl

purulent adj crawnllyd, gorllyd

purvey vb darparu lluniaeth, darmerth

purview n amcan, maes, cylch

pus n crawn, gôr

push vb gwthio ♦ n gwth, ysgwd; ymdrech

pushchair n coets

puss n titw, pws; ysgyfarnog

pustule n ploryn, llinoryn

put vb gosod, dodi, rhoddi, rhoi

putative adj tybiedig, cyfrifedig

putrefaction n pydredd, madredd

putrefy vb pydru, madru

putrid adj pwdr, mall

putty n pwti ♦ vt pwtio

puzzle n dryswch, penbleth, pos ♦ vb drysu, pysio

pygmy n corrach

pyjamas npl gwisg nos, gŵn nos

pyramid n pyramid, bera

pyre n cynnau angladdol, coelcerth

pyrotechnic adj, n (o natur) tân gwyllt

Q

quack n crachfeddyg, cwac

quack vi cwacian

quadrangle n pedrongl

quadrant n cwadrant

quadruped n pedwarcarnol

quadruple adj pedwarplyg

quadruplet n pedrybled

quaff vb drachtio, cofftio, yfed

quagmire n siglen, cors, mignen, sybwll

quail n sofliar

quaint adj od, henffasiwn

quake vi crynu

Quaker n Crynwr

qualification n cymhwyster; cymhwysiad

qualified adj cymwys

qualify vt cymhwyso, cyfaddasu

quality n ansawdd, rhinwedd

qualm n petruster, amheuaeth

quandary n penbleth, cyfyng-gyngor

quantity n swm, maint, mesur

quarantine n cwarant, neilltuaeth

quarrel n ymrafael, ffrae, cweryl ♦ vi ffraeo

quarry n chwarel, cloddfa, cwar ♦ vb cloddio

quarry n ysglyfaeth

quart n chwart, cwart

quarter n chwarter, cwarter; cwr, man; trugaredd; (pl.) llety. **a q. of an hour** chwarter awr. **q. final** rownd gogynderfynol. **quarter-sessions** n llys chwarter

quartet, -te n pedwarawd

quarto adj, n (llyfr) pedwarplyg

quartz n creigrisial, cwarts

quash vt diddymu, dirymu

quaver vi cwafrio, crynu ♦ n cwafer

quay n cei

queen n brenhines

queer adj od, hynod, digrif, ysmala

quell vt llonyddu, gostegu, darostwng

quench vt diffodd, dofi, torri

quern n llawfelin, breuan

querulous adj cwynfanllyd, blin

query n holiad, gofyniad ♦ vb holi, amau

quest n ymchwil, ymchwiliad, cwest

question n gofyniad, cwestiwn ♦ vt holi, amau

questionable adj amheus

question mark n gofynnod

questionnaire n holiadur

queue n cynffon, cwt, ciw

quibble n geirddadl, mân-ddadl ♦ vi geirddadlau, mân-ddadlau, hollti blew

quick adj byw; buan, cyflym, clau. **to the q.** i'r byw

quicken vb cyflymu

quicksilver n arian byw

quid n punt

quiescent adj distaw, llonydd, digyffro

quiet adj llonydd, tawel, distaw ♦ n llonyddwch, tawelwch ♦ vt llonyddu, tawelu

quill n pluen, plufyn, cwilsyn

quilt n cwilt, cwrlid ♦ vt cwiltio

quintet n pumawd

quintuplet n pumled

quip n gair ffraeth, ateb parod

quit vt gadael, symud ♦ adj rhydd

quits adj yn gyfartal

quite adv cwbl, llwyr, hollol

quiver n cawell saethau

quiver vi crynu, dirgrynu

quixotic adj mympwyol, gwyllt

quiz vt holi, pysio, profocio

quoit n coeten, coetan

quondam adj wedi bod, gynt, hen

quorum n nifer gofynnol, corwm

quota n rhan, cyfran, dogn, cwota

quotation n dyfyniad; prisiant

quote vt dyfynnu; nodi (prisiau)

quoth vt meddai, ebe

R

rabbi n rabi

rabbit n cwningen

rabble n ciwed, tyrfa ddireol

rabid adj cynddeiriog

rabies n y cynddaredd

race n ras, gyrfa, rhedfa ♦ vi rasio

race n hil

racial adj hiliol

racism n hiliaeth

rack n rac, clwyd, rhestl; arteithglwyd ♦ vt arteithio, dirdynnu

racket n twrf, mwstwr; raced (tennis etc.)

racy adj blasus; arab, ffraeth

radiant adj disglair, llachar, tanbaid

radiate vb pelydru, rheiddio

radiation n ymbelydredd

radiator n rheiddiadur

radical adj gwreiddiol, cynhenid; trylwyr ♦ n rhyddfrydwr, radical

radio n radio

radioactive adj ymbelydrol

radio station n gorsaf radio

radish n rhuddygl, radis

radius (-ii) n cylch; radius

raffle n raffl

raft n cludair, ysgraff, rafft

rafter n tulath, ceibren, trawst

rag n carp, clwt

rag doll n doli glwt

rage n cynddaredd ♦ vi terfysgu, cynddeiriogi

ragged adj carpiog, bratiog

raid n rhuthr, cyrch ♦ vb anrheithio, ysbeilio

rail n canllaw, cledren, rheilen ♦ vb cledru

rail vi difrïo, difenwi, cablu

raillery n difyrrwch, cellwair

railway n rheilffordd. r. station n gorsaf reilffordd

raiment n dillad, gwisg

rain n glaw ♦ vb glawio, bwrw glaw

rainbow n enfys

raincoat n cot law

rainy adj glawog

raise vt codi, cyfodi, dyrchafu

raisin n rhesinen

rake n cribin, rhaca ♦ vb cribinio, crafu, rhacanu

rally vb atgynnull; adgyfnerthu, gwella ♦ n cynuliad

ram n hwrdd, maharen ♦ vt hyrddio, pwnio

ramble vi gwibio, crwydro ♦ n gwib

rampant adj uchel ei ben, rhonc

rampart n caer, rhagfur, gwrthglawdd

ramshackle adj bregus, candryll

rancid adj â blas cryf arno, drewllyd

rancour n digasedd, chwerwder

random n antur, siawns, damwain ♦ adj damweiniol

range n amrediad; cwmpas; ystod; lle tân â ffwrn ♦ vb rhestru, cyfleu; crwydro

ranger n coedwigwr, ceidwad parc

rank n rheng, gradd ♦ vb rhestru. the r. and file y bobl gyffredin

rank adj mws; gwyllt, bras; rhonc, noeth

rankle vi gori, madru; cnoi, llidio

ransack vt chwilio, chwilota, ysbeilio

ransom n pridwerth ♦ vt prynu, gwaredu

rant vi bragaldian, brygawthan

rap n cnoc, ergyd ♦ vt cnocio, curo

rap n gronyn, mymryn, blewyn

rapacious adj rheibus, ysglyfaethus

rape vt treisio ♦ n trais

rapid adj cyflym, buan, chwyrn, gwyllt

rapist n treisiwr

rapture n perlewyg, gorawen, afiaith

rare adj anaml, prin; godidog; tenau

rascal n dihiryn, cnaf, gwalch, cenau

rash adj byrbwyll, rhyfygus, anystyriol

rash n brech, tarddiant

rasher n ysglisen, sleisen, tafell, golwyth

rasp vb rhasglio, crafu, rhygnu

raspberry n afanen, mafonen

rat n llygoden fawr, llygoden ffrengig ♦ vi llygota

rate vt ffraeo, dwrdio, dweud y drefn

rate n cyflymder; treth; cyfradd *(of interest)*

rateable value n gwerth trethiannol

ratepayer n trethdalwr

rather adv braidd, hytrach, go, lled

ratify vt cadarnhau

ratio n cyfartaledd; cymhareb

ration n dogn, saig ♦ vt dogni

rational adj rhesymol

rationale n rhesymwaith

rationalization n rhesymoliad

rationalize vb rhesymoli

rattle n rhuglo, trystio ♦ n rhugl, rhwnc

raucous adj cryg, garw, aflafar

ravage vt anrheithio, diffeithio, difrodi

rave vi gwallgofi, ynfydu, gwynfydu

ravel vb drysu; dad-weu, datod

raven n cigfran

ravenous adj rheibus, gwancus

ravine n hafn, ceunant

raving adj ynfyd, dwl, gwallgof

ravish vt treisio, cipio; swyno, hudo

ravishing adj deniadol iawn

raw adj amrwd; crai, cri; noeth, dolurus, garw; dibrofiad ♦ n cig noeth, dolur

ray n paladr, pelydryn

ray n cath fôr

raze vt llwyr ddymchwelyd, dileu

razor n ellyn, rasal ♦ vt eillio. **r. blade** n llafn ellyn

re prep ym mater, mewn perthynas â

re- prefix ad-, ail-

reach vb cyrraedd, estyn ♦ n cyrraedd

react vi adweithio

reaction n adwaith

reactionary adj adweithiol

reactor n adweithydd

read vb darllen

readable adj darllenadwy

reader n darllenydd

readily adv yn barod, yn ddiffwdan

reading n darllen

readjustment n atgywiriad, addasiad

ready adj parod, rhwydd

reafforestation n ailfforestiad

real adj gwir, real, go-iawn

reality n gwirionedd, sylwedd; dirwedd, realiti

realize vt sylweddoli; troi yn arian

really adv gwir, hollol, mewn difrif

realm n teyrnas, gwlad, bro

reap vb medi

reappear vb ailymddangos

rear n cefn, pen ôl, ôl

rear vb codi, magu; codi ar ei draed ôl

reason n rheswm ♦ vb rhesymu

reasonable adj rhesymol

reassurance n calondid

reassure vt calonogi, cysuro

rebate n ad-daliad

rebel vi gwrthryfela ♦ n gwrthryfelwr

rebellion n gwrthryfel

rebound vi adlamu ♦ n adlam

rebuff n nacâd, sen ♦ vt nacáu, sennu

rebuke vt ceryddu ♦ n cerydd, sen

rebut vt gwrthbrofi, gwrthddywedyd

recall vt galw yn ôl; galw i gof, cofio

recant vb datgyffesu

recapitulate vt ailadrodd (yn gryno)

recede vi encilio, cilio yn ôl

receipt n derbyniad; derbynneb

receive vt derbyn

receiver n derbynnydd

recent adj diweddar

receptacle n llestr; cynheiliad

(llysieueg)

reception n derbyniad, croeso. **r. desk** n man croeso, man derbyn
receptionist n croesawferch, croesawydd
recess n cil, encil; cilfach; gwyliau
recessional adj, n (emyn) ymadawol
recipe n cyfarwyddyd; rysáit
recipient n derbyniwr, derbynnydd
reciprocal adj cilyddol
reciprocate vb cael yn ôl, cydgyfnewid; cilyddu
recital n adroddiad, datganiad
recitation n adroddiad
recite vb adrodd
reck vb gofalu, ystyried
reckless adj anystyriol, rhyfygus, dibris
reckon vb cyfrif, barnu, bwrw
reclaim vt adennill, diwygio
recline vb lledorwedd, gorwedd, gorffwys
recluse n meudwy, ancr
recognition n adnabyddiaeth, cydnabyddiaeth
recognize vt adnabod, cydnabod
recoil vi adlamu, gwrthneidio, cilio
recollect vt galw i gof, atgofio, cofio
recommend vt cymeradwyo, argymell
recompense vt ad-dalu, gwobrwyo, talu
reconcile vt cymodi, cysoni
recondite adj dwfn, cudd, cêl, tywyll
recondition vt atgyflyru, ail-wneud
reconnaissance n rhagwiliad
reconnoitre vt chwilio, archwilio
record vt cofnodi, recordio ♦ n cofnod, record
recorder n (LAW) cofiadur; (MUS) recordydd
recording n recordiad
recount vt adrodd

re-count vb ailgyfrif
recoup vb digolledu
recourse n cyrchfa. **to have r. to** mynd at, defnyddio
recover vb cael yn ôl, adennill; ymadfer; adferiad
recreation n difyrrwch, adloniant
recruit n recriwt; newyddian ♦ vt codi gwŷr; adennill
rectangle n petryal
rectangular adj petryalog
rectify vt adennill, cywiro; puro, coethi
rectilinear adj unionlin
rector n rheithor
rectory n rheithoriaeth; rheithordy
recuperate vb adfer, ymadfer, cryfhau, gwella
recur vi ailddigwydd, dychwelyd
recurrence n ail-ddigwyddiad, ail-ymddangosiad
recurring adj cylchol
recusant n anghydffurfiwr
red adj, n coch, rhudd
redeem vt prynu (yn ôl), gwaredu
redemption n prynedigaeth
redeploy vb adleoli
redeployment n adleoliad, trawsgyflogaeth
red herring n (met) ysgyfarnog
redirect vb ailgyfeirio
redo vb ail-wneud
redolent adj yn sawru o
redoubtable adj i'w ofni; pybyr
redress vt unioni ♦ n iawn (am gam)
Red Sea n: **the R.S.** n Môr Coch
reduce vb lleihau, gostwng; rhydwytho
reduced adj gostyngol
reduction n lleihad, gostyngiad
redundancy n anghyflogaeth
redundant adj gormodol; anghyflog, digyflog
reed n cawnen, corsen, calaf; pibell
reef n plyg hwyl, riff ♦ vt plygu

hwyl

reef n creigle (yn y môr), creigfa, riff

reek n mwg, tarth, drewdod ♦ vb mygu, drewi

reel n rîl ♦ vb dirwyn

reel vi troi, chwyldroi ♦ n dawns

refectory n ffreutur

refer vb cyfeirio, cyfarwyddo

reference n cyfeiriad; geirda

refill n adlenwad ♦ vt adlenwi

refine vb puro, coethi

reflect vb adlewyrchu; myfyrio

reflection n adlewyrchiad, myfyrdod, ailfeddwl

reflex n adweithred, atgyrch

reflexive adj atblygol

reform vb diwygio, gwella ♦ n diwygiad

reformation n diwygiad

reformatory n ysgol ddiwygio

refrain vb ymatal

refrain n byrdwn

refresh vt adfywio, dadebru, adlonni

refresher course n cwrs adolygu

refreshing adj adfywiol

refreshments npl ymborth, lluniaeth

refrigerate vt rheweiddio, cadw'n oer

refrigerator n rhewgell, oergell

refuge n noddfa, lloches

refugee n ffoadur

refund n ad-daliad ♦ vb ad-dalu

refurbish vb adnewyddu

refusal n gwrthodiad, nacâd

refuse vb gwrthod

refuse n ysbwriel, gwehilion, sothach

refute vt gwrthbrofi, datbrofi

regal adj brenhinol

regard vt edrych ar, ystyried ♦ n sylw, parch, hoffter

regarding prep ynglŷn â, ynghylch

regardless adj heb ofal, diofal

regenerate vt aileni

régime n trefn, cyfundrefn

regiment n catrawd

region n ardal, bro, gwlad

regional adj rhanbarthol

register n cofrestr ♦ vt cofrestru

registered adj cofrestredig

registrar n cofrestrydd

registration n cofrestriad. **r. number** n rhif cofrestru, rhif trethiant

registry n cofrestrfa

regret vt gofidio, edifaru ♦ n gofid

regular adj rheolaidd, cyson

regulate vt rheoleiddio, llywio, rheoli

regulation n rheol, trefniant

rehabilitate vt adfer i fri neu fraint, ailsefydlu

rehabilitation n adferiad

rehearsal n rihyrsal, practis

rehearse vt adrodd; ymarfer ymlaen llaw

reign vi teyrnasu ♦ n teyrnasiad

reimburse vt talu yn ôl, ad-dalu

rein n awfyn, awen ♦ vt ffrwyno

reindeer n carw

reinforce vt atgyfnerthu

reinstate vt adfer i safle neu fraint

reiterate vt ailadrodd, mynychu

reject vt gwrthod, bwrw ymaith

rejection n gwrthodiad

rejoice vb llawenhau, gorfoleddu

rejoin vb ateb, gwrthwaberb

rejoinder n ateb, gwrthwaberb

rejuvenate vb adfywiogi, adnewyddu

relapse vi ailglafychu, ailymhoelyd, atglafychu

relate vb adrodd, mynegi; perthyn

related adj yn perthyn; wedi ei ddweud

relating to prep yn ymwneud â

relation n adroddiad; perthynas

relationship n perthynas

relative adj perthnasol ♦ n perthynas. **r. pronoun** n rhagenw perthynol

relax vb llacio, llaesu, ymollwng

relaxing adj ymlaciol

relay n cyfenwad newydd, cyfnewid; darlledu ♦ vb ailosod. **r. race** n ras gyfnewid

release vt rhyddhau, gollwng ♦ n rhyddhad

relegate vt alltudio, deol, darostwng

relent vi tyneru, tirioni, llaesu

relevant adj perthnasol

reliable adj y gellir dibynnu arno, dibynadwy

reliance n ymddiriead, dibyniaeth, hyder, pwys

relic n crair, (pl) gweddillion

relief n cynhorthwy; gollyngdod, ymwared; tirwedd

relieve vt cynorthwyo; esmwytho, ysgafnhau; rhyddhau, gollwng

religion n crefydd

religious adj crefyddol

relinquish vt gollwng, gildio, gwadu

relish n blas; enllyn, mwyniant ♦ vb blasio, hoffi

reluctance n amharodrwydd, anfodlonrwydd

reluctant adj anfodlon, anewyllysgar

rely vi hyderu, ymddiried, dibynnu

remain vi aros, parhau, gorffwys

remainder n gweddill, rhelyw

remains npl olion, gweddillion

remand vt aildraddodi. **r. home** n cartref i droseddwyr ifanc

remark vb sylwi ♦ n sylw

remarkable adj nodedig, hynod, rhyfedd, syn

remedial n adferol; meddyginiaethol

remedy n meddyginiaeth ♦ vt meddyginiaethu, gwella

remember vt cofio

remembrance n cof, coffa, coffadwriaeth

remind vt atgofio, atgofia, cofio

reminiscence n atgof

remiss adj esgeulus, diofal, llac

remission n maddeuant

remit vb maddau; arafu, peidio; anfon

remittance n taliad

remnant n gweddill, gwarged

remonstrance n cwyn, gwrthdystiad

remonstrate vi ymliw, gwrthdystio

remorse n edifeirwch, gofid, atgno

remote adj pell, pellennig, anghysbell

remotely adv o bell

removable adj symudadwy, y gellir ei symud

removal n symudiad, diswyddiad

remove vb symud, dileu; mudo

remunerate vt talu, gwobrwyo

renaissance n dadeni

rend vb rhwygo, dryllio, llarpio

render vt talu; datgan; gwneud; troi, cyfieithu

rendezvous n cyrchfa, man cyfarfod

renegade n gwrthgiliwr

renew vt adnewyddu

renounce vt ymwrthod, ymwadu, gwadu

renovate vt adnewyddu

renown n clod, bri, enwogrwydd

rent n rhwyg

rent n ardreth, rhent ♦ vt ardrethu, rhentu

rental n rent

repair vi cyrchu, mynd

repair vi atgyweirio, trwsio ♦ n cywair

reparation n iawn, ad-daliad

repartee n ateb parod

repatriate vb adfer i'w wlad ei hun

repeal vt diddymu ♦ n diddymiad

repeat vb ailadrodd, ailgyflawni

repel vt bwrw yn ôl

repent vb edifarhau, edifaru

repentance n edifeirwch

repetition n ailadroddiad
repetitive adj ailadroddus
replace vb ailosod, dodi'n ôl; cymryd lle (arall)
replacement n un sy'n cymryd lle arall
replay vb ailchwarae
replenish vt ail-lenwi, diwallu
replete adj llawn, cyflawn, gorlawn
replica n copi cywir, cyflun
reply vi ateb ♦ n ateb, atebiad
report vt adrodd, hysbysu ♦ n adroddiad; swn ergyd
reporter n gohebydd
repose vb gorffwys ♦ n gorffwys
repository n ystorfa, trysorfa
reprehend vt ceryddu, argyhoeddi
represent vt portreadu; cynrychioli
representative adj yn cynrychioli ♦ n cynrychiolydd
repress vt atal, gostegu, llethu
repression n ataliad, darostyngiad, gwrthodiad
reprimand n cerydd ♦ vt ceryddu
reprisal n dial
reproach vt ceryddu, gwaradwyddo, edliw ♦ n gwaradwydd
reproduce vt atgynhyrchu, epilio
reproduction n atgynhyrchiad, copi; epiliad
reproof n cerydd
reprove vt ceryddu, argyhoeddi
reptile n ymlusgiad
republic n gweriniaeth, gwerinlywodraeth
repudiate vt diarddel, diarddelwi, gwadu
repugnant adj croes, atgas, gwrthun
repulse vt bwrw'n ôl; nacáu ♦ n gwrthergyd
repulsion n gwrthnysedd
repulsive adj atgas, ffiaidd
reputable adj parchus, cyfrifol
reputation n gair, cymeriad, enw da
repute vt cyfrif, tybied ♦ n parch, bri
request n cais ♦ vt ceisio, gofyn
requiem n offeren dros y meirw; galargerdd
require vt gofyn, mynnu
requisite adj gofynnol, angenrheidiol
requisition n archeb ♦ vb hawlio
requite vt talu, gwobrwyo, talu'r pwyth
rescind vt diddymu, dirymu
rescue vt achub ♦ n achubiad
research n ymchwil, ymchwiliad ♦ vb ymchwilio
resemblance n tebygrwydd
resemble vt tebygu i
resent vt tramgwyddo, digio, cymryd yn chwith
resentful adj digofus, llidiog
resentment n dig, dicter
reservation n cadw, cadfa
reserve vt cadw yn ôl, cadw wrth gefn ♦ n yr hyn a gedwir, cronfa; swildod
reserved adj swil; wedi ei gadw; **r. seat** sedd gadw
reservoir n cronfa, llyn
reshuffle vb aildrefnu
reside vi preswylio
residential adj preswyl
residue n gweddill
resign vb rhoi i fyny, ymddiswyddo, ymddeol
resignation n ymddiswyddiad; ymostyngiad
resilience n hydwythder, ystwythder
resilient adj hydwyth, ystwyth
resin n ystor, rhwsin
resist vb gwrthsefyll, gwrthwynebu
resistance n gwrthwynebiad, gwrthsafiad
resolute adj penderfynol
resolution n penderfyniad
resolve vb penderfynu ♦ n

penderfyniad
resonant *adj* atseiniol
resort *vi* cyrchu ♦ *n* cyrchfa;
ymwared
resound *vb* atseinio, diasbedain
resource *n* sgil, dyfais; *(pl)*
adnoddau
respect *vt* parch ♦ *n* golwg; parch
respectable *adj* parchus
respectful *adj* boneddigaidd, yn
dangos parch
respective *adj* priodol, ar wahân
respite *n* oediad, saib, seibiant,
hamdden
resplendent *adj* disglair,
ysblennydd
respond *vi* ateb, ymateb; porthi
response *n* ateb, ymateb
responsibility *n* cyfrifoldeb
responsible *adj* atebol, cyfrifol
responsive *adj* ymatebol
rest *n*, *vb* gorffwys ♦ *n (music)*
tawnod
rest *vi* aros, parhau ♦ *n* gweddill
restaurant *n* tŷ bwyta, bwyty
restful *adj* tawel, llonydd, esmwyth
restitution *n* adferiad; iawn
restive *adj* ystyfnig, ystranclyd,
noglyd, diamynedd
restless *adj* aflonydd, rhwyfus
restore *vt* adfer; atgyweirio
restrain *vt* atal, ffrwyno
restrained *adj* cynnil, gochelgar,
cymhedrol
restraint *n* atalfa, ffrwyn,
caethiwed
restrict *vt* cyfyngu, caethiwo
restriction *n* cyfyngiad
result *vi* deillio, canlyn ♦ *n*
canlyniad
resume *vt* ailddechrau
résumé *n* crynodeb
resumption *n* ailddechreuad
resurgent *adj* yn ailgodi, yn ailfyw
resurrection *n* atgyfodiad
resuscitate *vb* adfywhau, dadebru
retail *vb* manwerthu, adwerthu ♦ *n*

adwerth
retailer *n* mân-werthwr
retain *vb* cadw, dal; llogi
retaliate *vb* talu'n ôl, talu'r pwyth,
dial
retaliation *n* dial
retard *vb* rhwystro, oedi
retch *vi* cyfogi, chwydu
retentive *adj* yn dal heb ollwng;
gafaelgar
reticent *adj* tawedog, distaw
retina *n* rhwyden y llygad, retina
retinue *n* gosgordd, gosgorddlu
retire *vi* ymneillltuo, encilio, cilio,
ymddeol
retired *adj* wedi ymddeol
retirement *n* ymddeoliad
retiring *adj* swil
retort *vb* gwrthateb ♦ *n* ateb
parod; ritort (cemeg)
retrace *vt* mynd yn ôl dros yr un
ffordd, olrhain
retract *vb* tynnu'n ôl
retrain *vb* ailhyfforddi
retreat *vi* cilio, encilio, ffoi ♦ *n*
encil, ffo
retrench *vb* cwtogi, cynilo
retribution *n* ad-daledigaeth, cosb,
dial
retrieve *vt* olrhain; adennill, adfer
retrogress *vi* mynd yn ôl, dirywio
retrospect *n* ad-drem, adolwg
return *vb* dychwelyd ♦ *n*
dychweliad; elw, enillion. **r.
(ticket)** *n* tocyn dwyfordd
reveal *vt* datguddio, amlygu,
dangos
revel *vi* gloddesta; ymhyfrydu ♦ *n*
gloddest
revelry *n* miri
revenge *vb*, *n* dial
revenue *n* cyllid, enillion, incwm
reverberate *vb* taro'n ôl; atseinio
revere *vt* parchu, anrhydeddu
reverence *n* parch, parchedigaeth
reverend *adj* parchedig
reverent *adj* parchus, gŵyl,

gwylaidd
reversal n dymchweliad, cwymp
reverse adj gwrthwyneb, chwith ♦
  vb troi, gwrthdroi ♦ n gwrthdro,
  aflwydd. **r. charge call** n galwad y
  telir amdani'r pen arall. **r. (gear)**
  n gêr ôl
revert vb troi yn ôl, dychwelyd
review vt adolygu ♦ n adolygiad
reviewer n adolygydd
revile vt difenwi, cablu,
  gwaradwyddo
revise vt cywiro, diwygio
revision n cywiriad; adolygiad
revival n adfywiad, diwygiad
revive vb adfywio, adnewyddu
revoke vb galw yn ôl, diddymu,
  dirymu
revolt vb gwrthryfela ♦ n
  gwrthryfel
revolting adj gwrthnaws, atgas,
  ffiaidd
revolution n chwyldro, chwyldroad
revolutionary adj chwildroadol ♦ n
  chwildrowr
revolve vb troi, amdroi, cylchdroi
revolver n llawddryll
revulsion n atgasedd
reward n gwobr ♦ vt gwobrwyo
reword vb ailysgrifennu,
  ailddweud
rhapsody n hwyl, ymfflamychiad
rhetoric n rhetoreg, rhethreg
rheumatism n cryd cymalau,
  gwynegon
rhinoceros n rhinoseros
rhombus n rhombws
rhubarb n rhiwbob
rhyme n odl, rhigwm ♦ vb odli,
  rhigymu
rhythm n rhythm, rhediad
rib n asen, eisen
ribald n maweddwr ♦ adj
  masweddol
ribbon n rhuban, ysnoden
rice n reis
rich adj cyfoethog, goludog, bras

riches npl cyfoeth, golud
richness n cyfoethogrwydd,
  braster, ffrwythlonrwydd
rick n tas
rickets npl y llech(au)
rickety adj simsan, bregus
rid vt gwared
riddle n dychymyg, pos
riddle n rhidyll ♦ vt rhidyllio,
  gogrwn
ride vb marchogaeth, marchocáu
rider n marchogwr; atodiad
ridge n grwn, trum, cefn, crib
ridicule n gwawd ♦ vt gwawdio,
  chwerthin am ben
ridiculous adj chwerthinllyd
riding n marchogaeth
riding school n ysgol farchogaeth
rife adj aml, cyffredin, rhemp
riff-raff n gwehilion y bobl, dihirod
rifle vt anrheithio, ysbeilio
rifle n dryll, reiffl
rig n agen, hollt, rhwyg
rig vb rigio, taclu ♦ n rig
right adj iawn, uniawn; deau ♦ adv
  yn iawn ♦ vt unioni, cywiro ♦ n
  iawnder, hawl. **r. angle** n ongl
  sgwâr. **rights and customs** braint
  a defod. **r. wing** (POL) asgell dde
righteous adj cyfiawn
righteousness n cyfiawnder
rightful adj cyfreithlon, iawn, teg
rigid adj anhyblyg, manwl, caeth
rigmarole n ffregod, rhibidirês
rigour n llymder
rile vt cythruddo, ffyrnigo, llidio
rim n ymyl, cylch, cant
rind n pil, croen, crawen, rhisgl
ring n modrwy, cylch ♦ vb
  modrwyo
ring vb canu cloch, atseinio;
  modrwyo ♦ n swn cloch, tinc.
  wedding r. n modrwy briodas.
  road n cylchffordd
rinse vt golchi, trochi
riot n terfysg, gloddest ♦ vi
  terfysgu

rip vb rhipio, rhwygo, datod ♦ n rhwyg. **r.-off** n lladrad amlwg

ripe adj aeddfed

ripple n crych ♦ vb crychu

rise vi codi, cyfodi ♦ n codiad

risk n perygl, enbydrwydd ♦ vt peryglu, anturio, mentro

rite n defod

ritual adj defodol ♦ n defod

rival n cydymgeisydd ♦ vb cystadlu

river n afon

rivet n rhybed, hem, rifet ♦ vb rhybedu, hemio, rifetio

rivulet n afonig, nant, cornant

road n ffordd, heol; angorfa. **map** n map ffyrdd, map moduro. **r. works** n gwaith cynnal y ffordd

roam vi crwydro, gwibio

roar vi rhuo ♦ n rhu, rhuad

roast vb rhostio, crasu, pobi, digoni

rob vt lladrata, ysbeilio

robber n lleidr, ysbeiliwr

robbery n lladrad

robe n gwisg, gŵn

robin n brongoch

robust adj cadarn, cryf, grymus

rock vb siglo

rock n craig

rockery n gardd gerrig

rocket n roced

rocky adj creigiog; sigledig

rod n gwialen, llath

rodent n cnofil

roe n iyrches, ewig

roe n grawn pysgod, gronell

roebuck n iwrch

rogue n gwalch, cnaf

role n rhan, tasg, cymeriad

roll vb rholio, treiglo ♦ n rhôl. **r. call** n galw enwau (ar restr). **r. pin** n

rolling adj tonnog. **r. stock** n rholstoc

Roman n Rhufeiniwr ♦ adj Rhufeinaidd, Rhufeinig. **R. Catholic** n Pabydd

romance n rhamant ♦ vi rhamantu

Romania n România

romantic adj rhamantus

Rome n Rhufain

romp vi rhampio ♦ n rhamp; rhampen

rood n rhwd; y grog, y groes

roof n to, nen ♦ vt toi

rook n ydfran, brân

room n lle; ystafell. **r. service** n gwasanaeth ystafell

roomy adj helaeth, eang

roost n clwyd ♦ vi clwydo

rooster n ceiliog

root n gwraidd, gwreiddyn ♦ vb gwreiddio; diwreiddio

rope n rhaff ♦ vt rhaffu, rhwymo

rosary n paderau, llaswyr

rose n rhosyn. **r. hips** npl egroes

rosette n ysnoden

rostrum n llwyfan, areithfa

rosy adj rhosynnaidd, gwritgoch, disglair

rot vb pydru, braenu ♦ n pydredd; lol

rota n rhod, trefn

rotate vi troi, cylchdroi, chwyldroi

rote n tafod-leferydd

rotten adj pwdr, pydredig, sâl

rouge n lliw coch, gruddliw

rough adj garw, gerwin, bras

round adj crwn ♦ n crwn, cylch, tro, rownd ♦ adv, prep o glych, o amgylch ♦ vb crynio, rowndio

roundabout n cylchdro, cylchfan, cylch ogylch; ceffylau bach ♦ adj o amgylch, cwmpasog

rouse vb dihuno, deffroi, cyffroi

rout n rhawt; ffo, dymchweliad ♦ vb ymlid, dymchwelyd

route n ffordd, llwybr, hynt

routine n defod, arfer

rove vb crwydro, gwibio

roving adj crwydrol

row n rhes, rhestr

row vb rhwyfo

row n terfysg, cythrwfl, ffrae

rowan n criafol

rowdy adj trystiog, afreolus
rowel n troell ysbardun, rhywel
rowing boat n cwch rhwyfo
royal adj brenhinol
royalty n brenhiniaeth; toll, tâl, breindal
rub vb rhwbio, rhathu, iro, crafu
rubber n rwber
rubbish n ysbwriel, sothach; lol. **r. bin** n bin ysbwriel. **r. dump** n tomen ysbwriel
rubble n rhwbel
ruby n rhuddem ♦ adj coch, rhudd
ruck n pentwr, crynswth, haid, ysgarmes
rucksack n rhychsach
ruction n helynt, terfysg
rudder n llyw
ruddy adj coch, gwridog, gwritgoch
rude adj anfoesgar; anghelfydd, garw
rudiment n egwyddor, elfen
rue vt galaru, gofidio, edifaru
rueful adj trist, truenus, gresynus
ruffian n adyn, anfadyn, dihiryn
ruffle vb crychu, cyffroi, aflonyddu
rug n hugan
rugby n rygbi
rugged adj garw, gerwin, clogyrnog
ruin n distryw, dinistr; adfail ♦ vb difetha, andwyo
rule n rheol, llywodraeth; riwl ♦ vb rheoli, llywodraethu; llinellu
ruler n llywodraethwr; pren mesur, rhiwl
ruling n dyfarniad, barn ♦ adj llywodraethol, mewn grym
rum n rym ♦ adj od, rhyfedd
rumble vi trystio, tyrfu, godyrfu
rummage vb chwalu a chwilio, chwilota
rumour n chwedl, gair, sôn, achlust
rump n tin, bôn, cwman, cloren
rumple vt crychu, sybachu

rumpus n helynt, terfysg
run vb rhedeg, llifo ♦ n rhediad, rhedfa. **in the long r.** yn y pen draw
rung n ffon ysgol
rupture n rhwyg; tor llengig ♦ vb rhwygo
rural adj gwledig, gwladaidd
ruse n ystryw, dichell
rush n brwynen, pabwyryn
rush vb rhuthro ♦ n rhuthr. **r. hour** n awr brysur
russet adj llwytgoch
Russia n Rwsia
rust n rhwd ♦ vb rhydu
rustic adj gwladaidd, gwledig ♦ n gwladwr
rusticate vt anfon adref am dymor
rustle vi siffrwd, chwithrwd, rhuglo
rusty adj rhydlyd
rut n rhych, rhigol
ruthless adj didostur, diarbed, creulon
rye n rhyg

S

Sabbath n Sabath, Saboth
sabotage n difrod bwriadol ♦ vb difrodi
sacerdotal adj offeiriadol
sack n sach, ffetan ♦ vt sachu; difrodi; diswyddo
sackcloth n sachlen, sachliain
sacrament n sacrament, ordinhad
sacred adj cysegredig, glân, sanctaidd
sacrifice n aberth, offrwm ♦ vb aberthu
sacrilege n halogiad, cysegr-ysbeiliad
sad adj trist, athrist, prudd, digalon
saddle n cyfrwy ♦ vt cyfrwyo; beichio

saddler n cyfrwywr

sadness n tristwch, prudd-der

safe adj diogel, dihangol, saff ♦ n cell, cist, cloer

safety n diogelwch. **s. belt** gwregys diogelwch. **s. pin** pin cau

saffron n saffrwm ♦ adj melyn

sag vb segio, segian, sagio, ymollwng

sage adj doeth ♦ n gŵr doeth

sage n saets

Sahara n Sahara

sail n hwyl ♦ vb hwylio, morio, mordwyo

sailing n hwylio. **s. boat** n llong hwylio

sailor n morwr, llongwr

saint n sant

sake n mwyn. **for the s. of** er mwyn

salary n cyflog

sale n gwerth, gwerthiant, arwerthiant

salient adj amlwg

saline adj heliaidd, hallt ♦ n heli

saliva n haliw, poer, dŵr anadl

sallow adj melyn afiach

salmon n eog, gleisiad, samwn

saloon n neuadd, salŵn

salt n halen, halwyn (cemeg) ♦ adj hallt ♦ vt halltu. **s. cellar** n llestr halen. **s. water** n dŵr hallt, dŵr y môr

salty adj hallt

salute vt cyfarch; saliwtio ♦ n cyfarchiad; saliwt

salvation n iachawdwriaeth. **S. Army** Byddin yr Iachawdwriaeth

salve n eli, ennaint ♦ vt elïo, lleddfu; achub

same adj yr un, yr unrhyw, yr un fath

sample n sampl, enghraifft ♦ vt samplu, samplo

sanctify vt sancteiddio

sanctimonious adj ffug-sanctaidd, sych-dduwiol

sanction n caniatâd; cosb; sancsiwn (moeseg) ♦ vt caniatáu; cosbi

sanctity n sancteiddrwydd

sanctuary n cysegr; noddfa, nawdd

sand n tywod ♦ vt tywodi. **s. castle** n castell tywod

sandpaper n papur gwydrog

sandpit n pwll tywod

sandwich n brechdan

sandy adj tywodlyd; melyngoch

sane adj iach, call, synhwyrol

sanitary adj iechydol. **s. towel** n tywel misglwyf, tywel iechydol

sanitation n iechydiaeth

sanity n iechyd meddwl, iawn bwyll

Santa Claus n Siôn Corn

sap n nodd, sudd, sugn ♦ vt sugno, hysbyddu

sap vb tangloddio, diseilio

sapling n pren ieuanc

sapphire n saffir ♦ adj glas

sarcasm n gwawdiaith, coegni, gair du

sarcastic adj gwawdlyd, coeglyd, brathog

sardine n sardîn

sash n gwregys; ffrâm ffenestr

satchel n sachell, cod lyfrau

sate vt digoni, llenwi, diwallu

satellite n canlynwr, cynffonnwr; lleuad; lloeren

satiate vt digoni, diwallu, syrffedu

satin n satin, pali

satire n dychan, gogan

satirize vb dychan, goganu

satisfaction n bodlonrwydd; iawn

satisfactory adj boddhaol; iawnol

satisfy vt bodloni, diwallu, digoni

saturate vt trwytho, mwydo

Saturday n dydd Sadwrn

sauce n saws; haerllugrwydd

saucepan n sosban

saucer n soser

saucy adj digywilydd, haerllug

Saudi Arabia n Saudi Arabia
saunter vi rhodianna, ymdroi, swmera
sausage n selsig, selsigen
savage adj gwyllt, ffyrnig, milain, anwar ♦ n dyn gwyllt, anwariad, anwarddyn
save vb achub, arbed, gwaredu; cynilu ♦ prep oddieithr, ond
saving adj achubol, darbodus
savings npl cynilion
saviour n achubwr, gwaredwr, iachawdwr
savour n sawr, blas ♦ vb sawru
savoury n blasusfwyd; adj sawrus
saw n llif ♦ vb llifio
sawdust n blawd llif
sawmill n melin llifio
say vb dywedyd, dweud
saying n dywediad, ymadrodd, gair
scab n crachen, cramen; clafr
scabies n y crafu
scaffold n ysgaffald; dienyddle
scald vt ysgaldio, sgaldan(u) ♦ n ysgaldiad
scale n clorian, tafol, mantol
scale n graddfa ♦ vb dringo
scale n cen ♦ vb cennu; digennu, pilio
scallop n gylfgragen; gwlf ♦ vt gylfu, minfylchu
scalp n copa, croen y pen ♦ vt penfflingo
scamp n cnaf, gwalch, dihiryn
scamper vi ffoi, carlamu, brasgamu
scan vt corfannu; sganio, edrych, chwilio
scandal n tramgwydd, gwarth, enllib
Scandinavia n Llychlyn
scanner n sganydd
scant, -y adj prin
scapegoat n bwch dihangol
scapegrace n dyn diras, oferwr, dihiryn

scar n craith ♦ vt creithio
scarce adj, adv prin
scarcely adv prin, braidd, odid, nemor
scare vt brawychu, tarfu ♦ n dychryn
scared adj wedi cael ofn, wedi rhuso, wedi brawychu
scarf n crafat, sgarff
scarlatina n y dwymyn goch
scarlet adj ysgarlad
scarp n llethr
scathe vt deifio, anafu, niweidio
scathing adj deifiol, miniog
scatter vb gwasgaru, chwalu, taenu
scavenger n carthwr, carthydd
scene n lle; golwg, golygfa
scenery n golygfa
scenic adj hardd, golygfaol
scent n arogl, aroglau, trywydd; perarogl ♦ vt arogli
sceptic n amheuwr
sceptical adj amheugar
sceptre n teyrnwialen
schedule n atodlen, cofrestr, taflen
scheme n cynllun; cynllwyn ♦ vb cynllunio
schism n rhwyg, ymraniad, sism
scholar n ysgolhaig, ysgolor
scholarly adj ysgolheigaidd
scholarship n ysgolheictod; ysgoloriaeth
scholastic adj athrofaol
school n ysgol, ysgoldy ♦ vt disgyblu
schoolbook n llyfr ysgol
schoolboy n bachgen ysgol
schoolchildren npl plant ysgol
schooldays npl dyddiau ysgol
schoolgirl n merch ysgol
schoolmaster n athro
schoolmistress n athrawes
schooner n ysgwner
sciatica n clunwst
science n gwyddor, gwyddoniaeth
scientific adj gwyddonol

scientist n gwyddonydd

scissors npl siswrn

scoff n gwawd ♦ vi gwawdio, gwatwar

scold vb dwrdio, tafodi, ceryddu, cymhennu ♦ n cecren

scone n sgon

scoop n lletwad ♦ vt cafnu, cafnio

scope n ergyd, bwriad; cylch, cwmpas, lle

scorch vb deifio, llosgi, greidio, rhuddo

score n hac, rhic; cyfrif, dyled; sgôr; ugain

score vb rhicio, cyfrif, sgori(o)

scorn n dirmyg ♦ vb dirmygu, gwatwar

scorpion n ysgorpion

Scot n Ysgotyn, Albanwr

scotch vt hacio, darnio, trychu

Scotch adj Ysgotaidd, Albanaidd

scot-free adj croeniach, dianaf

Scotland n Yr Alban

Scottish adj Albanaidd

scoundrel n cnaf, dihiryn

scour vt carthu, ysgwrio

scour vb rhedeg; chwilio

scourge n fflangell, pla ♦ vt fflangellu

scout n sgowt, ysbiwr ♦ vt sgowta, ysbïo

scowl vb cuchio, gwgu ♦ n cilwg, gwg

scraggy adj esgyrnog, tenau, cul, salw

scramble vi, n ciprys, ymgiprys.

  scramble egg n cymysgwy

scrap n tamaid, tameidyn, dernyn

scrapbook n llyfr lloffion

scrape vb crafu ♦ n helynt, helbul, crafiad

scratch vb crafu, cripio

scrawl vb ysgriblo, ysgriblan

scream vi ysgrechain ♦ n ysgrech, gwawch

screech vi ysgrechain ♦ n ysgrech

screen n llen, cysgod; sgrîn ♦ vt

cysgodi

screw n sgriw, hoel dro ♦ vb ysgriwio

screwdriver n tyrnsgriw

scribble n ysgribl ♦ vb ysgriblo, ysgriblan

script n llawysgrif, ysgrif, sgript

scripture n ysgrythur

scroll n rhôl, plyg llyfr

scrub n prysgwydd; ysgwrfa ♦ vt ysgwrio

scruff n gwar, gwegil

scrum(mage) n sgrym, ysgarmes

scruple n petruster (moesol) ♦ vi petruso

scrupulous adj gwyliadwrus, manwl

scrutinize vt chwilio, archwilio

scrutiny n archwiliad

scuffle vi, n ymgiprys, ymryson

scull n rhwyf unllaw, rhodl ♦ vb rhodli

scullery n cegin fach, cegin gefn

sculptor n cerflunydd

sculpture n cerfluniaeth; cerflun ♦ vb cerfio, torri

scum n sgum; gwehilion, sorod

scurf n cen, mardon

scurrilous adj bustladdd, brwnt, difriol

scurry vi ffrystio ♦ n ffrwst, ffwdan

scurvy adj crachlyd, crach ♦ n llwg

scutter vi ffoi, diengyd

scuttle n llestr glo

scuttle vt tyllu llong i'w suddo

scuttle vi heglu ffoi, dianc

scythe n pladur

sea n môr, cefnfor; moryn. **s. water** n dwr y môr

seaboard n morlan, glan y môr

seafood n bwyd môr

seagull n gwylan

seal n morlo

seal n sêl, insel ♦ vt selio

sea level n lefel y môr

seam n gwniad, gwrym; haen, gwythien; craith

seaman n morwr, llongwr

seamstress n gwniadwraig, gwniadyddes

seamy adj annymunol

seance n seawns

seaplane n awyren fôr

sear adj sych, crin, gwyw ♦ vt serio, deifio

search vb chwilio, profi ♦ n ymchwil

seashore n glan y môr

seasickness n salwch y môr

seaside n glan y môr

season n tymor, amser, pryd, adeg ♦ vb tymheru; halltu. **high/low s.** n tymor prysur/llac

seasonal adj tymhorol

season ticket n tocyn tymor

seat n sedd, sêt, eisteddle ♦ vi eistedd

seat belt n gwregys diogelwch

seaweed n gwymon, gwmon

seaworthy adj addas i'r môr, diogel

secede vi ymneilltuo, encilio; torri'n rhydd, ymwahanu

secession n ymneilltuad, enciliad; ymwahaniad

seclude vt cau allan, neillltuo

second adj ail ♦ n ail; eiliad ♦ vt eilio. **s. class** adj ail ddosbarth, isradd

secondary adj eilradd, uwchradd. **s. school** n ysgol uwchradd

second-hand adj ail-law

secret n dirgel, cyfrinachol ♦ n cyfrinach

secretary n ysgrifennydd. **S. of State** n Ysgrifennydd Gwladol

secretive adj yn celu, tawedog

sect n sect, enwad

sectarian adj enwadol, cul

section n toriad, trychiad; rhan, adran

sector n sector

secular adj bydol; lleygol; seciwlar

secure adj sicr, diogel ♦ vb sicrhau, diogelu

security n diogelwch, sicrwydd, gwystl

sedate adj tawel, digyffro ♦ vb rhoi i gysgu, tawelu

sedative adj lleddfol, lliniarol

sedge n hesg

sediment n gwaelodion, gwaddod

sedition n terfysg, brad, gwrthryfel

seduce vt llithio, hudo, twyllo

seductive adj llithiol, deniadol

see n esgobaeth

see vb gweld, canfod

seed n had, hedyn ♦ vb hadu, hedeg

seedy adj hadog; salw; sâl, anhwylus

seek vb ceisio, ymofyn, chwilio

seem vi ymddangos

seemly adj gweddus, gweddaidd, addas

seep vb diferu, gollwng

seer n gweledydd

seesaw n siglenydd

seethe vb berwi, byrlymu

segment n darn, rhan, segment

segregate vt didoli, neillltuo, gwahanu

seize vb gafael mewn, atafaelu, dal, achub

seizure n daliad; strôc

seldom adv anfynych, anaml

select vt dewis, dethol

self (selves) n hun, hunan ♦ prefix hunan-, ym-

self-catering adj hunan arlwy

self-conscious adj hunanymwybodol, swil

self-contained adj annibynnol, ar wahân

self-control n hunanlywodraeth

self-employed adj hunangyflogedig

self-evident adj amlwg, eglur

self-government *n* ymreolaeth
self-interest *n* hunan-les
selfish *adj* hunanol
self-possessed *adj* hunanfeddiannol
self-respect *n* hunan-barch
self-sacrifice *n* hunanaberth
selfsame *adj* yr un, yr unrhyw
self-satisfied *adj* hunanddigonol
self-service *n* hunanwasanaeth
self-sufficient *adj* hunanddigonol, hy
sell *vb* gwerthu; siomi ♦ *n* siom
seller *n* gwerthwr
sellotape *n* selotáp
semblance *n* tebygrwydd, rhith
semi- *prefix* hanner, lled, go
semicolon *n* gwahannod (;)
seminary *n* athrofa, ysgol
sempiternal *adj* bythol, tragwyddol
senate *n* senedd
send *vt* anfon, danfon, gyrru
senile *adj* hen a methedig, heneiddiol
senior *adj* hŷn ♦ *n* hynaf
seniority *n* blaenoriaeth
sensation *n* ymdeimlad, teimlad; cyffro, ias, syndod
sensational *adj* iasol, cyffrous
sense *n* synnwyr, pwyll, ystyr
senseless *adj* dienaid, disynnwyr, hurt
sensible *adj* synhwyrol; teimladwy
sensitive *adj* teimladwy, croendenau; hydeiml
sensual *adj* cnawdol; trythyll, chwantus
sensuous *adj* teimladol, synhwyrus
sentence *n* brawddeg; barn, dedfryd ♦ *vt* dedfrydu
sententious *adj* doetheiriog
sentiment *n* syniad, teimlad
sentry *n* gwyliwr, gwylgadw
separate *adj* ar wahân ♦ *vb* gwahanu, neilltuo, ysgar; ymwahanu

separation *n* gwahaniad
sept- *prefix* saith, seith-
September *n* Medi
septic *adj* braenol, pydrol, madreddol
sepulchre *n* bedd, beddrod
sequel *n* canlyniad
sequence *n* trefn, dilyniad
sequester *vt* neilltuo; atafaelu
serenade *n* hwyrgan, nosgan ♦ *vt* hwyrganu
serene *adj* teg; tawel, digynnwrf
sergeant *n* rhingyll, sarsiant
serial *adj* cyfresol, bob yn rhifyn ♦ *n* stori gyfres
series *n* rhes, cyfres
serious *adj* difrifol
seriously *adv* yn ddifrifol
sermon *n* pregeth
serpent *n* sarff
serrated *adj* danheddog
serum *n* serwm
servant *n* gwas; morwyn
serve *vb* gwasanaethu, gweini
service *n* gwasanaeth, oedfa; llestri. **s. charge** *n* tâl am wasanaeth
serviceable *adj* gwasanaethgar, defnyddiol
serviette *n* napcyn
servile *adj* gwasaidd
session *n* eisteddiad; sesiwn; tymor
set *vb* gosod, dodi; plannu; sadio; sefydlu; machlud ♦ *n* set; impyn, planhigyn
settee, settle *n* sgiw, setl
setting *n* lleoliad, safle; machludiad
settle *vb* sefydlu; penderfynu; cytuno, setlo; plwyfo; talu
settlement *n* cytundeb; gwladfa
seven *adj, n* saith
seventeen *adj, n* dau (dwy) ar bymtheg, un deg saith
seventh *adj* seithfed
seventy *adj, n* deg a thrigain,

saith deg
sever *vb* gwahanu, datod, torri
several *adj* amryw; gwahanol
severance *n* gwahaniad,
datgysylltiad
severe *adj* caled, tost, llym,
gerwin
severity *n* llymder, gerwindeb
sew *vb* gwnio, pwytho
sewage *n* carthffosiaeth, carthion
sewer *n* ceuffos, carthffos
sewing machine *n* peiriant gwnio
sex *n* rhyw
sex education *n* addysg ryw
sextet *n* chwechawd
sexton *n* clochydd; torrwr beddau
sexual *adj* rhywiol
shabby *adj* carpiog, gwael, aflêr
shack *n* caban
shackle *n* hual, gefyn, llyffethair
shade *n* cysgod; ysbryd ♦ *vt*
cysgodi
shadow *n* cysgod ♦ *vt* cysgodi
shadowy *adj* cysgodol, rhithiol
shady *adj* cysgodol; amheus
shaft *n* paladr, saeth; llorp,
braich; pwll; gwerthyd
shaggy *adj* cedenog, blewog
shake *vb* ysgwyd, siglo, crynu
shaky *adj* ansad, crynedig
shallow *adj* bas ♦ *n* basle, beisle
sham *vb* ffugio ♦ *adj* ffug, gau,
coeg ♦ *n* ffug, ffugbeth
shambles *npl* galanastra
shame *n* cywilydd, gwaradwydd,
gwarth ♦ *vb* cywilyddio,
gwaradwyddo
shamefaced *n* cywilydd, gwaladd
shameful *adj* cywilyddus,
gwarthus
shampoo *vt* golchi pen ♦ *n*
siampŵ
shank *n* coes, gar, esgair; paladr
shanty *n* caban, bwthyn, penty
shape *n* siâp, llun ♦ *vt* siapio,
llunio
shapeless *adj* afluniaidd, di-lun

shapely *adj* siapus, lluniaidd,
gosgeiddig
share *n* rhan, cyfran ♦ *vb* rhannu;
cyfranogi
share *n* swch aradr
shareholder *n* cyfranddaliwr
shark *n* siarc, morgi; twyllwr
sharp *adj* siarp, llym, miniog ♦ *n*
llonnod (cerdd)
sharpen *vb* hogi, minio, awchlymu
sharpener *n* naddwr
sharper *n* siarpwr
sharply *adv* yn sydyn
shatter *vb* dryllio, chwilfriwio;
ysigo
shave *vb* eillio, torri barf; rhasglio
shavings *npl* naddion
shawl *n* siôl
she *pron* hi ♦ *adj*, *prefix* benyw
sheaf (**sheaves**) *n* ysgub
shear *vt* cneifio; siero
shears *npl* gwellau
sheath *n* gwain; (*contraceptive*)
maneg atal cenhedlu
sheathe *vt* gweinio
shed *n* penty, sied
shed *vt* tywallt; gollwng; colli;
dihidlo, bwrw
sheen *n* disgleirdeb, llewyrch,
gwawr
sheep (**sheep**) *n* dafad
sheer *vi* gwyro o'r ffordd, cilio
sheer *adj* pur, glân, noeth, syth,
serth
sheet *n* llen; cynfas; hwylraff;
taflen
shekel *n* sicl
shelf (**shelves**) *n* silff, astell
shell *n* cragen; plisgyn, masgl;
tân-belen
shellfish *npl* cregynbysg
shelter *n* cysgod, lloches ♦ *vb*
cysgodi, llochesu; ymochel;
llechu
shelve *vi* llechweddu, llethru
shelve *vt* gosod naill ochr, troi o'r
neilltu

shepherd n bugail ♦ vt bugeilio

sheriff n sirydd, siryf

sherry n sieri

Shetland n Shetland

shield n tarian ♦ vt cysgodi, amddiffyn

shift vb newid, symud; ymdaro ♦ n newid; tro, stem, shifft

shilling n swllt

shilly-shally n anwadalwch

shimmer vi tywynnu, caneitio, rhithio

shin n crimog, crimp coes

shindy n helynt, ffrwgwd, terfysg

shine vb disgleirio, llewyrchu, tywynnu ♦ n disgleirdeb, sglein, llewyrch

shingle n graean, gro

shingle n peithynen; estyllen

shingles npl yr eryr, yr eryrod

shiny adj gloyw, disglair

ship n llong ♦ vt trosglwyddo

shipping n llongau (gwlad)

shipshape adj, adv taclus, trefnus, twt

shipwreck n llongddrylliad

shire n sir

shirk vt gochel, osgoi

shirt n crys

shiver vi crynu

shiver vb dryllio, chwilfriwio

shoal n haig ♦ vi heigio

shoal n basle, beisle

shock n sioc, ergyd, ysgytiad ♦ vt ysgytio; tramgwyddo

shocking adj arswydus, ysgytiol

shoddy n brethyn eilban ♦ adj ffug, gwael

shoe n esgid; pedol ♦ vt pedoli

shoehorn n seisbin, siasbi

shoelace n carrai/lasen esgid

shoemaker n crydd

shoe shop n siop esgidiau

shoot vb tarddu, blaguro; saethu ♦ n ysbrigyn, blaguryn

shooting n saethu

shop n masnachdy, siop ♦ vb siopa

shopkeeper n siopwr

shopper n prynwr

shopping n siopa

shore n glan, traeth

short adj byr, cwta, prin

shortage n prinder, diffyg

short circuit n cylchedd byr

shortcoming n diffyg, bai

short cut n llwybr tarw, llwybr llygad, ffordd fer

shorthand n llaw-fer

shorts npl trowsus cwta

shot n ergyd; saethwr

shoulder n ysgwydd, palfais ♦ vt ysgwyddo. **s. blade** n sgapwla, pont yr ysgwydd

shout vb bloeddio, gweiddi ♦ n bloedd, gwaedd

shove vb gwthio

shovel n llwyarn ♦ vt rhofio

show vb dangos, arddangos ♦ n arddangosfa, sioe, siew

shower n cawod, cawad ♦ vb cawodi, bwrw

shred n llarp, cerpyn ♦ vb rhwygo, torri'n fân

shrew n cecren, gwraig anynad; llyg

shrewd adj ffel, craff, call, cyfrwys

shriek vb ysgrechian ♦ n ysgrech

shrill adj llym, main, meinllais

shrimp n berdysen ♦ vi berdysa

shrine n ysgrin; creirfa; cysegr, seintwar

shrink vb crebachu, tynnu ato, cilio

shrivel vb crychu, crebachu

shroud n amdo, amwisg; (pl) rhaffau hwylbren ♦ vt amdoi, cuddio, celu

Shrove Tuesday n Mawrth Ynyd

shrub n prysgwydden, llwyn

shrug vb codi'r ysgwyddau

shudder n crynfa, echryd, arswyd ♦ vi crynu, arswydo

shuffle vb siffrwd; llusgo; gwingo,

gwamalu

shun vt gochelyd, osgoi

shunt vb troi o'r neilltu, symud o'r ffordd, siyntio

shut vb cau ♦ adj caeëdig

shutter n caead, clawr, gwerchyr

shuttle n gwennol (gwëydd)

shuttlecock n gwennol

shy adj swil ♦ vi osgoi, rhusio

siblings npl plant

sick adj claf; yn chwydu, â chyfog arno; wedi diflasu

sickbay n canolfan iechyd

sickening adj atgas, diflas, cyfoglyd

sickle n cryman

sickly adj afiach, nychlyd

side n ochr, ystlys; tu, plaid ♦ vi ochri

sidestep vb ochrgamu

sidetrack vb troi o'r neilltu

sideways adv tua'r ochr, yn wysg ei ochr

sidle vi cerdded yn wysg ei ochr, gwyro

siege n gwarchae

sieve n gogr, gwagr, rhidyll, sife

sift vt gogrwn, nithio, hidlo, rhidyllio

sigh vb ochneidio ♦ n ochenaid

sight n golwg, golygfa ♦ vt gweld

sightseeing n taith i weld y wlad

sign n arwydd, argoel ♦ vb arwyddo, llofnodi

signal adj hynod ♦ n arwydd

signatory adj arwyddol ♦ n arwyddwr

signature n llofnod

significance n arwyddocâd, ystyr

significant adj arwyddocaol; o bwys

signify vb arwyddo, arwyddocáu

signpost n mynegbost, arwyddbost

silence n taw, distawrwydd ♦ vt rhoi taw ar

silent adj distaw, tawedog, mud

silhouette n llun du, cysgodlun,

silwet

silicon n silicon. **s. chip** sglodyn silicon

silk n sidan

silky adj sidanaidd

sill n sil

silly adj gwirion, ffôl, disynnwyr

silt n gwaelodion, llaid ♦ vb gwaelodi, tagu

silver n arian ♦ vt ariannu. **s. paper** n papur arian

silversmith n gof arian

silvery adj ariannaid(d)

similar adj tebyg, cyffelyb

simile n cyffelybiaeth, cymhariaeth

simmer vi lledferwi, goferwi

simper vi cilwenu, glaswenu

simple adj syml, unplyg; gwirin, diniwed

simplicity n symlrwydd, unplygrwydd

simplify vt symleiddio

simulate vt ffugio, dynwared

simultaneous adj cyfamserol, ar y pryd

sin n pechod ♦ vb pechu

since conj gan, yn gymaint ♦ prep er, er pan

sincere adj diffuant, didwyll, pur

sinew n gewyn, giewyn

sing vb canu

singe vt deifio

singer n canwr, cantwr, cantores

singing n canu

single adj sengl, dibriod, gweddw. **s. bed** n gwely sengl. **s.-minded** adj unplyg, cywir. **s. room** n ystafell sengl

singlet n gwasgod wlanen, crys isaf

singular adj unigol; hynod

sinister adj ysgeler; chwithig

sink vb soddi, suddo ♦ n sinc

sinner n pechadur

sinuous adj dolennog, troellog

sip vt llymeitian ♦ n llymaid,

llymeidyn
siphon n siffon
sir n syr
siren n corn, seiren
sirloin n llwyn eidion
sissy n cadi(ffan)
sister n chwaer
sister-in-law n chwaer yng nghyfraith
sit vb eistedd
site n safle, lle ♦ vb lleoli
sitting n eisteddiad
situated adj yn sefyll, wedi ei leoli
situation adj n lle, safle; sefyllfa
six adj, n chwech
sixteen adj, n un ar bymtheg, un deg chwech
sixth adj chweched
sixty adj, n trigain, chwe deg
sizable adj gweddol fawr
size n maint, maintioli
sizzle vi ffrio
skate n cath fôr
skate n sgêt ♦ vb ysglefrio
skateboard n bwrdd sglefrio
skein n cengl, sgain
skeleton n ysgerbwd; amlinelliad
sketch n llun, braslun ♦ vb braslunio, tynnu
skewer n gwaell, gwachell
ski n sgi ♦ vb sgio
skid vb llithro (naill ochr)
skier n sgïwr
skiff n ysgafnfad, ceubal, sgiff
skill n medr, medrusrwydd
skilled adj medrus, crefftus
skim vb tynnu, codi (hufen)
skimmed milk n llaeth glas, llaeth sgim
skimp vb crintachu, cybydda
skimpy adj crintach
skin n croen ♦ vb blingo
skinny adj tenau; prin, crintach
skip vi llamu, sgipio
skipper n capten llong
skipping-rope n rhaff sgipio
skirmish n ysgarmes

skirt n godre, sgyrt ♦ vt dilyn gyda godre
skit n gogan
skittish adj nwyfus, gwantan, anwadal
skittles npl ceilys
skulk vi llechu, techu
skull n penglog
skunk n drewgi
sky n wybren, wybr, awyr
skylark n ehedydd
skylight n ffenestr do
slab n llech
slack adj llac, diofal, esgeulus ♦ n glo mân
slacken vb llacio, llaesu
slag n sorod, slag
slake vt torri (syched), slecio
slam vb cau yn glats, clepian
slander n enllib ♦ vt enllibio
slang n iaith sathredig, slang ♦ vt difrio
slant vb gwyro, gogwyddo ♦ n gogwydd
slanting adj ar oledd/osgo
slap vt clewtian ♦ n clewt(en), palfod
slapdash adj ffwrdd-â-hi, rhywsut-rywfodd
slash n slaes, hac ♦ vt slasio, chwipio
slate n llech, llechen
slate vt sennu, difrio
slattern n slwt, slebog, sopen
slaughter n lladdedigaeth, lladdfa ♦ vt lladd
slaughterhouse n lladd-dy
slave n slaf, caethwas ♦ vi slafio
slavery n caethiwed, caethwasanaeth
slay vt lladd
sled, sledge, sleigh n car llusg, sled
sledgehammer n gordd
sleek adj llyfn, llyfndew, graenus
sleep vb cysgu, huno ♦ n cwsg, hun

sleeper n (person) cysgwr; pren neu ddefnydd arall i ddal y cledrau

sleeping bag n sach gysgu

sleeping pill n pilsen gysgu

sleepy adj cysglyd

sleet n eirlaw

sleeve n llawes

sleight n deheurwydd, cyfrwystra, dichell

slender adj main, eiddil, prin

slice n tafell, ysglisen ♦ vt tafellu, ysglisio

slick adj llyfn, tafodrydd, slic

slide vb llithro, sglefrio ♦ n llithren, sleid

slight adj ysgafn, eiddil, prin ♦ vt diystyru ♦ n diystyrwch, sarhad

slightly adv ychydig; ychydig

slim adj main, eiddil

slime n llaid, llaca; llys, llysnafedd

sling vt taflu, lluchio ♦ n ffon dafl

slip vb llithro, dianc; gollwng ♦ n slip

slipper n llopan, sliper

slippery adj llithrig, diafael, di-ddal

slipshod adj anniben

slipway n llithrfa

slit vb hollti, agennu, rhwygo ♦ n hollt

slither vb ymlusgo, llithro

slobber vb glaferio, slobran

sloe n eirinen ddu fach, draenen ddu

slog vb gweithio'n galed

sloop n slŵp

slop n (pl) golchion ♦ vb gwlychu, trochi

slope n llethr, gogwydd ♦ vb gogwyddo

sloppy adj lleidiog, tomlyd; meddal, masw; anniben

slot n agen, twll

sloth n diogi, seguryd, syrthni

slouch vb llaesu, ymollwng;

cerdded yn aflêr

sloven n dyn aflêr, slebog

slovenly adj anniben

slow adj araf, hwyrfrydig, hwyrdrwm ♦ vb arafu

slowly adv yn araf (deg)

sludge n llaid, llaca

slug n gwlithen, malwoden

sluggish adj diog, dioglyd, swrth

sluice n llifddor

slum n slym

slumber vb hepian, cysgu ♦ n cwsg

slump n cwymp, gostyngiad; dirwasgiad

slur vb difrïo ♦ n llithriad, cyflusg (cerdd.); anffri

slush n llaid, llaca, eira gwlyb

slut n slwt, slebog

sly adj cyfrwys, ffals, dichellgar, tan din

smack n blas ♦ vi blasu, blasio, archwaethu

smack n smac, palfod ♦ vb smacio, chwipio

smack n llongan, smac

small adj bach, bychan, mân, main

smallholder n tyddynnwr

small-pox n y frech wen

smart vi gwynio, dolurio, llosgi ♦ n gwyn, dolur ♦ adj llym, bywiog; ffel, ffraeth; crand

smash vb torri, malu, chwilfriwio

smattering n gwybodaeth fas, crap

smear vt iro, dwbio

smell n arogl, aroglau ♦ vb arogli

smile vb gwenu ♦ n gwên

smirch vt llychwino, difwyno

smirk vi cilwenu, glaswenu ♦ n cilwen

smith n gof

smithy n gefail (gof)

smog n smog, mwgwl

smoke n mwg ♦ vb mygu, ysmygu, smocio

smoked adj wedi ei fygu

smoky adj myglyd

smooth adj llyfn, esmwyth ♦ vt llyfnhau

smother vb mygu, llethu

smoulder vi mudlosgi

smudge n baw, staen, smotyn ♦ vb difwyno, trochi

smug adj hunanol, cysetlyd

smuggle vt smyglio

smut n parddu, huddygl, smotyn; siarad aflan

smutty adj aflan, brwnt

snack n tamaid, byrbryd. **s. bar** n lle am damaid

snag n rhwystr, maen tramgwydd

snail n malwoden, malwen

snake n neidr

snap vb clecian, torri'n glats; tynnu llun ♦ n clec

snare n magl, croglath ♦ vt maglu, rhwydo

snarl vi ysgyrnygu, chwyrnu

snatch vb cipio ♦ n cip, crap; tamaid

sneak vi llechian ♦ n llechgi

sneaking adj llechwraidd, cachgïaidd

sneer vb gwawdio, glaswenu ♦ n gwawd, glaswen

sneeze vi tisian

sniff vb ffroeni, gwyntio

snigger vb glaschwerthin

snip vb torri, cynhinio ♦ n demyn, toriad

snipe n gïach

snippet n tamaid, cynhinyn

snob n crechyn (pl. crachach), snob

snobbish adj crachaidd, snoblyd

snooker n snwcer

snooze vb hepian ♦ n cyntun

snore vi chwyrnu

snort vi ffroeni, ffroenochi

snotty adj cas

snout n trwyn anifail, duryn

snow n eira, ôd ♦ vb bwrw eira, odi

snowball n pelen eira

snowdrift n lluwch

snowflake n pluen eira

snow plough n aradr eira

snub vt sennu ♦ n sen

snub adj pwt, smwt

snub-nosed adj trwyn smwt

snuff vb ffroeni, snwffian ♦ n trwynlwch, snisyn

snug adj cryno, clyd, diddos

snuggle vb ymwasgu at; llochi, anwesu

so adv, conj fel, felly; mor, cyn

soak vb mwydo, sucio; slotian

soap n sebon ♦ vb seboni. **s. opera** n opera sebon. **s. powder** n powdr golchi

soapy adj sebonllyd

soar vi ehedeg, esgyn

sob vi igian, beichio ♦ n ig, ebwch

sober adj sobr, sad ♦ vb sobri

sobriety n sobrwydd

so-called adj dywededig

soccer n pêl-droed, y bêl gron

sociable adj cymdeithasgar

social adj cymdeithasol. **s. club** n clwb cymdeithasol. **s. security** n nawdd cymdeithasol. **s. work** n gwaith cymdeithasol

socialism n sosialaeth

socialist n sosialydd

society n cymdeithas, cyfeillach

sociology n cymdeithaseg

sock n hosan

socket n twll, crau, soced

sod n tywarchen

soda water n dŵr soda

sodden adj wedi mwydo, soeglyd

sofa n glwth, esmwythfainc, soffa

soft adj meddal, tyner; distaw; gwirion. **s. drink** n diod ysgafn

software n meddalwedd

soggy adj gwlyb, lleidiog

soil n pridd, daear, gweryd

soil vt difwyno, baeddu ♦ n baw, tom

solace n cysur, diddanwch ♦ vt cysuro, diddanu

solar adj heulog, solar
solder n sawdring, sawdur, sodr ♦ vt asio, sawdurio, sodro
soldier n milwr
sole adj unig, unigol, un
sole n gwadn ♦ vt gwadnu
sole n (fish) lleden chwithig
solemn adj difrifol, dwys
sol-fa n sol-ffa ♦ vb solffeuo
solicit vt erfyn, ymofyn; llithio
solicitor n cyfreithiwr
solid adj caled, sylweddol, solet, cadarn
solid n solid
solidarity n undod
solitary adj unig; anghyfannedd
solitude n unigedd
solo n unawd
soloist n unawdydd
soluble adj toddadwy, hydawdd
solution n dehongliad, esboniad; toddiant
solve vt datrys, dehongli
solvent adj yn gallu talu, di-ddyled ♦ n toddfa
sombre adj tywyll, prudd
some adj rhai, rhyw, peth, ychydig ♦ pron rhywrai, rhywfaint ♦ adv ynghylch, tua, rhyw
somebody pron = someone
somehow adv rywfodd, rhywsut
someone pron rhywun
somersault n trosben ♦ vb troi tin tros ben, pen dra mwnwgl
something n rhywbeth
sometime adv rywbryd, gynt
sometimes adv weithiau, ar brydiau, ambell waith
somewhat adv go, lled, braidd
somewhere adv (yn) rhywle
son n mab
song n cân, cathl, cerdd
sonic adj sonig
son-in-law n mab yng nghyfraith
sonnet n soned
soon adv buan, ebrwydd, clau
sooner adv (time) ynghynt, yn

gynt; (preference): **I would s. do** byddai'n well gennyf wneud; **s. or later** yn hwyr neu'n hwyrach
soot n huddygl, parddu
soothe vt lliniaru, lleddfu, dofi, tawelu
sop n tamaid (wedi ei wlychu)
sophism n soffyddiaeth
sophist n soffydd
sophistical adj soffyddol
sophisticated adj soffistigedig
sopping adj gwlyb diferu
soppy adj teimladol; mwydlyd
soprano n soprano
sorcerer n swynwr, dewin
sorcery n swyngyfaredd, dewiniaeth
sordid adj brwnt, cybyddlyd, gwael
sore adj tost, blin, dolurus ♦ n dolur
sorrow n tristwch, gofid, galar ♦ vi tristáu, gofidio
sorry adj drwg gan, edifar; salw
sort n modd; math, bath ♦ vt trefnu, dosbarthu
sortie n cyrch
sorting office n swyddfa ddosbarthu
so-so adv gweddol
sot n diotyn, meddwyn
soul n enaid
soul-destroying adj yn fwrn llethol
sound n sain, swn, trwst ♦ vb seinio
sound vb plymio, chwilio
sound n culfor, swnt
sound adj iach, iachus, dianaf, cyfan, dilys. **s. effects** npl effeithiau sain
soundboard n seinfwrdd
soundly adv yn drwm, yn llwyr
soundproof adj yn gwrthsefyll swn
soup n potes, cawl
sour adj sur ♦ vb suro
source n ffynhonnell, tarddiad

south n deau, de. **S. Africa** n De Affrica

southern adj deheuol

souvenir n cofrodd

sovereign adj pen ♦ n penadur; sofren

Soviet adj Sofietaidd

Soviet Union n: the **S.U.** yr Undeb Sofietaidd

sow n hwch

sow vt hau

soya n soya. **s. beans** npl ffa soya

space n lle, gwagle, gofod, encyd, ysbaid

spaceman n gofodwr

spaceship n llong ofod

spacious adj eang, helaeth

spade n rhaw, pâl

Spain n Hisbaen

span n rhychwant ♦ vt rhychwantu

spaniel n adargi, sbaniel

Spanish adj Sbaenaidd ♦ n Sbaeneg

spank vt slapio, smacio, palfodi, chwipio tin

spanner n sbaner

spar vi cwffio, paffio

spar n polyn, cledren, ceibren

spare adj prin; tenau; sbâr ♦ vt arbed; hepgor

sparerib n sbarib, asen-frân

sparing adj cynnil, prin

spark n gwreichionen

sparkle vi gwreichioni, serennu, pefrio

sparkling adj gloyw, llachar; byrlymog

sparrow n aderyn y to

sparse adj tenau, prin, gwasgarog

spasm n pwl, gwayw, brath

spate n llifeiriant sydyn

spatter vb tasgu

spawn n grawn, gronell; grifft; sil ♦ vb silio, bwrw grawn

speak vb llefaru, siarad

speaker n llefarydd, siaradwr

spear n gwaywffon, picell ♦ vt trywanu

special adj neilltuol, arbennig

specialist n arbenigwr

speciality n arbenigrwydd

species (**species**) n rhywogaeth

specific adj priodol, penodol, pendant

specify vt enwi, penodi

specimen n enghraifft, cynllun

specious adj teg yr olwg, rhithiol

speck n brycheuyn, ysmotyn

speckle vt britho, brychu

spectacle n drych, golygfa; (pl) sbectol

spectator n edrychwr, gwyliwr

spectre n drychiolaeth

spectrum (**-ra**) n spectrwm

speculate vi dyfalu; anturio, mentro

speculation n dyfaliad; antur, menter

speech n llafar, lleferydd, parabl, ymadrodd; araith

speed n cyflymder, buander ♦ vb prysuro, cyflymu. **s. limit** n ataliad cyflymder

speedometer n mesurydd cyflymdra

spell n cyfaredd, swyn

spell n sbel, hoe, ysbaid

spell vt sillafu

spend vb treulio, gwario, bwrw

spendthrift n afradwr, oferwr, gwastraffwr

sperm n had

spew vb chwydu

sphere n cronnell, sffêr, pêl; cylch, maes

spice n perlysiau, peraroglau, sbeis

spick-and-span adj fel y pin

spicy adj blasus; ffraeth, diddorol; coch

spider n cor, corryn, pryf copyn

spike n pig, hoel, cethren

spikenard n ysbignard, nard

spill vb colli, tywallt

spin vb nyddu, troi, troelli

spinach n pigoglys, sbinais

spindle n gwerthyd; echel

spin-dryer n trowasgwr

spine n asgwrn cefn; draen, pigyn

spinner n nyddwr

spinning top n top tro

spinning-wheel n troell

spin-off n mantais

spinster n merch ddibriod, hen ferch

spiral adj fel cogwrn tro, troellog

spirant adj llaes ♦ npl llaesion

spire n meindwr, pigwrn, pigdwr

spirit n ysbryd; gwirod

spirited adj calonnog, nwyfus, ysbrydol

spiritual adj ysbrydol

spiritualist n ysbrydegydd

spit n bêr

spit vb poeri

spite n sbeit, malais ♦ vt sbeitio

spiteful adj maleisus, sbeitlyd

spittle n poer, poeryn

spittoon n llestr poeri

splash vb sblasio, tasgu

spleen n y ddueg; pruddglwyf; natur ddrwg, gwenwyn

splendid adj ysblennydd, gwych, campus

splendour n ysblander, gwychder

splint n dellten, ysgyren, sblint

splinter vb ysgyrioni ♦ n ysgyren, fflaw

split vb hollti, rhannu, gwahanu

spoil n ysbail, anrhaith ♦ vb ysbeilio, ysbwylio, difetha

spoke n adain olwyn, sbogen, braich

spokesman n llefarwr, llefarydd

spoliation n ysbeiliad, ysbwyliad

sponge n sbwng ♦ vb ysbyngu

sponsor n mach, hyrwyddwr, noddwr; tad bedydd, mam fedydd

spontaneous adj gwirfoddol, digymell

spook n ysbryd, bwgan, bwci

spool n gwerthyd

spoon n llwy ♦ vb llwyo; caru

spoonful n llwyaid

spoor n brisg, ôl

sporadic adj achlysurol, gwasgarog

spore n had (rhedyn, etc)

sport n sbort, chwarae, difyrrwch, cellwair, hwyl

sportive adj chwareus, nwyfus

sports npl mabolgampau, chwaraeon

spot n man, lle, llecyn; brycheuyn, ysmotyn ♦ vt mannu, brychu, ysmotio ♦ adj ar y pryd

spotless adj difrycheulyd, glân

spotted adj brith, brych

spouse n priod

spout vt pistyllio, ffrydio ♦ n pistyll

sprain vt ysigo

sprawl vi ymdaenu, ymdreiglo, ymrwyfo

spray n gwlith, tawch, trochion ♦ vt taenellu; chwistrellu

spray n ysbrigyn, cainc; chwystrellydd

spread vb lledu, taenu, lledaenu, gwasgaru

spree n sbri

sprig n brigyn, ysbrigyn

sprightly adj bywiog, hoenus, nwyfus

spring vb tarddu, codi, deillio; llamu, neidio ♦ n ffynnon; llam; sbring; gwanwyn. **s.-clean** n glanhau'r gwanwyn

springy adj sbringar

sprinkle vb taenellu, ysgeintio

sprint vb gwibio

sprinter n gwibiwr

sprit n sbryd

sprite n ysbryd, bwgan, bwci

sprout vb tarddu, egino, glasu

sprouts npl (Brussels) ysgewyll Brysel

spruce adj twt, taclus, smart,

crand ♦ n pyrwydden
spry adj sionc, heini, hoyw
spur n ysbardun, swmbwl ♦ vb ysbarduno, symbylu
spurious adj ffug, gau, annilys
spurn vb cicio, dirmygu, tremygu
spurt n ysbonc
sputter vb poeri siarad, baldorddi
spy n ysbiwr ♦ vb ysbio
squabble vi cweryla, ffraeo ♦ n ffrwgwd, ffrae
squad n carfan, mintai
squadron n sgwadron
squalid adj brwnt, bawlyd, budr
squall vi ysgrechain ♦ n gwawch; storm o wynt
squalor n brynti
squander vt gwastraffu, afradu
square adj, n sgwâr, petryal
squash vt gwasgu, llethu ♦ n sboncen. orange s. sudd oren
squat vi swatio, cyrcydu
squawk vi gwawchio ♦ n gwawch
squeak vi gwichian ♦ n gwich
squeal vi gwichian
squeamish adj dicra, misi
squeeze vb gwasgu
squelch vt llethu, gostegu, rhoi taw ar
squib n tanen wyllt, fflachen; gogan, dychan
squint vb ciledrych, cibedrych ♦ n llygaid croes
squire n ysgweier, yswain
squirm vb gwingo
squirrel n gwiwer
squirt vb chwistrellu, tasgu ♦ n chwistrell, gwn dŵr
stab vb brathu, gwanu, trywanu
stable n ystabl
stable adj diysgog, sefydlog, safadwy, sad
stack n tas, bera; corn simnai, stac
staff n ffon; erwydd; staff
stag n carw, hydd
stage n pwynt; gradd, lefel;

llwyfan
stage-coach n y goets fawr
stagger vb honclan, gwegian; syfrdanu
stagnant adj llonydd, marw
stagnate vi cronni, sefyll
staid adj sad, sobr
stain vb ystaenio, llychwino ♦ n staen
stained glass window n ffenestr liw
stainless adj difrycheulyd, gloyw
stair n gris, staer
stake n polyn, pawl, ystanc; cyngwystl
stale adj hen, hendrwm; diflas, mws
stalk vb torsythu, rhodio'n benuchel, mynd ar drywydd
stalk n paladr, gwelltyn, coes
stall n côr; stondin; talcen glo ♦ vb stolio
stalls npl (in cinema, theatre) seddau; stondinau
stallion n march, stalwyn
stalwart adj cadarn, pybyr, dewr
stamen n brigeryn
stamina n saf, ynni
stammer vb bloesgi, siarad ag atal arno
stamp n stamp, delw, argraff ♦ vb stampio; curo traed
stampede n chwalfa, rhuthr
stanch vt atal, sychu (gwaed)
stanchion n annel, ateg, post, gwanas
stand vb sefyll, bod, aros ♦ n safiad; eisteddle; stondyn
standard n lluman, baner; post; safon
stanza n pennill
staple n prif nwydd; edefyn (gwlân, etc)
staple n ystwffwl, stapal
stapler n styffylwr
star n seren ♦ vb serennu
starch n starts

stare vb llygadrythu, synnu
stark adj syth, moel, rhonc ♦ adv hollol
starling n aderyn drudwy, drudwen, aderyn yr eira
starry adj serennog
start vb dechrau, cychwyn, codi, rhusio, tasgu
startle vt brawychu, dychrynu, rhusio
starvation n newyn
starve vb newynu; fferru, rhynnu
state n ystad, cyflwr, ansawdd; rhwysg; gwladwriaeth; talaith
state vt mynegi, datgan; penodi
stately adj urddasol, mawreddog
statement n mynegiad, datganiad, haeriad
statesman (men) n gwladweinydd
station n gorsaf, stesion; safle, sefyllfa
stationary adj sefydlog
stationer n gwerthwr papurau
stationer's n (shop) siop bapurau
stationmaster n gorsaf-feistr
statistics npl ystadegau
statue n delw, cerfddelw, cerflun
stature n uchder, taldra, corffolaeth
status n safle, braint, statws
statute n deddf, cyfraith, ystatud
staunch adj pybyr, cywir
stave n estyllen, erwydd ♦ vt astellu; dryllio. **s. off** cadw draw
stay vb aros; ategu; atal ♦ n arhosiad; ateg; (pl) staes
stead n lle
steadfast adj diysgog
steadily adv yn bwyllog, yn gyson
steady adj sad, diysgog; cyson, gwastad
steak n golwyth, stec
steal vb dwyn, lladrata, cipio
stealth n lladrad. **by s.** yn ddistaw bach
stealthy adj lladradaidd
steam n ager, anwedd, stêm, tarth

♦ vb ageru
steamer n agerlong, stemar
steed n march, ceffyl
steel n dur ♦ vt caledu
steelworks n gwaith dur
steep adj serth ♦ n dibyn, clogwyn, llethr
steep vt rhoi yng ngwlych, mwydo, sucio
steeple n clochdy
steer n bustach
steer vb llywio; cyfeirio
steering n llywio
steering wheel n llyw
stem n paladr, corsen, coes, bôn; ach; pen blaen
stem vt gwrthsefyll, gwrthladd, atal
stench n drewdod, drycsawr
stenography n llaw-fer
step vi camu; cerdded ♦ n cam; gris
step- prefix llys-
stepdaughter n llysferch
stepfather n llystad
stepmother n llysfam, mam wen
stepsister n llyschwaer
stepson n llysfab
stereotype n ystrydeb ♦ vt ystrydebu
sterile adj diffrwyth, sych
sterilize vb diffrwythloni, diheintio
sterling adj ysterling; diledryw, diffuant
stern adj llym, penderfynol
stern n starn, pen ôl llong
stethoscope n corn meddyg
stevedore n llwythwr a dadlwythwr llongau
stew vb araf ferwi, stiwio ♦ n stiw
steward n stiward, goruchwyliwr, distain
stick n pren, ffon, pric, gwialen
stick vb glynu; gwanu, brathu
sticky adj gludiog, glynol; anodd
stiff adj syth, anystwyth, anhyblyg, ystyfnig

stiffen vb sythu, ystyfnigo

stifle vt mygu, tagu, diffodd

stigma n gwarthnod, stigma

stile n camfa, sticil, sticill

still n distyllfa, stil

still adj llonydd; marw ♦ vb llonyddu

still adv eto, er hynny; byth

stilt n ystudfach

stilted adj annaturiol; mawreddog

stimulant n symbylydd; gwirod

stimulate vt symbylu

stimulus (-li) n symbyliad, swmbwl

sting vb pigo, brathu, colynnu ♦ n colyn

stingy adj crintach, cybyddlyd

stink vi, n drewi

stinking adj drewllyd

stint vt cynilo, cybydda ♦ n prinder

stipend n cyflog, tâl

stipulate vb amodi, mynnu

stir vb cyffroi, cynhyrfu, symud ♦ n stŵr, cynnwrf

stirrup n gwarthol

stitch n pwyth; gwayw, pigyn ♦ vt pwytho, gwnïo

stoat n carlwm

stock n cyff; stoc, ystôr. **stocks** npl cyffion

stock exchange n cyfnewidfa stoc

stocking n hosan

stocky adj cadarn, cryf, cydnerth

stodgy adj toeslyd, trymllyd, diflas

stoke vb edrych ar ôl tân, tanio

stole n ystola

stolid adj swrth, digyffro

stomach n cylla, stumog

stone n carreg, maen ♦ vt llabyddio

stool n ystôl

stoop vb plygu, crymu, gwargrymu, ymostwng

stop vb atal, rhwystro; stopio, cau; aros, sefyll ♦ n atalfa; atalnod

stoppage n (pay) ataliad, (strike) streic

stopper n topyn, caead

storage n stôr, storfa

store n ystôr, ystorfa ♦ vt ystorio

storey, story n uchdwr, llofft, llawr

stork n ciconia, chwibon

storm n (y)storm, tymestl

stormy adj stormus, tymhestlog, garw

story n hanes, chwedl, stori; celwydd

stout adj tew, ffyrf; pybyr, gwrol, glew

stove n stof, ffwrn

stow vt pacio, dodi o'r neilltu

stowaway n teithiwr cudd

straddle vi bongamu, lledu'r traed

straggle vi crwydro, gwasgaru

straggler n crwydryn

straight adj union, syth

straighten vb unioni

straightforward adj syml; didwyll, gonest

straightway adv yn y fan, yn syth

strain vb straenio, streiffio, ysigo; tynhau; hidlo ♦ n straen

strainer n hidl(en)

strait n cyfyng, cul, caeth ♦ n cyfyngder; culfor

strand n traeth, traethell, tywyn

strand n cainc (rhaff), edau

strange adj dieithr, estronol, rhyfedd

stranger n dyn dieithr, estron

strangle vt tagu, llindagu

strap n strap, cengl

strategic adj strategol

strategy n strategaeth

stratum (-ta) n haen

straw n gwellt; gwelltyn, blewyn

strawberry n mefysen, syfien

stray vi crwydro, cyfeiliorni

streak n llinell, rhes, rhesen; stremp ♦ vb gwibio

stream n ffrwd ♦ vb ffrydio, llifo

streamer n rhuban, baner

street n heol, ystryd

strength n cryfder, nerth, grym

strengthen vb cryfhau, nerthu

strenuous adj egniol, ymdrechgar

stress n pwys, straen, caledi

stretch vb estyn, tynhau ♦ n estyniad

stretcher n trestl, stretsier

strew vt gwasgaru, sarnu, chwalu, taenu

strict adj cyfyng, caeth, llym

stricture n cyfyngiad; cerydd, sen

stride vb camu, brasgamu ♦ n cam

strife n cynnen, ymryson, ymrafael

strike vb taro; gostwng ♦ n taro, streic

striker n streiciwr

striking adj trawiadol, hynod

string n llinyn, tant, cortyn

stringent adj caeth, llym, tyn

strip n llain, llafn, llefnyn. **film s.** striplun, stribed ffilm

strip vb diosg, ymddiosg, ymddihatru

stripe n rhes, rhesen; gwialennod

striped adj rhengog, rhesenog; â llinellau amliw ar hyd-ddo

stripling n glaslanc, llanc, llencyn

strive vi ymdrechu; ymryson

stroke n dyrnod, ergyd, trawiad; llinell

stroke vt llochi, dylofi, pratio, canmol

stroll vi crwydro, rhodianna

strong adj cryf, grymus, cadarn

stronghold n amddiffynfa, cadarnle

structure n adail, adeilad, saerniaeth, adeiledd, strwythur

struggle vi gwingo; ymdrechu ♦ n ymdrech

strut vi torsythu

stub n bonyn

stubble n sofl

stubborn adj cyndyn, ystyfnig

stuck-up adj ffroenuchel

stud n boglwm, boglyn, styden

stud n gre

student n myfyriwr, efrydydd

studio n stiwdio

study n astudiaeth, efrydiaeth, npl efrydiau; myfyrgell, stydi ♦ vb myfyrio, efrydu, astudio

stuff n defnydd, stwff ♦ vb stwffio, gwthio

stuffing adj (bed) fflocys; (CULIN) stwffin

stuffy adj myglyd, trymllyd, trymaidd

stumble vb tramgwyddo, baglu, syrthio

stump n bonyn, boncyff

stun vt syfrdanu, byddaru, hurtio

stunt vt crabio

stunted adj crablyd

stupefy vt syfrdanu, hurtio

stupendous adj aruthrol

stupid adj hurt, pendew, dwl, twp

stupor n syfrdandod, syrthni

sturdy adj talgryf, pybyr, cadarn, cryf

stutter vi siarad ag atal arno, bloesgi

sty n cwt, cut, twlc

style n dull, arddull; cyfenw, teitl ♦ vt cyfenwi

stylish adj dillyn, trwsiadus

stylus n (of record player) nodwydd

suave adj mwyn, tirion, hynaws, rhadlon

sub- prefix tan-, is-, go-

subconscious n isymwybod ♦ adj isymwybodol

subdue vt darostwng; lleddfu

subject n darostyngedig; caeth; ufudd ♦ n deiliad; pwnc, testun; goddrych

subject vt darostwng, dwyn dan

subjective adj goddrychol

subjugate vt darostwng

subjunctive adj dibynnol

sublime adj aruchel, arddunol

submarine adj tanforol ♦ n llong

danfor
submerge vb soddi, suddo
submission n ymostyngiad;
ufudd-dod; cyflwyniad
submissive adj gostyngedig, ufudd
submit vb ymostwng,
ymddarostwng; datgan barn;
cyflwyno
subnormal adj isnormal
subordinate adj israddol ♦ vt
darostwng
subpoena n gwŷs
subscribe vb tanysgrifio, cyfrannu
subscription n tanysgrifiad,
cyfraniad
subsequent adj canlynol, dilynol
subsequently adv wedyn, ar ôl
hynny
subside vi soddi, ymollwng;
darfod
subsidiary adj israddol;
ychwanegol, atodol
subsidy n arian cymorth,
cymhorthdal
subsist vb byw, bod, bodoli,
ymgynnal
subsistence n cynhaliaeth
subsoil n isbridd
substance n sylwedd, defnydd; da
substantial adj sylweddol
substantiate vt profi, gwirio
substitute n eilydd, dirprwy, un
yn lle arall ♦ vt rhoi yn lle
subterfuge n ystryw, cast
subterranean adj tanddaearol
subtle adj cyfrwys, craff
subtract vt tynnu ymaith
suburb n maestref
subvert vt dymchwelyd, gwyrdroi
subway n isffordd
succeed vb dilyn, canlyn, llwyddo,
ffynnu
success n llwyddiant, llwydd,
ffyniant
successful adj llwyddiannus
successfully adv yn llwyddiannus
succession n dilyniad, olyniaeth

successive adj dilynol, olynol
succinct adj byr, cryno
succour vt swcro, ymgeleddu ♦ n
swcr, ymgeledd
succulent adj ir, iraidd, noddlyd
succumb vi ymollwng dan, ildio,
marw
such adj cyfryw, y fath, cyffelyb
suck vb sugno, dyfnu; llyncu, yfed
suckle vt rhoi bron, sugno
suction n sugn, sugniad,
sugndyniad
sudden adj sydyn, disymwth,
disyfyd
suds npl trochion sebon, sucion
sue vb erlyn; erfyn, deisyf
suede n swêd
suet n gwêr, swyf, siwed
suffer vb goddef, dioddef, gadael
sufferer n dioddefydd
suffering n dioddef
suffice vb bod yn ddigon, digoni
sufficient adj digon, digonol
suffix n olddodiad
suffocate vb mygu, tagu
suffrage n pleidlais
suffuse vt taenu, gwasgaru,
ymledu
sugar n siwgr ♦ vt siwgro
suggest vt awgrymu
suggestion n awgrym, awgrymiad
suicide n hunanladdiad
suit n cwyn, cyngaws, hawl;
deisyfiad, cais; siwt, pâr ♦ vb
ateb, siwtio, gweddu, taro
suitable adj addas, cyfaddas,
cymwys
suitably adv yn addas
suitcase n bag dillad
suite n cyfres; gosgordd, nifer
suitor n cwynwr; cariadfab
sulk vi sorri, pwdu, mulo
sullen adj sarrug, cuchiog, blwng
sully vt difwyno, llychwino
sulphur n sylffwr
sultan n swltan
sultry adj mwrn, mwll, clòs

sum n swm ♦ vt crynhoi, symio

summarize vb crynhoi

summary adj byr, cryno ♦ n crynodeb

summer n haf

summerhouse n tŷ haf

summit n pen, copa, crib

summon vt gwysio, dyfynnu

summons n gwŷs, dyfyn

sump n swmp

sumptuous adj moethus

sun n haul ♦ vt heulo

sunbathe vb torheulo, bolaheulo

sunbeam n pelydryn

sunburn n llosg haul

Sunday n dydd Sul

sunder vt ysgaru, gwahanu

sundry adj amryw, amrywiol

sunflower n blodyn yr haul

sunglasses npl sbectol haul

sunny adj heulog

sunshine n heulwen

sunstroke n ergyd (yr) haul

suntan n lliw haul

sup vb llymeitian; swpera, swperu ♦ n llymaid

super- prefix uwch, goruwch, gor-, tra-, ar-

superannuation n ymddeolaeth, pensiwn

superb adj ysblennydd, godidog

supercilious adj balch, ffroenuchel

superficial adj arwynebol, bas

superfine adj coeth

superfluous adj gormodol, afreidiol

superintend vt arolygu

superintendent n arolygwr, arolygydd

superior adj uwch, gwell, rhagorach; uwchraddol ♦ n uchafiad, uwchradd

superiority n rhagoriaeth

superlative adj uchaf; eithaf

supermarket n archfarchnad

supernatural adj goruwchnaturiol

supersede vt disodli

superstition n coelgrefydd, ofergoeliaeth

superstitious adj coelgrefyddol, ofergoelus

supervene vi digwydd

supervise vt arolygu

supervision n arolygiaeth

supine adj diofal, didaro, swrth

supper n swper

supplant vt disodli

supple adj ystwyth, hyblyg

supplement n atodiad ♦ vt atodi

supplementary adj atodol, ychwanegol

suppliant n ymbiliwr, erfyniwr

supplicate vb erfyn, ymbil, deisyf

supplier n cyflenwr, cyflenwydd

supply vt cyflenwi, cyflawni ♦ n cyflenwad

support vt cynnal ♦ n cynhaliaeth

supporter n cefnogwr, cefnogydd

suppose vt tybio, tybied, bwrw

suppository n tawddgyffur

suppress vt llethu, gostegu; atal; celu

suppurate vi crawni, gori

surcharge n gordal, gordoll ♦ vb codi gormod

sure adj, adv siwr, sicr; diamau, diau

surely adv yn sicr, yn ddiau

surety n mach, meichiau, gwystl

surf n traethfor, beiston; gorewyn ♦ n brigo, brigdonni

surface n wyneb, arwynebedd, caen

surfeit n syrffed ♦ vb alaru, syrffedu

surge vi ymchwyddo ♦ n ymchwydd

surgeon n llawfeddyg

surgery n llawfeddygaeth; meddygfa, llys meddyg

surgical adj llawfeddygol

surly adj sarrug, afrywiog

surmise n tyb ♦ vt tybied, amau

surmount vt mynd dros, gorchfygu, trechu

surname n cyfenw ♦ vt cyfenwi

surpass vt rhagori ar, trechu

surplice n gwenwisg

surplus n gweddill, gormod, gwarged

surprise n synodd ♦ vt synnu

surprising adj syn, rhyfedd

surrender vb traddodi, ildio

surreptitious adj lladradaidd, llechwraidd

surrogate n dirprwy, rhaglaw esgob

surround vt amgylchu, amgylchynu

surroundings npl amgylchoedd

surveillance n arolygiaeth, gwyliadwriaeth

survey vt edrych, arolygu; mesur ♦ n arolwg

survival n goroesiad

survive vb goroesi

survivor n goroeswr

susceptible adj parod i, tueddol i

suspect vt drwgdybio, amau ♦ n un a ddrwgdybir

suspend vt crogi; gohirio, atal

suspended sentence n dedfryd wedi'i gohirio

suspense n pryder, petruster, oediad

suspension n ataliad. **s. bridge** n pont grog

suspicion n drwgdybiaeth, amheuaeth

suspicious adj drwgdybus, amheus

sustain vt cynnal; dioddef, goddef

sustained adj parhaus, cyson

sustenance n cynhaliaeth, ymborth, bwyd

swagger vb rhodresa, torsythu, swagro

swallow n gwennol

swallow vt llyncu ♦ n llwnc

swamp n cors ♦ vt gorlifo, boddi

swan n alarch

swank vi bocsachu, rhodresa ♦ n bocsach

swap vb ffeirio

swarm n haid ♦ vi heidio, heigio

swarm vb dringo

swarthy adj melynddu, croenddu, tywyll

swat vt taro

swathe vt rhwymo, rhwymynnu

sway vb siglo, gwegian; llywio ♦ n llywodraeth, swae

swear vb tyngu, rhegi

sweat n chwys ♦ vb chwysu

sweater n cot wlan, sweter

sweaty adj chwyslyd

swede n rwden, sweden

Swede n Swediad

Sweden n Sweden

Swedish adj Swediaidd

sweep vb ysgubo ♦ n ysgubiad; ysgubwr

sweeping adj ysgubol

sweet adj melys, pêr, peraidd ♦ n pwdin

sweeten vb melysu; pereiddio

sweetheart n cariad

sweetmeat n fferin, melysyn

swell vb chwyddo ♦ n chwydd, ymchwydd; gŵr mawr

swelling n chwydd(i)

swelter vi crasu; lluddedu, dyddfu

sweltering adj llethol, tesog

swerve vi gwyro, osgoi, cilio, troi

swift adj cyflym, buan, chwyrn, clau

swift n gwennol ddu

swig n llymaid, dracht ♦ vb drachtio

swill n golchion; bwyd sur ♦ vb golchi; slotian

swim vb nofio ♦ n nawf

swimmer n nofiwr

swimming n nofio

swimmingly adv yn braf, yn hwylus

swimming pool n pwll nofio

swimsuit n dillad nofio, gwisg nofio

swindle vb twyllo, hocedu ♦ n twyll

swine (swine) n mochyn

swing vb siglo ♦ n sigl, siglen, swing

swinge vt llachio, baeddu

swirl vb troi, chwyldroi, chwyrndroi

swish vb chwipio

switch n swits, botwm ♦ vb troi, newid

swivel n arwyddlun ♦ vb troi

swollen adj chwyddedig, wedi chwyddo

swoon vt llewygu, llesmeirio ♦ n llewyg

swoop vb dyfod ar warthaf, disgyn

swop vt cyfnewid, ffeirio

sword n cleddyf, cleddau, cledd

sycamore n sycamorwydden

syllable n sillaf

syllabus n rhaglen, maes llafur

syllogism n cyfresymiad

symbol n arwyddlun, symbol, symlen (estheteg)

symbolism n symboliaeth

symmetrical adj cymesur

symmetry n cymesuredd

sympathetic adj cydymdeimladol

sympathize vi cydymdeimlo

sympathy n cydymdeimlad

symphony n symffoni

symposium (-ia) n trafodaeth, cynhadledd

symptom n arwydd

synagogue n synagog

synchronize vb cyfamseru, cydamseru

syncopation n trawsacen (cerdd)

syncope n marwlewyg; syncopé

syndicate n cwmni

synod n cymanfa, senedd, synod

synonym n (gair) cyfystyr

synopsis (-ses) n cyfolwg; crynodeb

syntax n cystrawen

synthesis (-ses) n cyfosodiad, synthesis

Syria n Syria

syringe n chwistrell ♦ vt chwistrellu

syrup n sudd; triagl (melyn)

system n cyfundrefn; trefn, system

systematic adj cyfundrefnol

systematize vb cyfundrefnu

T

tab n tafod, llabed

tabby n cath frech, cath fenyw

tabernacle n tabernacl, pabell

table n bwrdd, bord; tabl, taflen

tableau n golygfa (ddramatig)

table-cloth n lliain bord (bwrdd)

tableful n bordaid, byrddaid

tablespoon n llwy fwrdd

tablet n llechen, llech; tabled

table tennis n tennis bwrdd, ping pong

taboo n ysgymunbeth; gwaharddiad, tabŵ

tabular adj taflennol

tabulate vt tablu, taflennu

tacit adj dealledig (ond heb ei grybwyll)

taciturn adj tawedog

tack n tac, pwyth, brasbwyth ♦ vb tacio

tackle n taclau, offer, tacl (mewn rygbi), tacliad ♦ vb ymosod ar, taclo

tackler n taclwr

tact n tact, callineb, doethineb

tactful adj doeth, pwyllog, synhwyrol

tactician n tactegydd

tactics npl cynlluniau, tactegau

tactile adj cyffyrddol

tactless adj di-dact, annoeth

tadpole n penbwl, penbwla
tag n pwyntl; clust, dolen
tail n cynffon, llosgwrn, cwt
tailback n cwt, tagfa
tailor n teiliwr
taint vb llygru, heintio, difwyno ♦ n llwgr, ystaen, mefl
take vb cymryd, derbyn, cael
talcum n talcwm
tale n chwedl, hanes, stori, clec, clep
talent n talent
talisman n swynbeth, swyn, cyfaredd
talk vb, n siarad
talkative adj siaradus
tall adj tal, hir, uchel
tallness n taldra
tallow n gwêr
tally n cyfrif ♦ vb cyfateb, cytuno
talon n ewin, crafanc (aderyn)
tambourine n tambwrin
tame adj dof, gwâr ♦ vt dofi
tamper vi ymhél(á), ymyrryd(á)
tampon n tampwn
tan vb trin lledr; llosgi, melynu
tangent n tangiad, llinell gyffwrdd
tangible adj cyffyrddadwy, sylweddol
tangle vb drysu, cymysgu ♦ n dryswch, cymhlethdod
tank n dyfrgist, tanc
tankard n diodlestr, tancr
tanker n tancer, llong olew
tannery n barcerdy, crwynfa, tanerdy
tantalize vt poeni, poenydio, pryfocio
tantamount adj cyfwerth, cyfystyr
tantrums npl cyfwerth, nwydau
tap vb taro yn ysgafn
tap n tap, feis ♦ vt tapio, gollwng
tape n tâp, incil
tape measure n tâp mesur
tape-recorder n recordydd tâp, peiriant recordio, arnodydd
taper n cannwyll gŵyr, tapr ♦ vb

meinhau, tapro
tapestry n tapestri
tape-worm n llyngeren
tapioca n tapioca
tar n tar; llongwr, morwr
tardy adj hwyrfrydig, araf, diweddar, ymarhous
target n nod, targed
tariff n toll; rhestr taliadau, rhestr prisiau
tarmac n tarmac
tarnish vb pylu, cymylu, llychwino
tarpaulin n tarpolin
tarry vb aros, oedi, tario; trigo, preswylio
tart n tarten, pastai
tart adj sur, surllyd
tartan n brithwe, plod
task n gorchwyl, tasg ♦ vt rhoi tasg, trethu, llethu
tassel n tusw, tasel
taste vb chwaethu, blasu, profi ♦ n blas; chwaeth
tatter n rhecsyn, cerpyn
tattered adj carpiog
tattle vb clebran, clegar ♦ n cleber, baldordd
tattoo n tatŵ ♦ vb torri llun (yn y croen)
taunt vt edliw, dannod, gwatwar ♦ n gwaradwydd, sen
taut adj tyn
tautologous adj ailadroddiad, cyfystyrol
tautology n tawtologaeth, ailadrodd, cyfystyredd
tavern n tafarn, tafarndy, tŷ tafarn
tawdry adj coegwych
tawny n melynddu, melyn
tax n treth ♦ vt trethu; cyhuddo
taxi n tacsi. **t. rank** n lloc dacsi
taxidermist n stwffiwr anifeiliaid
tea n te
tea-bag n bag te, cwdyn te
teacup n disgl de, cwpan te
tea-leaves n dail te

tea-party n teparti
teach vt dysgu, addysgu
teacher n athro
teaching n dysgeidiaeth; dysgu
teak n tîc
team n gwedd, pâr, tîm
teapot n tebot
tear n deigryn, deigr
tear vb rhwygo, llarpio ♦ n rhwyg
tearful adj dagreuol
tease vt pryfocio, plagio, poeni
teaser n poenwr, poenydiwr
teaspoon n llwy de
teaspoonful n llond llwy de
teat n teth, diden, bron
technical adj technegol
technician n technegydd
technique n techneg
technological adj technolegol
technology n technoleg
teddy (bear) n arth anwes, tedi
tedious adj blin, anniben, poenus
tedium n diflastod, blinder
teem vb epilio, hilio, heigio
teenager n un yn yr arddegau
teens n arddegau
teethe vi torri dannedd
teetotaller n llwyrymwrthodwr, titotal
telecast n telediad
telecommunication n cysylltiad trwy'r teliffon, telegyfathrebaeth
telegram n teligram
telegraph n teligraff ♦ vb teligraffio
teleology n dibenyddiaeth
telepathy n telepathi
telephase n olgyfflwr
telephone n teliffon, ffôn. **t. box** n bocs ffonio. **t. call** n galwad ffôn. **t. directory** n cyfeirlyfr ffôn
telescope n ysbienddrych, telisgob
televise vb teledu
television n teledu
tell vb dweud, traethu, adrodd, mynegi; cyfrif, rhifo
telltale n clepgi, clepiwr,

clepwraig
temerity n rhyfyg, hyfdra
temper n tymer, naws ♦ vt tymheru
temperament n anianawd
temperamental adj gwamal, oriog, di-ddal
temperance n dirwest
temperate adj cymedrol; tymherus
temperature n tymheredd
tempest n tymestl
tempestuous adj tymhestlog
temple n teml
temple n arlais
temporal adj tymhorol
temporary adj dros amser, tymhoroi
temporize vi oedi, anwadalu
tempt vt temtio, profi
tempter n temtiwr
temptation n temtiad, temtasiwn
ten adj, n deg
tenable adj daliadwy, y gellir ei ddal; diffynadwy
tenacious adj tyn ei afael, gwydn, gludiog, cyndyn
tenacity n cyndynrwydd
tenant n deiliad, tenant
tench n tens
tend vb tendio, gweini
tend vi tueddu, cyfeirio, symud
tendance n sylw, gofal, tendans
tendency n tuedd, gogwydd
tendentious adj pleidiol, pleidgar
tender adj tyner, tirion, mwyn; meddal
tender vb cynnig, cyflwyno ♦ n cynnig
tenderness n tynerwch
tendon n gewyn
tendril n tendril
tenement n annedd, rhandy
tenet n daliad, barn, tyb
tenfold adj dengwaith
tennis n tennis. **t. ball** n pêl dennis. **t. court** n cwrt tennis. **t. racket** n

raced tennis
tenon n tyno
tenor n cyfeiriad, tuedd, rhediad;
  tenor
tense adj tyn, dirdynnol, dwys,
  angerddol
tense n amser (berf)
tension n tyndra, pwys, tyniant
tent n pabell
tentacle n tentacl, braich
tentative adj arbrofiadol, dros dro;
  ansicr
tenter-hook n bach deintur. **on
  tenter-hooks** ar bigau'r drain
tenth adj degfed
tenuous adj tenau, main, prin
tenure n deiliadaeth
tepid adj claear
tercentenary n trichanmlwyddiant
term n terfyn; term; teler, amod;
  tymor ♦ vt galw, enwi
terminal adj terfynol, termol
terminate vb terfynu
termination n terfyniad
terminology n termynoleg
terminus n terfyn
termites npl morgrug gwynion
tern n môr-wennol
terrace n rhes dai, teras
terrain n tir, bro, ardal
terrestrial adj daearol
terrible adj dychrynllyd, ofnadwy,
  arswydus
terrier n daeargi
terrific adj dychrynllyd, arswydus
terrify vt brawychu, dychrynu
terrifying adj brawychus,
  dychrynllyd
territorial adj tiriogaethol
territory n tir, tiriogaeth
terror n dychryn, braw, arswyd,
  ofn
terrorise vb dychrynu, brawychu
terrorist n terfysgwr, brawychwr
terror-stricken adj wedi ei
  ddychrynu
terse adj byr a chryno

terseness n byrdra
test n prawf ♦ vt profi
testament n testament, cyfamod,
  ewyllys
testator n cymynnwr
tester n profwr
testicle n caill, carreg
testify vb tystio
testimonial n tysteb, tystlythyr
testimony n tystiolaeth; profiad
testy adj afrywiog, ffrom, croes
tetanus n gên glo, tetanws
tether n rhaff, tennyn ♦ vt clymu
text n testun, adnod
textbook n gwerslyfr
textile adj gweol
textual adj testunol
texture n gwe, gwead,
  cyfansoddiad
Thailand n Gwlad Thai
than conj na, nag
thank vt, n diolch
thankful adj diolchgar
thankless adj diddiolch
thanks npl diolch, diolchiadau
thanksgiving n diolchgarwch
that pron dem hwn (hon) yna
  (acw), hwnnw, honno, hynny ♦ rel
  a, y(r) ♦ adj hwn, hon, yma, yna,
  acw ♦ conj mai, taw
thatch n to, to gwellt ♦ vt toi
thatcher n tôwr (â gwellt, etc)
thaw vb dadlaith, dadmer,
  meirioli, toddi
the adj yr, y
theatre n theatr, chwaraedy;
  maes, golygfa
theatrical adj theatraidd
thee pron ti, tydi, tithau
theft n lladrad
their pron eu
theirs pron yr eiddynt, eiddynt hwy
theism n duwiaeth, theistiaeth
theist n un sy'n credu yn Nuw
them pron hwy, hwynt, hwythau
theme n testun, pwnc, thema
themselves pron eu hunain

then adv y pryd hwnnw, yna ♦ conj yna

thence adv oddi yno, o hynny

thenceforth adv o'r amser hwnnw ymlaen

theocracy n theocratiaeth

theologian n diwinydd

theological adj diwinyddol

theology n diwinyddiaeth

theorem n theorem

theoretical adj damcaniaethol, mewn theori

theorise vb damcaniaethu

theory n damcaniaeth, tyb

therapeutic adj iachaol, meddygol

therapy n therapi

there adv yna, yno, acw; dyna, dacw

thereafter adv wedyn

thereat adv ar hynny, yna

thereby adv trwy hynny

therefore conj gan hynny, am hynny

therefrom adv oddi yno

therein adv yno, ynddo

thereupon adv ar hynny

therewith adv gyda hynny

thermal adj thermol, gwresol, brwd

thermometer n thermomedr, mesurydd gwres

these adj pl y rhai hyn, y rhai yma

thesis (-ses) n gosodiad; traethawd, thesis

they pron hwy, hwynt, hwynt-hwy

thick adj tew, praff, trwchus

thicken vb tewhau, tewychu

thicket n prysglwyn, llwyn

thick-headed adj pendew, hurt, twp

thickness n trwch, tewder

thick-skinned adj croendew

thief (thieves) n lleidr

thieve vi lladrata, dwyn

thigh n clun, morddwyd

thimble n gwniadur

thin adj tenau, cul, main; anaml, prin ♦ vb teneuo

thine pron eiddot ti; dy

thing n peth, dim

think vb meddwl

thinker n meddyliwr

third adj trydydd, trydedd

thirst n syched ♦ vi sychedu

thirteen adj, n tri (tair) ar ddeg, un deg tri (tair)

thirty adj, n deg ar hugain, tri deg

this adj, pron hwn, hon, hyn

thistle n ysgallen

thither adv yno, tuag yno

thong n carrai

thorax n y ddwyfron, y frest, thoracs

thorn n draen, draenen; pigyn, swmbwl

thorny adj dreiniog, pigog

thorough adj trwyadl, trylwyr

thoroughbred adj trwyryw, o rywogaeth dda

thoroughfare n tramwyfa

thorough-going adj trwyadl

thoroughness n trylwyredd

those adj pl y rhai hynny, y rhai yna

thou pron ti, tydi, tithau

though conj er, pe, cyd

thought n meddwl

thoughtful adj meddylgar, ystyriol

thoughtless adj difeddwl, anystyriol

thousand adj, n mil

thraldom n caethiwed

thrall n caethwr, caethwas

thrash vt dyrnu, ffusto, curo

thread n edau, edefyn

threadbare adj llwm, treuliedig, wedi treulio

threat n bygwth, bygythiad

threaten vt bygwth

threatening adj bygythiol

three adj, n tri, tair

three-cornered adj trichornel

threefold adj triphlyg

three-legged *adj* teircoes
threepence *n* tair ceiniog, pisyn tair
thresh *vt* dyrnu, ffusto
thresher *n* dyrnwr, ffustwr
threshold *n* trothwy, rhiniog, hiniog
thrice *adv* teirgwaith
thrift *n* darbodaeth, cynildeb
thriftless *adj* gwastraffus
thrifty *adj* darbodus, cynnil, diwastraff
thrill *vb* gwefreiddio ♦ *n* ias, gwefr
thriller *n* stori iasoer
thrilling *adj* cyffrous, gwefreiddiol
thrive *vi* llwyddo, ffynnu; prifio
throat *n* gwddf
throb *vi* dychlamu, curo
throe *n* dolur, poen, gloes, gwewyr
thrombosis *n* clot mewn gwythien, thrombosis
throne *n* gorsedd, gorseddfainc
throng *n* tyrfa, torf ♦ *vb* tyrru, heidio
throstle *n* bronfraith
throttle *n* corn gwynt, corn gwddf, sbardun ♦ *vt* llindagu
through *prep* trwy ♦ *adv* trwodd
throughout *prep* trwy, trwy gydol ♦ *adv* trwodd
throw *n* tafliad ♦ *vb* taflu, bwrw, lluchio
thrower *n* taflwr
thrush *n* bronfraith
thrush *n* llindag, gân
thrust *vb* gwthio, gwanu, brathu ♦ *n* gwth
thud *n* twrf, sŵn trwm
thug *n* llindagwr, dihiryn
thumb *n* bawd ♦ *vt* bodio
thump *vb* dyrnodio, pwnio, dulio
thumping *adj* aruthrol
thunder *n* taran(au), tyrfau, trystau ♦ *vb* taranu
thunderbolt *n* llucheden
thunderstorm *n* storm dyrfau
Thursday *n* dydd Iau

thus *adv* fel hyn, felly
thwart *vt* croesi, gwrthwynebu
thwart *vb* rhwystro
thy *pron* dy, 'th
thyme *n* teim
thyroid *n* thiroid
tiara *n* talaith, coron, coronig
tibia *n* asgwrn y grimog
tick *vi* tipian, ticio ♦ *n* tipian, tic
tick *vt* marcio, ticio ♦ *n* nod, marc, tic
tick *n* lliain gwely, tic
ticket *n* tocyn, ticed. **t. collector** *n* tocynnwr. **t. office** *n* swyddfa docynnau
tickle *vb* goglais, gogleisio ♦ *n* goglais
ticklish *n* gogleisiol; anodd, dyrys
tide *n* llanw, teid; amser, pryd. **high/low t.** *n* penllanw, trai
tidiness *n* taclusrwydd
tidings *npl* newyddion, chwedlau
tidy *adj* taclus, twt, trefnus, destlus
tie *vt* clymu, rhwymo ♦ *n* cwlwm, cadach
tier *n* rhes, rheng
tiff *n* ffrae fach
tiger *n* teigr, dywalgi
tight *adj* tyn, cryno, twt; cyfyng
tighten *vb* tynhau
tightness *n* tyndra
tights *npl* teits
tigress *n* teigres
tile *n* priddlech, teilsen
till *prep, conj* hyd
till *vt* trin, amaethu, llafurio
tiller *n* coes llyw; llafurwr, triniwr
tilt *vb* gogwyddo; gosod (â gwayw)
tilth *n* triniaeth tir, âr
timber *n* coed, pren
time *n* amser ♦ *vt* amseru
timely *adj* amserol, prydlon
timepiece *n* cloc, wats
timetable *n* amserlen
timid *adj* ofnus, ofnog, llwfr
timidity *n* ofnusrwydd

timing n amseriad

timorous adj ofnus, ofnog

tin n alcam, tun

tincture n lliw

tinfoil n ffoel alcam

tinge vt lliwio, arlliwio ♦ n arlliw, gwawr

tingle vi ysu, llosgi, merwino

tinker n tincer; eurych ♦ vb tincera

tinkle vb tincian

tinned adj mewn tun, tun

tint n lliw, arlliw, gwawr ♦ vt lliwio

tinted adj wedi ei lliwio

tinworker n gweithiwr tun, gweithiwr alcam

tiny adj bychan, bach, pitw

tip n blaen, pen ♦ vt blaenu

tip vb troi, dymchwelyd; gwobrwyo ♦ n tip, tomen; cyngor; gwobr, cil-dwrn

tipple vb llymeitian, diota

tippler n diotwr, meddwyn

tipsy adj meddw, penfeddw, brwysg

tiptoe n: **on t.** ar flaenau ei draed

tip-top adj campus, penigamp

tirade n araith lem

tire vb blino, lluddedu, diffygio

tire, tyre n cant, cylch, teiar

tired adj blinedig

tiredness n blinder

tireless adj diflino

tiresome adj blin, diflas, plagus

tiro, tyro n newyddian, dechreuwr

tissue n gwe, meinwe; defnydd cnawd

tissue paper n papur sidan

titanic adj cawraidd, anferth, aruthrol

titbit n tamaid blasus, amheuthun

tithe n degwm ♦ vt degymu

titivate vt pincio, ymbincio

title n teitl, hawl, hawlfraint

titled adj â theitl

title-deed n dogfen hawlfraint

title-page n wyneb-ddalen

titmouse n gwas y dryw, yswidw

titter vi cilchwerthin, chwerthinial

tittle n gronyn, mymryn, tipyn

tittle-tattle n cleber

titular adj yn rhinwedd teitl; mewn enw

to prep i, at, hyd, er mwyn, wrth, yn

toad n llyffant du dafadennog

toadstool n caws llyffant, bwyd y boda, madarch

toady n cynffonnwr ♦ vt cynffonna

toast n tost; llwncdestun ♦ vb tostio, crasu

toaster n tostiwr

tobacco n tybaco, baco

tobacconist n gwerthwr tybaco

toboggan n tybogan, sled fach, car llusg

today adv heddiw

toddle vi cropian

toddler n plentyn bach

toe n bys troed; blaen carn ceffyl

toe-cap n blaen esgid

toffee n taffi, cyflaith

together adv ynghyd, gyda'i gilydd

toil vi llafurio, poeni ♦ n llafur

toilet n trwsiad, gwisgiad; ystafell ymolchi, tŷ bach. **t. paper** n papur tŷ bach. **t. water** n dŵr Groeg

token n arwydd, argoel; tocyn

tolerable adj goddefol; gweddol, symol, cymhedrol

tolerant adj goddefgar

tolerate vt goddef

toleration n goddefgarwch

toll n toll, treth

toll vb canu (cloch, cnul)

tollbooth n tollfa

tomato n tomato

tomb n bedd, beddrod

tomboy n hoeden, rhampen

tom-cat n gwrcath, cwrcyn

tome n cyfrol (fawr)

tomfool n ynfytyn, pen-ffŵl

tomfoolery n ynfydrwydd, ffwlbri

tomorrow adv yfory

tomtit n gwas y dryw, yswidw

ton n tunnell

tonality n tonyddiaeth

tone n tôn, oslef ♦ vb tyneru, lleddfu

tongs npl gefel

tongue n tafod; tafodiaith, iaith

tonic n meddyginiaeth gryfhaol, tonic. **t. water** n dŵr tonig

tonnage n pwysau llwyth (llong); toll

tonsil n tonsil

tonsillitis n llid y tonsil

tonsure n corun, tonsur

tonight adv heno

too adv rhy; hefyd. **t. much** gormod

tool n arf, erfyn

toot vb canu corn

tooth (**teeth**) n dant

toothache n dannoedd

toothbrush n brws dannedd

toothed n danheddog

toothless adj diddannedd, mantach

toothpaste n sebon dannedd, past dannedd

toothpick n pic dannedd

toothsome adj danteithiol, blasus

top n pen, brig, copa ♦ vt tocio; rhagori ar

top n cogwrn, top

top-heavy adj pendrwm

topic n pwnc

topical adj amserol

topography n daearyddiaeth leol

topple vb syrthio, cwympo, dymchwel

topsyturvy adv wyneb i waered, yn bendramwnwgl

torch n fflach, tors, ffagl

torch-light n golau tors

torment n poen, poenedigaeth ♦ vt poeni, poenydio

tormentor n poenydiwr

torn adj wedi ei rwygo, rhwygedig

tornado n hyrddwynt, corwynt

torpedo n torpedo

torpid adj marwaidd, cysglyd, swrth

torrent n cenllif, llifeiriant, rhyferthwy

torrential adj llifeiriol, trwm

torrid adj poeth, crasboeth

torso n corff (heb y pen a'r aelodau), torso

tortoise n crwban

tortoise-shell n cragen crwban, trilliw (am gath)

tortuous adj troellog, trofaus

torture n dirboen, artaith ♦ vt arteithio

torturer n arteithiwr

tory n tori, ceidwadwr ♦ adj toriaidd

toryism n toriaeth

toss vb taflu, lluchio, bwrw

total adj hollol, cyflawn ♦ n cyfan, cyfanswm

totalitarian adj totalitaraidd

totalitarianism n totalitariaeth

totality n cyfanrwydd

totally adv yn llwyr, yn gyfan, yn ei grynswth

totter vb honcian, siglo, gwegian

touch vb teimlo, cyffwrdd ♦ n teimlad

touched adj dan deimlad

touching adj teimladwy

touch-line n yr ystlys

touchstone n maen prawf, safon

touchy adj croendenau

tough adj gwydn, caled, cyndyn

toughen vb gwneud yn wydn, cryfhau

tour n tro, taith

tourism n twristiaeth

tourist n teithiwr, ymwelydd, twrist. **t. office** n swyddfa twristiaid

tournament n twrnamaint

tourniquet n offeryn i atal gwaed

tousle vt dragio, anhrefnu

tousled adj anniben

tout vi poeni pobl am archebion, gwasgu ar

tow n carth

tow vt llusgo, tynnu

toward, -s prep tua, tuag at

towel n lliain sychu, tywel

tower n tŵr ♦ vi esgyn, ymgodi, sefyll yn uchel

town n tref. **t. centre** n canol(y) dref. **t. clerk** n clerc y dref. **t. council** n cyngor y dref. **t. hall** n neuadd y dref

township n trefgordd

toxic adj gwenwynig

toy n tegan ♦ vi chwarae, maldodi

trace n tres; ôl, trywydd

trace vt olrhain, dilyn ♦ n ôl

tracery n rhwyllwaith (maen, etc)

trachea n breuant, corn gwynt, pibell wynt

track n ôl, brisg; llwybr ♦ vt olrhain

tracksuit n tracwisg

tract n ardal, rhandir

tract n traethodyn

tractable adj hydyn, hydrin, hywedd

traction n tyniad, tyniant, llusgiad

trade n masnach; crefft ♦ vb masnachu

trade-mark n nod masnach

trader n masnachwr

trade-union n undeb llafur

trade-wind n gwynt y dwyrain, cylchwynt

tradition n traddodiad

traditional adj traddodiadol

traduce vt cablu, difenwi, enllibio

traffic vb masnachu, trin ♦ n masnach, trafnidiaeth. **t. jam** n tagfa. **t. warden** n warden traffig

traffic-lights npl goleuadau traffig

tragedy n trasiedi, trychineb

tragic adj trychinebus, alaethus

trail n llusg, brisg, ôl ♦ vb llusgo

trailer n ôl-gerbyd, ôl-gart; cart;

rhaglun (ffilm)

train vb hyfforddi, ymarfer ♦ n gosgordd; godre; trên, cerbydres

trained adj hyfforddedig, cymwys, wedi ei hyfforddi

trainer n hyfforddwr

training n hyfforddiant, disgyblaeth. **t. shoes** npl esgidiau ymarfer

trait n nodwedd, (pl) teithi

traitor n bradwr, teyrnfradwr

trajectory n taflwybr

trammel n rhwyd; hual ♦ vt llyffetheirio, hualu

tramp vb crwydro, trampio ♦ n crwydryn

trample vb sathru, sangu, mathru

trance n llewyg, llesmair, perlewyg

tranquil adj tawel, llonydd, digyffro

tranquility n tawelwch, llonyddwch

tranquillizer n tawelyn, tawelydd

trans- tran-, tra- prefix tros-, tra-

transact vt trafod, gwneud, trin

transaction n trafodaeth

transactions n trafodion

transcend vt rhagori ar, trarhagori

transcendent adj tra-rhagorol

transcendental adj trosgynnol

transcribe vt copïo

transcriber n adysgrifiwr, copïwr, copïydd

transcript n copi, adysgrifiad

transept n croes (eglwys)

transfer vt trosglwyddo ♦ n trosglwyddiad

transference n trosglwyddiad

transfiguration n gweddnewidiad

transfigure vt gweddnewid

transfix vt trywanu, gwanu

transform vt trawsffurfio

transformation n trawsffurfiad

transformer n newidydd

transfusion n trosglwyddiad (gwaed), trallwysiad (gwaed)

transgress vt troseddu
transgression n trosedd, camwedd
transgressor n troseddwr
transient adj diflanedig, darfodedig
transit n mynediad dros, trosiad
transition n trosiad, trawsgyweiriad
transitional adj ar newid, tros dro
transitive adj anghyflawn (gram)
transitory adj diflanedig, darfodedig
translate vt cyfieithu
translation n cyfieithiad
transliterate vt trawslythrennu
translucent adj tryloyw
transmigrate vi trawsfudo
transmission n trosglwyddiad
transmit vt anfon, trosglwyddo
transmitter n trosglwyddydd
transmitting-station n gorsaf drosglwyddo
transmute vt trawsnewid
transparency n tryloywder
transparent adj tryloyw
transpire vb dyfod yn hysbys, digwydd
transplant vt trawsblannu
transport vt trosglwyddo; alltudio ♦ n trosglwyddiad; cludiant; perlewyg, gorawen
transpose vt trawsddodi, trawsgyweirio
transubstantiation n trawssylweddiad
transverse adj croes, traws
trap n trap, magl; car bach ♦ vt dal, maglu
trapeze n trapis
trappings npl harnais, gêr
trash n sothach, gwehilion, ffwlbri, ysbwriel
travail vi trafaelu ♦ n trafael, llafur
travel vb teithio, trafaelio ♦ n teithio, (pl) teithiau. **t. agent** n asiant teithio
traveller n teithiwr, trafaeliwr. **t.'s**

cheque n siec deithio
travelling adj teithiol
traverse vb mynd ar draws, croesi
travesty n parodi
trawl vb llusgrwydo ♦ n llusgrwyd
trawler n llong bysgota
tray n hambwrdd
treacherous adj twyllodrus
treachery n brad, bradwriaeth
treacle n triagl
tread vb sathru, sengi, troedio ♦ n sang
treadmill n troell droed
treason n brad, bradwriaeth
treasonable adj bradwrus
treasure n trysor ♦ vt trysori
treasurer n trysorydd
treasury n trysorfa, trysordy, y Trysorlys
treat vb trin; tretio; traethu ♦ n gwledd, amheuthun
treatise n traethawd
treatment n triniaeth, ymdriniaeth
treaty n cyfamod, cytundeb
treble adj triphlyg ♦ n trebl ♦ vb treblu
tree n pren, coeden
trefoil n meillionen, meillion
trek vi mudo ♦ n mud, mudo
trellis n delltwaith
tremble vi crynu, echrydu, arswydo
tremendous adj dychrynllyd, ofnadwy, anferth
tremor n crynfa, cryndod, ias
tremulous adj crynedig
trench n ffos, rhigol, rhych ♦ vb ffosi
trenchant adj llym, miniog
trencher n trensiwr, treinsiwr, plat
trend vi tueddu ♦ n tuedd, gogwydd
trepidation n cryndod, ofn, dychryn
trespass vi troseddu ♦ n trosedd
trespasser n tresmaswr
tress n cudyn gwallt, tres

trestle n trestl

tri- prefix tri

triad n tri, (pl) trioedd

trial n prawf, profedigaeth, treial

triangle n triongl

triangular adj trionglog

tribal adj llwythol

tribe n llwyth, tylwyth, gwehelyth

tribulation n trallod, cystudd

tribunal n brawdle, llys, tribiwnlys

tributary adj dan deyrnged ♦ n rhagafon, isafon, cainc

tribute n teyrnged, treth

trice n munudyn, chwinciad

trick n tric, cast, ystryw ♦ vt castio

trickery n dichell, twyll, ystryw

trickle vi diferu, diferynnu

trickster n twyllwr, castiwr

tricky adj ystrywgar; anodd

tricycle n treisigl

trident n tryfer

triennial adj bob tair blynedd

trifle n gronyn, mymryn; gwaelbeth ♦ vt ofera, cellwair

trifling adj diwerth, dibwys

trigger n cliced, triger

trigonometry n trigonomeg

trill vb crychleisio, cwafrio ♦ n crychlais

trillion n triliwn

trilogy n cyfres o dair (nofel, drama etc)

trim adj taclus, twt, del ♦ vb taclu, trwsio ♦ n diwyg, trefn

trinity n trindod

trinket n tegan, tlws

trio n triawd

trioxide n triocsid

trip n tripio, maglu; disodli ♦ n trip, tro

tripartite adj teiran

tripe n tripa

triple adj triphlyg

triplet n tripled

tripod n trybedd

trite adj cyffredin, sathredig

triumph n gorfoledd, buddugoliaeth ♦ vi gorfoleddu; buddugoliaethu

triumphal adj buddugol

triumphant adj buddugoliaethus

triumvirate n llywodraeth tri (Rhufain)

trivet n trybedd

trivial adj distadl, dibwys, diwerth

trolley, -y n trol

troop n byddin, torf, mintai ♦ vb tyrru. **troops** npl lluoedd, minteioedd

trooper n milwr (ar farch)

trophy n gwobr, tlws

tropic n trofan

tropical adj trofannol

trot vb tuthio, trotian ♦ n tuth, trot

troubadour n trwbadŵr, bardd telynegol

trouble vt blino, trafferthu ♦ n blinder, trallod, helbul, trafferth

troubled adj aflonydd, anesmwyth, pryderus, ofnus, dyrys

troubles npl trafferthion, helbulon, pryderon, ofnau

troublesome adj blinderus, trafferthus

trough n cafn

trounce vt ffonodio, cystwyo, baeddu

troupe n mintai o berfformwyr

trousers npl llodrau, trowsus, trwser

trousseau n dillad priodasferch

trout n brithyll

trow vb tybied, meddyliwd, credu

trowel n trywel

truant n triwant, mitsiwr

truce n cadoediad

truck n trwc, gwagen

truck vb cyfnewid, ffeirio

truckle vi plygu, ymostwng, ymgreinio

truculent adj ffyrnig, milain

trudge vb cerdded yn ffwdanus, trwmgerdded

true adj gwir, cywir

truism n gwireb, gwiredd

truly adv yn wir, yn ddiau, yn gywir

trump vb utganu; twyllo, ffugio ♦ n trwmp

trumpery n sothach, ffwlbri ♦ adj coeg, gwacsaw

trumpet n utgorn, corn, trwmped

truncheon n pastwn, trensiwn

trundle vb treiglo, rholio

trunk n cyff, cist; corff; duryn, trwnc

trunks npl trons

truss vb gwneud bwndel; gwaellu (ffowlyn)

trust n ymddiried, ymddiriedaeth, coel; ymddiriedolaeth ♦ vb hyderu, ymddiried, coelio

trustee n ymddiriedolwr

trusteeship n ymddiriedolaeth

trustworthy adj y gellir dibynnu arno

trusty adj ffyddlon, cywir, teyrngar

truth n gwir, gwirionedd

truthful adj geirwir

truthfulness n geirwiredd

try vb profi, cynnig, ceisio, treio

trying adj poenus, anodd, blin

tryst n oed

T-shirt n crys-T

tub n twba, twb, baddon

tuba n tiwba

tube n pib, pibell, tiwb, corn

tuber n cloronen, taten

tuberculosis n darfodedigaeth, dicáu, diclein

tubular adj tiwbaidd. **t. bridge** ceubont

tuck vt cwtogi, plygu ♦ n plyg, twc

Tuesday n dydd Mawrth

tuft n cogyn, tusw, cudyn

tug vb llusgo, tynnu

tuition n addysg, hyfforddiant

tulip n tiwlip

tumble vb cwympo ♦ n codwm, cwymp

tumbler n gwydryn

tumid adj chwyddedig

tummy n bola

tumour n chwydd, casgliad, cornwyd

tumult n terfysg, cynnwrf

tumultuous adj terfysglyd

tuna n tiwna

tune n tôn, tiwn, cywair ♦ vb cyweirio

tuneful adj soniarus

tunic n crysbais, siaced

Tunisia n Tunisia

tunnel n ceuffordd, twnnel

turban n twrban

turbid adj afloyw, cymysglyd, lleidiog

turbine n twrbin

turbot n twrbot

turbulence n terfysg, cynnwrf

turbulent adj terfysglyd, afreolus

turf n tywarchen

turgid adj chwyddedig

Turk n Twrc

turkey n twrci

Turkey n Twrci

Turkish adj Twrcaidd

turmoil n trafferth, ffwdan, berw

turn vb troi ♦ n tro, trofa

turncoat n gwrthgiliwr

turner n turniwr

turning n tro; trôedigaeth

turning point n trobwynt

turnip n erfinen, meipen

turnout n cynulliad

turnover n cyfanswm busnes

turnpike n tollborth, tyrpeg

turnstile n camfa dro

turntable n trofwrdd

turpentine n twrpant, turpant

turpitude n gwarth, ysgelerder

turquoise n maen glas (gwerthfawr)

turret n twred, tyryn

turtle n crwban môr

turtle, -dove n turtur

tusk n ysgithrddant, ysgithr

tussle n ymgiprys, ysgarmes
tut excl twt!
tutelage n hyfforddiant, nawdd
tutor n athro, hyfforddwr ♦ vt hyfforddi
tutorial adj tiwtorial
twaddle n lol, ffiloreg
twang vb clecian, swnio ♦ n swn, llediaith
tweed n brethyn gwlân, twid
tweezers n gefel fach
twelfth adj deuddegfed
twelve adj, n deuddeg, un deg dau
twentieth adj ugeinfed
twenty adj, n ugain
twice adv dwywaith
twiddle vt chwarae bodiau, cellwair
twig n brigyn, ysbrigyn, impyn
twilight n cyfnos, cyfddydd
twill n brethyn caerog
twin n gefell
twine n llinyn ♦ vb cyfrodeddu, cordeddu
twinge n cnofa, brath, gwayw
twinkle vi serennu, pefrio
twinkling n chwinciad, amrantiad
twirl vb chwyrndroi, chwyldroi, nydd-droi
twist vb nyddu, nydd-droi, cyfrodeddu; troi, gwyrdroi ♦ n tro; edau gyfrodedd
twit n dannod, edliw; un ffôl
twitch vb tymhigo, brathgnoi ♦ n tymig
twitch n gwayw, brath, plwc ♦ vb brathu, tynnu'n sydyn, plycio
twitter vi trydar
two adj, n dau, dwy
two-faced adj dauwynebog
twofold adv deublyg
two piece n deuddarn
tympan n tabwrdd, tympan
type n math, teip
typescript n teipysgrif
typewriter n teipiadur, peiriant teipio

typhoid n twymyn yr ymysgaroedd
typhoon n corwynt
typhus n twymyn heintus, teiffws
typical adj arwyddol, nodweddiadol
typify vt arwyddo, nodweddu
typist n teipydd
typographical adj argraffyddol
typography n argraffwaith
tyranny n tra-arglwyddiaeth, gormes
tyrannize vb gormesu, treisio
tyrant n gormesteyrn, gormeswr
tyre n teiar
tyro n newyddian, dechreuwr

U

ubiquitous adj ym mhob man, hollbresennol
udder n pwrs, cadair, piw
ugh excl ach! ych y fi!
ugly adj hagr, hyll
ugliness n hagrwch, hylldra
ulcer n casgliad, cornwyd, wlser
Ulster n Ulster
ulterior adj tu draw i, tu hwnt i, pellach; cudd
ultimate adj diwethaf, olaf, eithaf
ultimately adv o'r diwedd
ultimatum n y gair olaf, y rhybudd olaf
ultra adj eithafol ♦ prefix tu hwnt i, gor-
ultramodern adj modern iawn
umbrage n tramgwydd
umbrella n ymbrelo, brela, ambarél, ymbarél
umpire n dyfarnwr, canolwr
un- prefix an-, am-, ang-, af-, di-, heb
unable adj analluog
unaccented adj diacen
unacceptable adj anghymeradwy, annerbyniol
unaccompanied adj heb gwmni;

heb gyfeiliant
unaccountable adj anesboniadwy
unaccustomed adj anghyfarwydd, anghynefin
unacquainted adj anghyfarwydd
unadulterated adj pur, digymysg
unaffected adj naturiol; heb ei effeithio gan
unanimity n unfrydedd
unanimous adj unfrydol
unanimously adv yn unfryd
unarmed adj diamddiffyn, heb arfau
unassailable adj diysgog
unassuming adj diymhongar
unattainable adj anghyraeddadwy
unavoidable adj anorfod
unaware adj anymwybodol
unawares adv yn ddiarwybod
unbearable adj annioddefol
unbecoming adj anweddus, anweddaidd
unbeliever n anghredadun, anffyddiwr
unbelieving adj anghrediniol
unbiassed adj diduedd
unblemished adj di-nam, dinam
unbounded adj diderfyn
unbridled adj heb ei ffrwyno
unbroken adj di-dor
unbutton vb datod, datfotymu
uncalled (**for**) adj di-alw-amdano
uncanny adj rhyfedd, dieithr, annaearol
uncle n ewythr
unclean adj brwnt, aflan
uncomfortable adj anghysurus
uncommon adj anghyffredin
uncompromising adj di-ildio, digyfaddawd, cyndyn
unconcerned adj difater, didaro
unconditional adj diamod
unconfirmed adj heb ei gadarnhau
unconquerable adj anorchfygol
unconscionable adj digydwybod, afresymol
unconscious adj anymwybodol

unconstitutional adj anghyfansoddiadol
uncontaminated adj di-lwgr, pur
uncontrollable adj aflywodraethus
unconventional adj anghonfensiynol
uncouth adj trwsgl, lletchwith, garw, amrwd
uncover vb datguddio
unction n eli; eneiniad, arddeliad, hwyl
unctuous adj seimlyd; rhagrithiol
uncultivated adj heb ei feithrin
undamaged adj heb ei niweidio
undecided adj petrus, mewn penbleth
undefended adj diamddiffyn
undefiled adj dihalog, pur
undefined adj amhenodol, annelwig
undeniable adj anwadadwy
under prep tan, is, islaw ♦ adv tanodd, oddi tanodd ♦ prefix is-, tan-
undercurrent n islif
underestimate vb prisio'n rhy isel
undergraduate n myfyriwr israddedig
underground adj tanddaearol
underhand adj llechwraidd, tan din
underline vb tanlinellu, pwysleisio
undermine vb tanseilio
underneath adv oddi tanodd ♦ prep tan
underpass n ffordd danddaearol, tanffordd
underrate vb tanbrisio, iselbrisio
understand vt deall, dirnad
understanding n amgyffred, dealltwriaeth
undertake vb ymgymryd
undertaker n ymgymerydd; saer (coffinau)
undertaking adj ymrwymiad
undertone n islais
underworld n annwn

undeserved adj anhaeddiannol

undesirable adj annymunol

undeveloped adj heb ei ddatblygu

undeviating adj diwyro

undignified adj anurddasol, diurddas

undisciplined adj diddisgyblaeth

undisputed adj diamheuol

undisturbed adj llonydd, tawel, digyffro

undo vt dadwneud; datod; andwyo, difetha

undoing n distryw, dinistr

undoubted adj diamheuol

undress vb dadwisgo

undue adj amhriodol

undulate vi tonni

unearned adj heb ei ennill

unearthly adj annaearol

uneasiness n anesmwythder, pryder

uneasy adj anesmwyth, aflonydd, pryderus

unedifying adj di-fudd, anadeiladol

uneducated adj annysgedig

unemployed adj di-waith, segur

unemployment n diweithdra, anghyflogaeth

unending adj diddiwedd

unendurable adj annioddefol

unequal adj anghyfartal

unequalled adj digymar, dihafal

unequivocal adj diamwys

unerring adj sicr

uneven adj anwastad

uneventful adj diddigwyddiad

unexpected adj annisgwyliadwy

unfailing adj di-feth

unfair adj annheg

unfairness n annhegwch

unfaithful adj anffyddlon

unfamiliar adj anghyfarwydd

unfasten vb datod

unfathomable adj annealladwy

unfavourable adj anffafriol

unfeeling adj dideimlad

unfettered adj dilyffethair

unfinished adj anorffenedig

unfit adj anghymwys; afiach

unfitting adj amhriodol

unflinching adj diysgog, dewr

unfold vb datblygu

unforseen adj heb ei ragweld

unforgiving adj anfaddeugar

unfortunate adj anffodus

unfortunately adv yn anffodus

unfounded adj di-sail

unfrequented adj anhygyrch, unig

unfriendly adj anghyfeillgar

unfrock vb diarddel

unfulfilled adj heb ei gyflawni

unfurnished adj diddodrefn

ungainly adv afrosgo, trwsgl

ungentlemanly adj anfonedigaidd

ungodly adj annuwiol, drwg

ungrammatical adj anramadegol

ungrateful adj anniolchgar

unguarded adj ar awr wan

unguent n ennaint, eli

unhallowed adj halogedig

unhappiness n anhapusrwydd

unhappy adj anhapus

unharmed adj dianaf

unhealthy adj afiach

unheeding adj diofal

unhesitating adj dibetrus

unhorse vb taflu oddi ar geffyl

unicorn n uncorn, uncorn

unification n uniad

uniform adj unffurf ♦ n gwisg swyddogol

uniformity n unffurfiaeth

unify vt unoli, uno

unilateral adj unochrog

unimpaired adj dianaf

unimpeded adj dirwystr

unimportant adj dibwys

uninspired adj diawen

unintelligent adj anneallus

unintelligible adj annealladwy

unintentional adj anfwriadol

uninteresting adj anniddorol

union n undeb; uniad

unionism n undebaeth

unionist n undebwr; unoliaethwr (Iwerddon)

unique adj dihafal, digymar

unison n unsain, unseinedd

unit n un, rhif un; uned; undod

Unitarian n Undodwr ♦ adj Undodaidd

Unitarianism n Undodiaeth

unite vb uno, cyfuno, cyduno, cydio

united adj unol, unedig. **U. States (of America)** n yr Unol Daleithiau

United Kingdom n: **the U.K.** y Deyrnas Unedig

unity n undod

universal adj cyffredinol

universe n bydysawd

university n prifysgol

unjust adj anghyfiawn, annheg

unjustly adv ar gam

unkempt adj heb ei gribo, aflêr, anniben

unkind adj angharedig

unknown adj anadnabyddus, anenwog

unlace vb datod

unlawful adj anghyfreithlon

unlearned adj annysgedig

unless conj oni, onid

unlettered adj anllythrennog

unlike adj annhebyg

unlikely adj annhebygol

unlimited adj diderfyn

unload vb dadlwytho

unlock vb datgloi

unlucky adj anlwcus

unmanageable adj aflywodraethus

unmannerly adj anfoesgar

unmarried adj dibriod

unmask vb dinoethi

unmatched adj digymar

unmerciful adj didrugaredd

unmistakable adj digamsyniol

unmixed adj digymysg

unnatural adj annaturiol

unnecessary adj dianghenraid

unobserved adj heb ei weld

unobtrusive adj anymwthiol

unoccupied adj gwag

unopened adj heb ei agor

unopposed adj yn ddiwrthwynebiad

unorthodox adj anarferol, anuniongred

unpack vb dadbacio

unpaid adj di-dâl, didal

unparalleled adj digyffelyb

unpardonable adj anfaddeuol

unpatriotic adj anwlatgar

unpleasant adj annymunol

unpolluted adj dihalog, pur

unpopular adj amhoblogaidd

unpopularity n amhoblogrwydd

unpractical adj anymarferol

unprejudiced adj diragfarn

unprepared adj amharod

unprincipled adj diegwyddor

unprofitable adj amhroffidiol

unprotected adj diamddiffyn

unpublished adj anghyhoeddedig

unqualified adj heb gymhwyster

unquestionable adj diamheuol

unready adj amharod

unreasonable adj afresymol

unrelated adj amherthnasol; heb berthyn

unremitting adj dyfal

unrestrained adj afrywiog

unripe adj anaeddfed

unrivalled adj digymar

unruffled adj tawel

unruly adj afreolus

unsafe adj anniogel

unsatisfactory adj anfoddhaol

unsatisfied adj anfodlon

unsatisfying adj annigonol

unscathed adj dianaf

unscrew vt agor; llacio; datroi

unscrupulous adj diegwyddor

unseasonable adj annhymorol

unseat vb troi o'i swydd; taflu (ceffyl)

unseemly adj anweddaidd

unseen adj anweledig

unsettled adj ansefydlog

unshaken adj diysgog, cadarn

unsighted adj heb allu gweld

unsightly adj diolwg, blêr

unskilful adj anfedrus

unskilled adj anghelfydd

unsociable adj anghymdeithasgar

unsolicited adj heb ei ofyn

unsound adj diffygiol, cyfeiliornus

unsparing adj diarbed, hael

unspeakable adj anhraethol

unstable adj ansefydlog

unstained adj dilychwin

unsteadiness n ansadrwydd

unsteady adj ansefydlog

unsubstantial adj ansylweddol

unsuccessful adj aflwyddiannus

unsuitable adj anaddas

unsullied adj dilychwin

unsurmountable adj anorchfygol

unsurpassed adj diguro

unsuspecting adj heb amau dim

untainted adj di-lwgr, pur

untangle vb datrys

unthankful adj anniolchgar

unthinking adj difeddwl

untidy adj anniben

untie vb datod

until prep, conj hyd, hyd oni, nes, tan

untimely adj anamserol

untiring adj diflino

unto prep i, at, hyd at, wrth

untold adj di-ben-draw

untoward adj anffodus, cyndyn

untrodden adj disathr

untrue adj celwyddog

unusual adj anarferol, anghynefin; anghyffredin; newydd; dieithr

unutterable adj anhraethadwy

unvarying adj digyfnewid, cyson

unveil vb dadorchuddio

unversed adj anhyddysg

unwarranted adj heb ei warantu

unwary adj diofal

unwell adj anhwylus

unwholesome adj afiach

unwieldy adj afrosgo

unwilling adj anfodlon, amharod

unwise adj annoeth

unwittingly adv yn ddiarwybod

unworthiness n annheilyngdod

unworthy adj annheilwng

unwounded adj dianaf, cyfan

unyielding adj di-ildio

up adj, prep i fyny, i'r lan

upbringing n magwraeth

upheaval n cyffro, terfysg

uphill adj i fyny

uphold vb cynnal

upholsterer n dodrefnwr, clustogwr

upkeep n cynhaliaeth

upland n ucheldir, blaenau

uplifting adj dyrchafol

upon prep ar, ar warthaf, ar uchaf

upper adj uwch, uchaf

uppermost adj, adv uchaf

upright adj syth, union, unionsyth

uprising n terfysg, gwrthryfel

uproar n terfysg, cythrwfl, dadwrdd

uproot vt diwreiddio

upset vb troi, dymchwelyd, cyffroi, gofidio

upshot n swm, canlyniad, diwedd

upside-down adj, adv (â'i) wyneb i waered

upstairs n llofft

upstart n crach fonheddwr

upward adj, adv, **upwards** adv i fyny

uranium n wraniwm

urban adj dinasol, dinesig

urbane adj hynaws, mwyn, boneddigaidd

urbanize vb gwneud yn drefol

urchin n draenog; crwtyn

urethra n bibell ddŵr o'r bledren

urge vt cymell, annog

urgency n brys

urgent adj taer, pwysig, yn gofyn brys

urine n troeth, trwnc, piso

urn n wrn

us pron ni, nyni, ninnau; 'n

usage n arfer, defod, triniaeth

use n iws, arfer, defnydd, gwasanaeth, diben ♦ vb iwsio, arfer, defnyddio

used adj arferedig, mewn arfer, cynefin; (car) ail-law

useful adj defnyddiol

useless adj diwerth

user n defnyddiwr

usher n rhingyll; isathro; tywysydd ♦ vt arwain i mewn, dwyn ymlaen

usual adj arferol, cynefin

usurer n usuriwr

usurp vt trawsfeddiannu

usurper n trawsfeddiannwr

usury n usuriaeth, ocraeth

utensil n offeryn, llestr

uterus n croth, bru

utilitarian adj defnyddiol

utilitarianism n llesyddiaeth

utility n defnyddioldeb, budd, lles

utilization n defnydd

utilize vt defnyddio

utmost adj eithaf, pellaf

utopia n gwlad ddelfrydol (ddychmygol)

utopian adj delfrydol, anymarferol

utter adj eithaf, pellaf; hollol, llwyr

utter vt yngan, traethu, dywedyd

utterance n parabl, ymadrodd, lleferydd

uttermost adj eithaf, pellaf

U-turn n tro pedol

uvula n tafod bach, tafodig

uvular adj tafodigol

V

vacancy n lle gwag, swydd wag, gwacter

vacant adj gwag; syn, synfyfyriol, hurt

vacate vt ymadael â, gadael yn wag

vacation n seibiant, gwyliau

vaccinate vt brechu, bufrechu, torri'r frech

vaccination n y frech, brechiad

vaccine n brech

vacillate vi anwadalu, bwhwman

vacuous adj gwg, syn, hurt

vacuum n gwag, gwagle, gwactod

vacuum cleaner n sugnydd llwch

vacuum flask n thermos, jac

vagabond n crwydryn, dihiryn

vagary n mympwy

vagrancy n crwydro

vagrant adj crwydrol ♦ n crwydryn

vague adj amwys, amhenddol

vagueness n amwysedd

vain adj balch, coegfalch; ofer

vale n dyffryn, glyn, bro, cwm, ystrad

valediction n ffarwel

valentine n falant, folant

valet n gwas

valiant adj dewr, dewrwych, gwrol, glew

valid adj digonol, dilys, cyfreithlon, iawn

validate vb cadarnhau, dilysu

validity n dilysrwydd

valley n dyffryn, cwm, glyn

valour n dewrder, gwroldeb, glewder

valuable adj gwerthfawr

valuation n prisiad

value n gwerth ♦ vt gwerthfawrogi, prisio

valuer n prisiwr

valve n falf

vampire n sugnwr gwaed

van n blaen cad, y rheng flaenaf

van n men, fan

vandal n fandal

vandalism n fandaliaeth

vane n ceiliog gwynt

vanguard n blaen cad, blaenfyddin

vanilla n fanila

vanish *vi* diflannu, darfod
vanity *n* gwagedd, gwegi, coegfalchder
vanquish *vt* gorchfygu, trechu
vanquisher *n* gorchfygwr
vantage *n* mantais
vapid *adj* diflas, merf, marwaidd, egr
vaporize *vb* anweddu
vaporous *adj* llawn tarth
vapour *n* tawch, tarth, ager, anwedd
variable *adj* cyfnewidiol, anwadal, oriog
variable *n* newidyn (rhifyddiaeth)
variance *n* anghytundeb, anghydfod, amrywioldeb
variant *n* amrywiad
variation *n* amrywiad
varicose *adj* chwyddedig (am wythiennau)
varied *adj* amrywiol
variegated *adj* brith, brithliw
variety *n* amrywiaeth
various *adj* gwahanol, amrywiol
varnish *n* barnais, farnais ♦ *vt* barneisio, farneisio
varnisher *n* farneisiwr
vary *vb* amrywio; newid
vase *n* cwpan, cawg
vaseline *n* faselin, eli
vassal *n* caethddeiliad, taeog, aillt, deiliad
vast *adj* dirfawr, anferth
vastness *n* mawredd, ehangder
vat *n* cerwyn
Vatican *n* plas y Pab
vaticinate *vb* proffwydo, darogan
vaticination *n* proffwydoliaeth, darogan
vault *n* daeargell, claddgell; cromen ♦ *vb* neidio, llamu
vaulted *adj* bwaog
vaunt *vb* ymffrostio, bostio, brolio
veal *n* cig llo
vector *n* fector
veer *vb* troi, cylchdroi;

trawshwylio

vegetable *adj* llysieuol ♦ *n* llysieuyn ymborth
vegetarian *n* llysieuwr
vegetate *vi* tarddu, tyfu; ofera
vegetation *n* tyfiant llysiau, llystyfiant
vehemence *n* angerdd
vehement *adj* angerddol, tanbaid
vehicle *n* cerbyd; cyfrwng, moddion
veil *n* gorchudd, llen ♦ *vt* gorchuddio
vein *n* gwythien
velar *adj* felar
veldt *n* anialdir, maestir
vellum *n* memrwn
velocity *n* buander, cyflymder, buanedd (mathemateg)
velvet *n* melfed
venal *adj* llygredig, anonest
vend *vt* gwerthu
vendor *n* gwerthwr
veneer *n* argaen, wynebiad; rhith, ffug
venerable *adj* hybarch
venerate *vt* parchu, arhydeddu
venereal *adj* gwenerol
Venetian blind *n* llen Fenis
vengeance *n* dial, dialedd
vengeful *adj* dialgar
venial *adj* maddeuadwy, esgusodol
venison *n* cig carw, fenswn
venom *n* gwenwyn
venomous *adj* gwenwynig
venous *adj* gwythiennol
vent *n* agorfa, twll, arllwysfa ♦ *vt* arllwys, gollwng
ventilate *vt* awyru, gwyntyllu
ventilation *n* awyriad, gwyntylliad
ventilator *n* awyrydd, gwyntyllydd
ventriloquism *n* tafleisiaeth
ventricle *n* bolgell y galon, fentrigl
venture *n* anturiaeth, mentr ♦ *vb* anturio, mentro
venturesome *adj* mentrus, anturus
venue *n* man cyfarfod

Venus n Gwener, duwies serch
veracious adj cywir, geirwir, gwir
veracity adj geirwiredd
verandah n feranda
verb n berf
verbal adj berfol; geiriol
verbally adv mewn geiriau, gair am air
verbatim adv air am air, air yng ngair
verbiage n amleiriaeth, geiriogrwydd
verb-noun n berfenw
verbose adj amleirig
verbosity n geiriogrwydd
verdant adj gwyrddlas, gwyrdd
verdict n dyfarniad, dedfryd, rheithfarn
verdure n gwyrddlesni
verge n min, ymyl ♦ vi ymylu
verger n byrllygsydd, eglwyswas
verification n gwireddiad
verify vt gwiro, gwireddu
verily adv yn wir, yn ddiau
verisimilitude n tebygolrwydd
veritable adj gwirioneddol
verity n gwir, gwirionedd
vermilion n fermiliwn, lliw cochlyd
vermin npl pryfed, pryfetach; llygod, etc
vernacular adj cynhenid, brodorol ♦ n iaith y wlad
vernal adj gwanwynol
veronica n feronica, llysiau Llywelyn
versatile adj amryddawn
versatility n amlochredd
verse n gwers, adnod, pennill; prydyddiaeth
versed adj cyfarwydd, hyddysg
versify vb mydru, prydyddu, prydu
version n cyfieithiad, trosiad; esboniad
vers libre n gwers rydd
versus prep yn erbyn
vertebra (-brae) n un o gymalau'r asgwrn cefn

vertebrate n anifail ag asgwrn cefn
vertex (-tices) n pen, crib, copa
vertical adj syth, unionsyth, plwm
vertigo n y bendro, y ddot
vervain n llysiau hudol, y ferfain
verve n bywyd, egni, asbri
very adj, adv iawn, pur, tra; diamheuol
vespers npl gosber
vessel n llestr
vest n gwasgod, crys isaf ♦ vb arwisgo, cynysgaeddu
vestal adj gwyryfol ♦ n lleian, gwyry
vested adj yn ymwneud ag eiddo
vestibule n porth, cyntedd
vestige n ôl, ôl troed, brisg
vestigial adj gweddilliol, ôl
vestment n gwisg, defodwisg
vestry n festri
vesture n gwisg, dilledyn, dillad
vet vb arholi, archwilio ♦ n meddyg anifeiliaid
vetch n pys llygod
veteran n un hen a chyfarwydd
veterinary adj milfeddygol. **v. surgeon** meddyg anifeiliaid, milfeddyg
veto (-oes) n gwaharddiad ♦ vt gwahardd
vex vt blino, poeni, poenydio, cythruddo
vexation n blinder, gofid
vexed adj blin, dig
vexing adj blin, plagus
via prep trwy, ar hyd
viable adj abl i fodoli, dichonadwy
viaduct n pontffordd, fforddbont
vial n ffiol
viand n bwyd, ymborth
vibrant adj dirgrynol
vibrate vb crynu, dirgrynu
vibration n dirgryniad
vicar n ficer
vicarage n ficeriaeth; ficerdy
vicarious adj dirprwyol, mechniol

vice *n* drygioni, drygedd, bai, gwŷd
vice *n* gwasg, feis
vice- *prefix* rhag-, is-
vice-admiral *n* is-lyngesydd
vice-chairman *n* is-gadeirydd
vice-chancellor *n* is-ganghellor
vice-president *n* is-lywydd
viceroy *n* rhaglaw
vice-versa *adv* i'r gwrthwyneb
vicinity *n* cymdogaeth
vicious *adj* drygionus, gwydus
viciousness *n* drygioni, sbeit
vicissitude *n* cyfnewidiad, tro
victim *n* aberth, ysglyfaeth
victimise *vb* erlid, gormesu
victor *n* gorchfygwr
victorious *adj* buddugol, buddugoliaethus
victory *n* buddugoliaeth
victual *n* (*pl*) bwyd, lluniaeth ♦ *vt* bwydo
victualler *n* gwerthwr bwyd. **licensed v.** *n* tafarnwr
vide *vb* gwêl
videlicet (**viz**) *adv* sef, h.y.
vie *vi* cystadlu, cydymgais
Vienna *n* Wien
Vietnam *n* Fietnam
view *n* golygfa, barn ♦ *vt* edrych
viewer *n* gwyliwr (teledu)
viewpoint *n* safbwynt
vigil *n* noswyl, gwylnos
vigilant *adj* gwyliadwrus
vignette *n* addurn, llun
vigorous *adj* grymus, egniol
vigour *n* grym, nerth, egni, ynni
viking *n* môr-leidr (o Lychlyn gynt)
vile *adj* gwael, brwnt
vileness *n* brynti
vilify *vt* pardduo, difrio
villa *n* fila
village *n* pentref
villager *n* pentrefwr
villain *n* cnâf, adyn, dihiryn
villainous *adj* anfad, ysgeler

villainy *n* anfadwaith
vim *n* grym, ynni
vindicate *vt* amddiffyn, cyfiawnhau
vindication *n* cyfiawnhad
vindictive *adj* dialgar
vindictiveness *n* dialedd
vine *n* gwinwydden
vinegar *n* finegr
vineyard *n* gwinllan
vintage *n* cynhaeaf gwin
vintner *n* gwinwr, gwinydd
viola *n* fiola
violate *vt* torri, troseddu, treisio, trochi
violation *n* treisiad, trosedd
violence *n* ffyrnigrwydd, trais
violent *adj* gwyllt, tanbaid, angerddol
violet *n* fioled, crinllys
violin *n* ffidil
violinist *n* feiolinydd, ffidler
violoncello *n* basgrwth
viper *n* gwiber
viper's bugloss *n* tafod y bwch
virago *n* cecren
virgin *n* gwyry, morwyn
virginal *n* fyrginal ♦ *adj* gwyryfol, morwynol
virile *adj* gwrol, egnïol
virility *n* gwroiaeth, gwroldeb
virtual *adj* rhinweddol
virtually *adv* i bob pwrpas
virtue *n* rhinwedd
virtuoso *n* un celfyddyd, carwr celfyddyd
virulence *n* gwenwyn, casineb
virulent *adj* gwenwynig, ffyrnig
virus *n* gôr, crawn; gwenwyn, firws
visa *n* fisa
visage *n* wyneb, wynepryd
vis-à-vis *adv* wyneb yn wyneb, gyferbyn
viscid *adj* gwydn, gludiog
viscount *n* is-iarll
visible *adj* gweladwy, gweledig
vision *n* gweledigaeth, golwg,

gweled
visionary n breuddwydiwr ♦ adj breuddwydiol
visit vt ymweld, gofwyo ♦ n ymweliad
visitation n ymweliad, archwiliad
visitor n ymwelwr, ymwelydd
visor n miswrn, mwgwd
vista n golygfa
visual adj gweledol, golygol. **v. aids** cyfarpar gweld
visualise vb gwneud yn weledig, disgrifio, dychmygu
vital adj bywiol, bywydol, hanfodol
vitality n bywyd, bywiogrwydd
vitalize vb bywiocáu, bywiogi
vitamin n fitamin
vitiate vt llygru, difetha, dirymu
vitreous adj gwydrol, gwydraidd
vitriol n fitriol, asid sylffurig
vitriolic adj fitriolaidd, atgas, chwerw
vituperate vt cablu, difenwi, difrïo
vituperative adj difrïol
vivacious adj bywiog, heini, nwyfus
vivacity n hoen, nwyf
viva voce adv ar lafar
vivid adj byw, clir, llachar, tanbaid
vividness n eglurder
vivify vt bywhau, bywiocáu
vivisection n bywdrychiad, bywddiffyniad
vixen n cadnawes, llwynoges
viz. adv sef (talfyriad o videlicet)
vizier n swyddog gwlad (Mohametanaidd)
vocable n gair
vocabulary n geirfa
vocal adj lleisiol, llafarol, llafar
vocalist n lleisiwr, cantor
vocalize vt llafarseinio; llafarogi
vocally adv â'r llais
vocation n galwad, galwedigaeth
vocative adj cyfarchol
vociferate vb crochlefain, gweiddi
vodka n fodca

vogue n arfer, ffasiwn, bri
voice n llais, lleferydd; stad (gram.)
voiced adj llafarog, lleisiol
voiceless adj dilais, mud
void adj gwag; ofer, di-rym ♦ n gwagle ♦ vt gwagu, gollwng; gwacau
volatile adj hedegog, anwadal, gwamal, ysgafn, cyfnewidiol
volcanic adj folcanig
volcano n llosgfynydd, mynydd tân
vole n llygoden y maes
volition n ewyllysiad, ewyllys
volley n cawod o ergydion; taro pêl yn yr awyr
volt n uned grym trydan, folt
voltage n grym trydan
voluble adj rhugl, ymadroddus
volume n cyfrol; swm, crynswth, folum (cemeg), cyfaint (mathemateg)
voluminous adj mawr, helaeth
voluntary adj gwirfoddol
volunteer n gwirfoddolwr ♦ vb gwirfoddoli
voluptuary n pleserwr, glythwr
voluptuous adj glwth, trythyll
voluptuousness n trythyllwch
vomit vb chwydu, cyfogi
voracious adj gwancus, rheibus
vortex n trobwll, chwyldro
votary n addunwr, diofrydwr; pleidiwr
vote n pleidlais ♦ vb pleidleisio
voter n pleidleisiwr
votive adj addunedol, addunol
vouch vb gwirio, gwarantu
vouchsafe vt caniatáu, rhoddi
vow n adduned, diofryd ♦ vb addunedu
vowel n llafariad. **v. affection** affeithiad. **v. mutation** gwyriad
voyage n mordaith ♦ vb mordeithio, mordwyo
voyager n mordeithiwr
vulcanize vb caledu rwber

vulgar adj cyffredin; isel, di-foes, aflednais

vulgarism n ymadrodd aflednais

vulgarity n diffyg moes

Vulgate n Y Fwlgat

vulnerable adj archolladwy, hyglwyf, hawdd ei niweidio

vulture n fwltur

W

wad n sypyn, wad

wadding n wadin

waddle vi siglo, honcian

wade vb beisio, rhydio

wader n rhydiwr

wadi n gwely afon (sy'n dueddol i sychu)

wafer n affladen

waft vt chwifio, cludo, dygludo

wag vb ysgwyd, siglo, honcian

wag n cellweiriwr, wag

wage vt gwneuthur, dwyn ymlaen

wage n cyflog, hur

wager n cyngwystl ♦ vt cyngwystlo

waggish adj cellweirus

waggle vb siglo

wagon n men, gwagen

wagtail n sigl-i-gwt

waif n plentyn digartref

wail vb cwynfan, wylofain, udo

wainscot n palis

waist n gwasg, canol

waistcoat n gwasgod

wait vb aros; gweini ♦ n arhosiad

waiter n gweinydd

waiting n aros, sefyll

waiting room n ystafell aros

waitress n gweinyddes

wake vb deffro ♦ n gwylmabsant; gwylnos

wake n ôl, brisg

wakefulness n anhunedd

waken vb deffro, dihuno

Wales n Cymru

walk vb cerdded, rhodio ♦ n

rhodfa; tro

walker n cerddwr

walkie-talkie n set radio symud a siarad

walking n cerddediad; cerdded. **w. stick** ffon gerdded

walkover n goruchafiaeth hawdd, digystadleuaeth

wall n mur, gwal, pared ♦ vt murio

wallaby n cangarŵ bach

wall-cress n berwr y fagwyr

wallet n ysgrepan, gwaled

wallflower n llysiau'r fagwyr, blodau'r fagwyr, blodau mamgu

wallop vt curo, llachio, wado

wallow vi ymdreiglo, ymdrybaeddu

wallpaper n papur wal

walnut n cneuen Ffrengig

walrus n morfarch

waltz n wols

wan adj gwelw, gwelwlas, llwyd

wand n gwialen, llath, hudlath

wander vb crwydro, gwibio, cyfeiliorni

wanderer n crwydryn

wandering adj ar grwydr

wanderlust n elfen grwydro

wane vi darfod, treio, cilio, lleihau

wangle vb dyfeisio

want n angen, eisiau, diffyg ♦ vb bod mewn angen

wanting adj yn eisiau

wanton adj anllad, trythyll; diachos

wantonness n anlladrwydd

war n rhyfel ♦ vb rhyfela

warble vb telori

warbler n telor

ward n gwart, gward; gwarchodaeth ♦ vt gwarchod, amddiffyn

warden n gwarden, gwarcheidwad

wardenship n gwardeniaeth

warder n gwarchodwr, gwyliwr

wardrobe n cwpwrdd dillad,

gwardrob

ware n nwydd; llestri, wâr

warehouse n ystordy, ystorfa, warws

warfare n milwriaeth, rhyfel

wariness n pwyll, gwyliadwriaeth

warlike adj rhyfelgar, milwraidd, milwrol

warm adj cynnes ♦ vb cynhesu

warmonger n rhyfelgi

warmth n cynhesrwydd

warn vt rhybuddio

warning n rhybudd

warp n ystof, dylif ♦ vb gwyro, lleddfu

warrant n gwarant, awdurdod ♦ vt gwarantu, cyfreithloni

warrantor n gwarantydd

warren n cwningar, parc cwningod

warrior n rhyfelwr

warship n llong rhyfel

wart n dafad, dafaden

wary adj gwyliadwrus, gochelgar

was vi oedd, bu

wash vb golchi ♦ n golchiad, golchfa; golchion

washable adj golchadwy

washing n golch

washing machine n peiriant golchi

washing powder n powdr golchi

washing-up liquid n sebon golchi llestri

wasp n cacynen, gwenynen feirch

wassail n gwasael

waste vb difrodi, gwastraffu, treulio ♦ n gwastraff, traul

wasteful adj gwastraffus

wastepaper basket n basged sbwriel

wastrel n oferwr, oferddyn

watch vb gwylio, gwylied, gwarchod ♦ n gwyliadwriaeth; oriawr, oriadur, wats

watchful adj gwyliadwrus

watchmaker adj oriadurwr, trwsiwr watsys

watchman n gwyliwr

watch-night n gwylnos

watchword n arwyddair, cyswynair

water n dwfr, dŵr ♦ vb dyfrhau

water-cock n tap

watercolour n paent (i'w gymysgu â dŵr); dyfrliw

watercress n berwr dŵr

waterfall n rhaeadr, pistyll, cwymp dŵr, sgwd

waterhen n iâr fach y dŵr

watering place n lle i anifeiliaid gael dŵr; tref ffynhonnau

waterlogged adj llawn dŵr

watermark n dyfrnod

waterproof adj diddos

watershed n trum, gwahanfa ddŵr

water skiing n sglefrio ar ddŵr

watertight adj diddos, heb ollwng dŵr neu leithder

water wagtail n sigwti fach y dŵr

watt n wat, uned pŵer trydan

wattle n clwyd, pleiden; tagell ceiliog

wave vb chwifio; tonni ♦ n ton

waver vi anwadalu, petruso, gwamalu

wax n cwyr ♦ vt cwyro

wax vi cynyddu, tyfu

wax-candle n cannwyll gŵyr

waxworks npl arddangosfa delwau cwyr

way n ffordd, modd, arfer

wayfarer n ffordddolyn, teithiwr, tramwywr

wayfaring tree n ysgawen y gors

waylay vt cynllwyn, rhagod

wayside n ymyl y ffordd

wayward adj cyndyn, ystyfnig, gwrthnysig

we pron ni, nyni, ninnau

weak adj gwan, egwan

weaken vb gwanhau, gwanychu

weakling n un gwan, edlych, ewach

weakly *adj* gwanllyd
weak-minded *adj* diniwed, gwirion
weakness *n* gwendid
weal *n* llwydd, llwyddiant, lles
weald *n* fforest; gwlad agored
wealth *n* golud, cyfoeth, da
wealthy *adj* cyfoethog
wean *vt* diddyfnu
weapon *n* arf
wear *vb* gwisgo, treulio ♦ *n* traul; gwisg
weariness *n* blinder
weary *adj* blin, blinedig ♦ *vb* blino
weasel *n* gwenci, bronwen
weather *n* tywydd, hin ♦ *vt* dal, dioddef
weather-beaten *adj* ag ôl y tywydd arno
weatherglass *n* barometr
weathervane *n* ceiliog gwynt
weave *vb* gwau, gweu
weaver *n* gwehydd
web *n* gwe
webbing *n* webin
web-footed *adj* â thraed gweog
wed *vb* priodi, ymbriodi
wedding *n* priodas
wedge *n* cŷn, gaing, lletem ♦ *vt* cynio; gwthio i mewn
wedlock *n* ystad priodas, priodas
Wednesday *n* dydd Mercher
wee *adj* bach, bychan, pitw
weed *n* chwynnyn, chwyn ♦ *vb* chwynnu
week *n* wythnos
weekday *n* diwrnod gwaith
weekend *n* dros y Sul, penwythnos
weekly *adj* wythnosol ♦ *n* wythnosolyn (cylchgrawn) ♦ *adv* yn wythnosol
weep *vb* wylo, wylofain, llefain
weevil *n* gwyfyn yr ŷd
weft *n* anwe
weigh *vb* pwyso; codi (angor)
weight *n* pwys, pwysau
weighty *adj* pwysig, trwm
weir *n* cored

weird *adj* annaearol, iasol
welcome *excl*, *n* croeso ♦ *vt* croesawu ♦ *adj* derbyniol; dymunol
weld *vt* asio
welfare *n* llwydd, lles
welfare state *n* gwladwriaeth les
well *adv* yn dda ♦ *adj* da, iach ♦ *excl* wel
well *n* ffynnon, pydew
well-balanced *adj* cytbwys
wellbeing *n* lles, budd
well-bred *adj* boneddigaidd
well-fed *adj* mewn cas cadw da
wellingtons *npl* esgidiau glaw
well-off *adj* cefnog, da ei fyd
Welsh *adj* Cymreig (o ran teithi); Cymraeg (o ran iaith) ♦ *n* Cymraeg
Welshman *n* Cymro
Welshwoman *n* Cymraes
welt *n* gwald, gwaldas
welter *vi* ymdrybaeddu
wen *n* wen
wench *n* geneth, llances
wend *vt* mynd, cerdded
werewolf *n* bleidd-ddyn
Wesleyan *adj* Wesleaidd
west *n* gorllewin ♦ *adj* gorllewinol. W. Germany *n* Gorllewin yr Almaen. W. Indies *npl*: the W.I. India'r Gorllewin
westerly *adj* gorllewinol, o'r gorllewin
western *adj* gorllewinol
westwards *adv* tua'r gorllewin
wet *adj* gwlyb ♦ *vt* gwlychu ♦ gwlybaniaeth
wetness *n* gwlybaniaeth
wetting *n* gwlychfa
wether *n* mollt, gwedder
whack *vb* llachio, baeddu, ffonodio
whale *n* morfil
wharf *n* porthfa, llwythfa
what *adj*, *pron* yr hyn; pa beth, pa faint
whatever *pron* beth bynnag

whatsoever pron pa beth bynnag
wheat n gwenith
wheedle vt denu, hudo, llithio, truthio
wheel n olwyn, rhod, troell ♦ vt olwyno, powlio
wheelbarrow n berfa (drol), whilber
wheelchair n cadair olwyn
wheelwright n saer troliau
wheeze vi gwichian ♦ n gwich
wheezy adj gwichlyd
whelk n chwalc, gwalc
whelp n cenau
when adv pan, pa bryd
whence adv o ba le, o ba un
whenever adv pa bryd bynnag
where adv ym mha le; yn y lle, lle
whereabouts adv ymhle
whereas conj gan, yn gymaint â
whereby adv trwy yr hyn
wherefore adv paham, am hynny
wherein adv yn yr hyn
whereof adv y ... amdano
whereon adv ar yr hwn
wheresoever, wherever adv pa le bynnag
whereto adv y ... iddo
whereupon adv ar hynny
wherewithal n modd, arian
wherry n ysgraff, ceubal, porthfad
whet vt hogi, minio, awchlymu
whether conj ai, pa un ai
whetstone n carreg hogi, hogfaen, agalen
whey n maidd, gleision
which pron pa un, pa rai; a ♦ adj pa
whichever pron, adj pa un bynnag
whiff n chwiff, pwff, chwyth, chwa
Whig n Chwig, Rhyddfrydwr
while n ennyd, talm, amser ♦ vt treulio ♦ (hefyd **whilst**) adv cyhyd, tra
whim n mympwy, chwim
whimper vb swnian crio

whimsical adj ysmala, mympwyol
whimsicality n bod yn fympwyol
whin n eithin
whinchat n clochdar yr eithin
whine vb swnian crio, cwynfan
whinny vi gweryru
whip vb chwipio, ffrewyllu, fflangellu ♦ n chwip, ffrewyll, fflangell
whiphand n llaw uchaf
whippet n corfilgi
whipping n chwipiad, fflangelliad
whir vi chwyrndroi, chwyrnu
whirl vb chwyrlio, chwyrnellu, chwyrndroi
whirligig n chwyrligwgan, chwyrnell
whirlpool n pwll tro, trobwll
whirlwind n trowynt, corwynt
whisk n tusw ♦ vb ysgubo; chwyrlio
whiskered adj blewog, barfog
whiskers npl blew, barf
whisky n chwisgi
whisper vb, n sibrwd, sisial
whist n chwist
whistle vb chwibanu ♦ n chwiban, chwibanogl, chwit
whit n tipyn, gronyn, mymryn
white adj gwyn, can, cannaid
whiten vb gwynnu, cannu
whiteness n gwynder, gwyndra
whitewash n gwyngalch ♦ vb gwyngalchu
whither adv i ba le
whiting n gwyniad
whitlow n ffelwm, ffalwm, ewinor, bystwn
whitlow grass n llysiau'r bystwn
Whit Monday n Llungwyn
Whitsun(day) n Sulgwyn
Whitsuntide n dros y Sulgwyn
whittle vt naddu, lleihau
whiz vi sio, chwyrnellu, chwyrlio
who pron a, pwy
whoever pron pwy bynnag
whole adj cyfan, holl; iach,

holliach ♦ n cyfan
wholehearted adj â'i holl galon
wholemeal adj â'r grawn cyfan, cyflawn
wholeness n cyfanrwydd
wholesale n cyfanwerth ♦ adj yn y crynswth
wholesaler n cyfanwerthwr
wholesome adj iach, iachus, iachusol
wholly adv yn hollol, yn gyfan gwbl, yn llwyr
whom pron a (y, yr)
whomsoever pron pwy bynnag
whoop vi bloeddio, banllefain ♦ n bloedd
whooping cough n pas
whop vt ffusto, baeddu
whopper n un mawr
whopping adj mawr iawn
whore n putain, hŵr
whorl n tro, troell, sidell
whortleberry n llus, llusi duon bach
whose pron y ... ei, eiddo pwy? pwy biau?
whosoever pron pwy bynnag
why adv paham, pam
wick n pabwyr, pabwyryn, wic
wicked adj drwg, drygionus, ysgeler
wickedness n drygioni
wicker n gwaith gwiail
wickerwork n plethwaith, basgedwaith
wicket n wiced, clwyd, llidiart
wide adj llydan, eang, helaeth; rhwth
wide-awake adj effro, ar ddihun
widely adj yn eang
widen vb lledu, llydanu
widespread adj cyffredinol
widgeon n wiwell
widow adj gweddw ♦ n gwraig weddw, gwidw
widowed adj gweddw
widower n gwidman

widowhood n gweddwdod
width n lled, ehangder
wield vt llywio, rheoli; ysgwyd, arfer, trin
wife (**wives**) n gwraig, gwraig briod, priod
wig n gwallt gosod, perwig, wig
wigging n cerydd
wild adj gwyllt ♦ n diffeithle ♦ adj anialwch
wilderness n anialwch
wildfire n tân gwyllt
wildness n gwylltineb
wile n dichell, ystryw, cast
wilful adj gwirfoddol, bwriadol; ystyfnig
wilfully adv o fwriad
wilfulness or U.S. **willfulness** n ystyfnigrwydd
wiliness n dichell, cyfrwystra
will vt ewyllysio, mynnu ♦ n ewyllys
willing adj ewyllysgar, bodlon
willingly adj o wirfodd
willingness n parodrwydd
will-o'-the-wisp n jacolantern
willow n helygen, pren helyg
willowherb n helyglys
willowy adj helygaidd, gosgeiddig
willpower n grym ewyllys
willy-nilly adv bodlon neu beidio, o fodd neu anfodd
wily adj cyfrwys, dichellgar
wimple n gwempl
win vb ennill
wince vi gwingo
winch n wins
wind n gwynt
wind vb dirwyn, troi
windbag n clebryn
windfall n lwc, ffawd dda
windflower n anemoni, blodyn y gwynt
windless adj di-wynt, llonydd
windmill n melin wynt
window n ffenestr
windowpane n cwarel
windpipe n breuant, y bibell wynt

windscreen n ffenestr flaen
windscreen wiper n braich law
windward adj tua'r gwynt
windy adj gwyntog
wine n gwin
wineglass n gwydr gwin
wing n adain, asgell; asgellwr (rygbi)
wing-commander n asgell-gomander
winged adj adeiniog
wing-forward n blaenasgellwr
wink vb wincio, cau llygad ♦ n winc; hunell
winner n enillydd
winning adj enillgar, deniadol
winnings npl enillion
winnow vt nithio, gwyntyllio
winnower n nithiwr
winsome adj serchog, deniadol
winter n gaeaf ♦ vb gaeafu
wintry adj gaeafol
wipe vt sychu
wire n gwïfr, gwïfren
wireless n radio
wirepulling n cynllwyn, dylanwadu, 'tynnu gwifrau'
wiring n weiro
wiry adj gwydn, caled
wisdom n doethineb
wise adj doeth
wiseacre n doethyn, ffwlcyn
wish vb dymuno, chwennych ♦ n dymuniad
wishbone n asgwrn tynnu
wishful adj awyddus. **w. thinking** breuddwyd gwrach
wishywashy adj gwan, di-asgwrn-cefn
wisp n tusw
wistful adj awyddus, hiraethus
wit vb: **to w.** sef, hynny yw, nid amgen
wit n synnwyr; arabedd; gwr ffraeth
witch n dewines, gwrach
witchcraft n dewiniaeth

with prep â, ag, gyda, gydag, efo, gan
withdraw vb tynnu yn ôl, encilio; codi arian
withdrawal n enciliad
withe n gwden, gwialen helyg
wither vb gwywo, crino
withering adj gwywol, crin
withers npl ysgwydd march
withhold vt atal, cadw yn ôl
within adv, n, prep i mewn, o fewn
without prep heb, di- ♦ adv, n tu allan
withstand vt gwrthsefyll
witless adj disynnwyr, ynfyd, ffôl
witness n tyst; tystiolaeth ♦ vb tystio
wits npl synhwyrau
witticism n ffraethair, ffraetheb
wittiness n ffraethineb
wittingly adv trwy wybod, yn fwriadol
witty adj arab, arabus, ffraeth
wizard n swynwr, dewin
wizardry n dewiniaeth, hud
wizened adj gwyw, crin, sybachog
woad n glaslys
wobble vi siglo, honcian, anwadalu
wobbly adj sigledig
woe n gwae
woebegone adj athrist
wolf n (**wolves**) n blaidd
wolfsbane n llysiau'r blaidd
woman (**women**) n gwraig, merch
womanliness n rhinweddau benywaidd
womanly adj gwreigaidd, benywaidd
womb n croth, bru
wonder n rhyfeddod, syndod ♦ vi rhyfeddu, synnu
wonderful, wondrous adj rhyfeddol
wont vb, n arfer ♦ adj arferol
woo vt caru; deisyf
wood n coed, coedwig; pren

woodbine *n* gwyddfid
woodcock *n* cyffylog
woodcutter *n* torrwr coed
wooded *adj* coedog
wooden *adj* o goed, o bren; trwsgl, trwstan
woodland *n* coetir
woodlark *n* ehedydd y coed
wood-louse (*-lice*) *n* gwrach y lludw, mochyn y coed, tyrchyn llwyd
woodpecker *n* taradr y coed
wood-pigeon *n* ysguthan
wood sage *n* chwerwlys yr eithin, saets gwyllt
wood sorrel *n* surran y coed
woodwind *npl* chwythoffer pren
woodwork *n* gwaith coed, gwaith saer
woof *n* anwe
wool *n* gwlân
woollen *adj* gwlanog, gwlân
woolly *adj* gwlanog
woolsack *n* sedd yr Arglwydd Ganghellor
word *n* gair ♦ *vt* geirio
wording *n* geiriad
wordy *adj* geiriog, amleiriog
work *n* gwaith, gweithred, gorchwyl ♦ *vb* gweithio
worker *n* gweithiwr
workhouse *n* tloty, wyrcws
working *adj* yn gweithio, gwaith
workman *n* gweithiwr
workmanlike *n* gweithgar, diwyd
workmanship *n* saernïaeth, crefft
workshop *n* gweithdy
world *n* byd
worldly *adj* bydol
worldwide *adj* byd-eang
worm *n* pryf, abwydyn; llyngyren ♦ *vb* ymnyddu
wormwood *n* wermod
worn-out *adj* wedi blino; wedi treulio
worried *adj* pryderus, gofidus
worry *vb* cnoi, baeddu, blino,

poeni, poenydio ♦ *n* pryder, blinder
worse *adj* gwaeth
worsen *vb* gwaethygu
worship *n* addoliad ♦ *vb* addoli
worshipper *n* addolwr
worst *vt* gorchfygu, trechu
worsted *n* edafedd hirwlan, wstid
worth *n* gwerth, teilyngdod
worthless *adj* diwerth
worthy *adj* teilwng ♦ *n* gŵr o fri
wound *n* archoll, clwyf ♦ *vt* archolli, clwyfo
wraith *n* cyhiraeth, cyheuraeth
wrangle *vb* cecru, cweryla, ffraeo ♦ *n* ffrae, ymryson
wrap *vt* plygu, amdoi, lapio
wrapping paper *n* papur lapio
wrasse *n* gwrachen y môr
wrath *n* llid, digofaint, soriant
wrathful *adj* digofus, llidiog, dig
wreak *vt* tywallt, dial (llid)
wreath *n* torch
wreck *n* llongddrylliad ♦ *vb* llongddryllio
wren *n* dryw, dryw bach
wrench *vt* rhwygo ymaith, tyndroi ♦ *n* tyndro
wrestle *vi* ymgodymu, ymaflyd codwm
wrestler *n* ymgodymwr, taflwr codwm
wretch *n* adyn, truan; gwalch, dihiryn
wretched *adj* truan, truenus, gresynus
wriggle *vb* gwingo, ymnyddu
wright *n* saer
wring *vt* troi, gwasgu
wrinkle *n* crych, crychni ♦ *vb* crychu
wrinkle *n* awgrym, hysbysrwydd
wrinkled *adj* crychiog
wrist *n* arddwrn
wristband *n* rhwymyn llawes
wristwatch *n* wats arddwrn, wats fraich, oriawr

writ n: Holy W. yr Ysgrythur Lân
write vb ysgrifennu
writer n ysgrifennwr, awdur
writhe vb ymnyddu, gwingo
writing n ysgrifen; ysgrifennu
writing paper n papur ysgrifennu
wrong adj cyfeiliornus, cam, anghywir, o'i le ♦ n cam ♦ vt gwneud cam â, niweidio, drygu
wrongdoing n trosedd, camwedd
wrongful adj anghyfiawn, ar gam
wroth adj dig, dicllon, digofus, llidiog
wrought adj: w. iron haearn gyr
wry adj cam, gwyrgam

X

xenophobia n senoffobia
X-rays npl pelydrau X
xylophone n seiloffon

Y

yacht n llong bleser, iot
yachtsman n hwyliwr iot
yap vi clepian, cyfarth
yard n llath, llathen; hwyl-lath
yard n iard, buarth, cadlas, clos
yarn n edau, edafedd; stori, chwedl
yawl n bad mawr, cwch llong
yawn vi dylyfu gên, agor ceg
ye pron chwi, chwychwi; chwithau
yea adv ie, yn wir
year n blwyddyn, blwydd
yearling n anifail blwydd
yearly adv blynyddol
yearn vi hiraethu, dyheu
yearning n hiraeth
yeast n burum, berem, berman
yell vi ysgrechain ♦ n ysgrech, nâd
yellow adj, n melyn
yellowhammer n y benfelen, melyn yr eithin

yelp vi cyfarth, gogyfarth, cipial
yeoman n gwrêng, iwmon; amaethwr
yeomanry n meirchfilwyr
yes adv ie, do, oes, etc
yesterday n, adv doe
yet conj, adv er hynny, eto
yew n yw, ywen
Yiddish n Almaeneg Iddewaidd
yield vb ildio, gildio, ymroddi, rhoddi ♦ n cynnyrch
yoghurt n iogwrt
yoke n iau, gwedd ♦ vb ieuo
yokefellow n cymar
yokel n lleban, gwladwr, taeog
yolk n melyn wy, melynwy
yonder adj acw, draw ♦ adv dacw, acw, draw
yore n y dyddiau gynt, y cynfyd
you pron chi, chwi, 'ch; chwychwi; chwithau
young adj ifanc, ieuanc
younger adj iau
youngest adj ieuaf, ifancaf
youngster n bachgennyn, plentyn
your pron eich, 'ch
yours pron eiddoch. yr eiddoch
yourself pron eich hun(an)
yourselves pron eich hunain
youth n ieuenctid, mebyd; llanc. y. hostel n gwesty ieuenctid
youthful adj ieuanc, ieuengaidd
Yugoslavia n Iwgoslafia
Yule n Nadolig
Yuletide n tymor y Nadolig

Z

Zambia n Zambia
zeal n sêl, aidd, eiddgarwch, brwdfrydedd
zealot n gwynfydwr, penboethyn
zealous adj selog, eiddgar, brwdfrydig
zebra n sebra
zenana n gwragedd-dy, gwreicty

zenith *n* entrych; anterth
zephyr *n* awel dyner (o'r gorllewin)
zero *n* dim, diddim, gwagnod (0), sero
zest *n* awch, blas, afiaith
zigzag *adj, n* igam-ogam
Zimbabwe *n* Zimbabwe
zinc *n* sinc

zip *n* sip
zither *n* sither
zodiac *n* sidydd
zone *n* gwregys, cylch, rhanbarth
zoo *n* sw
zoological *adj* swolegol
zoologist *n* swolegydd
zoology *n* milofyddiaeth, swoleg